March 1980

Indonesia: The Possible Dream

HOWARD PALFREY JONES

Indonesia:

PUBLISHED UNDER THE AUSPICES OF
THE HOOVER INSTITUTION

The Possible Dream

HARCOURT BRACE JOVANOVICH, INC.
NEW YORK

The excerpts from *Sukarno: An Autobiography, as told to Cindy Adams,* copyright ©
1965, by Cindy Adams, are reprinted by permission of the publishers, The Bobbs-
Merrill Company, Inc. The material reprinted from Bernhard Dahm, *Sukarno and
the Struggle for Indonesian Independence,* translated from the German by Mary F.
Somers Heidhues, © Alfred Metzner Verlag, Frankfurt am Main, Berlin, 1966, copy-
right © 1969 by Cornell University, is used by permission of Cornell University
Press. Permission was also granted by Harper & Row, Publishers, Incorporated, for use
of material in *Just Friends* by Robert F. Kennedy, and in *The Story of Indonesia* by
Louis Fischer; The Macmillan Company of Canada, St. Martin's Press, Inc., New
York, and Macmillan and Company Limited, for use of material in *The History of
South-East Asia* by D. G. E. Hall; W. W. Norton & Company, New York, for use of
material in *Letters of a Javanese Princess* by Raden A. Kartini.

Library of Congress Catalog Card Number: 78–142090

Printed in the United States of America

A B C D E

With love to

MARY LOU

who was always there

*The author wishes to express
his especial gratitude to the Hoover
Institution on War, Revolution
and Peace, Stanford University,
whose grant of fellowship,
including financial assistance and
facilities for research, permitted his
undertaking of this work.*

Contents

Illustrations

Between pages 204 and 205

Foreword

My first acquaintance with Indonesia came about quite by accident when I was a boy in high school in Milwaukee, Wisconsin. The class was studying about the Crusades, and our teacher suggested that if we wanted to see the armor worn by the Crusaders, we should visit Milwaukee's excellent museum. I was fascinated by the rows of shining, armor-clad figures: Knights of Saint John of Jerusalem, Teutonic knights, Knights Templar, Scottish knights; some were in chain mail, some in armor plate. At the end of the rows was a showcase containing several curious, daggerlike weapons. One was reptilian in shape, with intricate designs etched on the steel blade; it slid into a highly decorated, bejeweled gold scabbard. The hilt was smooth and beautifully carved wood. Underneath was the legend, "Javanese *Kris*, 14th century."

I knew from geography class that Java was an island somewhere in Asia, and I had seen pictures of attractive, sarong-draped men and women in some magazines. That was the extent of my knowledge of Java. But an interest in Indonesia took root—and destiny, in its own curious ways and without my conscious assistance, so directed my path that some of my richest years were spent in that country.

What follows is not only a narrative of my personal experiences at a crucial point in U.S.-Indonesian relations; it is also the story of Indonesia —its ancient history, its colonial past, its turbulent career since independence. Above all, it is an intimate record of how a nation, brought to the brink of chaos and written off by most experts as lost to Communism, managed the most dramatic turnabout in recent history, rejecting an alien ism, repudiating a charismatic leader, renewing its commitment to freedom, and rebuilding its shattered society.

Repeatedly, Americans ask me, What possible claim has Indonesia to be a nation? What have these thousands of islands in common except the fact that they were Dutch colonies for 350 years? These questions demonstrate the ignorance of Westerners generally about lands and peoples across the Pacific. To many of us who grew up before World

War II, Southeast Asia remains an unknown quantity; our education encompassed only half the world. The difficulties Americans face in understanding a nation like Indonesia are partly a result of the fact that they have never delved deeply into its cultural heritage. Both the American and Indonesian cultures are rich, and they represent a blending, borrowing, and perfecting of the diverse cultures of older civilizations. The sources from which each has drawn its basic institutions, however, differ considerably.

The main elements of the American political and economic system have all flowed from the great mainstream of European civilization—from Greece and Rome, from the medieval scholars of France and Italy, from the English judges and parliamentarians who compiled the great body of common law. And this ideological system has brought to Americans such immense material and spiritual benefits that they might perhaps be pardoned for sometimes falling into the error of thinking of it as universal, rather than only one of several rewarding systems. But Indonesia's culture, political, and social heritage flows from equally exalted albeit very different sources—from the age-old civilization of Java and the India of Buddha and Asoka; from the laws of Manu and the splendid empires of Sriwidjaya and Madjapahit; from the teachings of the prophet Mohammed.

A particularly striking contrast in the ideological evolution of the two countries has come in the past 200 years. Since 1776, Americans have been the masters of their own destiny, free to draw on their cultural heritage in shaping their society, with virtually no interference from the rest of the world. But during those same 200 years, Indonesians were under the domination of what was to them a totally alien culture.

It must be remembered that only in the brief twenty years since Indonesia's struggle for independence met with success in 1949 have the Indonesian people been able to address themselves to the great task that has engaged our energies for the past 200 years—forging a political, ideological, and cultural heritage into a unique national identity. Moreover, they have had to face this task not in the remote world of the eighteenth and nineteenth centuries—when it might take half a year for a letter to travel from Djakarta to Washington—but in the full glare of the present world of instantaneous communication and all-pervasive ideological conflict.

Freedom from colonial domination has brought many an important by-product to Southeast Asian countries; one of the most significant is a sudden awakening of interest in one another, a growing realization that they have many common concerns, political and economic, as well as military. The recent organization of ASEAN (Association of Southeast Asian Nations) by Indonesia, Malaysia, the Philippines and Thailand, the activities of ECAFE (Economic Commission for Asia and the Far East), the Asian Development Bank—these are just some of the regional efforts reflecting the growing sense of an Asian neighborhood, which includes eight free nations and the two great entrepôt cities of Singapore, which became a separate state in August 1965, and Hong Kong. In any assessment of the area's future, this new awareness, the seed perhaps of a burgeoning unity, must be taken into account.

The burning desire on the part of the Indonesian people to shape their own national identity is a salient factor in Indonesia's relations with the United States. Whether Indonesia will be able to solve its problems, feed its people, and play its proper role in the free world will depend largely upon what Americans do. The world cannot exist half poor and half rich. Yet the gap between the developed and the less-developed nations is year by year becoming greater rather than less.

There is an alternative to accepting today's world conflicts merely on a political level: to explore and to understand the social and economic pressures that are the source of the conflicts and have their roots in a contrasting culture. Which brings me to my reasons for writing this book.

First, Indonesia offers a prime example of the interplay of complex historical, cultural, political and economic forces—internal and external—ignorance of which can lead to disastrous decisions.

Second, the story of Indonesia's recent history demonstrates the need for clear definitions of objectives in dealing with an Asian nation, for persistence in the pursuit of these objectives, and, however strong the contrary evidence, for confidence in the common sense of ordinary people, who, however misguided by their leaders, in the end defend their own most cherished values.

Third, Indonesia presents a totally different picture from other Southeast Asian countries in that it alone has the potential to become a major power in Asia. The world's sixth most populous nation, after Pakistan, strategically located, Croesus-rich in resources largely unexploited, except in the case of oil, it is the pivot around which the future of Southeast Asia revolves.

Fourth, the United States has a role to play in Asia. Peace depends on whether we play that role well or badly. Lessons learned at great cost in Indonesia have application to other situations we face on that troubled continent.

It is my desire now to share my experience, especially with the American people, so much of whose blood and treasure has been lost in Asian lands.

HPJ

Acknowledgments

Although this book is the story of American diplomacy in one nation as seen through the eyes of one man, accomplishments in the diplomatic service are never the work of only one. I feel a little like the youngster sitting at his grandfather's knee, listening to stories of World War I. Finally he asks, "Grandpa, did anybody help you fight the war?" Thus I am first and foremost indebted to the members of that elite corps, the Foreign Service of the Department of State. Through trial and triumph, through ordeal, failure, and some successes, the dedicated men and women who make up that Service are the real heroes of this narrative. Without their unflagging devotion, their highly developed skill in the art of diplomacy, and the political and economic dissection that forms the raw material from which policy decisions are made, many events described herein would not have taken place, and this book consequently would never have been written. To them I owe a debt of gratitude that can never be repaid. Most of necessity will remain nameless in these pages, but I want them to know how much I have appreciated their friendship and unfailing support through troubled years. The same must be said of professionals from other departments of the government —the military attachés, the members of the economic aid missions, the U.S. Information Service, the intelligence community, the agricultural and commercial attachés, and other government representatives. To friends from other embassies who have shared insights with me through the years, appreciation is also due.

I am especially indebted to Professor George McT. Kahin of Cornell University, Frank J. Miller of the Ford Foundation, Dr. W. Glenn Campbell of The Hoover Institution at Stanford University, and Alexander C. Herman of New York City for encouragement and support. The Hoover Institution, the Ford Foundation through Cornell University, and Thomas L. Brook of Calgary, Canada, supplied financial support that eased the way. Among my American colleagues to whom a special word of appreciation is due, both for their stanch support in what seemed to be crises at the time, and their assistance in reconstructing events and reviewing manuscript are: W. Averell Harriman, Roger Hilsman, U.S. Ambassador Francis J. Galbraith, U.S. Ambassador James D. Bell, John M. Allison, Edward E. Masters, Country Director for Indonesian Affairs at the Department of State, John W. Henderson, Robert G. Rich, Jr., Lewis M. Purnell, Edward Ingraham, Samuel P. Hayes, Colonel George O. Benson, Walter J. Levy. Indonesians who generously assisted me are too numerous to mention, but I should acknowledge my debt to Dr. Mohammed Hatta, General Abdul H. Nasution, Johannes Leimena, Ambassador Soedjatmoko, Anak Agung Gde Agung, Oejeng Soewargana and B. M. Diah. I also wish to thank Dr. William M. Franklin, director of the historical division of the Department of State, and Wilmer P. Sparrow, Mildred F. Nash and the staff of RS/R at the Department of State for their help in locating and providing my old cables, from which I drew heavily for this book.

Special appreciation is also due Professor Frederick C. Bunnell, of Vassar College, and his wife, Alice, who were with me all the way; Arthur Goodfriend, author, whose editorial input was inspired, as always; Julian Muller, Vice-President of Harcourt Brace Jovanovich, Inc., for encouragement, inspiration, and unfailing wise counsel and guidance at critical points, and Miss Gloria Hammond, peerless copy editor, who manicured the manuscript gently but firmly for redundant hangnails and surplus verbiage; also to Cindy Adams, whose persistence overcame overwhelming odds in her *Sukarno, An Autobiography*, and to her husband, Joey for special insights. Finally, my gratitude goes to Miss Judi Mason, my enthusiastic and tireless research assistant, who worked long and hard bird-dogging elusive facts and typing manuscript. Any sins of omission (of which there are many) or commission are, of course, mine.

And of President Sukarno himself, although he shall never read these pages, I should like to say that I valued his friendship and appreciated his many courtesies; that I have made every effort to portray him as he was—a human being of great warmth and magnetism, a leader of vision who lost himself in self-glorification, forgetting that the truly great are humble, and in so doing betrayed his people. He was nevertheless a man who, when the chips were down, stuck by the precepts of unity in which he had always believed, even though this meant pulling the pillars of his temple down upon his own head. I hope that he understood the sadness with which my wife and I viewed the tragic events that brought him down but for which he must bear major responsibility.

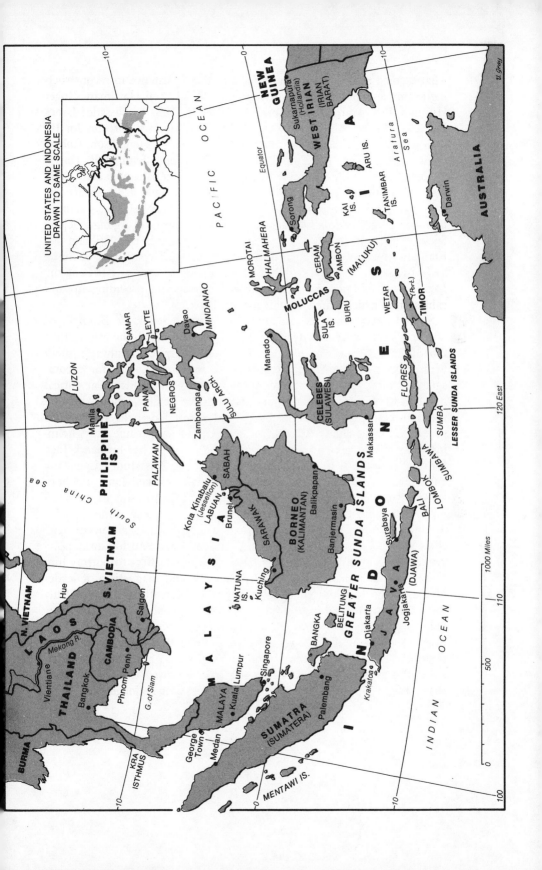

PART I

Toward Understanding Indonesia

Even so the tongue is a little member, and boasteth great things. Behold, how great a matter a little fire kindleth!
—JAMES 3:5

A nation can only be saved from oblivion by men whose spirit is made up of the elements of lightning and thunder.
—VIVEKANANDA

What is man? Man is that force which ultimately cancels all tyrants and gods.
—ALBERT CAMUS

CHAPTER 1

Footprints in Stone

There are in Java at least twenty live volcanoes, and as many more on Sumatra and Bali. Their grayish yellow fumes drift lazily upward and stain the blue sky. Islands come and go in this part of the world. In 1883, the island of Krakatoa, just off the coast of Java, blew up and disappeared—with its 30,000 inhabitants—below the surface of the sea. Now Krakatoa is again emerging, shouldering its way upward out of the sea at the rate of several feet a year. There are two islands—mother and child, the Indonesians call them, the mother's peak now some 1,500 feet above the sea. A few fishermen beach their boats on the dark sands, but there are as yet no permanent settlers. They will come; human memory is short.

Geologists believe that much of what comprises Indonesia's 4,000 islands today was a solid land mass thousands of years ago, with no sea separating Java and Sumatra from the Asian mainland, and that the great migrations were over land. The Indonesians call their country "*Tanah Air Kita*" ("Our Land and Water"), and may be the only people in the world who think of water as an integral part of their homeland.

There are ten nations in Southeast Asia. With one exception, Thailand, which has been independent for more than 700 years, they are new nations, all former colonies of the French, British, or Dutch, with a few Portuguese colonial remnants in Macao and Eastern Timor. Indonesia is by far the largest of these, both in population and area. An interesting and even somewhat startling fact is that Indonesia's horizontal sweep exceeds that of the United States, reaching all the way from California in the West to Bermuda in the East—an observation readily apparent when a map of Indonesia is superimposed over a map of the U.S. Separating Australia from Asia and Europe, and lying between the Indian and Pacific oceans, the archipelago is of critical strategic importance.

More than half of Indonesia's 115 million people live on the fertile island of Java, which has a population density averaging 1,235 persons per square mile, one of the highest in the world. Most of the remaining 4,000 islands are underpopulated. Thus Indonesian Borneo, as big as Texas, contains slightly more than 4,000,000 people; one can fly for many hours over green mountains and jungles without seeing a sign of habitation. Rich Sumatra, four times the size of Java, has only 19,000,-000 people. West Irian, Indonesia's half of New Guinea and still largely unexplored, is half the size of Texas in area but smaller than Rhode Island in population. In wealth of natural resources Indonesia ranks third in the world.

Indonesia is a country of immensely varied physical beauty, presenting to the world an appropriately symbolic setting for its history.

The fast-flowing Tjiaruten River tumbles over rocks and boulders as it winds through the lush green countryside of West Java and near the pleasant red-roofed little city of Bogor, at the foot of the great green pyramid that is the mountain called Salak, which means "snake." This is rice and cassava country, and the rice fields are rich here—silver mirrors reflecting the sun when the rice is newly planted, a thicket of green growth high as a man's waist at its peak, towheads nodding and beckoning when ripe for the harvest. A man can do a day's walk through the hot, humid paddies, along the foot-wide ridges that separate them, without coming to a village, although he will pass innumerable small kampongs huddled in the shade of great yellow bamboos and towering coconut palms.

The river is one of the numerous tributaries that feed the greater river called Tjisadana, which in turn spills into the Java Sea at Tangren, just west of Djakarta. One of the boulders over which its water froths is a great granitic rock as tall as a man. Impressed into it, as though a man had walked there eons ago when the boulder was moist sand, are the footprints of Java's earliest recorded ruler. The Sanskrit inscription below the footprints—the first written record of man on Java—proclaims:

> These are the two footprints of King Purnawarman, like the footprints of the God, Vishnu.

Guarding the footprints are two spiders carved into the granite, faintly showing. Another inscription, in rolling characters several inches high, is in a language still to be understood.

King Purnawarman left no date in his inscription. But archaeologists say he reigned in the fifth or sixth century A.D. His kingdom was called Tarumanegara. It is the oldest kingdom known in Java, the second oldest—after that of King Mulawarman in East Kalimantan (Borneo)—in Indonesia. Purnawarman was a great king, the Javanese say, because the footprints are only one of five records, separated by great distances, that he left in stone. He was a builder. An inscription found near Tandjong

Priok, the harbor of Djakarta, apparently carved in the twenty-second
year of his reign, states that King Purnawarman "dug a river." This canal
was presumably the forerunner of the system of canals built by the
Dutch in the same area centuries later. But it was footprints we had
come to see one steaming Sunday morning, accompanied by Mohammed Buchari, head of the Department of Epigraphy of the Archaeologi-
cal Institute of Indonesia, and Uka Tandrasumita, head of the Department of Islamic Archaeology at the same institute.

I had read somewhere that the footprints of King Purnawarman's elephant were also embedded in a rock in the vicinity. Buchari regarded me
curiously when I inquired about this. "If you want to ford the river, we
can return another way," he said. "It is longer but we will pass the rock
with the elephant's footprints." The heat was intense—we all were dripping with perspiration. I could see that he was wondering why on earth
an American official would go to such trouble to see an elephant's footprints carved in a rock!

The elephant rock was not in the river bed but on the crest of the
embankment. We reached it after a stiff climb. On the gray top of a
boulder similar to the one bearing the footprints of the King were the
clearly defined footprints of a huge elephant. I had never seen such an
elephant, but perhaps in those days the greater the King, the greater the
elephant. In diameter, the footprints measured twenty-two inches. Perhaps the sculptor had exaggerated somewhat, a reasonable speculation,
although the footprints of the King were not overly large.

Again, an inscription, clearly legible, was carved below the footprints.
It read in Sanskrit:

> These are the footprints of the elephant of King Purnawarman, which
> look like the footprints of the elephant of Indra.

I asked Buchari how he accounted for the fact that the King's footprints were in the river bed, while those of his elephant were on top of
the bank some distance away. Buchari, a true scholar, would not venture
an opinion. However, he and his colleague were a mine of information. I
learned that the King's name means "perfect armor," so he was clearly a
warrior. Buchari described fifth-century West Java as a society based on
autonomous villages, all of which paid tribute to the King once a year.
Some of the artifacts discovered in a later period show that payment for
land was in gold—and also that there were more than a hundred different titles for tax collectors, not counting, one may assume, some of the
other names these persons may have been called.

Buchari had the impression of a happy people in this early kingdom,
not oppressed by autocratic government. He disagreed with the many
authorities who contend that the great eighth-century Borobudur temple
in Central Java was built by forced labor. Our guide was convinced that
the Buddhists of the period built the temple as a labor of love, and he

cited the humorous touches at the corners of the great building as evidence of the spirit of the craftsmen. He also noted the present-day Balinese custom whereby all the people of a village join together to build a temple, or a town hall, or a recreation center, and concluded that such cooperative practices may have had their origins in fifth-century West Java.

Although the granite inscriptions of King Purnawarman make up the first written record of man on Java, the ethnologists and anthropologists, the linguists, historians and other scholars combine to tell us a good deal of what went on before.

A traveler today, if he is in a hurry, can have dinner in Honolulu, breakfast in Tokyo, and dinner in Djakarta. During the course of that trip, he flies over part of the trail that the ancient Indonesians took eons ago to find their new homeland. Indonesian man was on this trail for many hundreds, probably thousands of years, learning as he moved, and followed by others like him. He came from somewhere in East Asia—the first wave from Yunnan in South China, scholars are convinced—through those areas now known as Laos, Vietnam, Thailand, and Cambodia. He wandered south along the great rivers and through the jungle, propelled perhaps by changing climate as the great icecaps moved southward in the middle Paleolithic time, by the pressure of hostile tribes to the north, by the shortage of game, or, as he learned how to till the soil, by the search for fertile land.

Early man followed the rivers and seacoast. One can see him on the flood plains, following the muddy sweep of that mightiest of all rivers in Southeast Asia, the Mekong, which cleaves its way out of the Himalayan heights from China through northern Thailand, and today separates Laos from Cambodia and Vietnam as it moves relentlessly seaward to the Gulf of Siam. Somewhere along that trail of 3,000 miles, he lingered for the thousands of years needed for him to become a farmer instead of a hunter, to learn how to grow rice in paddies, work metals in a small way, and make pottery. Also along that route, the early Indonesian must have learned about the wheel. The dense jungles of Malaya most likely held back his southward progress for many centuries—unless more hospitable terrain available to him in his southward passage has since disappeared beneath the sea. Even after he had reached Sumatra and Java, he was too preoccupied with the problems of living to record much about himself, if, indeed, he had learned to write. Apparently he had not, if the cave drawings of 20,000 years ago are his.

Thus Indonesia, long before it was exposed to later Indian and Chinese cultural influences, had already developed a distinct culture of its own, and henceforth the impact of foreign contacts, great as it might be, would nevertheless be considerably muted. By the time exposure to outside influences had taken place, Indonesians had developed sophisticated cultivation of irrigated rice fields, domesticated the ox and buffalo, acquired some skill in bronze and iron, and could be rated as good navigators. They also had their own theater, highly developed music in the form of the gamelan orchestra, and were producing fine batik textiles with intricate designs and patterns by a complicated process involving the use of dyes and wax.[1] They were an artistic people, and their homes were decorated with delicate carvings.

The many similarities of the wajang legendary tales to early Indian classics have been the subject of considerable controversy. Did these similarities arise from the impact of Indian culture, or from the fact that both the Indonesians and Indians stemmed from a common source? One theory asserts that western China, now generally conceded to have been the place of origin of the Indonesian stream of migration, was also the home of early Indian culture.

What did the ancestors of today's Indonesians find when they crossed from what is now the mainland into Java or Sumatra? It is still an unanswered question; but some form of two-legged being has lived in this part of the world since time immemorial. The fragmentary skeleton of Java man, *Pithecanthropus erectus*, discovered in the Solo Valley in 1890, led to the conclusion that Java was the original home of man as we know him today, and consequently is the site of the Garden of Eden. Even if that is not true, it should be; for it would be difficult to find anywhere in the world a paradise surpassing this land of lush beauty, literally a garden. Although modern scholars tend to place the origin of man farther north and west, the idyllic quality of the Indonesian archipelago lends itself appropriately to the legend of *Genesis*.

Java man lived about half a million years ago, and is considered to have been a primitive type—not to be classed either as the "missing link" or *Homo sapiens*. The first skulls of the latter were found in eastern Java. They were people who lived perhaps 10,000 years ago. When today's Indonesians arrived, in waves beginning about 3,000 years before Christ, it is possible that they were greeted by a type similar to the primitives, generally referred to as aborigines, who still inhabit the forests of Sumatra and the mountain fastness of the eastern islands. These aborigines may have been still earlier arrivals from the Asian mainland; in any event, they are not to be confused with Java man. Whether he was still around when the early arrivals came from the mainland seems highly unlikely. Indonesian legends, however, are full of conflicts between the good princes and the "giants" who inhabited the jungles; one might speculate that these stories have some basis in fact, and were not simply horror inventions to make children behave.

There may have been two great waves of these peoples, some scholars

1. Cf. D. G. E. Hall, *A History of South-East Asia*, 3rd ed. (London: Macmillan & Co., 1968), p. 9.

think—the proto-Malays, so termed because they came first, about 3500 B.C., and the deutero-Malays, who arrived perhaps 2,000 years later. They had progressed during those millenniums. They brought with them manufacturing and the use of metals, principally bronze and later iron, and possessed the tools and arms to conquer the fauna and jungles of Java. They were great seafarers, too, traveling as far as the southern shores of Japan and migrating across the Indian Ocean to Madagascar. This, it must be remembered, was at a time when all Europe was in a state of neolithic civilization; the island of Britain was still "inhabited by painted savages," to use Captain Cook's description.

The Gajo and Alas peoples of northern Sumatra and the Toraja group in Sulawesi are generally considered by scholars to belong to the first wave, and all other Indonesians, save the primitive peoples in the mountains and jungles, to the second. It is a curious fact that the earliest Indonesians, these so-called primitives, played no role on the stage of Indonesian history.[2] Time passed them by, leaving them as it found them. They are still there, living the life they lived thousands of years ago, retreating before the advancing thrusts of modern civilization to their own mountains and forests. Like the American Indian, they have been hostile to change. Unlike him, change has not yet been forced upon them. From the jungles of Sumatra through the wild mountains of Ceram to the rain forests of West Irian, I have seen many of them—strong, vigorous, well-muscled people, happy in the ways of their ancestors. I have met a head-hunter chief in West Irian, armed with a long bow and poisoned arrows as well as a wicked curved sword, a highly polished skull hanging from his neck.

Buchari's comment about a happy people is understandable to those who know Java for, despite the fact that the density of population in this beautiful island is one of the highest in the world, the fertile soil and the equable climate make it one of the most desirable places in the world to live. In the green valleys, towered over by equally green mountains upthrust by the restive giants beneath the earth, the Javanese people early organized one of the most concordant forms of government known to man.

The Javanese village was designed for harmony. It subsisted by acting as "one extended family."[3] The land on which the farmer worked was owned by the village and allotted to the villagers on the basis of shares distributed "as equitably as possible." The village claimed a small share of each farmer's produce to meet its communal requirements; the remainder he sold for what he could get.

2. Bernard H. M. Vlekke, *Nusantara, A History of Indonesia* (Chicago: Quadrangle Books, Inc., 1960), pp. 8–10.
3. Bienti Karmawan, "The Economy of Indonesia" (unpublished manuscript, 1967).

When fire, flood, earthquake, volcano or other disaster struck, the community reacted to the need. A house was rebuilt, a well repaired, a road fixed by the villagers, who donated their services spontaneously, without compensation. There is a word for this kind of cooperation in Indonesia—*gotong-rojong*. The philosophy of helping each other is still deeply embedded in the life of the Javanese villages. In Bali, which has a similar system, I once asked a villager what would happen if one member of the village failed to do his share. He looked at me strangely and said, "That would almost never happen."

"Why not?" I asked.

"Because every child is brought up to be a member of the village and learns to do his part from an early age. You see, a village is like a club, only it is a club that is necessary for survival. If a man is banished from his village, he has nowhere to go. No other village will accept him. He is literally an outcast. This is a terrible fate. That is why crime is almost unknown here."

"But can't a man go to a big city and get along?"

My friend nodded. "Yes, that is possible today. But you see, our people love their villages so much, love the idyllic life they lead, that this is a great hardship. A man's heart remains in his village. He needs a village to go back to."

Skeptics of the practicability of applying democracy in an Asian country like Indonesia will be surprised to know that traditionally in many parts of Indonesia, the *lurah*, who is the head of the village, is elected by the secret ballot of all those over eighteen who have lived continuously for a minimum of three months in the village. The ballots are in the form of palm-leaf ribs (*lidi*), and a bamboo tube serves as the ballot box.

There are few more heartwarming experiences than watching a Javanese village come to life. It has a pulse all its own. As the first rays of light spray skyward and the rooster crows, the bird kingdom suddenly awakes, not with a few chirps or the soothing sound of a flute startling the silences, as in the West, but in full chorus as if at the signal of a baton. And if the village be in dense jungle or rain forest, when the bird symphony ceases, the monkeys open up with their daily greeting of the miracle of the sunrise. Immediately the red sun breaks over the horizon, the chorus stops. For a moment, all is quiet as the awakened Moslems pray to the muezzin's call. Then the village is alive. Water splashes in a thousand homes. The lazy clop, clop of oxen hooves are muffled hammers moving toward the marketplace. The murmur of voices and the laughter of children start a rhythm of their own. People are on the streets, greeting each other gaily, with shining eyes and contagious smiles. This is Java, the home of a happy people blessed by Allah.

The Javanese village, or *desa*, includes not only the farmhouses, barns and community meeting places but also whatever fields, fishponds, forests and other areas are claimed by the village or its residents. It is thus not merely a place where people live; it is the entire productive community, embracing the means of production as well as the producers. Its unit is the family farm, including irrigated rice fields, a bamboo house, some cattle and poultry, a few fruit and fiber trees such as papaya, mango, guava, coconut and other palms, and kapok. The Javanese farmer is relatively self-sufficient. He has always needed the cooperation of his neighbors to manage the irrigation of his rice paddies, and from outside the village he requires metals for tools, and salt. As in the case of American pioneers, the great contribution of Javanese forebears was the clearing of the jungle and the building of the rice terraces. The Javanese are eternally grateful to these ancestors and invoke the "Grandfather Spirit" at the opening of most ceremonies.

The village is traditionally governed by a council of elders. But every member of the village is equal to every other member, and in that respect the system resembles the New England town meeting. One important distinction between Indonesian democracy and American democracy must be made, however. The Indonesian believes there is nothing sacred about a majority plus one. He therefore does not ordinarily put an issue to a vote; instead, the village council discusses it until there is what the head of the council of elders can proclaim without opposition as the consensus. The process is called *musjawarah*; the decision when reached unanimously is called *mufakat*. In Afro-Asian meetings in recent years, much has been heard of *musjawarah*, since the Indonesians have taken the lead in stressing that Afro-Asian decisions must be taken as a result of unanimity of view, a desirable although often difficult end to achieve.

And so life has gone on in Java for thousands of years, ever since man learned the art of the rice terrace and no longer had to roam, a life of peace and stability that survived war and famine.

Surrounded by magical beauty of land, sea, and sky, Indonesians felt close to God in nature, and accordingly their religion was originally animistic and mystic in character. It is not difficult to understand that the Indonesian would feel a presence behind all this beauty, that he first saw in every living thing a soul, or "life energy." Indeed, cannibalism and head-hunting had their origin in the attempt to possess the life energy of an enemy. The soul dwelt in the body throughout life, survived the body after death and customarily remained near the location of its bodily existence, continuing to take an interest in the affairs of the living.[4]

A special sacred character was attached to the great waringin, or banyan tree, which replants itself in the earth with its drooping branches and presumably never dies. These trees reach a great height, but even more impressive is their breadth. Tied to the earth by the umbilical cords of their branches, they appear to have one great trunk. In girth

---

4. Cf. Vlekke, *Nusantara*, pp. 14–15.

they may spread for thirty or forty feet. Powerful spirits dwell in these trees, which must never be cut down.[5]

Fifteen hundred years before Christ, Indonesian contacts with India brought Hinduism to the archipelago, with its belief that God and the universe are one and that the material world is an illusion to be dispelled in a manner as yet unrevealed. And Indonesia remained Hindu until the arrival of Buddhism, also from India, with its sevenfold path leading to enlightenment. It dominated Java and Sumatra from the fifth century to the fourteenth, at which time Islam took over as the major religion.

Of the islands, Bali alone remained Hindu. All of Java became Moslem except one interesting enclave in the highlands of West Java. The Baduis, deeply committed to their own austere religion, swore that they would never become Moslems. To ensure constancy of themselves and later generations, they built a wall around their village, and have so maintained their isolation since the fifteenth century.[6] In the course of time, to prevent overpopulation and for various other reasons, many members of the village have left. They are not allowed to return, but the village elders in some mysterious way keep track of major happenings to their people outside. One of my friends,[7] a member of a prominent Djakarta family whose progenitor had come from this village, told me the following.

Her father was very ill, and it appeared he had not long to live. The day before he died, there was a ring at the door. She answered it, to find five men dressed in Badui black. Before she had a chance to say anything, their leader asked anxiously, "Tell me, are we in time?" The young woman nodded soberly and answered, "Yes, you are in time." The

---

5. Animism has never been completely displaced in Indonesia. I knew one Western-educated Sundanese who, upon returning home, would park his car in the garage at night but never dream of entering his house and going to bed without saying a polite "Good night" to the two ghosts or spirits who inhabited the great waringin in his garden. Once a member of the family, in her hurry, forgot. She fell seriously ill the next day.

6. There is a story of a Dutch professor of anthropology who, armed with authorization from the Dutch government, attempted in the latter part of the nineteenth century to enter the village. When he reached the gate, he was refused admittance. When he showed the official papers he carried authorizing entry, he was strongly warned not to come in. He inquired whether the people would harm him. The Baduis said no, but still they insisted he not enter lest "something happen" to him. The professor did enter, and spent two weeks in the village, making copious notes on the customs. Two weeks after he left the village, and before he had an opportunity to transcribe his notes into writing, he died suddenly of a mysterious malady. Since then, no outsider has entered the village.

7. Wietje Djajadiningrat, daughter of Pangeran Aria Achmad Djajadiningrat. She is a direct descendant of a Badui leader who left the village in the seventeenth century to see the outside world.

men asked to see her father and spent several hours talking with him. He died the next morning, and the Baduis stayed for the funeral.

Now one of the strange customs of these people is that they will not use any modern form of technology. They reject all modern means of travel, and will not use the telephone, which they consider (and they may not be alone in their view) the invention of the devil. Thus my friend knew that they had walked more than 250 miles to reach the house. When the time came for them to depart, she said to them, "Would you please answer one question for me? How did you know that my father was ill?" "We have a series of jars representing each branch of the family that has gone out of the village," the Baduis replied. "We watch these jars, which are filled with water. When a jar suddenly becomes empty and the grass at the bottom of it turns black, we know that the head of one of the branches of the family is about to leave us. We try to be on time in order to pay our respects."

The Hindu religion as practiced in Badui country, or for that matter in Bali, would not be recognized by a Hindu from India.

The first time I visited a Hindu temple in Bali, one of my companions was the Indian Ambassador. He shook his head when he saw the Balinese altars, which are of plain stone with no images to worship. We watched a procession of beautiful Balinese girls marching erect with gilded towers of food, fruit and flowers on their heads. They went to the altar, deposited their burdens, and knelt in prayer for perhaps fifteen or twenty minutes. Then they arose, picked up the glittering towers of fruit and food in gold and silver wrappings, replaced them on their heads, and marched out.

"Where are they going, to another temple?" I asked a Balinese friend who was with us.

"No," he laughed, "they are going home to eat. After a holy day, they all have a feast."

"I don't understand," I said. "I thought these were offerings to the gods. But they take them home and eat them?"

My Balinese friend smiled patronizingly (thinking, no doubt, These stupid Americans!). "The gods, of course, are spiritual. They have no need for material sustenance. The offering is placed on the altar. The girls pray. When they feel deep inside themselves that their gift has been accepted and that the god has absorbed its essence, they have a sensation of exaltation and upliftment. Then they are free to leave. They return home and consume the material portion of it." I thought, What a practical religion!

These were offerings, not sacrifices. But when the wind blows too fiercely and the sea roars, when the god of the volcano rumbles and threatens, then the Balinese will make sacrifices to the gods—the god of the wind, the god of the sea, the god who lives in the volcano—sacrifices of fowl or pig, depending on the seriousness of the situation.

The offering to the gods is characteristic not only of Hindu Bali but also of Moslem Java. To understand the principle that the gods or spirits absorb the essence of an offering and not its material manifestation is to understand the *slametan*,[8] the ritual ceremony practiced throughout Indonesia.

As one Javanese described it, "At a *slametan* all kinds of invisible beings come and sit with us and they also eat the food. That is why the food and not the prayer is the heart of the *slametan*. The spirit eats the aroma of the food. It's like this banana. I smell it but it doesn't disappear. That is why the food is left for us after the spirit has already eaten it." [9] One might think of it as "the Javanese version of what is perhaps the world's most common religious ritual, the communal feast, and, as almost everywhere, it symbolizes the mystic and social unity of those participating in it." [10] Such a ceremony is held to celebrate any or all occasions, and is a must for important ones, like the dedication of a new building, a birth, or a harvest, in order that the spirits will be placated and the future harmonious.

Such old customs persist, and a Westerner must be ready to bow to them. A caribou head was ceremoniously planted in the foundation of the new American Embassy in Djakarta when I made a speech laying the cornerstone. There was also the case of the leaky swimming pool. William E. Palmer, a representative of the American motion-picture interests and beloved by Indonesians and Westerners alike, had a beautiful mountain bungalow in the Puntjak area of West Java. He decided that he wanted a swimming pool in his lovely garden and contracted for it to be built. Unfortunately, when the pool was finished, it would not hold water. Palmer called the contractor and had the pool rebuilt. A few days later, the pool was empty. Exasperated, he again called the contractor, who shook his head and assured him that this time he would certainly fix it. But again the pool was empty after a few days. At his wit's end, Palmer asked one of his servants what to do.

"I think you should ask the Hadji[11] to come," the servant replied. "Perhaps he can find out what's wrong." The Hadji! A religious man! Bill was incredulous but called for the Hadji. He came, spent some time in meditation by the pool, and returned to Palmer to report that it was "the little men. They're angry. They say there was no *slametan* when the pool was built, and they are insulted. They refuse to hold up the pool."

"So what do we do now?" asked Palmer.

---

8. Cf. Arthur Goodfriend, *Rice Roots* (New York: Simon and Schuster, 1958), pp. 65–70.
9. Clifford Geertz, *The Religion of Java* (Glencoe, Ill.: The Free Press, 1960), p. 15.
10. *Ibid.*, p. 11.
11. A religious leader who has made the pilgrimage to Mecca.

"I think if we have a *slametan* and plant the head of a rooster in each corner of the pool, then everything will be all right."

Palmer, though skeptical, gave the instructions. The *slametan* was duly held, the fowl sacrificed, the red-combed heads planted, the earth replaced. There was no further trouble with the pool; ten years later, it was still as good as new.

The faith of today's Indonesian, a devout and sincere believer in God, is built upon the layers of several religions; it is a strong and rich blend that serves him well and accounts for the depth of his convictions and his tolerance of other faiths and points of view. Islam came to Indonesia in the late thirteenth century. It was a gentle Islam, and it became a kind of veneer over the animism, Hinduism, and Buddhism preceding it. The Indonesians embraced Islam, softened as it was by the blending. The quality of love that had built the great Borobudur was transmitted to the new religion.

What has often been called "the Moslem invasion" was no invasion at all, in the usual sense of the word, but rather an import brought by the foreign trader—Indian, Persian, Arabian, Turk—along with the goods he had to sell. The simplicity of Islam, with its one God, its direct and personal relationship between God and man, the sense of man's equality before God, and its lack of a priestly hierarchy with special privileges, appealed to the Indonesians—especially to the kings of the islands. The concept of a god-king was indigenous to Indonesia; but a king who was also a sultan acquired religious authority in addition to his temporal power and, more important, a particular aura as the direct representative of the deity. Indeed, the first major conversion of a Javanese potentate occurred when the King of Mataram, who, as his empire expanded, had bestowed upon himself the title of "Susuhunan," or Emperor, embraced Islam and obtained a set of documents from the Caliphate of Turkey officially conferring upon him the title of "Sultan." Thus Islam had a political as well as a religious attraction for the early Indonesian rulers, particularly after the decline of the Madjapahit Empire, when rival kings and petty chieftains were endeavoring to consolidate their hold.

To the people, however—and the people in the fourteenth century were the peasants in the fields, except for a few artisans, clerks, traders and sailors—Islam carried a special message. There was only one God, and man was beholden only to him. A peasant could kneel and pray five times a day and know that he had just as much right to talk with God as the most powerful potentate in the land. To him, in a world full of gods and goddesses, good and evil, princes and potentates, the revelation of one all-powerful God to whom he was responsible for his deeds and with whom he could communicate directly, came as a new light in the heavens.

The Indonesian did not wholly desert his own traditions. Islam was a valued import, a garment, if you will, to be worn with or thrown over his traditional garments. Perhaps an understanding of Indonesia in religious, social and attitudinal terms can best be gained from the wajang, the age-old epic shadow play of Java. For it is from the wajang that the majority of Indonesians derive their sense of values, their feelings about right and wrong, their concepts of relationships with their fellow man, and finally, their mystical approach to communicating with the deity.[12] The all-pervasive influence of the mythology presented in the wajang may be appreciated when it is realized that, until the relatively recent arrival of the motion picture, the wajang play represented the major form of entertainment for all Indonesians, peasant and President alike. It was Sukarno's favorite form of amusement. He and his invited guests would sit enthralled at all-night performances.

The wajang was traditionally presented as a shadow play in which elaborately designed and beautifully decorated leather figures (wajang *kulit*) were manipulated behind a screen by the narrator (*dalang*). Eventually, two additional forms developed—the puppet play, in which magnificently carved, gilded and colored puppets (wajang *golek*) were seen on a miniature stage, and the wajang *orang*, in which men and women actors put on a standard theatrical performance, combining the drama of the epics with the classical Javanese dances that had developed out of the wajang and become an integral part of the art form.

The legends themselves represent a blend of the Indian Ramayana and Mahabharata with Indonesian prehistory. Although it has been generally assumed that the inclusion of the Indian epics signifies a separate influence in the wajang, the disposition of some modern scholars to believe that the Indian and Indonesian cultures had a common origin suggests that the wajang may have been part of the cultural heritage brought by the proto- or deutero-Malays from the ancestral home of the Aryans. Be that as it may, the wajang represents a complete set of mores and social values.

The wajang is fascinating in its glittering array of some 168 diverse characters. President Sukarno's favorite was the popular figure of Gatutkatja, with whom, I always felt, he tended to identify himself. Sukarno never tired of watching Gatutkatja's triumphs over his enemies with his remarkable combination of physical prowess, courage, and guile.

Instead of being brought up on Mother Goose, *Grimm's Fairy Tales*, or Snoopy, the young Indonesian lives and breathes the wajang. By the time he is fairly launched in school, he knows intimately the virtues and vices of every one of the characters, as well as the conflicts and complexities that enter into decisions they are required to make. These are no simple contests between good and evil, but a series of situations in which

---

12. For an interesting exploratory study of the wajang, see Benedict R. O'G. Anderson, *Mythology and the Tolerance of the Javanese* (Ithaca, N.Y.: Cornell Modern Indonesia Project, Monograph Series, 1965.)

a character has to choose what is for him the right thing to do—and this right thing varies with his station in life and the class to which he belongs.

I never saw a young Indonesian with an inferiority complex, and I think it is due to the fact that, as Anderson expresses it, the child growing up "is presented with a wide choice of models for his own personality, which he can be sure will win approval anywhere in Javanese society . . . both the heavily-built, active, but inarticulate boy and the delicately-boned, introspective child have acceptable ways in which their personalities and physical traits can evolve without unneccesary spiritual violence being done to them." [13]

The wajang is drama, tragedy, comedy and romance mingled in one grand epic. It even includes a generous element of political cabaret in the beloved comic figures, clowns who comment ironically, in current slang instead of old Javanese, on happenings of the day, poking fun at political figures from the President down. From these plays, the young Indonesian acquires the basis of his philosophy—in which the good and the beautiful are distinguishable from each other only insofar as they represent different "aspects of the appropriate or harmonious" [14]—and develops his personality.

The extent of involvement of Indonesian life and culture in the wajang may also be gauged by the dance, which is a part of the training of every well brought up Indonesian boy or girl. It is based on the wajang, and tends to develop not only an extraordinary physical grace, dignity of posture and sense of rhythm, but also an understanding of and identification with the characters enacted in the course of learning the dance. This is not social dancing, or even folk dancing, but a highly sophisticated, stylized art form deeply rooted in and symbolic of Indonesian tradition and culture. Each dance tells a story; its language is the intricate movements of fingers, hands, arms, shoulders, eyes, hips, feet and head.

Indonesia cannot be understood without some insights into the particular aspect of the Indonesian attitude toward life whereby existence on this planet is considered to be merely an interim, a wayside stop on a long journey. Man lived before mortal birth, and he continues to live after the experience called death. Indeed, the patience with which the Indonesian, the Indian, and other Asians put up with intolerable conditions of life traces back directly to their conviction (regardless of what creed they profess) that life after death will be better, that they will enter through "the gates" into spiritual bliss.

The Indonesian is deeply mystical. "The religious and cultural history

13. *Ibid.*, pp. 25–26.
14. *Ibid.*, p. 24.

of Java consists in the successive integration into its closed world of animistic magic of the spiritual techniques and occult formulas of each of
the religions that have come from the Asian continent: the cults of Shiva,
Vishnu, Buddha, and Mohammed. The successive 'conversions' of the
Javanese courts to the new religions . . . were never anything more
than adoptions of new rituals designed to win over the cosmic forces to
the side of the initiate." [15] This is well said but goes perhaps too far.
The Indonesian believes deeply in God. His occult trappings are carried
along with him as baggage, which he thinks helps him communicate
with the Infinite. When man-made problems defy solutions or burdens
become too great to bear, the Indonesian turns to the source of all wisdom and energy for solace or solution. Thus spiritual healing is not uncommon in Indonesia, which brings us to the *dukun*.

There are many gradations of *dukun*, varying from what we would
think of as witch doctors or conjurors of black magic to spiritual leaders
of a high order. The typical *dukun* uses herbs and incantations to accomplish physical healing; some accept payment for attempting to weave
a spell for good or ill.[16] A higher order uses water, as did John of the
Wilderness, in a kind of symbolic cleansing of the spirit. Other *dukuns*
simply pray, and do not deserve the somewhat belittling connotation
that frequently accompanies the term.[17]

I knew several Indonesian religious leaders of this higher order as
deeply spiritual, dedicated men—like Abdurachim, for instance, who
was known for years as Sukarno's spiritual adviser, and had hundreds of
physical healings to his credit.[18] I once asked him how often he prayed.
"Why," he answered, "I pray all the time. I'm praying right now!" As

---

15. Herbert Luethy, "Indonesia Confronted (II)" *Encounter*, vol. 26, no. 1
    (January 1966), p. 77.
16. Mysticism is often popularly identified with magic practices and occult
    phenomena, but this is an adulteration. True mysticism involves a close
    relation between man and the divine, its objective being unity with God.
    This is normally achieved by a kind of quietism or meditation involving
    extinction of human will and withdrawal from worldly interests and
    thoughts. Certain occult phenomena, however, represent offshoots or lower
    forms of mysticism, best known in the wizardry and necromancy of the
    Old Testament of the Bible but still practiced to some extent in Indonesia,
    India and other parts of Asia and the Middle East.
17. For a comprehensive discussion of this phase of Indonesian life, see Geertz,
    The Religion of Java, chapter 8.
18. As Sukarno turned his course leftward, he no longer consulted Abdurachim.
    When the latter was dying in 1966, he asked to see Sukarno once more.
    He was bedridden and had to be carried into the palace. He told the
    President he was embarked on the wrong course. He urged him to turn
    away from Communism and to work with Generals Suharto and Nasu-
    tion. Sukarno refused and stuck to the way that brought him down.
    Suharto, Indonesia's current President, also has a spiritual adviser whom
    he consults regularly.

was the case with spiritual leaders and prophets in the Bible, this man each year went up into the mountains for a period of prayer and fasting. His influence, I am sure, was entirely for good. He loved much.

Another experience that has to do with faith in God involved the wife of one of the ambassadors in the diplomatic corps in Djakarta. Critically ill, she could not eat, and was reduced to skin and bones. The doctors had given her up. One day she had a visitor, the wife of a prominent Indonesian diplomat, who said to her, "My father heals people through prayer. Would you be interested in having him help you?" The woman said she would try anything.

The father, who lived in Central Java, answered his daughter's letter by saying that although he could not come to Djakarta for several months, it did not matter because, "God's power is not limited by space. Tell me what is the trouble and I will pray." The ambassador's wife wrote to him. Three days later, as she described it to me, she suddenly began to feel better. There seemed to be a glow of light in the room where she lay in bed. She felt hungry, and that night she joined her amazed family for dinner. Within a week she was completely well.

Months later, I talked with the man who had healed her. "I don't heal," he said, "God heals. I simply pray."

Indonesia has always harbored within itself the seeds of a remarkably egalitarian spirit. Despite the economic ascendancy of the aristocracy, by the time of Sukarno and the Javanese leaders, Indonesian society was, within the simple framework of village activity, both a political and economic democracy. The people were not rich in the goods of this world; they had other riches. Their love for the life of the village was so strong that even when, in the course of time, problems of overpopulation and decreasing land pressed upon them, they could not move to neighboring islands where land was plentiful. The urge to find new horizons was not in them. They were content.

Content, that is, save for one thing: they were not free. For 300 years, they had been forced to submit to alien rule.

CHAPTER 2

The Legacy

But even in the midst of alien occupation, every Indonesian, whether prince or pauper, fawning courtier or sturdy farmer, soldier or sailor, teacher or trader, knew that he was the inheritor of an ancient culture that had had its own great period—indeed, periods—of empire before the white man came.

The first of these was the Sumatran-based Sriwidjaya Empire. "The development of a direct sea route to China by the beginning of the fifth century A.D. brought new importance to the southeast coast of Sumatra, which had long traded with India and Ceylon."[1] I Tsing, the famous Chinese Buddhist pilgrim, stopped there enroute to India. In 671 A.D., he spent six months at what had become a Mahayanist intellectual center and the seed of Buddhism, studying Sanskrit grammar before proceeding to India. In 685, he returned to Palembang, the principal port of South Sumatra, and "spent some four years there translating Buddhist texts from Sanskrit into Chinese." His comments, plus the discovery of a series of old Malayan inscriptions, confirmed the existence at Palembang "of a Buddhist kingdom which had just conquered the hinterland of Malayu and was about to attack Java."[2]

Thus, long before the Battle of Hastings, in 1066, the Sriwidjaya Empire in Sumatra dominated the stage of Southeast Asia in the seventh to ninth centuries. Seldom has the world seen a more brilliant collection of scholars than was gathered at the court in the city of Palembang. They came from China, India, Persia, and the Middle East; probably also from Greece and Rome, though their great days were past. The capital of this empire was known as a scintillating center of Buddhist scholarship. Here the great Buddhist leader of Tibet, Atisha, studied from 1011 to 1023 and received much of his inspiration and education. This

---

1. D. G. E. Hall, A *History of South-East Asia*, 3rd ed. (London: Macmillan & Co., 1968), p. 41.
2. *Ibid.*, p. 42.

empire is said to have enjoyed the perhaps dubious distinction of employing the first economist as consultant to an established government. This empire, too, the territory of which spanned approximately the same portion of the globe as that of its Javanese successor some four centuries later, contributed much to the perspective of past glory preserved in the hearts of Indonesians today; it is also responsible in part for the sense of unity that has enabled this archipelago to have achieved "*Bhinneka Tunggal Ika*," the "Unity in Diversity" that is its motto.

The reason for the decline of the Sriwidjaya Empire is a matter of speculation. Indeed, we do not know how the Sumatran dynasty came to control Java, but only that there were recurring quarrels between Javanese and Sumatran rulers, and that the Javanese vigorously resisted Sumatran rule.

The final blow to the power of the empire was delivered by the Indians in 1025. Details were recorded by the Chola ruler, Rajendra, in an inscription in Tanjore, India, in 1030. It reads in part:

> [Rajendra] having despatched many ships in the midst of the rolling sea and having caught . . . the king of Kadaram, together with the elephants in his glorious army, [took] the large heap of treasures which [that king] had rightfully accumulated; captured with noise [the arch] . . . at the war-gate of his extensive capital, Srivijawa, with a jewelled wicket-gate adorned with great splendour and the gate of large jewels. . . .[3]

While Sumatra was the center of Buddhist scholarly culture, Java under the Shailendra dynasty[4] became the artistic center. The great Buddhist monuments of the eighth and ninth centuries are the precursors of those at Angkor Wat in Cambodia by at least two centuries. The famous Borobudur temple, near Jogjakarta in Central Java, represents the highest expression of the artistic genius of the time and is a major cultural contribution and tourist attraction today. It is a beautiful and impressive stupa, rising 150 feet and crowning a great hill that commands the entire countryside. To read this textbook in stone requires a walk of more than three miles. The walls of the galleries are adorned with bas-reliefs illustrating the life of Buddha and the principles he taught. Mingled with Buddhist concepts are Shivaist figures, indicating clearly that the Javanese were digesting the two religions together. In addition to furnishing an impressive presentation of Buddhism, the

---

3. *Ibid.*, p. 58. Inscription dated 1030–31.
4. Vlekke writes, "The glory of the Shailendras lived on . . . in Javanese tradition. Ideologically all later Javanese rulers claimed to be the legitimate successors of the great Shailendra dynasty." See *Nusantara, A History of Indonesia* (Chicago: Quadrangle Books, Inc., 1960), p. 34.

monument also presents a remarkable picture of Javanese life and customs of the time.

The Borobudur is by no means the only artistic work of this sort. Sir Stamford Raffles wrote in about 1815, "In the whole course of my life I have never met with such stupendous and finished specimens of human labour, and of the science and taste of 'ages long since forgot.' " [5] He describes in detail the Hindu "Chandi Sewu," or "Thousand Temples," many of which have been restored in all their brooding beauty, and can be seen at Prambanan, near Surakarta in Central Java. And these are not the only outstanding artistic remnants of Hindu worship and culture. In Raffles' time, the whole of the plain was "covered with scattered ruins and large fragments of hewn stone . . . [where] traces of the site of nearly four hundred temples were discovered, having broad and extensive streets or roads running between them at right angles." [6]

And on the Dieng plateau, 6,000 feet up on the slopes of the Prahu mountain in Central Java, with stone staircases leading up the site, the Javanese in the seventh and eighth centuries constructed temples of classic simplicity dedicated to the Hindu god, Shiva.

Indonesia had its second period of glory in the Madjapahit Empire, based on the island of Java. From roughly 1293 to 1389,[7] the empire spread over much of Southeast Asia, rubbing shoulders with China on the north, apparently reaching to West New Guinea on the east. The unity of vast territories thus obtained must have had its own substantial influence on the development of the language that today is still spoken from the southern borders of Thailand to and including parts of New Guinea.

The rise of Madjapahit followed several centuries of struggle by one ruler after another for dominance over Java and the neighboring islands. Prior to the rise to power of the Buddhist house of Shailendra, which controlled the Sumatra-based Sriwidjaya Empire, only one King after Purnawarman is mentioned in inscriptions: Sanjaya, King of Mataram in 732, glorified in Sundanese legend as a great conqueror who united Bali, Sumatra, Cambodia, India, and even China.

Airlangga, King of East Java, was the first monarch after the Buddhist Shailendra dynasty to emerge as a definite figure on the Javanese historical horizon. His career was not unlike that of King Alfred of England. The son of a local Bali ruler, he endeavored to assume the throne of East Java, but resistance was too great and he spent years hiding in the jungle, living among the hermits. It was this experience that he credited with

---

5. Sir Stamford Raffles, *History of Java*, 2nd ed. (London: John Murray, 1830), vol. II, p. 16. See pp. 6–35 for Raffles' survey of the temples of Java.
6. *Ibid.*, p. 34
7. After the death of Ayam Wuruk, grandson of Madjapahit's founder, King Vijaya, the empire lost most of its significance.

providing him the magic force that ultimately brought him to power.[8]

Joyoboyo, King of Kadiri, next thrust himself into the pages of Indonesian history. It seems that Airlangga had two sons whom he loved equally. Personal considerations all too often motivate the acts and overpower the judgment of the otherwise great and wise. And Airlangga, moving against the needs of the time, which called for consolidation of principalities and the creation of larger entities of government, divided his kingdom into two parts, Kadiri and Janggala. Joyoboyo, a wise ruler who was credited with the gift of prophecy, was King of Kadiri from 1135 to 1157, and may have extended his power far beyond the boundaries of the kingdom, but of this we have no certain knowledge. We do know that he arranged for the famous Indian epic, the Bharatayuddha (a part of the Mahabharata) to be translated into Javanese.[9] His fame, however, rests upon his prophecies, of which more will be discussed later.

Kadiri yielded its supremacy to Singhasari in the first half of the thirteenth century, when its last King was defeated by an extraordinary character named Angrok. Javanese history in this period is an interesting combination of fact and legend in which the gods play, as in Greek history, an important role.

Angrok, it seems, rose from not merely a humble but a criminal background. The story goes that he offered himself as a sacrifice to the gods, hoping to improve his position in life. The gods accepted his proposition, and from that moment his fortunes altered dramatically. He fell in love with the Queen of Singhasari and promptly arranged to kill the King. The method of assassination was as ingenious as it was shameful. He ordered a powerful sword made, then lent it to a friend, who was very proud of it and showed it everywhere. Angrok secretly retrieved it, murdered the King and left the sword in the body. The friend was executed as the killer, Angrok married the Queen and became King.

He made one serious mistake, however. The smith who made the sword was not a fast enough workman to suit Angrok, and he, impatient at the delay, slew the smith with the sword. The dying smith put a curse on the sword: "Through this sword your children and grand children shall die. Seven kings shall die by this single sword." The curse was fulfilled. Angrok himself was slain by the stepson of the King he had murdered, and this young man became the next King to fall.[10]

The last King of the Javanese kingdom of Singhasari, Kertanagara (1268-1292), steps into the pages of history because it was he who in effect thumbed his nose at the great Khan and brought the Mongol forces

---

8. Vlekke, *Nusantara*, pp. 44–45. Cf. Hall, *South-East Asia*, pp. 69–71.

9. Vlekke, pp. 47–50.

10. *Ibid.*, pp. 54–57.

pouring into Java. The invasion would never have taken place had it not been for Kertanagara's rash and unnecessary insult.

The first Westerner to reach Indonesia mounts the stage for a brief moment at this point. Marco Polo visited northeastern Sumatra in 1292 as the ambassador of Kublai Khan. He was unfavorably impressed by the cannibals he found there and advised the Khan not to bother with Java. The Khan nevertheless sent emissaries to Southeast Asia to accept homage from the rulers of the area. When his envoys reached Singhasari, Kertanagara arrested them and "sent them home with mutilated faces." [11] Such an insult was not one to be taken lightly, and the Khan mounted an expedition of 1,000 ships and 20,000 soldiers to demand satisfaction. By the time his army reached Java, the man he was after, Kertanagara, was dead, killed by the King of Kadiri, his ancient rival.

A young prince of the royal blood of Singhasari, Vijaya, outwitted both the King of Kadiri and the Chinese invaders. He offered his help to the Chinese on righting the wrong, with the result that they invaded and destroyed Kadiri. Vijaya in turn managed to escape from the Chinese, and organized a guerrilla force against them.

The Khan's generals, who had never intended permanent occupation of the country, concluded that, having avenged their emperor, they could withdraw with honor, neatly disregarding the ironic fact that the King they had destroyed had killed the malefactor, and that by withdrawal they were restoring the dynasty of the ruler who had caused the trouble in the first place.[12] One year after Polo's visit and shortly following the exodus of the Khan's army, Prince Vijaya established himself on the throne of what was to become the Madjapahit Empire.

Among Marco Polo's comments about Sumatra is the interesting report that the people living in the town of Perlak on the northern tip of Sumatra "had been converted to Islam," apparently the first such conversion. It is known that at about the same time there were Chinese settlements in Indonesia, some of them undoubtedly established by soldiers from the Khan's army who, impressed with the country, elected to remain.[13] Thus the arrival of the first European in Indonesia, the beginnings of the Islamic takeover of the country, and the early Chinese settlements marked the emergence and convergence of the major non-Indonesian forces that would influence the future of the country for centuries after the Madjapahit Empire had ceased to be.

As Bismarck was the real creator of Kaiser Wilhelm's powerful Germany of World War I, so was Gadja Mada the real architect of the Madjapahit Empire. Gadja Mada was an officer of the royal bodyguard.

---

11. *Ibid.*, p. 64.
12. *Ibid.*, pp. 65–66.
13. *Ibid.*, pp. 67–68.

Singlehanded, he is reputed to have quelled a rebellion among the soldiers of the guard and saved King Vijaya's son, Jayanagara (1309-1328). His reward was promotion to Prime Minister in 1331.

Gadja Mada swore he would not participate in *palapa*, probably the pleasant and sensual Tantrist rites introduced by Kertanagara, until the realm had been restored to its past glory. Scorn and ridicule by the courtiers for what they considered vain boasting only made him more determined. After years of combat and intrigue, Gadja Mada succeeded in his ambition, embracing a long list of vassal states of Madjapahit, including Bali, Sumatra, Borneo, Makassar, Timor, and the Moluccas. Palembang was also conquered and placed under Madjapahit rule, but was not allowed to exist as a vassal state. Instead, it was made into a province and governed by Javanese representatives.

In the process of building an empire, the Javanese incurred the undying enmity of the Sundanese, who made up the major population of West Java, by an action that is still remembered with anger today. Young King Ayam Wuruk wanted to marry the beautiful daughter of the King of Sunda. The latter was agreeable, assuming his daughter was to be the official Queen of this prestigious monarch. But the Prime Minister informed the Sundanese King that his daughter would merely be accepted as a gift to the royal harem, a tribute from a vassal to his overlord. The Sundanese proudly refused, and and a battle ensued in which the King of Sunda and all his retinue were slaughtered.[14]

The measure of a great statesman is not the territory he conquers but what he does with it. Gadja Mada made a general survey of laws and customs and codified them. He established rules for internal administration; district chiefs and village elders were exhorted to:

> Serve faithfully your Lord and King! Take care to neglect nothing that may add to the welfare of your district; take good care of the bridges, the roads, the *waringins*, the houses, and the sacred monuments, so that our ricefields and all that is planted may flourish, be protected, and well tended. Look after the dikes of the *sawahs*, so that the draining water does not run off and the people have to leave for better sites.[15]

Madjapahit had become one of the great powers of Asia. It had diplomatic relations with China, Champa, Cambodia, Annam and Siam. Its court was brilliant and luxurious. The royal stables were filled with horses, elephants, oxen, and "assorted exotic animals." In the royal plaza the King held great banquets for thousands of his followers. Court jesters sang and danced. Even the King participated in the entertainment.[16]

In terms of broad economic and social development, Java in 1300 was

---

14. *Ibid.*, pp. 68–71.
15. *Ibid.*, p. 77.
16. *Ibid.*, pp. 72, 77–79.

centuries ahead of Europe. The individual farmer did not appear as the basic economic unit of Europe until the beginning of the Middle Ages, after the breakup of the Roman Empire and the consequent splitting up of the large estates tilled by slave labor. Long before the time of Madja-pahit, however, Java had a strong peasantry and the beginnings of a middle class.

The Hindu priests were the custodians of all that was precious in Javanese history and culture. The Brahmins were more often than not the poets, architects, engineers, painters, physicians, scientists. The same could be said of the Buddhist priesthood in Sumatra.

Economically, however, Sumatra was different. The early settlers in this large island found their wealth not in rice paddies but in the hills and jungles. They located gold and tin, found pepper growing wild, elephants in the jungles, valuable for their ivory, and timber in apparently limitless quantities. The Sumatrans became traders and seafarers. The market was their life, and they built and lived in cities. Their labor was slave labor. This was not true of Java. The aristocracy of Java owned slaves, but slavery was not the basis of their agriculture.

The history of the two Indonesian empires is a vital part of the psychological heritage of the Indonesian. Tradition is an important priestess at the altar of national pride; if a nation lacks tradition, it perforce must create one. Indonesia, however, has a great tradition. Again and again during my tenure there, various actions of national consequence were to seem bizarre by Western standards; the recollection of Indonesia's past furnished me with insights and explanations that informed my mind and steadied my course.

CHAPTER 3

The White Buffalo

Joyoboyo, King of Kadiri in the twelfth century, was known for his gift of prophecy. According to Javanese legend, he predicted that a white buffalo will come to rule Java and will remain for a long time; he will be supplanted by a yellow monkey who will remain only the time it takes maize to ripen; then, Java, after a period of chaos, will come back to its own people.[1]

The white buffalo came to Indonesia in the fifteenth century. In the time of the great search for a short-cut to the Indies, contact between the brown man of Indonesia and the white man resulted from the great Portuguese voyages of exploration—save for occasional intrepid travelers such as Marco Polo. Riches in spice and silk were the prize. Vasco da Gama and Francis Magellan came close but did not quite make a landfall. Neither did Columbus.[2] But now, a certain white man, the first to land on the shores of Indonesia, sailed under a favorable wind and was

---

1. Various versions of this myth exist. This is the most popular; it appeared in a pamphlet issued in the Indonesian language and widely circulated during the Japanese period. There is some reason to believe that the legend was an eighteenth-century creation ascribed to Joyoboyo to lend color and authenticity to its message that the Dutch would not forever remain in Indonesia.

2. History records that the new continent was named America after Americus Vespucius, but they think differently in that part of the world where white and brown first met. I met the Sultan of Bone in Pari-Pari, in the Buginese area of Sulawesi. He was a knowledgeable patriarch of eighty-five who said he was glad to meet an American—and thought I might be interested in the real origin of my country's name. For thousands of years, long before the beginning of written history, the sailors of Bugi had whistled up a favorable wind by crying out to the elements an appealing call, like the cry of a sea gull, "Ameriki, Ameriki." And the god of the skies would answer. So "America" means "favorable wind." The Portuguese explorers brought the expression back from their travels. Columbus used it as he approached the strange shores of an unknown land, and so America was named. Thus spoke the Sultan.

borne along that exquisite necklace of islands that make up the Moluccas, the famous Spice Islands of Eastern Indonesia. Antonio d'Abreu, under instructions from Albuquerque, the Portuguese explorer who had occupied Malacca in 1511, "to do everything possible to establish friendly relations with the islands, and to observe the customs of the people," visited the Moluccas in 1511 and 1513. He established relations with the islands' rulers; in many cases, he claimed territory in the name of Portugal or secured a monopoly of the spice trade by treaty.[3] But the claims were short-lived. In the course of a century-long competition for the spice trade, the Spanish moved into the Philippines. King Philip II took over both Portugal and the Moluccas in 1580.

The British and the Dutch were late-comers to the colonial feast. They had been preoccupied with resisting the ambitions of a Spain bent on conquest. The defeat of the Spanish Armada in 1588 freed both nations to enter the competition for the silks and spices of the Orient.

At the same time, the Dutch were far ahead of the British in shipping and trade; but despite this superiority, the British beat them to the Spice Islands. Sir Francis Drake, sailing for Queen Elizabeth I, brought England directly into conflict with the Portuguese when he landed at Ternate in the Moluccas in late 1579 or early 1580. He was warmly welcomed by the Sultan of Ternate, who was in the midst of war with the Portuguese. The Sultan sold Drake several tons of cloves and promised that other English traders would have the right to buy spices.

The Dutch, meanwhile having found their way around Africa, followed closely on the heels of the British. In 1595, four ships, with crews totaling 249 men under the command of Cornelis de Houtman,[4] set out on a voyage that was to take more than a year and a heavy toll in lives. Sailing along the north coast of Java, they visited the town of Sunda Kalapa, or Jacarta, later to be settled by the Dutch as their capital in Indonesia.

The Dutch and British, at this point friendly competitors because of their cooperation in Europe, intensified their efforts to establish trade with the East when Mediterranean and Atlantic Portuguese ports were closed to them by the Spanish takeover of Portugal. The latter, unable to

---

3. D. G. E. Hall, A *History of South-East Asia*, 3rd ed. (London: Macmillan & Co., 1968), pp. 240–243.
4. Bernard H. M. Vlekke, *Nusantara, A History of Indonesia* (Chicago: Quadrangle Books, Inc., 1960), pp. 107–108. Vlekke describes de Houtman's background as follows: "This Cornelis de Houtman had spent many years in Lisbon. He pretended to be well informed on all matters relating to the Indies and to know everything about the navigation of the Eastern waters. On his two trips to the Indies he proved to be a boaster and a ruffian. Nevertheless, he had succeeded in obtaining the support of a group of wealthy merchants in Amsterdam. These merchants had equipped the first expedition to Indonesia." The second expedition left Holland in 1598, and was closely followed by expeditions financed by other groups of merchants.

defend herself, and with the Spanish unwilling to help, lost most of its empire in the East between 1600 and 1640 to Britain and Holland. After the defeat of the Armada, Spain settled for control of the Philippines.

In 1602, the United East India Company was formed and given by Dutch law a right to sovereignty over the Indonesian islands and "a monopoly over all commerce in Asia." [5] In 1618, Jan Pieterszoon Coen, who is responsible for laying the foundation of the Dutch colonial empire in Indonesia, was appointed Governor-General; by the following year he had established the headquarters of the Dutch East India Company in Jacarta (renamed Batavia by the Dutch).

Coen was ambitious for the Company's interests, which he felt could be best secured by the establishment of Dutch settlements. He planned to obtain possession of key territories such as Ambon and Banda in the Moluccas, establish a fortified port in Jacarta, and drive out not only the British from Indonesian waters but also the Spanish and Portuguese from the China Sea by conquering Manila and Macao. Coen envisaged a great commercial empire with its capital in Batavia, and he had the determination to see it through. His brutal and impatient character can best be seen by his own communication with the Company headquarters in Amsterdam: "I swear that no enemies do our cause more harm than the ignorance and stupidity existing among you, gentlemen!" [6]

Such a man naturally aroused violent opposition. His detractors sarcastically wrote, "Is it the intention to possess all trade and shipping and even all agriculture in the Indies? If so, how will the Indians be able to make a living? Will you kill them or starve them? You would not find any profit in it, for on empty seas, in empty countries and with dead people little profit can be earned." [7] The point is interesting as a clear demonstration that at this stage, the relation with Indonesia was in no sense a colonial one.

To hold his fortress at Batavia, Coen had to fight off the British by sea, the Prince of Jacarta and the King of Bantam by land. Desperate, he sailed to the Moluccas for reinforcements. Luckily for him, his enemies fell out among themselves, and when Coen returned, he found the Dutch still holding out in the fortress. Two days later, in May 1619, he launched a successful attack on the town of Jacarta, burned it down, and ordered the construction of a new and larger fortress. When this was finished, he built a carbon copy of a Dutch town, with canals and bridges, in the swampy land of what is now the capital of Indonesia.

The Molucca Islands were next on his list. His objective was complete domination of the Banda Islands, with a monopoly of the nutmeg and clove trade. The Bandanese, guessing his purpose when he put his troops

---

5. *Ibid.*, pp. 118–119.
6. *Ibid.*, p. 139.
7. *Ibid.*, p. 137.

ashore, resisted valiantly but in vain: Coen's men were merciless, and the little population was almost exterminated.

This brutal action again aroused criticism in Amsterdam. One ex-officer of the Company wrote, "We should realize that the Bandanese fought for the freedom of their country, in exactly the same way as we have done in Holland for so many years. Greater justice could have been done towards them . . . But that was not permitted, some people wanted to have their name recorded and remembered to the end of all times. Posterity, however, will condemn them as the Spaniards have been condemned for their cruelty in the West Indies . . . Things are carried on in such a criminal and murderous way that the blood of the poor people cries to heaven for revenge." [8]

Sultan Agung of Mataram, who regarded himself as the legitimate successor of the Madjapahit Empire, launched attack after attack upon Batavia, but without success. The Javanese were not beaten in battle but were starved out. The Sultan could not transport sufficient food overland through the dense jungles to maintain his forces, and when he tried to send supplies by ship, his rice-laden vessels were sunk by the Dutch.

The conflict between the Dutch and the British throughout Indonesia over control of the lucrative spice trade lasted until the Massacre of Ambon in 1623, when the Dutch Governor of the island had ten Englishmen put to death.[9] This ended the British attempts to gain a share in the spice trade; from then on, they were to concentrate on building up their position in India.

Coen died in 1629, but his ambitious program was carried on by his successors. They moved against the Portuguese and in 1641 captured Malacca, their last stronghold in the area. The Dutch were now the undisputed masters of the Indonesian seas. With the exception of the period of the Napoleonic Wars, from 1812 to 1816, when the British moved against the Dutch and occupied Java, the Dutch held exclusive possession of Indonesia until the outbreak of World War II.

Part of the Dutch technique to dominate Indonesia was the vicious *idjon* system, by which money was advanced to producers at planting time to purchase harvests yet to come, naturally at low prices. As the hapless farmers fell more and more into debt, the Company moved in, confiscated the plantations, and reduced the heretofore independent farmers to a virtual state of bondage. Not content with that, the Company, bribing the Sultan of Ternate to keep his eyes closed, forced the small proprietors outside its own territory to destroy their clove-tree gardens and instead plant rice and sago palms to provide food. This was impractical in these small mountainous islands, so the Company then sold imported rice to the inhabitants. Caught between the high prices

---

8. *Ibid.*, p. 141.
9. Cf. Hall, *South-East Asia*, p .310.

charged them for rice and the low prices the Company paid for spices and other products, the once thriving population was gradually squeezed into poverty.[10] By the middle of the seventeenth century, Coen's dream of an Asian commercial empire based in Jacarta had been well nigh realized. The Company controlled the trade in cinnamon and cloth of India, Japanese copper, sugar from China, Persian silk, and spices from the Moluccas.[11] Guilders flowed into Amsterdam. Holland became the mistress of the eastern seas and the banker of Europe.

Although the objectives of the Dutch East India Company did not include colonization, internal pressures, conspiracies, and attacks against its outposts forced the Company to seek internal allies and actively participate in military campaigns in an effort to divide and conquer. It was only a matter of time before the Indonesian Susuhunan at Mataram had become practically a vassal of the Dutch—the same kingdom to which the Dutch had been paying tribute only a few years earlier.

In Java and Sumatra, the Company's policies were not so ruthless as in the Moluccas—there was no wholesale slaughter of peasants—but the effect was almost as serious in that "merchants and ship-builders lost their occupation, and the fisheries and forests were no longer profitable. The Javanese became a people of cultivators, and the economic content of their social life was stunted." [12]

It was only a step now to full-fledged colonialism. From 1680 on, the Dutch controlled Indonesia and treated it as a colony, although it was not until 1799 that the demise of the Dutch East India Company led to direct control of Indonesia by the Netherlands government.

Practices developed that imposed increasingly heavy burdens upon the peasantry. Appanage was one evil custom. A lord would grant authority over a certain area to a relative or friend, who in turn "leased his rights over the area to another Indonesian or to a Chinese." [13] In areas controlled by the Company, Indonesian or Chinese subordinates would be appointed with similar authority. Increasingly unreasonable demands were made upon the peasants. They were, for example, forced to make deliveries of a large portion of their crops and "to perform nonagricultural forced labor on an extensive scale." [14] What this came to was that the village, which heretofore had been able to market all the crops raised by its farmers, was allowed to keep "just enough of its produce to sustain its inhabitants as a labor force." [15]

10. Vlekke, *Nusantara*, pp. 158–159.
11. *Ibid.*, pp. 159–160.
12. J. S. Furnivall, *Netherlands India, A Study of Plural Economy* (Cambridge: At the University Press, 1944), pp. 43–44.
13. George McTurnan Kahin, *Nationalism and Revolution in Indonesia*, 3rd printing (Ithaca, N.Y.: Cornell University Press, 1955), p. 6.
14. *Ibid.*, p. 7.
15. *Ibid.*

The Chinese were extensively utilized by the Company as cat's-paws; it contracted with Chinese for the collection of taxes, for which a commission based on a percentage of the amount collected would be paid. This practice extended to road tolls, bazaar fees, the collection of customs duties. The Chinese ultimately dominated the internal commerce of Java, acting as both distributors and the moneylenders. It was only a matter of time until there were few if any small independent farmers left in Indonesia. They were in perpetual debt to the Chinese, who either charged usurious interest rates or bought the crops cheaply before they were planted, or both. The perniciousness of this system was such that once held in its clutches, a farmer could never free himself. A Chinese would buy his crop before planting. This money would finance the purchase of seed and support him and his family through the growing season. But at the end of the growing season, his crop taken by the Chinese, he would have to borrow money to live until the next crop could be planted and sold in advance.[16]

Inevitably, the standard of living of the average Indonesian dropped steadily from the entry of Europeans on the scene in the sixteenth century to independence in 1949. The character of the society was gradually altered, becoming more authoritarian. The strength and economic independence of the peasantry was undermined to such an extent that many of the farmers became little more than serfs. Finally, the beginnings of a middle class were gradually annihilated by the Dutch monopoly of all trade and commerce and by their internal economic policies.

The policy of the Company, and the policy of the Netherlands government after it had taken over from the Company, was to rule feudalistically through the aristocracy. With Dutch guns behind them, members of the aristocracy had a previously unknown control over the people within their territory. More and more, they ruled not in their own right, but as agents of a foreign power. In this way colonialism in Indonesia produced feudalism.[17]

Through the long centuries, one reprieve from that system came about as a result of the Napoleonic Wars. When Napoleon's armies overran the Netherlands, and Holland thus became an enemy of England, the British navy moved in to cut off the resources of Indonesia and frustrate the plans of the ambitious Corsican to encircle India. At that point, the British redcoats marched into the capital of Indonesia to receive the surrender of the Dutch commander—and one of the most romantic and colorful figures in Indonesia's long history strode in with them.

---

16. W. J. Cator, *The Economic Position of the Chinese in the Netherlands Indies* (Oxford: Kemp Hall Press Ltd., 1936).
17. Cf. Kahin, *Nationalism and Revolution*, chapter 1. I agree with Kahin that it was a completely different sort of feudalism than was experienced in Europe.

From 1811 to 1816, Sir Stamford Raffles was to be British Lieutenant-Governor of Java and introduce reforms that would make the Indonesians sing his praises ever after. He was a determined young man of thirty, with burning ambition and a history of passionate interest in Indonesia.

Starting his meteoric career with the British East India Company's London offices as a clerk at the age of fourteen, he was sent to the new settlement of Penang, in Malaya, in 1805 as assistant secretary. He made quite an impression when, shortly after his arrival, he was found speaking the Malayan language fluently—he had studied intensively on the outward voyage. With this advantage, he soon became an expert on Malayan history and culture, a rare thing for those times.[18]

On August 31, 1810, Lord Minto, the Governor-General of India, received a communication from the board of the British East India Company confirming his view "as to the expediency of endeavouring to expel the enemy from their settlement in the Island of Java, and from every other place which they may occupy in the Eastern Seas." [19] He sent for Raffles, of whom he had heard from Dr. John Leyden, his colleague and also a Malayphile.[20] Minto and Raffles had entirely different ideas of the purpose of British occupation of Java. The British government had no interest in the inhabitants and still less in the island, having no intention of permanent occupation. Not so Raffles. Both he and Leyden were imbued with the idea that Dutch rule in the East was "utterly pernicious," and should be replaced by British "justice, humanity and moderation" to provide a better life for the Indonesians.[21] And Raffles set about to do just that.

As soon as British authority had been established in the area, he moved fast to introduce a general tax on land to replace all the forced labor and deliveries of the Dutch system. The tax was levied not on individuals but on villages (desas), and varied according to the productivity of the land. The peasant's crops were his own, to dispose of as he pleased, and he could pay his tax in either money or rice. Thus, in one stroke, Raffles freed the Javanese farmer from the burdens he had been carrying for nearly 200 years.

However, since part of Raffles' objective was to induce the British government to keep Java, he knew that he would have to demonstrate that occupation of it was a paying proposition. For this he needed coffee, and could not take the chance of altering the deeply rooted system by which coffee was grown. It was Raffles' ace in the hole. When war was over, a boom in coffee from Java was anticipated. If he could sell his at

---

18. Hall, *South-East Asia*, p. 479.
19. Vlekke, *Nusantara*, p. 255.
20. Hall, *South-East Asia*, p. 479.
21. *Ibid.*, p. 480.

high prices on the world market, he had a chance of achieving his objective.

His other reforms were legion. He took steps toward the abolition of slavery, abolished torture in the judicial process, reorganized the administration of the area, restored the Borobudur—and wrote a two-volume *History of Java*, still the best history in the English language. But dreaming his dream of substituting British humanity for Dutch cruelty, Raffles ran headlong into the policy of his government under Lord Castlereagh: to create a strong Netherlands as a barrier to further French aggression on the continent, Napoleon or no Napoleon. When the war ended and Napoleon was banished to Elba, the Netherlands again became an independent country. Meanwhile, the British government had signed a convention in 1814 promising to restore Java to Holland, which was done in 1816, much to Raffles' dismay. But he was not the kind of man to give up. He long pestered his government to retain a foothold on Sumatra, and when that failed, he moved into an unlikely-looking jungle off the tip of the Malayan coast. It turned out he had founded Singapore.

It was not long after the Dutch returned to Indonesia that the worst abuses of the old Dutch East India Company were reinstated, albeit this time under a new name, the "Culture System." It was "in many ways . . . the old system of forced deliveries and contingencies with a new look." [22] However, with the improvement of communications, the good burghers of Holland began to hear about the intolerable situation of the Indonesian people under Dutch rule. The voice that prodded their Calvinist conscience and sense of justice was in the form of a novel by Edward Douwes Dekker, a former Dutch official in Indonesia. *Max Havelaar, Or the Coffee Auctions of the Dutch Trading Company* (1861), presumably largely autobiographical, told the story of a well-motivated official whose efforts to stop the exploitation of the peasants were blocked at every turn by his white superiors.

Dekker's words echoed through Holland. Press, Parliament, and the public took up the cry for reform. The year before his book was published, the Dutch Parliament had banned slavery in the Indies. The King's power was no longer absolute, for in 1848 a new constitution had been wrested from royalty, and Parliament had acquired powers that it was beginning to employ with some effect. A new attitude on the part of Dutch business helped the reformers. Indonesian markets had moved closer to Dutch suppliers and stirred a new kind of interest in the colony on the equator. Henceforth, Indonesia would be seen as not only the producer of raw materials and scarce consumer goods but a prospective customer.

In 1862, a year after Dekker's book was published, the Dutch government decided to end the Culture System. One by one, state agricultural

---

22. *Ibid.*, p. 546.

monopolies were abolished. However, government domination of the sugar industry held on until 1890, state coffee cultivation until 1917.

Dekker watched the trend of events at first with satisfaction, and then with growing alarm. Suddenly he saw that free enterprise and free labor, unrestricted, could bring abuses greater than the old system, as the state monopolies passed into private hands. Wealthy Europeans would quickly snatch up Indonesian land. Indonesia could become a country of landless peasants. Fearing that his novel might have done his beloved peasants more harm than good, he rushed into print a pamphlet, *Once More Free Labor,* pointing out the dangers and urging legislation to ensure that no one could deprive the peasants of their land.

The liberals and the reformers won. Agrarian laws were passed that protected the small farmer. If he cleared jungle land, it became his. Individual land holdings in Java rose from forty-seven per cent of the total farmed acreage in 1882 to eighty-three per cent in 1932.[23]

The restoration of title to land, however, was relatively meaningless unless the opportunity for improvement in living standards accompanied it. True, if one owns a piece of land that he is not permitted to sell (in order to protect him from foreign exploiters) or borrow money on, there is still some psychological satisfaction in being owner instead of tenant, but it does not pay bills. The Indonesian peasant continued to work not for himself but for the moneylender, and was eternally in debt.

In 1901, Queen Wilhelmina announced the "Ethical Policy," designed to remedy this evil by making credit facilities available to the peasant; but they were far from adequate and the evils persisted. Holland began to contribute approximately 40,000,000 guilders a year for the "amelioration of economic conditions in Java and Madura." [24] That the reaction to practices in Indonesia should have gone this far was a tribute to the Dutch conscience, but it came too late.

The impact of colonialism upon society in Indonesia was generally similar to its impact elsewhere in Asia. The gaps in the rather rigid social structure between the royal aristocracy on the one hand and the peasantry on the other widened as the peasants' position deteriorated. The development of urban centers became more extensive after the establishment of large-scale enterprises by Western initiative. This in turn led to what has been termed a plural society, in which both labor and wealth are divided along racial and ethnic lines.

Contributing to this division were not only European elements but Chinese. From an early period, the Chinese had come as scholars, traders, and, in the greatest numbers, as common laborers. They settled in North Borneo and were industrious, enterprising, well-behaved, law-

---

23. Louis Fischer, *The Story of Indonesia* (New York: Harper & Brothers, 1959), pp. 45–48.
24. *Ibid.,* p. 49.

abiding people. Their immigration was encouraged by the Dutch. Before long, they had worked their way up the economic ladder to become the retailers, wholesalers and moneylenders of Indonesia. Owing in large part to their success at trade and finance, they became a separate cultural enclave in Indonesian society. As time went on, the Dutch more and more used the Chinese as their go-betweens, replacing the Indonesian aristocracy. Ultimately, this was to cause problems for the Chinese, who, as tax collectors and moneylenders, became a hated group.

There were other ways in which the Indonesian became a second-class citizen in his own country. Such colleges and universities as existed in the country were for the education of the sons of the Dutch. There were exceptions: the sons of the sultans and princes who cooperated with the colonial power were permitted to go to Holland to be educated; but their experience was uniformly the same. As one of my friends expressed it, "A Dutch education turned us into Dutchmen. It took years of being pushed around after we returned to our own country to turn us into Indonesians again."

For even an educated Indonesian had no future. "I could not get a job," my friend explained, "not because I was uneducated, but because I was educated! All the jobs for which I was qualified were held by Dutchmen." This man was a lawyer. He finally eked out a meager living by being appointed by the court to represent defendants who had no money to pay a lawyer. Three years after he had returned to his country, embittered and disillusioned, he lost his faith in the Dutch and joined the independence movement.

When I first arrived in Indonesia in 1954, the Indonesian peasant was still suffering from the impact of the colonial past.

"Let me tell you what happened to an uncle of mine," one Indonesian Cabinet minister told me in the days when the Communist Party was making striking inroads among the peasantry as well as the workers.

"It was at planting time, and my uncle was wondering where he could borrow the money to buy his seed. A man stopped by his small farm, talked a while, asked him if he had any problems. My uncle shrugged his shoulders. 'The usual ones,' he replied.

" 'How much money do you need?' the man asked. My uncle told him.

" 'Don't do anything for a few days. Wait until I come back,' the man said.

"Several days later he returned. 'I've got the money you need,' he told my uncle. 'I will loan it to you at five per cent interest.' This was at a time when interest rates were running as high as forty per cent—if you could borrow money at all. The only other recourse was the infamous *idjon* system.

"My uncle was overjoyed. For the first time in generations he would be out of debt at the end of the crop season. It turned out that his saviour was a representative of the Communist Party. What do you think my uncle did? He joined the Communist Party!"

Such was the time of the white buffalo in Indonesia. It taught me how deep were the wellsprings of Indonesia's urge for independence.

CHAPTER 4

From Berlin to Djakarta

The conquest of the China mainland by the Communists in 1949 was the single most significant political development on the international scene since World War II. It had immediate repercussions upon American policy, beginning an involvement in Asia that was to preoccupy America from that time forward and shift our immediate concern from West to East. The Marshall Plan had saved Europe. Communist pressure on Berlin had been withstood. The Communist drive to take over Greece had been thrown back. Now new urgencies were developing in Asia as the Communists probed for soft spots following their victory on the Chinese mainland.

Henceforth Asia, not Europe, would be the principal focus of our aid programs. The objective would be containment of Communist China by assisting the nations of Asia in maintaining their independence. These developments brought about a prompt movement to Asia of personnel who had been involved in the cold war in Europe. I was among the group moved from Europe to the new front line in the world conflict.

By 1954, after lengthy postwar experience in West Germany and two and a half years as Deputy Chief of Mission, part of the time as chargé d'affaires, in the American Embassy in Taipei, I was on my way to Djakarta as Chief of the Economic Aid Mission, then called the United States Operations Mission—a bad title because no Asian wanted to be "operated on" by Americans. The job to be done was a reorganization of the mission and a redesign of the program.

The task intrigued me. Despite Dutch propaganda, I knew that the leaders of the new nationalist revolutionary movement were not Communists. I knew also that our policy in Asia at the time was widely misunderstood by Asians, who had had little reason to look for altruistic help from the West. Throughout the area, the dynamism of revolution and change in the air was combined with a suspicion of the West and all its works. In Indonesia, this was especially true, despite the help America had given the Indonesians in achieving their independence from the

Dutch in 1949. Three and a half centuries of colonialism had left their scars. American assistance was cautiously welcomed but scrutinized carefully at every point for evidence of "strings." But the potential of the country and its people convinced me that unless Indonesia lost its way, it would emerge within the next quarter of a century as a leader in economic development among Asia's newly independent nations.

Nineteen fifty-four was the fateful year of Dien Bien Phu and of the Geneva agreements on Vietnam, to which the United States was not a party but at which we were a most interested and active observer. For the time being, the agreements had halted the southward flow of Communism in Southeast Asia.

There were two theories in Washington as to the next move of the Communists in that area. According to the "domino theory," the fall of a single country would cause the collapse of the rest. The second, or "leap-frog theory," meant that the Communists would focus their next effort not on Thailand or some other country of Southeast Asia where their moves could well be anticipated, but instead would leap-frog the rest of the Southeast Asian mainland and concentrate on Indonesia. If this big country fell to Communism, the theory ran, the rest of Southeast Asia would be caught in a pincers between Communist China and Indonesia, and the entire area's capitulation to Communism would be simply a matter of time.

Enroute to Djakarta, I met a wise and understanding Indonesian.

"Your task will not be an easy one," he said. "My people feel they have won the right to make their own mistakes. They fought, bled, and died for their independence, as did your forebears, but my people lived through more than three and a half centuries of colonialism. This has left its emotional residue. I am afraid my people will make mistakes willfully, do things that inside themselves they know are wrong, just as a young boy kicks out at his father when he is angry. If your country can exercise sufficient forbearance during this growing-up period, it will be able to help us. Then, I think that we may avoid making the fatal mistake of going Communist, but the road will not be smooth."

I was destined to spend the remaining decade and a half of my diplomatic career in dealing with Asian affairs. In those fifteen years, I was often to reflect on the wisdom of the words uttered by my Indonesian friend.

Early in the morning of July 14, 1954, we reached Djakarta—a teeming, steaming tropical metropolis of about 3,000,000 people. From a placid little city of some 600,000 at the beginning of World War II, it had mushroomed into a vast conglomerate of squatters' shacks, streets jammed with coolies balancing huge loads on their poles, *betjas*—the Indonesian name for pedi-cabs in which a seat for passengers is attached to a bicycle—motor bikes, bicycles, weary-looking trucks left over from World War II, most of them sagging from overloading, and thousands of automobiles of varying quality, including the shiny American cars of most members of the diplomatic service.

The Dutch had built thousands of pink and white houses on tree-lined streets, reproducing as far as possible in the humid tropics their homeland on the North Sea. Stanch-walled and small-windowed, with even the roofs in mimicry of cold and blowy Holland, they were built to withstand the pressure of heavy snow, in obedience to a building code that itself had been transported 10,000 miles without change of a comma. The languid coconut palms in the gardens, however, reassured the visitor that this was, indeed, a city on an island splashed almost across the equator. The canals, constructed perhaps also to relieve nostalgia for the waterways of Amsterdam—but more likely in order to drain the marshlands of an early Batavia—once may have lent a freshness to the drab dustiness of the streets. Now they were more like open sewers in which sweating humanity bathed, washed, and defecated.

Djakarta, observed on that first drive from the airport, seemed to be four cities in one. There were the *kampongs*, in which the great mass of Indonesian inhabitants lived—tight clusters of small houses that looked as if they had all been built onto one another. The small yards were noisy with the shrill cries of children. It was dusk, and smoke from charcoal fires hovered in the heat and clogged the nostrils. Here and there, one could see small kerosene stoves.

A world apart was the second city, Chinatown, or Glodock. Like its counterparts in Singapore or Saigon, Hong Kong or Bangkok, it was a tumultuous area of hand carts and bicycles, narrow streets, and thousands of shops, red banners announcing their wares to the milling throng that shouldered its way in all directions. In the center of Glodock was the Chinese Embassy, a large area of imposing buildings set off by barbed wire and forbidding gates.

Then there was the city of the elite. The shaded residential streets that had once been exclusively Dutch were now occupied by well-to-do Chinese and Indonesian businessmen, important public officials, the Caucasian community, and, of course, Embassy Row. Housing pressures were pushing residential growth out into the rice paddies, and an attractive suburb called Kabajoran had recently been born.

Finally there were the squatters, hundreds of thousands of them, living in shantytowns wherever they could find space. Great streams of them had flowed in from the countryside when Indonesia became a nation, partly for security reasons as combat menaced their farms, partly because Indonesia was free, and Djakarta was now their country, their government, and their capital. The squatters had become a major problem for the government, as well as for the city's residents. Woe betide the householder who went off for a weekend without a guard on his house. Upon his return, he would find it full of nonpaying tenants, comfortably ensconced and difficult to dislodge.

It was as if in these four cities that made up Djakarta, Indonesia's past, present and future were revealed.

In 1954, the Indonesian government official responsible for handling all foreign assistance was Dr. Djuanda, head of the Planning Bureau, who was later to become Prime Minister. Former Ambassador to the United States Ali Sastroamidjojo was Prime Minister of a government that had taken office in August 1953. (It was to remain in power for two years, until August 1955, the longest up to that time in the life of this new nation.) Ali headed a coalition Cabinet in which the Nationalist Party, the PNI, was the major element, but which also included representatives of one of the major Moslem parties, the NU (Nahdatul Ulama), and several of the smaller parties. The big Moslem party, the Masjumi, the Socialist and the Christian parties were in opposition. The Communists had only a handful of representatives in Parliament, but this handful had bargaining power out of all proportion to its numerical strength because of the narrow margin—occasionally only one or two votes—by which the Ali government maintained power.

A new polarization began to evidence itself in Indonesian politics, with President Sukarno, the PNI, the NU and the Communist Party cooperating to reduce the influence of the Masjumi. The seeds of rebellion and of the Communist increase in strength and influence were sown in this period.

Hugh S. Cumming, Jr., was the U.S. Ambassador deftly dueling in a difficult situation with the anti-American, antidemocratic forces in the country. We worked closely together. I wore two hats—head of the economic aid mission and economic counselor of the embassy, an unusual arrangement that worked well in the coordination of all economic policies and programs.

The free rein given the Communists by the government was evident to me my first day in Djakarta. In Merdeka Square, across from the U.S. Chancery, every tree was plastered with a poster bearing the hammer and sickle. The same was true in the circle in front of our house, and telephone poles in important sectors of the city were thus decorated. I was to discover on my first drive through Java that all across the island, one's automobile passed under arches of hammer-and-sickle streamers fastened to trees on either side of the highway.

As "Pepper" Martin, perceptive correspondent for *U.S. News and World Report* and regarded at that time as the dean of foreign correspondents in Asia, put it to me after a few days in Indonesia, "It looks as if it's all over but the shouting, doesn't it?" It wasn't all over, but it represented the start of the big drive by the Communists, defeated and discredited by a premature putsch at Madiun a few years earlier, to regain power.

I made one or two false starts in my efforts to revise the aid program. Examination of the government budget revealed a definite need for tax and revenue modernizing. Even without curtailing expenditures, the budget could be balanced by updating the tax system and the machinery of tax collection. When I suggested this to Dr. Djuanda, I touched a politically sensitive nerve. He made it clear that the Indonesian government would brook no foreign interference in its internal financial administration. I protested that I had no thought of interference but was simply noting that the Indonesian government might gain by the experience of other nations and that it might be useful to have one or two consultants in this field who could make suggestions for tax revision. The Indonesian government could take them or leave them. I argued to no avail.

A conversation I had in Manila a few months after I arrived made me realize more keenly the handicaps under which our Economic Aid Mission in Indonesia had been operating. In October 1954, a conference of aid missions' chiefs throughout East Asia and the Pacific was held in Manila. Dr. Raymond D. Moyer was the director of the Far Eastern bureau for the equivalent of the Agency for International Development (AID) at the time. Over lunch, I touched on the emphasis and direction of our assistance program in Indonesia. "Just the other day," I said, "Dr. Djuanda and I had luncheon together and reached some conclusions. . . ."

Moyer interrupted me, "What did you say?"

I repeated what I had just said and started on the substantive part of the conversation.

"Wait a minute," Moyer stopped me again. "Did you say that you had lunch with Djuanda?"

"Yes," I answered, and again endeavored to get back to discussion of the program. But Moyer seemed interested only in that luncheon. "How did it happen? Where was it held?"

I said there was nothing remarkable about the circumstances of the luncheon. "I had been anxious to have a talk with him, and he suggested that we meet for luncheon, that's all."

"Where did you meet?"

"At the Djakarta Club."

"Is the Djakarta Club a public place? Were there others there? Did you have a private room or meet in a public dining room?"

"It was a public room. I suppose there were seventy-five or a hundred there, mixed Indonesian and continental businessmen and government officials, for the most part." Nonplused and close to impatience, I asked, "What are you after? A man asks me out to luncheon. I go. What's all the excitement about?"

Moyer settled back in his chair. "Well," he said, "you've just given me the best news I've heard in a long time! You have been there three months. Somehow you've broken through. I don't know how you did it. But I can tell you that this is the first time a prominent Indonesian public official has had a meal in public with a member of the American Aid Mission for years. Not since the Cabinet fell in Cochran's time." [1]

It was my turn to be surprised. I was adding to my Indonesian education.

There were politically sensitive areas where we could not help Indonesia for the time being. Government finance and internal governmental administration were taboo. Structures of government and the whole democratic process, except for the mechanics of elections, were also off limits. But Djuanda did recognize American pre-eminence in technology —physics, chemistry, engineering, medicine, agriculture, industrial management, public administration—education, and industry. And these were just the areas most underdeveloped in Indonesia. Four years after independence, Indonesia's major problem was a paucity of trained personnel: there were only 1,200 doctors in the entire country, and only 120 engineers. The literacy rate at independence was somewhere around five per cent. In the big Ministry of Agriculture, with 40,000 officials and employees, there were just two college graduates.

We agreed on a formula for the U.S. aid program. To the extent that our own aid budget made it possible, America would assume as its primary responsibility the technical education of Indonesians. Both Djuanda and I were keenly if tacitly aware of the important by-products that would result, namely, understanding of the United States by Indonesians, who presumably would return to their country not merely with increased technical knowledge, but also with an appreciation of what a free society was like and, in particular, some comprehension of the American dynamic.

I have always had a deep conviction that exposure to a free society leaves a lasting impression on people, and I felt this with particular keenness about Indonesians, whose magic word was *merdeka*, encompassing all that we Americans think of in our own magic word "liberty." I knew, too, that our own Revolution had been in part the inspiration for Indonesia's. The Dutch-educated Indonesian revolutionary leaders had seen democracy at work in Holland; they had studied and been stirred by the American Revolution, for the American dream had caught fire in Indonesia. Years later Sukarno was to say, "The shot that was fired at Lexington on the nineteenth of April, 1775, was heard around the world. It echoes still in the hearts of peoples who still struggle against their colonial bonds. . . . Over half the world the burning words

---

1. The Indonesian Cabinet fell on the issue of a secret aid agreement signed by the Foreign Minister and the U.S. Ambassador in 1952.

which fired the American War of Independence have been closely studied as a source of inspiration and a plan of action." [2]

I believed strongly that living and studying in America would generate an understanding that we still lived by the principles that had motivated us nearly two hundred years ago; and I was convinced that if enough Indonesians who might be expected to play leadership roles in the future could visit America long enough to understand us, not only would our relations with this important country benefit, but Indonesia might be less likely to abandon democratic concepts.

What I considered the ideal form of American aid was currently being applied in the construction of Indonesia's first cement plant at Gresik, a small village near Surabaya in East Java. The project was financed through a dollar loan from the Export-Import Bank and the contract awarded to an American construction firm. Simultaneous with the assurances of financing, our Economic Aid Mission sent young Indonesian engineers to the United States to study cement engineering, partly in universities, partly in on-the-job training at American cement plants. Three years later, when the plant was finished, Indonesians were ready to take over every job in it. For one year, the construction firm of Morrison-Knudsen had a management contract to supervise the operation of the plant and assist the Indonesian staff. At the end of the year, the plant was turned over to the Indonesians to run. It was well run, and for years thereafter exceeded its standard rated capacity in cement production.

As the gears of our aid program began to mesh, our relations with the Indonesians improved. It was not that we were giving them any more aid. It was that we were working with them, abjuring the attitude that "Papa knows best." The Indonesian, who had been treated as a second-class citizen for so long, resented the slightest tinge of paternalism—and he was very adept at recognizing it. When he did, the result would be the substitution of passive resistance for cooperation.

The Indonesian attitude toward aid was pointed up one stifling evening by a touch of melodrama. My wife and I were in the midst of having coffee when suddenly the curtains of the French doors parted and a young man stepped into the room. Not knowing what to expect, I instantly rose and confronted him. He turned out to be no ordinary intruder.

"I apologize for entering your house this way," he said. "But I'm a newspaper reporter, and I've been trying to see you for weeks without success. I can't seem to get by your secretary," he added, half belligerently.

I laughed. "She has her own ideas of guarding me," I said. "I am sorry.

2. Text of Sukarno's address before a joint session of Congress, New York *Times*, May 18, 1956.

My door is always open to reporters. Since you are here, come join us in a cup of coffee and we'll talk now."

The young man plied me with questions about American policy and our aid program for about an hour. Just as he was about to leave, he said, "I'd like to ask you one more question. *What is America after in giving us this aid?* What does America want? Are you trying to get us to change our neutralist foreign policy?"

"To the latter question, the answer is no," I replied. "Not that we would not like to have you on our side. Naturally, we would prefer to have you agree than disagree with us. But no, we are not trying to influence you in this respect with our aid. Our motivation is very simple, and I think it is one you can readily understand. We consider that we have a basic identity of interest with Indonesia. We are convinced that your most precious possession is your independence. You fought, bled and died for your independence, as we did. We think you would do so again, if necessary. Am I right?"

The young man nodded a vigorous assent. "Now it so happens that we Americans consider it in our interest for you to maintain your independence. We don't want to see you swallowed up by the Communist bloc. And we know that to preserve your independence, you will have to be economically stable.

"I think you will concur that in your country today, economic stability is a prerequisite to political stability. I also think you will agree that your country needs help in achieving economic stability—and I am not talking stability in the sense of staying where you are. But to progress economically, to develop, you have to have a solid foundation on which to build. Your people want a better life and this depends upon economic development. Economic stability and political development are Siamese twins—they can't be separated and are essential to maintaining independence in the world. Since we consider that your independence is in our interest, we stand ready to help."

The reporter nodded thoughtfully, as if to remember each word I had used, thanked me and departed, this time by the front door.

Two months later, he came to see me again.

"Repeat what you told me the last time I saw you," he asked. "I've been talking to a lot of my friends about what you said and I'm confused. They keep talking about American imperialism, and I'd like to get your side of the story clear in my mind." I complied. (The episode illustrates the importance of what Communist propagandists long since discovered—the necessity of repetition.) A few months later, he had the opportunity to attend a seminar at one of American's best universities. He was gone three months. When he returned, he called at my office.

"I've got it!" he exclaimed enthusiastically.

"What have you got?"

"I understand America! I see now what America is all about! Why, you people mean what you say. Freedom means something. It is important to you. People say what they think. They criticize American policy. They even criticize the President. And Americans *do* believe in independence for others. You're not trying to dominate the world but to free the world!"

I thought I had seldom heard a better definition of our objectives.

"From now on, believe me," he said, "I'm on America's side!"

He made good his word, writing editorials in his newspaper in support of American policy. Years later, when pressure was exerted to keep him quiet, he refused to yield. Ultimately, his paper was closed down for taking a strong line in opposition to the government's soft policy toward Communism.

During 1954, pressures were building up to force the government to hold a parliamentary election. In a country the size of Indonesia, with its many islands and a populace that had never participated in an election or known the machinery of national democracy, it was a tremendous administrative task, calling for a nationwide educational campaign. Our aid mission assisted in the production of motion pictures demonstrating how an election worked and how to deal with the problems of influence and corruption.

The elections, held in 1955, resulted in one big upset—the Communist Party, the PKI, came in fourth, with approximately seventeen per cent of the votes cast. The party had spent millions to bring this about, working hard and skillfully to win over the underprivileged. Typical of its activities was its shrewd squatters-aid program, part of which was to introduce legislation in Parliament that would provide free government land for the squatters. When they finally succeeded in getting it through, party organizers helped the squatters make application for their land. After title had been secured, party representatives approached the squatters with the proposition that they would arrange for the sale of this land, buy its equivalent in another, lower-priced area, and build a house on it to boot. With this kind of program, the squatters' vote for the PKI was forever assured.

Nineteen fifty-five saw another significant event, one that temporarily added to the prestige of the Ali government. In April, the first Asian-African Conference was held in Bandung. President Sukarno is credited with the idea, the first attempt of the Asian-African nations to get together in an effort to help each other solve their problems. Sukarno saw the meeting as a move toward the formation of an Afro-Asian bloc, a third force in the world committed to progress and the overthrow of the *status quo*.

Although these nations were divided in their economic and political interests, they had at least two things in common: except for Japan, they represented the less-developed areas of the world and therefore had an interest in upgrading their standard of living; and the majority of them had been colonies, and so had a built-in anticolonial, anti-imperial bias. They were also nonwhite. But while color might have contributed a certain community of interest, it had much less significance than has generally been thought. The Bandung conference was not antiwhite; it was concerned with finding solutions to mutually shared problems.

The conference put Indonesia on the world stage. Bandung, a lovely little city nestled in the hills of West Java on the site of a prehistoric lake, became world famous as a symbol of Asian-African unity. From now on, Sukarno would ensure that Indonesia was a nation to be reckoned with.

I had been in Indonesia just one year when, in June of 1955, I received a telegram summoning me back to Washington as Deputy Assistant Secretary for Far Eastern Economic Affairs. It had been a good year, and I had learned much. My wife and I had come to love Indonesia; we were leaving a host of friends behind. Hundreds turned out at the airport to say *"Selamat Djalan"*—"Go with God." I had no premonition, as we flew away over the jade-colored Java Sea, that within three years I would be returning, this time as Ambassador, to share in a more turbulent period than the country had known since its revolution.

CHAPTER 5

Sukarno

Well, frankly I tell you: I belong to the group of people who are bound in spiritual longing by the romanticism of revolution. I am inspired by it, I am fascinated by it, I am completely absorbed by it, I am crazed, I am obsessed by the romanticism of revolution. And for this I utter thanks to God, who commands all Nature!

—SUKARNO
August 17, 1960

There are two prerequisites for an effective movement toward a country's independence. The first is unity; the second, a leader around whom to rally. The second must come before the first. A young man born of a Balinese mother and a Javanese father became Indonesia's man of the hour.

He cut a handsome and jaunty figure garbed in a tropical officer's uniform replete with decorations, a black *pitji* on his head, dark sunglasses, and sporting a small black and silver swagger stick. These were his stage props. Although he never served in the armed forces, he thus identified himself with the military and underlined his role as commander-in-chief.

I first met Sukarno in 1954, when he was at the height of his powers. My impression was of a man with enormous brilliant brown eyes and a flashing smile that conveyed an all-embracing warmth. To meet him was like suddenly coming under a sunlamp, such was the quality of his magnetism.

Our first talk was about the economic aid program to Indonesia, but it was also about the world, the flesh, and the devil; about movie stars and Malthus, Jean Jaures and Jefferson, folklore and philosophy. Sukarno asked about my family. When I said I had one beautiful daughter and two granddaughters who took after her, he laughed.

"You're no Indonesian," he said. "Indonesians breed like rabbits.

47

Ten, twelve, fourteen children. This is usual, and we have a big country." He waved his arm expansively. "Plenty of room to grow. Like America used to be. But our young men don't have to go West."

Sukarno was a vital man, expressing exuberance and enthusiasm in everything he did. He had an extraordinary boyishness and, in those early years of his power, was warm, responsive, casual, and always ebullient. His face lighted up with an infectious smile when greeting a friend or a new acquaintance. He was not easily disturbed unless his overweening vanity was touched or his emotions were aroused; then he could become explosive. He was, in brief, a dynamic, magnetic leader, a self-professed egotist, an effervescent extrovert. His amazing energy and vitality were the talk of the diplomatic corps. After a day in which he addressed mass meetings for hours—on one occasion I heard him make three two-hour speeches within an eight-hour period—he would wolf down an enormous dinner and then dance until after midnight, enjoying every moment.

He was vain—and admitted it. But his sense of humor had a disarming quality that tended to soften his vanity. On one occasion, when Prince Sihanouk was scheduled to visit Djakarta, a few of us were talking with Sukarno.

"I was Ambassador to Cambodia for two years," one of my colleagues said. "Do you mind if I caution you, Mr. President? You will have to handle this young man with kid gloves. You will have to warn your people to be careful. Mr. President, this man is terribly vain."

Sukarno sat up like a pouter pigeon, struck an attitude, pounded himself on the chest, surveyed the group. "Is he as vain as I am?" he asked.

Once I asked him why he ate so fast—he had finished his entire meal one evening before I had fairly started the main course. I apologized for being so slow. He waved an airy hand.

"Pay no attention to me," he said. "I can't help it. Shall I tell you why? Because all those years in prison, I was allowed just six minutes to eat. The plate was pulled away if I had not finished in six minutes." He sobered. "I learned to eat fast," he said grimly, "and I can't get over it. Twelve years is a long time."

It was hard to get him to talk about those years. He preferred to talk about palaces, villas, airplanes, art collections, literature, philosophy, religion, his goals for the nation, international affairs—the things that had come to him with success. He had a memory like an elephant's. In those years in prison, he had read and read, and he seemed to have not forgotten a thing. He could quote authors at length and by the score—on socialism and revolution, most of them well-known writers, French, German, English, Italian, Czech, Russian, Dutch, American, Japanese. In the same speech he would quote from Thomas Jefferson and Lenin, particularly in the period when he was steering a neutral course and wooing both sides alike.[1]

The charismatic, megalomaniac quality of Sukarno blossomed through the years. And always he showed the strong streak of mysticism that is not uncommon in Indonesians, especially in the Javanese and Balinese. It showed up in numerous ways. He refused to have surgery when his doctors advised it. Whether he felt that it would affect some of his near-magical powers, or whether, as some alleged, he had once been told by a fortuneteller that he would die by the blade of a knife, no one knew. When he had to make an important decision, he waited for some inner voice. And I shall never forget the morning after an attempt had been made on his life.

The would-be assassin had chosen a Moslem holyday when Sukarno was praying in the mosque in his palace with several hundred invited guests. At a moment when all were in the position of prayer, heads bowed to the floor, the assassin, not eight feet from Sukarno, rose to his knees and fired five shots point-blank at the President. Every shot hit a mark. Five people were severely wounded. Sukarno was untouched.

"There is only one thing I can think after yesterday," the President said, shaking his head soberly when I expressed relief over his narrow escape from death. "That is that Allah must approve of what I am doing, otherwise I would long ago have been killed." It was the seventh time that assassins had narrowly failed.

Sukarno was all too often the victim of his own faith in people. He had, for all his Oriental sophistication in politics and his understandable skepticism of Western motivations, a naïve trust in individuals and an almost mystical faith in the people of Indonesia and their love for him. It was to Sukarno unbelievable that any Indonesian could wish to do him harm. Assassins' attempts were put down, at least at first, to foreign instigation. When he finally did face up to the fact that some Indonesians did indeed want to get rid of him, he went to the other extreme. There was to come a time when his suspicions of everybody even caused him to have his food tasted before he consumed it.

Once asked to describe Sukarno to an intimate group session in Washington, I said, "In terms of personality, he is a charmer. He is a combina-

---

1. Once for his birthday, I presented Sukarno with a beautiful leather-bound copy of *The Federalist Papers*. He thanked me, then laughed loudly as he glanced through it. I suddenly realized that Sukarno's allergy to a federal state was such that he could hardly be expected to give the book an unprejudiced reading. I told him that I was not indulging in propaganda; but it had occurred to me that he might be interested in the basic philosophy of the American form of government. He never referred to them after that, and I doubt he ever read them. Thomas Jefferson was the only American of that period whom he ever quoted.

tion of Clark Gable and Franklin Roosevelt." Somehow, the description was reported back to Sukarno, who apparently was pleased. He quoted my words in a speech to the American community in Djakarta. He slyly observed that he hoped there was more of Gable than Roosevelt in him.

But perhaps the description of himself that Sukarno liked best was that of Louis Fischer. "The best key to Sukarno is love," Fischer wrote. "He is the great lover. He loves his country, he loves women, he loves to talk about women, he loves himself." [2] Sukarno would quote this passage on the slightest provocation, winding up with great guffaws. One of his most redeeming and disarming qualities was that, up to a point, he enjoyed a joke on himself.

An early riser, normally at 5:30, it was his custom as a Moslem to pray for a quarter of an hour or more at sunrise, then stroll around the beautifully landscaped grounds of the Presidential Palace. Sometimes he scheduled appointments as early as 6:30, but customarily by 7:00 he would be found having coffee on his ample veranda overlooking the green velvet lawn, huge, gracefully symmetrical rain trees, luxuriant lavender bougainvillaea, and the lily pond in the distance.

Here the President's friends would gather. Cabinet ministers dropped in to chat and do business. Lovely Javanese ladies in colorful *kain* and *kabaya* sought his blessing for their marriage or the bestowal of a name on a newborn baby. Occasionally, a favored ambassador joined in the cheerful banter of this morning ritual in the hope of obtaining a few precious moments alone with the President. Movie stars, department-store managers, highway engineers, military officers, police officers, politicians, architects, artists, labor-union officials, old cronies from more revolutionary days, businessmen, travelers from abroad, university students and professors, philosophers, religious leaders, scientists—a catalogue of Sukarno's visitors would list these and many more. Customarily dressed in a sport shirt and slacks, with sandals on his feet, Sukarno would greet his guests, see to it that they were served coffee or tea, then whisk rapidly through a stack of a dozen morning newspapers, in Indonesian and English, commenting good-humoredly as he came across an item of interest.

"Ha! The Beatles arrive in Australia!" the President said on one occasion, looking around and motioning as if to pull his hair down over his brows. "I have forbidden Beatle haircuts in Indonesia. You know what? If an Indonesian boy wears his hair like that, the police are ordered to clip off all his hair." The President guffawed. "No, no Beatles. No rock and roll. No twist." A man with hair almost white joined the group. (This is unusual since most Indonesians have black hair; few gray-haired men or women are seen. Some unkind suggestions have been heard to

---

the effect that this is not entirely nature's work.) Sukarno stretched out a welcoming hand, introduced the newcomer. "He is my political philosopher—that is why he has gray hair! Haw, haw, haw!"

A beautiful young woman in green and gold, with golden ornaments in her shining black hair and a white flower behind one ear, leaned over and asked "Bapak" (Indonesian for "Papa," which most Indonesians called the President) to give her new baby a name. "Boy or girl? When was it born?" the President asked. He thought a moment, wrote out a name on a piece of paper, handed it to the young woman. The name usually had some significance relative to the date and place of birth. "Read it," the President commanded. She read it out loud. The President nodded enthusiastically. "Its a good name," he confirmed. One morning while I was there, he named six babies.

A secretary arrived with a pile of papers a foot high for the President to sign. He slapped his knee exuberantly. "Ho! That is a table. Put them there!" he said boisterously. For fifteen minutes Sukarno concentrated intensely, reading rapidly through the papers, asking quick, sharp questions about them, signing them with a broad pen and his legible signature, "Soekarno."

"People are always misspelling my name," he complained. "*Soekarno* —that is not my name. That is my signature. My name is spelled *Sukarno.*"

"Why the difference?" I asked him.

"*Soekarno*—that is the Dutch spelling. I don't want my name spelled with the Dutch spelling! No! But my signature—that's the way I started out. I don't want to change it."

On one occasion the conversation turned to the GANEFO (Games of the New Emerging Forces, organized as a rival to the Asian and Olympic games). "Did I ever tell you about the Egyptian dancer I wanted to have come here?" the President asked. "Well, when I asked the UAR representative to send her to Djakarta as part of the international entertainment, he said, "but Mr. President, you don't want her, she is already an old established force!" Much laughter.

Shortly after 8:00, the lively chatter of children was heard, as an open-air kindergarten began its day in the pavilion in the center of the garden. "You know why I have a kindergarten in my garden?" the President asked. He answered his own question, "Because the mothers who bring children to kindergarten are still young and beautiful." He laughed.

"You know," he continued, mischievously regarding the ladies who were present, "why a woman is like a rubber tree? Because a rubber tree is no good after thirty years!"

To Sukarno, the story of his life was the story of Indonesia's independence, and he never ceased to meditate upon it before he made a major speech. He personalized the history of the Indonesian revolution. And the Horatio Alger story of his rise from "rags to riches" was the inspiration of all his people who were reaching for the sky.

Born near Surabaya, East Java, on June 6, 1901,[3] Sukarno was a "child of the dawn," and it is related that his birth was marked by the eruption of a volcano near his home that had been regarded as extinct. People later said a new explosive force had been released in the world on that day. Whether fact or fiction, the legend is appropriate in light of his career.

There are various superstitions in Indonesia connected with a "child of the dawn": that such a child is especially favored and will make his mark in the world; that he must be kept out of the jungle, presumably because evil forces are lurking and ready to consume a promising human destined for leadership.

Sukarno's father, Sosrodihardjo, was born about 1869, apparently in East Java. Although he possessed the common *priyaji* title of *"Raden,"* [4] he does not seem to have been directly linked to any of the major court or even *bupati* ("county manager" or "official") families. After attending an elementary school for "natives," he was admitted to a Teacher Training School in Probolinggo, East Java, which prepared teachers for Dutch/Indonesian education. It was designed primarily for the sons of middle-level Indonesian officials; few others could gain admission to the three-year course then provided, particularly since instruction was given, up to 1885, in the Dutch language.

Sosrodihardjo did very well, and after graduating, took up a teaching job in East Java. Meanwhile, the Dutch had begun looking for Indonesian teachers for their newly conquered territories in North Bali. (In 1882, the Balinese kingdoms of Ganjar and Karangasem had capitulated to a Dutch military expedition and been placed under Assistant Residents—although military occupation continued in the face of persistent Balinese resistance, which prevented the subjugation of South Bali until

---

3. This is the official date given by Sukarno himself. However, some questions surround its accuracy. Sukarno was born no later than 1901—and possibly as early as 1899—in Surabaya, where his father was teaching. Although it is not known if his parents lost some children prior to Sukarno's birth, the tendency for Javanese to have children rapidly after marriage suggests that he may well have been born at the earlier date. At least two scholars have reached this conclusion—Professor Roger K. Paget of the University of Colorado and Professor Benedict R. O'G. Anderson of Cornell—based on interviews with Sukarno's contemporaries.

4. Equivalent to "prince." Originally the hereditary aristocracy of Indonesian society, *priyaji* evolved into the ascendant group of social elite from which members of the bureaucracy were recruited—and to which an impressive list of connotations can be ascribed: *"politesse," "noblesse oblige," "superiority to any given situation," "untouchable by fear," "intuitive intellectualism."*

about 1908.) [5] As a bright young man apparently anxious to advance quickly in his profession, Sosrodihardjo presumably calculated that his career would be furthered if he responded to the Dutch need for teachers on the neighboring island. So he went to Bali, where he worked as a teacher and where also he found his life partner. Named I. Njoman Rai, she is said to have been the daughter of a Balinese Hindu priest who had been banished to Sumatra by the Dutch. Her name would indicate that she was not of the high caste of nobles (*satria*), although Sukarno always referred to her as of high caste (Brahman) and said that the last King of Singaradja in Bali was his mother's uncle. In any event, she was a remarkable woman whose strength, affection and wisdom were at least in part responsible for the guidance of her son's early precociousness into serious channels.

The date of the marriage is not known, but it was surely before Sosrodihardjo left Bali, in about 1893, to return to East Java. There he resumed his teaching career, finally settling in the Blitar area in East Java. Serving long after the normal pension age, he did not retire until 1935. At that time he had attained a position of considerable prestige as vice-director of the Teacher Training School at Blitar. Even at that juncture there were only five such schools in all of the Dutch East Indies, and only three in Java. Achievement of such a relatively high academic position for an Indonesian at that time again points up the fact that Sukarno's father was undoubtedly one of the better-educated Indonesians of this period. It also suggests how he was able, apparently with the help of a friend, to arrange his son's admission to the very privileged Dutch high school [6] in Surabaya in 1916, and to make the financial sacrifice necessary to maintain him there.

At birth the baby was called Kusnososro. But the young boy was unhealthy and suffered from one disease after another. His father decided that the name was ill-fated. He renamed his son "Karna," after the hero in the Hindu classic, Mahabharata. But Javanese names end in *o* rather than *a*. And many of them have the prefix *Su*, which means "good" or "best." Thus the young boy became "Sukarno."

Sukarno described his boyhood frequently as poverty-stricken. "I did

---

5. For a dramatic account of this tragic episode in Balinese history, see Vicki Baum, *Tale of Bali*, trans. Basil Creighton (New York: Doubleday, Doran and Co., Inc., 1937). See also Cindy Adams, *Sukarno, An Autobiography as Told to Cindy Adams* (Indianapolis: The Bobbs-Merrill Company, Inc., 1965).

6. Although the first of the Dutch high schools had been founded in Djakarta in 1867, and the second in Surabaya some years later, they remained not only small in number but very exclusive because of the stiff entrance requirements. That barrier effectively denied entrance to all but a few Indonesians who, like Sukarno, enjoyed the benefit of at least a partially Dutch-educated father, and one who had achieved considerable status within the Indonesian official class.

not own a pair of shoes," he often said. "Even when I attended the university, sometimes I had to attend classes barefoot. I had to study by a flickering oil lamp. We had no electricity, no running water. We were so poor we could eat rice only once a day. And this was rice that my mother bought as paddy, with the husk still on it. She had to pound it every morning." Except when the young Sukarno took over this chore.[7]

But his parents were not ordinary people or poor people. And neither was he part Dutch, although a rumor to that effect persisted for a long time, it having been difficult for many Caucasians (not only Dutch) to believe that an Indonesian of such extraordinary qualities did not have some white blood in him.

At his mother's knee, the boy Sukarno heard stories of the Balinese defense of their land against the Dutch, learned of those Balinese heroes who dressed themselves in white and, armed only with the Balinese dagger, the kris, marched in suicidal, serried ranks against Dutch cannons and rifles.

He became steeped in Javanese culture, which was to remain an asset to him throughout his political career. He had natural leadership qualities and was nicknamed "Djago," which means "rooster" or "champion." He was the kind of boy who climbed the tallest tree, led his companions on youthful adventures and was, at that stage, perhaps a desultory student. He was fascinated by the classical puppet plays, the wajang, and apparently spent a great deal of time watching these nightlong performances, a practice he maintained during his presidency. I have often thought that the key to Sukarno was in the wajang—its heroes, its villains, and its romanticism.

At six years of age, Sukarno was enrolled in the school of his grandparents, and later he attended his own father's school at Modjokerto. Neither of these schools, however, taught Dutch, and at the age of twelve he entered a Dutch elementary school. He must have been a reasonably good student since he received his clerkship diploma at fourteen, making him eligible for positions in the lower governmental service. At this time, he also came under the influence of his father's friend, a Surabaya businessman, journalist, teacher, and national political leader named Raden Umar Said Tjokroaminoto, who was to be Sukarno's mentor. This man was then head of the influential Moslem organization known as Sarekat Islam.[8] Impressed with young Sukarno's leadership potential, Tjokroaminoto took him under his wing and acquainted him with the leading Indonesian political figures of the time. Tjokroaminoto was widely read, and gave Sukarno his first introduction to the masters of political philos-

---

7. Cf. Adams, *Sukarno, An Autobiography*, p. 23.
8. See Bernhard Dahm, *Sukarno and the Struggle for Indonesian Independence*, trans. Mary F. Somers Heidhues (Ithaca, N.Y.: Cornell University Press, 1969), pp. 12–20, 32–39.

ophy. Sukarno credited this tutelage as his principal inspiration in launching him on a political career.

Tjokroaminoto, who must have come to love Sukarno like a son, arranged for him to enter the Dutch high school in Surabaya, a school attended almost exclusively by Dutch children and the children of a few high-ranking Indonesian officials.

With great gusto, Sukarno told me the story of his first serious love affair, which occurred at this time. The girl was an attractive blonde, blue-eyed Dutch girl, and she and Sukarno were very much in love. There came the time when Sukarno called at her home to take her to a dance. The father for the first time realized that his daughter was going out with a brown boy. Enraged, he threw the young Sukarno out of the house.

Years later Sukarno saw the girl again. "I realized how much I owed to her father," he noted with relish. "She was no longer the slim, beautiful girl I had known. She was five by five!" he laughed, stretching his arms wide.

Good-humored as he could be about this incident later, his treatment at the hands of the Dutch father must have reinforced Sukarno's youthful determination to fight for Indonesian independence so that Indonesians would no longer be second-class citizens in their own country. For it was at this time that he joined the Young Java[9] organization, where he began to attract attention both as an orator and as a writer.

When Sukarno completed high school in 1921, he entered the Bandung Technical College in West Java, established for the training of Dutch engineers and architects, where he joined one of the first classes the Dutch had permitted Indonesians to attend.

Sukarno was awarded a degree five years later in civil engineering and architecture. He was reputed to have been a brilliant student—one of his professors is alleged to have said he was the most brilliant student he had had. It was certain that he was the leader of the Indonesian group on the campus, and even while a student he was elected as the first secretary of the Algemeene Studieclub ("General Study Club"), which was founded January 17, 1926. The chairman was Mr. Iskaq Tjokrohadisurjo, who had studied in Holland and was a rising political leader. The members of this club, in July 1927, formed the Indonesian Nationalist Party, or PNI,[10] which ultimately became one of the most influential political parties in the nation.

Sukarno told me he worked as an architect for a short period after

---

9. Cf. Dahm, *Sukarno*, pp. 39–40. Sukarno was active in the Young Java's Surabaya section, which was founded February 1, 1920.

10. Established July 4, 1927, it was originally called "Perserikatan Nasional Indonesia," or "Indonesian National Association." In May 1928, after its first party congress, the PNI came to stand for Partai Nasional Indonesia.

graduating from college, and his interest in architectural design never left him; but within six months he was spending all his time on politics. There were numerous small Indonesian nationalist movements at the time. He made up his mind that there should be only one objective: Indonesian independence from Dutch rule. On fire with the idea of Indonesian independence, he alone among the young leaders saw the masses as the key to its success.

The fact that Sukarno had not been educated in the Netherlands not only set him somewhat apart from his colleagues in the nationalist movement, most of whom had Dutch educations; it also gave him the political advantage of being regarded as a son of native soil. And it was to the people of that soil that he appealed.

In his emphasis upon a broad political foundation based upon support from the masses, Sukarno was unique among his colleagues. He was unique, too, in his insistence upon unity. He rejected the limitations inherent in basing a movement upon any single religion or political doctrine. Since more than ninety per cent of his countrymen were Moslems, this must have been a great temptation. But he resisted it, stressing instead the need for unity as the means of realizing Indonesia's independence and self-development. No philosophy, creed or culture should divide the people. This idea became an obsession that remained with him to the end of his career.

In October 1928, he said, "It must be understood that we are to think above all of the great question, we are to think continually of the first goal of our movement—that is, of Indonesia's independence. Yes, no more and no less than that: an independent Indonesia, by the quickest way possible. Therefore we must strive for independence not merely by reforming the disordered living conditions in our land; rather, we must strive first for Indonesian independence, so that our living conditions may then be improved. Independence is the first, it is the primary goal." [11]

Sukarno swept aside all subsidiary goals of social and economic reform, for at the time he felt they would interfere with and hinder the drive for independence. Time and time again in the 1960's, I heard Sukarno insist on the doctrine of "historical necessity," which he believed was moving Indonesia along the road of progress and freedom. He had believed this as a young man, and had even criticized Mahatma Gandhi in December 1928 for forgetting that ". . . politics, if it is to bear sound fruit, must rise on the basis of actual, concrete, substantial conditions, and not lose itself in the vague clouds of philosophy and abstraction; still less can it oppose the iron laws of social evolution." [12]

In November 1926 and January 1927, the Communist Party launched

---

11. Dahm, *Sukarno*, p. 106.
12. *Ibid.*, p. 107.

abortive revolts against the Dutch government. They were premature and sternly crushed, and the Communist Party was banned. Seeking a new home, many of its members joined the budding PNI. Led by the magnetic Sukarno, the PNI abandoned the idea of compromise or co-operation with the Dutch in some form of union and aimed for complete independence for Indonesia.

Sukarno was moving rapidly toward success in mustering mass support when outside forces intervened. The PNI was fast becoming the strongest nationalist political party in Indonesia, and the Dutch government was watching it with growing apprehension. On December 29, 1929, the Dutch decided it was time to act, and Sukarno and several other leaders of the PNI were arrested.

It was in this period that the young Sukarno began to generate the convictions that never left him. He was not an originator of ideas; he was an absorber and an adapter. He was also a packager and a salesman. Under the tutelage of his mentor, Tjokroaminoto, he began to see that Indonesia would be great only through the dynamics of its people, and that that prescription was only possible through unity of concept and action. Since people were divided on so many issues, it was necessary to pierce through to the one thing on which they were united—a desire for independence. Prince and pauper, patrician and coolie, Moslem and Christian—all could be united in a passionate drive for a single goal, Sukarno saw. This goal was liberty, or *merdeka*, a word that became the rallying cry of the cause.

Sukarno was steeped in the legends and mysticism of his time. The Indonesians were awaiting the arrival of a kind of messiah figure on horseback, Ratu Adil. This "just prince" would lead them out of the wilderness of slavery into freedom and establish a kingdom based upon justice and prosperity. Considering what the Indonesian felt about the Ratu Adil, it is not impossible to see how Sukarno could gradually begin to think of himself as "the great prince" who would rescue his people. It is not difficult to imagine the idea being fostered by a wise and politically sophisticated elder statesman who saw in the young Sukarno the buds of the essential qualities of leadership that this country would one day need. And it was becoming clear to Tjokroaminoto that that day was not far off.

To do Tjokroaminoto justice, however, he had long since endeavored to turn the preoccupation of his people away from the ancient notion that one heroic individual was the answer to their prayers, and instead had tried to teach them that the power for change lay in their hands. In 1921, he put the idea into these words:

> We await a new messenger of God, the successor of Moses, Jesus, and Mohammed, who will drive all evil desires from the hearts of men. This is the messenger called Ratu Adil. All of us, whatever our religion, await him. But this Ratu Adil will not appear in human form; rather,

he will appear in the form of socialism. It is to this that the SI [Sarekat Islam] looks forward.[13]

Self-government in the form of socialism was Tjokroaminoto's enlightened interpretation of the ancient legend.

But Sukarno, who personalized everything, also, I am convinced, did so here. He became to himself the Ratu Adil in this early period, as he later became the personification, or so he thought, of his nation and his people. And his guide through the jungles of political theory was too old a hand not to know that concept and charisma must join in the leadership that moves nations.

Sukarno chose to defend himself at the trial, which opened August 18, 1930. As he later told me, it was his chance "to get my message to my people. The court record was privileged. Nobody could be punished for publishing a court record. The Dutch handed me an opportunity of which I took full advantage"—as anyone who heard him speak or has read the transcript can testify. It is easy to picture the scene of December 1930. The young, flashing-eyed Sukarno. The excited, crowded courtroom. The dignified Dutch officials, outraged, yet perhaps listening half against their will and with secret admiration to the stirring tones of the youthful speaker, some in their hearts grudgingly admitting the justice of his cause.

"The Indonesian people speak with one voice! They cry out for independence." This was the burden of his closing plea before the Dutch court. Sukarno placed himself and his codefendants in the company of great national leaders who, like Tilak of India, willingly sacrificed themselves for "the sacred principle, ideal, and right of national freedom." In the rolling, rhythmic, emotion-rousing golden voice that would continue to inspire Indonesia's masses for decades to come, Sukarno spoke not so much to his Dutch judges as to his people—whose awakening political consciousness would be deepened and inspired by his words:

"We . . . are devoted to sacred and glorious ideals, *we* also are striving to restore the *right* of our land and people to a free life. Three hundred years, even a thousand years, cannot wipe out the *right* of the country of Indonesia and the people of Indonesia to that freedom. For the fulfillment of that *right* we are willing to suffer every hardship demanded by our country, willing to endure whatever misery is required at any time by Mother Indonesia." [14]

Then, after stressing that no sacrifice would be wasted, because of the inevitability of Indonesia's achieving its freedom, Sukarno returned to what perhaps has always been his most cherished theme—his oneness with his people:

---

13. *Ibid.*, p. 19.
14. "Indonesia Excuses: Bung Karno's Address to the Colonial Court, December 1930" (Djakarta: Department of Information, 1961).

"We who stand here stand as part of the tormented Indonesian people, loyal and faithful sons of Mother Indonesia. Our voice sounded within this courtroom at this moment is not confined merely within its walls—our voice is also heard by the people whom we serve, echoed in every direction, across plain, mountain and sea. . . . The Indonesian people who hear our voice feel that they are listening to *their own* voice. . . . And now, united in spirit with the Indonesian people, faithful and obedient to our beloved Mother Indonesia—confident that the Indonesian people and Mother Indonesia will one day achieve unending glory, whatever our fate may be, we are ready to hear the verdict of the Honorable Judges."

Knowing in his heart what that verdict would be, this thirty-one-year-old prisoner was seeking the verdict of history. His defense was of his country, not himself. It was really no defense at all, but an attack upon the colonial system that had kept Indonesia captive.

Sukarno was sentenced to four years in prison. He was released a year later (December 31, 1931), the Dutch apparently reasoning that the young man had learned his lesson.

The loss of Sukarno's leadership even for a year, however, effectively destroyed the dynamism of the PNI. Shortly after his imprisonment, it splintered into several factions. One, Partai Indonesia, or Partindo, the old PNI's successor, maintained the PNI's radical opposition to the Dutch and continued to demand complete independence. A second drifted into the more moderate course of seeking independence through cooperation with the Dutch. Meanwhile, a new group emerged, led by Sjahrir and Hatta, both of whom had recently returned from study in Holland. Smaller, more elitist and intellectual than the mass-based PNI, they formed the Indonesian National Education Club ("PNI-Baru"—Pendidikan Nasional Indonesia) and concentrated on training cadres for nationalist activity. They were convinced that political education of the Indonesian people was the road to follow toward independence. Sukarno had been preaching non-cooperation and passive resistance. "Independence now!" was his goal. Attempts by Sukarno and others to merge these divergent strands into a single movement failed.

The Dutch guessed wrong about Sukarno. His year in prison had hardened his resolve. After his release, he at once plunged into renewed political activity. Failing to unite his splintered PNI, he joined and led the more radical group in July 1932, and was officially elected chairman in April 1933. Within a year, Sukarno's personal popularity and his vigorous campaigning had built up his group, the Partai Indonesia, to a membership of 20,000. The Hatta-Sjahrir faction had only about 1,000 adherents, chiefly among the intellectuals.

The Dutch were again watching the soaring star of the young Sukarno with much concern. It seemed clear that he was the fire of the independence movement, and they were determined that this fire be extinguished. The government arrested him again, on August 1, 1933, and exiled him to the island of Flores, this time without a trial. Later he was transferred to Bengkulen in Western Sumatra, where he remained until released by the Japanese forces in 1942. Most of the twelve years from the age of twenty-nine to forty-one, the years most men consider the best in their lives, Sukarno was either in jail or in confinement in exile. The years in prison and exile were hard years. They toughened the fiber of his spirit.

In an effort to stamp out the independence movement entirely, the Dutch also arrested the other two outstanding nationalist leaders, Hatta and Sjahrir, on February 26, 1934. They, too, were exiled without trial.

Again the Dutch had guessed wrong. Sukarno, Hatta and Sjahrir were out of sight but not out of mind. For the next almost nine years, wherever Indonesians met and talked of independence, they talked of Sukarno. He became a legend.

The years in prison and exile were years of education. No matter where Sukarno was confined, friends smuggled books to him. He read and read —everything he could get his hands on. But he wanted books on socialism and revolution mostly; books that would teach him how to organize against the Dutch, that would supply a philosophy of revolution, that would teach him how to build a nation out of 4,000 islands with disparate cultures, and how to instill a spirit in the people of these islands that would make them unite against the occupier.

Years later, Sukarno described his prison-reading experience: "I met in the world of the mind with Tom Paine. I met and spoke in the world of the mind with the leaders of the French Revolution. I met with Mirabeau; I met with Moreau; I met with Danton; I met with the leader of the revolutionary women in Paris. And in the world of the mind I met also with the leaders of Germany. I met with Herr Alterfritz, Frederick the Great. I met with Wilhelm Lieplat and, yes, then I met also Marx, Karl Marx. I met with Adolf Bernstein. I met with Friedrich Engels.

"I met with Mazzini, with Garibaldi, with Plekhanov, with Trotsky, with Lenin, with Gandhi, with Mustafa Kemal Ataturk, with Ho Chi Minh, with Sun Yat-sen, with Saygo Takamori. I met with Nehru, with Mohammed Ali Jinnah, with José Rizal Mercado, who was shot dead by the Spanish in 1903. I met with Thomas Jefferson and Abraham Lincoln.

"Well, after having met—after having spoken with all those great leaders—I became convinced that mankind is one."

The great Indian philosopher Vivekananda was another source of inspiration to Sukarno. In the foreword to an edition of *The Voice of Vivekananda*,[15] Sukarno wrote, "He was one of the men who gave so much inspiration to me—inspiration to be strong, inspiration to be a ser-

---

15. Published by the Indian Community of Indonesia to commemorate the birth centenary of Vivekananda, April 1963.

vant of God, inspiration to be a servant of my country, inspiration to be a servant of the poor, inspiration to be a servant of mankind. He it was who said, 'We have wept long enough; no more weeping, but stand on your feet, and be men!' "

One can speculate at great length as to whether Sukarno was the force that welded Indonesia together, or whether it was the forces, pressures and dynamics of the Indonesian people that produced Sukarno. Certainly Sukarno emerged as not only the symbol of the aspirations of the Indonesian people, but as the quintessence of their emotionalism, their requirement for self-respect, and their insistence that the world see them for what they were—a proud people of ancient culture who had been subjugated and humiliated by a colonial power. In this sense, Sukarno represented his people in a special way; he was indeed, as he kept insisting, their mouthpiece; he voiced their aspirations as no one else had.

In 1934, Dr. Sutomo, not a partisan of Sukarno, wrote that Sukarno "had been the motor, the driving force of the left-oriented movement; it was he above all others who had sowed the spirit of nationalism in all classes of the people and in all parts of the land. It was he who had demolished the crumbling walls that divided the various groups of the people from one another: Javanese, Sumatran, Ambonese, Menadonese, etc. Marhaens and nobles greeted him as their champion. For them he was Bung Karno and nothing more. They did not see his leftist tendencies, they saw in him only the prophet of freedom. In him was the rallying point of all the feelings and longings that ruled in the hearts of the Indonesians." [16]

Sukarno's policies through the years were designed, consciously or unconsciously, to meet the overwhelming hunger of his people for internal reassurance through recognition and prestige. His division of the world into the "old established forces and the new emerging forces" was a direct reflection of Indonesia's colonial experience. His embracing of a neo-Marxist view of the world, dividing it into the exploiters and the exploited, was the natural result of his own and his country's struggle. He saw the great world conflict as the inevitable strife between "the haves and have-nots," represented by the Western capitalist nations on the one hand, and the socialist and underdeveloped states on the other. He saw himself as not only the great revolutionary leader but also the man who had been tapped by Allah to lead all the captive countries out of bondage and through the wilderness of post-independence chaos to the goal of ending, once and for all, the *"exploitation de l'homme par l'homme."* Finally, he saw the restoration of these nations to their entitled "place in the sun" as a victory of right over wrong; in effect, an international "redress of grievances."

The difficulty the West had in understanding Sukarno derived not

16. Dahm, *Sukarno*, p. 166.

merely from the inadequacy of our knowledge of Indonesian culture and history, but also from the antithetical concept of power held by the Javanese, which was in contradistinction to Western ideas. Professor Benedict Anderson, of Cornell University, is responsible for a revealing analysis of the Javanese concept that clarifies much of Sukarno's behavior, heretofore inexplicable to Western observers.[17] Power to the Javanese is a reality related to the cosmos or God, and not merely a definition of human, or international, or socio-economic relationships, as in the West. Thus power is divine energy to be sought and acquired by ambitious mortals. Once possessed, it must be carefully tended. It is an immortal fire that gives to its possessor qualities enabling him to dominate people and events. As Soedjatmoko expressed it, "a central concept in the Javanese traditional view of life is the direct relationship between the state of a person's inner self and his capacity to control his environment." [18]

Sukarno's conviction that he could reconcile the irreconcilable, that he could resolve contradictions and harmonize opposing forces in the society, that he could mix political oil and water, was an important aspect of his possession of power. "The most obvious sign of the man of power is . . . his ability to draw into himself power previously external to his person, and . . . to concentrate within himself conflicting and antagonistic opposites." [19]

As one of the Indonesian Cabinet ministers once told me of his President, "This man does not admit there are contradictions that cannot be resolved. He believes he can unite conflicting social forces. He believes he can merge Communism and anti-Communism." This was said in no spirit of derision, but to explain apparent inconsistencies in Sukarno's positions.

Sukarno's irrational (to us) maintenance of his Crush Malaysia campaign, which began in 1963, was another example of the Javanese concept of power. Sukarno was determined to impose his will to a point of advantage. This did not mean he had to crush Malaysia. But he did have to extract from his strong stand some positive advantage for his country; otherwise, he had, in Javanese terms, no choice but to go down fighting. Westerners tended to think of this in terms of face saving, as did some Malaysians. I used to argue that the Malaysia dispute could be settled if we could give Sukarno something by which he could save face. Those who disagreed with me had no intention of providing Sukarno with an out. I felt that an exit for the Indonesian President could be provided that

17. Benedict R. O'G. Anderson, "The Idea of Power in Javanese Culture" (unpublished manuscript, Cornell University, 1970).
18. Soedjatmoko, "Indonesia, Problems and Opportunities," *Australian Outlook*. vol. 21, no. 3 (December 1967), 266.
19. Anderson, "Idea of Power," p. 20.

would benefit the entire region. But this was not to be. However, the point here is that something more than face was at issue—the Javanese concept of power, mystical, quasi-religious, and intensely personal, which mandated Sukarno to stand his ground. If this be understood, much that was obscure in the Indonesian leader's reactions through the years becomes explicable.

Much has been made by Sukarno's detractors of his peccadilloes. Many Indonesians felt that their leader's conduct downgraded their country in the eyes of foreigners. Others felt that the frequency of his casual affairs was setting a bad example in a nation where emphasis was placed upon an individual's religion, family affection and responsibility, dignity, and sobriety. Still others noted that virility and sexual potency were historical attributes of Javanese legend and leadership. Sukarno, they admitted, was unquestionably overplaying the role, but the masses probably did not resent this, but in fact took a certain measure of pride in their leader's vaunted capacity.

Many Westerners were startled to find that Sukarno had four wives. Under Moslem law, this is permissible provided a husband treats his wives equally—economically as well as in terms of affection. When Mohammed so ruled, the problem in the deserts of the Middle East was how to *reduce* the number of wives a man took unto himself. He settled on four, presumably because there was a surplus of women in a land where men did the fighting and ran the hazards of desert life.

However, Indonesia, after 1950, was moving at a dizzy pace into the modern world, and the women of the nation who had fought side by side with their men during the revolution were having none of polygamy. They felt let down by Sukarno when he abandoned Fatmawati, his wife of the revolution. But Sukarno, like a deer hunter in Maine, was determined to fill his quota, not counting those shot out of season. Since the Koran allowed four, he took four. Not counting his two earlier wives from whom he was divorced, the three he maintained were Hartini, the beautiful Javanese wife with whom he normally spent every weekend; Dewi, the exquisite Japanese wife, for whom he built a villa on the outskirts of Djakarta and who is one of the most beautiful women I have ever seen in any land; and Hariati, a lovely young Javanese girl. He also continued to provide amply for Fatmawati after their separation.

Sukarno cannot be brushed off, however, as merely a woman-chaser or playboy. In his visits to other countries, he insisted on staying at hotels rather than luxurious private villas. This was not, as so many of his critics assumed, primarily for the purpose of having easy access to night life. Indeed, on the one occasion when I accompanied him to a well-known restaurant-nightclub in San Francisco, Sukarno was more interested in talking with people than in the leg show. He was fascinated by people, art, sculpture, education. He invariably wanted to visit colleges and universities, stores, markets, art galleries—anyplace that gave him contact with human beings and provided fresh insights into what made a country tick. A protocol officer in a European country Sukarno once visited told me, "We were disgusted by his immediate demands for women. But we were charmed by his enthusiasm and excited interest in our educational institutions, our art, our sculpture, our music. It was not the interest of a dilettante, but of one who knew much and had a deep feeling for all that was vital."

Such was the man, then, with whom I would be carrying on a continuous dialogue; and this was the country in which I would be living for eight and a half years.

PART II

Return to Indonesia

The Ambassadors said further, that the people were ready to burn their houses.

—FLAVIUS JOSEPHUS
(37 A.D.–100 A.D.)

The victories of diplomacy are won by a series of microscopic advantages; a judicious suggestion here, an opportune civility there, a wise concession at one moment and a farsighted persistence at another; of sleepless tact, immovable calmness and patience that no folly, provocation, no blunder can shake.

—LORD SALISBURY

Of all the dangers which encompass the liberties of a republican state, the intrusion of a foreign influence into the administration of their affairs is the most alarming.

—JOHN QUINCY ADAMS

CHAPTER 1

Storm Over Java

On February 21, 1958, I stood in the wood-paneled reception room at the Department of State in Washington to be sworn in as American Ambassador to Indonesia. In wishing me God's speed, Secretary of State John Foster Dulles said soberly, "We are giving you one of the toughest assignments in the world today. Good luck!"

At this time in Indonesia, Djuanda Kartawidjaja was Prime Minister and Sukarno was President. Hatta had resigned as Vice-President on December 1, 1956. Popular demand would have had him appointed as Cabinet formateur in March 1957, but Sukarno turned to Suwirjo, chairman of the PNI, with the mandate that all major political parties, including the PKI, should be included in a coalition Cabinet. Suwirjo failed, whereupon Sukarno, bypassing the large Masjumi Party, appointed himself "Citizen Sukarno" as *formateur* of a Cabinet of "experts." He was successful. He selected Djuanda, a nonparty civil engineer who was widely respected and had been a member of previous Cabinets, as Prime Minister. As for the rest of the Cabinet, no Communists were admitted, but two nonparty Ministers—Agriculture and Mobilization of National Strength for Reconstruction—were sympathetic to the PKI.

Relations between Indonesia and the United States were at a low point. The tensions dated back to 1952. The fall of the Sukiman Cabinet on the issue of the secret U.S. aid agreement had created an atmosphere of suspicion and distrust that was exacerbated by what the Indonesian President regarded as our unhelpful attitude on the West Irian dispute, as well as by what we regarded as his dangerous encouragement of the expansion of the Communist Party within the country. My immediate predecessors, Hugh S. Cumming and John M. Allison, had both done their utmost to improve relations while at the same time endeavoring to take measures directed toward curbing the increasing power and influence of the Communists. Unconcealed U.S. sympathy for the Sumatran and Sulawesi "Colonels' Revolt" in 1957 and 1958, and widespread criticism of Sukarno in America, however, had made any real *rapprochement* impossible and brought the dialogue almost to a close. Also, President Sukarno was convinced that Washington, working through the CIA, was endeavoring to bring him down, and that we were actively helping the rebellion.

In addition, the Indonesians were fearing the worst in the appointment of a new ambassador. Apprehension over my appointment had its roots in speculation as to the reasons for the transfer to Prague of my well-regarded predecessor, Ambassador Allison, after only about eight months in Djakarta. One Washington columnist had heralded my nomination as evincing the adoption by the Administration of a new pro-Dutch policy in the bitter Dutch-Indonesian dispute over West New Guinea. Although nothing could have been farther from the truth, this and other comments had caused a stir in Djakarta; in Parliament and the newspapers, attacks on the new appointment had been launched even before my arrival.

Prior to my departure from Washington, Secretary Dulles told the press:

> The U.S. would like to see in Indonesia a government which is constitutional and which reflects the real interest and desires of the people . . . the present 'guided democracy' trend in Indonesia does not entirely satisfy large segments of the population. I think that there has been a growing feeling among the Moslems, particularly in the islands other than Java, a feeling of concern at growing Communist influence in the government of Java and a feeling that the economic resources of these outer islands, like Sumatra, are being exploited contrary to the best interests of the entire Indonesian people. We doubt very much that the people of Indonesia will ever want a Communist-type or Communist-dominated government. Most of them are Moslems and they would not want, I think, to be subjected to a type of government which everywhere, I would say, where it does have power, maintains itself only by coercive methods and does not respond to the will of the people.[1]

One of the rules of international diplomatic usage is that a new envoy to a country cannot do business or participate in official activities of any kind until he has presented his credentials and been officially recognized. Normally, his first few days in a country are devoted to getting settled. If for any reason the presentation of his credentials is delayed for an inordinate period, it can be a lonely time. It is not considered "correct" for him to make calls upon his colleagues; consequently, he is invited to no functions of any kind and is, in fact, subjected to a sort of diplomatic Coventry.

In my case, however, all rules were off. I had landed in Djakarta almost on the day that civil war broke out, and there were things that needed doing and doing fast. It was Wednesday, March 5, the day that the Gov-

---

1. New York *Times*, February 12, 1958.

ernment of the Republic of Indonesia had selected to launch an expeditionary force by ship through the Straits of Malacca for the purpose of attacking rebels who had established a revolutionary government headquarters in the jungles of Central Sumatra. It was quite clear from military and intelligence reports that American lives and property would be endangered by the approaching conflict. The American oil firm, Caltex, the overseas exploration and development arm of Standard Oil of California and the Texas Company, had a large oil camp at Rumbei, near Pakanbaru. Several hundred Americans, including women and children, were living there. This installation, located near the Siak River, one of the few deepwater rivers of Sumatra navigable for a hundred miles into the interior, might well be directly in the path of the oncoming invasion.

After a day of extensive briefing, on March 7 I telephoned the Prime Minister, Dr. Djuanda, and sought an appointment on an urgent basis. He greeted me warmly and arranged for us to meet that same afternoon at his home. I asked H. H. Arnold, Jr., former head of Caltex in Indonesia and then vice-president of all Caltex worldwide operations, to come with me; also Robert Harding, who had succeeded Arnold as general manager for Indonesian operations.

Minister Djuanda received us cordially; we were glad to see each other again after almost three years. But there was an ominous note of warning in his welcoming remarks. "I hope that nothing will happen to disturb our friendship in the days which lie ahead," he said. The remark was grimly prophetic.

Djuanda faced a difficult problem in social and personal ethics, as well as a matter of serious national concern to both our governments. The central government's plan of attack was, of course, top secret. If he told us to evacuate American personnel, it would be a dead giveaway that the attack was to be launched in the Caltex area; should this information leak out, the rebels would be prepared and the surprise element lost. Aware of the U.S. government's sympathy for the rebel cause, he was obviously wondering whether he could trust us not to pass information to the opposing force. On the other hand, if he led us to believe the attack would be launched in a different area, and American lives and property were destroyed as a result, serious international repercussions were inevitable.

I realized full well that once I had his answer, my government would also face a hard choice. Should it pass this information through whatever channels it might have to the rebel leaders? Or keep faith with a man of integrity who was a top official of a government with whose policies we were unsympathetic? Of such stuff is the warp and woof of diplomacy made.

"I am going to trust you," Djuanda said finally, his manner heavily serious. "I shall require your word of honor that what passes between us will not reach outside sources. If it should, many of our soldiers' lives might be sacrificed. This is a grave responsibility for me and for you." He then outlined in very general terms the plan of campaign, not in sufficient detail to give away any military secrets, but enough to reassure me that the Indonesian government was taking every precaution in its plans to ensure that the Caltex oil-producing installations would be protected. At the end, however, he advised us to evacuate all women and children to cover any unforeseeable eventualities.

On March 10, 1958, I presented my credentials to President Sukarno in a brief but dignified ceremony at Merdeka Palace in Djakarta. I expressed the United States government's desire to continue cordial relations with the Government of the Republic of Indonesia, and our interest in assisting Indonesia in maintaining its independence. I assured the President that the U.S. had no intention of interfering in Indonesian internal affairs.

Sukarno's response emphasized Indonesia's adherence to the *Pantjasila*—the Five Principles upon which the government rested—its active independent foreign policy, taking no sides with either major world bloc, and the necessity for completing Indonesia's revolution by effecting the return of West Irian. Significantly, he noted that Indonesian–United States relations would continue to be tested by the realization of those principles and goals. He also recalled favorably his 1956 visit to America and noted the many similarities between the American and Indonesian revolutions. He said he "would not wish at this moment to withdraw a single word" of the speeches he made in the United States— speeches that quoted Thomas Jefferson and Abraham Lincoln, praised America, and emphasized nationalism as a progressive, constructive world force.

The Indonesian press gave wide coverage to the occasion, which shared headlines with the SEATO meeting scheduled for the next day in Manila. The majority of the press played up my assurances of noninterference in internal affairs, but the Communist and extreme left-wing newspapers commented that there would be no change in U.S. policy and that the "Allison meddling" would be continued.

Cameras flashed as we raised champagne glasses filled with orange juice and exchanged toasts to the health of the Presidents of both countries. Sukarno, like most Moslems, did not drink alcohol. The apparently friendly, albeit somewhat formal congeniality of the occasion, tended to conceal the reality of my being an unwelcome ambassador to a nation whose leader and policies my government opposed. At almost that very moment, Indonesian regular army troops were hacking their way through Sumatran jungles and making their way up the Siak River in an effort to confront the rebel forces.

The United States government had made its sympathies amply clear. Any doubt about this had been laid to rest by Secretary Dulles on

March 9, in a statement to the House Foreign Affairs Committee. "We should be very happy," Dulles said, "to see the non-Communist elements who are really in the majority there . . . exert a greater influence in the affairs of Indonesia than has been the case in the past where President Sukarno has moved toward this so-called guided democracy theory, which is a nice-sounding name for what I fear would end up to be Communist despotism." In answer to a question concerning the rebels' chances of success "if they have no air umbrella and if Sukarno continues to use American-bought planes to bomb them," Dulles replied: "I think there is a fair chance that out of this will come a curtailment of the trend toward Communism. I don't want to be more precisely detailed at the moment than that." [2]

The release of these comments the day before I presented my credentials added perceptibly to the official restraint and incipient suspicion that undercut the personal cordiality of my formal reception. Like subsequent Washington statements of a similar stamp, this was regarded not only as an expression of sympathy for the rebels but a blatant attempt to interfere in Indonesia's domestic quarrels.

The convening of the annual SEATO meeting in Manila the day following the credentials ceremony compounded Djakarta's resentment and suspicion of the United States and its anti-Communist allies. Convinced that the meeting was hatching plans to support the rebels, politically conscious Indonesians continued to give vent to their highly volatile nationalistic sentiments through fiery editorials and a massive demonstration at the American Embassy on March 25. Predictably, the demonstrator's placards called for the dissolution of SEATO on the ground it was aiding the rebels.

Thus, at the outset of my assignment, I was confronted with perhaps the most conspicuous feature of the Indonesian political landscape—a sensitive nationalism easily aroused at the slightest hint of an encroachment on Indonesia's precious sovereignty by a foreign power.

I had my work cut out for me.

Settlement of Indonesia's rebellion took almost as long as our own Civil War. It appeared as though each side, at least in the beginning, was reluctant to shoot at the other. Neither had wanted the differences between them to come to physical conflict; each had anticipated that, faced with substantial physical force, the other would back down. But once force is applied, the consequences are usually grimly predictable. To the outside world, the conflict was pictured as anti-Communist rebels against a pro-Communist government in Djakarta. In fact, it was a much more complex affair, involving anti-Communists on both sides.

For years prior to the outbreak of the rebellion in February 1958, cen-

---

2. New York *Times*, March 10, 1958.

tralization of the government in Djakarta had increasingly concentrated business, finance, trade, as well as purely governmental functions such as education, public health, public works, and police, in Javanese hands. Loud was the complaint that officials in Djakarta were ignorant of conditions outside Java; anti-Javanese feeling in the outer islands gradually mounted. Economic grievances were also behind the clamor that had led to active revolt. Leaders from Sumatra and Sulawesi complained, with some basis in fact, that their production was largely responsible for financing the government: approximately seventy-one per cent of the foreign exchange the nation received was produced by Sumatran exports, but only twelve per cent of it was spent in Sumatra. Central-government policies appeared to be favoring the Javanese importer as against the outer-island exporter. The Sumatrans felt that not only was the region losing foreign exchange, which it produced, but the producer himself was being hurt by Djakarta's fiscal and monetary policies, such as over-evaluation of the rupiah. This rich island, four times the size of Java, badly needed schools, roads, harbor facilities, power plants. With Sumatran rubber, oil, coffee and other products paying for the importation of rice and various consumer goods to populated Java, it was inevitable that Sumatrans would rise to claim a larger share of the fruits of their efforts.[3]

It was to have been anticipated that issues affecting so vital a nerve as the pocketbook would ultimately explode into open defiance on the part of the outer-islands population. Smuggling became the standard means of showing this defiance of Djakarta, particularly in North Sumatra and North Sulawesi, where a large part of the profits were used to effect improvements that the central government could no longer manage. In mid-1956, for example, Colonel Simbolon, head of the North Sumatra military command, organized a large-scale smuggling operation out of one of the small ports in East Sumatra, with the ultimate purpose of improving conditions for his soldiers. The military housing and health situation in Sumatra was so serious that soldier morale was threatened. The central government was not providing sufficient funds to meet the problem, and Simbolon courageously notified officials in Djakarta of his intention. Between May 15 and June 5, seven ships of foreign registry called at a port in East Sumatra and moved out some 5,000 tons of rubber and coffee under army protection. When the Cabinet instructed Simbolon to stop the smuggling, he went to Djakarta, assumed personal

3. For more detailed discussions of the causes of rebellion, see Herbert Feith, *The Decline of Constitutional Democracy in Indonesia* (Ithaca, N.Y.: Cornell University Press, 1962); Daniel S. Lev, *The Transition to Guided Democracy: Indonesian Politics, 1957–1959* (Ithaca, N.Y.: Cornell Modern Indonesia Project, Monograph Series, 1966); James Mossman, *Rebels in Paradise: Indonesia's Civil War* (London: Jonathan Cape, 1961); Ruth T. McVey, ed., *Indonesia*, rev. ed. (New Haven, Conn.: HRAF Press, 1967).

responsibility for the action, and worked out a settlement with the civil and military authorities. By 1957, it was estimated that one-third of Indonesia's annual rubber crop was being exported by smugglers, resulting in considerable loss of revenue to the government.[4]

Equally, if not more important from the standpoint of viable nationhood, was the diminution in central government authority. People were beginning to thumb their noses at Djakarta with impunity. Still, government officials refused to compromise. The impasse precipitated a power struggle between Djakarta and regional, outer island officials, as well as a parallel conflict within the army as powerful territorial commanders challenged the authority of headquarters.

Internal division over economic policy was nothing new for Indonesia. From the earliest days, Sukarno had advocated the removal of what he termed the "stranglehold" of the Dutch on the economy of the country. Political independence was not enough, he insisted. Indonesia would not be genuinely independent until the Dutch were thrown out.

Hatta, Sjafruddin, Natsir, most of the leaders of the powerful Masjumi Party, disagreed with him. So did Sjahrir and key leaders of the Socialist Party. Sjafruddin, then Governor of the Central Bank, later to become Prime Minister of the so-called Revolutionary Government, told me as far back as 1954, "We are moving in the wrong direction. We badly need the Dutch capital and know-how."

Nineteen fifty-seven was a fateful year in the history of the young nation, economically as well as politically. It was the year the Dutch were thrown out of Indonesia, and the year in which Sukarno announced his plan for "Guided Democracy." In the opinion of many, this was nothing more or less than the first step toward dictatorship, and something must be done before it was too late. What made the 1957 climate even more ominous was that of the nation's political parties, the Communist appeared to emerge as the strongest. Local elections held in June, July and August resulted in the PKI's winning 27.4 per cent of the votes cast. It seemed possible for a time that this shock might tend to bring greater unity among the elements opposing Communism in Indonesia. The rebels in the outer islands and their Djakarta sympathizers might present a common front to the enemy. Three of the non-Communist parties, the NU (the conservative Moslem scholars' party), the PNI and the Masjumi, held discussions with a view to effective cooperation in opposition to the PKI, but the effort fell apart before it had got really under way.

As the year progressed, tensions between Djakarta and the regions increased, and lines on both sides hardened, in spite of vigorous efforts by Hatta and Dr. Roem, Masjumi leader, to bring the opposing elements together. In Djakarta, demands grew for strong action to bring the rebel-

---

4. Feith, *Decline of Constitutional Democracy*, pp. 496–499.

lious regional leaders to their knees. In the outer islands, people began to talk about open confrontation with Djakarta and to initiate contacts for overseas support. In September, the central government, belatedly but genuinely alarmed by the situation, brought together military and civilian representatives from the regions and central government officials at a national consultative conference called in Djakarta by Prime Minister Djuanda. Although committees were appointed to deal with various aspects of the conflict, no agreement was reached, partly because events moved too fast from this point on, partly because top rebel leaders suspected that they would be trapped and arrested if they went to Djakarta for high-level meetings.

As if the situation were not complex enough, two other developments influenced the course of events in this period. In November 1957, a number of states friendly to Indonesia proposed a resolution calling upon the Netherlands and Indonesia to negotiate a settlement of the West Irian dispute. The climate at the UN, however, was not promising for its passage. As this became more and more apparent, the attitude of Sukarno and his followers became more and more threatening. If the resolution were defeated, Sukarno warned on November 8, "We will use a new way in our struggle which will surprise the nations of the world."

The defeat of the resolution on November 29 would have been enough to ignite passions in Djakarta. But on November 30, an attempt was made to assassinate President Sukarno as he was leaving a ceremony at Tjikini grammar school in Djakarta, where two of his children were enrolled. Surrounded by an admiring throng on his way to the car, he became the target for two hand grenades suddenly hurled from a short distance away, both of which burst close to him. Three more grenades exploded in quick succession. The President and a wounded aide dashed across the street to seek shelter in a house. Recognizing it as a Dutch dwelling, they turned away and ran into the house next door, an Indonesian home. There was a grim touch of irony in the President's choosing to risk his life rather than be saved in a Dutch home.

The grenades took a terrible toll. Nine people were killed, six of them children, and 150 wounded. But Sukarno emerged untouched.

Four of the assassins, fanatical Moslems, were apprehended and tried. At the trial, they publicly denounced Sukarno as "a mere orator," and the "chief protector of the Communists." They called him a "*kafir*," or nonbeliever, and even criticized Sukarno's marriage to Hartini. When the judge asked one of them if he felt any remorse, he replied, "For the many victims, but not if Bung Karno had been hit."

The trial disposed of the considerable speculation that the assassination had been Dutch-inspired. One of the defendants admitted that his political and religious teachings had come in part from Colonel Zulkifli Lubis. The anti-Sukarno Lubis, who was hiding out somewhere in Java, boldly went on the radio and, denying he had any part in the plot, boasted, "I would have succeeded!" Lubis was apparently moving around in Java attempting to drum up support for the rebel position. He subsequently joined the rebels in Sumatra.[5]

By January 1958, rumors were flying thick and fast that Djakarta was planning military action against the regions. As part of counterpreparations, regional leaders made contact with Western powers to obtain political, diplomatic and military support for their struggle against Sukarno. The pressure was on. Much to everyone's surprise, in the midst of all this hubbub, President Sukarno, reportedly shaken by the Tjikini affair, left the country for a "much-needed" six week rest trip overseas.

Apparently thinking they had Sukarno on the run, the dissident groups moved fast. Strenuous efforts were made to induce a change of government in Djakarta while he was gone. But central-government officials hesitated. Finally, on February 10, 1958, six days before Sukarno was to return home, Lieutenant Colonel Hussein, army commander in Central Sumatra, issued an ultimatum to the central government to the effect that unless a new Cabinet were set up in five days, led by Hatta and/or the Sultan of Jogjakarta, a new government would be formed in Sumatra.

The complete text of the ultimatum was carried in the Indonesian official press bulletin, having been broadcast by Radio Padang at repeated intervals following its announcement. The ceremony at which the ultimatum was made public was attended by dissident military officers, most notably the former North Sumatra commander, Colonel Simbolon; several top leaders of the Masjumi, including Mohammed Natsir, Sjafruddin Prawiranegara, and Burhanuddin Harahap; local officials from Central Sumatra, and other leaders. The ultimatum was significantly called "The Charter for Defending the State." There was no hint of secession; but it peremptorily demanded that:

> within five times twenty-four hours following the publication of the ultimatum, the Djuanda Cabinet should return its mandate to the President (Acting President) and a new cabinet should be formed. Dr. Hatta and the Sultan of Jogjakarta should be designated by the President to form a national business cabinet consisting of 'honest and non-atheistic' leaders who command full authority with the task of safeguarding the state from disintegration, of preventing a calamity which might befall the state, and of laying down strong foundations for the country's development.

Sukarno was asked to return to his position as constitutional President, to stop violating the provisional constitution, and also "to afford opportunity to a cabinet to be led by Hatta and Hamengku Buwono to work until the next general elections." The ultimatum carried the threat

5. This incident is recorded in greater detail in Louis Fischer, *The Story of Indonesia* (New York: Harper & Brothers, 1959), pp. 227–229.

that if points one and two were not complied with, "we shall take our own steps."

The Charter further stated that the ultimatum was based on the consideration that the Republic of Indonesia was a law-abiding national state with a faith in "the one and only God, humanity and democracy." It warned that the Republic of Indonesia was threatened with "total collapse" because the President had violated the Constitution in forming the Karya ("working") Cabinet and the National Council, and because of the infiltration of atheists in the central administration, a decline of moral values, and destruction of "the people's living resources."

The issuance of the ultimatum at a time when events in Djakarta were moving in a direction favorable to a peaceful solution of the controversy was a major mistake on the part of the Sumatran rebels. It was inconceivable that the Djakarta government would bow to an ultimatum. Sukarno would never back down in the face of a threat. And so it proved. Furthermore, the ground was cut out from under the rebels' Djakarta friends and those seeking a compromise as opposition elements coalesced.

Years later I asked Sjafruddin what had motivated that decision. "It was Colonel Hussein's decision. I opposed it," he replied. "I pleaded with Hussein to wait at least two weeks. But he was adamant. 'I'm going ahead,' he told us. 'With you or without you.' Both Natsir and I were against its issuance. But there was nothing we could do. It was too late to withdraw. However, you will note that I did not sign the ultimatum. Hussein signed it."

On February 15, the Revolutionary Government of the Republic of Indonesia (PRRI) was proclaimed in Padang, with Sjafruddin Prawiranegara as the Prime Minister. The Cabinet included men from various parts of Sumatra as well as two from Java. The Revolutionary Government denounced Sukarno, Guided Democracy, and Communism, and demanded regional autonomy and a state truly based on faith in God.

Desperate last-minute efforts were made by Hatta to stave off a military clash. Sukarno returned to Djakarta; Hatta met with him on February 20 and again on March 3 to try to find a way out. Had a Sukarno-Hatta government been formed, even at so late a stage, civil war might still have been averted. But the two leaders could not agree on terms. With the landing of the central government forces at Bengalis on the east coast of Central Sumatra in early March, hope for a peaceful settlement vanished.

The issues sparking the rebellion were not primarily drawn on Communist versus anti-Communist lines, but involved economic, social and political factors on which anti-Communists and non-Communists were divided. There was no division, of course, among the Indonesian Communists, who had long since learned the lesson of "united we stand, divided we fall." The fact that Sukarno was sheltering, even nurturing the expansion of the Communist Party, that the base of Communist strength was in Java, and finally that the rebel leadership was solidly anti-Communist lent color to the conviction, widespread in Washington, that the major issue was the Communist issue. It was simply not so, however. This is not to say that those who supported the rebels on the basis that Sukarno's leftist leanings would inevitably lead Indonesia toward Communism were wrong. As it turned out, they were right.

But in 1958, Sukarno was a fact of life. There was no one who had the leadership capacity to counter that golden voice and strong will. And the attempt to wring concessions out of the Government of Indonesia and topple Sukarno by the threat of force was simply a bad guess as to the parameters of the possible.

In the latter part of 1957, there was, as far as Washington was concerned, a very real possibility of Indonesia's, or at least Java's being lost to the Communists in the immediate future. During the previous year, Indonesia had fallen into an advanced state of political confusion and economic deterioration. The growing Communist strength, particularly in Java (of the thirty-nine Communist representatives in Parliament, thirty-five came from Java), was alarming. By 1955, the PKI had become the fourth-largest political party; in 1957, it had remarkable successes in local elections. The Communist labor organization, SOBSI, had spearheaded a move to take over the Dutch properties, and was well organized and well financed. In contrast, the non-Communist political parties were ineffective, unable or unwilling to cooperate with each other, to rise above factionalism and a concentration of interest on political patronage. Sukarno seemed to have been drawn more and more into the Communist net.

However, it was recognized that the non-Communist forces throughout Indonesia, while of differing motivation, were still in the majority, although far stronger in the outer islands, particularly Sumatra, than in Java. Consequently, the most promising approach to the Indonesian situation was considered to lie in the direction of exploring the potential political and economic resources available in the outer islands, particularly in Sumatra and Sulawesi. The U.S. government therefore decided to employ all feasible means to strengthen the determination and cohesion of the anti-Communist forces there, with two objectives in mind: first, to affect the situation in Java through their pressure; and second, to encourage the formation of a rallying point for the forces of freedom if, as seemed possible, the Communists should take over Java.

As for the question of whether sanctions should be applied through aid programs, three alternative approaches were discussed: (1) continue the assistance programs in the hope that the Communist gains per se would arouse and unify non- and anti-Communist forces enough to reverse the trend; (2) terminate the programs in the hope of producing a shock reaction that would alert the non-Communist elements to the seriousness with which we regarded the situation; (3) continue the existing pattern of formal relations with the government in Djakarta but adjust our policy so as to emphasize our support for the anti-Communist forces in the outer islands.

In December 1957, it was decided that the situation had become sufficiently serious to warrant the United States government's taking steps toward the implementation of the third alternative. This would have the advantage of enabling communication to be established with those elements in the outer islands opposing the central government, so that in the event of Java's being suddenly lost to Communism, the outer islands might be salvaged. It was hoped that a focal point of opposition to Sukarno and his policies would result in sufficient pressure on the central government to bring about a change in those policies, if not a step down by Sukarno himself. To those of us familiar with the Indonesian situation, the former was certainly a possible outcome; the latter was wishful thinking.

An outstandingly able officer, Gordon Mein,[6] was then head of the Office of Southwest Pacific Affairs in the Department of State. Mein did his utmost to resist a U.S. course of action that would encourage the rebels to launch armed rebellion against the central government. Assistant Secretary Robertson supported Mein in this and, as Robertson's deputy, so did I.

American sympathy with the rebel cause was understandable. The military leaders involved were among the most capable in the Indonesian Army. The civilian leaders included some of the most outstanding personalities in the country, and most of the men who had stood for what represented, in the eyes of the U.S. government, sound policies. They were men of personal and intellectual integrity. I knew them all well as a result of my previous service as Chief of the Economic Aid Mission.

The prejudice against Sukarno in Washington was so great as to blind some of the most responsible officials to the realities of the power situation. In intelligence circles, there was a conviction that an overthrow of Sukarno by the rebels was possible; there was also the hope on the part of some of the Sukarno-haters that even if he could not be overthrown, Sumatra, the oil-rubber-tin–producing powerhouse, might secede from Indonesia—and American and other foreign properties would be salvaged. Some false hopes were also entertained that the army, commanded by a Sumatran, General Nasution, might cooperate with the rebels in forcing changes in Indonesian government policies upon Sukarno.

Among the rebels, as well as in some Washington circles, there was

---

6. Later assassinated by left-wing elements in Guatemala, where he was United States Ambassador from 1966 to 1968. He was a close friend and a dedicated diplomat; his murder represented a real loss to the country.

virtual contempt for the executive and administrative capacity of the central government in Djakarta. Sukarno, it was said, did not have the intestinal fortitude to order the Indonesian military into action since it would split the country. Sukarno had worked all his life to unite his country; he was the last man to take an action that would result in a division that might be irrevocable. It was argued that even if Sukarno were inclined to take strong measures against the rebels, the pro-insurrectionist elements within the government would be able to dissuade him or throw roadblocks in his way. Finally, there was the conviction that the central government would never take the economic risk involved in military action, not merely because of its cost, but also because such action would cut off the vitally needed foreign exchange that Sumatran production provided. This last argument overlooked the fact that Sumatra was already diverting large amounts of foreign exchange from Djakarta by trading directly with other countries.

The Indonesian government's decision to suppress the rebellion by force made it clear that none of these assumptions and hopes were valid.

I myself felt a strong identification with the rebel cause in terms of the issues dividing the rebels from the central government. But I held from the beginning an even stronger conviction that these issues were not of such a character as to justify force of arms on either side. Patience and forbearance from both could have brought about a peaceful settlement. I was reinforced in this conviction by the positions that I knew men of vision in Indonesia had taken, among them Dr. Hatta, the former Vice-President, Dr. Sjahrir, former Prime Minister, Dr. Roem, the Masjumi leader, the Anak Agung, former Foreign Minister. Knowing personally the leadership on both sides, I had hoped to reach Indonesia in time to play a role in encouraging a peaceful solution; unfortunately, I was too late.

My first talk in depth with Sukarno following my arrival was on Tuesday, March 18, at the white-pillared palace in Bogor, some forty miles from Djakarta. The President was his old informal self, enthusiastic, bouncy, jubilant. His face was more rugged and lined than I remembered it, although not so haggard as a recent *Time* magazine cover portrait had made him out to be. He welcomed me with great cordiality and chatted volubly during the first few moments while cake and coffee were being served. When he grew suddenly serious and asked, "Well, how are things?" I parried by answering in a personal vein and returned the question regarding Indonesia.

The President referred to his response to my credentials presentation: "Indonesia is strategic in place and in time—politically, militarily and economically," and the United States should recognize this. "Relations between us are not and have not been what they should be," he said. He regretted this lack of understanding and cited the failure of the United States to support Indonesia's claim to West New Guinea, complaining that the American people's general impression of him, as seen in the American press, was that he was a Communist and that the present government was Communist inclined. As examples of possible reasons for this impression, he referred to Minister of Education Prijono's receiving the Stalin Peace Prize. Prijono, said Sukarno, was not a Communist. He also referred to Minister of Veteran Affairs Chairul Saleh, whom he described as a left-wing nationalist but not a Communist, and to Minister Hanafi, who was the only one in the Cabinet that could really be called a "fellow traveler" though not, he felt certain, a member of the PKI. Sukarno mentioned that another factor in this lack of understanding was Indonesia's request for arms a year or two earlier, to which there had been no response.

Sukarno insisted he stood firmly, and Indonesia stood firmly, on the principles of the *Pantjasila*. Sukarno said that though he was referred to as the "creator of *Pantjasila*," it had really "been dug out of the soil of Indonesia"; he was only the tool that unearthed it. He said he recognized two political elements in Indonesia endeavoring to destroy the *Pantjasila*: fanatical Moslems and the Communists.

Sukarno pointed out that Indonesia was striving to cover centuries within a few years. On his trip to the United States, Soviet Russia and Communist China in 1956, he had found the U.S. so far advanced economically and industrially that Indonesia had no hope of catching up within his lifetime. Soviet Russia was similarly developed industrially. Communist China, which had been "a miserable country" only eight years ago, had made tremendous advances, and he had been greatly impressed by what he had seen there. His conclusions, he emphasized, were shared by Hatta and Minister of Public Works Noor of the Masjumi Party, who had also visited Communist China after seeing the United States.

"When I say that methods adopted by Communist China in achieving this development may hold lessons for Indonesia, I do not include their political doctrine," he said. "This I reject!"

"Americans do not seem to understand this," he complained. "I am called a Communist by the American press, and even Secretary Dulles said that Indonesia was drifting toward Communism. I am not a Communist. Every word I said in America I still stand by. I tried to point out that nationalism was the fire that was sweeping Asia, and this is true. I am a nationalist, but no Communist."

I interjected with the observation that Communist China was a country in which individual freedom had been lost—*merdeka* had been destroyed—and where only one and three-quarters per cent of the people were Communists, led by a handful of leaders who were forcing their will upon the vast majority. I stated I was confident Indonesia did not want to follow this road, and that I was one American who was convinced Sukarno was not a Communist. I said it was difficult for Americans to understand the rapid growth of Communism within Indonesia, his sympathy with it, and why steps had not been taken to curb expanding Communist influence.

Sukarno countered by saying that the United States must share the responsibility for this. Our position on West Irian was a major factor in the growth of the PKI; Indonesians did not understand America's failure to help Indonesia achieve one of its basic national aspirations. On the other hand, Soviet Russia and other Communist countries supported Indonesia on this issue right down the line. Not only that; this was colonialism and America claimed to be anti-colonial. He then repeated what he had said frequently in the past—if the United States would change its position on West Irian, he would throw out the Communists. He snapped his fingers to emphasize this point. "This is true and yet America stands mute!" he said. "Mute! And why? Why can't America change its position on this one issue?"

I retorted that he knew our position quite well—we regarded the West Irian issue as a bilateral dispute between two of our friends, Indonesia and the Netherlands. This was a matter on which we must remain neutral.

"This I do not understand," he shouted. "If you changed your position, little Holland would be annoyed—yes? But how do you balance that against the annoyance of Indonesia?"

I admitted that Indonesia was a bigger country with greater resources, but I said there was a principle here that one did not desert one's old friends. I pointed out, however, that we were not supporting the Dutch, either. Sukarno must understand our position—cases of this kind, in which it is difficult for a country to take sides in a bilateral controversy, occur not infrequently. I pointed out that in the Kashmir dispute, Indonesia had, despite much pressure from both India and Pakistan, refused to take sides. West Irian was a parallel case.

Sukarno quickly changed the subject and reverted to the status of Communism within Indonesia. The Indonesian people are not Communists, he insisted. Even most of those who voted for the PKI are not Communists. They are left-wing nationalists. He cited the case of what is called the "Holy City," that section of Surabaya in which is located the Sacred Mosque of Ampel. "These people are one hundred per cent Moslem," he said. "They pray five times a day. But the Holy City voted one hundred per cent Communist!" He also cited the case of two leaders he knew in the PKI who were strict Moslems.

I observed that Islam and Communism seemed to me as oil and water, and I found it difficult to understand how the PKI leaders referred to could rationalize their position. The dialectical materialism of Communism left no place for God. In the case of Moslem Surabaya, I was confident that the voters had no idea of what Communism meant. I pointed out that PKI orators in Surabaya made a pretense of believing in God. It was the old story of the wolf in sheep's clothing. The fact that most Indonesians who voted for the PKI were not Communists but nationalists did not reduce the danger of a Communist takeover, since a vote for the PKI had the same value whether cast by a Communist or non-Communist. We did not believe the Indonesian people would ever willingly go down the road to Communism. Our fear was that if Communist power within the country were permitted to grow, ultimately the time would come when, even though a minority, the Communists would take over. It was a familiar tactic; witness Czechoslovakia.

Knowing Sukarno had been brought up with the other side of the story, I recalled that President Beneš had felt it necessary in the reconstruction of Czechoslovakia after World War II to have all elements of the political community, including the Communists, represented in the government. In the period from 1945 to 1948, I emphasized, the Communists posed as the champions of national liberty and an independent foreign policy. They took great care to operate within the framework of Czechoslovak national psychology, making no moves that were not generally politically acceptable. When they were strong enough, however, they moved quickly to take over. I paused a moment for the point to sink in, then added soberly, "I am certain your Excellency knows that Jan Masaryk was found dead outside the Foreign Office, generally believed to have been assassinated by the Communists, and that President Beneš, broken in body and spirit, his influence gone, retired to the country." Sukarno nodded, his expression thoughtful, and it was clear the parallel was not lost upon him.

Sukarno then asked why we were so worried about Indonesia's percentage of Communist votes. "You aren't worried about France and Italy's, yet theirs is higher." I pointed out that the Communist vote in France and Italy was decreasing as compared with earlier years, whereas in Indonesia it was increasing.

"We were worried about Communism in these countries," I said. "That is what the Marshall Plan was all about: to enable European countries to rehabilitate themselves after the war, regain lost standards of living and give people hope once more. We think it accomplished its purpose."

Sukarno referred to Dulles' remarks on the subject of Guided Democracy, complaining that it had been generally misunderstood in the United States. "This is my idea to correct a trouble from which we suffer—over-democracy," he said, pointing out that there were some forty-seven political parties in Indonesia, each representing special points of view or special interests. "This is nonsense!" he shouted, his fist pounding the table. "No country can function with its people so divided. No government can act." His concept of Guided Democracy was designed to correct the evils in the body politic—not to destroy democracy—by reducing the number of political parties.

He insisted the central government was not using a great deal of force and did not wish to, but it must reestablish its position and authority in Sumatra. He had tried to settle the controversy as soon as he returned from Japan, but the actions of the rebels in laying down an ultimatum and proclaiming a revolutionary government had made this impossible. He then said that the head of the NU had come to him with a request for a conference of all political party leaders, including the PKI, he added significantly, and Hatta. He said he was considering this but had not yet made up his mind.

Responding to Sukarno's complaints about the American press, I suggested that he himself could take one step to improve the situation. American correspondents representing reputable media had complained to me that they were unable to see him, whereas they had no difficulty in seeing Nehru in New Delhi and other national leaders in other countries. They could not understand this. More important, this prevented them from hearing Sukarno's views from his own lips.

"But aren't these men prejudiced?" Sukarno queried.

"They are trying to be objective," I replied, "but if they have no way of getting your side of the story, you yourself are placing them under a handicap." I pointed out further the outstanding success he had enjoyed in dealing with the American press in the United States, mentioning his speech before the National Press Club in Washington, and his skillful handling of questions and answers on that occasion. Sukarno looked at the ceiling, pursed his lips, and said he would think about it.

I took advantage of the appearance of the President's aide, indicating that other visitors were waiting, to say that I felt we had a great many things to discuss, and I hoped this would be one of a series of conversations. Sukarno seemed pleased and readily agreed, adding that he had intended to suggest this had I not done so. I assured him that I considered the establishment of a close understanding between our two countries the most important aspect of my mission. Nodding, Sukarno said he wanted to see me often.

As he accompanied me to the door, I mentioned that when I had been in Indonesia previously I had, of course, known Vice-President Hatta and planned to call on him in due course, but wished that Sukarno be informed in advance. The President responded quickly that he had no objection. He hesitated for a moment, then added with a slight smile, "There are others, of course, who in the light of this current situation will charge you with playing a game." I indicated that I understood this. He was referring to Hatta's contact with the rebels and his effort to settle the rebellion peaceably.

As I thought about this conversation, I was struck by the fact that although we had not agreed on anything, we had been able to discuss controversial issues frankly and without heat. It seemed probable that my tenure as Ambassador to Indonesia was destined to be a short one, considering the state of affairs. It had always been difficult to carry water on both shoulders, and this is what the American government seemed to be trying to do. It was important that this new nation become a viable entity, able to stand on its own feet. This was our objective. It was vital to our national interest, and even more vital to the Indonesian people. But how to get across to them that we were sincere in this?

Certain facts of life struck me in the situation with which I was faced. One was Sukarno's hold on the hearts of his people. Regardless of the bitter divisions among the Indonesian elite, there was nothing to suggest in 1958 any diminution in Sukarno's popularity among the masses. If the central government succeeded in putting down the rebellion, Sukarno's personal power and prestige unquestionably would be heightened. If the rebels won, the best Sukarno could hope for would be to remain as a figurehead President; or he might lose out altogether. But as of the moment, his image was still that of the great revolutionary leader.

Second, it was apparent that the rebellion differed fundamentally from our own Civil War in that there was neither threat of nor desire for secession. The rebels were aiming at more regional autonomy and a change in the government in Djakarta, but insisting on the maintenance of Indonesia as a united nation.

Third, Indonesia now had a divided army and a divided territory. Two important areas—much of Sumatra and all of North Sulawesi—were in the hands of rebel forces.

Aside from the rebellion, there was a multiplicity of problems facing this eight-year-old nation; it seemed to need everything at once. The economy was in poor shape, with a badly balanced budget and an inadequate tax and revenue system. The value of Indonesian currency on the black market was four times the official rate.

The paucity of educated and trained personnel was appalling. Cabinet decisions often were not carried out owing to the lack of technical competence at secondary and lower levels of the bureaucracy. The people had a burning desire for education, but resources to meet the demand were almost nil.

The country was only potentially rich because it lacked the capital and skill to exploit its resources. In throwing out the Dutch entrepreneurs in late 1957, the Indonesian government had literally killed the goose that laid the golden eggs. Though they hated to admit it, Dutch capital and expertise were desperately needed by the new nation.

With fertile soil, favorable climate, and millions of acres of cultivatable jungle, Indonesia did not raise enough food to feed its people, and was using sparse foreign exchange to import rice.

Nationalism and xenophobia were so intense and widespread, partly owing to continuing Communist influence, that foreign investment was not welcome. The shortsighted petroleum policy of the government was to keep the oil in the ground except for the amount needed to meet the internal requirements of the country.

The governmental structure was weak and poorly adapted to the needs of a new nation. Its political parties were too numerous, too divided and self-seeking, for the most part, to provide essential stability.

An effective, fast-growing, well-financed Communist Party was rapidly penetrating the bureaucracy and other key areas of the society.

Thousand-year-old rivalries between island peoples threatened the unity of the country. Java and Sumatra were hereditary enemies. Sulawesi and the Moluccas had long been antagonistic to dominant Java.

It was an appalling catalogue of ills. Perhaps the nation's most important asset was its will to survive and the determination of its leaders that come what might, they would never again surrender their independence or allow Indonesia to disintegrate. "What was the Indonesian nation in 1945?" Sukarno thundered at mass meeting after mass meeting. "It was a song and a flag, that's all." The nation had come a long way since that time. Again to quote Sukarno, it was "the burning fire for freedom within the breasts of the Indonesian people" that had brought them this far.

Shortly after my arrival in Djakarta, I received the standard request from the Department of State for a situation estimate predicting political developments over the next six months. I cabled back that I was unable to predict what would happen during the next six hours, much less six months!

There are times when human beings can control, or at least influence the course of history. There are other times when events themselves take over—precipitated perhaps by earlier human decisions—and this seemed to be one of them.

CHAPTER 2

The Rise of
the Nationalist Movement

Before I could indulge in the risk-ridden exercise of political prediction—and certainly before I could recommend initiatives to be taken by the United States government—I needed to know much more about the motivations of the dramatis personae and what had been going on behind the scenes prior to my arrival. The situation I found had not developed overnight. In part its roots lay in the glory of the ancient empires; more urgently, it derived from events occurring within this century—the persistent growth among the people of anti-colonial sentiment; the impact of World War I with its aftermath of Marxism, Leninism, and Wilsonian liberalism; the rout of the Dutch by the Japanese and the opportunities opened by World War II to nationalist leaders. I did not ignore the daily press of problems at the embassy, but it was to the recent past that I gave a great deal of my time.

I quickly learned that the Indonesian people, gentle and patient as they are, had not been passive under colonialism. They fought back whenever they got the chance. During the centuries of occupation, more than thirty revolts broke out against the Dutch. Of these, the rebellion the Dutch refer to as the Java War (1825–1830) was the most prolonged and most serious from their standpoint because it constituted a direct assault upon already established authority in Java, the seat of their operations. Most of the other revolts were regional in character. The Balinese and Atjehnese fought off the Dutch for generations, and were not brought under effective control until well into the twentieth century.

The Java War was the result of tactless Dutch behavior in insulting the influential Prince Diponegoro, a religious mystic and advocate of a national purification program at a time when all sorts of immoral excesses were being practiced at the court, apparently by both the Dutch and native rulers. The proud Prince gathered support from the masses of the peasantry, from those elements of the Javanese aristocracy who agreed with him, and from others who wished to throw off the Dutch yoke. Using skillful guerrilla tactics, Diponegoro inflicted defeat after defeat upon well-trained Dutch armies, until finally the arrival of rein-forcements and a new strategy adopted by Dutch General de Kock paci-fied the countryside and wore down the resistance of Diponegoro's forces.[1]

Dutch perfidy in finally disposing of Diponegoro occupies an impor-tant page in Indonesian history. The prince was invited to Batavia by the Dutch to discuss an armistice. During the discussions, when Diponegoro wanted more time to consider the Dutch proposals, General de Kock had the meeting place surrounded by troops, and took Diponegoro pris-oner. He was first exiled to Menado on the island of Sulawesi, and later brought to Makassar, where he spent the rest of his life in ascetic prac-tices and meditation. He is one of the most revered national heroes, and his example has remained an inspiration to his countrymen ever since.

World War I was a European war. Its impact on Asia was through its by-products. Wilson's clarion call to "make the world safe for democ-racy" raised the hopes of people everywhere. Sun Yat-sen's nationalist revolution was already underway in 1911, and the seeds of India's move-ment for independence had been sown in the writings and actions of men like Gandhi, Tagore, and Tilak. The success of the October Revo-lution in Russia created a new crusade to establish societies based on Marxism throughout the world. Japan's modernization and ascending power made a tremendous impression on Indonesians.

Indonesians had their chance during World War I to make a break for independence but the young nationalist movement was not yet strong enough or sufficiently cohesive. The Dutch government, faced with the problem of security at home as war raged all around them, was in no position to do much about an Indonesian independence move-ment, but there was fear of Japan. The colonial army of about 25,000 in Indonesia was too small to resist an invader. If Indonesia were to be defended, Indonesians would have to defend it. The Dutch raised the question of conscription with Indonesian leaders. The answer was: "No obligatory military service without some measure of self-government and, first of all, without parliamentary representation." [2]

This was too much for the Dutch. They had no intention of sharing power with Indonesians. The problem of defending Indonesia suddenly lost some of its urgency. But the Indonesians were quick to perceive the

---

1. Justus M. van der Kroef, "Prince Diponegoro, Progenitor of Indonesian Nationalism," *Far Eastern Quarterly*, vol. VIII, no. 4 (August 1949).
2. Bernard H. M. Vlekke, *Nusantara, A History of Indonesia* (Chicago: Quadrangle Books, Inc., 1960), p. 354.

new bargaining power they possessed, and the Dutch began to realize they would have to make some concessions if the Indonesians were to be kept in line.

They yielded an almost meaningless minimum, grudgingly agreeing to the establishment of a representative body with purely advisory powers. At the same time, through the liberal-minded Dutch Governor-General Van Limburg Stirum, they held out promises of a greater degree of self-government after the war if the Indonesians behaved themselves. In 1918, Van Limburg Stirum specifically pledged that the powers of the body would be enlarged in the near future, but these promises were not kept. Shortly after the War, Van Limburg Stirum was transferred to Berlin as the Dutch Ambassador to Germany. His son, John, who was on my staff years later in postwar Berlin, told me that his father was extremely bitter about this. He felt to the end of his days that he, as well as the Indonesians, had been betrayed by his own government in failing to fulfill pledges made in good faith.

The advisory body, called the People's Council (*Volksraad*) was set up in 1916, although it did not meet until May 18, 1918. To the Indonesians, it was a travesty. The Council was composed of elected and appointed members, the latter named by the Governor-General. Its racial composition included Indonesians, Europeans, Indo-Arabians, and Indo-Chinese, the majority being not Indonesians but Europeans! [3]

The Indonesian nationalists were bitter over having acquired not much more than a sounding board. They had no hope even of inducing the Council to furnish advisory opinions on the many problems with which they were concerned, for it was dominated by the colonial society. Even the elected members were chosen by regional and city councils, and since the franchise was still extremely limited, there was little opportunity for reflection of Indonesian public or group opinion.

The end of the war, in November 1918, removed the basic pressure on the Dutch to be responsive to Indonesian demands, but the wave of postwar liberalism, with its emphasis upon self-determination, forced the Dutch to make a gesture in this direction. Two years later, the number of members in the People's Council was increased to provide for somewhat greater Indonesian representation. This was a poor palliative, however, and finally, spurred by the liberals, public opinion in the Netherlands demanded more meaningful action. Under this pressure, the Dutch Constitution was amended in 1922 to permit the introduction of democratic reforms. The reforms guaranteed broader Indonesian representation in what was a purely advisory body; they did not move in the direction of self-government. For that, the Dutch were determined to wait until the Indonesian people were "ripe for a larger measure of self-

---

3. *Ibid.*, pp. 361–362.

government." [4] What this meant no one knew, but the Indonesians were certain it meant indefinite postponement of their right to govern themselves. And it appeared they were right.

The disillusionment resulting from unkept Dutch promises and the lack of response to initial good will from the Indonesian side brought the beginning of radical trends in the nationalist movement after 1918.[5] Henceforth, noncooperation and agitation for independence would be the levers used by Indonesians to pry open their colonial society.

The Dutch reaction to the increased frustration of the Indonesians and the mounting political unrest was to tighten the bonds even more. While providing the appearance of greater Indonesian participation in the People's Council on the one hand, the Dutch took more repressive administrative measures on the other. In 1923, the Governor-General restricted the right of assembly and made it an offense to incite strikes. For all practical purposes, the rights of freedom of speech, press and assembly were nonexistent. The Indonesians were not specifically denied these rights, but the Dutch authorities had wide latitude in dealing with any dissident element in the population.

The Dutch Governor-General was vested with so-called exorbitant rights by which he had almost complete dictatorial powers. Dutch authorities could imprison or exile without trial Indonesians considered dangerous to law and order. And "dangerous" was interpreted by the Dutch authorities to mean anyone found criticizing in speech or in writing the colonial government, its members, or its regulations.

In its determination to quell the rising tide of Indonesian nationalism, the Dutch government even forbade the use of the word "Indonesia" in the colony and made clear that the right of freedom of speech in the Netherlands Constitution did not apply to Indonesian efforts toward self-government, not to mention independence.

By the early twenties, despite all the Dutch could do, a strong nationalist movement had developed in Indonesia. It originally gained impetus from the need for education, and it was a heroine, not a hero, who launched the first Indonesian cultural program in 1902. Raden Adjeng Kartini, the daughter of the Javanese regent, was the Joan of Arc of Indonesian nationalism. She founded a school for the daughters of Indonesian officials and preached the importance of Western education to Indonesian national progress. That a woman should have been the initiator of such a movement in an Asian Moslem country might come as a surprise to some. It was testimony to the influence of women in Indonesian society, which had not been wholly eroded by the Islam religion.[6] In parts of

---

4. *Ibid.*, p. 364.
5. Cf. George McTurnan Kahin, *Nationalism and Revolution in Indonesia*, 3rd printing (Ithaca, N.Y.: Cornell University Press, 1955), pp. 73–74.
6. *Ibid.*, p. 64.

Sumatra, matriarchal societies still existed. In Java, however, the position of women, particularly noblewomen, was historically one of seclusion until after marriage. They were not given the educational opportunities available to their brothers. Kartini revolted against this. She wrote:

> I am the eldest of the three unmarried daughters of the Regent of Japara, and have six brothers and sisters . . . the youngest of my three older brothers has been studying for three years in the Netherlands, and two others are in the service of that country. We girls, so far as education goes, fettered by our ancient traditions and conventions, have profited but little by these advantages. It was a great crime against the customs of our land that we should be taught at all, and especially that we should leave the house every day to go to school. For the custom of our country forbade girls in the strongest manner ever to go outside of the house. We were never allowed to go anywhere, however, save to the school, and the only place of instruction of which our city could boast, which was open to us, was a free grammar school for Europeans.[7]

Kartini was critical of the Dutch colonial policy regarding education. "As early as 1895 there was a decree, that without the special permission of his Excellency the Governor-General no native child (from six to seven years old) who could not speak Dutch would be admitted to the free grammar school for Europeans. How can a native child of six or seven years learn Dutch? He would have had to have a Dutch governess, and then before he is able to learn the Netherlands language, the child must first know his own language, and necessarily know how to read and write." [8] She resented the Dutchman's treatment of the Javanese people: "There are many, yes very many Government officials, who allow the native rulers to kiss their feet, and their knees." [9] She continued, "In many subtle ways they make us feel their dislike. 'I am a European, you are a Javanese,' they seem to say, or 'I am the master, you the governed.' Not once, but many times, they speak to us in broken Malay; although they know very well that we understand the Dutch language." [10] She was equally critical of the overbearing Javanese aristocracy.

Kartini's initiative was carried on by Mas Wahidin Sudiro Husodo, a retired Javanese physician. Between 1906 and 1908, he unsuccessfully toured Java to raise scholarship money for Javanese boys. However, his efforts moved to action three students at the medical college in Batavia, and on May 20, 1908, Dr. Sutomo, Dr. Mangunkusumo, and their associates founded an organization called Budi Utomo ("Pure," or "High,"

---

7. Raden Adjeng Kartini, *Letters of a Javanese Princess* (New York: W. W. Norton & Company, 1964), p. 32. Kartini's letters were published in 1911, seven years after her death at the age of twenty-five.
8. *Ibid.*, p. 56.
9. *Ibid.*, p. 60.
10. *Ibid.*, p. 61.

"Endeavor") that advocated a combination of Western and traditional education for Indonesians in order to "guarantee them the life of a dignified people." [11] Initially set up as a cultural society, it later adopted a political program to obtain for Indonesians the same status in their country as the Dutch had.

The first important nationalist, and frankly political organization, the Sarekat Islam, was organized in 1912, and its dramatic expansion testified to the fact that it was successfully responding to the popular will. Four years after it had been launched, its membership had reached 360,000, and by 1919, with a membership of nearly 2,500,000, it was advocating complete independence for Indonesia, and the utilization of force, if necessary, to achieve its objective.[12]

It was at this point that Marxism first entered the lists in Indonesia. A Dutch socialist, Hendrik Sneevliet, embraced it after the success of the Russian Revolution and saw in the Sarekat Islam an organization ready made for infiltration of his Marxist views and takeover. Aided by the reaction against the hard-nosed Dutch policy after 1918, he and his associates, notably Semaun, were extraordinarily successful—so much so that his tactics were later suggested as a model for Chinese Communist tactics *vis-à-vis* the Chinese nationalist movement, the Kuomintang.[13]

His efforts precipitated a bitter struggle within the party. He failed in his objective, primarily because of the initiatives taken by a young and articulate leader, Hadji Agus Salim. At the Sixth National Congress of Sarekat Islam in 1921, Salim introduced a motion demanding party discipline and ruling that no member of the party could hold membership in any other. Control over the growing trade-union movement in Indonesia was the real battle issue because the Sarekat Islam had been successful in uniting some twenty-two Indonesian trade unions under its banner. After bitter debate, the Communists resigned. The fight, however, was fatal to the Sarekat Islam, which gradually went into a decline.[14] Its Moslem members moved into a nonpolitical organization, the Mohammadijah, as a more effective medium to accomplish their purposes.[15] The nationalist feelings of the Indonesians had been demonstrated, however, and the simmering was soon to come to a boil.

An effective nationalist movement depended upon the development of an Indonesian elite capable of launching such a movement and governing the nation if it were successful. The Dutch had always carefully discouraged the creation of such an elite; now a new cloud appeared on

---

11. Kahin, *Nationalism and Revolution*, p. 65.
12. *Ibid.*, pp. 65–66. Cf. Bernhard Dalm, *Sukarno and the Struggle for Indonesian Independence*, trans. Mary F. Somers Heidhues (Ithaca, N.Y.: Cornell University Press, 1969), pp. 13–14.
13. Kahin, *Nationalism and Revolution*, p. 72.
14. *Ibid.*, pp. 75–76.
15. *Ibid.*, pp. 87–88.

the horizon to give the Dutch concern, the Pan-Islam movement. The danger they underestimated, however, lay in the ideas and teachings of a Cairo leader named Mohammed Abduh, which were incorporated into the Modernist Islamic Movement.

Abduh's ideas, first put forward at the turn of the century, spread widely in Indonesia at the hands of religious leaders who had made the pilgrimage to Mecca and been influenced by the modern Islamic thinkers in Cairo. Abduh was convinced that Islam would survive only if its adherents adopted Western progressive methods, and he advocated a major shift toward Westernization of Islamic education. This fitted in with the growing Indonesian conviction that education was the route to independence.

To counter what they considered the growing menace of Egyptian-based Islamic influence, the Dutch decided to educate a limited number of Indonesians. They had been induced by the Dutch expert on Islam, C. Snouck Hurgronje, to develop a Western-educated Indonesian elite with the objective of turning Indonesians away from cultural associations with Cairo and toward Holland. He was wise enough to stress that Indonesians who acquired a Western education must be guaranteed positions in the government service.[16] But the Dutch government neglected the second part of Hurgronje's advice. Had they followed his counsel, the history of Indonesia might well have been different. For, ironically enough, it was the few Dutch-university-educated Indonesians who formed the elite necessary to give life to the latent revolutionary spirit in Indonesia. The contrast between the freedom they found in Holland and the situation in Indonesia stimulated their desire for independence and sharpened their realization that the Dutch, having fought for independence from outside interference throughout their history, nevertheless had no intention of applying the Golden Rule to Indonesia.

------

16. *Ibid.*, pp. 47–48.

CHAPTER 3

World War II and Merdeka

Although World War II deeply affected the Indonesians, in that their country was occupied by a crueler and harsher regime than the Dutch had ever imposed, it, too, was not their war. They saw it only as a conflict between foreign forces; they took full advantage of it in training their people for government and in planning their own independence struggle, which began in 1945, when World War II ended, and continued for four more bloody years.

When Japanese tanks rolled into Djakarta in 1942, they were welcomed as liberators from Dutch colonialism. The warmth of the welcome was soon stamped out by the brutality of the Japanese war machine.

Sukarno, sleeping in a friend's house in Padang, Sumatra, was awakened by the thunder of the Japanese advance. To him, it meant the end of Dutch imperialism in Indonesia. Watching the marching columns, he told his friend Waworunto, "We must be grateful to the Japanese. We can use them. [This will bring] the result for which I have sacrificed my whole life." [1]

Hatta and Sjahrir met in Djakarta and discussed what they would do under the Japanese occupation. "It was agreed that I would do what I could for our people in the open," Hatta told me, "and Sjahrir would lead the underground." Hatta was promptly put in charge of an advisory bureau on relations between the Japanese and Indonesians. He insisted that Sukarno be brought to Djakarta from Sumatra, and the Japanese acceded. The three met in Hatta's home in Djakarta, on tree-lined Djalan Diponegoro. Sjahrir wrote later that Sukarno regarded the Japanese "as pure fascists, and felt that we must use the most subtle countermethods to get around them, such as making an appearance of collaboration." [2]

---

1. Cf. Cindy Adams, *Sukarno, An Autobiography as Told to Cindy Adams* (Indianapolis: The Bobbs-Merrill Company, Inc., 1965), p. 157.
2. *Out of Exile*, trans. Charles Wolf, Jr. (New York: John Day, 1949), p. 246.

Sukarno, impressed by the Japanese war machine, thought the war might last ten years. Sjahrir was more optimistic. A program of underground resistance and the appearance of collaboration to prepare the way for independence was agreed upon.

Sjahrir set up his headquarters at his sister's house in Tjipanas, a little village in the picturesque Puntjak mountain area about two hours from Djakarta. A radio was installed to permit monitoring of world events. He traveled widely, establishing and keeping in touch with guerrilla bands and underground units. His aim was not so much to sabotage the Japanese war effort as build an organization that could strike for Indonesian independence when the moment was ripe. That moment came in August 1945.

The tide of Japanese fortunes had turned by the fall of 1944. The success of MacArthur's forces in the Pacific was ensured by the island-hopping campaign, although bitter fighting would take place for another year. This coincided with the liberation of Belgium in September 1944, as the German panzer divisions began to fall back after the successful Channel crossing of D-Day in June. Japanese leaders recognized that Indonesian cooperation had become vital to them if they were to hold that key anchor point in Southeast Asia. On September 7, 1944, Premier Koiso announced that Indonesia would be granted independence at an unspecified time in the future.

In early 1945, the Indonesians began pressing hard for some realization of this promise of independence, and in February the Japanese formed the Committee for the Investigation of Indonesian Independence (Baden Penjelidik Kemerdekaan Indonesia, or BPKI), which held its first meetings from May 28 to June 1. Sukarno's *Pantjasila* emerged from these meetings, and was accepted. Apparently, the Japanese had meant this primarily as a gesture, but the Indonesians were not about to miss an opportunity for which they had long waited. Ignoring the Japanese minority on the committee, the Indonesian majority moved ahead with determination, and by July 17, 1945, had produced a draft constitution for the new Indonesian state.[3]

The surrender of the German armies and the end of the war in Europe in June 1945 hit Asia with the impact of a hurricane. And then, on August 6, the first atomic bomb was dropped on Hiroshima. The end had come.

On August 7, the day before Russia declared war on Japan, the Japanese moved fast to retrieve their political position in Indonesia, an-

---

3. See: John R. W. Smail, *Bandung in the Early Revolution, 1945–1946* (Ithaca, N.Y.: Cornell Modern Indonesia Project, Monograph Series, 1964); Benedict R. O'G. Anderson, *Some Aspects of Indonesian Politics Under the Japanese Occupation: 1944–1945* (Ithaca, N.Y.: Cornell Modern Indonesia Project, Interim Reports Series, 1961).

nouncing the formation of a Committee for the Preparation of Indonesian Independence (Panitia Persiapan Kemerdekaan Indonesia, or PPKI). Originally, the Tokyo plan intended that independence be declared in the name of the Emperor as soon as Russia had entered the war; Japan apparently hoped Indonesia would fight with them against the invasion forces. The next day, Sukarno, Hatta, and Dr. Radjiman, chairman of the research committee, were flown to Saigon to meet General Terauchi, the Commander of Japanese forces in Southeast Asia. Terauchi told them that if the new committee could finish its work in time, Indonesian Independence Day would be August 24.[4] Sukarno, Hatta, and Dr. Radjiman returned to Djakarta on August 14 with the good news.

Sjahrir met them soon after their arrival. He had urged Sukarno and Hatta to proclaim Indonesia's independence, promising them the support of the underground and many PETA (Pembela Tanah Air, or "Defender of the Fatherland," Indonesia's first army)[5] units. Sukarno, however, was convinced the Japanese would not surrender for several months. Now Sjahrir informed him the Japanese had requested an armistice, and he again urged immediate issuance of a proclamation of independence—which he had ready, a strongly worded anti-Japanese document that he and his co-workers had prepared. He told Sukarno he already had begun to organize the underground and Djakarta students for mass demonstrations and "military eventualities." He had circulated copies of an anti-Japanese statement throughout Java, to be published immediately "upon the expected announcement of the fifteenth" by Sukarno.[6] He did not want Indonesian independence on a Japanese platter.

Sukarno and Hatta continued to stall; not convinced the underground had sufficient strength to overthrow the Japanese, they feared a "useless bloodbath." Furthermore, they had had no confirmation locally of Japan's surrender.

Sjahrir had counted on action on the fifteenth. It was too late to reach all the leaders of his organization to inform them of the delay, and an isolated revolt broke out in Cheribon on August 15 under Dr. Sudarsono, but was suppressed by the Japanese.[7]

Djakarta was tense on that day. Rumors of Japan's surrender to the Allies were flooding the city. Leaders of the Indonesian independence movement were desperately trying to find out the truth in order to de-

---

4. Smail, *Bandung*, p. 19; George McTurnan Kahin, *Nationalism and Revolution in Indonesia*, 3rd printing (Ithaca, N.Y.: Cornell University Press, 1955), p. 127; cf. Anderson, *Aspects of Indonesian Politics*, pp. 62–63.
5. Cf. Harry J. Benda, *The Crescent and the Rising Sun* (The Hague: W. van Hoeve, Ltd., 1958), pp. 138–141.
6. Kahin, *Nationalism and Revolution*, pp. 134–135.
7. *Ibid.*

termine their course of action. Sukarno, Hatta, and Achmad Subardjo[8] called on Vice Admiral Mayeda, Japanese Navy chief in Java and head of Naval Intelligence for Indonesia.

Mayeda had evinced sympathy for the aims and aspirations of the Indonesians, and it was from him, the leaders decided, that they could learn the truth. But Mayeda, whatever he may have known, said he could neither confirm nor deny the rumor of the Japanese surrender. He promised to let them know. In view of the pressing need to finish the work of the Preparatory Committee, Sukarno, Hatta and Subardjo decided to call a meeting of the committee members for the following day, August 16, at 10:00 A.M. The meeting was to be held in the former headquarters of the Advisory Council of the Dutch government, the *Raad van Indie*. The committee was composed of twenty-one members, all outstanding nationalists: twelve from Java, three from Sumatra, two from Sulawesi, one each from Bali, Kalimantan and the Moluccas, and one from the Chinese community. Attempts were made to ascertain the true situation before the committee convened, but no news was obtained.

Late that night, a meeting was held at Sukarno's house. It was a stormy one, with the Indonesian pemudas demanding that the proclamation be issued at once, and Sukarno and the elders wanting to sound out the Japanese attitude first. The word *pemuda* means youth, but as commonly used at the time, it referred to the revolutionary youth, militant and well organized, who were the cutting edge of the revolutionary movement. This same group—of which Chairul Saleh, Adam Malik, Sukarni, B. M. Diah and many others whose names would one day make Indonesian history were the principals—later became known as the "Generation of '45," and for more than a decade wielded considerable political influence.

Wikana, the leader of the youth group, demanded that Sukarno announce on the radio that Indonesia was free. Sukarno refused and insisted they were not ready to move that night—a meeting of the Preparatory Committee had been called for the following day, and it was necessary that the full committee be consulted and lend their support to

---

8. Later to become Foreign Minister in the first Cabinet, August 31 to November 14, 1945, and in the Sukiman Cabinet, 1951 to 1952. The account of events immediately leading up to the issuance of the Proclamation of Independence is largely taken from Subardjo's unpublished manuscript, "A Short History of the Indonesian Revolution." Subardjo had worked with Mayeda closely, and knew him well as a man of liberal bent. Under Subardjo's direction, Mayeda sponsored the establishment of a school to educate Indonesian youth in the problems of government and politics or, as Subardjo described it, "in Indonesian patriotism in the context of Asian solidarity." Many prominent political personalities came to lecture there, including Sukarno, Hatta, Sjahrir, and Hadji Agus Salim. There seems to be no evidence for the accusation that this was a Communist-inspired effort.

whatever course of action was taken. Hatta supported Sukarno's position and further emphasized: "Japan belongs to the past; we have to face the Dutch now, who will try to come back as the old masters of our country. If you do not agree with what I say, and [you want to go ahead], why do you not proclaim independence by yourselves?"

At one point Wikana threatened that if Sukarno failed to announce Indonesia's independence that night, he could expect blood and murder on a large scale the next day. Sukarno, furious, exclaimed he was not to be considered a coward. "You pemudas have not to wait until tomorrow. If you want my neck [offering his neck with both hands around it], drag me to the lawn and take my life!" Surprised by this outburst, the pemudas backed down, but were not satisfied. There were further angry exchanges. Then tense silence. Finally, the meeting broke up without agreement.

That night, Sukarno and Hatta were kidnaped.

Subardjo was notified at eight o'clock the morning of the sixteenth by his secretary, Sudiro, that Sukarno and Hatta were missing. He immediately communicated with the Japanese naval authorities (for if Sukarno and Hatta had been arrested by the army, the sympathetic navy could have secured their release), and then proceeded to Admiral Mayeda's residence and told him of the kidnaping. Mayeda, surprised by the news, promised his assistance.

Meanwhile, a few pemudas were meeting in Subardjo's office. It was they, backed by the PETA, who had kidnaped the two leaders. Subardjo finally talked them into taking him to Sukarno and Hatta. Subardjo, Sudiro, Jusuf Kunto, the messenger who had come from the place where Sukarno and Hatta were kept in hiding, then drove to PETA headquarters in the small city of Rengasdengkok on the Java Sea north of Djakarta. Sukarni, a left-wing youth leader with a reputation for recklessness, received them. He and the other youth leaders had endeavored unsuccessfully to convince their captives that the Japanese had surrendered and the time had come to issue the proclamation. Sukarni maintained that 15,000 armed youths were waiting on the outskirts of Djakarta to march against the Japanese as soon as the proclamation was made. Sukarno and Hatta both believed that this was an exaggeration, and that the Japanese would easily suppress them. Furthermore, both were hopeful, Hatta told me later, that it would be possible to reach an understanding with the Japanese so the Indonesians would not be opposed by military force when the declaration was made.

Sukarno and Hatta also felt that the proclamation should emphasize "its all-Indonesia source" and therefore be issued through the Indonesian Preparatory Committee.[9] Subardjo was then asked by Major Su-

---

9. Cf. Kahin, *Nationalism and Revolution,* p. 135.

beno of PETA whether he could guarantee to proclaim independence before midnight if Sukarno and Hatta returned with him. Subardjo replied that was impossible.

"We have to go back first, then summon all members of the Preparatory Committee for a meeting. It requires much time. We shall have to work all night long, I'm afraid, before we are ready."

"What about 6:00 A.M. tomorrow?" the major asked.

Subardjo promised to be ready by noon the following day.

"If not, what then?"

"Major, if everything fails, I will bear the responsibility. You can shoot me to death!" Subardjo replied impulsively. (He later told a friend his life depended on the Proclamation of Independence!)

The major was convinced, and they were taken to see Sukarno, who had just finished his evening meal with his wife, Fatmawati, his baby son, Guntur, and Hatta. As Subardjo tells the story, he rushed up to the group and said, "Quick, quick, we have to go back to Djakarta. The Preparatory Committee cannot continue its work without us. They waited in vain this morning."

"Has Japan surrendered?" Sukarno asked.

"I have come here to tell you the news," Subardjo replied. "I was informed this morning by Mayeda himself. He asked me to communicate it to you, as he had promised. He knows about your absence from town."

Subardjo, Sukarno, Hatta, Sukarni and the others then left for Djakarta. It was already around 9:00 P.M.

The Preparatory Committee worked most of the night in Admiral Mayeda's residence. Shortly before daybreak, all questions had been resolved. The proclamation would be signed by Sukarno and Hatta. Its final text was simple and direct. It read:

> We, the Indonesian people declare herewith our independence. Matters regarding the transfer of power and other affairs will be arranged in an accurate manner and within the shortest time possible.

B. M. Diah, a young newspaperman, seized a copy before the ink was dry and rushed off to a printing shop so as to have thousands of copies distributed all over Indonesia by the morning trains. A few minutes past ten the next morning, Sukarno read the proclamation. After 350 years, Indonesia was free! The popular response was tremendous. The Japanese reaction was harsh: Mayeda and his entire staff were arrested, and all armed Indonesian organizations were banned the next day.

But nothing could stop the Indonesians now. On August 19, Sukarno and Hatta addressed tens of thousands of wildly cheering Indonesians in Djakarta's central park, soon to be rechristened Merdeka Square. Japanese tanks and armored cars had rolled up and encircled the area, apparently with the intention of breaking up the celebration, but changed their minds—probably because the high command was anxious to leave behind as much good will as possible.

The Japanese, accustomed to the discipline of a rigid society, now found themselves in a difficult position. They were occupying Indonesia on behalf of the victorious Allies and were responsible for maintaining law and order, the presumption being they would hand over to the Allies the Indonesia of prewar days, that is, a Dutch colony. Japanese response to the new situation consequently was not uniform. In some areas, they attempted to block the Indonesians as they assumed new governmental powers. In others, they cooperated, at least to the extent of bowing before an Indonesian show of force. In Bandung they did both, first yielding to the pressures of the pemudas, and then suddenly counterattacking and restoring Japanese military control of the city.[10] At first, they banned the flying of the Indonesian flag; but within six weeks the famous *Merah Putih* ("Red and White") was flying from nearly every public building in Java, as the Indonesians, led largely by the pemudas, moved in and took control of government agencies.

The day following the Proclamation of Independence, the Preparatory Committee met. By acclamation, Sukarno was chosen President and Hatta Vice-President of the new nation before the Constitution had been finished. For a transition period of six months, regulations were adopted that suspended the Constitution, gave the President extraordinary powers, and provided that until a Parliament and other instrumentalities could be established, their powers would be exercised by the President with the assistance of a National Committee (Komite Nasional). Its formation became the subject of controversy between the youth groups and their seniors. Three Djakarta pemudas, Sukarni, Wikana, and Chairul Saleh, who had been added to the Preparatory Committee to make it more representative, demanded that the latter be disbanded because it was a Japanese creation. In its place they wanted a National Indonesian Committee, broadly representative, which would meet in public, "among the people." [11]

This demand was rejected by Sukarno, and the three pemudas promptly resigned. The Preparatory Committee continued its work and completed the final draft of the Indonesian Constitution within a week. On August 29, utilizing his new powers, Sukarno dissolved the committee. Apparently taking his cue from the youth leaders, he replaced it with the Central Indonesian National Committee (Komite Nasional Indonesia Pusat). This advisory body became popularly known as KNIP.[12]

---

10. Smail, *Bandung*, pp. 62–63.
11. *Ibid.*, p. 25.
12. *Ibid.*, p. 26. Cf. Kahin, *Nationalism and Revolution*, pp. 139–140.

On August 31, the first Indonesian Cabinet was appointed:

Minister of Foreign Affairs	Mr. Achmad Subardjo
Minister of Internal Affairs	R.A.A. Wiranata Koesoema
Minister of Justice	Professor Soepomo
Minister of Economic Affairs	Ir. Soerachman
Minister of Finance	Dr. Samsi
Minister of Education	Ki Hadjar Dewantara
Minister of Social Affairs	Mr. Iwa Kusuma Sumantri
Minister of Information	Mr. Amir Sjarifuddin
Minister of Health	Dr. Boentaran Martoatmodjo
Minister of Communications	Abikusno Tjokrosujuso
Minister of State (without portfolio)	Dr. Amir
Minister of State (without portfolio)	Wachid Hasjim
Minister of State (without portfolio)	Mr. Sartono
Minister of State (without portfolio)	Mr. A. A. Maramis
Minister of State (without portfolio)	Otto Iskandar Dinata
Minister of State (without portfolio)	Soekardjo Wirjopranoto[13]

Every new nation faces serious problems of structure, organization, and administration. The new Indonesia faced, in addition to these, the unique problem that the country was still occupied by the Japanese, who were charged with preserving the *status quo* until the colonial power could return. As Sukarno expressed it in a speech on August 23:

> To proclaim independence is easy. To make a constitution is not diffi-cult. To elect a President and a Vice-President is easier still. But to establish the organs and offices of authority for the administration of the state, as well as to seek international recognition, especially under conditions such as the present, in which the Japanese government is still obliged by the international status quo to remain in this country to run the administration and maintain public order—these tasks are not easy.[14]

Indeed, they were not easy. And the men of the new fledging govern-ment knew that they had still to face the return of the Dutch.

---

13. Kahin, *Nationalism and Revolution* p. 139; cf. Anderson, *Aspects of In-donesian Politics*, pp. 112–113.
14. Smail, *Bandung*, p. 27; cf. Anderson, p. 117.

CHAPTER 4

Four Years of Revolution

But it was the British, not the Dutch, who came first to accept the Japanese surrender and act as caretakers until the Dutch could arrive. It was an ironic position. After their nearest base at Singapore had collapsed in one of the most inglorious defeats of World War II, they had had nothing to do with Indonesia or the island operations of MacArthur, but were concentrating on India and Burma. It was Franklin D. Roosevelt who, in one of his sudden flashes of intuition, had arranged with Churchill the transfer of this area to Mountbatten's Southeast Asia Command from MacArthur's Far Eastern Command. Averell Harriman, who told me this, pointed to the move as the result of one of Roosevelt's many brilliant insights. He had no intention of letting the United States become involved on the wrong side of a colonial dispute!

The Dutch, remembering Britain's historical interest in Java and Sumatra, were not sure this was to their liking. On the other hand, if the Americans remained in the Indies, who was to know whether the American bias against colonialism might result in resistance to the Dutch return?

In any event, British Rear Admiral Patterson, Mountbatten's deputy, arrived in Djakarta on September 16, 1945, accompanied by Dr. Charles van der Plas, the Netherlands' representative on Mountbatten's staff, and a company of Seaforth Highlanders. Patterson shortly announced that his troops were there "to maintain law and order until the time that the lawful government of the Netherlands East Indies is once again functioning." [1]

About this time, Dr. Hubertus J. van Mook, Dutch Minister of Colonies during World War II and now Lieutenant-Governor-designate of

---

1. Louis Fischer, *The Story of Indonesia* (New York: Harper & Brothers, 1959), p. 81. Cf. George McTurnan Kahin, *Nationalism and Revolution in Indonesia*, 3rd printing (Ithaca, N.Y.: Cornell University Press, 1955), pp. 141–142.

the Netherlands Indies, cabled The Hague that "it is of the utmost importance to imprison the leadership of the so-called Republic of Indonesia immediately, because apprehension of the leading persons and a show of force will strip the movement of its strength"; Patterson, pressed by van der Plas, issued orders to the Japanese Command to arrest all "terrorist" leaders in Java.[2] But the British had little stomach for an operation that was to hold the territory until the Dutch could take over and re-establish colonialism. Patterson was told by Mountbatten to avoid interference in Indonesian internal politics. This was easier said than done. The British leadership, already caught in the middle, was determined to discharge its responsibilities without compromising itself with either the Dutch or the Indonesians.[3]

The Dutch would neither recognize nor hold discussions with the Indonesian leaders. With difficulty, Mountbatten persuaded van Mook to meet Sukarno on October 23. At this informal meeting, the British policy, as Fischer aptly puts it, was one "of recognizing a government that was not governing and refusing recognition to one that was." [4]

Up to this point, relations between the Indonesians and the British had been friendly. But when, on the afternoon of October 27, British planes showered leaflets on Surabaya calling for Indonesians to deliver up all their arms immediately, the Indonesians were convinced the British forces were simply paving the way for Dutch reoccupation. Their reaction was fast and fierce: "One [British] infantry brigade, dispersed in various parts of the city, found itself attacked by about 20,000 Indonesians armed and trained as regular troops by the Japanese and supported by tanks, and by an uncontrolled mob of about 120,000 men armed with rifles, swords, poisoned spears, clubs and daggers." [5] Indonesians who were there, and with whom I have talked, saw the conflict somewhat differently—a huge mob of Indonesians, armed for the most part with bamboo spears, daggers, and Indonesian-type hoes, desperately attacking well-armed British troops and being mowed down by them. Sukarno said later, "On October 5, the People's Army of the Republic was born. Its vital statistics were five men to every gun." [6]

Both versions undoubtedly bore truth. Certainly, it was a savage affair, with brutal atrocities committed by both sides.

Within twenty-four hours the situation of the British and Indian troops was desperate, and there was "serious danger of the whole Brigade

2. Fischer, *Story of Indonesia*, p. 81.
3. *Ibid.*
4. *Ibid.*, p. 82.
5. David Wehl, *The Birth of Indonesia* (London: George Allen & Unwin Ltd., 1948), pp. 54–55.
6. Cindy Adams, *Sukarno, An Autobiography as Told to Cindy Adams* (Indianapolis: The Bobbs-Merrill Company, Inc. 1965), p. 227.

being annihilated." [7] A truce was agreed upon, and the British arranged for Sukarno and Hatta to fly from Djakarta to Surabaya to attempt to calm the aroused population.

"I drove around all day and night shouting, 'Stop fighting,'" Sukarno related later. "'The terms of agreement are to cease fire and stand fast. Don't shoot. Those are my orders. Stop fighting instantly.'" [8] Sukarno's golden voice fell on deaf ears. Within hours after he had returned to Djakarta, General Mallaby, the British Commander, was killed while endeavoring to implement the truce.

The worst fighting was still to come. The day following Brigadier Mallaby's death, Lieutenant General Sir Philip Christison issued a strong warning to the Indonesians:

> These direct and unprovoked attacks upon British Forces cannot in any circumstances be permitted, and unless the Indonesians who have committed these acts surrender to my forces, I intend to bring the whole weight of my sea, land and air forces and all the weapons of modern war against them until they are crushed.[9]

Moderate Indonesian leaders were endeavoring to quiet the populace. But the extremists were calling for blood. A famous woman broadcaster, called by the British "Surabaya Sue," continued to incite the population, demanding a "Holy War" to drive the Allies into the sea. "Surabaya Sue" was an interesting character whom I came to know some years later. A Hollywood writer who had been born on the Isle of Man, she had become enamored of Bali and had adopted an Indonesian name, "K'Tut Tantri." She joined the Indonesian guerrilla forces and spent some time in a Japanese jail. Freed at the outbreak of the revolution, she remained with the Indonesians until their independence was won.[10]

But the Fifth Indian Division had planes to strafe and bomb the disorganized and by now frenzied Indonesians, who were shouting the Indonesian equivalent of "Liberty or death!" The carnage was frightful. Fanatical self-sacrifice marked Indonesian resistance. Thousands of men armed with the Indonesian *kris* (a small dagger) launched themselves against Sherman tanks. It was estimated that many thousands were killed before the Indonesian resistance ended.

The Battle of Surabaya was a tragic and unnecessary conflict deplored by leaders on both sides. It did, however, change stubborn Dutch minds on the subject of negotiations, and the first Prime Minister of Indonesia, Sutan Sjahrir, concentrated his attention on getting these going. British General Christison finally managed to organize an informal conference between the Dutch, Indonesians and British on November 17. Sjahrir

---

7. Wehl, *Birth of Indonesia*, p. 56.
8. Adams, *Sukarno*, p. 229.
9. Wehl, *Birth of Indonesia*, p. 62.
10. See K'Tut Tantri, *Revolt in Paradise* (London: Heinemann, 1960).

was his usual composed, quiet self at the meeting. According to Wehl, who was there representing British intelligence, "Occasionally he made one clear statement . . . repeated as though he were mildly surprised he had not been heard and understood before. It was to the effect that Indonesia was an independent country, and he was really not interested in any meetings or discussions or arguments that assumed Indonesia was anything else." [11]

But the Dutch had no intention of letting the Indonesians become independent. Sixteen months of stormy discussions took place before an agreement was signed by the Dutch and Indonesians, called the Linggadjati Agreement after the attractive hill station in northeastern Java where the talks took place. Initialed on November 15, 1946, it was not signed until March 25, 1947, at the palace in Djakarta. The main provisions, as summarized by Charles Wolf, Jr., were:

1. That the Netherlands Government recognize the Republic as the *de facto* authority in Java and Sumatra;
2. That the Netherlands and Republican Governments cooperate toward the setting up of a sovereign democratic federal state, the United States of Indonesia, to consist of three states, the Republic of Indonesia, embracing Java and Sumatra, the state of Borneo, and the Great Eastern State;
3. That the Netherlands and Republican Governments cooperate toward the formation of the Netherlands–Indonesian Union, to consist of the Kingdom of the Netherlands—including the Netherlands, Surinam, and Curaçao—and the U.S.I., which Union would have as its head the Queen of the Netherlands;
4. That the Netherlands–Indonesian Union and the U.S.I. be formed not later than January 1, 1949, and that the Union set up its own agencies for the regulation of matters of common interest to the member states, specifically, the matters of foreign affairs, defense, and certain financial and economic policies;
5. Finally, the Agreement provided for a mutual reduction in troop strength and a gradual evacuation of Dutch troops from Republican areas as quickly as possible consistent with the maintenance of law and order, and for the recognition by the Republic of all claims by foreign nationals for the restitution and maintenance of their rights and properties within areas controlled by the Republic.[12]

As Wolf points out, the agreement had within it the seeds of its own destruction. It was based upon cooperation between two parties who were not yet ready to cooperate; in effect, it set up two competing gov-

---

11. Wehl, *Birth of Indonesia*, p. 72.
12. Charles Wolf, Jr., *The Indonesian Story* (New York: The John Day Company, 1948), pp. 43–44.

ernments in Indonesia. This could not last, particularly since about eighty-five per cent of the total population lived in Java and Sumatra, which "accounted for between four-fifths and nine-tenths of the total export and import trade of the whole Indonesian archipelago." [13]

That the Dutch had no serious intention of abiding by the letter of the agreement seems clear. Van Mook, the Dutch Governor-General at the time, told Louis Fischer later that the ink on the agreement was hardly dry when the Netherlands began making a series of doubtful interpretations that "torpedoed the whole thing." [14] Dr. J. Jonkman, former Minister of Colonies, told me later of the problem that the Dutch had faced: "The agreement had to be approved by Parliament. In order to obtain this approval, it was necessary to interpret the agreement in the light of the Netherlands Constitution. Otherwise, it would not have been endorsed."

But words have no meaning when minds do not meet. Such a tense situation, with two governments sitting in the same country, each claiming jurisdiction, led inevitably to physical conflict. Four months after signing the agreement, the morning of July 21, 1947, Dutch troops and armor rolled into the territory of the Republic. In simultaneous actions, Dutch military forces invaded Java, Madura and Sumatra.

To justify what it called a "police action," the Government of the Netherlands charged that Sukarno's government had deliberately failed to supply the Dutch-administered parts of Java with rice; also, that in violation of the agreement, the Republic was seeking diplomatic recognition from foreign governments. To Sukarno and his colleagues, of course, the Dutch action represented a deliberately planned attempt to regain their former colony. Their views tended to be substantiated by the fact that the Government of the Republic of Indonesia, now headed by Amir Sjarifuddin, made proposals on July 8 that more than met the Dutch complaint. The Republic offered to desist from sending diplomatic representatives abroad, permit Holland to post a Dutch official inside the Republican Government, and expressed its willingness to include Dutch officials in the future provisional Government of Indonesia.

The Dutch government and press reported the rebellion as Communist-dominated. Nothing could have been farther from the truth. The nationalist movement, composed of many divergent elements, was united in its opposition to the return of Dutch colonial rule. Reading from right to left, these were the parties that emerged after the dawn of independence: the Masjumi, a federation of Islamic parties constituting the largest single political party in the Republic and claiming about 10,000 adherents; the Catholic Party; the Protestant Party; the PNI, second to the Masjumi in political strength and holding the balance of

---

13. *Ibid.*, p. 45.
14. Fischer, *Story of Indonesia*, p. 96.

power between the right and left; the Indonesian Socialist Party, headed by Sjahrir and generally regarded as the third-largest party, being aligned with the Federation of Indonesian Labor (Gabungan Surikat Buruh Republik) and several smaller groups; the Communist Party and its left-wing coalition groups. As time marched on, they would split on many issues; but they were united against reversion to colonial status.

Within two weeks, Dutch tanks, armor and infantry were holding most of the chief cities and towns in West and East Java, had obtained some control over the communication links between them, and occupied all the Javanese deepwater ports. Republican forces withdrew to the hills and mountains, and the government established itself in the cultural center of Java, the city of Jogjakarta.[15] World reaction to the Dutch initiative was swift. On July 30, India and Australia placed the Indonesian conflict before the UN Security Council. The British simultaneously prohibited the selling of war materiel to the Dutch for use in Indonesia; the United States shortly followed suit. The British also offered to mediate the dispute, but the Dutch refused. On July 31, the United States government offered its "good offices" to both parties. Kahin comments dryly, "The Dutch, already having attained most of their geographical objectives and undoubtedly in the hopes of removing the dispute from the U.N. arena, agreed on August 3 to accept the American proposal." The proposal, however, was rejected by the Indonesians, apparently in the belief that the Republic's "interests would be better protected by the United Nations." [16]

Had the United Nations not intervened at this critical moment, in the opinion of Van Mook, the Republic would have passed out of existence within three or four weeks.[17] The Security Council called upon both parties on August 1 to "cease hostilities forthwith" and to "settle their disputes by arbitration or other peaceful means." The Dutch paid little attention, continuing mop-up operations.[18]

But world opinion had been aroused; speeches of protest were ringing in the halls of America's Congress. The United Nations established a Committee of Good Offices. This was pressure Holland could not ignore. The Committee would be made up of two member nations, one each to be selected by the two antagonists; the first two selected would in turn choose a third. Holland picked Belgium and Indonesia chose Australia. The two representatives, Dr. Paul van Zeeland, former Prime Minister of Belgium, and Justice Richard C. Kirby of the Australian Court of Arbitration, selected the United States as the third country,

---

15. Kahin, *Nationalism and Revolution*, p. 213.
16. *Ibid.*, p. 214.
17. Fischer, *Story of Indonesia*, p. 101.
18. *Ibid.*, pp. 101–102.

and Dr. Frank P. Graham, President of the University of North Carolina, was appointed by the State Department as its representative.

Precious time passed in futile argument over where to meet—until Dean Rusk, then Assistant Secretary of State for Far Eastern Affairs, proposed a meeting aboard the United States Navy transport *Renville*, a neutral vessel. The result was an unhappy mixture of so-called principles, based upon what the Dutch called a "plebiscite" and the Indonesians called "free elections."

The Netherlands went into the *Renville* meeting holding high cards. They had set up an East Indonesian state of which the Anak Agung of Bali was the head; it embraced the Celebes, Bali, Bangka and Billiton, and the islands to the East. They had formed two autonomous states in Borneo and moved to establish eleven more. They had captured the Indonesian capital and reduced the Indonesian Army to guerrillas in the hills. There were more than 90,000 Dutch troops in the Republic. It was clear from beginning to end of the conference, which lasted from December 8, 1947, to January 17, 1948, that the embattled Dutch had no notion of yielding the ground they had won or establishing an independent Indonesia. They proposed a federal arrangement for Indonesia, bypassing the already established Republic and, incidentally, thereby giving the federal concept the kiss of death. The Dutch presented the conference with twelve principles that offered "independence for the Indonesian peoples" within a framework certain to enable them to frustrate that independence. The new United States of Indonesia would be tied to a union with Holland. This was an ultimatum. If not accepted within five days, the Dutch would resume "liberty of action." Everyone knew what that meant.[19]

America came to the rescue. Dr. Graham, after consulting with the Indonesians, countered with six principles that were accepted by the Committee of Good Offices; they were concerned with the inclusion of the Republic, a plebiscite, and a continuing role for the United Nations in supervising events to come. By this time the Dutch were hardly speaking or listening to the Good Offices Committee. Graham then passed the ball to Washington, and Secretary of State Marshall let the Dutch know that he favored the new proposal.

To everyone's amazement, agreement was reached, the six principles drafted by Graham being included as "additional." But nobody was happy. The Dutch felt that a plum within their grasp had just been plucked away. And the Indonesians found themselves controlling only one-third of Java, with the future dependent upon a plebiscite and the United Nations.[20] Nevertheless, the *Renville* meeting had saved Indone-

---

19. *Ibid.*, pp. 102–103.
20. *Ibid.*, pp. 103–106.

sia, for without it, as Dr. Graham told me later, the Indonesian freedom fighters would have been reduced to guerrilla warfare in the jungles.

The Dutch did not give up. The Linggadjati Agreement was not the only one they did not keep. The fighting stopped, but tactics described by Dr. Graham as "delay and attrition" were resorted to by the Dutch, *i.e.*, holding up the discussions while they starved out the Indonesians.

Meanwhile, the Indonesians were having internal problems. Sjahrir was accused of being too pro-Dutch following his negotiation of the Linggadjati Agreement. Amir Sjarifuddin, a Christian Batak from North Sumatra, had succeeded him as Prime Minister of Indonesia in June 1947. Now Sjarifuddin was forced out because he was held responsible for negotiating the unpopular Renville Agreement. Dr. Hatta succeeded him on January 29, 1948. Bitter and frustrated, Sjarifuddin allied himself with Communist Party leaders Musso and Alimin, recently returned from exile, in the formation of a National Democratic Front (Front Demokrasi Rakjat). The conflict between the rival forces in the new government sharpened as a polarization developed between Musso and the moderate elements, led by Sukarno, Hatta and Sjahrir. The vital issue was whether the Indonesian revolution was "a part of the world revolution," as Musso claimed—"and to be in the right path Indonesia must side with Russia" [21]—or a genuine nationalist revolution leading to independence.

The lines were sharply drawn. Hatta's view was that "we must not be an object in international political controversies but must remain a subject entitled to determine our own attitude and entitled to struggle for our goal of a completely independent Indonesia." [22]

Charges and countercharges were hurled. Sjarifuddin was called a "lackey of the imperialist van der Plas who must be hanged" by one of the rival groups, the Republic of Indonesia Rebel Troop (BPRI), led by Dr. Mawardi. Sjarifuddin admitted that he had received 25,000 florins from van der Plas "because the Comintern has advised us to cooperate with colonial rulers in the common front against Fascism." [23] To do Sjarifuddin justice, his alliance with the Communists was apparently the result of his conviction that a policy of negotiating with the Dutch, to which both the Sjahrir and Hatta governments were firmly committed, was leading the nation into a blind alley. But the confusion was confounded by the revelation that he had taken money from the Dutch.

There was not one army at this time but three: a government army, a Communist left-wing army (PKI/FDR), and a neutral army. Nasution, leader of the Siliwangi—called "Wilhelmina's Shock Troops" by the

---

21. A. H. Nasution, *Menegakkan Keadilan dan Kebenaran* (Djakarta: Seruling Masa, 1967), vol. I, p. 15.
22. *Ibid.*, p. 16.
23. *Ibid.*, pp. 16–17.

Communists—was determined to merge the three groups into a single Indonesian National Army (TNI). Disorders increased; the commander of the Fourth Division, Colonel Sutanto, was murdered; one of the battalions of the Siliwangi was attacked. What made the situation especially intolerable was the fact that this divided army was facing a strong and determined enemy.

The government appointed Colonel Gatot Subroto, Military Governor of the Solo area, with the responsibility of stopping the conflict one way or another. Subroto, a black-bearded, good-natured gorilla of a man, was a no-nonsense commander. He issued an order that shooting between units must stop and called upon all commanders to pledge their loyalty to the Republic of Indonesia. When some of the commanders failed to respond, he announced that they had disobeyed his order and so were considered "rebels against the Government of the Republic of Indonesia." [24]

Moving fast, the Communist coalition seized the little city of Madiun in Central Java on September 18, 1948. The commanders of regular army units were killed or captured. The Communists appointed new officials and announced plans for setting up an Indonesian Soviet State that would fly a red flag. Musso would head the new government.

The Sukarno-Hatta Cabinet met and gave full authority to Commander-in-Chief General Sudirman to crush the rebellion and restore order. Sukarno announced on September 19:

> Yesterday morning the Musso-PKI staged a coup, seized power in Madiun, and set up there a Soviet government under Musso's leadership. They consider this seizure of power to be the beginning of an attempt to take over power throughout Indonesia. It is obvious that the Solo and Madiun affairs are not unrelated events but links in an action to topple the R.I. government. . . . You and we all are confronted with the most serious trial in determining our own fate and have to choose between following Musso and his PKI, or following Sukarno-Hatta, who, with God's help will lead an independent R.I., not dominated by any power whatsoever.[25]

When Sjarifuddin's office was raided, the rebel plans were found. The Solo area was to be turned into a "Wild West" that would divert public attention from the real storm center, Madiun. Communist-controlled units were to be withdrawn from the front facing the Dutch. An illegal army was to be set up. Large-scale demonstrations accompanied by a general strike and violence were to be mounted. "Burglaries and thefts at night as well as in the daytime" were encouraged to create trouble.[26]

But the rebels were up against stanch commanders, Subroto and

---

24. *Ibid.*, pp. 17–19.
25. *Ibid.*, p. 21.
26. *Ibid.*, p. 19.

Nasution, and others like them. The rebellion was crushed in two weeks. Later, Subroto, by then advanced to a general, told me grimly, "Yes, the Communist leaders were executed by my order. I only made one mistake. Aidit got away." Forever after, the Indonesians would call this action by the Communists the "stab in the back" of the new Republic.

The referendum provided by the Renville Agreement never did take place. On the heels of the PKI revolt, the Dutch struck again, in what they termed a "second police action," in December 1948. The Dutch action was a fierce and determined effort to take over the third of the country still in the hands of the Republic. Dutch planes bombed Jogjakarta. Dutch armor rolled into Djakarta. The President and other officials were captured. The Indonesian army took to the mountains and jungles.

The surprise attack was a direct violation of the Renville Agreement. The Dutch had informed Merle Cochran, a career Foreign Service Officer who had succeeded Dr. Graham in August 1948 as the U.S. representative on the UN Committee of Good Offices, that within eighteen hours the Government of the Republic of Indonesia must accept their demands for unlimited powers for the Dutch High Commissioner and the unlimited right of the Dutch army to go anywhere in the archipelago.

Cochran refused to transmit the Dutch proposal, "because it calls for a non-negotiated blanket assent." Just before midnight on December 18, the Dutch representative in Djakarta notified Cochran that his government was denouncing the Renville Agreement as of midnight. The Indonesian government representative in Djakarta was notified fifteen minutes later. The Dutch had cut all wires leading to Jogjakarta. The first news to reach the government in Jogjakarta was bombs and rockets falling on the local airport.

Professor George McT. Kahin, who was in Jogjakarta at the time, described the attack in the early morning of December 19:

> After the small Indonesian force defending the airport had been eliminated by an hour of heavy bombing and rocket fire, some 900 Dutch parachutists were dropped. They quickly secured the area, and soon a steady stream of Dutch transports began funneling troops and supplies from the Dutch airbase at Semarang, some eighty miles away. Thereupon, Dutch bombers [American Mitchells] and rocket-firing P-51's and Spitfires began softening up Jogjakarta. . . . Bombs and rockets were loosed at various objectives, mostly of military value, . . . and planes strafed the streets both lengthwise and crosswise.[27]

In England, America and Asia, public and official opinion was outraged. On December 27, the Committee of Good Offices reported unanimously to the UN that "Netherlands forces crossed the status-quo line

---

27. *Nationalism and Revolution*, p. 337. Cf. Fischer, *Story of Indonesia*, p. 119.

and initiated hostile military action against the Republic while the obligations of the Truce Agreement were still fully operative." The bitterness of the Indonesians was reflected in a comment from the Republic's New York office: "Holland, home of Kris Kringle and good cheer, timed its murder for Christmas, when the world's leaders had conveniently dispersed. The UN General Assembly had adjourned. So had the United States Congress." [28]

"For the second time the Dutch have repudiated a signed agreement" the *Manchester Guardian* wrote, "and resorted to force in the hope of suppressing the Indonesian nationalist movement." [29]

Dr. Sumitro, Indonesian Minister of Trade and Finance, protested to Acting Secretary of State Robert Lovett in Washington, calling the Dutch action a second Pearl Harbor. He told newspapermen, "Money received from the United States, for the purpose of reconstruction in Holland, has been diverted at the rate of one million dollars a day to maintain an army of 130,000 in Indonesia. . . . I predict that the Dutch will find no peace in Indonesia no matter how many so-called victories they win. . . . The fact that the Dutch were able to capture Republican leaders was due to the fact that our government believed that negotiations were still going on. With unheard-of treachery, the Dutch launched a sneak attack." [30]

Lovett replied in writing that the United States would not endorse or condone the Dutch military action. The American press was up in arms. The Chicago *Tribune* shouted that the Queen and top Dutch officials deserved hanging. The New York *Times* and the *Christian Science Monitor* criticized the Dutch action.

India, whose leader charged the Dutch with "naked and unabashed aggression" moved into the breach. In New Delhi, Prime Minister Nehru called a meeting of nineteen nations, including Australia and New Zealand, to protest the action.[31]

Secretary of State George C. Marshall committed himself to the Indonesian cause. And the UN Security Council, fortuitously meeting in Paris, adopted a resolution the night before Christmas calling upon both sides in Indonesia "to cease hostilities forthwith." But when the Council instructed Holland to release the Republican leaders, restore the Government of the Republic in Jogjakarta, and transfer sovereignty to the United States of Indonesia by July 1, 1950, the Dutch Foreign Minister rejected the resolution as "unacceptable."

Nothing made any impression upon the Dutch until the United States made it quite clear that no Marshall Plan aid would be forthcoming

---

28. Fischer, *Story of Indonesia*, p. 121.
29. *Ibid.*, pp. 119–120.
30. *Ibid.*, p. 120.
31. *Ibid.*, p. 121.

until the Dutch settled with the Indonesians. It happened that the roughly $400 million worth of aid allocated to the Dutch represented just about the annual cost of Dutch military operations in Indonesia.[32] The United States had suddenly discovered it was in the awkward position of indirectly financing a colonial operation designed to block Indonesian independence aspirations.

Money talked. On April 22, the Dutch announced that action would be taken to re-establish the Republic, and that the political prisoners would be released on condition that guerrilla warfare was halted. Discussions between the Netherlands representatives and the Republic of Indonesia began in Djakarta on April 14, 1949, and resulted in the Roem—Van Royen Agreement on May 7, which followed almost identically the terms of the UN resolution earlier rejected by the Dutch.

The end was in sight. After months of jockeying, the Round Table Conference in The Hague decided that the Netherlands would transfer sovereignty to the independent Republic of the United States of Indonesia no later than December 30, 1949. The sense of joy and triumph was well nigh overwhelming. Millions thronged into Djakarta. People danced in the streets.

The Republic was saved; opponents of colonialism and the subjection of peoples everywhere rejoiced. The world was in a new era. No longer could the will of one nation be imposed upon another by force. To Indonesians, their new nation had been born after a struggle that would ever live in their minds and hearts. After this, no obstacle would ever seem too great for them to surmount.

---

32. Cf. Kahin, *Nationalism and Revolution*, p. 403.

CHAPTER 5

Rebellion in Paradise

However high a priority I had given to understanding Indonesia's revolution—to knowing its leadership, to feeling the pulse of the people —the commanding fact of my first days and weeks as Ambassador was the rebellion in Sumatra.

Two seemingly contradictory developments took place the week of my arrival: as the army began preparations for crossing the Straits and mounting a land invasion of Central Sumatra, Hatta and Sukarno were conferring in an attempt to reach a peaceful solution to the dispute between Sumatra and Java. Reports were conflicting as to the results of these discussions. But Tamzil, director of the President's Cabinet and ordinarily a reliable source of information, reported progress in the negotiations. He informed us that the two leaders found themselves in general agreement but had as yet reached no decision on three key points— the dissolution of the rebel government, the extension of amnesty to the rebels, and how to bring about a reconciliation. Sukarno, he reported, was opposed to all-out military operations against the rebels, a course of action favored by General Nasution and some of the top army staff. Talks between the two leaders would be resumed in the near future, Tamzil said.

A significant little item crept into the news on March 7: the announced results of the regional elections in South Sumatra on December 1, 1957. These were elections for the provincial legislature and city and regency councils. The Masjumi held its position as the leading political party but failed by a small margin to capture a majority. The PKI, however, rose from third to second position in the area, a thirty-three and one-third per cent vote increase accounted for by the Communists' intensive cultivation of workers in the oil fields of Standard Vacuum and Shell, employees of the two big refineries at Palembang, and other estate workers and peasants.

On the same date, as military preparations progressed, the Government of Indonesia announced a strict control of news, reflecting the increasing irritation of Sukarno and the government leadership with foreign correspondents and the press. Indonesian news commentators began a barrage of charges of SEATO involvement in the rebellion, and rumors were spreading of U.S. government subversive involvement. Despite strict government control of pro-rebel news, an increasing number of Javanese intellectuals were favoring the rebels as the only possible saviors of Indonesia from the corrupt, autocratic, and left-leaning central government. The Communists, however, had the better of it. They were making hay out of the confusion, posing as honest nationalists indignant at the actions of Central Sumatra and North Sulawesi.

March 10, 1958, the day I presented my credentials, I had appointments both with Prime Minister Djuanda and Foreign Minister Subandrio. Djuanda, talking as an old friend, spelled out the situation as he saw it. The discussions between Hatta and Sukarno,[1] he predicted, would result in the formation of a new government with Sukarno as President and Hatta as Vice-President, following the lines of the 1945 to 1949 Cabinets of the early revolutionary period. All non-Communist elements in Java were in accord with this plan, he said, and Cabinet changes acceptable to Hatta had been agreed upon. The decision, however, would not be announced for two weeks in order to allow time for the central government to exert its authority in Sumatra and thus not be in the position of losing face by seeming to have yielded to a threat of force. In order to solve the dilemma with which they were presently confronted, a solution must be reached that would preserve President Sukarno from the appearance of defeat, and at the same time re-establish the authority and influence of Hatta in an anti-Communist government.

"We are all against Communism," Djuanda insisted. 'We know that if we permit the growth of Communism within our country, it will destroy us. Sjafruddin and I think alike, too, on the importance of protect-

---

1. Washington continued to be skeptical, as I was, about the Sukarno-Hatta discussions. In view of Sukarno's hold on the masses, it was difficult to see how he could be separated from the exercise of power. Any major reorientation of the central government would therefore appear to involve either changes in Sukarno's own outlook, which apparently was not a prospect, or Sukarno's retirement from an active political role. Even in retirement, Sukarno would be dangerous in view of the almost messianic image he had of himself and because of his love of power. These the Communists had shown a continuing capacity to exploit. If Hatta and Sukarno could actually get together, I had some hope of positive results. Recognizing Sukarno's capacity for political maneuver, I also knew Hatta's character and point of view. He would not agree to anything that did not give him clear-cut responsibility, which he would use intelligently and effectively, countering Sukarno's predictable attempts to circumvent him. Hatta's problem would be his integrity and rigidity. He thought in straight lines; Sukarno was a master of the curved ball.

ing Sumatran oil installations and foreign personnel." [2] Djuanda's warm tone as he spoke of Sjafruddin, the Prime Minister of the rebel government, reflected their long-standing friendship.

To seize Padang, the Sumatran west coast city that housed the rebel headquarters, was the government's goal. Djuanda informed me that the government forces had already occupied Bengalis Island at the mouth of the Siak River; he stated without qualification that no plans to occupy the oil installations were under consideration. The decision to take military action in Sumatra, Djuanda said sadly, was the hardest decision he had ever had to make in his life because it might involve the shedding of Indonesian blood. But he had come to the conclusion that it was necessary to preserve the Republic.

I saw Subandrio late in the afternoon. He was to figure largely in my life for the next seven years. An East Javanese of average build and supercharged with nervous energy, his career was marked by chameleon changes—of profession, political affiliation, and outlook on international affairs. He was agile, vocal, opportunistic, and highly ambitious. During the course of our extraordinarily frank conversation that day, he said, "Sukarno is an element in the present situation. He can't be disposed of." He described Sukarno as a sensitive man, brilliant orator, superb political maneuverer, but one who so loved the fleshpots that he might destroy himself. "Let him remain and have his pleasure," Subandrio said. The implication was that others would rule, presumably including Subandrio, and that the pleasure-mad President would become a figurehead.

On March 9, two days after I had unofficially seen the Prime Minister, the Indonesian government formally requested Caltex to suspend operations and evacuate their dependents. Padang, on the West Coast of Sumatra, was shelled by the Indonesian Navy on March 10. Two days later Pakenbaru, the little city in North Central Sumatra closest to the Caltex

---

2. Reports from all sources on March 10 indicated that the evacuation of foreign nationals from the Sumatran combat area was proceeding without a hitch; both the central and rebel governments were cooperating. One of my staff, William Kelly, was aboard a Caltex motorboat maintaining communication with the U. S. Navy in case additional vessels were needed for evacuation. We thought this highly unlikely, however, since we had received word that the British Navy was sending a destroyer from Singapore to assist with the evacuation, if necessary. Needless to say, all this foreign naval activity in the area was making the Indonesian government nervous. It, too, was making what moves it could to strengthen its position. Djakarta Radio reported that Foreign Minister Subandrio and Shipping Minister Nazir had discussed with the Soviet Ambassador the possible purchase of some 35,000 tons of Soviet ships. On Sumatra, Prime Minister Sjafruddin of the revolutionary government was expressing confidence in his ability to beat off the approaching assault. "Invasion," he predicted, "would be President Sukarno's last breath! When it fails, he has nothing."

oil operations, was captured by government forces, and at the same time substantial quantities of "foreign arms" were seized, left behind by the retreating rebels. On March 16, the Indonesian Foreign Ministry announced that Caltex could safely resume operations the following day. So rapidly did the military situation change.

Events were moving fast in Washington, too. On March 14, Secretary Dulles, meeting with Foreign Minister Casey of Australia and British Secretary Selwyn Lloyd, raised the question as to possible recognition of the rebel regime in Sumatra. He suggested that the United States government might tell Sukarno that since an early military solution seemed unlikely, the United States must inquire as to the likelihood of a political solution, or, failing such a likelihood, the U.S would have to consider according belligerent rights to the rebels. If such an approach to Sukarno were accurately timed, he suggested, it might strengthen the hand of those seeking a political solution.[3] A few weeks later, I was instructed to raise this sensitive issue in my next talk with Sukarno. When I told the President that Secretary Dulles had asked me to alert him to the possibility that if hostilities continued, our government might have to give consideration to recognizing the belligerent status of the rebels, Sukarno bridled. "This is the way to hell," he said angrily, and threatened that such a move would bring a violent reaction not only throughout Indonesia but elsewhere. I pointed out that an early settlement of the internal conflict would avoid the necessity for facing this issue and asked Sukarno if he had anything to say on the subject. I prefaced my question by emphasizing the United States' strong conviction that dismemberment of the Republic of Indonesia would not be in the interest of the free world. At the mention of dismemberment, the President's eyes blazed, but he answered soberly. "Yes," he said slowly, "this would be against the interests of the whole world." He added, "We will reach a settlement as soon as the rebellion is quelled."

On March 15, Subandrio asked to see me. He wanted an explanation for the arms and ammunition that he alleged had been air-dropped (he did not say the planes were American) in the Pakenbaru area on February 26 and March 12. The drop of February 26 was still in unopened cases on the Pakenbaru airfield when the airport was captured. On March 12 a four-engine unidentified plane had dropped twenty cases of arms, including machine guns, sten guns and bazookas. One of the weapons, he said, bore the mark of a manufacturer in Plymouth, Michigan. He asked if I could give him any information concerning these drops. I said I could not, pointing out that American arms were available for purchase on the international market, particularly the older types. I

---

3. The rapid progress of the military action, however, destroyed any possibility of a successful *démarche* of this kind.

noted that both sides were using American weapons. The bombing operations by the Indonesian Air Force in Sumatra were also mounted with U.S. planes, guns, and ammunition.

The Foreign Minister backed off and said he did not intend to imply that the United States government was involved in supplying these weapons. However, several times during the conversation, he introduced the topic of foreign support for the rebels, noting that the Sumatran forces appeared to be equipped in the ratio of three weapons to one man, whereas the central-government forces had only one weapon for every three men. The ever-articulate Subandrio talked in and around the subject for some time, finally saying that the Indonesians were convinced of foreign participation in the rebellion by the way in which the whole matter had been handled. The laying down of an ultimatum followed by a proclamation was alien to the Indonesian way of doing things. He added that he had definite evidence of the involvement of Taiwan in support of the rebels, but he did not spell it out.

A few days later, on March 21, I called on Dr. Hatta. As an old friend, I knew that I would get straight answers from him. He responded to my questions in his usual precise, direct manner. He had been sympathetic to the rebel objectives, but strongly against resorting to force. His view matched my own that the issues were of such a character that they could and should have been handled by negotiations. Dr. Hatta had, therefore, not joined the rebels, but instead exerted strenuous efforts in a vain attempt to bring about a peaceful compromise solution. He was critical of the rebel impatience and precipitate delivery of an ultimatum, but even more critical of the central government's use of force. He included both Sukarno and General Nasution in his censure.

Hatta was optimistic regarding the possibility of reaching an agreement with Sukarno on the formation of a new government, but pessimistic about an early settlement of the rebellion. He and Sukarno had a fundamental disagreement on how to cope with the Communist problem, he said. Sukarno was concerned about the growing strength of the PKI, but believed that its gains were made entirely on the basis of promises it could not fulfill. He thought that the Communists must be brought into the government and forced to accept responsibility. Hatta entirely disagreed with this. The PKI, he insisted, would exploit their position in the government to burrow into the bureaucracy and the army and ultimately acquire real power.

The issue on which the previous talks foundered, Hatta explained, was the construction of a framework for the next government. This was no mere legal quibble, as he saw it, but a basic power problem. Hatta was unwilling to clear important questions with party leaders in Parliament after he had assumed responsibility, since the political party representatives tended to place patronage first. Unless he could bypass the parties in reaching decisions, he would be unable to take the necessary steps to eliminate corruption and lay the foundations for an orderly development of the economy.

Sukarno had told Hatta that he was not against a constitutional framework for the government that would bypass the political parties in the executive decision-making process; but he represented the PNI as having strong objections. They had agreed that Djuanda should remain in office until he and Sukarno agreed on a Cabinet. Hatta would not agree to the President's appointing the National Council, however, and also insisted that its function be purely advisory. When he had suggested to Sukarno that the members be selected from the regions by the provincial legislatures, Sukarno agreed.

On the economic front, Hatta saw many problems facing a government that would win the people's confidence. There had been extensive hoarding of currency, which would come out of hiding as soon as such a government were established and create additional inflationary pressures. There was the need for more effective rice distribution, and for the development of a program to raise the standard of living, which Hatta saw as the best way to fight Communism. He felt that the emphasis should be on creating a positive plan of economic development, and he recognized that substantial outside aid was needed for this purpose. Sukarno rejected Hatta's rationale. To him, the priorities in nation building were political, not economic.

He talked about the tactics of the PKI in dealing with the army. They were too clever to preach Communism to the soldiers. Instead, they showed interest in their welfare, commiserated with them about the poor pay, and generally bad living conditions, and promised, once the Communist Party got into power, to remedy these conditions. Even so, Hatta said, not more than ten per cent of the enlisted personnel were Communists.

Before leaving Hatta, I asked about General Nasution. "What kind of man is he and where does he stand?"

"From the standpoint of America, you could not have a better man as Chief of Staff of the Indonesian Army," he said positively. "I do not agree with him on many things. I did not agree that the army should launch an attack on the rebels. That was a mistake. But from your standpoint, Nasution is fine."

"Exactly what do you mean by that, Dr. Hatta?" I asked.

"The Communists call me their 'Enemy Number One,'" Hatta answered succinctly. "They call Nasution 'Enemy Number Two.'"

"I see," I said. "Then what has happened in Indonesia is that the anti-Communist army leadership has been split. Anti-Communists are fighting anti-Comunists. Communism is not the major issue of this dispute."

"Exactly," Hatta replied.

In this one significant statement, the rebellion and American policy took on a new perspective. If Hatta's words were true, and I had no reason to doubt him, American policy ought to be directed toward settling the rebellion as fast as possible. It would take unity among the anti-Communists to defeat the burgeoning Communist Party in Indonesia. Division could spell defeat.

The next day I called on Djuanda. Following up his previous conversation with me, he said the Government of Indonesia would move toward a settlement of the rebellion when Padang was captured. Considerable political maneuvering was going on behind the scenes to accomplish this. Among others, Wilopo of the PNI was working to achieve both a formula that the rebels might accept and a new Cabinet acceptable to all elements. This was good news because it was the first time I had heard of an active leader of the PNI associated with an attempt to solve these problems. Djuanda said that the NU was also working behind the scenes, but primarily in order to assure itself of a position in the next Cabinet that would bring more political patronage.

Reminiscing about the development of the crisis, Djuanda said that on February 8 he had sent a message via Roem to Padang pleading with the leadership not to take overt action. He had informed them that he would resign within two weeks of the return of Sukarno and pave the way for a Sukarno-Hatta government. He was confident that this could have been done, because it was only with the greatest reluctance that Sukarno had yielded to pressures to take military action. But Padang itself had destroyed the possibility of a peaceful settlement with the issuance of its ultimatum. After that, Djuanda said, he himself was as much responsible as anyone for the decision to take military action. He felt it was necessary to establish for all time in Indonesia that open rebellion and the use of force was not the way for societal groups to accomplish their objectives.

As I departed, he expressed some concern regarding SEATO. I reassured him that it was a purely defensive alliance and was not seized with the Indonesian affair.

The Indonesian crisis assumed a personal dimension for me when, during the afternoon of March 24, I received a telephone call from a neighbor who lived across the street from our home on Embassy Row. "There's a big crowd demonstrating outside your house," she said. "I thought you'd like to know. I've tried to get Mrs. Jones without success. It may be that the wire has been cut." I called for my car and hurried home. As I approached the residence, I could hear angry voices a block away, and as I turned the corner, I saw a crowd of perhaps a thousand outside the gates. They were shouting denunciations of SEATO and of American intervention in Sumatra. The crowd was too large to get through, so I drove around to the rear entrance and walked up onto the veranda.

I have always been proud of my wife, but I was especially so that day. In full sight of the mob, Mary Lou was calmly sitting on the veranda, reading a magazine. She arose, I kissed her, and asked her why she wasn't upstairs.

"Do you think I would let those people think I was afraid?" she asked. "Not on your life!"

I grinned. "Then let's both sit down," I said.

We had no sooner done so when the yelling became shriller and more menacing, winding up in a roar of triumph as the iron gate to the garden clanked open. The mob had forced it, shoved the guard [4] out of the way, and was swarming into the garden. Within seconds, hundreds were racing up the driveway toward the house. Some of them were tough-looking thugs, others obviously university students. I walked out to meet them. I don't mind admitting that my heart was in my mouth. But apparently I had taken them by surprise, for the crowd slowed down and came to a wary halt as I approached its front ranks. They were obviously nonplused as I smiled and held out my hand. I shook hands with half a dozen or more and asked them to select one man as their spokesman. I would be glad to listen to what they had to say, but I could not understand them when they all talked at once.

A handsome young man, who spoke good English and introduced himself as a university student, made a brief speech in a loud voice denouncing SEATO and American intervention on the side of the rebels. He had difficulty making himself heard because the crowd refused to remain quiet. He was interrupted by catcalls and shouts as men pushed and shoved each other, and shook their fists.

Still standing in the driveway, I held up my hand and said I wanted to say a few words. I explained that the Southeast Asia Treaty Organization was a collective defense arrangement aimed only at aggressors. It was certainly not intervening in the Indonesian rebellion. I asked them who they thought were members of SEATO. "Taiwan, Korea!" somebody yelled. At the mention of Taiwan, the mob roared angrily.

"You're wrong!" I tried to make myself heard above the din. "Neither is!" Then I named its members. I pointed out that the Philippines and Thailand were Asian members of SEATO and asked the crowd whether they feared an invasion from them. Some students laughed. Others glowered. Still others shook their fists and shouted, "Down with SEATO!" They had probably read reports of the alleged use of Philippine airbases by unmarked planes that were dropping arms to the rebels.

---

4. The so-called *Jaga* was really not much of a guard, just an unarmed Indonesian watchman who was supposed to see that unauthorized persons did not come in. No blame was attached to him. Afterward he said that the mob had snarled at him, "Get out of our way or we'll kill you." Later, the Indonesian government provided armed guards for the embassy residence.

After about half an hour of this, I suggested that it was time for them all to go home. I urged the protesters to think about what I had said and not be misled by unfair propaganda from the enemies of America. I wound up my remarks by saying that the United States government was interested in the preservation of Indonesia's independence, as I assumed they all were. Then I attempted to dismiss them. I shook hands with all I could reach, after which the crowd slowly broke up and departed, with a few final defiant cries. Halfway to the gate, several turned around and came back to shake hands with me, grinning as if to say "No hard feelings."

My only regret was that I had not invited them in for a cold drink, something I did the next time. Demonstrations came to be a way of life in Indonesia. At one point, Dr. Hatta sarcastically termed the new approach to government in Indonesia as "government by demonstration."

A few days later, I saw one of the demonstrators, a young man with wavy hair and a small mustache whom I knew to be a Communist, emerging from Foreign Minister Subandrio's office as I was entering. "I have just had a report from one of the demonstrators at your house," Subandrio said amusedly. "Apparently you made quite an impression. Congratulations!"

Convinced that in some way the wily Indonesian Foreign Minister had had a hand in the affair, I dryly acknowledged the compliment. Later, I learned that by Indonesian standards I had done the right thing, acting in the correct tradition of preserving at least an appearance of Javanese *priyaji* (aristocratic) nonchalance in the face of challenge or danger.

It now seemed self-evident that Washington policy makers had not been privy to all the facts nor really grasped the inwardness of the situation, but had proceeded on the assumption that Communism was the main issue. This was the all too common weakness of Americans—to view conflict in black and white terms, a heritage, no doubt, from our Puritan ancestors. There were no grays in the world landscape. There was either good or evil, right or wrong, hero or villain. Here was another case of predilections blinding us to facts, of prejudices blocking judgment, of the wish being father to the thought. It was another lesson testifying to the critical importance of diplomatic reportage in depth; however, even the best of reporting much too frequently encounters immovable objects—preconceptions in the minds of the readers. As one who was participating, albeit on a secondary level, in this policy making in 1957, I shared to some degree the responsibility for this failure.

If a break in relations between Indonesia and the U.S. were to come, the principal beneficiaries would be the Indonesian Communist Party and the Soviet bloc. The Russians had not been slow to exploit the widᵗning breach in U.S.-Indonesian relations. On March 11, 1958, when SEATO was meeting in Manila, Subandrio and the Soviet Ambassador met to discuss the purchase by Indonesia of Soviet ships. Thus began the build-up of the huge Soviet military assistance program to Indonesia. Together with economic assistance, it dwarfed our efforts, reaching a total of more than $1,400,000,000 over the next six years. It represented a gigantic drive to move Indonesia into the Communist bloc and exploit the opportunity that, for understandable if shortsighted reasons, we had passed up.

It should be noted that Indonesia never approached the Communist bloc for either economic or military aid until it had exhausted the possibility of help from America. As far back as 1955, the Soviets, copying our economic aid and technical assistance programs, offered substantial economic aid to the Indonesian government. At the time, the government, pursuing a neutralist policy, told the Russians it would not consider accepting any more than the Americans had given. Some years earlier, we had extended $100 million in credit from the Export-Import Bank for economic-development projects. So the Russians offered aid in that amount, but the Indonesian Cabinet could not agree on whether to accept. It was not until three years later, in the spring of 1958, that, convinced we were turning our backs on them, the Indonesians finally took up that option and accepted economic aid from the Soviet government.

On April 6, Indonesia announced the first step in the Soviet bloc military-aid program. It included deals with Poland, Czechoslovakia, and Yugoslavia for small arms, jet fighters and bombers, which were Soviet built. The reaction in Washington was immediate. State Department spokesman Lincoln White declared, on April 7, "We regret that Indonesia turned to the Communist bloc to buy arms for possible use in killing Indonesians who openly oppose the growing influence of Communism in Indonesia."

Considering the Indonesians had been pounding on our door for years requesting arms, White was on a bad wicket. Foreign Minister Subandrio protested that only when the United States had rejected Indonesia's request to purchase American weapons had Indonesia turned to the Communists. In 1955, when the Indonesians had submitted a shopping list totaling between $6,000,000 and $7,000,000, the U.S. had answered neither yes nor no.

Secretary Dulles acknowledged this the next day but said the Indonesians had been refused arms because of their apparent intention to use the weapons against the Dutch in West Irian. He added that "later when the [Sumatran] revolt broke out, . . . it did not seem wise to the United States to be in the position of supplying arms to either side of that civil revolution," and that it was "still our view that the situation there is primarily an internal one, and we intend to conform scrupulously to the principles of international law that apply to such a situation." [5]

The Foreign Minister followed up the arms issue with me on April 8. He stressed the vital importance of keeping internal law and order while the fighting was going on in Sumatra and Sulawesi. With the bulk of Indonesia's fighting men no longer in Java, the security situation gave his government concern. The Indonesian Army was expanding its personnel to ensure internal security, but small arms and ammunition were desperately needed to supply the new recruits. Subandrio said his government would pledge that any United States-supplied arms would not be used against the rebels; but, with Java denuded of fighting men, it must be anticipated that the Communists or the Darul Islam would attempt to exploit this opportunity. The latter, he noted, had already cost some 27,000 lives in Indonesia with their depredations of the past few years. His new request for arms aid made news throughout the world. In response to press queries in Washington, Secretary Dulles replied that a new request for military assistance to Indonesia, which had been presented to me by Subandrio on the same day, had not yet reached Washington.[6]

Increasingly, I sensed the importance of the role of General Nasution. His anti-Communism had been established by fire and sword. I put him down as a dedicated nationalist. But what was his philosophy of the army's role in Indonesia? And how did he view the rebellion, originating as it had in his own home island of Sumatra? At the first opportunity, I had lunch with two of my diplomatic colleagues, the British and Australian Ambassadors, and asked their opinion of the man. They looked at each other wryly. Dermit McDermit, the tall, lean Irishman who was the British Ambassador, was a man of few words but those always right to the point. He said, "We don't know."

"You don't know!" I exclaimed. "What is this? The good old British game of pulling the leg of the new boy?"

My Australian colleague, Jim McIntyre, dry, good-humored, down-to-earth, and with a real gift for political perception, was amused. "Dermit's right, Howard," he said. "We don't know him. You see, Nasution is a new kind of bird around here. He works around the clock. He does not attend dinner parties or receptions. He makes no speeches. He won't receive visitors. No member of the diplomatic corps, including the dean, has been given an appointment to call upon him. Of course, we have met him. Once or twice a year he attends a reception given by President Sukarno in the palace, and we have shaken hands with him and had a few words with him there. But know him? No, we don't."

---

5. Dulles' news conference of April 8, 1958. *The Department of State Bulletin,* vol. XXXVIII, no. 983 (April 28, 1958), p. 685.
6. *Ibid.,* pp. 684–685.

"I've got to see him!" I said.

My friends grinned maliciously. "We wish you luck," they said. "We've tried. But seriously," one of them added, "we do wish you luck. We all need to know more about Nasution. If you can get to him, it will help us all."

I returned to my office and sent word to General Nasution via the military attaché that I would greatly appreciate an opportunity to call upon him. The attaché returned with the curt message: "General Nasution is not interested in courtesy calls. If the American Ambassador has something of substance to discuss with him, General Nasution will be glad to receive him." I grinned at the attaché.

"Sounds like quite a man. Pass the word to his aide that I, too, am uninterested in courtesy calls and am glad to find a kindred spirit. Say that I will request another appointment when I have something of substance to discuss with him. I trust this will be soon."

On April 12, two significant approaches were made to us by top Indonesian military officials. Colonel Yani, First Deputy Chief of Staff, told an attaché of the embassy that American aid to the rebels, of which there was now no doubt, placed the pro-U.S. officers in the Indonesian Army in an intolerable position. Unless something were done, the influence of these officers would deteriorate seriously, he said. Another staff officer informed the embassy that reaction against the United States among the anti-Communist officers in the Indonesian Army was reaching alarming proportions. In Washington, Secretary Dulles was still considering the possibility of recognizing a state of belligerency in Indonesia, assuming, of course, that government forces failed to contain the rebellion.

With the U.S. government denying that it was giving aid to the rebels —although clearly indicating its sympathy with the rebel cause; with anti-Communists fighting each other in bloody civil war; with the anti-Communist army leadership becoming disillusioned with America, and with Sukarno clearly in command of the situation and turning more and more to the Communist bloc and away from the free world, it seemed time for a shift of emphasis in U.S. policy.

There were those in Washington who regarded Sukarno as a rising Asian Hitler and opposed him on the ground that he was "a dangerous man" not to be trusted, a description presumably based on his noticeable determination and demonstrated capacity to upset the *status quo*, and on the fact that he held Marxist views. The question American policy makers had to decide was a dual one: Were Sukarno's objectives for his country inimical to U.S. interests, and if so, what could we do about it? In the early spring of 1958, I would have answered "Not necessarily" to the first half of the question, and "Not much" to the second half. It seemed to me that we had three alternatives:

One, go all-out in support of the rebels in an effort to depose Sukarno;

two, let matters take their own course, viewing the rebellion as an internal matter in which we had an interest but in which we were not prepared to take sides; three, take positive steps to improve relations with the Indonesian government in the hope of being able to encourage a settlement of the rebellion and influence Indonesia toward a more constructive course, internally and externally.

We had done none of these, with the exception of giving lip service to the second. The first course was highly impracticable and undesirable for a number of reasons. Sukarno's hold on his people was such that an attempt on the part of a foreign power to force him out would have only generated greater mass support for him—and would have undoubtedly brought him active military support from both Communist China and the Soviet Union. Secondly, United States' pretensions to noninterference in internal affairs of Asian nations would have been completely discredited and the moral quality of our leadership, so recently established in Asia by our voluntary act in granting independence to the Philippines, would have been lost. Finally, credence would have been given to the charge by Communists and others that the United States was an imperialist power determined to impose its will upon others by force, if necessary.

The second course, viewing the rebellion as an internal matter, was in fact the United States' official policy, violated by some unofficial acts that had high official sanction. It was a "do nothing" policy and could only result in declining American influence and prestige.

I felt the time had come to adopt the third course of action as our only chance to influence the course of future events in Indonesia. At the least, it would encourage the considerable forces in the Indonesian government working along what were in our opinion constructive lines.

The political weakness of the rebels could be seen in their failure to enlist the support of such prominent anti-Communist, anti-Sukarno figures as former Vice-President Hatta, and Army Chief of Staff General Nasution—both Sumatrans and, one would have thought, logical spokesmen for the rebel cause. Why did men like these remain aside? There was, additionally, an impressive array of present and potential anti-Communist leaders and groups in Java, which, if effectively marshaled, might turn the Communist tide—moderate leaders of the Masjumi Party, including Natsir, Sjafruddin, Roem, Harahap, Isa, Abu Hanifah, active and astute men. Some of them, however, lacked resolution and seemed inclined to wait on events.

Key figures like General Gatot Subroto, Colonels Kosasih, Mokaginta, Sarbini, Suharto and "Andi" Jusuf (Makassar) were typical of the stanch anti-Communists in the army leadership. Colonel Zulkifli Lubis, contender for Chief of Staff when Nasution was appointed, was also a strong anti-Communist, but playing a lone hand.

In early 1958, there was still a vigorous, independent, anti-government press, including *Indonesia Raya, Abadi, Pedoman, Pia. Merdeka,* though nominally independent, was at this time generally supporting the government.

Prime Minister Djuanda, although supporting Sukarno, was also anti-Communist, and could be depended upon to resist Communist expansion in the government.

The leadership of the Socialist Party, the PSI, was solidly anti-Communist, including such men as Sjahrir, Soedjatmoko, Simatupang, General Sukanto, head of the police, and the PSI leader in Parliament, Subadio, as well as an outstanding woman, Maria Ullfah Santoso, former Minister of Social Welfare. The same could be said for the moderate PNI leadership, which included former Prime Minister Wilopo and the Secretary-General of the party, Hardi.

The Sultan of Jogjakarta, a member of no political party but a power in his own right, was strongly anti-Communist. This was also true of the Anak Agung, former Foreign Minister and once head of the early Federal State of East Indonesia, organized at a time when the Republic of Indonesia included only Java and Sumatra. (The Anak Agung was leader of the grouping that included all Eastern Indonesia after the Linggadjati Agreement.)

Finally, there was the Darul Islam, fanatical Moslems who were fighting in the hills as guerrillas, and were responsible for most of the attempts on Sukarno's life. They were avidly anti-Communist and anti-government, their objective being to establish Indonesia as a Moslem state, with which neither we nor the Indonesian government agreed.

The existence of such men, parties and press strengthened my hope that a political solution was possible. In terms of power politics, it would mean placing our bets squarely on the Indonesian army. The most to be hoped for from such a change in tactics was that it would induce Sukarno to shift direction on the ground that his country could make more rapid progress in this post-independence era by cooperation with the United States and the West. In the event of such a shift, which at the time was only a remote possibility, the rebellion could be settled without permanent damage to the elements in the society that had mounted it, and at the very least, we would be in on the discussions with a chance that our voice might be heard.

The alternatives were most unpalatable. I could see the inevitability of increasing Communist influence in the government. All the brakes on anti-Americanism in Indonesia would be removed by the evidence pointing to active U.S. support for the rebels; in cartoons and editorials, the Communist press was already having a field day. I could see myself on the way home in a matter of weeks unless some positive action were taken soon to improve our position.

While a shift in U.S. policy implementation of course carried no guarantee of success, nevertheless, it would at least tend to strengthen the hand of the anti-Communist elements in Indonesia by assuring them of the moral support of a powerful external ally. On April 15 I proposed to Washington that we make a bold move in this direction by telling the Indonesian government that we would provide military aid and expand our economic assistance if it would take positive steps to negotiate with the rebels and settle the rebellion.

In my cable to the Department of State, I said that the time had come to make some positive gesture of support toward the Indonesian military if we were to preserve the pro-American, anti-Communist loyalties of the top officer group in the army. Recent gestures toward the United States by Sukarno, government leaders, and army officers made it apparent that the Indonesians were opening the door to a *rapprochement* with the United States government. But at the same time, there was an increasing conviction on the part of the Indonesian military that the United States government was actually aiding the rebels. And this, if not remedied, might result in a deterioration of the long and carefully nurtured relations with the army. Anti-Communist officers friendly to America (not pro-American but convinced that it was in Indonesia's interest to cooperate with America rather than Russia) still held the balance of power in the army, but this could be upset.

"As I see it," I advised Washington at the time, "the Army is more and more likely to determine the future course to be followed by Indonesia. The Army is gathering more power, both in the political and economic spheres. If the Army remains anti-Communist, it can be counted upon to take positive action to prevent a Communist take-over. The Army does not regard the struggle with the rebels as a battle between Communists and anti-Communists since the Army leadership in Djakarta is as strongly anti-Communist as the Army leadership on the rebels' side. Neither do most influential Indonesians so consider it. To the Army, the issue is the simple one of discipline, and the Army shares Djuanda's view that it was necessary to re-establish for all time in Indonesia that open rebellion is not the way to accomplish the objectives of any group within the society."

I recommended, therefore, that (1) the United States government honor the long-standing request of the Indonesian government for military equipment, with the understanding that the arms be delivered after the resolution of the present conflict in Indonesia; (2) we invite top Indonesian officers to the Pentagon to discuss these arrangements; (3) we invite Indonesian officers to the Staff and Command School at Fort Leavenworth and offer additional training for officers and non-commissioned officers; (4) after hostilities ceased, we provide the parachutes the Indonesian Army had been requesting. I also recommended that we respond favorably to their request to replace cotton with rice in the surplus-commodity program.

My advocacy of this *démarche* has often been referred to as representing a major shift in American policy toward Indonesia. But I did not so regard it. The basic policy was to assist Indonesia in the development and maintenance of economic and political stability, with a view to ensuring its capability to preserve independence. Alterations in programs or modification of plans or turns in tactics are common in diplomacy as logical adjustments in the furtherance of major policy objectives. Only in this context did the proposal represent a radical change of direction and emphasis in our courses of action.

CHAPTER 6

U.S. Policy Shifts

The pleasant little city of Ambon, 1,700 miles east of Djakarta on an island in the blue Banda Sea, is the gateway to the Spice Islands. The people are gay and music loving. Singing and dancing are what Ambon is famous for—along with cloves and other spices.

But on Sunday morning, May 18, 1958, there was no laughter left in the city. Its residents, more than half of whom are Christians, were on their way to church when the roar of an airplane engine was heard overhead. There was no time for them to seek shelter; indeed, few of them would have believed the sound carried the threat of sudden death. Seconds later, bombs whined toward the earth. One dropped into the smokestack of an Indonesian naval vessel and sank it at the dock.

Ambon's antiaircraft batteries opened up. A plane burst into flame and traced a fiery path earthward. A figure plummeted for an instant; then a white parachute billowed above him, and he was swept by the wind toward a coconut grove. His chute was caught in the branches of a tall palm, where he was suspended for a moment before crashing to the ground.

The flier was an American named Allen Pope. His hip was broken in the fall, and he lay helpless until he was found and captured by Indonesian soldiers, who probably saved him from certain death at the hands of irate farmers.

Pope was the kind of man generally characterized as a "soldier of fortune." He had flown with the French forces at Dien Bien Phu prior to their defeat by the Communists. He was known as a skillful pilot, a man who sought danger and adventure wherever he could find it.

The bomb that hit the church may or may not have been dropped by Pope, for he was not alone on that raid. He denied it. But to the Indonesians, his name became synonymous with sudden death and foreign intervention in the internal affairs of Indonesia.

The news that an American had been captured flying a rebel plane spread rapidly, although the Indonesian government withheld official confirmation until nine days after the fact. It was suggested that fear for Pope's safety until he had been moved to Java dictated the delay; but there was also the possibility that the Indonesians wanted to probe U.S. attitudes before making an issue of the matter at a time when Washington seemed to be adjusting its position.

In any event, Pope was not identified as the pilot of the downed rebel plane until May 27. On that day, Lieutenant Colonel Herman Pieters, Commander of the Maluku and West Irian military command, who had escorted Pope and his Indonesian crew member to Djakarta from Ambon, told the press Pope had been a flier "with the Taiwan Aviation Company [Civil Air Transport], and had been seconded to the rebel regime." He said Pope had confessed to having received direct orders from the rebel leaders to strafe and bomb ships and locations in East Indonesia, for which he received the salary of $10,000 (U.S.) monthly.[1] "This town of Ambon has been attacked almost daily by rebel B-26 bombers over a two-week period and at least twenty-two civilians and nineteen soldiers have been killed during these raids," Pieters said.

A week following Pieter's announcement, the pro-Communist *Bintang Timur* came out with a cartoon on the front page illustrating what the Indonesians considered the dualism in our policy. It showed John Foster Dulles as a boxer in the ring. One of his gloves was labeled "Goodwill Jones," the other "Killer Pope."

Weeks before Pope's capture, the Indonesians had obtained what they felt was conclusive evidence of American support for the rebels. On April 30, Prime Minister Djuanda declared publicly that the government had "evidence of foreign aid in the bombing of several towns in the eastern part of Indonesia." He noted that the rebels had only two Indonesian pilots at their disposal, that in Menado, North Sulawesi and surrounding areas, there was no available stock of aviation gasoline and all fuel installations had been destroyed by government forces. It was obvious, he pointed out, that the gasoline used during the air operations must have come from outside Indonesia in some illegal manner. "From this we can draw the conclusion that the pilots and airmen used by the rebels are foreigners," he continued. "Reports received from Menado corroborate that the rebels are employing American and Formosan pilots in their operations," and there was also government evidence that between April 25 and 30, automatic weapons had been smuggled from Formosa into Indonesia. "A feeling of disgust and resentment has emerged among the armed forces and people of Indonesia against those countries," Djuanda said, "and if this situation is allowed to continue, it might badly affect the relations between Indonesia and the United States." That this might result in Indonesia allying itself with the Com-

---

1. Pope later denied this.

munist side in the world struggle was clearly implied in his statement that "the foreign intervention might have far-reaching repercussions not only between Indonesia and the world but also within the framework of the cold war.

"For the sake of good relations between the Indonesian and the American people," he urged that a positive effort be made to ensure that "American citizens do not give aid to the rebels in any form such as: (1) the sale or purchase of arms; (2) the use and sale of aircraft, ships, or other means of transport and communications; (3) the sending of their technicians for war purposes; (4) the providing of facilities for flights from airfields under their control." He wound up by appealing "to the world generally and to Asian and African nations particularly . . . to condemn this foreign intervention which contains elements that endanger peace in Asia and the whole world."

President Eisenhower and Secretary Dulles answered the charges in two separate press conferences. On April 30, Eisenhower stated, "When it comes to an intrastate difficulty anywhere, our policy is one of careful neutrality and proper deportment all the way through so as not to be taking sides where it is none of our business. . . . Now, on the other hand, every rebellion has its soldiers of fortune," who engage in foreign rebellions either for pay or enjoyment.[2] Dulles followed this up on May 1 by saying that the United States government could "not be sure Americans were involved" in the Indonesian civil war:

> There are Americans around the world who engage in such enterprises. I know today we are alerted to the fact that it may be possible that some Americans are flying Soviet arms into Yemen. I don't know whether they are or are not. But that is also a conceivably possible thing that we cannot control. And we have no legal obligation to control the activities of Americans of this character.[3]

The Communists moved fast to exploit the new developments. On May 1, PKI chief Aidit sent me a telegram threatening action against American economic interests in Indonesia if our aid to the rebels were not stopped. Since oil and rubber represented the principal U.S. investments in Indonesia, it could be assumed that the leader of the PKI had in mind action against the rubber estates and the oil fields.[4] In both

---

2. New York *Times*, May 1, 1958.
3. *The Department of State Bulletin*, vol. XXXVIII, no. 986 (May 19, 1958), 808.
4. The principal American rubber holdings were in the hands of Goodyear, with its Sumatra "Wingfoot" estate, the largest single rubber estate in the world with more than 3,000,000 rubber trees, and U. S. Rubber, with a complex of estates representing one of the largest groups of rubber-producing plantations in the world. The Standard Oil Company had important producing areas in Sumatra and a refinery at Palembang in South Sumatra. Caltex had greater production but no refinery. The other major oil

industries, the Communist-controlled roof organization, SOBSI, dominated the trade unions and was in a position to call strikes, stimulate sabotage and cause trouble generally. It had sufficient power to stop production if it were willing to go to those lengths.

The Department of State was greatly concerned over this threat, but I did not think the Communists would be so foolish as to endanger the flow of oil, which was not only essential to the economy of Indonesia but absolutely vital to the military effort supported by the PKI. If an army once moved on its stomach, today it rolls on rubber and oil. And rubber was also the leading foreign-exchange producer for the country at the time. If the estates were in rebel territory, the PKI might sabotage production, though the rebels would do their utmost to prevent this. But if the central-government forces controlled the territory, I could see little likelihood of the army permitting a shutdown of the rubber estates.

As a matter of principle, I lodged a protest with the Indonesian government, recognizing that a warning from the army, with the country under martial law, would help deter irresponsible actions. While I considered Aidit's telegram propaganda, I was quite aware that if the army were to stand aside, the Communist Party leader would be in a position to make good his threat.

Aidit also celebrated May Day by asserting that the United States government, after the defeat of the rebels, had as its objective the replacement of the Djuanda Cabinet by an anti-Communist one. America, he charged, "intends to use the Indonesian military to pressure Sukarno into agreeing to a Cabinet change." He declared that this "would be bitterly opposed by the people of Indonesia" and warned that the PKI "would never call for increased production in the nation if the Government was in the hands of persons unfriendly to labor and the Indonesian people." The only possible substitute for the Djuanda Cabinet, he insisted, was a *gotong-rojong* ("share-the-burden") cabinet—by which he meant one that included Communist representation.

President Sukarno, apparently taking his cue from Aidit, leaped into the fray on May 2 and warned Washington: "Don't play with fire." As for adventurers, "We could easily have asked for volunteers from outside. We could wink an eye and they would come. We could have thousands of volunteers, but we will meet the rebels with our own strength." He cautioned that if "some circles assist the rebels, others would assist us and the result would be a world war." Sukarno blamed Washington for the deterioration of United States-Indonesian relations. He asked the U.S. to reappraise its Indonesian policy and understand Indonesia.[5]

---

company was Shell, which was controlled by the British and Dutch, although it included a minority American interest.
5. New York *Times*, May 3, 1958. The allusion to "outside volunteers" referred to offers made to Sukarno by the Chinese Communists.

Also on May 2, Foreign Minister Subandrio, speaking in Bandung, pleaded with the United States to try to understand Sukarno. But he hailed the American statements as conciliatory, stating they "could be interpreted as very receptive to the suggestion to stop intervention in Indonesia by United States nationals." [6] Behind the scenes, however, Indonesian suspicions regarding the United States were not allayed.

In a two-hour conversation with me the following day, Subandrio sought American assistance in quelling the rebellion and halting the spread of Communism within the country. The press crowded around him as I left his office. He told them (not in my presence) that Indonesia would regard continued foreign military help to the rebels as "aggression endangering general peace" and would have no alternative but to take the case to the United Nations if the issue were not settled. The Indonesians could draw no conclusion from the existing evidence, he said, but that military equipment at the rebels' disposal had been received from American and Taiwan adventurers.

On May 5, I received an urgent request from the Prime Minister to come to his home that evening. The Foreign Minister was present; it was obvious something important was in the wind. Djuanda's manner in greeting me was, as I informed the Department of State, "graver and more serious" than I had seen before. He plunged at once into the burden of his message, saying that he feared "relations between the U.S. and Indonesia were at a crossroads and that the next few days might determine the outcome." Originally he had hoped the capture of Padang and Bukittinggi would make it possible to bring about a political settlement with the rebels, but the foreign bombings had "introduced a new element which had so aroused Indonesians that the Government was determined to push on with the military campaign."

Discussing the thoughts behind his April 30 speech, Djuanda emphasized to me that he had made every effort to draft his statement in such a way that no specific accusations would be made against the United States, but he implied he knew we were involved and said flatly that he could not understand our motives. It now looked to the Indonesian government as if the policy and purpose of the United States was to split Indonesia in two in order to ensure that at least one part of the country would remain non-Communist.

Such an intention on our part, he warned, would mean tragedy for Indonesia, as well as for the basic objectives of American policy, because it would play directly into the hands of the Communists. The PKI would be delighted by an estrangement between the United States and Indonesia over the bombing issue. Indeed, the PKI was already making

which he made public on May 19. Cf. The Washington *Post*, May 20, 1958.
6. New York *Times*, May 3, 1958.

every effort to capitalize on the increasing claims of American assistance to the rebels, with a view to pushing Sukarno and the Cabinet into taking "steps from which there would be no return." The President himself was so furious that it was "with the greatest difficulty" that Djuanda had been able to persuade him not to make a speech openly attacking the United States. Sukarno's speech at Bandung on May 2 had, in fact, come close to so doing.

At this point I broke in to assure Djuanda and Subandrio that the United States government was not aiming at a dismemberment of Indonesia; that would not be in the interest of Indonesia, the United States, or the free world. At the same time, we were greatly concerned about the growth of Communism in Java and that apparently nothing was being done about it.

Djuanda said that he, Subandrio, and others were aware of that, and he was glad to be able to tell me that "the PNI in its meeting in Semarang had decided to take positive steps." Djuanda and people like Vice Prime Minister Hardi would be working out a specific program to reduce PKI influence. But there was a caveat: the United States must do its part. Evidence of U.S. involvement in the current struggle could provide the PKI with the ammunition it needed to turn Indonesians against America. In this connection, he informed me of recently received information from the Indonesian embassy in Manila "that new preparations were being carried out at Clark Field for additional plane and MTB [motor torpedo boat] assistance to the rebels." I expressed shocked surprise at this, having no inkling that Clark Field was being so used.

Djuanda made a strong appeal for action by the United States government "to halt bombings and further aid to the rebels." If the Secretary of State were to publicly indicate that the U.S. intended to do what it could, it would help those within the Indonesian government interested in cooperating with the U.S. and help foil the Communist thrust in Indonesia. Djuanda, too, would be helped—in exerting influence toward a settlement of the rebellion and moving against the PKI internally. He stressed that America's friendship was so important to the future of Indonesia that he was willing to overlook past American support of the rebels; but he pleaded for "hands-off" in the future. "Let Indonesians settle their own internal conflicts," he concluded.[7]

Returning to the chancery, I drafted a long, urgent message to the Department. The following day a reply was on my desk, asking me to express my government's appreciation of the frankness of the discussion

7. Subandrio announced to the press on May 6 that he believed "current foreign intervention in Indonesia can be overcome before long." The same day, the Prime Minister somewhat cautiously confirmed that the government's military policy was to settle the rebellion in North Sulawesi as soon as possible, but added that his government "will not be frightened by foreign intervention from any side."

and tell both Djuanda and Subandrio that we would welcome any additional comments and suggestions they might wish to make, and agreeing that such frank, informal talks respresented the best method for eliminating any misunderstandings. I was also asked to say that the U.S. government had "no control over the rebel bombings or 'adventurers' hired by the rebels," and to reply to the allegations point by point. As for the evidence of U.S. involvement cited by the Foreign Minister: if C-47's were turned over to the regels in Singapore, "the U. S. Government had no knowledge of, and the U. S. Navy has not issued instructions for, such transactions in Singapore or elsewhere"; if the Indonesians had documents, I was authorized to assure them the documents were false. The Indonesians had mentioned 7.35 mm semi-automatic rifles; these were not manufactured in the United States or used by our armed forces. I was also to assure Djuanda that Clark Field was not serving as a base to assist the rebels.

Accompanying this message was a long-awaited response to my earlier recommendations for economic and military assistance to the Indonesian government. I was authorized to tell the Prime Minister that the United States was prepared to sell Indonesia 35,000 tons of rice, but further decisions by the U.S. government for other assistance would be more easily made if the Indonesian government took positive steps to curb Communist expansion within the country.

In a separate personal message from Assistant Secretary Robertson, I was asked to emphasize to Djuanda that for the U.S. government to be effective in restraining others from giving active assistance to the rebels, "we need a concrete demonstration it was the Indonesian Government's intention to deal effectively with the Communists."

The quandary faced by Washington was clear. Assuming that support for the rebels was coming from such anti-Communist neighbors of Indonesia as Taiwan, the Philippines and Singapore, those furnishing such assistance would have to be convinced the Indonesian government was not on its way to becoming a Communist country. The same consideration applied to United States policy. If arms were furnished to Indonesia and it later went Communist, we would be in the ironic position of having handed weapons to our enemies. The United States government wanted tangible evidence from Indonesian authorities that they had the will and the capability to stem the rising tide of Communist power and influence in the country. The requirement of action in this direction before aid would be forthcoming also represented a test of the strength of the anti-Communist elements within the government. We knew the Prime Minister was in favor of taking such action. We knew the army leadership was. We were doubtful about Sukarno, and the question was whether the forces within the government that were opposed to Communism and anxious to receive assistance from America could exert sufficient pressure upon Sukarno to induce him to act against a powerful political group that had been and continued to be politically useful to him, however dangerous it might be for the country—the PKI. The most desirable action was settlement of the rebellion; that would enable anti-Communist groups to reunify, eliminate the political, social and economic disruptions inevitably accompanying civil war, and permit the Indonesian government to get on with the job of economic development. We also wanted the government to curtail further Communist penetration of governmental apparatus and control the increasingly threatening actions and demonstrations against friendly powers endeavoring to assist the government.

This was, we thought, a reasonable, non-interfering position. We were simply seeking assurance that the government we were helping would continue to be in friendly hands.

I immediately sought an appointment with the Foreign Minister, who, when he learned that I had already received a reply to the questions raised the preceding evening, telephoned the Prime Minister. He asked that we come to his home at once. Both were pleased with the prompt response, which had proved timely since a special Cabinet meeting had been called for the next day to discuss the critical situation. "Pressures within the government are building up," Djuanda said; the PKI was engaged in feverish activity designed to force the Indonesian government "into an irrevocable anti-American position." The proffer of rice and the indication that we were willing to consider further economic and military aid was recognized as an earnest of our intentions and as a major shift in American tactics.

Nevertheless, Djuanda was emphatic that while the Indonesian government was appreciative of the U.S. offer, it "would not be willing to consider any offer which carried with it conditions affecting internal operations of the country." Indonesia would not bargain away its independence of action. I insisted that we assumed the Government of Indonesia would follow the course it deemed to be in its own best interests. While we had confidence that the course would be one we could support, we did need some assurance to that effect.

The Prime Minister acknowledged the fine distinction with a smile and said he was planning two moves in the near future: a reshuffle of the government, and more positive actions to curb the PKI. He added he "could tell me confidentially that he, as well as the army, was very much concerned about the current activities of the PKI." Djuanda also mentioned his concern for Java's internal security—since the main body of the Indonesian military was now outside Java—particularly if the Communists should step up their activities (as reports indicated) to stage a coup or continue disruption of the economy through strikes and boycotts. He added that "he had instructed the military to crack down on any action taken by the Communists against foreign interests."

The question of how to handle the Communists and the extent of the military capability on Java, he said, would be discussed with Nasution at the Cabinet meeting the following day. As for a Cabinet reshuffle to include Hatta, he was still hopeful that this could be accomplished. The first difficulty was Hatta's own rigidity and unwillingness to compromise; the second, the fear of some army leaders that Hatta might favor the Sumatrans to such an extent that control of the army might actually pass into rebel hands. The Sultan of Jogjakarta, however, was certain to be included in the Cabinet, either as Minister of National Defense or Minister of Economic Affairs. If Djuanda had his way, the new Cabinet would be anti-Communist in orientation, and its objectives would coincide with those of the U.S.

Djuanda said that I could be sure that no arms from the United States would be used against the dissidents. As I left, he expressed appreciation for the decision on our part to deliver a quantity of surplus rice, which was desperately needed, and for the other assurances I had given him.

Shortly after seeing Djuanda, I received word that General Nasution, whom I had never met, would like to see me at eight o'clock the following morning. My arrival at army headquarters was marked with full honors—even to the blare of trumpets. Nasution and his top staff received me formally in his impressive office. The figure before me was stocky, erect; he wore green combat fatigues, three gold stars gleaming from heavy shoulders. He was handsome, his eyes alight with intelligence, his smile open and friendly, his manner self-assured—a man who immediately inspired confidence, liking and respect.

I began with a question: What did he envisage the political role of the army to be in the Indonesian state?

"The Indonesian Army," he replied, "is the army of the revolution. We are still the army that fought for and won independence for our country. Our basic objective is to maintain that independence and ensure that the goals for which our soldiers fought, bled and died are not endangered. To accomplish this, the army must be unified."

"In the achievement of that objective," I asked, "would the army take control of the government?"

"We believe in constitutional government and civilian control of the armed forces," he answered. "The Indonesian Army is not like the armies of so many Latin American countries. What happens there? A military junta takes over, runs the country in its own interest, until it makes so many enemies it is thrown out and a new military faction takes over and does the same. The process is repeated over and over, and what happens to the people? They receive no benefit from the various changes in power. No! The Indonesian revolution was fought for the benefit of all the people of Indonesia, and as long as I have anything to say about it, the army will never take over the government in its own interest."

Whether Nasution or any other army leader, faced with an actual conflict between the interests of the professional military and a civilian group, could maintain such a stand, might be open to some question, I thought, but the philosophy was sound.

"Suppose that there is a threat from the left to take over the government," I suggested. "What would the army do then?"

"If there were a threat from the left—or a threat from the right—the army would act. We would move whenever we saw what we considered a threat to the goals for which we fought the revolution. But if the army had to take control of the government, it would be a temporary measure for the purpose of restoring constitutional government, not replacing it."

"Then the army considers itself the guardian of the constitutional government in Indonesia. But is there any constitutional provision for that?"

There was none, the General recognized, but he believed that there ought to be. In the meantime, if it should come to a matter of life or death for the new Republic, the army would do the necessary, provision or no provision.

I said I was aware that he was against the growing power and influence of the Communist Party in Indonesia, and was regarded by the Communists as an enemy. It seemed to me rather obvious that an unfortunate situation had developed in which the anti-Communist forces of the nation had become divided. If one assumed, as I did, that Communism represented a major threat to the independence of Indonesia and the goals of the revolution, the sooner the rebellion could be settled, the better. It was in this spirit that I was coming to him to suggest that the United States might be willing to provide some military assistance and additional economic aid to Indonesia if the rebellion were to be settled.

Nasution replied that he did, indeed, see a threat to independence from the left. But this was not the major issue of the rebellion. He, too, was anxious to have it settled; the question was how. He was, of course, vitally interested in military assistance and expanded economic aid. But the rebellion would have to be settled by the rebels' yielding, not by negotiation. There would be no negotiated settlement. If that was what we were asking, the answer was no. "Ever since we became independent, separate groups have been attempting to resist the authority of the central government," the General pointed out. "It is vital to our survival as a nation for us to have a unified army and a government strong enough to resist movements like that of the Darul Islam and guarantee the security of our territory. An army commander cannot feel free to oppose the carrying out of any order he doesn't like; that is basic to army discipline" —on this the General's attitude was uncompromising. In defying the authority of the central government and the military command, the rebels had become outlaws. If they laid down their arms and indicated a desire to return to the fold, they would be welcome. Otherwise there would be no dealing with them as equals. "We have to prove that the central government is strong enough to prevent this kind of thing,"

Nasution emphasized. "If any faction in the military or in the society becomes dissatisfied and thinks it can get what it wants by revolting, we will never build a nation." He recalled our own Civil War. "Even America had to go through this kind of internal struggle before you emerged as a nation."

I left with a fuller appreciation of Nasution. Though his rejection of my proposal raised serious questions for us, at least the air had been cleared. He was now aware that the U.S. was not unfriendly. The rapport we had established was a base on which to build.

Washington's view of the delicate situation was somewhat different, as aptly summarized in a personal message to me from Secretary Dulles:[8]

> The Communists are taking advantage of the fact that President Sukarno feels a need for greater authority at the top in the situation that confronts him. They are seeking to impose upon Indonesia a Communist-type 'dictatorship of the proletariat' which will end up by taking the Indonesian Republic into the Communist camp and making Sukarno in effect a prisoner. . . . It is utterly unrealistic for anyone to believe that Indonesia can in tranquility wend its way into the Communist camp. Once it became clear that that was the course, the now dying embers of revolution would burst into flames and it would not be possible for the United States, even should it so desire, to restrain the impulses of governments and individuals who are dedicated to freedom and some of whom would feel they were imperiled by the course Indonesia was taking.
>
> Furthermore, the economy of Indonesia is so fragile and is so dependent upon the free world and the West, that it would be impossible for long to maintain a viable government and prosperous society if the economic pattern were to be readjusted to dependence upon the Sino-Soviet bloc.
>
> The United States is exerting itself strongly to permit of an orderly and peaceful evolution of Indonesian policy in a direction which will avoid, and preclude, the danger of the Republic being captured by the International Communist movement. The situation cannot, however, for long stand still. We are hoping to see, concretely, the start of a new trend and some action responsive to our own.

The message constituted both a statement of the dangers the U.S. government saw in the situation and a hardly veiled threat of the turbulence in store if Indonesia were to move toward Communism. Needless to say, I used the statement with discretion. I did make a point of letting both the Prime Minister and Foreign Minister know the Secretary's views. If the Indonesians moved one way, they could expect our help. If they moved the other way, they could anticipate our opposition. Although never stated as bluntly as that—for such directness is beyond the Indo-

---

8. In this same message, I was authorized to quote him at my discretion in conversation with Indonesian officials.

nesian cultural frame—there was no misunderstanding of where America stood.

The extreme sensitivity of the Indonesians to American reactions was illustrated by the momentary uproar caused by a press dispatch from Copenhagen alleging that Secretary Dulles, in a restricted NAC (North Atlantic Council) session, had mentioned the possibility of Indonesian aggression against West Irian. The Ministry of Information stated that the United States could now no longer be considered neutral on the West Irian issue, and the press was hot on my heels. After checking with Copenhagen and Washington, I issued an official denial, characterizing the report as an "obvious fabrication." The denial was widely carried in the Indonesian press, and the furor died down as quickly as it had arisen.

Although the focus of suspicion and public attack on foreign aid to the rebels had been on the United States and Taiwan, the Indonesians had become increasingly wary of the Philippines. Violent official and press reaction greeted Philippine Defense Minister Vargas' accusation on May 10 that Soviet technicians and military experts were aiding the Indonesian government forces in their efforts to quell the rebellion. The Indonesian Army spokesman challenged Vargas to visit Indonesia to be convinced "that his charge is completely unfounded, so that he will cease acting as a mouthpiece for rebel leaders." Subandrio described the Indonesian people as conscious of the danger inherent in the use of foreign volunteers. Protesting officially to Manila, he noted ominously that should the Indonesian government be forced to accept such assistance, "such a development would not be conducive to the security of the Philippines." Vargas was subsequently reported as denying that his government was aiding the rebels.

Communists in Djakarta stepped up their pressure in this period with a constant barrage of speeches, editorials and demonstrations against America. A monster mass meeting to be sponsored by the Communist-dominated National Front was announced for May 16 in Merdeka Square, opposite the U.S. chancery. The call was for a *million* participants! We were somewhat concerned, as this could too readily have got out of hand, but the Indonesian Army, in a signficant action, stepped in and canceled the meeting.

It was at this point that Pope parachuted into Ambon. His capture dramatized the dichotomy in American policy and accentuated our difficulties in Djakarta. At one point, Subandrio presented me with evidence to substantiate Indonesian suspicions that Pope was an agent of the American government, or at least of the CIA. When captured, he had on his person military orders establishing him as a civilian of officer rank and entitling him to use the officers' mess and quarters at whatever American base he might land. When the Foreign Minister showed me a copy of these orders, I noted that they were almost a year old. They were the standard orders issued to CAT (Civil Air Transport) pilots who were servicing American bases in the Pacific. I explained that CAT was not only operating a regular passenger line from Tokyo to Taiwan and Hong Kong, but had contracts with the U.S. government for the transportation of freight and military personnel. All they proved, I said, was what we already knew: that Pope had worked as a pilot for CAT prior to becoming involved in the rebellion.

Pope was treated well and given excellent medical attention by the Indonesian Army. During the period of his recuperation from a broken hip, he was confined in house arrest in the resort area of Kaliurang in Central Java. His trial was delayed for nineteen months. Some Americans attributed this to Sukarno's interest in keeping him a hostage as insurance that America's new policy of *rapprochement* with Indonesia would be continued. Indonesians maintained that the delay was to let Indonesian tempers cool down, and privately admitted that the PKI would have a field day if Pope were tried while the whole matter was fresh in the minds of the public. Certainly from the standpoint of the American government, an early public trial of Pope would not have helped matters.

He was finally brought before a military court on December 28, 1959, accused of flying six bombing raids for the rebels and killing twenty-three Indonesians, seventeen of them members of the armed forces. For this offense, the maximum penalty was death. Pope pleaded not guilty. He maintained he had flown only one combat mission, that of May 18, 1958, when he was shot down. The other flights, he testified, were of a supply or reconnaissance nature, not involving combat.

All sorts of stories were circulating in Djakarta, and feeling, even so many months after the fact, ran high. One was that Pope had bombed the marketplace in Ambon when people were on their way to church and that the church itself had been destroyed. Civilian casualties were reported in the vicinity of 700. No correspondents and few foreign representatives of any kind had been there at the time. Shortly after the bombing, an American visiting the area reported that he could find no evidence of a church having been bombed, but it was true that an Indonesian destroyer had been sunk at the dock.

Pope had kept a diary of his activities; it contained detailed accounts of various bombing missions, and was introduced as evidence at the trial. He consistently maintained that the diary listed the activities of all the rebel pilots, not merely his own. When the court inquired what his real motive had been in joining the rebels, Pope replied, "Your Honor, I've been fighting the Communists since I was twenty years old—first in Korea and later at Dien Bien Phu." In his final plea, he asserted that "I am not responsible for the death of one Indonesian—armed or unarmed. I have served long enough as a target of a Communist press, which has been demanding the death sentence for me."

The court handed down the death sentence on April 29, 1960. The trial had taken four months. Pope appealed to higher tribunals without avail; the sentence was upheld both by the appeals court and the military supreme court. The sentence was never carried out, but Pope remained in prison, a kind of hostage, until his release on July 2, 1962, after much diplomatic pressure.

Mrs. Pope, an attractive former Pan American hostess, and a women's golf champion in her home state of Florida, flew to Indonesia to make a personal appeal to President Sukarno.[9] Sukarno told her he would give her plea every consideration, but made no promises. He gave the impression that it had been Mrs. Pope's emotional plea that finally moved him to pardon her husband. "Pope's wife . . . asked to see me and I received her," Sukarno is quoted as saying.[10] "She cried bitterly and begged me to pardon him. When it comes to women I am weak. I cannot stand even a strange woman's tears. Then his mother and sister visited me and those two sobbing was more than I could bear." [11]

However, Attorney General Robert Kennedy may deserve the credit for springing Pope. In February 1962, during a good-will visit to Indonesia aimed at stimulating a settlement of the West Irian dispute, the Attorney General, reminding Sukarno of his conversation with President Kennedy in Washington the year before, asked him to release Pope. The session was a stormy one, Kennedy accusing Sukarno of not having kept a promise to his brother, Sukarno maintaining that Pope would be released but not until the political climate improved. In the embassy, we followed up Kennedy's initiative, reminding the Indonesian President and Foreign Minister of this commitment. Finally Sukarno sent word to Pope. "By the grace of the President you are pardoned. But I do so silently. I want no propaganda about it. Now go. Lose yourself in the U.S.A. secretly. Don't show yourself publicly. Don't give out news stories. Don't issue statements. Just go home, hide yourself, get lost, and we'll forget the whole thing." [12]

Embassy military attachés, working with the Indonesian Army, made all the arrangements. Pope walked out of prison without fanfare, boarded a civilian automobile, which the embassy had standing by, and was rushed to the airport, put aboard an American military plane and flown off.

The Foreign Ministry requested secrecy on Pope's release and I prom-

---

9. However, even during this period, there were rumors that all was not well between the Popes, and in December Mrs. Pope filed for divorce, charging her husband with "extreme cruelty" and "habitual indulgence in a violent and ungovernable temper."

10. Cindy Adams, *Sukarno, An Autobiography as Told to Cindy Adams* (Indianapolis: The Bobbs-Merrill Company, Inc., 1965) p. 271.

11. *Ibid.*

12. *Ibid.*

ised both Subandrio and Sukarno, with Washington's concurrence, that within our power we would accede to their request. As it turned out, Pope's release was a well-kept secret. He kept his pledge of silence, and the Department of State did not reveal his release until August 22. As Pope resumed his normal life, the Department announced he had been freed as part of the improvement in the climate of our relations with Indonesia. The United States made no concessions to obtain his release, which came as part of a general amnesty that the Indonesian government had given to all those participating in the rebellion in Indonesia. The announcement had been delayed, the Department said, because Pope had requested that publicity be withheld to allow him a quiet time with his family.

Pope's participation in the rebellion and the arms drops to the rebels were widely assumed to have been the work of the CIA, and numerous accounts have been published that lend credence to that assumption.[13] In May 1958, however, neither the fact nor the extent of such support was known to us in the American Embassy, Djakarta. Allen W. Dulles, a good friend from post-World War II days in Germany, had promised before I left Washington to keep me informed of any CIA activity in Indonesia. I can only assume he thought either the cover was impenetrable and that the activity was being carried out by others, with the CIA only indirectly involved, or concluded that I could only be embarrassed by the knowledge. Nevertheless, the arms that dropped out of the sky had to come from some terrestrial origin. The Indonesians were not stupid. All they had to do was draw a circle around Indonesia with a radius representing the distance a plane could fly to and from a given point without refueling to know that the territory of neighboring nations was being used for takeoff. But that still did not necessarily mean that the CIA was involved. There were other pro-rebel, anti-Sukarno forces in the area. Indeed, Indonesia was in the unfortunate position of being surrounded by neighbors unsympathetic to the government in power. One of my staff, who visited Manila shortly after Djuanda's accusation that Clark Field was being used as a base for rebel operations, reported seeing a plane with wings painted black in one corner of the field, and that the gossip there was that these planes were ferrying supplies to the Indonesian rebels. The implication was obvious. Clark Field was an American base. The planes could not have landed without permission. If the gossip were correct, regardless of the origin of the aircraft (*e.g.*, Taiwan), the U.S. government must have some knowledge of the matter.

From the moment of my arrival, I had recognized the importance of

---

13. See for example David Wise and Thomas B. Ross *The Invisible Government* (New York: Random House, 1964) and James Mossman, *Rebels in Paradise: Indonesia's Civil War* (London: Jonathan Cape, 1961).

keeping the members of the American Embassy staff close together. They all needed to know what was going on; our thinking had to be on the same wave length. I held a "country-team" meeting every morning at eight o'clock in that fast-moving situation. Every top U.S. government agency representative in Djakarta attended, including the military attachés, the economic aid mission chief, the agricultural and commercial attachés, and the CIA station chief.[14]

The authority of an ambassador over representatives of U.S. agencies other than the State Department had been first enunciated by President Eisenhower. Conflicts had occasionally developed between ambassadors and Marshall Plan mission chiefs in the days when the latter were independent; clarification of authority was essential in order that the American government could speak with one voice. The growing independence and power of the CIA in the fifties, as illustrated by the role it played in Laos and other areas, was such that another serious threat to ambassadorial authority and prestige seemed to be developing. Eventually, in order to meet this head on, President Kennedy sent a letter of instructions to every ambassador on May 29, 1961, following the Bay of Pigs. It was blunt and to the point. The one I received read: "You are in charge of the entire United States Diplomatic Mission, and I shall expect you to supervise all of its operations. The Mission includes not only the personnel of the Department of State and the Foreign Service, but also the representatives of all other United States Agencies which have programs or activities in Indonesia."

From the time of my arrival, I had assumed I had such authority. Although differences of opinion often developed within the embassy, as was inevitable and desirable, no challenge of leadership had arisen. In no sense did I view the "country team" as a board of directors for the embassy, but rather as comparable to the President's Cabinet at a lower level. They were an outstanding group. I appreciated their input of information, advice and council, but I had the responsibility. We exchanged thoughts, ideas and news each morning. The discussions were full and frank, no holds barred.

Even in 1958, therefore, I was confident that members of my official family were not engaged in major activities of which I was not informed, and that this included the CIA station chief. I could not be sure that operatives outside Indonesia were not in some way involved in assisting the rebels. Inquiries to Washington brought nothing more than instructions as to what I was to tell the Indonesian government. Statements

---

14. The "country team" concept originated during the Eisenhower Administration. The idea was that the ambassador would have a team composed of the heads of all U.S. missions. In Indonesia, I broadened it to include all of my top staff and attachés.

from Washington were not helpful in reducing the credibility gap between the two governments. It looked to the Indonesians, as to others, as though one hand of the U.S. government did not know what the other was doing. Since this seemed incredible, those statements were read as sign language—not taken too literally. When the statements became more conciliatory and friendly, the Indonesians met us halfway.

It was quite clear to me that the Indonesian government was certain the U.S. government had a role in assisting the rebels, was indignant over what it considered our duplicity, but was pragmatic enough to recognize that righteous indignation would accomplish little or nothing. The important thing was to get us to stop. This they endeavored to do by tactfully making us aware of their knowledge or assumptions and giving us a clear signal that they were ready to let bygones be bygones.

The dilemma with which the Indonesians were confronted was clear. The active intervention of the United States in the conflict could determine the outcome. For us to be indirectly supplying arms to the rebels, as the Indonesians believed, was one thing and serious enough. For us to engage in direct military action on the side of the rebels was another, and greatly to be feared.

The Indonesians were not the only ones who were perplexed and disturbed at the confusion of events. I found myself in an awkward position as a result of what appeared to be conflicting statements from Washington, some of which were at variance with facts that emerged. I knew what everybody else knew—that the U.S. government favored the rebel position. I did not know that we were, either directly or indirectly, supplying military assistance to the rebels except as that information was revealed from Indonesian sources. It did not take long, however, for me to conclude that this was the case and that it was a self-defeating policy.

Roger Hilsman, discussing the concern in the Capitol regarding the CIA, reports that before "President Sukarno's visit to Washington in 1961, [President] Kennedy remarked in conversation that when you considered things like CIA's support to the 1958 rebellion, Sukarno's frequently anti-American attitude was understandable." [15]

At this point, however, let me say that I yield to no one in my appreciation of the importance of the role of the Central Intelligence Agency in America's current global strategy. There is a popular misconception that most of its employees are operatives of the James Bond type, involved in all sorts of subversive and clandestine activities. Actually, CIA has the responsibility for collecting, digesting, collating and interpreting the intelligence information that is required by the senior policy officers of our

---

15. *To Move a Nation* (Garden City, New York: Doubleday & Company, Inc., 1967), p. 363. See also p. 86 for a discussion of how Southeast Asian nations viewed U.S. policy.

government in making decisions.[16] Most of the Agency's personnel are engaged in this type of activity. These men and women, as well as the relatively few who are involved in cloak-and-dagger programs, are intelligent, dedicated people who suffer the strain of anonymity and are forbidden to discuss their work even with their families. They are making a great contribution to the security of the country. In common with other agencies of our government, the CIA sometimes makes mistakes. When it does, unlike other agencies, the operatives involved do not have the privilege of defending their actions.

Yet the questions I am dealing with here relate not so much to the role of the CIA, all too often a convenient whipping boy, but to the extent of intervention by any agency of the United States government in the internal affairs of other nations. It perhaps needs to be said that the CIA of course makes no policy and takes no actions that are not authorized by the government. The Foreign Intelligence Advisory Board exercises "a continuing review and assessment of all functions" of the CIA and reports to the President thereon;[17] also, Congress has subcommittees that review CIA's activities and provide for its appropriations. To the extent, then, that CIA is involved in operations, it is implementing policy decisions of the U.S. government, either by direct order or tacit acquiescence.

---

16. The Central Intelligence Agency was established by Congress under the provisions of the National Security Act of 1947. It reports to the National Security Council, of which the President of the United States is chairman.
17. Executive Order, May 4, 1961.

CHAPTER 7

The Thaw

It is customary for heads of intelligence departments to periodically make inspections of their operations abroad and obtain firsthand impressions of critical and difficult situations. Thus, on May 8, 1958, Admiral Laurence H. Frost, Chief of U.S. Naval Intelligence, arrived in Djakarta. I welcomed this visit, for it could help check my own conclusions as well as provide support for my recommendations.

The Admiral had frank talks with Nasution (May 9) and other leaders, which served to reinforce my *démarche*, convince the Indonesians of United States' sincerity, and allay suspicion that the U.S. Navy was aiding the rebels. Frost's conclusion was the same as my own: the Indonesian military leadership was the key to remedying the internal political situation. He found no indication that anyone was thinking of trying to unseat Sukarno; indeed, the President was still a potent symbol of Indonesian independence, and it was time for the United States government to accept this as a fact of life. Frost also supported my feeling that our government must now show the Indonesian military leadership tangible evidence of its willingness to support them.

The army's position had been made crystal clear in our talk with Nasution and in supplementary talks with Lieutenant Colonel Sukendro, Indonesian Deputy Chief of Intelligence. First, Nasution planned to bring about changes in the Cabinet to replace leftist-oriented members. Second, he was deeply concerned over the economic situation resulting from the rebel bombings of Indonesian shipping. Third, the bombings had completely upset his timing for taking action against the Communists; he "could not and would not make any such move until the rebel problem was solved." He pointed out that the PKI was exploiting the increasing economic difficulties.

Sukendro said that Nasution wanted to advise me of a rapidly approaching climax in U.S.-Indonesian relations; he could not hazard his chances of success in dealing with the current situation by acting against the Communists internally without having some idea of how to control them and at the same time solve the developing economic crisis. He needed arms, and he needed financial aid. In order to bring about Cabinet changes and move against the PKI, he must first know unequivocally —and soon—what the U.S. government intended to do. In view of the recent past, Sukendro said, he was skeptical of American motives and the sincerity of our intentions.

At this same time, cables were flashing back and forth between Djakarta and Washington on the basic policy question of arms aid to Indonesia. During these weeks, we in the embassy continued to actively advocate a readjustment of our policy toward support of the governmental elements that could be counted upon to resist the increasing Communist influence. These elements were the military—basically, the powerful army headed by Nasution, whose prestige had reached an all-time high— and those civilians interested in economic stabilization and development and represented in half a dozen key Cabinet Ministers led by Prime Minister Djuanda. Immediately after the nation's primary problem, security, had been solved, the latter was determined to concentrate on curbing the ever increasing inflation that threatened to engulf the nation.

I strongly advocated military aid, even if it was not much more than token assistance, to demonstrate our good will; increased technical help for the development of the minds and skills desperately needed to start this nation on its way; limited economic-development assistance on a loan basis for specific projects; and surplus-commodity shipments, which would not only help to feed the people but also contribute to development since it was standard practice to loan the receipts from the sale of these commodities for mutually agreed projects.

The unwillingness of Nasution and Djuanda to go ahead with their plan until the rebels had been defeated, or at least until it was clear that they were receiving no further outside support, gave us some concern. Washington felt the best course of action to be complete cessation of military activities in order to permit the anti-Communist elements in Djakarta to move toward the attainment of their objectives, which in essence were the same as those of the dissidents. On May 15, I was asked to explore this possibility with the Indonesian government. If it would agree to a cease-fire—"during which Nasution would be in a position to take such action as he contemplates"—we would be willing to take the initiative on the following basis: the Secretary of State would make a public statement to the effect that the United States government hoped for a quick settlement of the rebellion and, to this end, suggested that both parties agree to a cease-fire. The ideal response would be acceptance of a cease-fire by both sides—with no interim build-up by either—and the going forward of the Cabinet reshuffle and the curbing of Communist activity. I was authorized to tell the Prime Minister that if there were to be effective anti-Communist action, he could be assured of receiving U.S. military and economic support. A token shipment of military equipment totaling about $7,000,000 could be made on short order; in addition, we would be prepared to assist in other fields, such as shipping, civil aviation, and training in our service schools. Once action had been taken against the Communists, we would hope that "the Government of Indonesia and the dissidents would seek an amicable settlement of their differences."

Djuanda sharply rejected the idea (it had not yet reached the stage of a formal proposal), making clear that he regarded it as an attempt to interfere in internal affairs. In a speech at Modjokerto in East Java the following day, Sukarno vigorously supported Djuanda's position. "At this time we will not talk about the rebels; we are gathering strength to crush the rebellion," the fiery President said. In the same speech he took the position that Indonesia was facing not merely "foreign intervention," but "overt agression from the outside."

In Djakarta on the same day, Subandrio challenged the United States to voice publicly its disapproval of any adventurers flying bombing mis sions for the rebels. Such a statement would be "of tremendous significance" in clearing the air and improving relations between Indonesia and the United States, he told me. Somewhat doubtful about its reception, I nevertheless cabled this request and urged that we accede.

Reflecting Washington's new attitude, Dulles responded, on May 20, with a press statement, in which he said that the rebellion should be settled "without intrusion from without." The following day, Washington agreed to release a small supply of arms for the Indonesian police, and large new supplies of rice for sale to Djakarta. Djuanda received this as "a hopeful sign of a cessation of the activities of foreign adventurers." He quoted the Secretary's statement in full:

> I would say this: that the United States believes that the situation in Indonesia can be and should be dealt with as an Indonesian problem. The United States itself is a nation which has suffered civil war, and we have sympathy and regret when another country undergoes the losses in life and the economic dislocations that are incidental to civil war. But we do believe that the situation can be and should be dealt with as an Indonesian matter by the Indonesians without intrusion from without, and we do hope that there will be quickly restored peace and stability in the Indonesian Republic.[1]

Djuanda concluded that despite the unwarranted interference by foreign powers, the "Government is prepared to carry on normal relations with these countries, provided that its independent and active policy is not interfered with and the Indonesian people are allowed to arrange

---

1. *The Department of State Bulletin*, vol. XXXVIII, no. 989 (June 9, 1958), pp. 945–946.

their national life on the principles of the *Pantjasila* without any hindrance from whatever quarter."

Coming at a time when American-Indonesian relations were on the mend, Djuanda's statement was generally regarded as conciliatory in tone. Among Indonesians one sensed a general feeling of relief that the crisis was over. There was little disposition to indulge in recriminations.

This forerunner of a shift in U.S. policy toward Indonesia aiming at greater *rapprochement* brought an immediate favorable reaction in Djakarta. Its most dramatic manifestation was substantively small but highly significant. On May 22, Sukarno came to lunch.[2]

Sukarno was at his most gracious best. With him were his wife, Madame Hartini, First Minister Djuanda, Foreign Minister and Madame Subandrio, Minister and Madame Leimena, among others. In addition to my wife and I, the Americans included James Baird, the aid mission chief, and his wife, Counselors James D. Bell and John W. Henderson, and Mrs. Henderson.

Toasting Sukarno, I said that United States-Indonesian relations at this point reminded me of a young man proposing a toast to the girl with whom he was in love. "Here's to you and here's to me and here's to the space between! May one disappear: not you, not me, but the space between!" Sukarno laughed loudly and responded with a statement of how much he loved America and Americans, although sometimes "I don't like American policy." He expressed his hope that Indonesian-American relations would improve.

There had been other, more meaningful reactions. The PNI declared on May 13 that it would not join in a PKI-sponsored rally against foreign intervention, aimed at the United States, because it was against foreign intervention "in whatever manifestation and from whatever side." The PKI attacked this decision and accused Suwirjo, head of the PNI, of having talked with me about a compromise with the rebels, charging that "Jones had influenced the PNI decision not to join the demonstration."

If I had influenced the PNI decision at the time, I was not aware of it. However, Suwirjo and I had had a very satisfactory talk a day or two before, during which we discussed the growing influence of the PKI and the danger this represented to Indonesia's independence. I commented that I assumed the PNI had learned its lesson about the perils of cooperating with the PKI. I was referring to the parliamentary elections of 1955, when the PNI and the PKI agreed to concentrate their campaign fire on their mutual antagonists rather than on each other. To the

2. Sukarno had accepted my invitation prior to Pope's capture on May 18. It was significant, however, that Sukarno was ready to show the world that despite the Pope affair, at long last America and Indonesia could be regarded as moving toward each other. The event attracted wide press notice.

PNI's distress, the PKI appeared to gain the most from this alliance, particularly in the heavily populated provinces of Central and East Java, reputedly PNI strongholds. Accordingly, the PNI eschewed any co-operation with the PKI in the 1957 elections. In those contests, however, the PNI suffered even more gravely. Not only did the PKI emerge as Indonesia's largest party, but their vote gain was almost entirely drawn from the numerical strength of the PNI. The other parties retained more or less their 1955 strength.

Another piece was added to the jigsaw puzzle when the first shipment of MIG-17 jet trainers reached Indonesia on May 6. Ordered earlier in the year from Czechoslovakia, their arrival raised the specter of an Indonesia beholden to the Soviet bloc.

Despite the need and extended negotiations for additional arms, it should be noted that the military situation had developed rapidly in the government's favor. For all practical purposes, the back of the rebellion was broken in Sumatra by April 17 in a parachute-troop landing in Pakenbaru—an action that met no resistance from rebel soldiers. And on the same date central-government forces penetrated Padang itself, the headquarters of the rebel regime. The city was taken two days later with comparatively little fighting. On May 4, government forces captured Bukittinggi, the last rebel-held city in Sumatra. Henceforth the rebel action would be reduced to guerrilla harassment. In North Sulawesi, the octopus-shaped island on which resided the other wing of the rebellion (Permesta), government forces met determined resistance when they staged a landing the second week in June, but by June 26, they had taken the important harbor of Menado. By the end of July, the North Sulawesi branch of the rebel movement no longer controlled any major town, and the conflict there, too, deteriorated into guerrilla fighting.

The central government and the army, led by General Nasution, had won a major victory in less than five months, confounding the predictions of most foreign observers. Although guerrillas in both North Sulawesi and Sumatra continued to be active for nearly three years thereafter, any real threat from the rebel forces was eliminated in the spring of 1958.

It had long been my own contention that it made little sense to deny military aid to a neutral nation if that nation were in a position to procure the same equipment from other sources since, aside from the good will thus engendered, such provision carried with it the possibility of exercising some control over its use. As Soviet military aid entered the picture and the movement of events favored the central government, it became apparent that it was to our interest to be helping the Indonesians rather than permitting the Soviets to pre-empt the field, and on May 22, the day Sukarno came to lunch, the United States approved small-arms sales to Indonesia and we were on the way. Djuanda asserted on June 2 that the Indonesian government must give priority to the solution of internal problems, a point on which we wholeheartedly agreed.

Throughout the spring of 1958, one consideration that was ever present in the thinking of the American Embassy in Djakarta and in Washington was the danger of the Indonesian internal conflict's widening to involve other Asian nations. Although no one had taken him too seriously, Syngman Rhee on March 31 had criticized both the U.S. failure to recognize the rebel government and what he called the Dulles "hands-off policy" in Indonesia. At the same time he offered Korean volunteers to assist the rebels. More serious was Communist China's offer of volunteers to the Indonesian government forces. The Government of the Republic of China (Nationalist China) had responded at once with the warning that it would consider the presence of such volunteers in the South China Sea a threat to its security and would interdict their movement. What might have happened had the rebels been more successful can only be guessed at.

The issue of United States support for the rebels still continued to plague us. Thus Djuanda, on July 4, 1958, in a statement to Parliament, summarized the government's view of the events of the past six months. He charged that the "political factors which gave birth to the regional disturbances also had their origins with several foreign countries," who felt that their positions had been threatened by the outcome of the general elections in which the PKI had made such headway, and wanted to exert their influence on Indonesia, economically as well as militarily.

He claimed that these foreign elements had found groups that "styled themselves anti-Communists" with which to work, and also people who were "willing to betray the state . . . for the lure of money and arms." Djuanda reminded his audience that the rebels had openly sought SEATO assistance and availed themselves of the service of foreign pilots and officers. He noted that "modern arms were dropped in several areas," but he did not accuse any nation in particular, going on to say, "It is no wonder that the military rebellion which culminated in the proclamation of the revolutionary government greatly attracted foreign elements," especially as the rebels "made propaganda as if they were fighting for an anti-Communist cause."

After referring to the smuggling of arms to Central Sumatra and the fact that the fall of Pakenbaru greatly limited the opportunity for this kind of external assistance, Djuanda described "the intervention of the foreign elements in the eastern part of Indonesia" as being "even more dangerous in character." Here large-scale smuggling of arms could take place without hindrance. He pinpointed the places where aircraft "piloted by foreigners were used to attack," mentioning specifically Makassar, Balikpapan, Bandjarmasin, Ambon, Ternate, Djailolo and Morotai. "The government," he charged, "is also in possession of conclusive evidence that airfields abroad were used as bases to attack several places in Indonesia."

To counter these efforts, he said, the Indonesian government has attempted, through diplomatic channels, to convince countries "in any way related to the aforementioned foreign adventurers, that their interference will not enhance the chances of the rebels to win absolute victory," because the resulting disorder in Indonesia would automatically harm those countries. Diplomatic efforts also included appeals for support from friendly Afro-Asian nations. Djuanda cited the "favorable response" of Egypt, India, Pakistan, Ceylon, Burma and Japan in rendering "moral assistance in dealing with foreign intervention." In addition, Indonesia found gratification in the "favorable response" of Yugoslavia, the Soviet Union, and the Chinese People's Republic.

To avoid loss of momentum in the process of healing relations, we moved rapidly to follow up our initial gesture of military aid. After several weeks of analysis by our military experts, Subandrio and I signed an agreement on August 13 that put the final cap of confirmation on the United States policy shift. Washington, however, did not announce the military-sales agreement until August 19, two days after Indonesia's Independence Day.

Why the delay? Sound diplomacy must invariably be responsive to the sensitivities of the other party as well as reactions at home. Once a year, on August 17, it was President Sukarno's custom to make a major policy speech. While it was desirable for the agreement to be signed before this speech took place for whatever impact it might have on content, it was equally important that Sukarno have the opportunity to pave the way for the announcement. His Independence Day speech on August 17, 1958, was, as anticipated, studded with denunciations of capitalist and imperialist machinations. In dealing with the PRRI rebellion, he made several sharp attacks on "imperialists and counter-revolutionary circles abroad" who have "collaborated" with the rebels. But careful scrutiny of the text revealed one slight gesture toward the United States. Discussing the "five stages" of the PRRI conspiracy, Sukarno denounced the rebels' "ruse of anti-Communism which they spread," and continued, with heavy sarcasm, "The central government is a Communist government. Sukarno is an exponent of Communism, or to say the least, a tool of Communism! What is the truth? Everyone knows that we awe and uphold the *Pantjasila*; everybody knows that our policy is to seek friendship with all countries, including the U.S.A. Everyone knows that I am a nationalist—a revolutionary nationalist!"

Two days after Sukarno's speech, the following press release was issued by the Department of State:

> The United States and Indonesia have concluded an agreement for the sale to Indonesia of certain military equipment and services.
> American Ambassador to Indonesia, Howard P. Jones, has informed the Department of State that an exchange of diplomatic notes took

place in Djakarta on August 13 between him and Foreign Minister Subandrio, according to which the United States Government will sell military equipment, materials, and services to the Government of Indonesia for payment in dollars or in Indonesia rupiah. The types and quantities of equipment and services involved will be determined by mutual agreement between the two countries.

The Government of Indonesia affirmed that the equipment and services purchased will be used solely for the maintenance of internal security and the legitimate national self-defense of Indonesia in accordance with the purposes and principles of the UN Charter. Indonesia also undertook not to relinquish title to any of the equipment or services purchased under the agreement except by mutual consent of the two Governments.

While the signature of the arms agreement marked a turning point in relations, Djakarta remained skeptical of American intentions. Suspicion was widespread that the U.S. would drag its feet on delivery of arms until the rebellion was settled. To offset this, a proposal to airlift a token shipment of arms was put forward, to which the Pentagon quickly responded. Between August 15 and 29, fourteen loads of equipment were delivered by huge Globemasters, the largest planes yet seen in Djakarta. And in order to further dramatize the new cordiality, I invited President Sukarno to take a ride in one of them. (I counted on his spirit of adventure to override advice to the contrary, which he was certain to receive from some within his circle.) He accepted and, with most of the members of his Cabinet, joined embassy officers and others in a thirty-minute tour of Java in the three-story plane.

By the time six months had passed, we had re-equipped some twenty-one Indonesian battalions, representing approximately 16,000 men, with small arms.

In an address to the American Association in Djakarta on September 4, Subandrio spoke rather hopefully of America's ability to achieve a constructive relationship with the new world of developing nations. He concluded on this optimistic note:

> . . . we all welcome, certainly the American Ambassador and I do, the fresh wind which is blowing through the Indonesian-American relationship. We hope that this will be the beginning of better appreciation and more confidence in each other. The delivery of arms to Indonesia is an important fact in itself, but on the other hand the political evaluation which led to the new transaction is of more importance for the future relationship between our two countries.

As I looked back in August 1958, I realized that the six months of my tenure in Indonesia had witnessed significant changes in the anatomy of political power. Some of these were constructive, some not. The most notable shift was the expanded political role assumed by the Indonesian Army. Its power had grown immeasurably since the establishment of martial law in March 1957, which in effect provided the military with what Daniel Lev has termed a "political and economic charter," [3] a license to assume an influential position in both politics and economics.

In the economic area, the Indonesian seizure of Dutch properties in December 1957 had resulted in the assumption by the military of managerial control over the most important of the nation's foreign-exchange–earning enterprises. During the rebellion, the army demonstrated its professional competence and, at the same time, won applause for preserving the nation. Equally important, the rebellion enabled the army to get rid of its most vociferous dissidents—the colonels who led the regional revolts.

Until the spring of 1958, the PKI had been making great strides in its penetration of the government. This was not only because of presidential favor; it had been so active politically as almost to preempt the leadership of popular causes. It had vigorously supported the central government in the struggle against the dissident regions. It had played a role in inducing Poland and Czechoslovakia to sell arms to Indonesia after the United States had refused. It was riding high when outside military support for the rebels came to light and key governmental leaders denounced SEATO and Western assistance, specifically, the United States and Nationalist China.

The combination of martial law and the early evidence of ultimate victory over the rebels, however, gave the army an opportunity to play a major political role in Indonesia. Military restrictions on party activities and the daily press, and its arrest of civilians as well as army leaders for corruption, were clear signs that a new force had arisen. It was to become one of the three major power elements in Indonesia.

Some of the ablest leaders in Indonesia and their party organizations were political casualties of the period. The powerful modernist Islamic party, the Masjumi, had been the principal counterweight to the Communists. The influential Socialist Party, also anti-Communist, included many of the nation's intellectuals. Faced with the choice of disavowing their former leaders, including Natsir and Sjafruddin, and the virtual certainty of being banned, the Masjumi leadership refused to condemn those of its members who had joined the rebellion, and walked off the political stage, flags flying. Sjahrir and the Socialist Party leadership on Java attempted a compromise with the government, and did disown those members who sided with the rebel elements; nevertheless the party shared the fate of the Masjumi. Even so key a figure as Dr. Hatta was to

---

3. Daniel S. Lev, "The Political Role of the Army in Indonesia," *Pacific Affairs*, vol. XXXVI, no. 4 (Winter 1963–64), p. 351.

some extent discredited, or at least immobilized, by what some regarded as his temporizing position on the rebellion.

The disappearance of the Masjumi and Socialist parties from the Indonesian political scene, made official with their formal banning in August 1960, had a number of important consequences. At a time when the nation was suffering from a paucity of competent people, it eliminated from public service some of the ablest and most dedicated personalities. With a political vacuum thus created, a large segment of public opinion found itself deprived of any means of expression. But the Communist Party survived; indeed it was now the largest and most powerful in the country.

Sukarno's new political strength and confidence became obvious in the moves he began to make after it was apparent that the open challenge to his authority had been beaten. Step by step, he paved the way for the establishment of a highly personal authoritarian system of rule—Guided Democracy. To accomplish this, and to avoid becoming a captive of the now powerful army, Sukarno had to find a force strong enough to create a balance of power. This force was ready at hand in the Communist Party, which had been rapidly expanding in the sun of Sukarno's beneficence. The other parties were neither strong enough nor sufficiently dynamic to fulfill his purposes. Equally important, none were anti-army as were the Communists.

But Sukarno had no intention of sharing power. He would be the *dalang* who would tell the story and manipulate the puppets in this Indonesian shadow play. The Communist Party of Indonesia, under its leader, Aidit, had no intention of becoming a puppet. It, too, aspired to the *dalang's* role.

CHAPTER 8

The Communist Road
to Power

The Communist Party of Indonesia had had a stormy career. Founded May 23, 1920, a year before the Chinese Communist Party came into existence, it had made two major attempts to seize power prior to independence. In 1926 and 1927, apparently acting against advice from Moscow, it staged unsuccessful coups in West Java and West Sumatra against the Dutch colonial government, and was declared illegal. As such it operated until 1945, a splinter group, with most of its leaders in Moscow or Yenan, China. When Indonesia proclaimed its independence on August 17, 1945, with four years of bloody fighting still ahead, the PKI resumed legal activity. In 1946, there was an ill-fated attempt to seize power on the part of Tan Malaka, a dynamic national Communist of the Ho Chi Minh variety who had split with the PKI and organized the Murba Party. This was frustrated by the Sukarno-Hatta government, and Malaka was imprisoned. The exiled PKI leaders then returned from Moscow and Yenan and assumed direction of the PKI.

In 1948, these leaders decided the time had come to take over the new embattled Government of Indonesia. They had infiltrated and gained control of a sufficient number of military units to have expectations of success. From their base in Madiun in Central Java, they attempted a *coup d'état.* But the loyal forces, led by General Gatot Subroto, overwhelmed them. Eleven of the top PKI leaders were summarily executed, many others were killed, and some 36,000 jailed. Termed a "stab in the back" because it was staged at a time when the new nation was engrossed in combat with Dutch forces, the coup discredited the PKI for years.

But when I first arrived in Indonesia six years later, as Chief of the United States Economic Aid Mission, the Communists had staged a comeback, and were already one of the most powerful political parties in the country. By 1965, the Communist Party claimed a membership of 3,000,000, and a Communist takeover of Indonesia appeared imminent. Seldom if ever has history recorded so rapid a reversal of political fortune.

What accounted for this remarkable turn of the wheel? What appeal did the Communist ideology have to a people nearly 95 per cent of whom were Moslem with a fervent belief in God? The answer is a curious one: none. What happened represented the success of an extraordinary program of power politics in which Communist doctrine was never preached except to the faithful, but every trick in the political trade was employed to gain adherents. The operations of the PKI would make Tammany Hall appear amateurish by comparison.

The strategy and tactics were the design of the younger generation of Communist leaders who took control of the party following the failure of the 1948 coup. When Aidit, Lukman, Njoto and Sudisman seized party control in 1951, the membership numbered only about 8,000. They promptly altered the earlier strategy, which had been based upon a broad coalition of left-wing groups, to one aimed at establishing the Communist Party as not merely the vanguard of the Indonesian revolution but its essence and core. The revolution was far from finished in the view of the new men, and the PKI's role lay in direct leadership of the masses. This required a large membership and a plethora of mass-based front groups.

Even the official Communist Party program was couched in Indonesian nationalist terms: "The tasks of national emancipation and democratic changes have not yet been carried out in Indonesia. The yearnings of the Indonesian people for complete national independence, for democratic liberties and for an improvement in the living conditions have not yet been realized." [1] The theme, later to be taken up by Sukarno, repeatedly stressed that the Indonesian revolution had not ended with the achievement of political independence in December 1949. In Aidit's words, "the task of the anti-imperialist national revolution and the task of the democratic anti-feudal revolution" remained to be finished. [2]

Dipa Nusantara Aidit, the man who became head of the party in 1951 and was responsible for the phenomenal recovery and progress of the PKI, was one of a group of young men who had witnessed the failure of violent revolutionary tactics at Madiun. Born July 30, 1923, in Sumatra, he had been active in radical movements since his early youth. His education consisted of seven years in an elementary school, and then study at a commercial high school in Djakarta. He began his political career in

---

1. D. N. Aidit, *Problems of the Indonesian Revolution* (Djakarta: Demos, 1963), p. 34. Aidit used italics.
2. *Ibid.*, p. 38.

1939, when he became active in a left-wing youth organization; from 1940 until the Japanese occupation ended in 1945, he was one of the leaders of the Youth Corps of the Gerindo, then the major radical nationalist party of Indonesia and thought to have been controlled by the Communist Party, at that time underground.

President Sukarno repeatedly emphasized in conversations with me that Aidit was an "Indonesian Communist" rather than simply a Communist. "He is an Indonesian first, and a Communist second," Sukarno insisted. But Aidit told an American correspondent, "I think it is better to put it this way. We accept the general principles of dialectical materialism. And we seek to blend these with the concrete situation in Indonesia. Because we are good Communists, we are good Indonesians!"

His explanation as to how he could accept Sukarno's philosophy—and particularly the *Pantjasila*, when one of its principles was "Belief in God"—was pure double talk: "It is precisely because we are Marxists that we accepted *Manipol-*USDEK and the *Pantjasila*. For what is the task of a Marxist in a country like Indonesia? Is it not to mobilize all the forces that can be united against feudalism and imperialism? As far as the *Pantjasila* is concerned, especially with respect to that part about God, we agreed to that principle in the framework of all five principles. If you combine the first principle with the other four, the *Pantjasila* leaves it to all Indonesians to profess whatever belief or religion they want because in the *Pantjasila* there is also the principle of democracy, so that no one can be forced to accept religion." An apt example of Aidit's political sleight of hand.

It is true that Aidit adopted courses of action that he considered appropriate to the Indonesian situation, emphasizing that the PKI had no intention of copying the societal or governmental systems of the Soviet Union or Communist China.[3]

Aidit was his own man and not an order taker. His manner was self-confident to the point of being cocky, and it is certain that he intended to be Indonesia's next President. Aidit recognized his need for backing and for years worked closely with the Soviet representatives in Djakarta. His strategy of wooing Sukarno and cooperating with the bourgeoisie was endorsed by, if not actually made in Moscow, and he did not alter it when he turned toward Peking.

Aidit and his associates were confident of riding the democratic road to power, and their record supported that confidence. In the September 1955 parliamentary elections, the PKI received 6,176,000 votes, 16.4 per cent of all votes cast. During the summer of 1957, in the elections for re-

---

3. But this was, after all, in line with the Soviet Union's longstanding objective in Southeast Asia: nothing less than the area's Communization, with the local parties subordinate to Moscow in what was euphemistically called "democratic centralism."

gional assemblies in Java, Sumatra and Riau, the PKI won 7,760,000 votes, which, Aidit boasted, represented an increase of 34 per cent over its 1955 strength,[4] and many observers agreed with his estimate. By 1964, Aidit was predicting that when general elections were held, the PKI would win 50 per cent of the vote.[5]

The confidence of Communist leaders might have proved well founded if the elections scheduled for 1959 had been held. But in May 1958, the Indonesian Army, acting under its emergency powers, stepped in and postponed elections. This happened to coincide with Sukarno's determination to establish Guided Democracy, and he sided with the army, despite Aidit's advocacy of elections and his attempt to reassure the elements opposed to Communist domination of the country. In an interview published on May 22, 1958, Aidit said, "It is not true that one party will be able to get the majority of seats in Parliament through the forthcoming elections. . . . The PKI will not fight for more than it is struggling at present, *i.e.*, the formation of a National Coalition Cabinet."

In politics Moscow-bred but Chinese-weaned, Aidit early took the lessons of the Chinese Communist success to heart. He looked at the society of his own country. Eighty per cent of the people lived in villages and worked on the farms. Of the remaining 20 per cent, the majority were members of what the Soviets would call the proletariat—workers in factories, unskilled and semi-skilled laborers in the cities, the unemployed or underemployed, the homeless squatters who had flooded to the capital and other large cities in the wake of the revolution. To win the rural population and the urban proletariat became the primary goal of Aidit's program. He did not overlook the *petite bourgeoisie* or the molders of public opinion—the press, radio, teachers, and other media of communication—but the 80 per cent who had their living from the farms fascinated him. He saw them as serfs tied to the land by "the seven village devils, the loan sharks, the wicked landlords, the village bandits, the capitalist bureaucrats, and other exploiters of the people."

In the 1959/1962 Constitution of the PKI, the peasants were seen as the foundation upon which a Communist Indonesia would be built: "The strength to create the Revolution will come from labor, the peasants and the *petite bourgeoisie*, but the main strength is the peasant community." [6] A few paragraphs later, this point is again underlined.

---

4. Cf. Guy J. Pauker, *The Rise and Fall of the Communist Party of Indonesia* (Santa Monica, Calif.: RAND Corporation, February 1969), p. 5.

5. Statement at Pemuda Rakjat meeting, June 15, 1964, attended by embassy officers.

6. *Ad-Art (Konstitusi) Partai Kommunist Indonesia (Constitution and By-Laws of the PKI)* (Djakarta: Central Committee, PKI, 1962), p. 7. This Constitution was adopted at the Sixth National Congress in September 1959 and reaffirmed, with minor changes, at the Seventh Special National Con-

"The main strength is the peasantry under the leadership of the proletariat." [7] The politically sophisticated city dweller, the factory- or dock-worker, the estate workers—those capable of rapidly mobilizing large masses for purposes of pressure—would be in command, but the occupation forces would be those already physically in possession of the land, the peasants.

Aidit's challenging speech on February 10, 1963, "Dare, Dare and Dare Again!" illustrated his skill at riding more than one horse at the same time; it also marked Indonesia's lining up with Communist China in the Sino-Soviet dispute, something Aidit made unmistakably clear—albeit slightly disguised as an attack in turn on revisionism and dogmatism. So politically significant did Communist China regard this speech that they published it in English in the Foreign Language Press as a report to the first plenary session of the Seventh Central Committee of the Communist Party of Indonesia. Its contents also reveal the lengths to which Aidit was ready to go in supporting Sukarno. He quotes Sukarno's call for a "genuine vanguard party," and his statement that "there can be other parties, not as commanders . . . but only as sergeants . . . and corporals." Aidit insists the message is clear; that "there is no similarity whatsoever between Bung Karno's ideas and the ideas of Hitler or Mussolini, or their followers here in Indonesia, namely to make a reactionary bourgeois party and suppress the party of the working class. This becomes even clearer if we bear in mind what Bung Karno once wrote: 'Our army is indeed the army of the Marhaen, an army which draws much of its personnel from the peasants, but our vanguard is the corps of workers, the corps of the proletariat.'" In the Chinese edition, *marhaen* is defined as "an expression that refers to the common man."

The Communist Party will, in Aidit's words, "continue to struggle, with a rifle in one hand and a spade in the other. In other words, we are always ready to storm the enemies of the revolution by force and ready, too, to increase production." Aidit called for a *gotong-rojong* cabinet based on "balanced representation," and emphasized that the demand for a Nasakom Cabinet had the support now not only of the Communists but also President Sukarno, the progressive mass organizations, the nationalist religious parties, and the Indonesian Journalist Association. Among the parties listed in support were the PNI, Partindo, Moslem, Perti, and regional leaders of the NU and the PSI.

Discussing "the crack that has appeared in the present international Communist movement," Aidit made a strong plea for fraternal consultations and discussions. He quoted the Moscow statement of 1960, the most important joint document for the international Communist move-

---

gress of the PKI in April 1962. It was preceded by the PKI Constitutions of 1951 and 1954.

7. *Ibid.*, p. 8.

ment, that "whenever a party wants to clear up questions relating to the activities of another fraternal party, its leadership approaches the leadership of the party concerned; if necessary they hold meetings and consultations." This quotation in the pamphlet issued by Peking was emphasized in bold type, as was a statement that "loyalty and practice to the declaration and statement is the main yardstick of the purity of a Communist party," indicating that the Chinese had reached the point where they were using the Indonesians as a bludgeon to bring the Soviets around.

Indonesian Communists must make themselves Communists "who firmly uphold the principles of Marxism-Leninism, but are flexible in applying these principles," Aidit urged. He made a strong defense of the international Communist movement: "Indonesian Communists will continue to unceasingly struggle . . . to become active participants in this mighty movement and to practice its proletarian internationalism in words and in deeds, because they are convinced that a strong international Communist movement means a strong world peoples movement against imperialism, and for national independence, for democracy, peace, socialism and Communism." But he also emphasized that "Indonesian Communists are patriots and internationalists at one and the same time."

By 1961, Aidit's PKI had reached the point of powers at which, one American expert on the subject wrote, "without abandoning its international connections, it has gained a powerful claim to national legitimacy. In the light of this achievement, it would seem not unnatural to conclude that the PKI is well on its way to an assumption of control over Indonesian affairs." [8] By 1964, a perceptive analyst of Indonesian developments concluded "that the PKI had outmaneuvered all major rival political organizations and, because of Indonesia's urgent need for better government, would come to power in the near future, by a combination of three factors: Sukarno's active support, lack of political competitors within the framework of an increasingly radical political milieu, and gradual elimination of all effective opposition. . . ." [9] Those who took this view had much on their side, for "the prevailing atmosphere of radical nationalism, under a leadership pursuing an aggressive, ego-gratifying foreign policy," might well have induced "the military establishment to accept the PKI as partner in the common pursuit of national glory." [10]

Aidit's grand design for the achievement of his purposes involved a vast complex of front organizations, an extensive apparatus that the

---

8. Ruth McVey, "Indonesian Communism and the Transition to Guided Democracy" (Unpublished memorandum, 1961).
9. Pauker, *The Rise and Fall*, p. 19.
10. *Ibid.*, p. 20.

party leaders would control. (It is significant that none of these ever included "Communist" or "Communism" in their names or titles.) The Communists were extraordinarily effective in organizing these mass movements among labor, youth, peasants and women, as well as school-teachers and cultural groups. Shaking her head over Communist success, Maria Ulfah Santoso, a former Cabinet Minister, once said to me, "they are so inventive!"

The most powerful mass organization, charged with penetration and domination of Indonesian labor unions, was the roof organization SOBSI (Sentral Organisasi Buruh Seluruh Indonesia, or Indonesian Federation of Trade Unions). Openly committed to the support of the PKI, SOBSI became the largest federation of labor unions in Indonesia, in plan equivalent to the AFL-CIO superstructure in America. By 1957, it claimed a membership of 2,700,000 and was estimated to control about 60 per cent of organized Indonesian labor, with its greatest strength among the workers in large foreign enterprises.[11] Before 1957, many of these foreign enterprises were Dutch, and the unions had a powerful leverage in imposing their demands upon management and ownership regarded as "colonial."

SOBSI's thrust was not only in the cities. The rural areas, with the estate workers (SARBUPRI), sugar workers (SBG), and forestry workers (SARBUK-SI), offered an ideal proletariat for exploitation. Efforts to organize the independent peasantry were also outstandingly successful. By the end of 1964, the peasants' group (BTI) claimed a membership of 8,500,000.

By the time I returned to Indonesia as Ambassador in 1958, approximately 50 per cent of labor, including office workers and those in government enterprise, had come under SOBSI. Roughly half the workers of Indonesia, therefore, could be regarded as under the control of the Communist Party. SOBSI's strength in foreign enterprises reflected successful Communist exploitation of nationalistic feelings rather than response to depressed conditions. Generally speaking, workers' wages and welfare arrangements were much more satisfactory in foreign corporations than in national enterprises.

In 1957, army officers were appointed supervisors of the newly nationalized Dutch enterprises. As a result of this direct confrontation with the SOBSI unions, the army was stimulated into setting up a rival labor organization, which took its cue from Sukarno's Guided Democracy. To attract plantation workers away from SOBSI, labor welfare funds were established with the profits from the sale of firewood, vegetables, and other commodities. A new roof organization was formed, called SOKSI, which attracted substantial numbers from SOBSI. For three years, SOKSI had some success, but factionalism and accusations of corruption finally resulted in the breakup of the organization in 1963. There was also sus-

---

11. McVey, "Indonesian Communism."

picion that crypto-Communists had worked from the inside to destroy it.

SOBSI emerged unchallenged then as the dominant trade-union organization, exercising a critical degree of influence among the labor force in key national industries. It had tremendous political and economic power. With approximately forty member unions, it could have crippled the economy and confronted the government, should that have been necessary in order to further the domestic or international objectives of the PKI. For more than a decade, it demonstrated its capacity and flexed its muscles by turning out huge numbers in parades, mass demonstrations, and support for Sukarno's pet patriotic occasions such as Independence Day. In September 1964, more than 70,000 people were present at the closing session of SOBSI's national congress. That SOBSI strength was not utilized to its full effectiveness through strikes was due partly to the power of the military—its banning of strikes during critical periods when martial law was in force, and its capacity for retaliation if challenged directly—and partly to the Communists' policy of pandering to Sukarno, avoiding any extreme action that would offend or embarrass the President, tend to reduce his prestige, or be interpreted as a defiance of his authority.

SOBSI was strong and well organized at national, regional, provincial and local levels, and maintained effective discipline. The union was well financed not only with dues but with substantial contributions from the PKI and, presumably, other sources such as the Communist Chinese and, before Aidit's speech of February 1963, the Soviet Union. Although the latter cannot be proved, SOBSI's expenditures obviously exceeded the amount collected in dues; the money had to come from somewhere.

Of the 80,000 railroad workers, SOBSI's subsidiary union controlled at least half. Facing powerful opposition from PBKA, the strong anti-Communist railroad union led by Dr. Kusno, the PKI exerted strenuous efforts over many years to undermine the rival union and, through the National Front and the Ministry of Labor, have it banned or to take control of it. SOBSI dominated the harbors through its power over the stevedores and longshoremen, postal and telecommunications through its active postal workers union, transportation through its motorized transport workers and its airways workers union, and was in a position to exert strong pressure on oil installations, rubber and other estates. The action of the postal workers union in boycotting both incoming and outgoing U.S. mail over a period of months was a good example of the PKI's power to cripple a government operation for the purpose of bringing pressure against a specific group in the society.

SOBSI illustrated the "wolf in sheep's clothing" aspect of Communist political action in Indonesia. Its mass appeal was much broader and deeper than its Communist ideology. As Indonesia's first large indigenous union, it had acquired fame opposing the Dutch and playing an active role during the revolution. Most of its rank and file were not Communists, but above the local level, the organization was completely Communist dominated.

Another of the PKI's most powerful political tools was its youth organization, the People's Youth (Pemuda Rakjat), which in 1956 announced itself as an official arm of the PKI, thus becoming the only one of the Communist-sponsored mass organizations to identify itself directly with the party. The youth group, numbering in the millions, was one of the PKI's most effective organizers of mass demonstrations, supporting volubly and often violently whatever was ripe for exploitation at the moment. These issues ranged all the way from national aspirations, such as the recovery of West Irian, to the murder in Harlem of Malcolm X, when Americans were accused of persecuting and killing Moslems in the U.S.

Typical of Communist tactics in Indonesia was the participation of the Communist youth in the nationwide Indonesian Youth Front (Front Pemuda Indonesia), where their dynamism enabled them to assume much of the leadership. However, Communist influence was adulterated by the refusal of other youth leaders to accept the Communists' objectives and accede to some of their tactics.

Other important Communist mass organizations deserve special mention. The Veterans Association (Perbepsi) represented an instrument of great potential danger, for it could have become a private PKI army. Fortunately, its offer to supplement other military efforts in quelling the radical Moslem guerrilla groups from the Darul Islam was rejected by the government.

Lekra, the cultural group, played a special role. In its encouragement of cultural performances, it won the allegiance of many of Indonesia's top artists in various fields and was highly influential in the universities, sponsoring social and cultural evenings on campuses where nothing of the kind had existed before and organizing clubs for this purpose. It reached out into the villages, where life was somewhat dull after dark, only the more prosperous areas having electric lights and most farmers being too poor to spend money on kerosene to brighten their evenings. Lekra provided cultural entertainment, generally enriched everyday life —and won adherents for the Communist Party as an organization, if not for its ideology.

Then there was the feverishly active Women's League (Gerwani), which was found in the forefront of all the major Communist campaigns, staging demonstrations, sponsoring educational programs, arranging meetings, marching, adding its shrill voice to the Communist-controlled chorus. Led by Madame Suryadarma, the ambitious wife of the former head of the air force, Gerwani and Pemuda Rakjat raided the mountain residence of William Palmer, representative of the American Motion Picture Association in Indonesia, and took over the property after Palmer had been forced out of the country.

In the PKI's many-stringed orchestra, there were other groups of varying degrees of effectiveness—the teachers organization, a civil service organization, high school and college groups. On any and all occasions, special *ad hoc* groups were set up, some of these going beyond the national arena, such as the International Writers' Association. The ramifications of the Communist effort were bewilderingly—and intentionally —complex. Society was kept in a continual state of uproar and excitement. Such tactics could not have been better designed to appeal to Sukarno, who was never happier than when in the midst of agitation and turmoil.

What this all added up to was that, in addition to its membership, the PKI by 1965 had almost 20,000,000 supporters, including about 3,500,-000 in SOBSI, roughly 9,000,000 in the Indonesian Peasant Front (BTI), and at least 1,500,000 each in the youth and women's organizations.

It took Aidit and his colleagues, with the blessing and encouragement of Sukarno, only a few years to construct this vast political empire, which was placed at the disposal of Sukarno so long as the objectives of the two men coincided, as they did most of the time. It was a fair trade. Aidit and the PKI bought protection from the army and the chance to expand. Sukarno acquired an efficient organization that could turn out huge parades, demonstrations, rallies, and all the other paraphernalia of mass political control at an instant's notice.

As Sukarno became more and more involved in staging international conferences to accomplish his objectives, the expertise of the Communist manipulators of meetings became more and more useful to him. Their skillful floor management, mastery of ruthless tactics to overwhelm opponents, and adroit maneuvering of public relations to ensure that their position or point of view was made to appear the dominant one at any given session were invaluable to an Indonesian President determined to become the acknowledged leader of the Afro-Asian bloc, if not of all the "new emerging forces" of the world.

The appeal of the Communist program that enabled its leaders to make such phenomenal progress in so short a time lay not in Communist ideology but rather in nationalism, which was sustained by patronage, favors, self-interest, pressure, terror and intimidation. The flavor of a Communist meeting in Indonesia was described by an embassy officer in June 1964:

> In being physically present at a function like this, one is even more impressed than from reading the press with the high nationalistic content of PKI propaganda and minimal attention to classical Communist themes. The strong attacks on 'imperialists' were largely ritual and did

not seem to be identified with living human beings in the minds of the speakers and audience alike. Slogans like 'freedom' were repeated over and over, *ad nauseum*. Party songs were met with almost religious fervor. (An old man in front of us—apparently a member of the MPRS—dabbed at his eyes during the haunting refrain of *Peh-kah-ee, Peh-kah-ee*, which sounds like a sort of blend of 'The Old Rugged Cross' and 'Hail to Thee Our Alma Mater.') In other words, 'in-group' versus 'out group' is a particularly strong factor in sustaining PKI strength and fervor. The greater 'nationalistic' and 'team' content in real PKI ideology and the ritualistic nature of its anti-Americanism does not make the PKI any less inimical to our interests, of course, but on the contrary makes it more attractive to its adherents and to potential sympathizers and also makes it more difficult to erode.

Every effort was made to avoid open conflict with the military. Aidit repeatedly pressed the point that there must be unity between the two because the ranks of the army were filled with PKI adherents—if this were doubted, he challenged the army to take a vote, which he maintained would show the PKI had the largest representation of all parties in the armed forces.

Sukarno's tremendous prestige, coupled with his open support of the PKI was also an important factor in its growth. The Communists were mouthing the same slogans as Sukarno; the identification was so complete that it was difficult to know which was made in Djakarta and which in Moscow or Peking. The PKI was successful in making every national issue of any importance its own by being in the forefront of the campaign. West Irian, the Malaysia confrontation, anti-imperialism and anti-colonialism, more food and clothing—these and a host of other domestic and international issues dressed in the red and white garb of Indonesian patriotism were to a remarkable extent captured by the Communists.

Why, then, did the Communists fail in Indonesia?

Because they were all things to all men, and were found out; they themselves exposed the wolf inside the sheepskin. They failed because they employed every weapon in the political arsenal: when they did not get their way by persuasion, they used intimidation and terror. They failed because they came with favor and stayed with fear.

Demonstrations, riots, violence, agitation of all kinds, leading to destruction of property and even physical attacks and murder, were the stock in trade of the PKI. The Indramaju affair, which blew up a storm in November 1964 and set the PKI back on its heels for a time, is a good example of Communist tactics. The Communists had found what they wanted—a genuine issue involving large numbers of discontented people. To establish themselves as champions of the underdog, they were prepared to indulge in violence and challenge established authority. The larger good did not concern them.

To the south and west of the little town of Indramaju in West Java lie large state forest preserves, which had become partly deforested owing to the dislocations of war and revolution. Peasant squatters had apparently been tilling the lands for some years, although the legal status as state forest preserves had never been in question. A government program of reforestation was begun in 1963. This was essential to the protection of rice paddies in the area from erosion by the heavy tropical rains. Of some 35,000 hectares of destroyed forest in the district, 2,000 had been reforested by the time this incident took place, and another 4,000 were in process of reforestation.

PKI agitators started moving into the area in the summer of 1964, and began fomenting incidents between peasants and the authorities. The agitators incited hatred against the forestry police, who were described as "village devils," "rats of the forest," and "landlords." Some of the peasants were apparently cutting down new plantings and stealing wood from the state forest.

On October 15, 2,000 demonstrators moved into the forest area near Indramaju, carrying banners of the Communist peasant and youth organizations and the national flag. Men armed with scythes, knives, hammers and axes were caught in the act of chopping down two- to-four-year-old saplings by an eight-man police patrol. The patrol was quickly surrounded, threatened, and told to hand over their weapons. Two of the eight refused, were beaten into insensibility, and stripped of most of their clothing. The mob tied the hands of the policemen behind their backs and marched them twenty kilometers to the nearby village, where they demanded a hearing from the local magistrate. The trip took five hours, and the badly beaten police were exhausted and ill. The authorities told the mob to disperse and indicated that any complaints they might have should be presented through legal channels. The police prisoners were released, and the injured were hospitalized.

A second incident occurred on October 16 in the subdistrict of Leles, where another PKI mob of 2,000 felled trees in the state forest and then proceded to the homes of local forestry officials, who were absent. The families of the officers were questioned, and the mob milled around for some time. Considerable clothing was stolen, and 70,000 rupiahs were taken from one house. In another area about the same time, a forestry official was killed. Authorities promptly made wholesale arrests. The incident, described by Governor Marsudi of West Java as a clash between the land-hungry peasants and the need for reforestation, created a great deal of attention. The PKI was blamed for stimulating the violations of law and order, unpopular both because of the violence and the Javanese love of their cherished forests, vital in preventing erosion of their rice paddies.

The PKI was invariably found supporting the little man against established authority whenever an issue could be found or created. But its use of force and violence, intimidation and terror, as well as the domineering posture of its adherents as they gained power, turned people against it.

It was in the cities, however, that the PKI could exercise the most pressure because they were more effectively organized. Block leaders enforced their will by the use of goons and hoodlums, and there was little recourse as long as Sukarno's protecting mantle was present. Indeed, for its phenomenal expansion the PKI must thank Sukarno. The party paid a price for his support, of course, in its sacrifice of a certain independence of action. It became an instrument of presidential power, and as such found its freedom restricted and its hands slapped whenever it exceeded the bounds of policy established by Sukarno or went too far in its confrontation of the military.

The President himself was sacred territory. Criticism of Sukarno or even identification of the President with governmental policies of which the PKI was critical was taboo. Thus the party not only exploited its relationship with Sukarno but was exploited by him in return—to the point where its revolutionary fervor was considerably dimmed and the patience of elements within the party that were dubious of its policy of cooperation with bourgeois elements was sorely tried. Sarcastic references to the "Impala Communists" in Djakarta (the party leaders rode around in big cars) by the rank and file in Central Java reflected the fact that the life style of Aidit and his colleagues took some of its character from Sukarno's court. The "domestication" of the PKI [12] thus became the route to both success and failure. The PKI was harnessed to Sukarno; so long as he was galloping, they were traveling fast. But when he faltered, so did they.

---

12. See Donald Hindley, "President Sukarno and the Communists: The Politics of Domestication," *The American Political Review*, vol. LVI, no. 4 (December 1962).

CHAPTER 9

President Sukarno Comes For Coffee

In October 1958, my wife, Mary Lou, and I leased a bungalow in the Puntjak area of the mountains of West Java. Designed by an Italian and then owned by a Dutchman, the bungalow had been called "Mirasole." At the request of Indonesian officials, in order to harmonize with the new spirit of Indonesian nationalism, we renamed it with the Sanskrit equivalent of Mirasole—"Wisma Surja," literally "Home of the Sun." There might have been a more beautiful place in the world than Wisma Surja, but I had not seen it.

Here, a crystal blue mountain stream gushed out of the rich greenery of the tropical jungle to divide at the crest of the hill on which the bungalow rested and form a bejeweled necklace that circled and caressed seven acres of velvet lawn and deep, cool cedar groves and gardens splashed with color. The stream merged with itself again at the throat of the hill, flowing on toward the lovely breasts of lower hills, smoky soft in the distance, bringing life and love to the glistening mirrors of rice paddies, flaring banana trees, with their great leaves slashed by the gods, and the feathery cassava trees, which a strong man could lift from the red soil with one powerful tug of an arm. Wisma Surja was like an island on the side of a mountain, and to my wife and me it was an island of God, a retreat where we could leave the world and its storms behind and find peace of mind.

At luncheon with President Sukarno and Madame Hartini Sukarno at the Presidential Palace at Bogor one Saturday, my wife and I could not restrain our enthusiasm. "You must come and see us," we chorused, emphasizing that, humble as it might be in comparison with the splendors of the Presidential Summer Palace, our little mountain hideout nevertheless was a gem.

"Of course. We'd love to," Madame Sukarno responded.

"We'll drop in unannounced for coffee some Saturday or Sunday," the President said, flashing the famous Sukarno smile.

"Oh, no. Come for luncheon," Mary Lou insisted.

"We'd be honored to have you drop in any time," I added, "but it would be a pleasure to have you both for luncheon. Just let us know when it is convenient."

"All right, we'll come," the President said. "Provided it's just a little informal family affair." He said he would let us know. Perhaps the following weekend. "But we'll just drop in. Don't go to any trouble."

Toward the end of the week, a telephone call came from the President's aide. "If it is convenient," he said, "President and Madame Sukarno will drop in for coffee Saturday noon."

"We are highly honored," I replied. "Will the President bring other guests with him?"

"We don't know yet," the aide responded, "but you'd better be prepared for eight or ten. And," he added, "I think that the President would be pleased if you invited some other Americans."

A President's wish is a command. And, of course, we were delighted that he wanted to meet other Americans. Nevertheless, I gulped. We had one small two-burner kerosene stove. But when I relayed the news to my wife, she merely smiled. "We'll manage. We'll have to provide luncheon, of course, at that hour. We'll simply prepare things in Djakarta." The fact that this meant a hot eighty-mile drive after the food had been cooked disturbed her not in the least.

Our cook, Amah, was a wonder. Her bright, brown eyes crinkled with pleasure at the idea of serving her "Papa President." There would be no problem. Amah was a tiny, motherly, cheerful Sundanese who lived for two things—to spoil her grandchildren, of whom she had a baker's dozen, and to cook. She would prepare a buffet supper for a hundred and fifty with apparently no more effort than a meal for the two of us. Indonesian, Chinese, or American food, as one wished. The lunch would be one the President would like, she assured me. She knew his tastes. A special soup, *soto*, a miracle of meats, vegetables and mystic herb flavorings unknown to the West; *sate*, a kind of shish kebab roasted on bamboo skewers and dipped in a spicy sauce. She would make chicken and beef *sate*; also *"banjak"* ("much" or "many") vegetables because the President liked them. And, of course, great bowls of the tropical fruit with which Indonesia abounds: the queen of fruits, the purple mangasteen with its snowy insides, juicy golden mangos from Surabaya, huge orange-red papayas as big as small watermelons, the red-haired rambutan, pale yellow fruits of the huge *nangca*, beautiful smooth Ambon and Rajah bananas, and many others.[1]

---

1. Indonesia has many fruits unknown to the West. One of my friends, a horticulturist, kept a fruit calendar showing which fruits ripened in which

Plans moved apace. Friday night, before our departure for the mountains, the telephone rang. It was a major from the security police.

"You won't mind, will you," he said, "if we post a few of our guards in the environs of your property?"

"How many will there be?"

"Oh, not too many," he replied. "About eighty."

"They will have their own rations with them, I suppose," I observed hopefully while an inner voice warned me what to expect.

The major coughed apologetically. "No," he said, "they'll be on duty from early morning until the President leaves. If you could have a little coffee for them, and some rice, they would be very happy."

I nodded weakly. It was after dark. And we were leaving early the next morning. Then I realized that the major could not see my nod over the telephone. "Your men will be happy, Major. Have no fear," I replied. "You're sure there won't be more than eighty?"

"I'm sure," the major said. "Except, of course, for the drivers. There will be about twenty drivers."

The party was growing. Before he could increase it further, I hung up the phone and dashed for the kitchen. "Amah," I groaned. "There will be eighty police and twenty drivers!" Amah's bright eyes turned even brighter. She waved a hand at the great mounds of rice piled up in big kettles in the kitchen. Her lips wore a knowing smile. "*Tidah apa*," she said. No matter, she was ready for what might come.

The day of the luncheon was beautiful. The lavender jacaranda trees were shining like many jewels in the sun. Tropical birds were calling each other with their flutes, and I noticed one acacia tree flowered with a flock of small orange blossoms—which flew away at my approach! In the distance the green shoulders of the great mountain named Gedeh were wearing the white clouds like a fur. Promptly at noon, screaming sirens echoing in the hills heralded the motorcade turning into our driveway. The President prided himself on his promptness. He alighted from his car, nattily dressed, as usual, in a light tan uniform glittering with decorations. Two American Marines, in blue and red dress uniforms, clicked their heels and saluted smartly as he stepped forward. The President returned the salute, then insisted on shaking hands with them, asked where they were from "in the States," chatted with them a moment. You couldn't tell those Marines there was anything wrong with President Sukarno!

The luncheon went off well, and the President walked out into the kitchen to tell Amah how much he had enjoyed it. We had a small Indonesian orchestra, and some of the more talented members of our

---

months. One month during which I consulted it, thirty-seven different fruits were ripe for the picking!

American group sang songs. The Indonesians (who all appear to be talented singers) joined in. And then the President suggested dancing.

He wanted Moluccan music, which has a strong beat and requires drums. "Have you a couple of big pans or kettles in the kitchen?" Sukarno asked. Our meagerly supplied kitchen in the mountain bungalow was not up to it. So we sent a servant next door to borrow a couple of kettles. Then, with members of Sukarno's group singing and hammering the kettles with heavy spoons or the blunt end of a bayonet, we started dancing the "Tari Lenzo" on the lawn. It was hot in the middle of the day, and soon everyone was dripping with perspiration but having a wonderful time. Sukarno was at his best, laughing, joking with his dance partners, spontaneously singing with the orchestra, indeed, leading the orchestra when the tempo was too slow for him.

Sukarno took my wife on his arm out into the garden and pointed to a hundred-year-old cedar tree with a beautiful spread of limbs. "You must cut that down," he said.

"Why?" Mary Lou asked.

"It spoils the view," the President replied. "You should see more of the valley below."

"Mr. President," Mary Lou said, shaking her head. "We will never cut down that tree. After all, Mr. President, as Joyce Kilmer said, 'Only God can make a tree.' And there is plenty of beauty here already."

"Nevertheless, my dear, it would be more beautiful without that tree. The next time I come, I will hope to see that tree felled."

After the President had gone, we surveyed the damage. Our neighbor's pots and pans had been pounded so hard the bottoms had fallen out. Otherwise, everything was as it had been. The security police, hiding in the garden, had not stepped on a single flower. No one would have known they had been there—except Amah, who reported that she had fed 150!

The tree, of course, was never cut down. But it was an interesting illustration of Sukarno's character. He had to remake the world. Nothing could remain the same as he had first seen it.

CHAPTER 10

The Tail
That Wagged the Tiger

At the close of 1958, the "winter of our discontent" was over and a period of thaw had come. Enough warmth had been infused into American-Indonesian relations by the unexpected arrangements to supply the Indonesian army with assistance so that a start could be made at serious communication on the substantive political issues disturbing these relations.

The dialogue began with the West Irian issue.

Throughout the course of a nation's history, a single issue often punctuates its smooth flow and dominates its development, soaring like a Halley's comet through the political skies. Sometimes the issue is small in terms of human history, but nevertheless looms large in the minds and hearts of the people of the nation concerned. Regardless of its place in world history, the struggle of the Indonesians to recover from the Dutch what they considered was a piece of their territory—West New Guinea, or West Irian, to use the Indonesian name—was an overwhelming, all-absorbing issue that dominated Indonesian political thought and action during the new nation's first twelve and one-half years.

For more than a decade, the West Irian issue constituted Sukarno's measure of the friendship of foreign powers. Soviet Russia and Communist China early appreciated and exploited this by giving vigorous public support to Indonesia's claim to West Irian. Indonesia generally supported Soviet positions in the United Nations, and as time went on people said that Indonesia's neutralism was neutralism on the side of the Communists. The issue also had an impact on internal politics, and from 1961 on tended to reinforce the Indonesian government's growing rapport with the PKI. The West Irian argument, in brief, contributed greatly to the genesis of the long, steady movement of Indonesia away from the West and toward the Communist bloc.

174

What made this Stone Age territory assume such shattering importance? What was the essence of the controversy?

West Irian is half of a huge land mass about the size of Texas that stretches out like a snapping turtle for 1,000 miles north of Australia, its jaws reaching threateningly toward the Eastern Islands of Indonesia. It was a part of the Netherlands East Indies during the colonial period and became the subject of bitter controversy when the Dutch failed to turn it over with the transfer of sovereignty in December 1949.

The main operative article in the transfer document provided that the "Kingdom of the Netherlands unconditionally and irrevocably transfers complete sovereignty over Indonesia to the Republic of the United States of Indonesia and thereby recognizes said Republic as an independent and sovereign state." Since West New Guinea was unquestionably a part of the territory known as Indonesia, it would appear at first glance as though the matter had been settled. But it must be remembered that the area is a wild, sparsely settled jungle inhabited by some 800,000 primitive Papuans. The jungles of New Guinea are a paradise for ethnologists and anthropologists since they contain some of the few known tribes of Stone Age cultures left in the world; some are still cannibalistic.

During the discussions leading to the transfer of sovereignty, the Dutch argued successfully that the new Indonesian nation did not possess the civil service organization that would be required to take over, administer, and keep pacified this large undeveloped territory filled with warring tribes. They reasoned that the new Republic would have its hands full establishing authority over the vast territory of Indonesia.

The Indonesians frankly admitted the difficulty involved, but considered it a temporary one. Their view was that after consolidation of their government, they could take on West New Guinea, perhaps within a year. After months of argument, a provision was agreed to. It read: "In regard to the residency of New Guinea, it is decided . . . in view of the fact that it has not yet been possible to reconcile the views of the parties on New Guinea, which remain therefore in dispute . . . that the status quo of the residency of New Guinea shall be maintained with the stipulation that within a year from the date of transfer of sovereignty to the Republic of the United States of Indonesia, the question of the political status of New Guinea be determined through negotiations between the Republic of the United States of Indonesia and the Kingdom of the Netherlands."

The vagueness of the language was probably deliberate. It was immediately subject to two interpretations. The Dutch insisted that the meeting to be held within a year was to discuss *whether* sovereignty over West New Guinea should be transferred to the Republic of Indonesia. The Indonesians insisted with equal, if not greater vehemence that the paragraph meant that the discussions were to deal with the question of *how* administration should be transferred—since sovereignty had already been transferred to Indonesia with the rest of the Dutch East Indies at the time of independence.

The conflicting interpretations rested on two ambiguous aspects of the foregoing articles. First, the absence of a definition as to the extent of the territory referred to as "Indonesia." Although both sides agreed that "Indonesia" was equivalent in territory to the former "Netherlands East Indies," there was dispute as to whether or not "Netherlands East Indies" in fact included West New Guinea. On this legal-historical question, the Indonesian position seemed to be stronger than that of the Dutch. Even observers otherwise hostile to the Indonesian claim—like the New York *Times*—came to concede the validity of this particular point. As Robert C. Bone pointed out in one of the few scholarly analyses that have been made on the roots of the dispute,[1] the official statements by the Netherlands as to Indonesia's future seemed to indicate every intent to include West New Guinea in the successor state to the Netherlands East Indies.

The second ambiguity, in Article II, was the words "status quo," used to describe New Guinea during the period before the agreed-upon conference to resolve the question of its political status. Did "status quo" imply Dutch retention of sovereignty, or simply Dutch maintenance of *de facto* administrative control? Again, both the Dutch and the Indonesians were in a position to interpret the phrase in accordance with their own desires.[2]

Subsequent to Indonesian independence, the West New Guinea matter became the subject of bilateral talks between the Netherlands and Indonesia on several occasions. In March 1950, the Indonesians brought it up at the first ministerial conference held under the Netherlands-Indonesian Union before that arrangement was dissolved. These talks proved futile. From that point on, the respective positions hardened, and acrimony increased.

---

1. For an excellent discussion of the entire issue, see Robert C. Bone, Jr., *The Dynamics of the West New Guinea (Irian Barat) Problem*, 2nd printing (Ithaca, New York: Cornell Modern Indonesia Project, Interim Report Series, 1962).

2. Years later, I discussed this matter with Sukarno, Hatta and others, and also with Ambassador H. Merle Cochran, who was the American representative on the Good Offices Committee that aided the Dutch and Indonesians in drafting the Charter of Transfer of Sovereignty in 1949. The vagueness of the two controversial articles was in fact deliberate. Both sides attached priority to obtaining agreement on the fundamental question of Indonesian independence at a time when renewal of hostilities appeared inevitable if the negotiations broke down. Moreover, the emotional trauma for many Dutchmen of surrendering their largest and most cherished colony made it politically difficult for the Dutch government to agree publicly to the loss of West New Guinea—the last foothold of the Dutch in Southeast Asia.

Shortly prior to December 27, 1950, which would mark the end of the twelve months specified in the charter for determining the fate of West New Guinea, a second ministerial conference was held in the hope of reaching a last-minute settlement. Indonesia offered a seven-point guar-antee of Dutch rights and interests in West New Guinea as an induce-ment to the concession of sovereignty. The Dutch rejected this and countered with a proposal to transfer sovereignty to the Netherlands-Indonesian Union, under which, of course, the Dutch would exercise *de facto* control. Alternatively, negotiations would be continued under the auspices of the United Nations.

But Indonesian feeling was running high. They rejected the politically unrealistic Dutch counterproposal. The Dutch stuck to their guns. The Indonesians walked out of the meeting in high indignation, convinced they had been tricked out of territory rightfully theirs. Bitterness reached an all-time high in November 1951, when the Dutch nailed down their position by submitting a constitutional amendment to Parliament that included West New Guinea in the official geographic definition of the Kingdom of the Netherlands. To the Indonesians this action represented a unilateral decision to retain West New Guinea and end all discussion, for they believed that it would henceforth be unconstitutional for any Dutch government even to discuss the matter seriously. The heated indignation that this aroused in the Indonesians kept the issue alive; they were still talking about it when I first arrived in Djakarta in 1954.

Having failed in their attempts at bilateral negotiations, the Indone-sians turned to the United Nations. They submitted the issue to the General Assembly four times between 1954 and 1957 (though it was debated only three times), but never obtained the two-thirds majority needed to pass even the mildest resolution on the issue. In February 1957, a resolution sponsored by thirteen Latin American, African and Asian nations would have placed the General Assembly on record as requesting "the President of the General Assembly to appoint a Good Offices Commission consisting of three members, with a view to assist-ing in negotiations between the Governments of Indonesia and the Netherlands in order that a just and peaceful solution to the question may be achieved, in conformity with the principles and purposes of the charter." The resolution also provided that the Commission should re-port to the General Assembly at its next regular session.

A substantial majority voted in favor of this resolution, but its sup-porters were unable to muster the two-thirds required. Analysis of the vote reveals one of the major reasons why Indonesia began from then on consistently to move away from the West. Among the Western nations, only Greece cast a pro-Indonesian vote, whereas Nationalist China was the only Asian-African nation to vote against Indonesia, with Laos and Cambodia abstaining. The nineteen Latin-American nations present divided almost evenly, with six for and six against the resolution, seven abstaining. Bone comments that the Latin American vote "seems far more attributable to a general desire to remain in the good graces of the larger nations of the Western bloc, with the potential economic assistance they represented, than any sudden conversion to the Dutch viewpoint." [3]

The Indonesians blamed America for this line-up. Although the official position was one of neutrality, American government sympathies were with the Dutch. We would support what the Dutch wanted to the extent consistent with our public position of neutrality on the issue. This led us into what I regarded as an untenable position—opposition to a resolution aimed at merely bringing two parties to a dispute together!

John Allison, who had gone to Indonesia as U.S. Ambassador in the spring of 1957, was at the same time bombarding the Department of State with telegrams to the effect that if we were to exercise any influence in Indonesia, we must come to terms with Sukarno on this question. Allison submitted a proposal designed to solve the problem of West Irian as well as bring about a settlement of the economic and financial differences between the Dutch and the Indonesians. Under it, Indonesia would get West Irian, but Dutch investments would be salvaged. Security provisions were included, which Allison thought would satisfy the Australians. In addition to the provision for Dutch-Indonesian negotiations on a financial settlement (which Allison did not attempt to spell out), it provided for transfer of sovereignty over West Irian to Indonesia after five years. In the meantime the U.S. would provide economic aid and cooperate with Indonesia in a political program to enhance the stability of the country. The latter was designed to see whether or not Sukarno would live up to his promise to cut the Communists down to size if the West would support him on Irian. At the end of the five years, when sovereignty passed, Indonesia would "associate itself" with, not join, the ANZUS (Australia-New Zealand-U.S.) defense pact for the purpose of "assuring the territorial integrity" of the area. This would bring Australia into the picture and reassure them, it was hoped, against a Communist takeover. [4]

---

3. *West New Guinea*, pp. 150–151. Bone comments that Colombia was "apparently absent from the voting."
4. Discussing it later, Allison stressed it was a package plan, and if one part was not carried out the whole thing went by the board. He believed that "the 100 million Indonesians could be led into the Communist world . . . easily by their demagogic and charismatic leader but that the 13 million Dutch, although they probably would shout and scream and make threats, would in the end realize . . . they had no place else to go. And when the shouting had died down they would still be in Indonesia, although not in the monopolistic manner of former days. The head of Shell in Djakarta and the Dutch secretary of their local Chamber of Commerce agreed with our

The proposal was promptly turned down by Washington. Allison, frustrated by his inability to make any headway in a situation that presented a diplomat with an almost impossible set of circumstances, finally told the Department of State that we had a choice of two courses of action in Indonesia: "The first, which I preferred, was to work with the leader to whom I was accredited, but this would necessitate giving me something to work with, *i.e.*, agreement to my proposal or something like it which would help solve the Irian problem. However, if Washington was convinced Sukarno was too involved with the Communists to be rescued, then we could probably get him out of office. I made clear I was willing to do either provided Washington would follow one policy or the other 100 per cent." [5] Neither course was acceptable to Washington policy makers, and shortly thereafter, Allison was transferred by Secretary Dulles to Prague.

As the new American Ambassador to Indonesia, I inherited the West Irian impasse. It was not long before Sukarno was addressing me with the same words he had put to John Allison and Hugh Cumming before me. "If the United States Government will change its position on West Irian and support our claim, I will abandon neutrality between the two blocs and take sides with America—like that!" snapping his fingers. If Sukarno told me this once, he told me a dozen times. It was the refrain that ran through almost every interview I and other Americans had with him from 1958 until the settlement of the dispute more than four years later. Like the others, I was discouraging about the prospects of any such change in United States policy. I told Sukarno again and again, "We view this dispute, Mr. President, as a bilateral dispute between two friends, the Netherlands and Indonesia. We would like to see it settled, as we would like to see the Kashmir dispute between Pakistan and India settled, in the interest of international harmony." I pointed out that Indonesia was not taking sides in the Kashmir dispute, regardless of how strongly each party was urging its claim. "You can understand our position, Mr. President. You are doing precisely the same as in the Kashmir dispute."

But Sukarno was having none of this. To him, the West Irian issue was a matter of principle. "America is against colonialism, you tell me. Then why is America not taking sides with us? Why is America not taking sides with Algeria? Why is America not taking sides with Angola?" To Sukarno, as to many Indonesians, America was disowning its heritage. To most Asians, colonialism and imperialism was the great issue of the time. An individual, a nation, was judged by the position taken on this issue.

---

stand and pleaded with us to get Washington to persuade The Hague to be reasonable. But Washington was looking the other way at that time."
5. Letter from John M. Allison to Howard P. Jones, October 13, 1969.

During this period many people asked me whether the Indonesian people as a whole really felt strongly about West Irian or whether this was simply Sukarno talking. There seemed little doubt that the Indonesian people were united on the subject of West Irian. I talked with Indonesians all the way from North Sumatra in the West to Dobo, 4,000 miles to the East. In Dobo, a small island under the neck of the West Irian turtle, I encountered an interesting reaction, which also disposed of some other misconceptions I might have had. Sitting around with several of the residents of Dobo, I asked, "Are you people really interested in the recovery of West Irian? And if so, why?" They looked at me in some amazement. "Why," one of them said, "West Irian is right over there," pointing across the stretch of sea. "It's part of our country. I have relatives over there." Another man chimed in and said, "My father and brother are over there." Another said, "We go back and forth all the time."

These people were not Papuans, they were Indonesians. Many, over the centuries, had settled on West Irian's coasts, leaving the interior's forbidding jungles to the savage tribes they had found there. These Papuan tribes had no common language, but the people on the coast used the same language as was spoken throughout the islands of Indonesia. The Deputy Chief of Mission of the American Embassy in Djakarta in 1962 through 1965, Francis J. Galbraith, first learned to speak the Indonesian language when he was with MacArthur's forces in World War II in West New Guinea.

The question that I and the Administration in Washington had to ask and answer was, What position on our part represented the optimum in terms of the national interest? Here a balance of opposing considerations had to be drawn up. The Dutch were our partners in NATO. We needed their support in a variety of urgent issues before the United Nations. There had been only slightly veiled threats from the Dutch that they would pull out of NATO if we intervened in any way concerning West Irian—although I often wondered just where they would go. We had no such close ties with the Indonesians. The weight of tradition, history, culture and long friendship was on the side of the Dutch. The little nation on the North Sea had been a staunch and long-time ally of the United States. Why risk a Dutch withdrawal from NATO and a tested friendship for such an uncertain quantity as volatile Indonesia under Sukarno appeared to be?

There was still, however, the overriding question of what open support for the Dutch would do to American prestige in Asia and Africa at a time which new nations had been or were about to be born—all of which had suffered under colonialism. America in Asia was already being accused of having proved false to her own tradition with her policy of temporizing in such explosive colonial situations as Portuguese Goa and Angola, French Algeria, the Belgian Congo. Time after time, Indonesians and other Asians would say to me in genuine mystification, "We just don't understand America. You were once a colony. You know what colonialism is. You fought and bled and died for your freedom. How can you possibly support the status quo?" This was a hard question to answer, and our posture lent some color to the charge that we had become an imperial power ourselves.

In sum, we had sufficient foresight to realize it was out of the question for us to take a position in support of Dutch, or any other nation's, retention of a colony. In the view of John Foster Dulles and most men in the Administration in 1957–1958, however, it was not the job of American diplomacy to pass on the question of right or wrong in the issue of sovereignty over West Irian. American policy therefore followed what seemed a sound and pragmatic course in remaining neutral about an issue in which right and wrong were somewhat obscure and the national interest seemed not to be directly concerned. It was not a heroic policy. It was not a dynamic policy. We were content to be safe and sane. We did not like to admit it, but we were wedded to the *status quo*.

But Washington and the West reckoned without Sukarno. It was simple enough to sit around a well-polished mahogany table in London, The Hague, Paris or Washington, and reach conclusions as to the logical thing to do about a Dutch colony in the South Pacific. But "a lion was loose in the streets." The question was what to do about him. He did not fit the pattern of the kind of Asian leader with whom we liked to do business. He was something new on the horizon—an Asian leader who knew what he wanted, determined to have his way while skillfully playing both sides of the street, and unwilling to follow the leadership of Washington. President Eisenhower disapproved of Sukarno. It was not easy for him to go out of his way to please a man he instinctively disliked and distrusted.

He had made a good start with Sukarno when he invited him on a state visit to the United States in 1956. But a good deal of water had gone over the dam since then. Immediately following his Washington visit, Sukarno had gone to Moscow and Peking, and when he returned to Indonesia, he announced his famed concept of Guided Democracy, in Washington's eyes another name for a type of Communism guided by a would-be dictator whose leftist leanings and personal peccadilloes were becoming more widely known. In any event, by the time President Eisenhower had reached his decision to visit Asia in 1959, he had no stomach for paying a return visit to Sukarno.

It was not easy to explain President Eisenhower's failure to expand his trip to India a few more hours to include Indonesia, but I did it on the basis that it was difficult for an American President to be long absent from his country, since he was not only head of state but head of government and of his political party. That was taken with several grains of salt by Sukarno, but he accepted the explanation without comment. Later, however, President Eisenhower planned a visit to Seoul, Tokyo and Manila; Djakarta was only a step farther. When the President replied negatively in response to Sukarno's fifth invitation to visit his country, Sukarno called me in.

"There are only two reasons I can think of for your President not visiting Indonesia on this trip," he said grimly. "One is that he does not consider Indonesia, even though it is the fifth largest country in the world, important enough. The other is that he doesn't like its President. Mr. Ambassador, which is it?"

There are times when the most skillful diplomat (which I was not) finds himself at a loss for words, particularly when he has been arguing with his government on the other side. (I had been bombarding Washington with cables strongly urging the importance of President Eisenhower's visiting Indonesia.) I realized that now it was up to me not only to defend President Eisenhower but to save Sukarno's face in the process. There were, of course, good reasons for the decision, even though I thought the balance was the other way. "Mr. President," I said, "you are wrong." I reviewed the American domestic political situation and the delicacy of American-Dutch and American-Indonesian relations as a result of the increasing acrimony over the West Irian dispute.

"For President Eisenhower to visit Indonesia at this juncture would be taken as siding with Indonesia in the West Irian dispute," I pointed out. "Furthermore," I said, "there are other nations in this part of the world much more friendly towards us than Indonesia. You will recognize, Mr. President, from your own experience in traveling, that President Eisenhower could not visit Indonesia without stopping in Bangkok as well as other friendly capitals. It was, therefore, not a question of simply adding Indonesia to his itinerary. He would have had to visit several other countries as well if he had come to Djakarta. His doctors just will not permit him to take so long a trip. They say he must return." Sukarno had to recognize that what I was saying was true. But the explanation did not satisfy.

There was a third reason, which I did not mention. Washington believed such a visit would build up Sukarno's prestige, and this it did not wish to do. History was repeating itself. In the fall of 1957, Under Secretary Christian A. Herter visited Bangkok and, instead of stopping at Djakarta, asked Allison to come to Bangkok to brief him on the Indonesian situation. Allison asked Herter why he had not come to Djakarta, and was told that Washington felt a visit by the Under Secretary would tend to build up Sukarno. Of course, the fact on which Allison and I agreed was that nothing we did or didn't do at that time would have built up Sukarno or torn him down in the eyes of the Indonesian masses. "What our actions accomplished was to alienate the one man who, at that time, could have led the 100 million Indonesians into paths of cooperation with us," Allison wrote me later.[6] "Just about the same time," he added, "Eisenhower turned down a cordial invitation by Sukarno to visit Indonesia. This was shortly after Voroshilov's[7] visit, which had done much to increase the prestige of the PKI. Sukarno told me if Eisenhower would come to Indonesia, he would be received in such a manner that the people would forget all about the Soviet visitor. But . . . Sukarno was just not a nice man so we snubbed him."

When it became apparent that he would not succeed in inducing President Eisenhower to come, Sukarno suggested Vice-President Nixon. I had first met Nixon when he visited Asia in 1953, and three years later, I attended a Washington dinner he gave honoring Sukarno on his first U.S. visit. "I like Dick Nixon," Sukarno said. "He and I hit it off well." But the Vice-President did not come, although he had a greater appreciation of the importance of Asia in the scheme of things than many of his colleagues.

The climax in a series of irritations was reached when Sukarno went to New York to speak before the United Nations in September 1960. Here he was, the head of a friendly country, in the United States and less than an hour from Washington. Yet no invitation to visit the White House had been extended, despite the embassy's continuing admonitions from Djakarta that failure to extend such an invitation would be taken by Sukarno as a deliberate snub.

Finally, the day before Sukarno was scheduled to depart New York for Paris to meet with de Gaulle, an invitation from President Eisenhower came through. At that point, Sukarno had to choose between de Gaulle and President Eisenhower. He chose the latter. And then, according to accounts from members of the party, Sukarno was kept waiting in the anteroom ten minutes while the American President talked with a member of his own staff!

There was, of course, an explanation. The fault was not President Eisenhower's, it was Sukarno's. One of the members of his party at the United Nations was Aidit, then leader of the Communist Party in Indonesia, and the ever-mischievous Sukarno had brought him along to the White House. An embarrassed aide, aware of the sensation it would cause, hesitated to usher in the head of the largest Communist Party outside of the Sino-Soviet bloc to greet the President of the United States. He kept the Sukarno party waiting for a few minutes while he alerted his chief to the situation. To his credit, President Eisenhower decided to invite the entire party into his office, but the damage had been done. The sensitive head of state of a proud Asian nation had been kept waiting ten

---

6. *Ibid.*
7. Klimet Voroshilov, President of the Soviet Union, who visited Indonesia early in May 1957.

minutes in the anteroom of another head of state! He had never been treated that way in any other country. And Sukarno was a proud and vain man.

As he told me later, "Okay, Eisenhower didn't meet my plane—okay, he didn't greet me at the door of the White House; I guess that's still okay. But when he had me cool my heels for close to an hour"—certainly an exaggeration—"I spoke to the chief of protocol. 'Have I to wait any longer? Because if so, I am leaving right now.' The man went pale. 'Please, I beg of you, wait just a minute, sir,' he stammered, and raced inside. Out came Eisenhower." [8]

This was a far cry from the warmth of Sukarno's welcome on May 16, 1956. President Eisenhower's concept of foreign policy was based upon the brotherhood of man. At the Women's National Press Club annual dinner in 1956, concluding an evening of fun, he suddenly turned serious and pulled from his pocket a newspaper clipping which he termed "the finest story of the week—maybe of the entire year." It was a moving quotation from the speech by President Sukarno upon his arrival in Washington:

> Today I am in Washington for the first time in my life and I feel that here, and I am sure that in all America, democracy is a reality. I saw the faces of the people along the streets and the hospitality given me.
> Look here, I am a brown man, an Indonesian, an Asiatic. I am the son of a poor family, the son of a nation only recently emerged into the world of national existence. Yet you accept me as a friend, you accept me as a human being, and perhaps you accept me as a brother.

President Eisenhower commented, "If we, as a nation, can convince every other nation that when they refer to us as a brother, they won't have to say 'perhaps,' they will see a real democracy." [9] It was sad to see misunderstanding develop between the Indonesian and American leadership after so fine a beginning.

Sukarno did his best over a period of years to get Washington to change its position on the issue that concerned him most, but without success. In the fall of 1957, when our position of neutrality had in fact assisted the Dutch in beating down a mild UN resolution aiming at a renewal of discussions between the two contesting parties, it was clear Sukarno would retaliate by throwing all Dutch business out of the country.[10]

---

8. Also reported in Cindy Adams, *Sukarno, An Autobiography as Told to Cindy Adams* (Indianapolis: The Bobbs-Merrill Company, Inc., 1965), pp. 295–296.

9. *The Christian Science Monitor*, May 18, 1956.

10. Actually, Sukarno had made clear during the preceding summer that he would take "drastic action" if the Indonesian resolution were defeated at the next General Assembly session. It was because of this that Allison had presented his proposal to the State Department. Among other things, he told me, it was "designed to get talks started between the Dutch and the

Still the Dutch continued adamant, unwilling even to discuss the matter with the Indonesians. "The day of colonialism is over," I commented in 1957 to a prominent Dutch businessman. "Why do you people continue to hang onto West New Guinea when you know you are about to sacrifice billions of dollars of investment in Indonesia for a piece of real estate that is costing you money and that you can't keep anyhow?"

"I couldn't agree with you more!" the man replied, to my surprise. He was the head of one of the largest corporations in Holland. "I'll tell you this. We got together a committee of all the businessmen in the Netherlands engaged in operations overseas and waited on the Dutch Cabinet. We spent an entire morning pleading with them to change their policy and work out a compromise with Indonesia. When we were finished, they thanked us politely. We had no more effect upon them than we would have had on a stone wall. They said that the prestige of our country was at stake. The contrary is true, in my opinion. If we are driven out of Indonesia, where is our prestige then? But we can't get them to see it. Luns [the Foreign Minister] won't countenance any compromise with Sukarno."

Little did Luns and others who took this point of view realize that in denying West Irian to Indonesia, they were strengthening Sukarno. They were handing him an issue that not only provided the fuel he required to feed the fires of nationalism, but paved the way for his acquisition of well-nigh dictatorial power.

So, to the detriment of both nations, Dutch enterprise was thrown out of Indonesia late in 1957. The Indonesians lost the desperately needed capital and know-how of the Dutch. The latter lost upwards of $2 billion worth of properties, and more than 40,000 Dutch citizens were sent home. Sukarno's determination against the Dutch, economically as well as politically, represented a major difference between him and such men as Hatta and Sjafruddin. The economists and financiers of the nation, though few in number, were not mesmerized by fear of foreign capital. Rather, Hatta, Sjafruddin and other knowledgeable men took the opposite view; they knew Indonesia needed the Dutch.

Hatta and the other anti-Communist, anti-Sukarno Indonesian leaders, however, were convinced that American policy was contributing to the very result that it was designed to prevent in Indonesia—the strengthening of Communist influence. They were right. Hatta wrote in the April 1958 issue of *Foreign Affairs*:

> Indonesians cannot understand why the United States should assume such a halfhearted posture on this matter. The United States has been

---

Indonesians and thus get Sukarno off the hook of having to throw out the Dutch. Very few of the Indonesian leaders wanted to do this, but they all felt they would have to support Sukarno if the Dutch continued to refuse to talk." Letter of October 15, 1969.

the moving force in setting up NATO and SEATO to halt the spread of Communist influence and power in Europe and Asia. Yet to permit West Irian to continue indefinitely as a bone of contention between Indonesia and the Netherlands is to afford Communism an opportunity to spread in Indonesia. The claim to West Irian is a national claim backed by every Indonesian party without exception; but the most demanding voice, apart from that of President Soekarno himself, is that of the Communist Party of Indonesia. By putting itself in the vanguard of those demanding realization of this national ideal, and because it agitates about West Irian as a national claim—in line with President Soekarno's standpoint—and because it backs this up by good organizational work, the Communist Party of Indonesia is able to recapture the imagination of an ever-growing section of the population.
The West Irian question thus represents a tragedy.[11]

To most Indonesians, West Irian was not a matter of money, or even of territory. It was a matter of principle, patriotism, and completing their revolution. Sukarno's golden voice and flashing eyes carried conviction. With *merdeka,* the people were for the first time free from foreign masters. They had endured the Dutch for centuries, and then the Japanese for four cruel years. It was hard for the Indonesians to believe the Dutch would not return. If Sukarno said their economic hold must be broken, then it must. He was the Moses who had led them out of captivity.

A representative to the Indonesian Foreign Office was quite frank about his government's intentions. "There are five approaches to the settlement of this matter," he told me in private conversation. "One, through bilateral negotiations with the Netherlands. We are prepared to discuss compensation for the properties we have taken over, if the Dutch will discuss West Irian. But they have refused even to talk with us. Two, by United Nations action. We have been denied repeatedly this remedy when we sought it. We thought that was what the United Nations was for—to settle controversies peacefully. But we could not get our foot in the door. There are reports that the *Dutch* will take the issue to the United Nations, and if so, we hope that a satisfactory solution emerges. But no solution will be satisfactory to us which does not give us reasonable assurance that the territory will be returned to us. Three, mediation by a third power. No third power has been willing to mediate, and it is questionable whether such mediation could be successful under present circumstances. Four, economic pressures. We have tried that, again unsuccessfully. Had the Dutch settled with us earlier, we would never have taken over their properties. Five, military action. We have repeatedly stated, publicly and privately, that we would not resort to the use of force

---

11. "Indonesia Between the Power Blocs," vol. XXXVI, no. 3, pp. 486–487. Italics are mine.

to settle this dispute. But Indonesia is a live volcano on this question. It will explode someday."

In reporting this conversation to Washington, I stressed the last point: "The Indonesians, if denied what they consider justice in this matter, are almost certain at some time in the future to explode into military action."

Such was the nature of the controversy that so aroused the Indonesians as to lead them, after unsuccessful attempts to get the United Nations to consider the question, to nationalize all Dutch properties in 1957, to break off all diplomatic relations with the Netherlands on August 17, 1960, and finally, with the aid of Soviet weapons, to initiate a military assault to dislodge the Dutch from West Irian.

In my view, the only way to have slowed Sukarno down would have been to extract the issue that was his strongest card. The United States was the only nation in a position to do this, but opinions were divided. Many in high positions were inclined to feel that the world was moving too fast, that we were caught in the current of a Niagara. We knew that it made no sense to attempt to paddle upstream. We had to be abreast, if not ahead of the times. But we sat on our hands and did nothing. Again, events and Sukarno had taken over.

To many Americans, Sukarno's insistence on "regaining" West Irian was simply self-aggrandizement and self-glorification for Sukarno. To others, it was a sign that a new Hitlerlike aggressor had risen up out of the jungles of Java, and was making territorial expansion his goal. Still others regarded it as a diversionary issue to distract the Indonesians from their internal difficulties. The truth was otherwise, although Sukarno was not one to disregard collateral benefits. It was a nationalistic issue to which all Indonesians reacted alike. It was a nation-building issue; it brought Indonesians together. Finally, it was a powerful political weapon for Sukarno, allowing him to consolidate power in his own hands.

The West Irian issue should never have been permitted to reach the stage where war threatened. Monday-morning quarterbacking will not change the past, but it may help next week's game. Had there not been so much misunderstanding in the West regarding this entire matter, some one of several attempts on the part of the Indonesians to take the issue to the United Nations would have succeeded. For that is, after all, what the United Nations is for. Its Charter clearly sets forth the powers and responsibilities of the Security Council in connection with disputes likely to endanger the maintenance of international peace and security. Instead, the dispute turned out to be a long, painful, and mutually damaging experience. A controversy that hinged on two words, "how" and "whether," took twelve years to settle.

CHAPTER 11

Indonesia Turns to Force

In company with the rest of the diplomatic corps, I was present for Sukarno's Independence Day speech on August 17, 1960. As we took our places, we were handed printed copies of the President's speech. Rumors had been rife that some kind of action would be taken against the Netherlands—speculation ranged all the way from the imposition of an economic blockade to a declaration of war.

We riffled through the long speech rapidly to find out what was going to happen. After rehearsing the attempts of Indonesia to regain West Irian and stressing that the Republic of Indonesia had tried, without success, every peaceful means at its disposal, including economic pressures, Sukarno said the time had come to "carry out the policy for the liberation of West Irian in a *revolutionary* manner. . . . A country of small creditors like the Netherlands . . . still preserves a taste for colonialism and is now trying to send its bailiff called 'Karel Doorman' [a reference to a big aircraft carrier sent to defend West Irian against anticipated Indonesian attacks]." At this climactic point, there was a blank space in the copy. The President was keeping us in suspense! It was typical of his sense of drama.

Two and a half hours and forty-four pages later, the President reached that point in his address. He paused for emphasis, then raised his hand and, slowly and impressively, said, "Now listen to me, Brothers and Sisters! In those circumstances, there is no use any more having diplomatic relations with the Netherlands. This morning I instructed our Foreign Affairs Department to break off our diplomatic relations with the Netherlands!" A murmur went through the diplomatic section. The vast throng, estimated at 500,000, broke into cheers. In the press section, there was a stir and a scraping of chairs as correspondents rushed for the telephone.

The Dutch were given three days to close their diplomatic mission, although the limit was later extended. Their representation in Djakarta had been changed only a few weeks earlier, and an attractive couple, the

188

Vixseboxses, with understanding and sympathy for the new nationalism of Indonesia, had been exerting strenuous efforts to improve the state of Dutch-Indonesian relations. My wife and I were sad to see them go—we thought they might have accomplished much.

From the American Embassy in Djakarta, all during the period from 1960 to 1962, we continually hammered away at Washington, urging that positive action be taken to settle the West Irian dispute. To us, Sukarno's every action seemed to promise a troublesome future. In September 1960, he addressed the United Nations General Assembly in New York, and his words were hardly calculated to reassure the American government as to his motivation and intentions.

"This is a time of the building of nations and the breaking of empires," Sukarno said. "If there is a cause for conflict, then men will fight with pointed sticks if they have no other weapon. I know, because my own nation did that very thing during our struggle for independence." He spoke about the "necessity of cooperation to bring about the final inglorious end of imperialism," and then turned to West Irian. "Bordering that territory," he went on, "our own troops stand guard by land and sea. Those two bodies of troops [Dutch and Indonesian] face each other, and I tell you that is an explosive situation." He reviewed Indonesia's efforts to obtain a peaceful settlement of the dispute with the Netherlands. "We have tried bilateral negotiations. We tried that seriously and for years. . . . We have tried using the machinery of the United Nations, and the strength of world opinion expressed there. . . . Hope evaporates; patience dries; even tolerance reaches an end. . . . The Netherlands has left us no alternative but to stiffen our attitude. If they fail correctly to estimate the current of history, we are not to blame. But the result of their failures is that there is a threat to peace, and that involves, once again, the United Nations. West Irian is a colonial sword poised over Indonesia. It points at our heart, but it also threatens world peace."

With Sukarno flaunting such words, even the friends of Indonesia in Washington were foreclosed from helping it militarily when, in October 1960, General Nasution made a trip there in search of substantial arms aid. At that stage, I was urging that we give the Indonesian army some encouragement, that we at least provide equipment that could be used only for domestic purposes, such as riot control and construction. I thought it desirable to make clear our continuing confidence in Nasution and the Indonesian army. But Nasution returned empty-handed.

In January 1961, he arrived in Moscow, where his reception was of a quite different character. Nasution had not wanted to go; he had resisted Sukarno's original request because he was against Communism. But Sukarno insisted and, we gathered, actually ordered Nasution to go. He was received with open arms, given the red-carpet treatment, had talks with Khrushchev. He came back with $400 million of arms in his bag and a new respect for the Russians. Upon his return, Nasution told the press at the airport that the Soviet arms purchases meant a substantial increase in power for the Indonesian armed forces. He asserted it was difficult if not impossible to buy heavy modern arms from Western nations, owing either to their connections with the Dutch or unfavorable credit terms. The general said he had obtained renewed pledges of Soviet Union support for Indonesian efforts to regain West Irian, that India and Pakistan, where he had stopped enroute, had also provided similar assurances.

The Soviets, once they had decided to enter the game, did not hesitate to raise the ante. Their total arms assistance to Indonesia would reach more than a billion dollars before they were through. Unless we were willing and able to compete with stakes of this size, which we were not prepared to do, we were out of the game.

Apparently fearing an unfavorable reaction from the United States to all of this, Prime Minister Djuanda, in a conversation with me on January 11, expressed hope that Washington would not consider the Nasution mission as representing a further adjustment of the Indonesian government policy toward the Soviet bloc. He emphasized that his government had taken this action with great reluctance, and that more aid would have been sought from the United States had it not been concluded, in the light of past experience, that such an approach would be futile.

Sukarno, buoyed up by the prospect of Soviet military support, boasted to his cheering people on December 7, 1960, "Before the cock crows to ring in the new year, West Irian will be restored to Indonesian sovereignty, provided we stay truly united." [1] The statement caused a sensation in the diplomatic corps. Could he have meant January 1, 1961? Sukarno had left himself a way out by not being specific. But at the least this meant that Sukarno had set January 1, 1962, as his target date for winning West Irian. This, in turn, meant West Irian would be the major matter on Sukarno's agenda for 1961. Indeed, the government had already taken a carefully calculated first step in a series of maneuvers to gain the active support of world opinion for its case, as well as build up domestic emotions at home. His emphasis on the seriousness of the problem was well timed.

On December 28, 1960, the Foreign Ministry transmitted a letter to the Secretary-General of the United Nations, warning that the West Irian

---

1. There were two versions of this speech, although the above became the official one. Sukarno was quoted in the New York *Times* (December 8, 1960) as having said West New Guinea (the *Times* referred to the territory as Netherlands New Guinea) would be in Indonesian hands "before the cock crows January 1, 1961." Foreign Minister Subandrio later told newsmen Sukarno had not fixed any actual date, but had said "in 1961."

policy of the Dutch would inevitably lead to physical conflict, and thus constituted an imminent threat to world peace. The letter noted that Indonesia would be forced to adopt "more energetic measures to cope with the situation." There was talk in the diplomatic corps that the letter might be followed with a call for a full-scale UN discussion of the issue if the Government of Indonesia were satisfied it had made its case regarding the serious threat to peace.

Regardless of how the rest of the world viewed these developments— and the general reaction was to write them off as typical Sukarno bluster—it was clear to us in Djakarta that the Indonesians were not bluffing, that we had the makings of a major military crisis on our hands. I can remember John W. Henderson, Deputy Chief of Mission and political counselor of the embassy, shaking his head early that year and saying, "There's one New Year's resolution we've got to make and keep. We've got to settle the West Irian dispute. And the only way it will ever be settled will be if Indonesia gets it." He expressed the sentiments of most members of the embassy, including mine.

There was general recognition in the embassy that this would not be easy, for reasons already made clear. People in Washington with a European bias would have to be convinced, not merely of the inevitability of West Irian going to Indonesia, but that it was in the United States' interest to do something to implement it. The impact such action would have upon the internal situation in Indonesia was not enough of an argument; even the possibility (which most people, including myself, did not take too seriously) that Sukarno would reorient his foreign policy toward the free world would not sway those who felt any move toward giving Sukarno what he wanted was pandering to an Asian Hitler and deserting a stanch ally. Only a clear threat to the peace of the area, of such a nature as to force American involvement in a conflict in which we had no interest, would move Washington. We in Djakarta saw the hull of that threat looming gray on the horizon, but, for the policy makers in the American capital, it was too vague and distant to be believed.

The election of a new President, John F. Kennedy, was the main topic of my talk with Sukarno on January 29. Referring to Kennedy's inaugural speech, Sukarno noted the favorable Indonesian press reaction and requested me to inform Kennedy that the Indonesian people were "expecting great things from him." By this, of course, he meant support for Indonesia's claim to West Irian. He expressed confidence that he and President Kennedy would get along very well together.

In a subsequent conversation the same day, Subandrio emphasized that the West Irian issue was the biggest obstacle to satisfactory U.S.-Indonesian relations because it had forced Indonesians to reach an accommodation with the Sino-Soviet bloc, which he termed unavoidable. The government was aware of the risks, but the bloc offered political and material support on the issue, and there was no alternative available. He stated that Nasution and other anti-Communist army leaders felt just as strongly as Sukarno and other Indonesians regarding West Irian.

Subandrio observed that many in the United States, as a result of this accommodation, were beginning to feel that the Government of Indonesia was abandoning its active independent foreign policy, and was perhaps on the way to becoming a satellite. This bothered the Foreign Minister, and he vigorously denied the Soviet deal would result in any basic change in Indonesian policy. Subandrio insisted Indonesia was not headed toward Communism and that President Sukarno planned to reduce the PKI to "auxiliary status" after the establishment of the National Front. He wound up this conversation by repeating his oft-expressed conviction that Communist China offered the only military threat to the country.

Regardless of the consequences for Indonesia's foreign relations, it was clear that Nasution's pilgrimage to the Kremlin for arms would have a favorable long-range effect upon the prestige of the PKI internally. Aware of this, sensitive to American reactions, and determined to keep the PKI from getting "too big for its britches," the army moved against the party for the first time in months. The PKI newspaper, *Harian Rakjat*, was suspended beginning February 3, on the grounds that the paper had published a statement by PKI Chairman Aidit, given at the party's tenth anniversary celebration, demanding a change in the Cabinet.

The PKI was simultaneously harassed by police for an alleged technical violation of the license requirements for a public meeting. According to a police officer, Aidit had delivered a political speech at the tenth anniversary reception, which had been described at the time of the license application as a "social gathering." As a result, Aidit was interrogated by police on February 2, and a permit for subsequent cultural performances to celebrate the occasion was denied. The action was encouraging as concrete evidence that the army remained fundamentally opposed to the PKI and to a Nasakom cabinet as a result of the aid from Soviet Russia.

Attesting the army's concern regarding U.S. reactions to Nasution's Moscow trip, Generals Nasution and Yani asked me separately whether the United States was curtailing its military assistance to Indonesia. They pointed out only limited quantities of arms and equipment had actually been delivered to Indonesia in recent months. This was true, and it represented an understandable response by Washington to what appeared as a major *rapprochement* with the Soviet Union.

The new Soviet initiatives in Indonesia not only gave concern to the West; they disturbed Communist China as well. Peking and Moscow were competitors in Indonesia, at first friendly competitors, then less so as it became apparent that China regarded Indonesia as its own front yard. Historically, China's relative geographic isolation hindered close contact with other civilizations of comparable stature. The Chinese thus developed a tremendous cultural superiority complex early in their history. They came to believe China, the Middle Kingdom, was the only truly civilized state on earth. This attitude still lingers today.

In March 1961, without much advance notice, Chinese Communist Foreign Minister Chen Yi visited Indonesia, and on April 1 signed an amity agreement backing the Indonesian claim to West Irian. The Chinese, too, were getting on the bandwagon. It was an important milestone and marked the beginnings of a *rapprochement* in the wake of the bitter Chinese-Indonesian dispute over Indonesian persecution of Chinese in Indonesia in 1959 and 1960.

All of the events of 1960, 1961, and 1962 in Indonesia had West Irian as their common denominator. It was Sukarno's determination to obtain West Irian that was responsible for his dissatisfaction with us, for his turning to the Soviet Union for military assistance, for his welcoming the political support of Peking, even, to some extent, for his growing fondness for the PKI, which had proved the most able and enthusiastic adherent of the cause. The issue was also primarily responsible for our rejection of the Indonesian request for major military assistance, for the unpopularity of the Indonesian President, who was beginning to be regarded as a warmonger if not an out and out Communist, and for the unfavorable congressional attitudes toward Indonesia.

On the positive side, a new and engaging personality had entered the scene with the election of John F. Kennedy. During the election campaign of 1960, I had presented President Sukarno with a copy of Kennedy's book, *The Strategy of Peace*, containing texts of his more important policy speeches to date. One morning over coffee, Sukarno picked up the book and said, "Mr. Ambassador, I'm a politician. I know that politicians don't mean everything they say when they're running for office. But," he emphasized what he was about to say by shaking the book at me, "if President Kennedy means what he says in these speeches, then I agree with him. I agree with him completely!"

In the Senate as far back as 1957, in a speech criticizing the United States' support of the French in the Algerian conflict, Kennedy said, "The most powerful single force in the world today is neither Communism nor capitalism, neither the H-bomb nor the guided missile—it is man's eternal desire to be free and independent. . . . The war in Algeria . . . has affected our standing in the eyes of the Free World, our leadership in the fight to keep that world free, our prestige and our security; as well as our moral leadership in the fight against Soviet imperialism in the countries behind the Iron Curtain." [2] This was language Sukarno could understand.

On peace, John Kennedy spoke movingly, "We move from crisis to

---

2. John F. Kennedy, *The Strategy of Peace*, ed. Allan Nevins (New York: Harper & Brothers, 1960), pp. 66–68.

crisis for two reasons: first, because we have not yet developed a strategy for peace that is relevant to the new world in which we live; and secondly, because we have not been paying the price which that strategy demands —a price measured not merely in money and military preparedness, but in social inventiveness, in moral stamina, in physical courage. . . . Now as never before, hundreds of millions of men and women—who had formerly believed that stoic resignation in the face of hunger and disease and darkness was the best one could do—have come alive with a new sense that the means are at hand with which to make for themselves a better life . . . it is we, the American people, who should be marching at the head of this world-wide revolution, counseling it, helping it to come to a healthy fruition." [3]

Kennedy's ringing words touched a responsive chord in Sukarno. A new American President had opened opportunities for bridging the U.S.-Indonesian rift.

For weeks prior to Kennedy's inauguration, I had been urging upon the State Department the importance of the new President's visiting Indonesia as soon as possible, or extending an invitation to Sukarno to visit the White House. To the ebullient Sukarno, personal relations were vital in the field of international affairs. Rapport with President Kennedy could mean much. President Kennedy was responsive to my appeal. Within a month after taking office, he extended an invitation for President Sukarno to visit him at the White House. Sukarno was highly pleased and accepted the invitation at once. He said he would come to Washington in April, at the start of his world tour.

The visit went off well. I had told Kennedy that when Sukarno visited Communist countries, he was invariably welcomed on arrival by the heads of state, and that it might be a helpful gesture if a high American official could be at National Airport in Washington to welcome him. Kennedy was there himself. He welcomed Sukarno warmly. In his few words of official greeting, President Kennedy hailed him as the "George Washington of Indonesia."

At noon that day, President Sukarno, Foreign Minister Subandrio, Deputy Prime Minister Leimena, and Ambassador Zain on the Indonesian side, and Secretary Rusk, Chester Bowles, Walt Rostow, John Steeves and I were invited to luncheon at the White House by the Kennedys. Before luncheon, President Kennedy took President Sukarno by the arm and steered him out onto the lawn to take a look at the new White House helicopter. Prior to this, in a whispered aside to me, President Kennedy had shown his awareness of Asian customs. "I ought to have a present for him," he said. "Do you think he would like a helicopter?" I assured him I couldn't think of a better gift. It would be prestigious but useful. Sukarno badly needed a helicopter to commute the forty miles between

3. *Ibid.*, pp. 3–6.

Bogor, where he spent his weekends, and Djakarta. To have a duplicate of the American President's helicopter would warm his heart and tickle his vanity.

The two heads of state were gone perhaps fifteen minutes. When they returned, Sukarno was grinning broadly. "I showed him my new helicopter," the President told me later. "We climbed inside. The decor is well done. I asked him if he'd like one just like it. He said he would." This came under the heading of "competition with the Soviet bloc." A gift was in order, certainly. But what a gift! The President was aware, however, that Khrushchev was more than generous with the gifts he bestowed upon Sukarno. A present in this case was only meaningful if it made an impression. This one would.

I have frequently been asked what President Kennedy expected to accomplish by such a gesture. I think he had three things in mind: first, to convince Sukarno that he as President wanted to wipe the slate clean and start off on a basis of personal friendship; second, to begin the process of re-establishing in Sukarno confidence that the United States was not only not against him, but was also interested in helping his country; finally, to put Sukarno in a favorable mood against the time when the U.S. President would seek to persuade him to free Allan Pope, who was then still under a sentence of death.

The substantive talks covered a wide range of topics. The official joint communiqué noted the emergence of the new nations in Asia and Africa, "welcomed the newly found freedom of these countries and agreed that their genuine aspirations can best be fulfilled through mutual cooperation both within and without the United Nations." Sukarno managed to get in some of his language and the statement that "both presidents recognize that these new countries must be alert to any attempts to subvert their cherished freedom by means of imperialism in all its manifestations." The latter phrase represented a concession to the West and an admission that there were other kinds of imperialism besides Western.[4]

---

4. It was a journalist, not a diplomat, who first put the idea to Sukarno that there was such a thing as Soviet imperialism. Louis Fischer, in 1958, chided Sukarno about his limited view of imperialism. "If you don't take an anti-imperialist stand on Russia's colonies, Americans may think you are anti-colonial only because you want the Dutch out of West Irian and not because you are anti-colonial in principle," Fischer told him. He added, "Every time you attack only Western imperialism and capitalism, you make yourself sound like a Communist even though you are not a Communist." Fischer reminded him of the Polish and Hungarian revolutions of October 1956.

"At the Afro-Asian Bandung Conference in 1955, I was the one who proposed the words 'against colonialism in all its manifestations' in a resolution," Sukarno recalled. He promised Fischer he would use that formulation in his future comments. Although Sukarno kept his promise, it meant little in terms of either his thinking or actions.

The communiqué further recorded President Kennedy's recognition of the fact that the Indonesian Eight-Year Development Plan provided further opportunity for the two nations to get together, and also Presient Kennedy's offer to provide the services of a top-level economic team —the subsequent Humphrey Mission, led by Professor Don D. Humphrey—to consult with Indonesian counterparts about the best way for the United States to assist in achieving the goals of this plan.

We in the embassy placed little faith in the Eight-Year Plan as such, but I had been instrumental in placing the services of Bernard Bell, a well-known Washington economic consultant, at the disposal of the Prime Minister to whip some sense into the plan and focus on the priorities. The plan itself was the most monumental product I had ever seen. It made the Harvard Classics look like a minor production. The reports, which I am confident nobody, with the possible exception of its extraordinary chairman, Yamin, ever read in full, made a pillar six feet high.

The Kennedy offer of economic help was not a mere gesture. It was based upon the conviction that the chances of a politically stable government in Indonesia rested directly upon the solution of the nation's economic difficulties. There was no expectation of immediate political reward in the form, for example, of a toning down of Sukarno's ever more virulent West Irian campaign. But there was the hope, later proved forlorn, that Sukarno's great leadership capacity might be concentrated on economic development once he saw how that could benefit his people. A Communist takeover of Indonesia was more likely, it was argued, if inflation continued to force prices up, increasing public discontent. Finally, there was the expectation that American influence in Indonesia would tend to increase, with a consequent decrease in the Communist capacity to call the shots of government policy, if an American-sponsored assistance program showed tangible results. The West Irian issue, on which we were neutral, was on the back burner as far as the U.S. was concerned, although the Indonesians would soon move it up front.

The problem of disarmament was also discussed at the White House luncheon, and both Presidents agreed that the successful conclusion of the treaty ending nuclear tests, while not in itself a solution to the problem of disarmament, would be a first and most significant step.

Both Presidents strongly supported the goal of a neutral and independent Laos. This was an important diplomatic point for the United States since it identified Indonesia with a well-defined U.S. policy.

On the matter of Pope, Kennedy suggested informally that, since the new Administration was attempting to start fresh in American-Indonesian relations, it would be helpful if this continuing irritant to good relations were removed. He hoped Sukarno would be willing to release Pope. Sukarno agreed to do so, but he made it clear he must take his own time about it since Indonesian feeling still ran high on the subject.

It was typical of Indonesian tact that no mention of Cuba or the Bay of Pigs fiasco was made, although Sukarno arrived in the wake of that incident, and the Indonesians could hardly avoid drawing a parallel with the issue of foreign aid to the rebels in their own civil conflict.

But Sukarno was doomed to disappointment on the matter closest to his heart. He sought, of course, America's support in his campaign to regain West Irian, and told Kennedy what he had repeatedly told us in Djakarta—that he himself was "the best bulwark in Indonesia against Communism." The implication was clear that, as he had so often said in Djakarta, if we would help him regain West Irian, we could count on his disposing of the Communist problem in Indonesia. President Kennedy listened but made no comments.

Although Arthur M. Schlesinger, Jr., reported, "The meetings with Kennedy were no great success," [5] considerable progress was made in renewing the dialogue. The Indonesians left enthusiastic, convinced that here, at long last, was a United States President who understood them and knew what was going on in their part of the world. They viewed the meeting as having laid the groundwork for a new era in American-Indonesian relations. President Kennedy flew Sukarno to the airport in his helicopter following their second meeting. Foreign Minister Subandrio and I drove out together. This facile, articulate diplomat was as excited as I had ever seen him. "For the first time, the President of the United States and the President of Indonesia are using the same glossary!" he said, indicating that if communication of this kind continued, there was real hope for genuine understanding and cooperation between our two countries.

Kennedy also seemed to feel that working with Sukarno was not a hopeless prospect, and that there existed a possibility of steering him in useful, constructive directions that would not pose a threat to the free world.[6] He summed up his private impressions of Sukarno as "an inscrutable Asian," but expressed the hope to me that the visit had done some good. He had been particularly anxious to convince Sukarno that his Administration was taking a different view of Indonesia, and should not be blamed for the mistakes of the past. In this he succeeded, although it was certain that Sukarno's measure of any new American attitude would be the extent of its support for West Irian.

It was not difficult to detect where Kennedy's sympathies lay in any colonial issue, but the American President was in no position to make a commitment. His first question regarding a proposed policy or course of action invariably was, "What is in the national interest?" Accordingly, at a time when not irritating a stanch NATO ally, such as the Dutch, was given high priority, President Kennedy was not prepared to alter the

5. *A Thousand Days* (Boston: Houghton Mifflin Company, 1965), p. 533.
6. Cf. Roger Hilsman, *To Move a Nation* (Garden City, N.Y.: Doubleday & Company, Inc., 1967), p. 375.

long-standing policy of neutrality on the West Irian issue. At the same time, the President was genuinely interested in continuing the dialogue with Sukarno. The result was a frequent exchange of letters on important topics throughout the Kennedy Administration. These letters were useful in giving Sukarno a first hand view of President Kennedy's thinking on various situations and maintaining a cordial relationship between the two leaders, regardless of policy differences. The relationship had no major impact on the movement of events, but I am convinced it would have borne fruit had the young President's Administration not been so tragically ended.

Not much was heard on the subject of West Irian until President Sukarno's return to Indonesia July 2, following his two and a half months' world trip. His homecoming coincided with the arrival of two medium-range TU-16 bombers, delivered by the Soviets under the Arms Purchase Agreement. Sukarno emphasized the trip had resulted in highly satisfactory progress toward "regaining" West Irian. He also alleged that other countries were considerably impressed by Guided Democracy. The government's food and clothing program was already achieving good results, he insisted, although this was not borne out by First Minister Djuanda's factual review of economic conditions to Parliament. Apparently coordinated with Sukarno's statement was General Nasution's warning in Bonn that "nobody can expect we will wait for an indefinite time for the return of West New Guinea," despite their desire for a peaceful solution to the problem.

Shortly before President Kennedy took office, Foreign Minister Luns had come up with an alternative to continuing West New Guinea as a colony: convert it to a United Nations trusteeship, with the eventual goal of independence. The plan was submitted to the UN General Assembly in the autumn of 1961 but was rejected. Again, although Indonesia was able to muster enough votes to engineer this rejection, it did not have enough support to enable it to renew an initiative. Instead, Indonesia reaffirmed its 1958 decision not to submit the issue to the General Assembly again. Rejection of the Dutch plan left the Netherlands with the choice of attempting negotiations with Indonesia or facing a war in the jungles.

At about the same time, Sukarno's ear, ever to the ground, informed him that despite the reluctance of officials in the Netherlands to appear to be giving in to him, the Dutch public would not support a war and therefore negotiations were possible. But pressure would be required to bring the Dutch to the conference table.

Washington's evaluation of public opinion in Holland was somewhat similar, but the United States government saw little prospect of a change in the Dutch government's position. It was clearly recognized at the time, however, that the Netherland's decision whether or not to wage war would depend upon the attitude of its allies, particularly Australia and the United States. If we were prepared to back up Holland, the answer might be quite different than if it would have to face such a conflict alone. The Administration, while remaining unresponsive and unsympathetic to Sukarno's thunderings on the subject, nevertheless had no intention of being drawn into an armed conflict on what history would certainly declare to be the wrong side of the issue.

With the change of Administration, Dean Rusk's appointment as Secretary of State was good news to me in Djakarta. Rusk had been Assistant Secretary of State for Far Eastern Affairs when I first moved to Asia. He was familiar with the problems of this part of the world in a way that no Secretary of State before him had been. I knew him as a man of high intelligence, complete dedication, sound judgment and controlled reactions. His comment upon assuming office said a great deal about the man. Asked by a *Time* correspondent how he approached his new and difficult assignment, he replied in the words of an itinerant preacher he had known as a boy in Georgia, advice he had never forgotten, "Pray as if it were up to God; work as if it were up to you."

In our conversations at the time, Rusk pointed out that we had enough problems in Southeast Asia without adding another. But he cautioned against Sukarno's taking this position for granted. Historically, we had been against aggression and aggressors. "If Sukarno starts aggressing against his neighbors, he'll find us on the other side," Rusk warned. "We learned our lesson with Hitler. The time to stop him was at the beginning." And more than one American military leader shared Admiral Felt's view that "we've got the power to stop Sukarno. Let's stop him!"

Admiral Felt and his wife were close friends of ours, as the Stumps and the Radfords had been before them. To any ambassador in the Pacific area, close contact with the man who held the powerful position of Commander-in-Chief of the Pacific (CINCPAC), with responsibility for all army, navy, air force and marine operations in the area, was essential. The U.S. bases there—in Japan, Okinawa, the Philippines and elsewhere, and the Seventh Fleet patrolling the China Sea—these were the "guns behind the door," the force that guaranteed peace and security in the area, the shield behind which the new nations of Southeast Asia could develop without fear of aggression from the North. Most of them recognized this and considered the American presence a benevolent one. The Foreign Minister of Indonesia once told Admiral Felt and me that the time might come when his government would be forced, for domestic reasons, to attack publicly the presence of the Seventh Fleet in the area. "If we do," Subandrio said, "pay no attention to us. We won't mean it."

Every ambassador in the area knew that with CINCPAC in Honolulu, he was negotiating from strength. There was no necessity for elaborating the obvious.

Admiral Felt was a doughty bantam of a man with a relaxed, easy drawl that belied a triggerlike mind. He was a perfectionist, a man of strong convictions, and one of the hardest workers I had ever seen. Even when we would go swimming together at Keehi Beach in Honolulu, Admiral Felt invariably would cart a load of papers along, which he would peruse while lying in the sun. He insisted on knowing every detail of the vast operation for which he was responsible.

As the year 1961 progressed, it became more and more apparent that American mediation was the only alternative to war. At the end of November, during the UN General Assembly debate on the Luns plan, the United States missed its last opportunity to support United Nations action in the interest of a peaceful settlement of this dispute. To the satisfaction of the Dutch and the chagrin of the Indonesians, the United States delegation refused to support an Indian resolution calling for negotiations between the Netherlands and Indonesia under the aegis of the President of the General Assembly. Although this simple resolution paid no deference to the Dutch conditions of UN trusteeship and ultimate self-determination, it also refrained from any explicit endorsement of the Indonesian claim to sovereignty over West Irian. In short, it was a very mild resolution indeed, committing its supporters to little more than an appeal for negotiations.

The Malayan Ambassador to Indonesia, Senu, was the head of the Malayan delegation to the United Nations that year. Senu told me later he had pleaded in vain with the American delegation to vote in favor of the resolution on the ground that this was a critical moment in Indonesia's relations with the free world. The U.S. delegation had agreed to a Dutch-approved resolution that would have set up a UN commission to investigate conditions in West New Guinea and consider the possibility of organizing a plebiscite to register the wishes of the population concerning their future, as well as the desirability of bringing the territory under the UN for an interim period. But when the Netherlands resolution was defeated, our delegation had been too inflexible to accept a reasonable alternative.

The Indonesians were understandably bitter over our failure to support the Indian resolution. Hardly less critical were the Malayans, the Indians, and other Asians, who had hoped to see the UN take constructive steps toward the settlement of this dispute.

Sitting in Djakarta, watching the arena of the United Nations from a point halfway around the world, living in the midst of the pressures of a striving people, I found the action of the U.S. delegation most difficult to understand. It appeared to signal a lack of awareness on America's part of the problems facing the world, a blind preoccupation with the *status quo*, an outdated assessment of our national interest. Or perhaps it was a reflection and a sharing of the Dutch petulance with

Sukarno. Too often through the years did the distaste of many of our people for Sukarno blind them to the larger issues involved.

The Dutch could hardly be blamed at this stage for their determination not to deal with Sukarno. As they saw it, Sukarno, after all, had driven over 40,000 Dutchmen out of Indonesia and confiscated property estimated at upwards of two billion dollars in an effort to force them to turn over West Irian. They had not yielded then; they were not about to do so now. And as for the United Nations, it was none of their business. The Dutch had sovereignty over West Irian; they had not transferred that soveriegnty, and had no intention of doing so. They resisted vigorously any attempt on the UN's part to take up this question, and were successful in such resistance for more than a decade.

The U.S. interest in the situation was quite different, however, and it was difficult for me to understand how America could oppose or fail to support a peacemaking effort by the United Nations that committed us to neither side. Discussing the matter on a subsequent trip toWashington, I found no disagreement in the State Department with my own point of view. No instructions had been issued from Washington; there had not been time. The action had been taken by the U.S. delegation. It is understandable how, in the midst of a heated argument and faced with the necessity for a split-second decision as the result of a change of tactics, a position based upon faulty judgment or lack of consideration of all the factors can be taken.

Whatever the cause, it was a fateful mistake. For the UN's refusal to consider the dispute left this hot potato in Washington's lap.

CHAPTER 12

The United States as Peacemaker

From Djakarta, I strove to make Washington understand that the time had come to change our policy of passive neutrality on West Irian and take positive steps to settle the question. It seemed obvious, as military hardware continued to pour in from Russia and the bloc, that it was only a matter of time before Indonesia would be sufficiently well-equipped militarily to challenge the Dutch.

In 1961, as in the Eisenhower period, domestic pressures from all sides hindered positive action. In Congress there was considerable opposition to aid for Indonesia, and increasing hostility toward Sukarno. Senator Dodd objected to turning West Irian over to a government that, "of all the governments in the non-Communist world, risks, perhaps, the greatest chance of falling to Communism before the decade is out." And Congressman William S. Broomfield, senior Republican member of the House Foreign Affairs Committee, called Sukarno a "despot," a "Hitler," and an "international juvenile delinquent."

There was also a complete lack of sympathy for Sukarno's noisy nationalism. People knew little about Indonesia—when I was first assigned there, one of my Washington friends who should have known better asked me whether I spoke French well enough to handle that assignment!—and the impression persisted that it was just another one of the small Balkanlike countries of Southeast Asia blowing a big trumpet.

In the Department of State, the line-up continued to be between those who placed greatest stress on our European concerns and those who considered that explosive situations in Asia represented a serious threat to American security and an immediate challenge for United States policy makers. In the thoughts of the latter, situations such as Korea, Vietnam, and Laos were uppermost, and anything that tended to stir up more trouble in that part of the world was unwelcome. This created, if not sympathy for Indonesia's point of view, at least active concern for a peaceful settlement of the West Irian issue. But in the early part of 1961, the European view of passive neutrality, or "do nothing" policy, prevailed in the State Department. It was not until a major shake-up of personnel in November of that year, and Averell Harriman took over as Assistant Secretary of State for Far Eastern Affairs, that our recommendations from Djakarta began to receive a sympathetic hearing.

To Embassy Djakarta, Harriman was a tower of strength. He understood the Asian point of view. Roger Hilsman tells the story of Harriman's appearance on a TV show shortly after he had taken office. An interviewer asked him something about "that Communist, Sukarno." As Hilsman described the incident, "At his crocodile best, Harriman snorted back, 'He is not a Communist, he's a nationalist!' " [1]

When Harriman became convinced that there was a real threat to peace in the West Irian issue and that the United States was, at this juncture, the only nation with sufficient leverage to do anything about it, things began to happen. He had a major ally in changing American policy on the issue from passive to active neutrality. The Pentagon had been dealing with the Indonesian military from the time the new nation was born, and by now much understanding of Indonesian feelings and points of view had developed. Also, there were many in the Pentagon who had gone to school with the senior Indonesian commanders, almost all of whom were American trained. Indeed, most of the top army generals were graduates of Fort Leavenworth Staff and Command School. It was natural, then, that those in the Pentagon were better able both to temper their reactions to Sukarno's fulminations and have greater respect for the capability of the Indonesian armed forces than were those who lacked that closeness of contact with the Indonesians. Thus the Pentagon could be counted on to welcome a change in policy that would remove the possibility of another unwelcome conflict in Southeast Asia, particularly one that might find us arrayed against an army, navy, and air force in which we had made a substantial investment, and where we had many friends.

Sukarno understood the tactics of *Realpolitik*. He was a master at painting himself into a corner and waiting for someone to rescue him. In this situation, with the help of the Russians, he created a real threat of war. It was not a bluff.[2] As the year 1961 wore on, Soviet tanks and

---

1. Roger Hilsman, *To Move a Nation* (Garden City, N.Y.: Doubleday & Company, Inc., 1967), p. 378.
2. At one point in his Independence Day address, he tied the theme of unity to his West Irian campaign: "To weaken unity means to strengthen the enemy, to work for disunity means to work for the enemy!" And he shouted, "We are not going to waste any more words with the Dutch

planes began to pour into Indonesia. There was irony in this military build-up since the Soviets within the country were supporting the Indonesian army's principal antagonist, the PKI. The army thus began to be dependent upon a nation that it regarded as inimical to its interests. General Nasution at one point commented drily, "I can see what is going to happen. We will wind up with an American-trained, Soviet-equipped army."

On December 19, convinced that he now possessed the strength to challenge the Dutch militarily, Sukarno issued what he called his "Trikora Command"—the "People's Triple Command for the Liberation of West Irian." This decree called for total mobilization for the purpose of regaining West Irian. And shortly thereafter, an able young army officer named Suharto was appointed a major general to head the Mandala Command, a joint army-navy-marine-air force task force charged with conducting a military campaign against the Dutch-held West Irian. A build-up began as Suharto established his headquarters in Makassar. Patrol boats and air transports moved to East Indonesia. Dutch and Indonesian naval vessels clashed off the coast of West Irian on January 14, 1962; paratroopers dropped into the inhospitable jungles of New Guinea. Faced with this situation, the Dutch Cabinet modified its earlier attitude toward negotiations by indicating its willingness to hold talks on the issue without insisting that the principle of self-determination be accepted as a prior condition.

Then, in February 1962, Robert F. Kennedy came to Djakarta. He had been scheduled to make a good-will tour of Asia, and we had been urging the importance of a stop in Indonesia. We hoped that a friendly gesture, like a visit by the brother of the President, might slow Sukarno down; at least the possibilities of a peaceful settlement could be explored.

We had arranged for the Attorney General to address students at major Indonesian universities. Astute, vigorous, looking even younger than his thirty-six years, Robert Kennedy won the hearts of the students of Indonesia with his fresh, honest approach. He also hit it off well with President Sukarno and gave him a letter from President Kennedy, the burden of which was an appeal to settle the West Irian question peacefully.

At a time when "Dutch" was a naughty word in Indonesia, Kennedy courageously told the students at the University of Indonesia in Djakarta, "We have been a friend of the Dutch for a long time and we have no apology to make for it. The Dutch were among the first to come and

---

now!" Indonesia would enter negotiations only if they were "based on the transfer of West Irian to the territory under the authority of the Republic!" To this end, he said, "We are therefore *accumulating power*."

Balinese dancing girls

The *tari lenzo*. Sukarno made this difficult dance look easy

Ambassador Jones, Mme Sukarno (Hartini), President Sukarno, Mrs. Jones

The "Sunlamp Smile"

Mme Sukarno (Dewi) and Sukarno

Typical anti-American billoard murals, frequently as long as a Djakarta city block, July 1964

"Merdeka!" Ambassador Jones gives the shout "Freedom!"

Minister of Light Industries Suharto, Soviet Ambassador Michaelov, Ambassador Jones, Colonel Suharto (now President)

Foto: Puspen /

"Ipphos" copyright Indon

Lunch with Speaker of Parliament Sartono

AP

Subandrio as
Foreign Minister (left);
in military prison, 1968

Representing a favorite political stance: the Russian Ambassador, the
American Ambassador—with Sukarno in between

Mme Hatta and Vice President Hatta

General Yani, Indonesian Army chief of staff, Ethel Kennedy, Michael
Forrestal, Sukarno, Robert Kennedy, February 1964

President Suharto

Mayor of Djakarta Ali Sadikin

The Agung volcano, Karangasem, Bali

settle in our country. They founded our biggest city, New York City, then called New Amsterdam, but," he emphasized, "we also have a close friendship with the people of Indonesia. We vigorously supported Indonesia's struggle for independence during the late 1940s. We feel that our best role could be played in trying to bring the government of Indonesia and the government of Holland—two close friends of the United States —together so that they can resolve this problem peacefully. That is the policy of the United States."

Kennedy's ready wit and sense of humor helped. At one meeting, a student stood up and asked, "Do you mind if I ask you a question about the history of your own political party?"

Kennedy grinned. "Of course not," he said.

"Well," said the student, "in the elections of 1844, the slogan of your party . . ."

Kennedy saw what was coming and interrupted. "Maybe I do mind," he interjected good-naturedly, amid laughter.

"The slogan of your party in 1844," the student continued, "was, 'Fifty-four forty or fight!' How do you reconcile that with your opposition to our using force to regain territory that belongs to us?" The students loudly applauded.

This, incidentally, was an untimely illustration of the fact that most Indonesian students know more about American history than most Americans.

"That is a very unfair question," Kennedy responded amid much laughter. "First, I don't think, looking back on it, that there would be a great deal of support for the position of the Democratic platform at that time that we were justified in claiming up to 'fifty-four forty.' And I think it was realized by Thomas Benton and others, who were very vocal initially, that we really didn't have a very good position, and that it should be resolved in other ways.

"So then we went into discussions, and through peaceful negotiations we were able to resolve the matter, and to everybody's satisfaction. So we didn't have a war with the British at that time, and peaceful discussions won out, and I think it was most fortunate."

The same student brought up the Mexican War and queried, "When peaceful negotiations break down, what is the alternative?"

Kennedy, noting that some Texans might disagree, frankly replied, "I don't think that this is a very bright page in American history, the war with Mexico, and I don't think we were justified in getting involved in it." [3]

---

3. I was present at this occasion. But see also Robert F. Kennedy, *Just Friends and Brave Enemies* (New York: Harper & Row, 1962), pp. 114–115. The Attorney General's comments raised a storm in Texas, and the next day he

Another time, Bobby Kennedy was needled by a student who tried to get him to say that if Indonesia's demands were not met and it used force, the United States would side with the Dutch. Kennedy replied that he was hopeful that negotiations would not fail, but that if they did, the United States position would be determined by who was responsible for the breakdown.

The Kennedy visit was an outstanding success. And Ethel did her part. These two attractive and popular young people were literally mobbed as they traveled around Indonesia.

The Attorney General's discussions with Sukarno were frequently heated, but Sukarno liked the younger man's refreshing candor and his ready grin. We had several lengthy meetings with the President, Subandrio, Djuanda and others. Kennedy's principal objective was to get Sukarno to agree to withdraw preconditions for negotiation. These were based primarily upon the earlier argument with the Dutch, Sukarno taking the strong stand that he would not negotiate about *whether* West Irian was to be transferred to Indonesia, but *how* it was to be transferred. As Kennedy saw it, Sukarno was asking the Dutch to yield their position before the negotiations started. The Dutch were saying they would only negotiate on the basis of the principle of self-determination —the Papuans in West Irian must have the right to decide about their own future. At times, Kennedy was direct to the point of bluntness, and once the talks threatened to break off. But Sukarno seemed to enjoy the exchange, and Kennedy was successful in inducing him to agree to negotiations without preconditions if the Dutch would do the same.

Before he returned to Washington, Kennedy went to The Hague, where he found that the intransigence of Dutch leaders over West New Guinea equaled that of their opposite numbers in Indonesia.

Although Kennedy's mission did not lead to an immediate solution, it did call attention to the increasingly serious situation developing in the South Pacific. As military incidents caused by Indonesian forays into Dutch-held waters and islands increased in number, cables flew back and forth between our embassy in Djakarta and Washington, as well as The Hague, in an effort to find a formula that might promise a peaceful solution. Finally, the American effort to initiate talks bore fruit, and a proposal for secret preliminary discussions, to be held near Washington,

---

received a telegram from the White House saying, "Your remarks about Texas appear to be causing some fuss. If you are pressed on this matter, President suggests you attempt to make some humorous remarks. Good Luck. Pierre Salinger." Kennedy showed me the wire, but Indonesia is a long way from Texas and nothing came of it until his return to Washington. After meeting with the President, he told the press he had been instructed in the future to clear all his Texas speeches with the Vice-President.

was accepted by both sides.[4] It was clearly understood that these talks were not to be negotiations, but rather a means of determining whether it was possible to obtain a meeting of minds through formal negotiations later.

Both sides agreed on Ambassador Ellsworth Bunker, one of our most experienced diplomats, to act as mediator of the talks, on loan from the U.S. government to the UN for that purpose.[5] Washington had no intention of accepting the responsibility for whatever formula might emerge. In spite of earlier U.S. reluctance to support the United Nations resolutions aimed at a negotiated solution to the dispute, it was now agreed that the UN was, after all, the appropriate instrument for handling the affair. This conclusion was partly the result of some serious rethinking of the American position as Indonesian military strength built up. U Thant agreed to appoint a representative acceptable to both sides to chair the talks.

The discussions opened on March 20, 1962, at a secret site near Washington. The Netherlands was represented by its Ambassador to the United States, Dr. Jan H. van Roijen, and its delegate to the UN, C. W. A. Schurmann. Indonesia was represented by its Ambassador to the Soviet Union, Adam Malik, and Sudjarwo Tjondronegoro, Chief of the Directorate for European Affairs in the Foreign Ministry.

Ambassador Malik, who was later to succeed Subandrio as Foreign

---

4. The Netherlands government was the first to agree to the American proposal. In announcing the Dutch acceptance on March 12, 1962, Premier John deQuay made clear that the Netherlands would not send further reinforcements to West Irian for the time being, unless Indonesia continued to threaten military actions. Two days later, Foreign Minister Subandrio announced that he found the U.S. proposal acceptable, and he expressed the hope that the talks could be quickly concluded so as to begin formal negotiations for the transfer of administration. The same day, Australia's External Affairs Minister Sir Garfield Barwick welcomed the plan, supporting the Dutch on the self-determination issue, and defined Australia's major interest, after self-determination for the Papuans, as "the security of Australia by reducing the spread of Communism." He hoped that Australia would have "cooperation from Indonesia in deterring the southward thrust of Communism."

5. The selection of a man acceptable to both sides took some time. Ten names were submitted simultaneously to the Indonesian and Dutch governments. I took the list to Sukarno, who wanted to be sure that the mediator—or "Third Party," as he was called—was a man who had some understanding of the specific problems of people in new nations. He was most favorably impressed by Bunker's record. Could I guarantee, he asked me, that Ambassador Bunker, whom he had not met, had a sympathetic approach to Asian peoples and the problems arising from colonialism? I said I could. Would he understand the Indonesian position? I assured him that he could count on Bunker's being an impartial, fair-minded man who understood the forces at work in the world today.

Minister, had proved himself a diplomat of great intelligence and skill. The Dutch Ambassador in Washington, likewise an outstanding diplomat with a sympathetic personality—and not so hard bitten and uncompromising as his Foreign Minister—was an ideal choice as Malik's counterpart.

The nub of the argument emerged clearly and quickly—if the self-determination issue could be settled, the dispute could be settled. The Indonesians slyly pointed out that the Dutch interest in self-determination for the Papuans was of recent vintage. They referred not only to their own colonial status but to the fact that the mechanics for a Papuan plebiscite were not set in motion by the Dutch until 1960. But the Dutch held firm. Both delegations had rigid instructions as to their positions on self-determination, and there was no give on either side. Faced with what he considered an impasse, Ambassador Bunker called for a recess to enable the two delegations to obtain more flexible instructions.

After the recess, Indonesia's attitude, expressed earlier by President Sukarno as, "We do not want to make a compromise; we only want to discuss the procedure of the transfer of administration over West Irian to us," hardened. The Indonesians decided not to return to the conference table until the Dutch had agreed to surrender control of New Guinea's administration. Time after time, I discussed with Sukarno and the Foreign Minister various ways to break the deadlock, but to no avail. Sukarno would negotiate only the question of *how* administration would be transferred.[6]

In Djakarta, the Communists were leading the cry to settle the problem by force, and Sukarno was not far behind. On March 27, he described the implementation of the three-point people's command as a "rolling snowball," which would grow bigger and bigger. Aidit, head of

---

6. At one point Sukarno said, "There is no reason for the talks to take time. It can be done in five minutes! All the Dutch have to say is, 'We are ready to transfer administration of West Irian to Indonesia,' and then we discuss how this shall be done. That's all." The Indonesians frequently harked back to their earlier experience with the Dutch when, as they saw it, talks had been the cover for other moves designed to thwart Indonesian objectives. They suspected that the Dutch were planning to use the Bunker talks the same way—that is, keep the talks going until the Papuan nationalist movement had been built up to such a degree that the Dutch could exploit it to prevent the transfer of the territory to Indonesia.

One of my suggestions was a UN trusteeship. The Foreign Minister had not dismissed this as a possibility—if Indonesia would be the trustee. But Sukarno never went so far; his position was consistent throughout. Sovereignty, he insisted, had in fact been transferred to Indonesia in December 1949. The only remaining problem was a simple one: to work out details of administrative transfer.

the Communist Party, said that "Indonesia should only start negotiations after its troops have arrived in West Irian."

The deadlock persisted for several months. Meanwhile, Indonesian guerrillas continued to infiltrate the jungles of West Irian, and General Suharto was proceeding with plans for a major military campaign. The Dutch countered by increasing their defending units to a total of 10,000 men. There were almost daily reports of clashes, battles, and paratroop drops.

Finally, on April 2, Bunker proposed a plan whereby the territory would first be transferred to UN jurisdiction and then to Indonesia, with eventual self-determination for the Papuans. The Indonesians accepted the proposal immediately "in principle." The Dutch were not satisfied, claiming it was "vague" on the issue of self-determination. Bunker altered the wording to be more explicit, but the Dutch were still stalling when, on May 24, U Thant, Secretary-General of the UN, addressed an appeal to both sides to accept the Bunker proposal. The following day, Bunker announced revised proposals, which had been submitted simultaneously to Indonesia and the Netherlands. Finally, on May 27, the Dutch said that they were prepared to accept the Bunker proposals "as a basis for further negotiations." Three days later, U Thant requested an immediate cease-fire pending negotiations.

The Bunker proposals provided for the transfer of administrative authority over West Irian to a temporary executive authority under the Acting Secretary-General of the United Nations on a specified day. The Secretary-General would then appoint someone, mutually acceptable and non-Indonesian, to undertake the administration of the territory for a period of not less than one year, not more than two. This administrator would replace top Dutch officials with non-Indonesian and non-Dutch officials hired on a short-term-contract basis. He would also arrange for the termination of the Netherlands administration under circumstances that would give the inhabitants of the territory the opportunity to exercise freedom of choice.

At the beginning of the second year, the Acting Secretary-General would replace UN officials with Indonesian officials, it being understood that by the end of the second year, full administrative control would be transferred to Indonesia. Indonesia in turn would agree to make arrangements to provide the people of the territory with the opportunity of exercising freedom of choice "not later than (unspecified) years after Indonesia had assumed full administrative responsibility for West New Guinea." The Government of the Netherlands would receive adequate guarantees for safeguarding the interests of the Papuans, including the right of self-determination. Finally, Indonesia and the Netherlands would agree to share the costs involved.

The plan was an ingenious one, skillfully designed to meet the difficult and delicate political problems in both The Hague and Djakarta. But weeks passed before meetings were resumed. Although both parties were willing to accept the Bunker plan as a basis for negotiations, neither was willing to come to the table until certain of the other's position on the major issues.

Suspicion on both sides led to some odd quibbling over words. Thus Indonesia accepted the Bunker proposal "in principle," while the Dutch announced that they accepted it "as a basis for further negotiations with Indonesia." At the UN, correspondents pressed the late Ambassador Adlai Stevenson as to the significance of the difference. Stevenson's answer, suave and politic, illustrated the problem of getting the two parties together when every word had to be examined and re-examined by both sides.

"I cannot answer the question," Stevenson said. "I am not sure what is in the minds of the Dutch any more than what is in the minds of the Indonesians. I assume . . . that in both cases they meant they were accepting the proposals, at least in principle, as the basis for the commencement of negotiations. And such an answer," Stevenson added with a smile, "having included both words, I think, is consistent with the diplomatic practice!"

While the diplomats were talking, the soldiers were shooting. Dutch troops and Indonesian paratroopers clashed again and again in the jungles of West New Guinea. On June 24, a new landing was made in West Irian near Merauke, only about forty miles from the border of the Australian territory of Papua, by between 150 and 200 paratroopers. Merauke, made famous by Sukarno's constant reference to Indonesia as extending from "Sabang to Merauke," included about 500 Dutch and 2,500 Indonesian families, in addition to a small native Papuan population.

In Djakarta, we knew that in spite of the moves toward the conference table, the Indonesians were continuing their preparations for a major military assault on West Irian. I became convinced that war was just around the corner, for we in the embassy knew what was happening as a result of an operation that was then top secret—direct observation by U-2 planes, a fact later publicly revealed by Sukarno. The Indonesians had the troops and the equipment, and public opinion had been whipped up to the high-tension level.

As everyone who has had anything to do with military operations knows, once the order has been given to move, particularly in an area and with a force lacking adequate communications, it is difficult if not impossible to stop. Sukarno's figure of a snowball rolling downhill might have been trite, but it was accurate. There were influential elements in Indonesia that wanted war; certainly, the Communists did. And they were backed by Soviet Russia and China, both interested in fishing in the troubled waters of the Java Sea. The race between a peaceful solution and a military one was about to wind up in a photo finish.

Agreement was finally reached through diplomatic channels for a preliminary meeting between representatives of both countries to clarify their respective positions before negotiations were resumed. On July 12, Malik and van Roijen met in Washington. The exploratory talks went well. Malik made clear to van Roijen that Indonesia was willing to accept the principle of self-determination, provided the Dutch agreed to transfer administration to Indonesia. The Dutch accepted the terms. Details remained to be worked out, but intentions on both sides were sufficiently spelled out that Sukarno authorized Subandrio to fly to Washington with full power to negotiate a final accord.

The difficulties were not over, however. Conflict developed over the period of time of the proposed UN stewardship over the territory. The Indonesians were demanding that the UN stewardship be largely symbolic and the transfer of authority to Indonesia be completed by the following January. The Dutch refused to agree to this modification of the Bunker proposal and Subandrio threatened to go home. Involved here was more than met the eye, for Subandrio was under compulsion to honor Sukarno's pledge to recover West Irian before the cock crowed on January 1, 1963.

It was a critical moment. Bunker knew that if Subandrio carried out his threat, all the months of hard work would have gone for nought. He communicated with U Thant and with the White House, with the result that both President Kennedy and U Thant had private talks with Subandrio. President Kennedy minced no words in this conversation. In effect, he told the Indonesian Foreign Minister that the United States was "through" with Indonesia unless Subandrio was prepared to be reasonable. Subandrio told me later, making a gesture of wiping his brow, "Whew! Your President certainly laid down the law."

U Thant apparently also made clear that the onus of the breakdown in negotiations would be laid at Indonesia's door and that under no circumstances would he agree to a UN stewardship that was not a genuine one. He told Subandrio that an effective stewardship could not possibly be carried out by January 1. Subandrio changed his mind, remained at the conference table, and a compromise was worked out under which the transfer of authority would take place in about ten months.

After all the time and effort, one seemingly minor detail caused a last-minute flurry that threatened to upset the entire program. The question arose as to what flags should fly over the territory and when. The first proposal was that the Dutch flag should be flown alongside the UN flag until Indonesia took over administration of the territory the following May. This was unacceptable to the Indonesians. As they saw it, their sovereignty must be recognized from the moment the UN took over from the Dutch. The Netherlands would have none of this. They felt they had yielded all they could to the Indonesians. So long as one Dutch official remained, the Dutch flag must fly.

The argument became more and more heated, and Ambassador Bunker again stepped into the breach. He proposed that the UN flag would fly alongside the Dutch flag from October 1 through December 31, 1962. Then, on January 1, 1963—consistent with Sukarno's boast— the Indonesian flag would replace the Dutch flag. Finally, on May 1, the UN flag would come down, leaving Indonesia's Red and White.

On August 15, the long-awaited announcement came: the Indonesian and Dutch negotiators had reached agreement on a formula that would give Indonesia administrative control over Netherlands New Guinea on May 1, 1963. Thus the dispute that had represented a major conflict between Indonesia and the West for a decade was finally settled.

Under the provisions of the agreement, Indonesia promised to conduct, no later than 1969, a plebiscite under UN supervision to let the 700,000 Papuan inhabitants of the colony choose between annexation to Indonesia and independence. The formula met the main objectives of both sides. The Indonesians naturally desired control over the region for a sufficient number of years to build up a following and make their case for Indonesian sovereignty. The Dutch wanted to avoid yielding the territory directly to Indonesia, and made good their promise of self-determination for the largely primitive Papuan population.

The solution represented a major victory for American diplomacy. This did not mean, however, that everybody was happy. President Kennedy's comment of April 12 had proved accurate: that the role of a mediator is not a happy one, but that the U.S. government was prepared "to make everybody mad" if progress could be made toward a solution.

The Dutch felt that they had been bullied by the United States into accepting an agreement on Indonesian terms. In Indonesia, satisfaction that the matter had been settled was mingled with disappointment that the United States had not openly sided against the Dutch. The general reaction was that justice had at long last been done. There was no wild hilarity; instead, the Indonesians took it quietly and with a feeling of relief that hostilities had not gone farther. In announcing the agreement, Sukarno stated soberly, that with the completion of the revolution, Indonesia's territorial aspirations had been fulfilled.

There was widespread hope in Djakarta that the settlement would leave the Indonesian government free to concentrate on finding solutions to the nation's economic difficulties. Sukarno himself publicly promised as much on August 17, 1962. "With the finalizing of the security question, and with the finalizing of the West Irian question, our assets for solving the economic question will greatly increase," he told his people. In a speech that at times was almost plaintive, he said, "I can follow the sufferings here . . . and bow my head before those sufferings, saying 'Go ahead, please go ahead, be angry with me; go ahead, point your finger at me; go ahead, put your wrath upon me—and I will accept it all calmly. . . . It is indeed true that I gave priority to the settlement of the problems of security and of West Irian, although I realized that for them nearly three-quarters of the national activity would have to be spent.

"Was that policy of mine right? . . . History will bring a final judgment. . . . Is there any Indonesian who sees our successes in the political field . . . who does not feel proud that he is an Indonesian?"

But the President showed sensitivity to the economic difficulties and assured his people that he felt "able, God willing, to overcome the bottlenecks and the difficulties of economic problems in a short time."

These words of Sukarno's were encouraging, not only to the Indonesians but to the policy makers in Washington. Sukarno's words were taken as an indication that the Indonesian President was now ready to face up to the economic difficulties that plagued his country. I was authorized to indicate to the Indonesian government that we were ready and willing to follow up our earlier initiative in the economic field when the Humphrey Mission had been sent out. Hopes were high in Washington and the American Embassy Djakarta that our efforts to achieve a peaceful settlement in the West Irian dispute, which had in fact resulted in the territory being "restored" to Indonesia, would bear fruit in terms of more friendly relations between Indonesia and America, and economic assistance from the U.S. and the other nations of the free world. We had made progress on at least two counts: a war that might have involved the U.S. had been averted, and the process of Indonesia's drift away from the West had been slowed perceptibly. We had likewise won the opportunity to continue reinforcing our ties with the non-Communist Indonesian military and other elements that presumably would one day be in a position of greater national power and influence. The next months would be encouraging ones in the seesaw of our relations with Indonesia.

As I think back, however, there was one little flicker of doubt that persisted in the back of my mind. In his West Irian campaign, Sukarno had made much of the point that recovery of this territory was necessary to complete the Indonesian revolution. Our communications between Djakarta and Washington being so much faster than the Indonesian, I was the first to bear Sukarno the news that the documents had been signed. I received a telegram at 6:30 in the morning. Shortly thereafter, I took it to Sukarno, with whom I had a date for coffee. "Mr. President," I announced to Sukarno and the group of Cabinet members gathered on his veranda, "your revolution is complete. The transfer documents have just been signed in New York."

I had anticipated an enthusiastic, even exuberant reaction. Not so. Sukarno nodded thoughtfully, spoke quietly to those who were with him. It was not an exultant moment. I had an odd feeling, as though I were witnessing a scene in which a beloved member of the family were leaving home. Sukarno would miss West Irian, I thought. He had won a victory, but he had lost an issue.

The final chapter in the West Irian dispute was written in the United Nations Assembly on November 19, 1969, when the joint draft resolution from Indonesia and the Netherlands was adopted by a vote of eighty-four in favor, none against, with thirty abstentions.[7]

The large number of abstentions raised some eyebrows. They were mostly African countries who, while appearing to be generally in favor of Indonesian acquisition of the territory, objected to the fact that the principle of one man, one vote was not a factor in the "act of free choice" by which that acquisition was made. Instead, the Indonesian government had decided to place the choice in the hands of eight consultative assemblies, whose members were elected by *mushawarah*. This meant that the tribal chiefs and other community leaders in the territory, where the vast majority was illiterate, determined the representation. Predictably, as the Secretary-General reported, the answer of the consultative assemblies was unanimous: West Irian should remain with Indonesia.

Acknowledging the problems his country faced in connection with the act of free choice, Indonesian Foreign Minister Malik pointed out that it is easy "to criticize the implementation of a complex and even controversial political exercise—and that was indeed the case of the arrangements for the holding of the act of free choice, especially when one tries to measure the so-called international standards, which usually means the application of Western standards to conditions and situations in Asia, which those standards do not necessarily fit. And particularly for West Irian, known to be one of the most undeveloped areas in the world, one should have specific consideration for specific circumstances." And, Malik went on, "the Indonesia-Netherlands agreement of 1962 cannot be separated from the Indonesian struggle for the freedom and independence of the whole of Indonesia, the former 'Netherlands East Indies' of which West Irian was an integral part." It was therefore true that implementation of the agreement was not really the honoring of an international agreement with the Netherlands but "the end of a long road, the end of a long, difficult and thorny struggle for the freedom, unity and independence of a nation, the Indonesian nation." [8]

Mr. Fernando Ortiz-Sanz, representing the Secretary-General, agreed with Malik, and in the conclusion of his report said that "on the basis of the facts . . . and the documents referred to, it can be stated that, with

7. UN document A/PV 1813, 19 November 1969, pp. 102–105.
8. UN General Assembly document A/PV 1810, 13 November 1969, p. 3.

the limitation imposed by the geographical characteristics of the territory and the general political situation in the area, an act of free choice has taken place in West Irian in accordance with Indonesian practice, in which the representatives of the population have expressed their wish to remain with Indonesia." [9]

9. UN General Assembly document A/7723, 6 November 1969, p. 70, paragraph 253.

All Play and No Work

I regarded it as an unparalleled opportunity when, in November 1958, Sukarno invited me, among other members of the diplomatic corps in Djakarta, to accompany him on a two-week trip through the famed Molucca Islands in the eastern part of Indonesia. It was a rare chance to see some of the most fascinating country in the world, a region well off the beaten track, seldom visited by Americans. I accepted with alacrity.

Especially important to an American Ambassador would be the opportunity to see Sukarno in action at close range; to observe how Indonesians who had never met the President would react to their chief; to discover what Sukarno thought about his people and his job; to learn something of how he had been able to maintain his unchallenged leadership over the young Republic.

It was one of Djakarta's best days—blue skies softened by a few lazily floating clouds—when we took off from Kemajoran airport for the first leg of our journey. We would travel by plane 800 miles east to Makassar, thence again by plane to Ambon, another 800 miles east. Beyond Ambon, there were no more airports, only occasional small grassy strips; we would go by ship.

We were flying plush—the President, three Cabinet members and a dozen diplomats—on the President's private plane.

On our way to Makassar, we crossed the famous Wallace's line, which marks the sudden change in sea depth. Java, Bali, Sumatra and Borneo, as well as the thousands of smaller islands between them and the Asian mainland, apparently rest on a great submerged bank, seldom deeper than fifty fathoms, or 300 feet, and apparently an extension of the continent. East of this line some of the great sea deeps reach a measured depth of more than 3,500 fathoms, or 21,000 feet—nearly forty miles. Seen from a plane, the water turns a dark blue, in contrast to the light greens and sky blues of the seas nearer the Asiatic mainland. This famous line also marks the division between two great regions of the world, the Asian and the Australian, with distinctive characteristics in plant and animal life and, to a lesser extent, human.

Most of the conversation aboard the aircraft was pure banter, for the President, anticipating the trip, was in high and infectious good humor. Occasionally, the talk took a more serious turn, as when Ambassador Fuentebella, the seventy-four-year-old Philippine envoy to Indonesia, re-lated an interesting episode from his own history. For most of his life, he said, he had been regarded as the Number One anti-American in the Philippine Islands, and for forty years he had refused to learn English so as not to speak the language of hated occupiers. He did not believe the American promise that the Philippines would be given its freedom as soon as it was ready for self-government. The moment that a definite date was fixed for independence, he realized how wrong he had been, and that America, unlike many other nations, did mean what it said. Indonesia had nothing to fear from America, he emphasized. The President nodded and seemed impressed by these statements.

At Hasanuddin airport, Makassar, we were greeted by the first of a series of colorful welcoming ceremonies. After a twenty-one-gun salute for the President, we were received by a delegation of Sulawesi college girls, from the University of Hasanuddin, in billowing, bright red cos-tumes—in South Sulawesi the unmarried women wear bright red, the married women wear pink. In addition to the usual army, navy and air force troops drawn up for review, there was a military band in traditional Makassar blue tunics, white trousers, and blue and white hats with white plumes, somewhat reminiscent of the dress uniform of West Point cadets.

The road from the airport to Makassar, twenty-two kilometers, was lined with many thousands of cheering, flag-waving children. I traveled in a car with the Japanese and Canadian Ambassadors, and there was a small sign on the windshield indicating our nationalities. Shouts of "America!" "Canada!" and "Japan!" greeted us as we passed.

Then, as we were entering a section of the highway bordered by deep jungle, I heard the cough of a mortar three times in quick succession, followed by machine-gun fire. Our column screeched to a stop. A truck full of soldiers tore past us, machine guns at the ready. In a few moments the convoy started again. Later we found out that our column had actu-ally been under fire, but the President's guard had attacked and dis-persed a few Darul Islam rebels discovered in the jungle. Another at-tempt on Sukarno's life had failed. The Indonesian Army was taking no chances with its precious cargo of President and diplomatic corps.

We went to the Governor's Palace after high tea to hear Sukarno speak to the faculty and 3,000 students of the university. Although he spoke for three hours extemporaneously, the President held the audience enthralled, punctuating his talk with humor and drama. I decided that he was the best speaker I had ever heard—not excluding William Jennings Bryan, to whom I had listened several times as a schoolboy. A master of change of pace and contrast, Sukarno had a sense of drama that kept his audience in the hollow of his hand.

I understood enough Indonesian to know that the President was saying that Indonesia would find its own way. He quoted Thomas Jefferson, Abraham Lincoln, and the Declaration of Independence on one side, and Karl Marx on the other, acknowledging that the two philosophies, democracy and Communism, were the dominant schools of thought and action in the world today. But, he emphasized, Indonesia would not follow either one; instead it would take from each and create something purely representative of Indonesia's own identity.

The President introduced the Ambassadors individually to the audience. It was gratifying to note that the American Ambassador received enthusiastic applause; in this relatively remote area, America was apparently known and appreciated. When the President called on the Communist Chinese Ambassador, he was not present, obviously out conferring with some of his constituents in the large Chinese community in Makassar. Someone must have got word to him, because he arrived shortly, puffing and perspiring, and took his seat.

Although it was after midnight when we retired, we were up at dawn to tour the city of Makassar before leaving. It was much more attractive than I had anticipated, particularly in the residential sections. In the harbor, the early sun's rays slanted against the huge sails of half a dozen of the big Makassar *prahus* and a hundred smaller fishing and trading boats. These large sailing vessels, several hundred tons in size, with their awkward-looking square sails, still ply, as they have presumably for thousands of years, between the islands of the archipelago, carrying freight hundreds of miles to Djakarta, Surabaya, the island of Bali, even to Australia. I saw only one steamship at the docks—a Polish freighter awaiting cargo.

Arrival at Ambon was comparable to the welcome given visiting dignitaries in the early days of Hawaii or Tahiti. As we walked from the plane on a fresh green mat made of palm fronds, a hundred or more singing, dancing women, dressed in the pink-red Ambonese costume, advanced toward us bearing a long piece of white sheeting about three feet wide and perhaps 200 feet long. Dancing to the music of flutes and drums, they surrounded our visiting group led by a smiling Sukarno and corralled us within the fence of white sheeting. Thus, singing and swaying to the rhythm, the women convoyed us to the airport waiting room. This was the traditional welcome of Ambon, symbolically throwing a cordon of love and protection around the honored guest.

On the terrace of the waiting room we were served refreshments, while approximately 1,000 women danced and sang a welcome to the ever-present rhythmic beat of native drums. And the combinations of color—which would cause shudders on Fifth Avenue—were beautiful in the brilliant sunlight. Various shades of pink, coral, rose and red were worn together, and each woman carried one large white and one large red flower by their long green stems, waving them at us in the slow, graceful rhythm of the dance.

A fifteen-minute ride by jeep brought us to the famous Bay of Ambon —one of the great natural harbors of the world. During World War II it was suspected that the German raider *Graf Spee* was hidden in this magnificent harbor. Cupped in a giant horseshoe by two peninsulas, Hito and Litomor, which rise like green-helmeted bastions from the sea, the bay at its entrance is about five miles in width and continues within the horseshoe for ten miles, at which point the land contracts to form a narrow passage leading to an inner harbor three miles long and slightly over a mile wide. Lush green hills and mountains rise precipitately from the water's edge. The sea is calm and the water so clear that the colorful coral and marine life can be seen f   he surface.

A small ferryboat was waiting   t the dock that served the airport. This we boarded for the   rip across the bay to the city of Ambon, residence of the Go   f the Molucca Islands and headquarters of the commander of t..   ilitary forces of the area. The captain of our little boat informed me that the water of the bay reached a depth of more than 1,800 feet. Once on board, we could see that the water was alive with canoes and *prahus* decorated with palm fronds and flags. Paddles flashed in the sun as the Ambonese drove their swift, slim craft past our chugging, Diesel-driven boat. These *prahus*, with their colorful, carved bows and sterns, were something out of a past era—one boat had twenty-eight paddlers naked to the waist, and drummers sitting in the center beating out the rhythm to which the paddlers responded. With the hypnotic beat of the drums, one was transported back in time. As the first Portuguese sea captain might have been escorted down the bay in 1513, so were we.

At the Ambon dock, hundreds more women greeted us, again with song and dance. Sukarno received the welcome of a movie star. The enthusiastic throngs pressed against our car so hard that I thought it would be overturned. Nothing could stem the crowd—the police and soldiers were helpless as it surged forward, shouting "*Merdeka! Merdeka! Merdeka!*" But the people were happy and the atmosphere was a holiday one, so that we felt no real alarm.

Young high-school girls had been assigned to each car as guides. The attractive Moslem girl who had been assigned to ours said to me (within hearing of the Chinese Communist Ambassador), "We hate Communists here. No one wants anything to do with Communism!" This young lady of seventeen wore a tight-fitting black and white lace *kabaya* with a bright red scarf tossed over her shoulder and a Jogjakarta *kain* of brown and white. In Ambon, the type of dress indicates a particular religion rather than matrimonial status; the Christian girls wear a loose smock that does not accentuate the figure. Our attractive guide sang songs to entertain us as we rode along.

That evening we had our first taste of the kind of dancing for which the Moluccan Islands are famous. Several hundred people participated —in Ambon, we discovered, one does not refuse to dance or sing. If you don't know how, you learn fast! When two attractive young ladies present themselves before you, bow politely and ask you to join them, it is impossible to refuse. But if you should be such a cad as to do so, you will find the next instant that one young lady has you by one arm and the other young lady has your other arm, and willy-nilly, you are catapulted onto the dance floor. From then on, it is a case of survive or perish. The first hour or so, your hosts launch into nothing more complicated than a kind of scarf dance—one that any tyro can stumble through without feeling he is being too ridiculous. As a matter of fact, self-consciousness goes with the wind in this part of the world. Everyone has such a good time letting the music move them from within that, in spite of yourself, you actually begin to enjoy it!

Dripping with perspiration and utterly exhausted, I looked with longing toward a seat on the sidelines. But the dancing became even more strenuous. At the call of "*yuri, yuri*," everyone on the floor squatted on his haunches and carried on the rhythm there, with the weight first on one foot and then on the other, in turn moving from side to side and balancing. A slight added complication was that this had to be done with each dancer holding a scarf entwined with the scarves of perhaps a dozen others.

It was a picture for posterity—the President of Indonesia leading the pack like the leader of a grand right and left, the entire diplomatic corps strewn about on the dance floor, middle-age spreads and all, paunches popping, gasping for breath, soaked in perspiration, knees aching as if they would break off any minute.

"Is this what you thought you were in for when you became a diplomat?" one young newspaperman asked me from his haunch position. "If you don't think I'm serving my country, I'd like to know what I'm doing," I replied.

The truth is, of course, that everyone was enjoying himself hugely. By this time, knees were numb; legs were no longer attached to the body but moved by mechanical levers. When we could stand no more, a change of rhythm was heard. The dance was at long last coming to an intermission. Right? Wrong. Simply another variation. And so it went on and on for hours, this *tari lenzo*, until I was so exhausted I seemed to have left my body somewhere else and was floating in mid-air.

This first dance came to an end sometime between midnight and one o'clock, and what was left of the diplomatic corps staggered across the garden of the Governor's Palace and into bed. But not for long. We were roused at 4:00 A.M., after less than three hours sleep on a hot night under mosquito nets. I shared a room with Ambassador Amroussi of the United Arab Republic and Philippine Ambassador Fuentebella. Somehow we managed to get our feet on the floor, assume an upright position, take a splash bath and join President Sukarno at a predawn breakfast. Through half-closed eyes we could see a bright-eyed Sukarno enjoying himself thoroughly, the perfect host, cajoling his guests, a friendly word for each, fresh as a daisy.

At 5:30 A.M., we boarded the small 1,500-ton inter-island passenger vessel that would take us eastward. I shared a small cabin with the Japanese and Canadian Ambassadors. It was too hot to stay in our cabins, so despite our lack of sleep, we spent the day on deck, visiting, playing cards, and otherwise relaxing.

A few of us played twenty-one all morning with the President, who thoroughly enjoyed the game. He was a reckless player and at first won substantially, but later wound up only slightly ahead. I was lucky, became banker, and like all bankers accumulated a sizable fortune! "Now I see how you capitalists do it," Sukarno quipped. But we were playing only for matchsticks.

In the afternoon, we arrived in the harbor of Saumlaki on the island of Jamjesan in the Tanimbar Islands of the Banda Sea—romantic names to savor with the tongue. Again, about fifty *prahus* decorated with flags and palm fronds greeted us, accompanied by the thunder of drums. We boarded a white-canopied platform that had been built crosswise on two *prahus*. This was part of the traditional welcome—a visitor must be paddled into shore. Also traditionally, women must greet and accompany the distinguished guest. Thus, alongside our vessel, there was a large *prahu* with only women as the paddlers. The villagers had done everything they could with their limited means. We sat on comfortable armchairs; handwoven carpets had been placed on the floor of the craft.

This was the noisiest reception we had during the trip. The pier down which we walked was approximately half a mile long, and shouts and chants of "*Merdeka!*" from youths lined up on both sides of us clapped across the water. The furious beating of drums and the singing of a dozen groups of dancing women from different villages (all singing different tunes!) added to the clamor. Halfway down the pier, the President pointed out signs on the subject of West New Guinea and said to me, "Look! Have you seen? These people want us to invade Irian Barat [West New Guinea]!"

Since this was the first of the eastern islands I had visited, I was anxious to find out whether these people, isolated as they were, thought of themselves as Indonesians, Moluccans, Tanimbarites, or what. I had frequently heard it said that the people of the Moluccas wanted their own republic and were against Sukarno. The answer could hardly be supplied by the response of crowds to a magnetic person and experienced orator like President Sukarno—although to the skeptical comment of one newspaperman that these mass rallies were staged, Sukarno quietly re sponded, "You can prearrange a crowd but you cannot prearrange a smile."

I talked with many people. There was no variance in the response. They said they were proud of being Moluccans, but they were prouder of being Indonesians, of belonging to a great new nation. It was admitted that there were some dissidents in the Moluccas, but they were referred to as a small minority.

I was reminded of a young engineer I had met in Sumatra. Was he, I asked him, a Sumatran, a North Sumatran, a Batak? I deliberately avoided mentioning Indonesia. He looked at me and gave me a Yankee answer.

"How do you think of yourself, Mr. Ambassador? Where were you born?"

I replied I was born in Chicago, Illinois.

"Well, do you think of yourself as a Chicagoan, an Illinoisan, a Caucasian, or an American? I'm sure you think of yourself as an American! Just so, I'm an Indonesian!"

The population of the Tanimbar Islands is somewhere between 30,000 and 50,000. People came by the thousands, and there were many children among them. The President led the children in singing Indonesian songs, and then he launched into his speech.

Except when he delivered a major policy address, such as his annual Independence Day speech on August 17, Sukarno spoke extemporaneously. Thus, though every speech was different, the design of each was such that it accomplished an identification of the speaker with his audience, lifted up the people and gave them pride and hope. His oratory had the effect of making the millions who heard him feel important, for as they listened to him, they could share in the goals of the Indonesian revolution, become part of something big, something significant, outside of but including themselves.

Sukarno could stir a crowd, but without the screaming fanaticism of a Hitler, the boisterous boasting of a Mussolini, or even the passionate preaching of a Patrick Henry. He was warm, magnetic, personal; a teller of stories, but stories with a punch line. A literal translation of Sukarno's speeches fails completely to give the effect of the man; but freely rendered, this was the sort of thing with which Sukarno charmed his people.

"What was Indonesia in 1945?" he would ask. "What was our nation then?" A pause. Then, softly, "It was only two things, only two things. A flag and a song. That is all." Perhaps a brief reminiscence at this point. And then a sudden dramatic pause, a cock of the head, a precautionary finger held up to indicate an afterthought. "But no," Sukarno would continue, chiding himself, "I have omitted the main ingredient. I have missed the most important thing of all. I have left out the burning fire of freedom and independence in the breast and heart of every Indonesian. This is the most important thing—this is the vital chord—the spirit of our people, the spirit and determination to be free. This was our nation in 1945—the spirit of our people!"

"And what are we today?" Sukarno would lead skillfully up to this question. "We are a great nation," he would reply to his own question. And at this point he might turn to the diplomatic corps behind him on the stage and say, "We are bigger than Poland. We are bigger than Turkey. We have more people than Australia, than Canada, we are bigger in area and have more people than Japan. In population we are now the fifth largest country in the world. In area, we are even bigger than the United States of America!" He might then turn to me and say: "The American Ambassador, who is here with us, admits this. Of course, he points out that we have a lot of water in between our thousands of islands. But I say to him—America has a lot of mountains and deserts, too!" The crowd would laugh appreciatively.

At some point in his speech, the President would become suddenly grave: "And when I die . . . and we all must die sometime. You and you and you," pointing to various people in the audience. "You must die sometime. And I must die. When I die—don't write upon my tombstone, 'Doctor, Engineer Sukarno, first President of the Republic of Indonesia,'" his voice heavy with sarcasm. "Don't write all the titles and honors, my people. Only this—'Here lies Sukarno, the voice of the Indonesian people.' That's all. Nothing else. For this is Sukarno. I am your mouthpiece. I am nothing without you. Without you, I would be the man next door. But when I speak, I say what is in your hearts. I speak for you. I say what you want said."

This had the effect of magic on his listeners, perhaps because he was saying what they wanted to hear, or hearing it made them think so. Some said this was nothing but superb demagoguery. The fact remains that Sukarno was regarded by masses of his countrymen as the authentic voice of his people. Anyone who watched his audiences, who talked with Indonesians about him, who heard him called " 'Bung' Karno" by *betjak* (pedi-cab) boys and Cabinet ministers alike, and "Papa President" by the less forward, learned this. The people, in those days the majority of them, believed him and believed in him. This had its tragic side. Few placed the blame for unsolved problems at the President's door. He was still the revolutionary, leading his people to victory. The problems, to him and to them, simply were signs that the revolution was not yet complete.

As part of building national pride in the hearts of his audiences, Sukarno would refer to the fact that every important nation in the world now recognized Indonesia. He would then present each Ambassador to the audience. Standard operating procedure, as it developed through the years, was for each Ambassador to stand up, wave at the crowd, and good-naturedly shout *"Merdeka!,"* the Indonesian equivalent of "Liberty!" [1]

One hot afternoon, as our ship was steaming through beautiful blue seas, the President suggested that those of us who had been clamoring for a swim could be satisfied since we were about an hour ahead of schedule. We were within sight of the island of Ceram when the President spotted a beautiful sandy beach against a background of coconut palms. He ordered the ship to go as close into shore as possible, but we were still about a mile off the coast when the grind of the anchor chain was heard and the ship slid to a stop.

Colonel Pieters, then Military Commander for the Moluccas, hoisted his small shell of a speedboat into the water and took off to explore the area, followed by a dinghy load of soldiers. Then half a dozen Ambassadors in swimming trunks clambered into a life raft—probably for the first time in history—and with the help of an outboard motor, started chugging toward shore. The water was so clear that one could see the coral formations at the bottom, though they were at least thirty feet down. A couple of hundred yards from shore, one of the prop blades struck a protruding piece of coral and was so badly bent it could not be used. So we divided up the paddles for the rest of the way to shore.

News of the ship's arrival had apparently spread through the jungle, and the inhabitants of a nearby village at the top of the bluff were thronging to the beach. Sukarno had a pat on the shoulder for one, a cheery word for another, and within five minutes was leading a few hundred villagers in one of the native dances. By the time half an hour had passed and we had all had a swim, everyone was calling him "Papa President" and laughing and talking as though they had known him intimately for years, an extraordinary example of the personal warmth and magnetism of the man.

---

1. On one particular occasion, Sukarno's subject was the regaining of West Irian. Following the Soviet Ambassador and several others (I had not yet the seniority I later attained as Dean of the Diplomatic Corps, in which event I would have been called upon first), I greeted the crowd with a wave of my hand and a shout of *"Merdeka!"* The Dutch government protested the action as being unneutral. The Dutch press picked up the story and sarcastically queried whether Jones "Heiled Hitler" when he was in Germany. *Time* magazine checked its files, retorted the answer was no. Reason: I had been involved in an international incident in 1934 with Professor Albert Lepawski, then of the University of Chicago, now at the University of California at Berkeley. He and I were attacked by Nazi brown shirts (*Sturm Abteilung*) on the streets of Berlin for refusing to salute the Nazi flag. My government did not take the Dutch protest seriously (Could an American ever be penalized for endorsing liberty?), but the news was, of course, published in Djakarta, where it was greeted with much hilarity. The Indonesians promptly dubbed me "Merdeka Jones." Needless to say, my status in Indonesia did not suffer thereby.

My visit to the Moluccas was but one of many memorable trips I took with the President to the Outer Islands. One, to Atjeh, was especially memorable. Except for the electric lights, the numerous black *pitjies* (cap of overseas type, made of velvet), and the Western dress of some members of the audience, including the jaunty, beribboned, uniformed President Sukarno, the scene might have been enacted more than a thousand years ago, when the great Sriwidjaya Empire of Sumatra had splashed like a tidal wave over the Asian mainland, its outer reaches lapping at the southern borders of China. The ceremonial dancers, weaving in graceful dignity to the rhythm of gentle, plaintive music toward the guest of honor, wore the court dress of the earlier period; they were sartorial poems in green and gold and red silks, with glittering headdresses that dropped golden ornaments over their soft, smooth, amber brows and enchanting, dark liquid eyes.

This was the ancient siri ceremony, in which the honored guest, weary and travel-stained, is welcomed by the most beautiful girls of the court and offered, in silver bowls and ornamental goblets, the refreshing greenleaved siri which revives the spirit, makes the blood flow faster, destroys all sense of fatigue, and imparts to the recipient a dreamy, peaceful sense of well-being and comfort that banishes all memory of the trials of the trail. I have tried it and can testify to the results. The taste is somewhat acrid, a strange but not unpleasant flavor, refreshing and slightly astringent, so that the teeth and gums feel thoroughly brushed and cleansed from the chewing of the leaves. There is a slight shock to the taste buds at first, which is hard to describe but may be likened to the first taste of oysters, a slight metallic flavor, something odd and different, neither food nor drink, not quite welcome in the mouth but with an aftereffect wholly pleasing.

There followed on the stage the famous dances of the region, quite different from the slow, graceful *srimpi* of Java, or the sensuous movements of Bali, or the romantic and hypnotic rhythms of the Moluccas; different, too, from the merry, swinging *serampang duabelas* of Atjeh's Sumatran Batak neighbors to the south. At one point, the beautiful Javanese wife of the commissioner of police, who was sitting next to me, leaned over and asked in a whisper which one of the twelve dancers, all girls aged from twelve to fourteen, I thought was the best. I considered the dancers a moment and then replied, "The second from the left."

"You are right," she said. "She is not the most beautiful girl, but she is the best dancer. You can see she has given herself wholly to the dance. Her heart is in it. She has lost herself in the dance. This is the secret of great dancing."

"Or the secret of greatness in anything," I thought to myself. A few moments later we were treated to an Oriental example of this raised to the nth degree, a demonstration of mystic power, which the Western world, not understanding, refuses to accept and instinctively shrugs off as hocus-pocus.

The weird, pulsating whine of Atjehnese flutes and stringed instruments suffused the night. A young man glided onto the stage, a muscular figure in orange silk. Clasping a dagger, he plunged the point into his bare arm and into his naked thigh. These were no light jabs, but powerful, savage thrusts, which he repeated again and again and again, in mounting tempo and ferocity, as though his thigh and forearm were enemies he must slash and totally destroy. Once, the dagger bent with the force of a blow. I examined it afterward. It was made of strong metal. Exerting all my force, I could not straighten it again. My friend Apa Pant, the distinguished Indian Ambassador to Indonesia, kept the bent dagger as a souvenir of the occasion. No blood had flowed.

But that was only the beginning. Two men then took a sharp-bladed sword and, one at each end, held it between them like the rung of a ladder. The young man then climbed up, stood on the blade edge—which creased his bare feet—and walked back and forth across it. It was like balancing on the sharp edge of a razor.

Next, a man brought out a gunny sack, tossed its contents—broken glass and shattered bottles—onto the stage. The performer now walked back and forth on this broken glass with his bare feet, emerging with not so much as a scratch. I was sitting in the front row next to President Sukarno, the performer less than fifteen feet from us. But the Indian Ambassador wanted to be sure. He moved forward, squatted at the edge of the stage so that he could see without a shadow of a doubt that there was no trickery involved.

I had often heard of the flagellants, who believe in mortification of the flesh, and even had a glimpse of them parading one Good Friday in Manila—a bloody exhibition. The use of skewers through the cheeks and other parts of the body to inflict pain was, therefore, nothing new. But the exciting element in the next performance was that six-inch skewers were pierced through the performer's cheeks and lips, from one side to the other, and through the flesh of the stomach, but no blood flowed.

The crowning feat of the evening, however, came next. The young man was handed a kerosense torch, which he lighted. The torch threw a smoky tongue of flame at least a foot high. The man shed his orange tunic and bared his breast; then, as the audience sucked in its breath, ran the torch up and down his bare stomach and chest. The flames licked eagerly at his breasts, chin and lips. He raised the torch. The searing flames covered his face, his eyes, enveloped his hair. He thrust the flame into his mouth, closing his mouth over the end of the torch so that the flame disappeared for an instant. He opened his mouth, withdrew the still-burning torch slowly, his lips, his eyes, his nose, his face, his hair completely exposed to the intense blaze. We watched breathless, unbelieving. Were we really seeing this? Were we being hypnotized? The man did this several times, then held the end of the torch in his mouth long enough to put out the flames. The performance was over.

The Indian Ambassador and I visited the little room in the Governor's Palace to which the performer and the rest of his group had repaired. We wanted to examine him immediately and to talk with him. There was no sign on the man of the effect of the fire. Neither his eyebrows nor his eyelashes were singed. As had been reported true of Adrach, Meshach and Abednego in the Bible, there was not even the "smell of fire" about him. At my request, he opened his mouth. The only evidence of the experience he had just been through was black soot on the roof of his mouth, for the torch had smoked badly.

We then examined his cheeks and his stomach where the skewers had been inserted. There was not only no blood, there was no mark of any kind, no hole, no indentation. The skin was unbroken and smooth. On his left forearm, where the dagger had been repeatedly plunged, there was no sign of blood, no bruise, no scar tissue. There were, however, a few patches of skin that seemed oddly wrinkled, as if in resentment at the oft-repeated whipping from the dagger.

We asked how he had acquired this power, what kind of training he had had to go through. The young man belonged to the *dabus*, a Moslem sect with disciples at Atjeh and a few other places in Indonesia. Like the priestly fire walkers in India, they believe that spiritual advancement comes with the demonstration of the power of God, or Allah, over the flesh. This is not merely the mortification of the flesh but triumph over it, proof to the participants that the power of Allah to protect his own is greater than the physical laws that normally govern the life of man. The devotees of this religion believe that these laws can be set aside—not by man but by God—and spend their lives proving it. Power to do so can be obtained by man only through prayer and fasting.

The *dabu* said he had spent seven years in prayer and fasting alone in a cave. Suddenly, at the end of this time, he had heard a voice ask, "What do you want?" He had replied that he wanted power over his flesh. He had then been seized with a terrible shuddering over which he had no control. He felt transported, inspired, and found he had the power he had sought.

"What if you should be afraid when you thrust the torch into your mouth?" I asked him.

His answer was simple. "I would be burned," he said. He made clear that his faith must be absolute, neither doubt nor fear must tarnish the pure gold of his faith, not the slightest trace of either could be left in his heart or mind.

The Moluccas, Sumatra, Bali, Sulawesi—each contributed vibrant chapters to my Indonesian saga. Of them all, one sticks out above the others—my first night in Ambon.

The scene was a public square. The black night was punctured by the flares of a hundred torches. Seated in a small grandstand overlooking the square, we could see shadowy figures silhouetted against the uncertain flickering light, more than 1,500 of them, standing, awaiting a signal. On a platform in front of the throng, one man stood, baton upraised. He was dressed in a faded sport shirt and khaki trousers. The only sound in the night was the chirp of crickets and the metallic rhythm of cicadas as audience and performers waited expectantly.

The leader's arm swept down in a sudden arc. Instantly, a sweet, plaintive, overwhelming sound broke out that pierced the heart as if it were the cry of a whole people. It was a sound like none I had ever heard. It was music so beautiful, so enchanting, so moving, that a lump rose in the throat. It was music bursting from 1,500 flutes! Accompanied only by the beat of drums, the tones of the flutes brought tears to the eyes, swept excitingly through one's being and overpowered the senses. The music seemed to tell the story of an island race, a people in love with the sea and the sky and the sun and the moon and the stars, the feathered bamboo on sandy beaches, and the soft tropical breezes caressing the little city of Ambon that night. There was sadness and tragedy in it, too, which told of loved ones lost at sea, or torn by tiger, or crushed by python. Birth and love and ecstasy and death were in it. And the melody ended, as life ends sometimes—in no dramatic climax—just halted, seemingly in the middle, marked only by a final soft drumbeat.

There were gasps from the audience, a recovering moment of silence and then tumultuous applause. Nothing like it had ever been heard by those of us from the West. Probably nowhere else in the world had an orchestra of 1,500 flutes ever been assembled, flutes carved by their owners out of bamboo growing tall in the jungles.

We had traveled a thousand miles by air from our home in Djakarta to hear this. I would travel ten times as far to hear it again. The orchestra did not stop with one selection—it kept on and on to fill the evening with moving music such as I have never experienced. Most were Moluccan melodies, some with the sweet plaintiveness of Hawaiian songs, for the origin of the Hawaiian people is believed by some to have been the venturesome sailors of the Moluccas. Others, however, were selections from our own Western classics, beautifully rendered from memory.

The experience was symptomatic and symbolic, for it represented to me the opening of a new world—though of course it had been here long before the dawn of history—but a world breathing the romance of the fabled Indies, a world visited by few Americans, a world still difficult to reach.

Indonesia itself seemed to be symbolized by the great orchestra—so many simple people from so many walks of life, melding themselves together in one harmonious whole. Sukarno might have been the orchestra leader, endeavoring to unify the musical strands of Indonesia's 4,000 islands, so diverse, yet so drawn together by their common love of freedom and independence. The impression prevailed that evening of a people reaching for the stars. Never mind if the heavens be distant, it is perhaps the reaching that counts.

PART III

Indonesia Leans Left

You saw the injustice of our conditions to the point of being willing to add to it. Whereas it seemed to me that man must exalt justice in order to fight against eternal injustice, create happiness in order to protect against the universe of unhappiness.

—ALBERT CAMUS

Nationalism is too valuable a weapon to lend to a disloyal opposition.

—LOUIS FISCHER

I would rather be exposed to the inconveniences arising from too much liberty than to those arising from too small a degree of it.

—THOMAS JEFFERSON

CHAPTER 1

Guided Democracy

I was in Washington serving as Deputy Assistant Secretary for Far Eastern Affairs at the time of Sukarno's visit to Eisenhower in May 1956. The visit was an outstanding success. From the moment the twenty-one guns boomed their salute to the visiting head of state to the moment of his take-off for a two-week swing around the country, Sukarno was front-page news in Washington. His ebullience caused one newspaperman to quip, "Sukarno goes our politicians one better. They shake hands with the mother and kiss the babies. Sukarno shakes hands with the babies and kisses the mothers!"

Vice-President Nixon and his wife gave an official dinner for Sukarno at the Pan American Union building. Everybody who was anybody in Washington was present at this gala occasion. There was great curiosity about this new comet in the Asian skies. A hard-boiled Washington correspondent sitting next to me growled, "I suppose he's here for a hand-out." Just then Sukarno rose to his feet to respond to the Vice-President's toast. He looked around at the glittering audience, ladies in evening dress, men in white tie and tails. He seemed almost abashed, though he cut quite a figure in his natty uniform and colorful decorations.

He began to speak slowly, almost hesitatingly, in English. "I am just a little brown man," he said. "And I am wondering what I am doing here." He paused to take in the audience with a sweep of his arm. "Am I dreaming?" And then he went on to talk about his own country and its fight for independence, and as he talked, the struggle of his people to free themselves after three and a half centuries of occupation by a colonial power came through to that audience. For a few moments they relived those intense days with him.

His audience thrilled, too, to his conclusions. "Democracy in America is a reality," Sukarno said. "I saw it in the faces of people along the street."

At a luncheon at the White House, President Eisenhower gave him a

233

most appropriate gift. The Indonesian President had alluded to **Paul Revere** in the address with which he opened the Afro-Asian Conference in Bandung the previous year. The present was a copy of the handsome silver bowl made by Paul Revere in 1768 for fifteen members of the Sons of Liberty to memorialize a protest against British "oppressive acts." [1]

Sukarno's address before a joint session of Congress was a sensation. He criticized American military aid to Asian nations as inevitably leading to greater dependence of those countries upon America. In the same breath, however, he told Congress what it wanted to hear, that the primary aim for the people of Asia should be economic and political stability. The speech was a ringing plea for America to understand the new nationalism of Asia. He pledged Indonesia's dedication to democracy, expressed appreciation for "assistance from whatever quarter it might come," and added that "we are determined that no material advantage will buy from us any part of our hard-won freedom." The speech won enthusiastic acclaim. One Congressman called it "the best speech ever made by a visiting statesman, with the possible exception of Winston Churchill."

Following a whirlwind tour of the United States, during which he was welcomed everywhere with enthusiasm, Sukarno went to Soviet Russia and Communist China enroute home. It had been the hope in Washington that the visit of this colorful Asian leader would lay the foundation for enduring understanding and friendship between our two countries. Indonesia needed what we had to give—technical assistance and training and economic-development aid. It was the perhaps naïve expectation that Sukarno would not only like us but see advantage for his country in developing closer mutual ties. The United States government's definition of friendship was quite different from Indonesia's. We wanted Indonesia *on our side*. Indonesia was committed to neutrality between the two blocs. In that period, John Foster Dulles looked upon neutrality as well-nigh immoral—if a nation was not for us, it was against us.[2] It was Washington's hope that Sukarno's American experience would have made such an impression that Moscow and Peking would be an anticlimax. But the Russians and Chinese did not pass up this opportunity to woo the Indonesian leader. They turned out massive, enthusiastic crowds wherever he went. He addressed cheering throngs of people who could not understand a word he said.

On his return home, Sukarno announced his plan for Guided Democracy. In that one announcement, the good will generated by Sukarno's visit to the U.S. was dissipated. Washington's reaction was skeptical and

1. New York *Times*, May 17, 1956.
2. Cf. Richard P. Stebbins, *The United States in World Affairs 1958* (New York: Harper & Brothers, 1959), pp. 291–293.

cynical. The new concept was regarded as bearing a distinct "Made in Moscow and Peking" label. The natural question was, Guided by whom? and the answer was implicit, Sukarno, of course.

Numerous versions exist of how the concept of Guided Democracy originated. The popularly accepted one is that it was a matter of evolution in Sukarno's thinking, drawing upon various patterns of government in both the East and West. But there is also a report that a group of Indonesian students in Europe, meeting to discuss solutions to the ills from which their country was suffering, drafted a document that included what later became the main ideas of Guided Democracy; it was submitted to Sukarno by Chairul Saleh.

Subandrio told me an interesting story about the origin of the phrase. Indonesian leaders frequently spoke Dutch among themselves, particularly when they were discussing complex political phenomena for which the Indonesian language was at times inadequate. "The word in Dutch for 'guided' is the same as the word for 'planned,' " the Foreign Minister explained. "If we had translated it into English as 'planned democracy,' it wouldn't have created a ripple. Planning was popular even in the West. But of course Sukarno chose the more dramatic word, 'guided,' and it was front-page news all over the world."

Some time passed without much being heard about Guided Democracy. In Washington, we had begun to think that we had been unduly alarmed. Perhaps it was just one of Sukarno's trial balloons that, for reasons of his own not apparent to us, he was prepared to see sail away into the skies. Although the subject itself was not mentioned, however, various straws in the wind indicated he was searching for a feasible formula.

On October 28, 1956, he advocated the disbanding of all the political parties. Later he told me with a grimace, "But I came up against an iron wall of resistance so that I was forced to give up that idea."

A few months later, on February 21, 1957, he made another suggestion —to construct a so-called *gotong-rojong* (share-the-burden) Cabinet on the basis of representation of all the parties in Parliament. To balance the ills of internal conflict that this might tend to perpetuate, he proposed the creation of a "National Council," to be formed primarily from representatives of the "functional groups." He got the second but not the first.

"*Gotong-rojong*" is a term that has deep meaning in Indonesia. "Cooperation" or "help each other" are perhaps the closest Western concepts. The idea derives from the earliest roots of Indonesian culture, from a time when there was no paid labor, and everybody worked together to get a job done. In the political situation with which Indonesia was faced in 1957, it had special significance. If all parties represented in Parliament were also to be represented in the Cabinet, then the Communists would be included. Owing presumably to army opposition, this suggestion went unimplemented, although Sukarno would refer to it from time to time.

One of the first long talks I had with Sukarno in 1958 was on this subject. He had made a speech advocating the same idea but reducing the main Cabinet elements to representation of the four major political parties—the Nationalist Party, the two Moslem parties, the Masjumi and the Nahdatul Ulama, and the Communists. The Cabinet at the time represented only three. Sukarno dubbed it "a three-legged horse," scoffingly asking whoever heard of a horse running on three legs, and said it was time the Cabinet became "a four-legged horse."

"The graveyards of history are full of people who admitted Communists to Cabinets," I cautioned Sukarno. "Czechoslovakia had four parties, too, until it admitted Communists to its Cabinet. That was the beginning of the end. They bored from within until they were in a position to take over."

Sukarno shook his head. "I would rather have the Communists represented in the Cabinet," he insisted. "There they have to share responsibility for governing the country. They can't be criticizing all the time. They have to help answer the critics. Furthermore, they are in a position where I can watch them, see what they are doing, knock their heads together if I don't like their actions."

I could not have disagreed with him more, and I did my best—without success—to convince him that this was a dangerous course. His attitude demonstrated a degree of naïveté regarding Communist strategy and tactics that I had not anticipated in so shrewd a political leader; perhaps the result of his overweening self-confidence, of which I was well aware. But any student of modern history knew that inclusion of Communists in a Cabinet was the camel's nose under the tent. Their purpose was not to help the government achieve its objectives but to sabotage its efforts, force it to fail, and take its power. But Sukarno was convinced that he could handle the Communists, whom he saw as beholden to him for their very existence.

At this time, Sukarno was determined to lead his people but never to get so far ahead as to lose them. However, he wanted advice—not instructions. He saw himself as the strong executive who would make the decisions, but not without knowing beforehand what his people thought. He was constantly searching for new ways to get accurate readings of their views.

Although he did not establish a *gotong-rojong* Cabinet, largely owing to army opposition, Sukarno did, on July 12, 1957, inaugurate the idea of a sounding board for public opinion, the National Council, composed of members of so-called functional groups, that is, youth, labor, women, teachers, farmers, the military, the political parties, regional representatives. All were appointed by the President. He retained the permanent chairmanship of the Council but appointed former Foreign Minister Roeslan Adulgani as vice-chairman and operational head. Sukarno and the Cabinet henceforth referred important questions of policy to the Council for advice, on the theory that it was broadly representative of the people. It would, he thought, create more realistic contact between the government and the people, which the President felt was not a characteristic of the parliamentary membership. As he saw it, Parliament was composed of representatives of self-serving political organizations rather than persons genuinely interested in the people's welfare.

Djuanda, who was then Prime Minister, scented danger immediately; a body such as the National Council could readily become a supercabinet if not, indeed, a substitute for it. Some of the most powerful men in the country were on the Council, including the head of the Communist Party, Aidit, and, at the other end of the spectrum, General Nasution, Chief of Staff of the Army. Djuanda made clear to me that he had a definite understanding with Sukarno that the Council was to be only a sounding board for public opinion and advisory in nature. But once the Council had been established, the Cabinet rarely took an action in opposition to its advice.

Shortly before Djuanda's announcement actually establishing the Council, Sukarno, impatient at the lack of response to his suggestions, had thundered in an address in Djakarta, in October 1958: "Indonesia's democracy is not liberal democracy. Indonesian democracy is not the democracy of the world of Montaigne or Voltaire. Indonesia's democracy is not à la America, Indonesia's democracy is not the Soviet—NO! Indonesia's democracy is the democracy which is implanted in the breasts of the Indonesian people and it is that which I have tried to dig up again, and have put forward as an offering to you. . . . If you [speaking to the youth], especially the undergraduates, are still clinging to, and being borne along the democracy made in England, or democracy made in France, or democracy made in America, or democracy made in Russia, you will become a nation of copyists!" Sukarno's appeal was for democracy appropriate to Indonesia, and in his search he turned inward, to the traditions of Indonesian village life. He had been leading up to this for some time. Speaking on Independence Day in 1957, Sukarno dismissed parliamentary democracy as "talk and criticism," and asserted that "after our twelve years' experience," democracy had proved "not to have been of any benefit to Indonesia but has done, instead, damage to, and brought about a decline in, Indonesia." It was, therefore, of the "utmost importance" that a political system be found that would be "the best for, and the most appropriate to, the identity and the mental outlook of the Indonesian nation." Without discipline and guidance, democracy becomes merely "chatterbox," Sukarno said. "Democracy is only a means. It is not an end. The end is a just and prosperous society." He described American democracy as "a free-fight liberalism . . . where nothing is spared but Freedom itself."

"We must solve three basic problems in this period of transition," Sukarno said. "First: How and where can we acquire capital for the work of development that we must carry out?

"Second: How can we acquire, in the shortest possible time, the skill, the technical and managerial know-how, to build up?

"Third: What political system will be best for Indonesia, best suited to the mental outlook of the Indonesian people; will provide the right atmosphere for the Indonesian people during this period of transition?"

But he was not yet ready to define what he meant by Guided Democracy.

Most Indonesians thought a change was needed. Prime Minister Djuanda was one. He had been struggling with the parliamentary system in his various Cabinet posts ever since he had first taken office, and could see new hope in a streamlined executive form of government. Djuanda was a non-party man dedicated to the job of moving his country forward. "We need a government that can make decisions and get things done," he told me a few months before Sukarno's concept had taken shape and form. "And we somehow need to recapture the spirit of 1945, when we all were working together to win our independence." How to unite a people in time of peace! The problem was one that political leaders had wrestled with since the dawn of history.

Sukarno's sense of timing had always been good. The virtual crushing of the rebellion, with its elimination of regional opposition to Sukarno and of the strong Masjumi Party, had resulted in a situation in which the President could do anything he and the army agreed on. The army leadership historically had been disgusted by the bungling and bargaining of party politicians and wanted to see more positive government. It was consequently inclined to go along with Sukarno's vague concept of Guided Democracy in the expectation that a stronger central government would emerge.[3]

Djuanda announced Cabinet approval of the still undefined concepts of Guided Democracy following a special meeting held in the Presidential Palace at Tjipanas on November 7, 1958. He explained that the new system was designed to correct the evils of the old. These included "the excessive number of political parties and factions in the Parliament, the absence of a stable government, and the deviation in the cultural and economic fields."

3. See "Indonesia," in *Major Governments of Asia*, ed. George McT. Kahin, 2nd. ed. (Ithaca, N.Y.: Cornell University Press, 1963), pp. 643, 649–650; and Daniel S. Lev, *The Transition to Guided Democracy: Indonesian Politics, 1957–1959* (Ithaca, N.Y.: Cornell Modern Indonesia Project, Monograph Series, 1966).

That the alarm in the West over Guided Democracy was not entirely without foundation, however, may be judged from an exchange that took place when Sukarno was asked by National Council to give an example of some state that already had Guided Democracy. Sukarno explained that though there was no precise parallel, both Communist China and the Soviet Union had the kind of governmental apparatus he had in mind. He mentioned the "People's Representative Body and so-called Congress" in China and observed that there was "a stirring, a vibration, a movement" that appealed to him. He emphasized that this vitality was within a context of national unity represented by "the combination of the Communist Party with the intelligentsia, with the Armed Forces, with the farmers, and with the workers."

Sukarno pointed to the unity in the Soviet House of Representatives and throughout the nation as the result of a single political party, apparently not realizing the extent to which this apparent unity was based upon the use of force and intimidation. He noted the function of the Communist Party in the Soviet Union was to "imbue all activities with spirit and with enthusiasm" and suggested that something of this kind should be created in Indonesia, but with a different content—"uniquely Indonesia's self." He was emphatic that he had no intention to introduce either the Chinese or Soviet systems in Indonesia. "I say firmly and clearly, I do not wish to copy them here," he insisted, stressing that whereas the guiding principles of the Soviet Union were Leninism-Marxism, for Indonesia the basic philosophy was the *Pantjasila,* or Five Principles.

It was two years after its announcement before Sukarno's concept of Guided Democracy began to take definite shape and form at the meeting of the Constituent Assembly, convened on April 22, 1959, in Bandung. Sukarno delivered an impassioned speech in which he formally presented the government's recommendation that the 1945 Constitution be readopted in unamended form. Endowed with the symbolism of the revolution, the 1945 Constitution was well-suited to serve as the structural framework for Sukarno's evolving concept of Guided Democracy. It gave the President supreme power, thus changing the nature of the Indonesian presidency; it provided for a representative government based upon a free and general election with sovereignty residing in the people and exercised in part by Parliament and in full by a superparliament, the People's Consultative Congress.[4] The Congress was required to meet at least once every five years to elect a President and Vice-President for a five-year term and recommend such changes in the Constitution and structure of government as it deemed advisable. It was also

---

4. Hereinafter also referred to as the Consultative Congress, the MPRS or the Constituent Assembly. This body was composed of the members of Parliament, plus regional and functional representatives.

responsible for determining broad lines of state policy. The Congress could be convened at any time by the President or by a petition signed by a designated number of its members.

Under this Constitution, still in effect in Indonesia, the President has the power to appoint his assistants, who thus become the Cabinet. The President can also appoint a Supreme Advisory Council, which acts as a sounding board for public opinion and advises the President on current issues. The 1945 Constitution makes clear that the President is not responsible to Parliament, nor is his position dependent upon it; likewise, the Cabinet Ministers are not responsible to Parliament, but to the President.

The 1945 Constitution soon acquired an almost mystical aura as the solution to all the problems of the country, political leaders and groups reading into its adoption the potential realization of their respective goals. Thus Djuanda and some of the other government leaders felt that a strong executive form of government would reduce the power and influence of the PKI, which, through its skill in parliamentary maneuvers, had exercised an influence in the legislative body out of all proportion to its numbers. The former Foreign Minister, the Anak Agung, expressed the hope that the new framework would pave the way for Hatta's return to the government and a fresh approach to the settlement of the rebellion.

Despite Sukarno's impassioned plea, all did not go well in Bandung at the Constituent Assembly. The two big Moslem parties were willing to return to the 1945 Constitution but not on Sukarno's terms, "without any amendment at all." They insisted that the Preamble be amended to include, after the affirmation of "Belief in the One God," a statement requiring obedience to the laws of Islam for the adherents of that religion.[5] Roeslan Abdulgani, speaking for the Government at the Assembly, argued that the *Pantjasila* guaranteed freedom of worship and was alone capable of assuring a strong bond of national unity.

To a Westerner, the seriousness of the conflict in the Constituent Assembly was difficult to appreciate. But it was a fundamental issue in Indonesia. In essence, it was whether Indonesia was to be a Moslem state or not. Since more than ninety per cent of the population was formally Moslem, the seven words the Moslem parties wanted to add to the Constitution that required Moslems to adhere to the laws of their religion meant that Islamic law would take precedence over Indonesian civil law

---

5. This formulation was taken from a historic document signed by Indonesia's national leaders just two months before the August 17, 1945 Proclamation of Independence. Known as the Djakarta Charter (June 22, 1945), the document failed to be included in the Constitution proclaimed on August 18, 1945. Significantly, the controversial phrase was deleted to secure the broadest possible support for the newly proclaimed government.

for the overwhelming majority of the population. Many felt it would tend to erode the freedom of religion guaranteed by the *Pantjasila*.

Months of argument failed to resolve the differences. On June 2, 1959, the third vote on President Sukarno's request to adopt the 1945 Constitution again fell short of the necessary two-thirds majority. The lines were drawn and no compromise appeared possible. President Sukarno was out of the country. Prime Minister Djuanda was doing his utmost. He warned the members of the assembly of a possible military assumption of power if they did not approve the President's proposal. But there was no give on the side of the Moslem parties. Wahab Chasbullah, president of the Nahdatul Ulama, replied that "Islam's followers will not flinch from the consequences emerging from the rejection of the government proposal, including the possibility of a military junta."

The deadlock precipitated a government crisis. The same day, June 2, Nasution, acting as "Central War Administrator," prohibited all political activity in Indonesia until further notice. Rumors spread that the army was planning to seize control of the government, but Nasution denied them. From Los Angeles, Sukarno cabled Nasution to refrain from any drastic action in the current crisis. Abdulgani flew to Japan to confer with Sukarno when he arrived there on June 6. There was tension in the air. Everybody expected something to happen, but nothing did.

Nasution could have taken over the government at this time, but he knew such action might precipitate civil war. The army was unified and powerful, but there would have been division when it came to taking on Sukarno. Furthermore, as he told me, "Indonesia needs the political leadership of a man like Sukarno at this stage."

Sukarno, disdaining to hasten his return (or perhaps awaiting an assessment of the situation), arrived in Djakarta more than three weeks later, on June 29. He was firm and resolute in his speech to the nation, promising to act decisively, but not as a dictator, under the 1945 Constitution. He left no doubt that he was determined to revive the 1945 Constitution, one way or another. This was Sukarno's moment to consolidate his power. He took full advantage of the opportunity. The army was with him, and he moved with speed and resolution. The first ten days of July spelled the demise of parliamentary democracy in Indonesia and the establishment of Guided Democracy.

Yielding to his pressure, the Cabinet resigned after giving Sukarno full executive powers to run the government. The President, even while denying he had any intention of becoming a dictator, dissolved the membership of Parliament and the Constituent Assembly. On July 5, 1959, he announced by decree a return to the 1945 Constitution without the amendment desired by the Moslem parties. The action preserved only the appearance of legality, but Sukarno had no challengers. The Indonesian President now had what he wanted; he was running the country.

Three days later, on July 8, Sukarno announced his new Cabinet—Indonesia's eighteenth Cabinet in fourteen years. It was made up of Ministers regarded as anti-Communist. Djuanda continued as First Minister and Minister of Finance; Nasution as Minister of Security and Defense; Subandrio as Minister of Foreign Affairs. In a nationwide broadcast, Sukarno said the program of his "Working [Kerdja] Cabinet" was "to fulfill the food and clothing needs of the people in the shortest possible time; to safeguard national security; to continue the struggle against economic and political imperialism."

Once his new Cabinet was installed and functioning, Sukarno began to move step by step toward implementing Guided Democracy. Ominous to us was his action on July 30, 1959, in naming a number of Communist leaders to membership on two new state bodies, the Supreme Advisory Council and the National Planning Council. This was the first time known members of the PKI had been appointed to high-level official bodies, although in both councils—the forty-five member Advisory group and the twenty-seven member Planning group—they were heavily outnumbered.

The Supreme Advisory Council, in effect the successor body to the National Council mentioned earlier, had only limited powers. Headed by the President, it was obliged to answer questions submitted by the President; it also had the right to make proposals to the government.

Assigned two of the twelve seats on the Supreme Advisory Council, apportioned to leaders of nine political parties ranging from Communist to anti-Communist, were Aidit, head of the PKI, and his second deputy, Njoto. The Nationalists and NU received two seats each. Six smaller parties, including the Protestants and the Roman Catholics, got one seat apiece. Of the major parties only the Masjumi, which opposed Sukarno on many issues—like the 1945 Constitution—was left off the Supreme Advisory Council. Most of the Council's members represented regions and professional and civil groups.

The National Planning Council was a project Sukarno had been urging for two years. Its task was to draft national-development blueprints for a "guided economy" in Indonesia. Mohammed Yamin, extreme nationalist and Minister of Social and Cultural Affairs in the inner Cabinet, was appointed chairman of the NPC.

Showing his satisfaction with the way things were shaping up, Aidit came out publicly in support of Sukarno's program on July 30. Ever since Sukarno had dissolved Parliament, the Communist hierarchy had been in doubt as to where Sukarno was heading. Opposed to the dissolution of Parliament, the PKI had been clamoring for national elections. The appointment of Communist leaders to the two new agencies of government was the price Aidit exacted for his support. It was a real breakthrough for the PKI. At last they had penetrated officialdom.

Presumably as a counter to these Communist appointments, Nasution on August 16, 1959, publicly ordered the PKI to postpone indefinitely its sixth national congress, scheduled to open in Djakarta on August 22. But this decision was later reversed by Sukarno, and it met from September 7 to 14.

The next major move toward full-fledged Guided Democracy following adoption of the 1945 Constitution was the reorganization of the political-party system by the issuance of Decree No. 7 on January 12, 1960. It had a dual purpose: to reduce the number of political parties to a manageable quantity by eliminating the numerous small splinter parties, and to establish conditions that the major parties associated with the rebellion of 1958 would not be able to meet, thus becoming the instruments of their own destruction. The first objective was accomplished by specifying that to qualify, a party must have an organization with branches in at least six provinces and twenty-five per cent of the regencies, and must have received a certain percentage of the vote in past elections; also, a party must have existed prior to July 1959. To get at the Masjumi and the Socialists, the Decree required parties to subscribe to the *Pantjasila* as a basic national policy and to condemn all rebellions against the government since 1945. This was a two-edged sword, however, since the PKI had staged a major revolt against the government in 1948 at Madiun.

In one more step toward a monolithic system, all parties were required to join the National Front, a new and significant appendage of Guided Democracy. They were also required to submit regular financial statements to the government. All foreign funding, as well as foreign members or advisers, was prohibited. This was clearly aimed at the PKI, and represented the army's contribution to the brew.

The President was also given broad powers to investigate party finances and assets, and to dissolve a party after perfunctory consultation with the Supreme Court if it opposed "the principles and goals of the state" or failed to condemn party leaders who had sided with the rebels. The entire political-party machinery was, in effect, placed at the mercy of the President.

The Decree was manifestly unjust in that it was penalizing all members of political parties for the actions of a few. It represented Sukarno's shrewd exploitation of an opportunity to get rid of powerful organized opposition against him once and for all. The Masjumi and the PSI had been thorns in his side for a long time. Now, with the army leadership alienated by the support of some of the party leaders for the rebellion, there was no remaining power element with sufficient concern or strength to oppose Sukarno by defending these groups.

The Decree spread consternation in Masjumi and PSI circles. The NU, the second-largest Moslem party, was delighted, seeing itself no longer faced with Masjumi opposition and emerging as the Number One party in Indonesia. The PNI, of course, went along enthusiastically with Sukarno's program. So did the PKI, although the Decree presented problems for it.

Masjumi leaders Roem and Prawoto told me the party would not kneel to Sukarno—it would sacrifice neither principles nor loyalty by subscribing to the *Pantjasila* and condemning rebel leaders. If Sukarno was determined to destroy the party, let him act and accept the onus of his action. The PSI, hoping to survive and not being so closely identified with the rebellion since its leader, Sjahrir, had remained in Djkarta, did not take so strong a stand.[6] It did not matter. Sukarno banned both parties in August 1960.

Idham Chalid of the NU was optimistic enough to think the new line-up might result in the NU's replacing the PKI in Sukarno's kitchen Cabinet; he said Sukarno frequently sought his advice these days. Chalid described Sukarno's position *vis à vis* the PKI as somewhat naïve, believing that his continued placation of it stemmed from an old fear of burning his bridges, and also alarm over the possibility that the Moslems might unite against him.

Chalid also revealed that Sjafruddin, Prime Minister of the rebel government, had said in a recent letter that there would be no difficulty in reaching an accommodation if Chalid and the NU took over the Indonesian government. But Chalid saw no immediate likelihood of such an event, noting that positions on both sides were still too stiff for a compromise as long as the present Cabinet was in office. As to the rumors of a possible Cabinet reshuffle, including added NU participation, he said this was possible, but it certainly would not include the PKI. So long as he and Nasution could prevent it, no Communist would enter the Cabinet.

The Communists, skilled in the art of deceit, did not let the Decree bother them. They could in good faith neither accept the *Pantjasila*, with its first principle of Belief in God, nor the condemnation of previous insurrections. There was hope among some in Djakarta that the party had been trapped. But this proved to be naïveté. Aidit, expert in flimflammery and double talk, made a public statement supporting the *Pantjasila*. There is no evidence that he ever condemned previous rebellions, but then Sukarno was not out after the PKI—and his government was not known for enforcing the law without fear or favor.

Also on January 12, 1960, Presidential Decree No. 12 established the new "temporary" structure of the Constituent Assembly under the 1945 Constitution, with the President appointing all members. Equally if not

---

6. However, the best financial brain in Indonesia, Sumitro, prominent Socialist, and former Finance Minister, had joined the revolutionary government's Cabinet.

more important to Sukarno's objectives was the simultaneous announcement of the formation of the National Front. Described as a vertical mass organization based upon Guided Democracy, with the Political Manifesto as its program, its Central Board would be chaired by Sukarno. Finances were to come from government assistance, registration, subscription, and donations. Minister of Information Maladi referred to the Front as a "national movement," not a state party, open to organizations as well as individuals.

In contrast to the Supreme Advisory Council, which channeled public reactions to the President and churned out recommendations for his consideration, the National Front's purpose was to create organic totality, enabling the nation to speak with one voice. Conflicts between parties and other groups would be resolved behind the scenes, and the Front would speak for the state as did the Communist Party in the Soviet Union. Although Sukarno never said so publicly, he indicated to me that he saw the National Front as a vehicle through which to create a one-party state.

This was confirmed in the plans for popular elections, scheduled to be held within the year. It was proposed that the National Front would run its own candidates for Parliament against candidates of the major political parties. The power behind the National Front would be such that its candidates would almost certainly be elected, and the old-line political parties would wither on the vine. But this notion died aborning; the parties themselves were quite willing to have representation in the National Front but unwilling to bury their identities under what seemed certain to become a political tombstone. Alone among them, the PKI saw the Front as a vehicle it could ride to power; but behind the scenes, it strongly opposed Sukarno's concept of the Front as a single party with proportionate representation from all parties. The army, favorable as always to anything that would abort the political bickering and divisiveness it considered responsible for Indonesia's ineffective government, thought it could control the Front and quietly supported Sukarno's concept. But the combined opposition of the parties was too much even for Sukarno, and this idea was abandoned. The Front instead became the central propaganda agency for the government. Increasingly dominated by the Communists, it added one more unofficial but important link between the PKI and Sukarno's Guided Democracy.

It should be understood that Guided Democracy was not, as some have assumed, merely a cunning contrivance designed by Sukarno to enhance his own political power, although it had that effect. Serving Sukarno's selfish purposes, it nevertheless represented a genuine search for a solution to the political chaos that had engulfed the country ever since independence.

Guided Democracy was based squarely on the *Pantjasila*, first enunciated by Sukarno in a speech on June 1, 1945, two months before the declaration of Indonesian Independence. This Asian equivalent to our Bill of Rights bore a halo of mysticism; according to legend, the President "communed with God" under the stars for two nights before he enunciated the concept. As Sukarno would have it, the Five Principles are divinely inspired from the Prophet Mohammed: belief in God, internationalism, nationalism, sovereignty of the people, and social justice.[7] Each had special meaning for the revolutionary society. They were remarkably tailored to the Indonesian environment, representing a mixture of religion, nationalism, democracy, and the goals for which the revolution was fought.

Number four, "sovereignty of the people," experienced a considerable transformation in character over the years. In Sukarno's 1945 speech, the emphasis had been clearly and definitely on elections and representative bodies. Significantly, no one mentioned this at the time of the adoption of Guided Democracy; "people's sovereignty" became merely an empty abstraction only theoretically embodied in the rubber-stamp consultative bodies that replaced the previously elected Parliament and Constituent Assembly. Representative government was no more.

I had serious reservations about Guided Democracy from the beginning, specifically about whether it would become a complex apparatus to keep Sukarno in power by providing a mechanism through which his own will could be manifested, rather than a democratic mechanism to enable him and his government to respond to the will of the people. It could have moved either way, but the temptation to utilize such machinery to exercise power was too great for Sukarno's ego to resist.

The first clear indication that Guided Democracy was no longer a two-way street maintaining communication between the leader and the led came with that strange exercise in pseudo philosophy called *"Manipol-USDEK."* Straining the credulity of the most confirmed apostle of acronymics, the phrase was derived as follows: *Manipol,* an abbreviation of *manifesto politik,* referred to Sukarno's 1959 Independence Day address, which presented his basic thinking and attempted to justify the Decree of July 5, 1959, dissolving the Constituent Assembly and re-establishing the 1945 Constitution. USDEK was an acronymic representation of the five basic elements in the philosophy of Guided Democracy: the 1945 Constitution, Indonesian Socialism, Guided Democracy, Guided Economy, and the Indonesian Identity.

---

7. The Preamble to the Constitution adopted in 1945 states the concept in these terms: "Belief in the One, Supreme God, just and civilized Humanity, the unity of Indonesia, and democracy which is guided by the inner wisdom in the unanimity arising out of deliberation amongst representatives, meanwhile creating a condition of *social justice* for the whole of the People of Indonesia."

To a Western mind, the philosophical justification for a program involving readoption of the 1945 Constitution, establishment of a strong executive type of government, and a jerry-rigged governmental apparatus might appear somewhat tortured. But in Indonesia, *Manipol*-USDEK became the established philosophy of government, and was taught in all schools and in adult-education programs. The direct and indirect pressures to line up and swear allegiance to this new approach were such that an expression of disagreement or opposition was stigmatized as unpatriotic, with the Communists leading the hue and cry against anyone having the temerity to express doubts.

While criticizing Western imperialism and all its works, Sukarno was not above borrowing language from the West. He seized upon "retooling," a perfectly good capitalist word, and redefined it as follows: "Retooling means to replace the instruments, to change the tools and the apparatus which are not in accord any more with the thinking of Guided Democracy, and replace them by new tools, new equipment and new apparatus which are more in accord with the new outlook. Retooling also means economizing all equipment which can still be used, as long as these tools can still be repaired and resharpened." As time went on and people were dismissed from their jobs and Cabinet members were changed because they did not agree with the new philosophy, the word began to take on the connotation of "removal from office."

In the frenzy of exaggeration accompanying this imposition of Sukarno's political concepts, the meaning of "retooling" continued to expand. "Retooling means total mobilization, to gather together material strength totally, to collect spiritual power totally, and to make these powers ready to fight and capable of fighting in order to realize the task and the responsibility of the Working Cabinet, which in principle constitutes a programme for the entire Indonesian people," the President explained in his *Manipol* speech.

Guided Democracy, as represented by *Manipol*-USDEK, moved rapidly into a quasi-religious phase in which those who did not subscribe to its tenets were regarded as heretics. The President envisaged unity as the combination of national, religious, and Communist elements in society, and called it "Nasakom"; thus it was only a step to the point where criticism of the Communist Party became an unpatriotic attack on the unity of the country and the philosophy of the state. A kind of mass hysteria developed in the society, such as I have witnessed only in Germany during the Hitler period and in Communist countries, where "thought control" came close to realization.

The concept of Guided Democracy in its inception represented a reaching out for a philosophical base that would express the Indonesian character and personality, and a structure that would manifest that expression. It was also an attempt by the Indonesian leadership to find a way through the manifold difficulties inherent in the birth of a nation. A not unimportant by-product was that it paved a road to personal power for Sukarno.

As Guided Democracy flowered into neo-dictatorship, Sukarno was often compared to Hitler. But, while both were mystics, they were as unalike as two men could be. Sukarno, the Oriental, was wiser than Hitler, the Occidental. In Germany during the Hitler regime, I used to plague my German acquaintances with the question, "What of the succession? What happens when Hitler dies?" This was the signal for shocked reaction, a quick look around to see if anyone were listening, and a hushed admonition with finger to lips. One must not speak of the possibility of the Führer's ever leaving the stage. There was no provision for succession. He had no term of office; presumably, he would go on forever. Sukarno did not make that mistake. If he had, there were people around him too wise to leave so obvious a gap in the fabric of the nation's continuum. The 1945 Constitution provided for the popular election of a representative body that would choose Sukarno's successor. The flaw in the Guided Democracy period was the quasi-legitimate character of Sukarno-appointed bodies; what would be their status in a post-Sukarno age?

This period in Indonesian history reveals an interesting apparatus designed to provide guidance for the guider, enabling him to respond promptly and effectively to the will of the governed without the utilization of elections. Guided Democracy tested public opinion in ways that would theoretically permit a popular regime to remain popular and thus stay in power indefinitely. It should have worked. With a gifted, beloved, charismatic leader able to communicate with the masses as no other man in modern times has managed to do, with listening devices that should have enabled this leader to hear the slightest rumble of dissatisfaction in his constituency, the system should have held together longer than it did. Yet Sukarno's equivalent of a public-opinion poll broke down because it somehow failed to record the ground swell of dissatisfaction with the man and his policies that resulted in his overthrow.

Why?

Three basic reasons stand out. First and most important was the absence of free speech and free press after Guided Democracy got under way. Governmental pressure to enclose comment within the fences of approved doctrine jammed what might otherwise have been a clear signal. No longer was "consent of the governed" sought. Dialogue died. The flow of opinion was now only from the top down. The sounding board for public opinion became an echo of the leader.

The second reason is that Sukarno, dazzled by the dynamics of power, listened to the signals he *wanted* to hear. Only those views survived that were acceptable to those in power. Contrary opinions did surface from time to time; Sukarno was repeatedly warned by old friends that he was following a wrong course. But he continued to do so, disregarding, too, the cautions against the unpopularity of his course—particularly significant for a leader who repeatedly thundered to his people, "I am your lips, I am your mouth, I am your voice." Sukarno paid the supreme penalty for failure to keep in touch with his people. He wound up by disregarding his own maxims. "Earth's thousand voices" no longer reached him.

When a leader loses contact with his people, he loses contact with his god. This, too, happened to Sukarno. Sukarno's god had been his country. When he substituted himself for his land and his people, he lost his way. And that is the third reason for the failure of Guided Democracy. The earliest open break in this communication was the revolt in the Constituent Assembly against Sukarno's domination, the first such challenge to his authority. The President imposed his will, to be sure, but he had to dissolve the representative assemblies to do it. Many scholars have pointed out that this act meant the demise of democracy in Indonesia.[8] It was also the first step in the downfall of Sukarno.

To those of us in the embassy in daily touch with Indonesians, private indications of Sukarno's loss of contact with his people were becoming more and more frequent. His peccadilloes, to which many people objected because of the sullied image it gave Indonesia abroad; his cosiness with the Communists, which put off the vast majority of his people, who were mostly Moslem and non-Communist, if not anti-Communist; his preoccupation with grandiose politics and disregard of the state of the economy, which was daily bringing greater hardship to the poor; finally, his lavish living and flamboyant exhibitionism, one example of which was his charter of a Pan American jet for himself and his party every time he went abroad—these and other evidences of an ego lost in self-satisfaction were more and more the subjects of comment at private gatherings.

I remember the first time I began to realize that Sukarno was losing contact with the youth. I was talking with a student leader at the Bandung Technical Institute. As Sukarno was arriving the following day, the city was gaily bedecked with flags and portraits, and I commented that I supposed everyone was proud their President was visiting them. The young man gave me a skeptical side glance, as if to say "Who's kidding who?" Then, with a scornful wave of his hand, he said, "We know our President. We know how he acts." His tone made clear that he had lost all respect for Sukarno.

But there were other voices to which Sukarno's ear became attuned, those of the PKI. Thus Guided Democracy gradually became a transmit-

---

8. Cf. Herbert Feith, *The Decline of Constitutional Democracy in Indonesia* (Ithaca, N.Y.: Cornell University Press, 1962).

ter for the thoughts and purposes of the PKI; and they were well disguised, so well as to perhaps persuade the "great revolutionary leader" that they were his own.

It was a good deal for the Communists. It was an Oriental trade of the highest (or lowest) order. They had provided Sukarno with an Aladdin's lamp and had received a transmitter in return.

CHAPTER 2

A Closing Society

Democracy in Indonesia was dying, but it was not yet dead. A final challenge to Sukarno's authority came from the Parliament, which he had suspended in July, and groups who believed in representative government. When Parliament reconvened in the middle of February 1960, Speaker Sartono lashed out at the government for its failure to give the body a full role in governing the nation, insisted that Parliament still had the right to review executive decrees and alter them if necessary, and disputed the government's legal right to dissolve the Parliament. His fight to regain some of the power eroded over the previous six months by Sukarno's Guided Democracy came as a surprise. Sartono was an old revolutionary associate of Sukarno's, and his determination not to be used as a rubber stamp was unexpected. But the Speaker, although an aristocrat by birth, had a sincere belief in democracy, and was not about to be used as a tool in tearing down what he had fought for during the revolution. He demonstrated real courage, but his valiant fight came too late. By now there was little possibility that Sukarno would be willing to submit his acts to parliamentary review or limit the government's rule by decree. Indeed, the fate of Parliament itself remained in doubt. Its suspension had doomed representative democracy in Indonesia since it wiped out the last stronghold of the political parties and the principal source of legislative power. Centralization of formal authority in the hands of the President and the Cabinet was now complete. Real power lay, of course, primarily with the President and the army.

Predictions that Sukarno was aiming at a rubber-stamp Parliament proved accurate. On March 23, 1960, Sukarno announced that a new, 261-member Parliament would be established. Its political composition would include the PNI, NU, PKI, and six minor parties that would share 130 seats. The new National Front, including the functional representatives, would occupy 131 seats. The functional representatives would be apportioned in approximately the same ratio as the National Planning Council and the Supreme Advisory Council. The Masjumi and the PSI

251

were to receive no seats as political parties, although some members might be included in the functional groups.

The President's action created a furor. Sartono resigned as Speaker.[1] Party leaders met and were united, for the first time in years, by the formation of an anti-Communist Democratic League, including the NU, the Catholic Party, the Protestant Party, the Masjumi, and the PSI. There was talk of a boycott of the new Parliament and other forms of open opposition to Sukarno's increasing power. Demonstrating his complete scorn for such opposition, Sukarno told the press that he would leave Indonesia April 1 for a world tour that would include talks with Nehru, Nasser, and Tito, plus three days in San Francisco. In a nationwide broadcast on March 27, Sukarno announced the membership of the *gotong-rojong* Parliament but stated that it would not be installed until he returned.

Could the Democratic League halt the slide toward neo-dictatorship? Only with the support of the army, which remained the key to the situation. In the two weeks following Sukarno's departure, the Djakarta anti-Communist press embarked on an unprecedented series of editorial attacks on the new, Sukarno-appointed Parliament and on the President himself. The campaign was spearheaded by the Masjumi newspaper, *Abadi*, which went to the extraordinary length of comparing Sukarno to Hitler, far exceeding the limits formally permitted the controlled Indonesian press. But no action was taken against the paper or its editor.

Sukarno's two-month absence again opened the door for the army to take countermeasures. Seldom has history been so cooperative in providing two such opportunities for acquisition of power within so short a time. But the military leadership hesitated. It lacked the internal cohesion essential to decisive action. It was united against the Communists; it was not united against Sukarno. Rumors of a coup during Sukarno's absence nevertheless continued to circulate in Djakarta, with the last week in April reported as the target date. The U.S. Embassy was of the opinion that "the logic of the situation indicates that the period prior to Sukarno's return or shortly thereafter may be the last chance to take successful action." The army leadership appeared ready to move if assured of sufficient political support. It could be certain of the backing of the large but discredited Masjumi Party, the PSI, and the Christian parties.[2] But as a balance to the parties supporting Sukarno, it needed the wholehearted support of the NU, which, deeply divided by patronage and power considerations, was an uncertain quantity.

Vigorously arrayed against the Democratic League, the PKI was giving

---

1. Sartono told me that he had been offered the speakership, but had attached conditions unacceptable to Sukarno.
2. After months of restriction and repression, the Masjumi and PSI were finally banned in August 1960.

full support to the Sukarno-created Parliament and hinting broadly that they expected a corresponding change in the Cabinet upon Sukarno's return. While some differences of opinion existed in the PNI, it looked as though its leadership was ready to acquiesce in the new Parliament, and might even be prepared to accept the PKI in the Cabinet if its own members were given a sufficient number of portfolios.

Three outcomes to the turmoil seemed possible. The army and anti-Sukarno forces might seize power prior to or shortly after the President's return, evict palace supporters from the government, and either depose Sukarno or relegate him to a titular presidency. Or, the same forces might hesitate in the face of public apathy and opposition, and be unable to prevent the returning Sukarno from realizing his long-standing goal of a *gotong-rojong* Cabinet. And finally, the opponents might cancel each other out. Just the fracas kicked up by the army and the Democratic League might be enough to dissuade Sukarno from a radical Cabinet reshuffle. Knowing the Indonesian proclivity for compromise, I considered this alternative the most likely.

Ironically, the Dutch saved Sukarno from the first possibility. Announcing a plan for reinforcement of West Irian, they stirred up a sudden storm whose clouds blacked out everything else. Government and political leaders, armed forces chiefs, and newspaper editors vied with each other in issuing statements condemning the Dutch provocation and stressing the determination of the Indonesians to resist military threats. The issue of Indonesian democracy moved off the front page.

With the pressures off for the time being, the NU executive council announced a fence-straddling decision on Sukarno's program. It endorsed the new Parliament but opposed the allocation formula for membership. Rumors of an army coup died down as the end of April passed and nothing happened. The moment was lost. The pro-League press played up a statement by the Djakarta Military Commander, Colonel Umar, to the effect that no steps would be taken against the League so long as activities were within the existing regulations, and that, in fact, it was natural for groups dissatisfied with the new Parliament to form such a group. But there was no fire left in the movement. Political leaders favoring the League's cause commented privately that serious damage was being done to the anti-Communist effort. One of them commented that Sukarno was "a very lucky man" to have the Dutch hand him such a sure-fire means of countering the growing strength of the opposition. Press comment was violently anti-Dutch, with the pro-Communist newspapers utilizing the issue to attack the United States and the West as supporting the Dutch. The rightist press and Sukarno opponents were charged with furthering Dutch aims.

Diplomatic activity mounted in an attempt to line up other Afro-Asians actively behind Indonesia in the dispute and induce them to take steps to hinder the movement of Dutch warships to West New Guinea.

Acting Foreign Minister Leimena held a series of meetings with representatives of other Afro-Asian countries to discuss the West Irian issue. The Ambassadors of the UAR, Pakistan, and Iraq made public statements denouncing the Dutch actions.

But the PKI kept their eye on the ball. Communist youth in Surabaya, waving posters and shouting support for Sukarno and the new Parliament, stormed into a meeting of the Democratic League on May 15 and broke it up. A subsequent report in *Nusantara* claimed that fifty-two persons had been arrested.

Rival forces were bracing themselves for Sukarno's imminent return, when he himself seized the initiative. In a speech in Tokyo on May 28, he unleashed a bitter attack on the Democratic League, called its members "newcomers," charged them with sympathy for the rebels, unfamiliarity with the people's sufferings, and, of all things, with "trampling democracy underfoot." The League and its supporters took public issue with the President and expressed determination to continue the struggle. Their firmness in standing up to him was apparently based on the belief that the army would not let them down, and that Sukarno would retreat when confronted with such proof of their strength. It was not apparent what the League would do if Sukarno did not back down. It was clear that the military leadership was generally satisfied with the League's activities, but we heard from reliable sources that it had rejected League proposals for a government takeover by Nasution or the establishment of a military "caretaker Cabinet."

Sukarno returned to Indonesia on June 10 and resumed his duties as if nothing had happened. In his first public speech he ignored all the press, smilingly described the domestic situation as "tranquil," lashed out at "foreign quarters" and traitors who wished to see a change in the Indonesian leadership. He challenged: "I am the Chief Executive and no longer just a symbolic head of state." On June 15, convinced the opposition to his program could be overcome, he announced that the *gotong-rojong* Parliament would be installed on June 25.

The Democratic League, now fighting a rear-guard action, stated that it was less concerned with the composition of the Parliament than with the illegal manner in which it had been established, and called for the restoration of democratic norms in the country. Sukarno paid no attention. On June 17 he announced the appointment of twenty-two additional members to the new Parliament, the bulk of them apparently non-Communist. He also announced the replacements for former Speaker Sartono and several others who had declined the meaningless membership. But the Democratic League had made some impression. Sukarno decided against admitting Communists to the Cabinet, and First Minister Djuanda, after a brief meeting with the President, announced that "there would be no Cabinet reshuffle." This was gratifying to the U.S. Embassy. We had worked long and hard to impress upon Sukarno,

Djuanda, and other leaders that such a move would inevitably have an unfavorable effect on relations between our two countries.

Sukarno, however, had won his battle to establish a Parliament completely subservient to the executive. That the legislative body had been reduced to impotency was clearly indicated by the new ground rules. It was announced on June 20 that the new Parliament would no longer be permitted to make its own standing rules, which had already been drawn up by the Cabinet to incorporate the "President's wishes" regarding the body's activities. The President's appointment of the Speaker violated another of Parliament's traditional privileges.

There was one encouraging note in this gloomy picture. The indications seemed to be that there was now a working agreement between Sukarno and the Djuanda-Nasution forces, whereby the latter was willing to accept the new Parliament in return for at least temporary abandonment of Sukarno's plans to include Communists in the Cabinet.

The attitude of the U.S. government, while undoubtedly not the key element in Indonesian decision-making, nevertheless continued to concern the Indonesian leadership. In a talk with Chargé d'Affaires Henderson on June 18, Subandrio took pains to get across the message that Sukarno, rightly or wrongly, continued to feel that the United States was seeking a change in the regime in Indonesia and aiming at getting rid of Sukarno. He said the President was distressed over a recent unfavorable squib in *Newsweek* inspired, he was convinced, by the State Department. Nor was he pleased by the emphasis given in the U.S. press to his playboy antics during his recent visit. Sukarno was not a Communist and wanted to be friends with the United States, Subandrio said, but felt that the U.S. was not reciprocating.

The last nail in the coffin of parliamentary democracy in Indonesia was driven at the swearing-in ceremony for the new appointees on June 25. Sukarno stressed parliamentary subservience to the executive, confirming that the body was not to vote on matters of business but leave decisions up to the President if unable to reach unanimity. A presidential decree released simultaneously defined the tenure of members as subject to Sukarno's will. Parliament, the guardian of the people's liberty, had become the creature of the President.

The reconstitution of the MPRS completed the roster of governmental bodies called for by the 1945 Constitution and followed the parliamentary precedent under which all members were chosen personally by the President. On August 15, he announced that the membership of the People's Consultative Congress (MPRS) would consist of all 283 members of Parliament plus ninety-four regional representatives, and 232 additional functional-group representatives. The latter two groups were named by the President and included thirteen Cabinet ministers, forty-seven members of the armed forces, a number of former Constituent Assembly delegates, assorted politicians, labor-union leaders, and youth leaders. The political complexion of the new appointees appeared to parallel that of Parliament, without a significant increase in either the right or the left. Guided Democracy—that is, democracy guided by Sukarno—was now an established fact.

The first session of the *gotong-rojong* Parliament (1960) was addressed by Sukarno. His message was devoted largely to denials that he had "killed democracy" by dissolving the elected Parliament and appointing "yes men" to the present body. It also included his usual intemperate castigation of liberal democracy and capitalism, linking them this time with fascism.

On the same day, Sukarno appointed the sixty-two members of the National Front Central Board. They included eight Cabinet ministers, seven members of the armed forces, representatives of the PKI, PNI, NU, and other parties, and regional and functional representatives. More than a quarter of them were known PKI members or sympathizers; in a somewhat smaller proportion were the anti-Communists. There was no statement of what the actual function and powers of the new board would be, but its heterogeneous composition, ranging from PKI head Aidit to staunch anti-Communists, seemed to guarantee that instances of unanimous agreement on any issue would be few. If Sukarno planned to use the Front as a vehicle to replace political parties, it was obvious he would have to lodge its actual leadership elsewhere. As it turned out, the Front became more and more a vehicle for Communist propaganda. Skilled in behind-the-scenes manipulations and in playing Sukarno's favorite theme songs, the party leadership came to dominate the Front's activity. The combined opposition of the parties thwarted Sukarno's purpose of using the Front as a single national political party, although the army would undoubtedly have gone along with this.

Sukarno had hardly driven the last rivet into his Guided Democracy structure when the Dutch again handed him the kind of issue he took relish in exploiting. As a part of their military build-up, the Dutch had dispatched the aircraft carrier *Karel Doorman*, pride of the Dutch fleet, to West Irian, and it was lying quietly in the harbor of Hollandia. Now the Dutch, the first Westerners to visit Japan, proposed to celebrate the anniversary of their long history of cultural relations with Japan by sending this ship on a good-will visit. The Indonesians, viewing this as an anti-Indonesia move related to the West Irian dispute, were outraged.

Parliament, on August 31, passed two resolutions strongly protesting the visit and calling on the government to prepare resolute action against Japan in diplomatic, economic, and commercial fields. Foreign Minister Subandrio warned that the dispute was taking on the character of "a physical conflict," and suggested that the Japan visit might lead to the conclusion that the vessel was obtaining Japanese arms for use in West Irian. The protests reached such a peak of intensity that the Indonesian government made clear it was prepared to break relations with Japan if the visit were carried out. This was like shooting a rabbit with a cannon, but it was an excellent illustration of the explosive character of Indonesian emotional reactions regarding any issue that tread on the sensitive toes of Indonesian nationalism.

In an effort at mollification, the Japanese informed Subandrio that they were unable to cancel the visit, which had been planned long before, but that the Dutch had agreed the vessel would not subsequently return to West Irian. Asserting that the issue had become a "matter of principle," Subandrio publicly announced that the Government of Indonesia was still insisting on complete cancellation of the visit.

Earlier in the week Subandrio had sent the deputy secretary-general of the Foreign Office to Tokyo in an unsuccessful attempt to obtain cancellation of the visit. A story was leaked to the press that the Government of Indonesia was determined to withdraw its Ambassador from Japan if the visit were not canceled. An ever-mounting flood of protest against Japanese acceptance of the visit poured in from mass organizations, the press, party groups of all shades of opinion. Although PKI-controlled bodies were in the forefront, even the anti-Communist Moslem elements, including Masjumi leaders like former Premier Sukiman, joined the chorus. The Japanese, faced with a choice between Indonesia and the Netherlands, really had no choice. Anguished screams suddenly changed to a triumphal chorus when, on September 3, the Japanese government announced indefinite postponement of the *Karel Doorman* visit.

Some of us were inclined to view this curiously exaggerated issue as an effort on the part of Sukarno and the PKI to divert attention from the internal power struggle. They had good cause for a diversion. Wary of the increasing influence and activity of the PKI, army commanders began cracking down in South Kalimantan, South Sumatra, and South Sulawesi, banning activities of the PKI and its affiliates in the interest of peace and order. Commanders of these areas were promptly summoned by Sukarno to Djakarta. Meeting with him on August 31, they vigorously defended their actions. The President then requested Nasution to arrange a September conference with all Cabinet ministers, governors, regional commanders, and heads of armed forces for a complete airing of the matter.

The lines were drawn as the time for the meeting approached. There were reports that the army planned to extend the ban on the Communist Party to East and West Java (the former being one of the PKI's major strongholds). The PKI brought intense public and private pressure to bear on the President and the government, charging that the army move was illegal, that only the President had the power to ban parties. It began to look as though at long last a real showdown between the country's two strongest forces was about to take place. It was a dramatic confrontation that took place on September 12. According to eye witnesses, the President opened the conference with a strong defense of the PKI as a loyal political party. He called for national unity, apparently acquiescing in the pre-existing army ban in the outer-island provinces, though he did not order an extension of it. The regional commanders reportedly challenged the President sharply with instances of PKI subversion. Sukarno's answers were unsatisfactory. Djuanda and Nasution attempted to pour oil on the troubled waters. Sukarno, becoming more and more emotional, attempted to exploit a forthcoming UN appearance, winding up with a dramatic plea for unity to uphold the prestige of Indonesia on the world stage. Angry, harassed, his back to the wall, he broke into tears at the conclusion of the meeting.

A compromise was reached—unsatisfactory albeit face-saving to both sides—by means of a presidential decree whereby all political activities were banned through November 30, to be permitted thereafter only with prior authorization of the local army administrators. The decree specifically exempted government-created bodies like the National Front and prohibited outright banning of any party without the President's permission. The temporary ban was a cleverly designed concession to the army; at the same time, it helped the PKI by blurring the distinction between the parties. After the meeting, Djuanda publicly expressed "relief" that the conference had "cleared the air," but nothing really had been settled. The contestants were unreconciled, and the situation continued unstable. While forced to give some ground, Sukarno achieved his minimum goal—sidetracking the army campaign against the PKI—and bought time for further maneuvers.

After the meeting it was announced that the President, who had been scheduled to leave for a UN General Assembly appearance in New York after October 5, had advanced the departure date to September 26. A formidable array of notables would accompany him: Subandrio, General Nasution, Deputy Chief of Staff Gatot Subroto, PKI head Aidit, PNI Chairman Ali Sastroamidjojo, NU Chairman Idham Chalid, another Sukarno, head of the police, and a large number of other political figures. Selection of such a group was an obvious attempt by Sukarno to demonstrate the apparent breadth of popular support for his Guided Democracy and advance the theme of a Nationalist-Communist-Moslem unity. He hoped thus to muffle the army-PKI conflict, divert the populace from its economic woes, and re-create his own image as a world leader.

Prior to his departure, Sukarno moved swiftly and effectively against those he considered his enemies. Early in September he issued unpublicized instructions imposing severe controls on members of the now banned Masjumi and PSI, including supervision of their contacts with foreign diplomats, restrictions on their movements, and a continuing check on their private business activities. He followed this by a drastic move to muzzle the opposition press. Printing plants used by eight daily newspapers associated with the Democratic League were seized by the government, including the strongly anti-Communist *Pedoman,* and *Abadi,* and the Surabaya *Suara Rakjat.* By a separate personal order, apparently issued immediately prior to his departure and without the knowledge of Nasution, Sukarno had the anti-Communist *Nusantara* printing plant seized and its publication rights canceled. The government announced that the plants would be turned over to its Information Department for operation, that the affected newspapers might publish elsewhere if they could locate facilities (an empty gesture), and that later on they might be permitted to use the seized plants "under certain conditions," which, it was understood, would include pledges to refrain from criticizing the government.

In the same period, Sukarno knocked off another major anti-Communist effort when he refused to go along with Labor Minister Ahem's plans for developing a unified, government-dominated trade-union organization that would exclude the PKI's sobsi.

With the top leaders of the nation out of the country, the War Administration promptly watered down the government's seizure of printing plants, announcing that publication permits of all papers would be "reconsidered" in light of the temporary ban on political activity, and that *Pedoman, Abadi,* and *Berita Indonesia* would be permitted to resume publication. However, responding apparently to a direct order from Sukarno, the War Administration withdrew the publication permit of the opposition sparkplug, *Nusantara.*

During the ensuing political lull, one significant incident occurred in the departure from the country of Nasution's assistant, Colonel Sukendro, on Sukarno's orders. The President had long been determined to exile Colonel Sukendro, whom he considered hostile to his purposes and partly responsible for promotion of the Democratic League and other army moves against the PKI. Nasution defended his assistant in vain.

A critical Sukarno returned on October 15. The United Nations, he said, was still an arena for the cold war. If this situation continued, many countries, including Indonesia, would lose confidence in the organization. He favored a shift of UN headquarters and a revision of its structure, but advised the Indonesian people not to be disappointed if the proposals were not rapidly realized.

If there were any doubts as to Sukarno's determination to impose his will on the rubber-stamp legislative bodies he had created, it was resolved when he laid down the law to the mprs on November 10 in Bandung. Despite the constitutional provision giving the mprs the power to appoint the President and Vice-President, Sukarno told the delegates they had no power over him since the assembly had only provisional status. He told them to act with dispatch and issued a hardly veiled threat to dissolve the assembly if it did not heed his words. He also charged the body with determining the broad outlines of state policy no later than January 1, pointedly noting that such policy was ready-made in *Manipol*-USDEK, and urged prompt action on a new eight-year plan. The assembly clicked its heels and obeyed. The rubber stamp worked so fast that the third primary plenary session was concluded in thirty minutes!

Indonesian leaders and the non-Communist press generally reacted favorably to the U.S. election results of 1960, indicating their expectation that U.S. policy toward the Afro-Asian nations would become more flexible and understanding. The pro-PSI *Pedoman* applauded the election of the youthful President Kennedy as an indication of "the vitality of a democratic nation," and speculated that he would "mobilize prominent intellectuals in positions of leadership." The pro-Murba (the PKI split-off party) *Berita Indonesia* regarded the outcome as offering a new hope for easing East-West tensions but saw little prospect for a change of U.S. policy toward West Irian.

B. M. Diah's *Merdeka* saw little hope for alteration in U.S. foreign policy, but commented that if Kennedy wished to restore the international prestige of the U.S., he must improve its "approach toward Asian-African countries, support general disarmament and peaceful coexistence." PNI leader Ali Sastroamidjojo stated that evaluation of the Kennedy victory should wait on his attitude toward disarmament and recognition of Communist China, and his policy toward West Irian and the elimination of colonialism. The Communist press unanimously parroted the party line that there was little likelihood of change in U.S. domestic or foreign policies since the American voters had no real choice, both parties being dominated by monopolistic capitalists.

As the year 1960 came to a close, more and more was heard of the national-unity concept advocated by President Sukarno under Nasakom. Sukarno, who had long stressed the need for unity of the revolutionary forces, and had included the PKI in all government areas except the Cabinet, now appeared intent on overriding army opposition to acceptance of the PKI. The PNI was following Sukarno's lead; its chairman labeled the leaders of the PNI, NU, and PKI as the Nasakom group.

Increasingly strong rumors of inclusion of Communists in the Indonesian Cabinet continued to be of concern to the U.S. government; so much so, that I called on General Nasution in December 1960 in order to express that concern. Nasution told me that for the sake of Indonesian unity, he was willing to accept PKI participation in an advisory body, such as the Supreme Advisory Council, but participation in the executive branch of government was another thing altogether. He assured me the United States could count on this not happening.

Nasution also confided that at Sukarno's order he would be visiting Moscow at the end of the month for the purpose of accelerating navy-

and air-force–aid programs in the face of the Dutch reinforcement of West New Guinea.[3]

Ultimately, military action against West Irian was avoided. But the interplay of forces within Indonesia—the Sumatra rebellion, the West Irian issue, the PKI's thrust for power, the evolution of Guided Democracy—had conspired to delimit the parliamentary process and deliver to Sukarno total authority over the country's policies, at home and abroad. He was quick to employ it in a new, potentially explosive area.

---

3. Unmentioned but implicit in this conversation was the fact that the U.S. Government had rejected Indonesia's request for arms in October 1960.

CHAPTER 3

"Crush Malaysia"

On September 16, 1963, Malaysia was formally established as a nation. On the previous day, Indonesia and the Philippines had announced their refusal to recognize what Indonesia termed "this neo-colonialist creation"; whereupon Malayans marked the day of the new nation's birth by stoning the Indonesian Embassy in Kuala Lumpur. Djakarta mobs responded by attacking both the Malayan and British embassies. At the British Embassy, my doughty, bearded colleague, Sir Andrew Gilchrist, received them in the spirit of "There will always be an England." He met with a delegation of the rioters and explained that the United Nations Secretary-General's report had given its blessing to the formation of Malaysia. When the rioters departed with a shout of "*Hidup* [Long live] Sukarno!" the British Ambassador responded with "*Hidup* U Thant!" To make sure the crowd had no doubt about the British spirit, Gilchrist sent one of his military attachés to stride up and down the balcony playing his bagpipes. I have no doubt Sir Andrew meant the gesture in good fun, but the Indonesian mob did not appreciate the Scotsman's sense of humor. They broke through the gates, pushed over the Ambassador's big black Rolls-Royce, and set it on fire.

The next day, Malaysia severed diplomatic relations with Indonesia. Everyone anticipated some kind of an outburst in Djakarta, but the day passed quietly.

The morning of September 18 was blistering hot, with hardly a cloud in the intense blue sky. The rainy season had not yet begun, and the expanse of lawn fronting the embassy residence was as brown as the Montana prairie. Djakarta's black asphalt pavements were cushion soft to the feet. The slight breeze, hot and unrefreshing, stirred small eddies of dust in the bone-dry streets and seemed to charge the atmosphere with electricity. At eleven o'clock, my phone rang. An excited voice shouted, "My God, Mr. Ambassador, they're burning the British Embassy!" The caller was an American staying at the new Hotel Indonesia, directly across the plaza from the scene of the fire. From his room he could see the mob, which he thought numbered about 5,000. As the day wore on, reports poured in from one section of the city after another that British homes had been set ablaze. Gangs of Communist thugs toured the city in trucks carrying gasoline and kerosene. Their work had been carefully planned. Each truck had its own list of addresses of British residents.

At 7:00 the next morning, without an appointment, I called at the palace. Sukarno received me soberly, in the presence of several Cabinet members. I related the events of the previous day in detail, formally protested the complete lack of protection of British persons and property, which, I emphasized, was the Indonesian government's responsibility, and demanded that he as President give instructions to ensure the safe evacuation of British families. Sukarno agreed at once. He barked orders to his Minister of Labor, the Foreign Minister, and the head of police. Grimly he turned to me. "Are you satisfied, Mr. Ambassador?"

I thanked him and left to inform the British Ambassador of these assurances. By that evening, British families were boarding planes which would carry them to Singapore.[1]

There was considerable speculation in Djakarta as to whether President Sukarno had given his blessing in advance to the PKI plans. There was no doubt he was highly emotional on the subject of Malaysia. The prevailing opinion in the diplomatic corps was that Sukarno certainly had been consulted if, indeed, he had not had a part in the outrage. Of this I have never been convinced. There is no doubt in my mind that Sukarno had acquiesced in the Communist gangs' rampaging through the city streets—but I doubt that he approved the burning of the British Embassy. My interpretation of his glum mood on the morning of the nineteenth was that Sukarno felt the demonstration against the British had gone too far. And the alacrity with which he responded to my requests and the faithfulness with which they were carried out would tend to indicate he was not pleased with what had happened.

Immediately prior to these dramatic events, on September 16, Subandrio had told me he thought "things could be smoothed over in a few weeks." He suggested I urge Dato Hadji Kamaruddin, the Malayan Am-

---

1. Sukarno's response went farther than I had anticipated. Later in the day, he authorized the issuance of an official statement that said, in part, "The Indonesian Government naturally cannot condone and gravely regrets these incidents although it can very well understand the outburst of popular anger . . . as of this time the Government has taken all the necessary measures with a view to preventing the recurrence of these undesirable acts." The statement concluded with an appeal to the community to refrain from such "wild actions which have an adverse effect upon our struggle" and to have "full trust in the Government in implementation of the lines of policy as set down by the President and the Government in our struggle to oppose Malaysia." Despite the reference to understanding "popular anger," the statement had the desired effect.

bassador, not to return to Kuala Lumpur. In response to my comment that this obviously put the Ambassador in an anomalous position since, with the formation of Malaysia, there was no longer any such nation as Malaya, Subandrio urged patience, noting it always took time to work these things out. Kamaruddin could remain in Djakarta informally. It was important to have a contact. I conveyed this message. Kamaruddin was uncertain about the right course of action, but he was spared any dilemma for, on September 17, Kuala Lumpur broke diplomatic relations with Djakarta and ordered him to come home.

If Subandrio's comment to me may be taken at face value, it would seem to indicate that the Indonesian leadership had not yet made up its mind about its future course of action.

Nevertheless, events moved swiftly from that point on. Taking advantage of anti-British sentiment following the burning of the British Embassy, the Communist-controlled labor unions moved to take over British enterprises. In response to British protests, the Indonesian government, on September 20, assumed control of these enterprises to ensure their "safety." This was hardly calculated to reassure the British, who demanded to know when the properties would be returned to full British control and what the supervision involved. The government attempted placation, insisting that no nationalization of them was intended, and that the sole purpose was to ensure their protection and the continuation of normal operations. The reaction reflected a hard-headed realization that oil from Shell wells must continue to flow; that rubber, tobacco, tea, and palm oil from British estates was bringing in desperately needed foreign exchange; and that a policy of confrontation accentuated the nation's dependency on existing foreign enterprise. But in spite of this, Sukarno put his priorities on confrontation. On September 21, the government declared an economic blockade of Malaysia.[2]

The Malaysia confrontation (*konfrontasi*) was one of two major external issues to dominate the political life of modern Indonesia—the other being the conflict with the Dutch over West New Guinea. The fact that the issue was born in a period of intense, emotional nationalism and had as its progenitors pride and suspicion perhaps makes it understandable how such a meaningless dispute could arise.

---

2. There is some circumstantial evidence that Sukarno had made the decision to break economic ties with Singapore and Malaysia even before the burning of the British Embassy. [See Frederick Philip Bunnell, "The Kennedy Initiatives in Indonesia, 1962–1963" (Thesis, Cornell University, September 1969), p. 648.] If so, the Tunku (Abdul Rahman, Prime Minister of Malaya) inadvertently played into Sukarno's hands, for cooler heads in the government might well have restrained the impetuous President. Djuanda, among others, was sufficiently sensitive to American response to have known that any such action, with or without provocation, must mean the end of the economic-stabilization program on which he had staked his reputation.

As part of Great Britain's program of decolonization in Southeast Asia, the small nation of Malaya was to be federated with Singapore and the three Crown Colonies of northern Borneo—Sarawak, Brunei, and North Borneo (Sabah). This concept of nation-making through territorial combination had been invented specifically to save Singapore. With the establishment of Malayan independence in August 1957, this heretofore prosperous city had been cut off from its hinterland and was slowly withering on the economic vine. As such, it was ripe for Communist exploitation, and the Chinese were not slow in taking advantage of the opportunity. Within four years, the semi-independent Singapore began to show signs of slipping into Communist hands—despite all the efforts of the once dominant Democrat Socialist People's Action Party (PAP), led by the brilliant and aggressive, Cambridge-educated Lee Kuan Yew. A Communist Singapore would be a spear aimed at Indonesia and a den of subversion for its neighbors. Western control of the strategic Straits of Malacca might be seriously undermined. Alert to the threat, Malaya and Britain proposed rather abruptly, in May 1961,[3] the idea of a Malaysian federation incorporating the hitherto unwelcome Singapore.

Long the entrepôt and logical outlet for Malayan products, it had not been included in newly independent Malaya in 1957 because the addition of the Singapore Chinese population would have made Malaya virtually a Chinese state. This was the last thing the Malayans—as well as the Western powers—wanted. The addition of the British colonies of Borneo to the mix, however, would offset the Singapore Chinese and result in a state approximately forty-eight per cent Malay, thirty-six per cent Chinese, nine per cent Indian and Pakistani, seven per cent aboriginal—with a total population of about ten and a half million.

Meeting in August 1961 to discuss a merger, the Prime Ministers of the territories established the Malaysia Solidarity Consultative Committee (MSCC) for the purpose of exchanging views and making appropriate recommendations for the formation of Malaysia. When the Prime Minister of Malaya, the Tunku, went to London in November to discuss the tentative proposals with the British, it was decided that it would be essential to ascertain the views of the peoples of North Borneo and Sarawak. The Cobbold Commission, after the name of its chairman, was set up to accomplish this, with two British and two Malayan representa-

---

3. On May 27, 1961, the Tunku made a speech to foreign correspondents at the Adelphi Hotel in Singapore in which he said, "Malaya today as a nation realizes that she cannot stand alone and in isolation. Sooner or later, she should have an understanding with the British and the peoples of the territories of Singapore, North Borneo, Brunei and Sarawak." Lee Kuan Yew supported the concept. On October 16, the Malayan Prime Minister proposed the formation of Malaysia in principle. The annual meeting of native chiefs in Kuching approved the plan on October 24 without dissent (although there was one abstention).

tives.[4] It was also deemed necessary to consult the Sultan of Brunei, whose participation in the federation was already uncertain.

Defense was among the numerous questions to be resolved. The existing defense agreement between Britain and Malaya was to be extended to embrace the other territories involved, with the British continuing their bases in Singapore "for the purpose of assisting in the defense of Malaysia and for Commonwealth defense for the preservation of peace in Southeast Asia."

On August 1, 1962, Prime Minister Rahman again went to London, where it was agreed that Malaysia would be formed on August 31, 1963. Endorsement of the merger proposal came from the Malayan Parliament August 15, 1962; by the Legislative Council of Sabah on September 12; the Council Negri of Sarawak on September 26; and on September 1, from 397,000 of 625,000 voters in Singapore. In the local elections held between December 1962 and June 1963, Malaysia was the main issue of the campaign, and the plan received heavy endorsement.[5]

In August 1961, British Commissioner-General for Southeast Asia Lord Selkirk visited Djakarta for the purpose of consulting with the Indonesians regarding the formation of Malaysia. At the time, I was informed, the Indonesian Foreign Minister indicated that his country was agreeable to the plan. In a letter to the New York *Times* on November 13, 1961, and in a speech to the General Assembly on November 20, Subandrio said that Indonesia had no objections to the proposed merger based upon the will of the peoples concerned. In response to my query a few weeks later as to whether this was still the Indonesian position, Prime Minister Djuanda responded, "Of course, we would rather have an independent Asian nation on our northern borders instead of a British colony." The PKI, however, was bitterly opposed. In December 1961, the party adopted a resolution condemning the formation of Malaysia as "neo-colonialism" and an attempt to suppress "the democratic and patriotic movements of the peoples in these five territories which are aimed at the attainment of genuine national independence and freedom

---

4. From February 19 to April 17, 1962, the Cobbold Commission conducted fifty hearings at thirty-five centers, met 4,000 persons in some 690 groups, received 2,200 letters and memoranda from various organizations. The commission concluded that, subject to certain terms and conditions, two-thirds of the population favored the proposal for the formulation of Malaysia; one-third was divided—between a desire for independence and a preference for British rule continuing for some years.

5. In Sabah, endorsement of the Malaysia proposal in the December elections was unanimous: 113 out of 119 seats were won by political parties favoring the Malaysia plan; the other six by independent candidates who also supported it. In Sarawak, in a general election based upon universal adult suffrage, the plan also obtained heavy endorsement. The Sarawak United People's Party campaigned opposing it but won only 119 out of 429 seats.

from imperialism." The majority of the Indonesian press took its cue from the Communist campaign, and eventually it became an open secret in Djakarta that the Government of Indonesia was adopting a correct but cool approach to the concept. Apparently, the Indonesians hoped they might ultimately extend their influence over North Borneo, and were fearful lest a more prosperous Malaysia might at some future time serve as a magnet to ethnically related Sumatra. Neither the correctness nor the cool lasted long.

The Philippine attitude was bound up with the question of their claim to Sabah. President Macapagal had been identified with the original agitation for the extrication of North Borneo from British control and, as a member of Congress, had introduced a resolution calling for "restoration" of its ownership. The agitation was revived by Nicasio Osmeña, Mayor of Cebu, who had obtained power of attorney from the heirs of the Sultan of Sulu and founded the Kiram Corporation, the purpose of which was the exploitation of the commerce of North Borneo under Philippine sovereignty when attained.[6] The essence of the controversy was whether the Sultan of Sulu had leased or sold Sabah to the British in 1878. If leased, as Macapagal insisted, it could still be considered Philippine territory. The Philippine government, however, took no action toward recovering Sabah until June 22, 1962, when it rejected a stiff British note insisting there was no question about British sovereignty over the territory. Even so, the Philippine Foreign Minister assured the Malayan Ambassador on July 27, 1962, that the Philippine claim was not intended to obstruct the formation of Malaysia. Yet almost simultaneously, the Philippine President announced plans for a Malayan confederation—the Philippines, Indonesia, Malaya, Singapore, Sarawak and Sabah—later called the Maphilindo Plan. Malayans viewed the proposal as designed to prevent the formation of Malaysia and salvage the Philippine claim to Sabah, and relations between the two countries worsened. The Malayan Prime Minister was attacked by the Philippine press for standing in the way of the Philippines' recovering North Borneo.

In this atmosphere, Azahari, President of Brunei's People's Party (Partai Rakjat) arrived in Manila at the invitation of Osmeña and met with leaders of the Philippine government, including Vice-President Emmanuel Pelaez. Two days after his return to Manila for a second visit, on December 8, 1962, a revolt broke out in Brunei. From Manila, Azahari proclaimed the formation of the Unitary State of Kalimantan Utara (North Borneo), with himself as President.

---

6. Cf. Bernard K. Gordon, *The Dimensions of Conflict in Southeast Asia* (Englewood Cliffs, N.J.: Prentice-Hall, Inc., 1966), chapter 1; and Diosdado Macapagal, *A Stone for the Edifice, Memoirs of a President* (Quezon City, Philippines: Mac Publishing House, 1968), pp. 253–275.

The PKI announced its backing for the revolt immediately, and Su-karno followed two days later. Brunei handed him the excuse he wanted for departing from his earlier policy regarding Malaysia; the re-volt came to be viewed as generally symptomatic of Bornean sentiment, and encouraged many to believe the rest of Borneo would resist joining Malaysia. But Brunei had its own special reasons for being uninterested in the Malaysia tea party.

Although Brunei is so small it is hard to locate on a map, consisting as it does of only 112,000[7] people inhabiting an area of little over 2,000 square miles, it is important for its petroleum resources. Brunei has ac-quired the nickname "Shellfare State" because the large Shell Oil Com-pany operations there produce sufficient income to support a debt-free government—with no taxes. Education is free, and all citizens are cov-ered by health and pension plans. Malaysia would have been certain to demand a large royalty in line with the practice in other countries such as Indonesia, where at the time companies were endeavoring to hold the line at a fifty-fifty split. It was easy to see why neither the ruling powers of Brunei nor Shell desired to join a larger entity.

Azahari's revolt might have been entitled to little space in the history books, since it was quickly put down, but for the fact that it lit the fires of what was to become the "Crush Malaysia" movement in Indonesia. The first step was taken by Foreign Minister Subandrio on January 20, 1963, with the declaration of a policy of "confrontation." He had re-cently returned from a trip to Peking,[8] where he had joined with the Chinese Communists in praising the Brunei revolt; now he denounced the Malayans as "henchmen of neo-colonialists and neo-imperialists" and accused the Government of Malaya of having adopted a hostile pol-icy toward Indonesia, whose "patience was running out."

There had been one significant statement earlier, in September 1962. Subandrio was quoted in Singapore as stating that he could not remain indifferent to Malaysia's creation because both countries "share a com-mon frontier." He threatened that if Malaysia established a military base in North Borneo, "we are certain to take counteraction." If it were "an American base, for instance, we shall then arrange for a Soviet base on our part of Borneo. I don't say that this thing will happen or even that it is being contemplated, but I merely want to make it clear why Indonesia cannot remain indifferent to the formation of Malaysia." When I subse-quently expressed amazement and asked for clarification, Subandrio said he had been "misquoted" on the subject of military bases in Borneo.

Tunku Abdul Rahman reacted immediately to Subandrio's confronta-

---

7. 1968 census. The sultanate is a protectorate state in the British Common wealth, with Britain responsible for its foreign affairs and defense.
8. Subandrio's visit to Peking was reportedly concerned with finding a means to settle the Sino-Indian border dispute.

tion statement, calling it a virtual "declaration of cold war." Sukarno countered and raised the tempo by saying a "physical conflict" between Indonesia and Malaya might well become "unavoidable." And on February 13, 1963, Indonesia formally launched its campaign against Malaysia when Sukarno announced at a mass meeting in Djakarta, "I now declare officially that Indonesia opposes Malaysia," and, in English, stated that the Indonesian position on Malaysia was "a matter of principle." When Sukarno wanted a statement to be heard around the world, he used the most universal language. "We are being encircled," he went on. "We do not want to have neo-colonialism in our vicinity. We consider Malaysia an encirclement of the Indonesian Republic. Malaysia is the product of . . . neo-colonialism." [9]

The following day, in a press conference in Washington, President Kennedy commented:

> We have supported the Malaysia Federation, . . . and it is under pressure from several areas. But I am hopeful it will sustain itself, because it is the best hope of security for that very vital part of the world.[10]

Although Indonesia was not mentioned, this was a clear signal to Sukarno to simmer down; it put the Indonesian leader on notice as to the U.S. position—we were for Malaysia but would remain neutral in regard to physical conflict. The statement had no visible effect upon Sukarno, serving only to heighten tensions between the United States and Indonesia at a time when the going was relatively smooth. Following the Brunei revolt, the U.S. had been fairly silent on the Malaysia question. This statement put us squarely in opposition to Sukarno. I am not being critical—I had made a number of speeches supporting the formation of Malaysia and had not changed my mind—but I was aware that with Indonesia in opposition, it was a different ball game.

Although the Brunei revolt was quelled in a comparatively short time by British military action, the issue of self-determination for the peoples of Borneo remained. Sukarno thundered from across the border that if these people wanted to be independent, he would help them! The Indonesians repeatedly denied that they wanted the Borneo territories for themselves. The various reasons they gave for opposition can be distilled into four:

One, they were convinced that the Borneans wanted to be independ-

---

9. In the embassy, we regarded Sukarno's statement as mere bluster, seeing it in the context of his earlier statements in support of the Brunei revolt. The idea that Sukarno would be so foolish as to take military action was rejected as obviously not in either his or his nation's interest. We thought that the colonial remnant of Portuguese Timor was a more likely target for any other anticolonial, nationalistic issue he might want to create.

10. *Wall Street Journal*, February 15, 1963.

ent. Therefore, Indonesians would support them, true to the tradition of backing independence movements of colonies everywhere.

Two, Sukarno believed that the formation of Malaysia was a British plot to encircle him and had no intention of permitting what he regarded as a hostile nation to be established on his northern border.

Three, Sukarno scoffed at Britain's alleged decolonization plans, regarding them as "recolonization" and pointing out that economic power and military defense of Malaysia would still be in British hands.

Four, some prominent army leaders maintained that the reasons advanced for establishing Malaysia were specious. Instead of curtailing Communist opportunities, it would simply open up North Borneo to Communist penetration and ultimate subversion. One Indonesian Army officer said to me: "I don't understand why you Americans, who profess to be so anti-Communist, don't see that in supporting Malaysia you are running the risk of the establishment of a Chinese Communist state right in the heart of Southeast Asia." When I questioned him as to whether he thought the only other apparent alternative, a united independent state of North Borneo, would be any better in this respect, his reply was affirmative. He obviously believed that self-interest, accompanied undoubtedly by Indonesian influence, would produce a harder anti-Communist line than would be taken by Malaysia. When I pointed out that Tunku Abdul Rahman and those near him were considerably stronger anti-Communists than President Sukarno and his associates, he replied: "Think of the complexion of Malaysia. I am not looking at Malaysia today, I am looking at Malaysia tomorrow. Who is going to run a country in which about forty per cent of the people control eighty-five per cent of the wealth? Obviously, the forty per cent, whether they run it themselves directly or through a Malayan façade." To my rejoinder that the Chinese in Malaysia were uniformly anti-Communist, the response was, "Yes, there is a veneer of wealthy Chinese who are unquestionably anti-Communist. But look at the rank and file. It is the rank and file who have the votes. No, the formation of Malaysia is not in our interest—or in your interest, either."

To many military leaders, however, try as hard as they could to follow Sukarno, Malaysia was just not the enemy he made the little country out to be. Neither was Britain. For the Indonesian military leadership knew as well as did the American Embassy that it was Sukarno's confrontation policy that kept the British in Southeast Asia and required them to expand their commitments just at the time when a basic decision had been made in London to pull out of the area. Implementation of that decision was delayed for years by Sukarno's confrontation. At the same time, however, confrontation had its advantages for the army. It gave them a job to do, thus enabling them to continue justification of a sizable military budget and underline the importance of the military establishment in the preservation of the nation.

In any event, the Indonesian military, ambivalent as it might be on the danger of Malaysia to Indonesia, could not afford to oppose Sukarno on confrontation if they were to continue to be in the van of Indonesia's emotional nationalism. The army leadership was competing with the PKI for the nation's favor, and had no choice but to ride the Sukarno bandwagon.

Arguments continue to this day as to the real reasons for Indonesia's moving into so untenable a position as the waging of war to prevent an arrangement apparently agreeable to the parties concerned. Some of the theories are worth considering.

The "abandonment theory" [11] was hatched in Kuala Lumpur. Following the Bandung conference of 1955, some Malayan leaders were convinced that Chou En-lai and the Indonesians got together and agreed on respective spheres of influence in Southeast Asia. Indonesia would have hegemony over the island areas—the Philippines and Borneo particularly —in return for giving the Chinese a free hand on the mainland, including the Malayan peninsula. Thus Malaya would be "abandoned" to the Chinese. About this time, Malayans observed withdrawal of Indonesia from contact with Malaya. Plans for cultural exchanges were never carried out. Instead, the Indonesians began to emphasize differences between their country and Malaya, whereas earlier they had stressed their similarities. Some leaders in Kuala Lumpur concluded that the Indonesians had decided to desert their Malayan brothers in the interest of a political deal with Peking. The formation of Malaysia represented to Sukarno, then, not a direct threat to Indonesian security but an upsetting of a basic understanding with Communist China for splitting up the entire area. The Malayan speculations were reinforced by a Chinese map marking out these spheres of influence, acquired via intelligence channels.

With his preoccupation with national security, it is difficult to envisage Sukarno's acceptance of the substitution of Chinese hegemony in the Malay archipelago for Malay control of the area. Agreement or not, domination from Peking would manifestly represent more of a security threat to Indonesia than could possibly be inherent in the existing situation. If Sukarno did make this kind of deal, he must have accepted China in his own mind as the wave of the future and considered that the time had come to cement relations by a basic understanding with respect to spheres of influence. As the proponents of abandonment see it, this is exactly what happened. But it becomes a neat, almost too pat explanation of Sukarno's subsequent *rapprochement* with Peking.

The "diversionary theory" held that Sukarno seized on a pretext for a

---

11. This theory was not widely held, but officials in Kuala Lumpur put it forward as a logical explanation of the gulf between Malaysia and Indonesia.

quarrel over Malaysia to divert the attention of his people from their internal woes. It was an attractive explanation—and a popular one—but I considered it wholly inapplicable. For one thing, the beginning of confrontation coincided with a major American-backed program to stabilize Indonesia's chaotic economy, and there was real hope on the horizon for the solution of the country's economic and financial ills. At that moment there was no reason to divert attention from the nation's ills—and every reason to focus on the fact that they were being solved!

Another theory worth noting might be called the "nation-building theory," emphasizing Sukarno's awareness of the advantages of an external enemy in the process of nation building. He probably missed his old issue, West Irian, and his old enemy, the Dutch. Both had stimulated strong emotional reactions among his people, and the wily Indonesian leader had exploited them to the full as a conscious part of nation building. Bored with the lull after settlement in August 1962, Sukarno seemed to grab quickly at the new issue to reignite Indonesian passions.

To all these hypotheses, I would add another: Sukarno's emotionalism and preoccupation with colonial issues, which so often led him to adopt an irrational course of action. He was ready to fight for peoples' freedom anywhere, at any time; he was highly suspicious of British motivation; he saw a permanent threat to Indonesian influence in non-Indonesian Borneo, a contiguous territory where he felt his nation had legitimate concerns. I am convinced that Sukarno simply could not believe that people in Borneo would prefer identification with what he saw as British-dominated Malaysia to independence or even affiliation with Indonesia. Although the latter possibility was never mentioned, Borneo must have looked to Sukarno as a ripe plum about to elude his grasp. There was also an element of pique at Malaya's record of successful democratic government at a time when Indonesia was turning away from parliamentary democracy. Malaya's economic system of free enterprise had boosted the country, whose resources were similar to those of Indonesia, into second place in per-capita income in Southeast Asia. Finally, Malaya had achieved this success on the basis of cooperation with a colonial power, whereas Sukarno had thrown the Dutch out of Indonesia. Sukarno might have feared the contagion of this kind of success and the impact it would have on Indonesia's attitude toward his own philosophy for developing a national system. But beyond this lay something deeper. Sukarno's emotional involvement with an issue affected him like a drug. He had an addiction to the politics of excitement; he craved the stimulus of public conflict. Agitational politics satisfied his ego and fitted in appropriately with his quasi-expansionist aims.

Years later, I asked Hatta when the major differences between him and Sukarno had first developed. Prior to independence, Hatta said, there had been two important points of departure—how to deal with

Dutch economic interest in the country, and the actual geographical boundaries that should mark the future Republic of Indonesia. As to the first, Hatta felt Dutch investment and know-how were essential to the new nation, whereas Sukarno saw a continuing Dutch stranglehold in their pre-eminent economic position. Ultimately, Sukarno, who had little understanding of economics, agreed with Hatta's view. He was to alter this position when the Dutch refused to settle the West Irian issue.

On the territorial question, Mohammed Yamin had early proposed an enlarged Indonesia based on the territory of the Madjapahit Empire. He and Sukarno were encouraged in this by delegations from Malaya who urged that their territory be incorporated into the new Republic of Indonesia, because they feared that an independent Malaya would be dominated by the Chinese. Hatta opposed this concept, insisting that Indonesia must be established on the basis of the unifying factors present in the situation—that these factors existed in the territory formerly occupied by the Dutch and incorporated in the Dutch East Indies, and that the idea of expanding beyond this was unsound. After considerable argument, Hatta said, his views prevailed. Nevertheless, he felt Sukarno's nature was such that this concept of a greater Indonesia must have always remained in the back of his mind. Although no other responsible leadership in Indonesia accepted the idea, Hatta recognized that escalation of the military conflict over Malaysia could result in the growth of expansionist ideas among Indonesian nationalists.

Sukarno's suspicion of the British was unfounded, and I repeatedly told him so—they were simply reacting to his initiatives. Certainly they were unhappy with him, and with reason, but the accusation that the formation of Malaysia was a plot to encircle Indonesia was too absurd. What the British were thinking about in those days was revealed in a conversation I had with British Deputy High Commissioner Moore in Singapore, in June of 1963. He confirmed, among other things, the fact that the British had been giving serious consideration to reducing their commitments in the area. Now, however, owing to Sukarno's opposition to Malaysia, they were digging in their heels.

Moore wondered whether U.S. and British views might not ultimately diverge with respect to objectives in Southeast Asia. He questioned whether the presence of the British fleet in the long run might not prove an embarrassment to the United States as we pursued our policies regarding Indonesia, assuming the primary objective of Indonesian policy to be the elimination of the British base in Singapore. I said this made no sense whatsoever. We were not pursuing a policy in Indonesia of interest to the United States alone—we were endeavoring to preserve the freedom of Southeast Asia, and I assumed the British interest was the same.

The British had no plan to topple Sukarno, Moore said, but he wanted to know whether there was a possibility of a breakup of Indonesia owing to the antagonism between Sumatra and Java. This was not a realistic possibility, in my opinion. Although there was considerable anti-Sukarno sentiment in the outer islands, it was not organized; furthermore, I had discovered no secessionist attitudes anywhere; opposition to Sukarno was directed at obtaining a change of government in Djarkarta. This opposition, however, had not crystallized into an effective movement.

"What, in your opinion, would happen if Sukarno were no longer onstage?" Moore asked. I thought it would depend upon circumstances at the time. I said, "If we are talking about the present, the army would either take over or select his successor. Undoubtedly, the PKI would exploit temporary uncertainty in order to attempt a coup. In my view, they would not be successful."

As our discussion continued, I found myself outlining my views on the Indonesian situation. I told him I was aware of being criticized for taking a soft line with the Indonesians, and I felt this was a misinterpretation of my own and my country's attitude. I had found it necessary to take antithetical positions to the hard-liners in Washington, because I was concerned with steering Sukarno into constructive channels and was keenly aware that threats would be counter-productive. I felt we had gone as far as we could without reaching the point where our extremely limited leverage would be lost. Of course, I continued to spell out to Sukarno the consequences of his actions, actual or proposed. Aside from the Chinese and the Soviets, I told Moore, the United States and Japan were the principal nations that could get Sukarno's ear. Therefore, within the limits of what was politically possible in view of U.S. domestic reactions, I considered it important that we maintain a dialogue as long as possible. Moore agreed.

The disturbing question that remains regarding Indonesia's challenge to Malaysia is whether the Indonesian leadership had contemplated a policy of confrontation against Malaysia prior to the Brunei revolt, and consequently had had a hand in it as part of a conspiracy to prevent the formation of Malaysia. Significant is the fact that the PKI took a specific, strong stand against the formation of Malaysia as early as December 1961. The following September, Subandrio attacked the Malaysia plan; three months later, Azahari's revolt took place in Brunei. What happened between December 1961 and September 1962 to change the official Indonesian position on Malaysia? Was it PKI pressure? Did Subandrio know in September of Azahari's plans for a coup in December, and was he simply paving the way for a scheduled reversal of position? It is possible only to speculate on the answers.

The Communist press alone in Djakarta referred to Azahari's revolt as a "North Kalimantan" revolt. The inference might be drawn that the Communists—and presumably Sukarno and Subandrio—had anticipated

a wider uprising, perhaps misled by the overoptimistic estimates of Azahari himself. There were some reports that the Partindo Party, a PKI
front group, helped Azahari in training his revolutionaries. If true, both
Subandrio and Sukarno must have been aware of it. In any event, given
Sukarno's natural sympathy for a cause that appeared to represent a
struggle against colonialism, the PKI would not have expected to encounter opposition from him in adopting an anti-Malaysia stand; nor would
they have been surprised if he seized the first excuse to do likewise.

As I saw the situation in June 1963, there was a simple solution that
would draw the nettle. The basis for Sukarno's position was his conviction that the people of Kalimantan wanted to be free and that they did
not want to join Malaysia. He was against the British disposing of them
as though they were chattels, using the transfer of sovereignty as the
excuse. He had other reasons, of course, but these were the foundation
of his public position.

Our independent investigations of the attitudes in Borneo—grass-
roots assessments by experienced Foreign Service personnel—supple-
mented by conclusions reached by scholars in the area, convinced us that
the majority of people were not opposed to transfer to Malaysia, as elections previously held had tended to demonstrate. There were several reasons for this. The Dyaks were for the most part illiterate and unprepared
for self-government. Some of their leaders realized this, and would have
preferred the British to stay until their people could assume greater responsibility. But the most compelling reason for not wanting independence, we found, was fear of Sukarno's Indonesia. Since Sukarno would
never discover this or, if he did, would find it unbelievable, the obvious
answer to the problem was for the British to offer to hold some form of
plebiscite on the issue, with United Nations observers present. Such a
proposal was in the British tradition; it was also one that Sukarno, who
based his position on the principle of self-determination, would have to
accept.

I sounded out Lord Selkirk on the idea, making clear this was not an
official American proposal but my own thought, which I wanted to explore with him before I carried it further. He puffed on his pipe for a
moment, took a long draw and exhaled slowly. "I'm not so sure," he said,
looking up at the ceiling, his long chin extended. "How would you put
the question, eh? For or against the transfer, with no other alternatives?
That smacks of Hitlerism, 'Ja oder nein.'

"And if you presented alternatives, what would they be? To remain
with Britain? We don't want that. We've made up our mind to get out.
To be independent? Independence is heady wine, you know. But Borneo's not viable. These people might land in Sukarno's lap.

"No, we're sure of how they feel today. The elections proved that.
Our case is solid. No, I don't think we should make this kind of move as
a gesture to bring Sukarno around."

I reported the conversation to Washington and suggested they might wish to explore the matter further, but nothing came of it. Thus the question of how the confrontation could be cooled was left open. Sukarno's reaction to the outbreak of the Brunei revolt and his resultant opposition to the formation of Malaysia raised the specter of another disadvantageous conflict in Southeast Asia. Behind the scenes, quiet but intense diplomatic activity had begun.

CHAPTER 4

The UN Survey:
A Near Miss

Representatives of Malaya, Indonesia, and the Philippines gathered in Manila on April 9, 1963, to prepare the groundwork for a pre-summit Foreign Ministers' meeting. During the talks, on April 12, the Indonesians staged their first military action in Borneo, a tactic obviously designed to demonstrate what might happen if a compromise were not worked out.

In May and early June, however, Sukarno suddenly turned off the faucet of fury and invited the Malayan head of state to meet him in Tokyo. This was the result of considerable diplomatic maneuvering behind the scenes. I had been urging Sukarno for some time to talk directly with the Tunku in an effort to settle the dispute. The Thais were doing likewise, and the Australian Foreign Minister, Sir Garfield Barwick, visited Djakarta twice in an endeavor to calm things down, following up these talks with meetings in Kuala Lumpur and Manila. President Macapagal claimed credit for the final push that brought Sukarno and the Tunku together.

Sukarno had planned to be in Tokyo for rest and relaxation at the end of May, and also to participate in negotiations with American oil companies.[1] His sudden invitation to the Tunku to visit him in Tokyo meant

---

1. The oil negotiations, successfully completed in June 1963, illustrate another facet of American diplomacy in which U.S. business interests and Indonesian national interests appeared to be on a collision course. It was a matter of politics as well as economics, since the Indonesians would have had to turn to the Soviets for petroleum technology had the Big Three—Caltex, Standard Vacuum and Shell—either withdrawn from or been thrown out of Indonesia. U.S. government initiatives brought the two sides together, and a mutually satisfactory contract was negotiated with the assistance of a U.S. government team chaired by Wilson W. Wyatt and including Walter J. Levy, Abram L. Chayes and me.

that Sukarno would be involved in discussions of the two major issues of concern to the U.S. regarding Indonesia.

On May 31 and June 1, Sukarno and Rahman met at the residence of Foreign Minister Ohira. The meeting apparently resulted in the two leaders' agreeing to settle their differences peacefully. The Tunku went so far as to say, "Tell the people at home our prayers have been answered." Harmony continued to reign at the Foreign Ministers' meeting in Manila, held from June 7 to 11; it began to look as though Pelaez, Subandrio, and Razak were about to pull a rabbit out of a hat. They laid the groundwork for a meeting of the three heads of state to be held in Manila at the end of July. They also endorsed President Macapagal's proposal for a greater Malay confederation, Maphilindo (an acronym for the three nations represented), and hammered out drafts of the accords to be presented at the summit meeting. The ministers' most significant proposal was their reaffirmation of the principle of self-determination for territories without self-government. Indonesia and the Philippines specified that they would welcome the formation of Malaysia if the support of the Borneo territories were impartially ascertained by an authority such as the UN Secretary-General or his representative. The Federation of Malaya gave itself the task of consulting the governments of Britain and the Borneo territories with a view to inviting the Secretary-General to implement the ascertainment.

But there was no prescription as to how this ascertainment would be carried out and, like so many other agreements in principle, it presented serious difficulties in practice. Nevertheless, we were encouraged by the results of the Foreign Ministers' meeting. Despite British doubts and the skepticism of some observers, Washington concurred in my assessment that it seemed to provide an opportunity to introduce some measure of tranquillity in the situation.

The July meeting was almost wrecked on the shoal of an agreement signed in London on July 9 between Malaya and the United Kingdom on behalf of Singapore, Sarawak, and Sabah. Providing for the transfer of British sovereignty in the territories to Malaysia on August 31, the agreement was interpreted by Sukarno as foreclosing the questions he expected to discuss in Manila later in the month. He was furious. It was nip and tuck as to whether he would attend the Manila meeting.

On July 10, the day following the signature, in a voice choked with emotion, he publicly accused the Tunku of violating his word, allegedly given in their Tokyo meeting, to delay the formation of Malaysia until after a United Nations referendum in Sarawak and Sabah. For the next fortnight, the President stoked all the fires of confrontation, increasing military pressures, stepping up anti-Malaysia propaganda. He called off Indonesian participation in talks aimed at obtaining UN cooperation in the dispute, and publicly threatened not to go to Manila. Some members of the embassy staff and Washington critics of the Administration's policy of attempting to work with Sukarno saw this as certain evidence that he had no intention of settling the dispute. I still believed, however, that the Indonesian President could be induced to go to Manila and, once there, could be steered into accepting a face-saving formula—particularly if it opened up to him the possibility of expanding Indonesian influence in Southeast Asia. I read his stepped-up anti-Malaysia campaign as typical threat tactics for strengthening his position in the forthcoming Manila negotiations and for answering an implication of U.S.-aid withdrawal. That implication came not from the Administration but from Congress, a distinction that, however clear to Americans, hardly ever registered abroad.

On July 25, Congressman Broomfield, long a critic of Sukarno and of what he regarded as the Administration's appeasement of him, obtained House Foreign Affairs Committee approval of an amendment to the Foreign Aid bill requiring the suspension of military and economic assistance to Indonesia unless the U.S. President determined such assistance to be in the national interest. "Instead of curbing Sukarno, our nation's foreign policy appears to be to placate him," Broomfield said. "Some 11,000,000 Americans learned during World War II that it doesn't pay to attempt to appease a dictator suffering from delusions of grandeur." And he referred to Indonesian agents in North Borneo and Indonesian naval maneuvers as evidence that "President Sukarno is going all out to prevent the Federation of Malaysia, scheduled to take place August 31." [2]

The following day, I was scheduled to meet with Sukarno to induce him to go to Manila. It would not be an easy interview. I had to overcome three obstacles—Sukarno's reaction to the Malay-British moves, his pique at the fact that the invitation to the summit had been received at the last moment, and last but not least, his bridling at the impending U. S. Congressional action—which, by confirming this proud Asian in his confrontation policy, was certain to have the reverse effect of what was intended. He had announced a giant anti-Malaysia rally for July 27. He would show the world he could not be pushed around.

I opened the conversation by asking how he felt. "I am still angry," Sukarno replied, but with a boyish grin that softened the statement. I said I had given much thought to the problem he faced, as had Washington. We had come to the firm conclusion that his own interests required him to attend the summit. He could not afford to let personal pique govern. If he stayed home, world opinion would blame him for the resultant tensions. Sukarno must consider that Philippine-Indonesian relations would inevitably suffer since the Philippine President

---

2. New York *Times*, July 26, 1963.

would lose face in his own country. Sukarno's world image would be tarnished, the principle of self-determination disregarded, and the chance to form a Malay confederation lost.

There was another point he must consider: the effect his refusal would have on the economic program we had been working out together. If Sukarno failed to go to Manila, it would be a clear indication to all concerned that he was not interested in settling the Malaysia dispute, and I said I could not vouch for our continuing ability to assist Indonesia. I told him I knew President Kennedy wanted to help. I questioned whether it was in Indonesia's interest for Sukarno to take actions that would make it politically impossible for Kennedy to carry out his intention, expressed when the two heads of state met at the White House two years before, to provide economic assistance to Indonesia. We had gone a long way with Sukarno. We had had a team of experts survey Indonesia's economic and financial requirements; we were now prepared to help implement the recommendations of their report. Even while we were talking, American representatives at a meeting of the Development Assistance Committee (DAC) in Paris were endeavoring to organize a consortium of nations to assist Indonesia in its program. I presented this argument on a facts-of-life basis, careful to avoid any hint of threat. It came down to this: we wanted to help Indonesia. Sukarno alone could prevent us from doing so.

Sukarno only interrupted once. When I pointed out that we must not overlook the possibility that the late arrival of the invitations was the result of a boner by inept subordinates in the Malayan External Affairs Ministry, and that, in any event, the Tunku should not be held responsible since he had been out of the country at the time, Sukarno interjected hopefully, "Do you really think this might have resulted from clumsiness on the part of underlings?"

I replied that we both knew how frequently these things happened. It seemed to me obvious that Malaya's top officials would not have intentionally issued invitations only a few days prior to the summit; they must have realized how such an act would be interpreted in Djakarta.

"Don't you think they did this to nail down the deadline of August 31?" Sukarno demanded. I said no; in my opinion the timing of invitations was quite inadvertent and not designed either as a provocation or as a tactic.

Sukarno indicated he would give serious consideration to what I had told him. The matter of the late invitation was relatively trivial, but it pointed up the extreme to which Sukarno allowed his vanity to carry him. In an interview concerned with matters of vital impact on the future of Southeast Asia, Sukarno's attention seemed to be concentrated only on a fancied slight to himself.

Sukarno kept us waiting until the last minute for his decision. In

Washington and Djakarta we held our breath until the word came.[3] Two very different courses in Southeast Asia could hinge on this decision. On the one hand, a long, dreary military conflict, with the ever-present danger of escalation into something menacing to world peace; on the other, a constructive and cooperative approach to the regional problems of Southeast Asia, with its largest and most powerful nation committed to arrangements that held much promise.

Would this satisfy Sukarno's vision of the future? Or did he have some grand design involving territorial expansion? In Washington, Hilsman, agreeing with my assessment, saw Indonesia "teetering on the verge of a fundamental decision whether to turn toward co-operation with the Communist nations or toward more peaceable channels for achieving the goals of nationalism, and the evidence at that time was that the decision was in the direction of the peaceable." If this occurred, as we all hoped, Indonesia would emerge as one of the "new forces of Asian unity and economic strength." [4]

At the rally on the day following our talk, Sukarno thundered from the platform, "If God wills it, I will leave for Manila the day after to-morrow to carry on our confrontation to oppose and eliminate the neo-colonialist Malaysia." Not a statement calculated to encourage a settlement even if he did attend the meeting. Sukarno held off notifying me or anyone else of his decision until a few hours before his departure. It was affirmative.

The Manila summit meeting, held from July 30 to August 5, 1963, came close to producing a successful formula for the settlement of the Malaysia dispute. But alleged violations of the agreements reached at that time were ever afterward cited by the Indonesian government as justification for continuance of the "Crush Malaysia" campaign.

Though not in attendance at the meeting, I was in the wings. Both my government and the Indonesian government had thought my presence in the neighborhood might be helpful. My wife and I were relaxing in Baguio, near Manila, when I received a call from Subandrio asking me to meet him as soon as possible at his suite in the Manila Hotel, and to use the rear entrance to avoid newspaper reporters.

I caught the first plane to Manila. Subandrio greeted me enthusiastically with news that the heads of state were close to agreement on what he termed a "fresh approach" after having been badly deadlocked over the problem of how to satisfy Indonesian insistence on self-determination for the Borneo peoples. The British and Malayans were insisting

---

3. Cf. Roger Hilsman, *To Move a Nation* (Garden City, N.Y.: Doubleday & Company, Inc., 1967), p. 393.
4. *Ibid.*, p. 406.

that the Borneans favored joining Malaysia since, in the recent elections, pro-Malaysia candidates had generally been chosen. The British would not agree to a plebiscite, which they saw as pandering to Sukarno. Indonesia would not yield on what it considered a basic principle. Everything else in the preliminary drafts prepared at the June Foreign Ministers' conference had smooth sailing. But how to resolve this impasse was a tough problem.

"We've done it," Subandrio said excitedly. "We've got the answer." Half skeptically I listened to his outline of a plan to resolve the deadlock, the essence of which was to ask the Secretary-General of the United Nations to ascertain public opinion in Borneo through an inquiry, which would ensure compliance with the self-determination provisions of a UN resolution[5] "taking into consideration elections already held." If the Secretary-General complied, a working party, including observers from Malaya, the Philippines and Indonesia, would be sent to the territories immediately. Ascertainment, which would probably take about six weeks, would have to be determined prior to the establishment of the new state of Malaysia or, in any event, no later than September 30. Political prisoners in the territories would be released and have the right to be enrolled as electors, with the exception of the active rebel leaders, Azahari and his associates.

I asked Subandrio if he thought the British would accept such an arrangement inasmuch as it called for postponement of the date for formation of Malaysia. After all, Sabah and Sarawak still had the legal status of British colonies, and sovereignty still resided with the United Kingdom. The Foreign Minister said it was "his impression" that they would; the Tunku, having accepted the concept, led Subandrio to assume the British would go along.

Subandrio was going into session again as soon as he left me. He anticipated that the agreement, which had only a few sentences still in need of ironing out, would be initialed that night and a public communiqué issued the following day. A private communication from the heads of state would be sent to U Thant.

The answers to why Subandrio was so interested in informing me about what had happened can only be speculated. Subandrio wanted perhaps to drum up support for the proposal and try out the idea on me before he committed his own prestige to it. He was quite aware, as was I, that the British were a key factor in determining the Tunku's position. They could hardly be automatically sympathetic to Manila developments, since they had not been invited to participate in the conference, which was discussing a territory that was still a British responsibility. Subandrio assumed, of course, that the U.S. government, through one channel or another, would immediately inform the British—and support

---

5. United Nations Resolution 1541.

the proposal in the ensuing talks with them. Subandrio could also assume that I would welcome any reasonable settlement proposal. I had been working closely with him for months in an effort to bring about a summit meeting. I was conversant with every move that had been made.

After a good deal of pulling and hauling, an agreement was reached that embodied fairly closely the points outlined by Subandrio. Made public on August 5, 1963, it was divided into three parts, an Accord, a Statement, and a Declaration. The Accord represented the agreement of the Foreign Ministers ratified by the three heads of state. Its key point was that Indonesia and the Philippines would welcome the formation of Malaysia if the UN Secretary-General ascertained that the peoples of Sabah and Sarawak desired to be incorporated into Malaysia.

The Statement spelled out the method of ascertainment. There was to be a scrutinizing of the recent elections in Sarawak and North Borneo, which had resulted in the choice of officials favorable to Malaysia, to determine if they had in fact represented the will of the people. The Statement also contained the following significant points: the establishment of Maphilindo was confirmed, and national secretariats were to be set up to develop the necessary machinery for the new organization; assurances regarding the Philippines claim to Sabah were reiterated; Asian solidarity was emphasized, and there was an implication that the United Kingdom and the United States had covertly supported the 1958 rebellion with aid routed through their military bases in Malaya and the Philippines; the temporary nature of foreign bases was stressed, as was the caution that these bases should not be allowed to be used directly or indirectly to subvert the national independence of any of the three countries.

The Declaration, a statement of principles and purposes, reaffirmed the three nations' adherence to the principle of self-determination, expressed their intention to promote social and economic progress, repeated their opposition to "colonialism and imperialism in all its forms," identified the nations represented as a part of the "new emerging forces" of the world, pledged to cooperate in building a better world based upon national freedom and independence, and reiterated the intention of the participants to move ahead with the formation of Maphilindo through frequent and regular consultations. Much of it was pure Sukarno.

On the whole, American official opinion regarded the Manila Agreement favorably. Maphilindo was welcomed by Washington as an "encouraging development" and "a welcome indication of the desire of the three countries to work together to promote their common interest." We did not like the references to foreign bases or the implied American and British support for the rebellion. But the conference had come up with what had been regarded as impossible—a formula on which all parties were agreed—and the outlook for settlement suddenly appeared bright.

The British felt differently. To them, the Declaration represented intolerable concessions to Sukarno. This shines through the British white paper on the Manila conference, which notes:

> It was with considerable misgivings that Her Majesty's Government acceded to the earnest request of the Malayan Government for their cooperation in such an unprecedented scrutiny by outside investigation of internal elections in British territory. As what they hoped would be a final concession intended to complete a negotiated solution, Her Majesty's Government nevertheless informed the Secretary-General that they would be willing to admit his representatives for the purposes envisaged and that they assumed that the Secretary-General could complete this task in time to permit the establishment of Malaysia on August 31.[6]

Duncan Sandys, Minister for Commonwealth Relations, was outraged. His position was that the territories involved were British colonies, and her disposition of them was her own business. Britain had not been a party to the Manila accords nor a participant at the conference that had produced them. Sandys did not want to postpone the date for the formation of Malaysia, nor did he want the United Nations poking its nose into a British colony. But the three Southeast Asian heads of state had presented the British with a diplomatic *fait accompli* and the British, albeit with ill grace, bowed to it. Britain's Foreign Minister, Lord Home, asked U Thant to complete the survey by August 31, but U Thant considered that the minimum time required would be until September 15.

Meanwhile, the British press accused the Tunku of having conceded too much; he was, the press implied, a babe in the woods compared with the sophisticated Sukarno. Not only the British took a dim view of the extent to which the Manila conference had bowed to Sukarno's will. Important congressional opinion took its cue from Robert Trumbull, who wrote in the New York *Times* that Sukarno had "succeeded in establishing a new basis for sabotaging" Malaysia, SEATO, and the Western position in the Pacific.[7]

The Conference clearly represented a diplomatic victory for Sukarno. The question we were asking ourselves in Djakarta was whether Sukarno really saw Maphilindo as an instrument through which Indonesian ambitions for greater influence in the area could be realized. If so, the effort had been worthwhile. The West could afford to live with some Sukarno rhetoric if doing so meant that peace in the area might be preserved. It was a risk, certainly, but I, for one, considered that an attempt at har-

---

6. *Anglo-Indonesian Relations*, p. 5, as cited in Frederick Philip Bunnell, "The Kennedy initiatives in Indonesia, 1962–1963" (Thesis, Cornell University, September 1969), p. 500.
7. August 10, 1963.

nessing Sukarno to a frame of regional cooperation and reasonable objectives was far better than leaving him to his own devices, when he might, like a bull, charge all over the lot. If successful, it would manifestly serve the interests of his country, and of the world; indeed, as I saw it, his own legitimate purposes and ambitions also.

Reaction in Indonesia was generally favorable, with the exception of the PKI. Sukarno and Subandrio appeared elated, although whether this was a reflection of their interest in settling the dispute or of their conviction that sentiment in Borneo actually was against transfer to Malaysia, and that this would be revealed by an impartial survey, can only be guessed. Anti-Communists, including the army leadership, saw the Manila accords as possibly leading to the solution of a problem that had been exploited to the full by the Communist Party, although there was some skepticism on the part of anti-Sukarno elements that it was too good to be true.

The PKI, Peking, and Hanoi were a chorus of opposition. They attacked Maphilindo and urged Sukarno not to give up his efforts to "crush Malaysia." The Russians were not so vocal. A Soviet diplomat told me privately at the time that the Soviets saw no advantage in further strife in Southeast Asia and would be glad to see the conflict settled and Indonesia concentrate on the job of economic recovery and development. What he did not say but clearly implied was that he saw the conflict between Malaysia and Indonesia as one that could be exploited by China.

Subsequently, the PKI changed its position on Maphilindo and supported it, while continuing to fire a barrage of Crush Malaysia propaganda. These apparently inconsistent positions may be explained on the basis that an Indonesia-dominated regional confederation was suddenly seen by the PKI leaders to be in their interest.

Whether Sukarno took Maphilindo seriously or simply went along either as a face-saving arrangement to enable him to withdraw from confrontation or as a device to hoodwink his opponents as to his real intentions will probably never be known. The several times we discussed it, however, he appeared to see it as an important step toward regional cooperation.

"I'd like to expand it," he told me at one point, "not limit it to the Malay race. Thailand and other Southeast Asian nations should be included. And Australia and New Zealand to the East." But this may have been simply his telling me what he thought I wanted to hear.

The Malayans did not take the Maphilindo concept seriously, as Ghazali, the Malayan Permanent Secretary for External Affairs, told me later. To them, it was purely a matter of tactics; a confederation of this type would not be a workable arrangement since Sukarno would insist on dominating it. They did not trust him, but they were willing to give it a try if the confrontation were called off.

"Although at one point," Ghazali admitted, "I detected a momentary change in Sukarno. I was having a heart-to-heart talk with him alone after the Tunku and Subandrio had left the room. We were talking about China, and he suddenly seemed to realize that if we could all work together we actually could face the Chinese with confidence.

" 'Bapa,' I said to Sukarno, 'Why sell me to the Chinese?'

"For a moment there was a real feeling of brotherhood. Then Sukarno said, 'We'll talk about it tomorrow.'

"We never did, of course. Sukarno is the great betrayer of the Malay race," Ghazali added bitterly.

In New York, U Thant somewhat reluctantly agreed to perform the survey asked by the three heads of state. But he wisely laid down three conditions: (1) that the United Kingdom agree to such a survey; (2) that the three nations requesting it foot the bill; (3) that his findings would not be subject to ratification or confirmation by any government. U Thant notified Rahman that he planned to ascertain through the Michelmore Mission whether the Malaysian question had been the principal issue in the Borneo elections, and also whether they had been freely conducted. The task was to be completed by September 14.

When the mission arrived in Borneo on August 15, a dispute between the new Maphilindo partners delayed the official start of the survey of opinion until August 26. In the short time left, the mission did a highly conscientious job. The UN teams conferred with officials, political leaders, and representatives of religious, ethnic, labor, and business groups, and even tribal chiefs. In Sarawak alone, some 400 persons were interviewed.

The dispute over observers of the UN survey deepened suspicions among the nations involved, and particularly Indonesian suspicion of British machinations. It concerned the number of observers that Britain had agreed to allow in the Borneo territories. After considerable argument as to how many should be permitted to enter—the Indonesians and Filipinos first requested thirty—the British finally allowed eight, four observers and four junior assistants. Among the Indonesian "junior assistants" were two of obviously higher rank—Mr. Rudy Gontha of the Foreign Office and Colonel Abdurachman. Aware that both of these men had engaged in intelligence work, the British balked. The Indonesians insisted they had the right to name their own observers and that the British had no veto privilege. The United States strongly urged the British not to be so technical, and they finally came around. Again, the issue was ultimately compromised, but at the expense of much irritation and the loss of valuable time.

A further dispute arose as to how the observers would reach Kalimantan. The Government of Indonesia proposed to fly the observers to Kuching directly from Djakarta by military aircraft. The British objected, insisting that the Indonesian observers fly to Singapore, and then be transported to Kuching by either commercial or British military aircraft. Another argument made by the British against a large number of Indonesian observers, and against senior personnel filling junior positions, was that available accommodations were inadequate and the junior assistants would have to sleep in tents!

It was self-evident that Duncan Sandys, provoked by what he regarded as Indonesian duplicity, had determined to make it as difficult as possible for the Indonesians to observe anything. A more cooperative attitude might have been wiser, although Sandys undoubtedly feared Indonesian interference with the process of ascertainment. Unfortunately, the Indonesian and Filipino observers, owing to this delay, were not present for three of the six days the observation team spent in the North Borneo territory.

During this entire period, Subandrio's attitude in private communications with me was that Indonesian hostility was directed toward the British, not toward the Malayans. Indeed, he characterized Indonesia's anti-Malaysian policy as a product of the country's having become "a prisoner of its own history," meaning that it was bound to attack colonial remnants, whatever form they assumed. That the UN survey would be favorable to Malaysia he deemed a foregone conclusion. What Indonesia was after, he said, was a clear-cut decision that would justify its recognition of Malaysia and pave the way for renewal of closer regional associations such as Maphilindo. This was just too pat to be believed, but it seemed to indicate that Subandrio was preparing the way in the event the UN report went against the Indonesian expectation.

On August 29, two days before the originally scheduled date for the establishment of Malaysia, the Government of Malaya issued a proclamation fixing September 16 as the new date for the inauguration of Malaysia. In an official explanatory statement accompanying the proclamation, Malaya insisted that the fixing of a new date in no way conflicted with the Manila Agreements. "The position that Malaya has all along taken is that the ascertainment by the Secretary-General is not a condition which will determine whether Malaysia should be formed or not." The statement went on to express Malaya's confidence that the outcome of the United Nations inquiry would provide "confirmation of what is already an established fact." These remarks, coming while the United Nations survey was still in process, led the New York *Times* to headline its proclamation story from Kuala Lumpur: MALAYA PROMISES A FEDERATION REGARDLESS OF FINDINGS BY UN.[8]

That this was indeed the intention of Malaya and the other future members of Malaysia seems amply demonstrated by the statements of their leaders at this juncture. In its official explanatory statement, the Government of Malaya said the Tunku had declared this intention. And

---

8. August 30, 1963.

Donald Stephens, the Chief Minister in Sabah, used even more expressive and concrete language to make the same point. Upon his return to Sabah on August 29th—after conferring with Duncan Sandys in Kuala Lumpur on the 28th—Stephens said that he and the Chief Minister of Sarawak had been given "a firm promise and guarantee" in Kuala Lumpur that there would be no further change or postponement in the formation of Malaysia. He went on to echo the Malayans:

> If the UN report confirms the wishes of the peoples for Malaysia, then we will have Malaysia with the blessing of Indonesia and the Philippines.
> If, in the unlikely event the report says the majority doesn't want Malaysia, we will still go ahead with Malaysia, but without the blessings of Indonesia and the Philippines. And Sarawak will be in, too.

To the Malayans credit, they did make one conciliatory gesture to head off what would surely be a stormy reaction in Djakarta to violation of the spirit, if not the letter of the Manila Agreements. Following the decision of the Malayan Cabinet to proclaim the new date for Malaysia, the Tunku invited Subandrio to come to Singapore for a meeting with the Deputy Prime Minister, Tun Razak. When Subandrio declined on grounds of illness, Secretary Ghazali flew to Djakarta for a morning meeting with Subandrio. Thus, two hours before the official Malayan—and simultaneous London—release of the proclamation of September 16 as Malaysia Day, the Indonesian government was not only informed, but given a lengthy explanation of the constitutional and political pressures that necessitated it. Moreover, according to the Malayans, Subandrio indicated no surprise or alarm and even commented that he realized that the formation of Malaysia was a "foregone conclusion"—as he had privately indicated several times to me. Ghazali later commented privately that he did not understand Indonesia's violent reaction to the announcement.

Even on the basis of the Malayan version of the Ghazali-Subandrio conversations, there was an important qualification to Subandrio's apparent acceptance of Malaya's decision to fix a new date for Malaysia. Not only did he state that "Indonesia must reserve her position," but he asked that Kuala Lumpur make its announcement in such a way as not to "prejudge the UN mission's findings." But it was just this request that the careful language of the Malayan government's explanatory statement did not satisfy. There were official protests from Djakarta and Manila. Djakarta deplored the "reckless and premature" decision, while Manila complained that the decision "does not conform to the letter and spirit of the Manila Agreement."

However, to cite the official reactions of the Indonesian and Philippine governments to the August 29th announcement does not convey the full impact of this action on the course of events in that critical six weeks between the Manila conference and the September 16 target date for the formation of Malaysia.

What must be understood is the central role of one man in determining whether the Federation of Malaysia would be accepted by its militantly nationalistic neighbor. That man was Sukarno. In the last analysis, the positions of other political forces—including the powerful PKI and the even more powerful army, as well as the crafty Subandrio—were peripheral to the decision-making process at this juncture. All deferred to Sukarno, psychologically and politically. His dominance on the issue of Crush Malaysia was virtually complete.

On the night following the August 29 Malayan proclamation, he called me to his palace at Bogor, an hour from Djakarta. He strode up and down the room, his face black with rage. "I have been duped and humiliated by the British," he thundered. "I will not take it!"

Sukarno's public reaction was in line with the wrath he vented privately on me. The reaction was not to the establishment of a new date as such; it was rather to the challenge that Malaysia would be formed regardless of the survey's outcome. In his fury, he shifted from what appeared in mid-August to be a moderate course for him. In his August 17 speech, he had eschewed a splendid opportunity to renew his denunciations of Malaysia and instead implied full satisfaction with the method to be employed in the ascertainment of the Borneo territories' opinion on the subject. He crowed over Indonesia's growing influence. No matter what resulted from the ascertainment, Indonesia had proved that nothing could be done around its borders without its approval. "Indonesia is no longer treated like a dummy," he told the throngs gathered at the huge stadium to hear his message, "and allowed just to look on at alterations to the *status quo.* . . ." The country was now "recognized as having the right and primary responsibility to guard security and peace in the region together with . . . the Philippines and Malaya."

This somewhat surprising indication that he was prepared to honor the Manila Agreement and let his confrontation against Malaysia lapse seemed corroborated by his major attention in that same crucial speech to the need for Indonesia to stress economic development. He urged his people to "confront themselves" and improve their declining standard of living. "If we are unable to provide clothing and food in this rich country of ours, then in fact it is we ourselves who are stupid," he declared.

But complicating any analysis of Sukarno's intentions was always the uncertainty about what set of facts he was using in making his decisions. There was the possibility that Sukarno was convinced the UN mission would find that the people of the Borneo territories did not wish to join Malaysia, and consequently he felt safe in saying he would abide by the findings. Confirmation of this came from Nasution. During a private conversation with me at this time, the General expressed surprise when I told him that our informal, independent investigations of opinion in

North Borneo showed that a majority of the people did in fact wish to join Malaysia. Naustion commented that if accurate, this would be a great blow to Sukarno, who had been informed otherwise. I reminded the General that Sukarno's information and that of the Indonesian government probably came from prejudiced sources. Obviously, the government was in touch with elements that had supported the Azahari revolt. Inevitably, these elements would exaggerate the amount of opposition to Malaysia.

Whether or not one assumed that Sukarno thought the survey would show support for Malaysia, on balance it appeared that, prior to the August 29th announcement, he was willing to accept the UN verdict. Long convinced of the role of emotionalism in determining the timing and character of some of Sukarno's most dramatic actions, I attached great importance to his outburst at the Malayan announcement. Sukarno's resentment may indeed have been decisive in scuttling the Manila Agreement, as well as the hope of ushering in Malaysia with his blessing and channeling him into the more moderate course presaged by the Western stabilization program and Maphilindo.

Early on Friday the thirteenth, Sukarno and I discussed the impending survey report. He was in a good mood, and the first forty-five minutes were spent in banter while he disposed of requests from various petitioners. His first serious comment was to report the painting of a sign during the night by a Communist youth organization in which the Tunku was described as a "bandit." Sukarno said he wanted me to know that at 5:30 this morning, when he had received this news, he had immediately ordered the sign to be rubbed out. He made quite a point of this, apparently to convince me in the presence of others that he was ruling out name calling.

I urged him that morning to be temperate in his reaction to the United Nations report, whatever its tenor might be. Sukarno interrupted to say that if the report indicated the people favored Malaysia, he would challenge it on the ground the survey was not a fair test. He recalled that at Manila it had been agreed that all of the detainees—the political prisoners who were jailed at the time of the Azahari revolt—would be allowed to express their views, whereas his information was that only four had been contacted.

Brushing these aside as details, I endeavored to convince him that it was in his interest not to take any action that would destroy the opportunity embodied in Maphilindo. In this developing structure, I pointed out, Sukarno and his government could exert its rightful leadership in the area in a constructive way. It was certain, however, that intemperate reaction or vigorous renewal of his confrontation policy would inevitably result in wrecking Maphilindo, with the consequent loss of an opportunity for Indonesia created by his own leadership at Tokyo and Manila. I painted a somewhat glowing picture of what Maphilindo could mean to

Indonesia in the future, and to himself in terms of stature and prestige.

On September 14, as promised, U Thant rendered his verdict on the basis of the United Nations Mission Survey:

> Having reflected fully on these considerations, and taking into account the framework within which the Mission's task was performed, I have come to the conclusion that the majority of the peoples of Sabah (North Borneo) and of Sarawak, have given serious and thoughtful consideration to their future, and to the implications for them of participation in a Federation of Malaysia.
>
> I believe that the majority of them have concluded that they wish to bring their dependent status to an end and to realize their independence through freely chosen association with other peoples in their region with whom they feel ties of ethnic association, heritage, language, religion, culture, economic relationship, and ideals and objectives. Not all of these considerations are present in equal weight in all minds, but it is my conclusion that the majority of peoples of the two territories, having taken them into account, wish to engage, with the peoples of the Federation of Malaya and Singapore, in an enlarged Federation of Malaysia through which they can strive together to realize the fulfillment of their destiny.[9]

The reaction in Djakarta was one of shock and derision. The survey was described as a "farce." "How can anyone make a thorough survey of opinion in that huge territory, where communication is so difficult, in so short a time?" one Indonesian asked me. U Thant himself deemed it unfortunate that the survey had to be done within the framework of a deadline, although he insisted that more time would not have significantly affected the conclusions.

When the announcement reached Sukarno, he summoned me to the palace at Bogor. He was conferring with Subandrio as I entered his study. The Foreign Minister, usually so effervescent, seemed uncertain of himself. "I have just told Subandrio that I am going to ask for another survey," Sukarno said, after a brief word of greeting. "I want a new ascertainment of opinion. I do not think this one was properly conducted in accordance with our agreements at Manila."

I was thunderstruck. Here again was a characteristic quality of Sukarno—the inability, when his own interests were involved, to put himself in the place of others; indeed, to face reality. "Mr. President," I said, "you can't do that."

"Why not?" he asked.

"Put yourself in the place of the Secretary-General of the United Nations," I said. "You and two other heads of state requested him to make a survey of public opinion in Borneo. With some reluctance he agreed. He made that survey. He has certified on the basis of it that the majority

9. New York *Times*, September 15, 1963.

of the people of the territory actually do want to join Malaysia. He can't, Mr. President, turn right around now and conduct another survey. He would appear ridiculous before the world. And," I continued, "knowing he cannot accept such a request, you are in an untenable position in making it."

We argued for some time about this. Subandrio said little. I reminded President Sukarno of the several occasions when he had pledged to accept the survey's verdict. I told him I thought it was in his interest to do so now. I said I could understand how he felt about the way in which the formation of Malaysia had been announced, and also about the various unsatisfactory incidents connected with the implementation of the survey. But I urged that it was in Indonesia's interest to be able to move forward with Maphilindo.

Sukarno's face was blank. He heard but did not listen. Finally, he said, "No, I cannot accept it." "Think it over, Mr. President," I urged him.

He thought it over. But the following day he telegraphed U Thant, formally asking for a reascertainment. Subandrio announced that Indo-nesia would withhold recognition of Malaysia until the United Nations had "made corrections" in its recent survey in North Borneo and Sara-wak. It was an exercise in futility, illustrating how far off the track ego and frustration can lead even a politically sagacious head of state.

CHAPTER 5

Tragedy in Texas

I was one of the last official callers President Kennedy had at the White House. On Tuesday, November 19, I had an hour and ten minutes with him. When I arrived, accompanied by Roger Hilsman, Assistant Secretary of State for Far Eastern Affairs, and Mike Forrestal, White House staffer on Indonesia—both of whom had been most helpful on Indonesian problems—the President was playing with John-John, his two-year-old son, and his dog. He suggested that it was time for John-John to toddle along, and then he told the dog to go out. The dog looked up at him, as if to confirm that he really meant it, and then trotted obediently out through the French doors.

The President grinned. "What do you think of that?" he asked. "Responds a lot better than some of the politicians you deal with, I'll wager," I said.

The role of the White House in foreign affairs varies with the personality and method of operation of the incumbent. Franklin D. Roosevelt might be said to have been his own Secretary of State. President Eisenhower, who had for so long worked within an army-staff system, was accustomed to delegating responsibility and acting only on the basis of completed staff work. He relied heavily on his Secretary of State, John Foster Dulles, and it was only in times of crisis or the need for major policy decisions that the President got into the act. He was consulted and kept informed by Dulles, but the Secretary of State carried the ball. This meant, in turn, that the Assistant Secretaries of State in charge of the various regions, such as the Far East, Europe, Africa and Latin America, were major power centers of policy making.

President Kennedy, however, had spent a great deal of time abroad and had a deep interest in foreign affairs. He built up a White House staff of specialists to assist him in keeping current on international developments. One of his men on Far Eastern affairs was Michael V. Forrestal, perceptive young lawyer and son of the former Secretary of the Navy.[1] Mike was typical of the bright young men with whom Kennedy surrounded himself, and could hold his own in any company. It was with men like Forrestal, Robert Komer, James C. Thomson, Jr., and others of the White House staff, as well as with the top officials and desk men of the State Department, that an Ambassador had to maintain contact. Repeatedly, Komer, who had a "feel" for Asian affairs, and Forrestal, with his deep empathy for Indonesia, saved the American government from over-reacting to Sukarno's excesses by their understanding response to points made by Harriman, Hilsman, and me.

In this period, the co-ordination between the State Department and the White House staff, at least on Indonesian affairs, was outstanding. And President Kennedy kept himself so well informed that frequently some startled young desk officer picked up the phone to find the President himself on the wire! Dean Rusk was Secretary of State in his own right, but in the Kennedy Administration, the White House kept on top of events on a daily basis. It was thus standard practice at that time for an Ambassador returning to Washington to see the President, not merely to make a courtesy call, but to discuss the issues and do business.

Relations between the United States and Indonesia in the fall of 1963 hinged on the personal relationship between President Kennedy and President Sukarno, as well as on the divisive issues. The affinity between the two leaders consisted of a few threads that could be used to bind us together. Now there was the possibility of President Kennedy's returning Sukarno's visit to America by making an official visit to Indonesia early in 1964, for I was the bearer of a personal invitation from President Sukarno.

Sukarno's heart was set on it. He admired Kennedy, thought of him as a friend, and believed that he was endeavoring to provide America with genuinely progressive leadership; more important, that he understood the economic and social revolution taking place throughout the world and was in sympathy with it. Equally compelling, President Kennedy had taken the initiative that had resulted in the settlement of the West Irian dispute. Although Sukarno thereafter credited his own shrewd tactics with forcing Kennedy's hand, the American President had, after all, been responsive to Indonesia's plight in a way that recorded him as a friend in Sukarno's lexicon.

Aside from the desire for a bridge built of personal relations with President Kennedy, and for the self- and national aggrandizement that would result from such a visit, Sukarno undoubtedly was seeking an opportunity to influence the U.S. President on the subject of Malaysia. Sukarno also unquestionably wanted to sound out President Kennedy's

1. James Forrestal, who made such a great contribution during World War II and died tragically in office.

views on the direction in which the world was heading. Here the objective was to induce him to work with Sukarno in his self-appointed mission of transforming the world. From Sukarno's point of view, this was a natural. Regarding himself as the leader of not merely the Asian-African nations but all the "new emerging forces," I am sure he felt that an understanding, if not an alliance between himself and the man he considered the leader of the Western world, was possible. He was being wooed by Khrushchev and Mao—why, then, should not the leader of the other world bloc be equally interested in working with him, assuming a like-minded approach to the solution of the world's ills? And Sukarno, seeking advantage where he could find it, was not yet irrevocably committed to a deal with Peking and an anti-American posture.

I had been pressing for a presidential visit to Indonesia for some time, and Roger Hilsman now lent strong support. He agreed that Sukarno placed "so much importance on President Kennedy's visit to Indonesia that this possibility alone might bring him to recognize Malaysia where all other pressures fail."

Hilsman had first broached the idea of an Asian trip to President Kennedy on July 8, 1963. He and Forrestal, supported by Harriman, were convinced that the time had come for "a dramatic affirmation of America's presence and commitment to Asia." [2] It was Hilsman's thought to key the trip to an initiative in foreign policy in Asia directed toward encouraging a growing community of interest among the Pacific nations in which Asians would assume, in cooperation with the United States, more responsibility for the security and development of the area as a whole. This was in line with our major Asian policy of attempting to build "a functioning system of cooperative, free and viable nations." [3] Both Hilsman and I thought that Sukarno, stimulated by a personal visit from President Kennedy, might well respond constructively to such an initiative. Support from the leader of the largest non-Communist nation in East Asia could mean much.

In the first few minutes of our talk with President Kennedy, Hilsman handed him a memorandum to this effect.[4] I told the President of the personal invitation from President Sukarno, and that he had asked me to say that he wanted President Kennedy to be the first guest in a new palatial guest house he had built in Bali. I said I thought a personal visit represented the best prospect for improving relations with Indonesia. International relations were human relations to Sukarno, who set great store on personal contact between national leaders as a prelude to understanding.

---

2. See Roger Hilsman, *To Move a Nation* (Garden City, N.Y.: Doubleday & Company, Inc., 1967), pp. 405–406.
3. Memorandum from Hilsman to McGeorge Bundy and Michael V. Forrestal, November 19, 1963.
4. *Ibid.*

I suggested that I be authorized to tell Sukarno that President Kennedy appreciated the invitation very much indeed and was hoping to accept it. Sukarno, however, must recognize that an easing of tensions in Southeast Asia was an essential condition for the U.S. President's coming to Indonesia. Such a visit was politically out of the question under present circumstances; but I proposed that we offer Sukarno a package deal, which Hilsman, Forrestal, and I had discussed in advance, designed to establish a suitable political climate.

From Sukarno, the package required assurance of his willingness to take immediate steps toward peaceful settlement of the Malaysia dispute; engage in tripartite discussions for that purpose before the visit; withdraw his military forces from the Kalimantan border (except what would be reasonable for defensive purposes); and cease active support of guerrilla actions in Malaysian territory.

In return for this, the U.S. government would do four things: use its influence to bring about a tripartite meeting of representatives of Indonesia, Malaysia, and the Philippines to settle the dispute and restore normal relations among the nations concerned; immediately offer to provide up to 150,000 tons of rice to Indonesia; plan for a presidential visit if negotiations succeeded; and finally, assuming settlement, resuscitate the multilateral DAC program to assist in the stabilization of the Indonesian economy, which had been scrapped because of the Malaysia dispute.

Since Sukarno could not initiate a settlement of the dispute himself without loss of face, I said that Hilsman and I had discussed the desirability, if Sukarno's response were positive, of Hilsman's coming to Djakarta a week or two after my return and then proceeding on to Kuala Lumpur and Manila.

The President inquired what Sukarno would accept by way of a settlement of the Malaysia dispute. What was he after? No one knew what formula the three Asian leaders could agree upon, I replied. It was my opinion that the outlines of a viable solution could be determined only by discussion among them, and therefore a summit meeting of the three Asian heads should be the objective. The ground would have to be carefully prepared, for face would have to be saved on all sides. No one could guarantee the result, but I thought we might pull it off, particularly when it seemed clear that all concerned had everything to gain and nothing to lose.

As a possible formula, I suggested the West Irian precedent. In return for Sukarno's recognition of Malaysia, it might be suggested that the Tunku hold a plebiscite in Borneo after five or six years to determine whether the people wanted to remain in Malaysia. I thought both Sukarno and the Tunku could agree to this. The Indonesians could hardly turn down a formula based on the West Irian settlement, and it would have the virtue of saving Sukarno's face without giving him a victory.

From the Malaysian point of view, such an arrangement would stop confrontation, and the Tunku's government would be recognized. The Tunku and the British were committed to self-determination as a principle; they ought to be willing to buy a plebiscite in return for peace with their large neighbor.

I added that I thought Sukarno was ready to call it quits, but would never submit to humiliation. The prospect of a presidential visit would provide a powerful incentive to him to be reasonable.

The President indicated agreement with this general line of reasoning, said he would be willing to go to Indonesia in April or May of 1964 if a political settlement were reached, and authorized me to tell Sukarno. He also agreed to my proposal to supply up to 150,000 tons of desperately needed rice for Indonesia.

President Kennedy was pragmatic in his dealings with Sukarno and inclined to do whatever he could within the limits of the politically possible to steer him in the direction we wanted him to go. Kennedy had to be sensitive to congressional opinion—he had always to keep in mind the effect of any action on his own legislative program—but in my experience with him, he never failed to respond to a suggestion that he regarded as within the competence of the executive and geared toward improving relations with Indonesia, even though he might be skeptical as to its success. He once referred to Sukarno as an "inscrutable Asian."

I was fully aware, of course, that Indonesia did not, and could not, represent top priority on the President's agenda. Vietnam even then was the tail beginning to wag the dog of American policy in Asia. I have often thought that had it not been for Vietnam, Indonesia, the largest country in East Asia except for Communist China, would have had much higher priority in American concerns. President Kennedy was keenly aware of its vital importance to the future of Southeast Asia and did what he could—witness his unpopular initiative in the West Irian dispute—to help keep it on the right track.

At this time, I also raised the question as to whether he wanted me to continue to represent the U.S. government in Indonesia, pointing out that I had now been Ambassador there for more than five and a half years. "I hope you will be willing to remain another year," he replied. I remained longer than that, but it was to serve another President.

On Friday, November 22, Roger Hilsman and I were working out the details of the plan, for I was about to leave for Djakarta. I first heard the news of President Kennedy's assassination in Dallas while walking back to the Department from lunch. A motorist pulled up to the curb alongside me. His radio was on. He leaned out the window of the car and shouted, "My God, the President's been shot!" I have never seen people in the Department of State so shaken by any event. Politically sophisticated, accustomed to dealing with war and revolution, with coups and countercoups, with the tragedies and triumphs of men and nations, dip-

lomats and their staffs are seldom stirred out of their composure by unexpected events. But on this tragic day, men and women sat blind at
their desks, staring out into space. They passed each other unseeingly in
the corridors. Secretaries and stenographers wept unashamedly over their
typewriters. The light had gone out of the day.

The assassin's bullet put an end to our plans and disposed of the immediate prospects for settlement of the Malaysia dispute.

General Nasution, who was to see President Kennedy on November
26, arrived in time to attend his funeral. Two days later, President Johnson, pressed as he was and weighed down by the tragedy that had
brought him to office, nevertheless made time to receive Nasution. Harriman and I accompanied the General. The two men had a brief but
friendly exchange of views, the President urging Nasution to do all he
could to bring about a settlement of the dispute.

Routine governmental decisions by an American President are automatically carried out by his successor unless they involve areas of policy
disagreement. The plan Hilsman and I had discussed with President
Kennedy, however, called for a major personal diplomatic role on the
part of the President of the United States. Yet it was difficult to see how
President Johnson could play such a role, even if he were so inclined. He
could hardly leave the country during his first months in office. In addition to the weight of his new responsibilities, he would be facing an
election before he had been in office a year. I had no clue as to his grasp
of the Indonesian problem, his reaction to Sukarno or Sukarno's to him.
But I felt confident that, as a master of political tactics himself, he
would not underestimate Sukarno, and I hoped he would see the desirability of establishing communication with him. I recognized that Indonesia was not among the new President's most urgent problems, and I
was prepared not to reach any definite conclusions at my first meeting
with him, on December 18. Harriman and I went to the White House
together.

We made three main points in talking with the President. First, that
the extent of United States influence in Indonesia was apt to be measured by President Sukarno's feeling of personal rapport with the President of the United States. I suggested it might be helpful if he could
authorize me to tell Sukarno that he planned to visit Indonesia after the
fall election.

Second, I briefed the President on the Malaysia impasse. There were
two possibilities unless settlement were achieved: either a Southeast Asia
split, which would help only the Communists, or an explosion leading to
some kind of military action, with the very real possibility of American
involvement as a result of our obligations under the ANZUS treaty.

Third, referring to the sharp criticism of United States aid to Indonesia under Sukarno, I pointed out that, with the exception of commodi-

ties sent to Indonesia under Public Law 480, our aid was primarily an investment in the future, with more than half the total program devoted to training and education. We were not, I emphasized, giving economic-development assistance to Indonesia, which would be to shore up a government of whose actions we disapproved. I left a memorandum with the President, and urged the continuation of the current program.

Reaching the President at almost the same moment was the Broomfield Amendment to the Foreign Aid bill, requiring a presidential determination that aid to Indonesia was in the national interest. Congressional feeling against Indonesia was running high at the time. According to Hilsman, Senator Russell of Georgia, one of President Johnson's closest friends in Congress, was reported to have told him that if he signed the determination he ought to be impeached. President Johnson's failure to sign, however justifiable from the standpoint of those who advocated the use of the stick to make Sukarno behave, represented a major setback in our efforts to build a good-will bridge. Sukarno was keenly eying the new Administration. This decision was to him a clear tip-off that he would find understanding of the new Indonesian nationalism hard to come by. Not that he expected us to support him in his confrontation of Malaysia—we had made our position quite apparent—but he had hoped we would work with him in other areas, particularly economic. In Embassy Djakarta, the feeling about Johnson's decision would be that we were throwing away our few remaining cards, which might have been played to restrain Sukarno.

President Kennedy, I knew, would have signed the determination almost as a matter of routine. It was disappointing, though understandable, that President Johnson had been unwilling to do so. Still, the President was interested in the United States' taking the initiative in an effort to settle the dispute. He suggested that we think about how to bring the three heads of state together and asked me to extend his greetings to Sukarno.

As was customary, before I left I briefed the Far East Subcommittee of the House Foreign Affairs Committee. This had always been a good group, taking its responsibilities seriously. Congressman Clement J. Zablocki was chairman. This time, I found it out of patience with Indonesia.

On my arrival back in Djakarta, I discovered that the immediate problem of getting negotiations under way was going to be difficult. The Tunku was not about to sit down at the conference table with a gun at his head; first Sukarno would have to agree to a cease-fire and withdraw his guerrillas from Malaysia. But I had no card to play to induce Sukarno to do so, and he was giving no evidence of a conciliatory mood. The Indonesian propaganda and military campaign against Malaysia was stepping up. Guerrilla operations within Borneo territory were intensify-

ing. The Indonesians now had approximately 10,000 troops in Kalimantan. This gave the Indonesians a numerical and tactical advantage, although most of the troops occupied defensive positions.

More threatening was our information that Indonesian Army commanders in Kalimantan were mounting what appeared to be a major
program of training and arming of guerrillas. Their agents were recruit-
ing dissidents (they called them "refugees") from the other side of the
border, training them in paramilitary tactics, equipping them with modern, light weapons, organizing them into units, and sending them back.
It would take a major diplomatic *démarche* to slow down Sukarno.

President Johnson was a great believer in the philosophy of the carrot
and the stick. After our December 1963 meeting, he had asked Secretary
of Defense McNamara for a list of all the items the Indonesians were
still receiving under our aid programs. McNamara supplied the list, together with recommendations for a program of progressive curtailment
of aid. And thus began a shift of emphasis in American policy to a
harder line (not a change in policy—for we had long favored the Malaysia confederation).

Settlement of the Malaysia dispute continued to be the foremost matter on my agenda. Without that, there was no hope of improvement in
U.S.-Indonesian relations. I was pressing for action to bring a summit
meeting into being. Hilsman was resigning in order to return to academic life, so the plan for him to come to Southeast Asia went out the
window. A visit by a high-level presidential emissary seemed a logical
beginning, and I continued to ask for this. The Attorney General, Robert F. Kennedy, was picked for this assignment. He would visit the three
capitals concerned, Djakarta, Kuala Lumpur, and Manila, and then go
on to London. It would be his task to make clear to Sukarno that there
would be grave consequences for our mutual relations if he continued
military confrontation of Malaysia; that we were prepared to assist actively in promoting tripartite talks between representatives of the three
nations, in hopes that an "Asian solution" could be worked out. The first
step, we felt, was a cease-fire.

Kennedy was ideal for this assignment. He had established a warm
rapport with Sukarno, knew many of the people involved, was familiar
with the issue, and had proved his skill in delicate negotiations.

On January 14, after stopping in Manila to see U.S. Ambassador Stevenson and President Macapagal and pave the way for the Kennedy mission, I arrived in Tokyo and met with my old friend Takeo Oda, former
Japanese Ambassador to Indonesia and now Vice Minister for Foreign
Affairs, who briefed me on the arrangements for Sukarno's visit to Japan.
When the Indonesian President arrived the following day, he, U.S. Ambassador Edwin O. Reischauer and I had a preliminary talk to ensure
that everything was set for the Attorney General's meeting with him the

following day. Kennedy flew in that night, landing at Tokota Air Force Base. In spite of the fact that the base is located twenty miles west of Tokyo, a crowd of several hundred were on hand to greet him. I flew out by helicopter with the Reischauers and others of the official party. As Kennedy came down the steps of the plane, he and Ethel both looking as youthful, eager, and enthusiastic as ever, despite their burden of grief, a group of shouting American teenagers displayed a banner saying "We're with you, Bobby."

At our first meeting with Sukarno the next morning, the President greeted Kennedy cordially. Then, typically, he challenged, "Did you come here to threaten me?" He was smiling but half serious. The Attorney General grinned and said, "No, I've come to help get you out of trouble." Both men laughed, and a moment that might have been awkward paved the way for the friendly talks that followed, in which the Attorney General again demonstrated his capacity to present his case with force and wit.

Kennedy took the position that the interests of the United States were directly involved in preserving peace in Southeast Asia and urged that the jungle warfare between the Indonesian-based guerrillas and the Malaysian and British forces be halted as a first step toward peaceful solution of the dispute. It was unreasonable to expect the Malaysians to come to a meeting as long as they were being attacked. If he could obtain Sukarno's assurance that he would stop the shooting, Kennedy said, he was hopeful that a peace conference for Malaysia, Indonesia, and the Philippines could be brought about, and he would talk to the Tunku in these terms. Sukarno was ready to attend a summit meeting, he said, but would not withdraw support for his guerrillas or announce a cease-fire unless the other side agreed to do so. Kennedy said he would notify Sukarno of the results of his talks with the Tunku on Wednesday, January 22, through me. If all went well, he would return to Djakarta, when, it was agreed, Sukarno would issue instructions for a cease-fire.

The Attorney General's discussions with Macapagal and the Tunku were fruitful. When he reached Djakarta on January 22, he had in his pocket the Tunku's agreement to a cease-fire if Sukarno would agree. Both Macapagal and the Tunku were willing to come to a summit, but not until the shooting had stopped. Sukarno kept his word, and on January 23 the cease-fire was announced at a joint press conference. The Attorney General felt encouraged enough to tell the newsmen that it was "very possible" a new meeting of the three Southeast Asian leaders would take place in the relatively near future, but that a definite answer would have to await the outcome of his conferences in other capitals.

The Kennedy mission was a whirlwind affair. Following the successful meetings with Sukarno, the Attorney General flew first to Bangkok, since it had been agreed that the Thai government would act as a center of communication. There, Kennedy attempted to tie the strings together. After a dinner conference with Foreign Minister Thanat Khoman, he said:

> All the parties have agreed to preliminary meetings in Bangkok and they have asked me to request Mr. Thanat Khoman to make the necessary arrangements. The parties to the dispute have also asked me to tell the Foreign Minister that they expect all military activities in North Kalimantan to cease by the end of this month and the meeting in Bangkok will therefore take place during the first week in February. At the request of the three parties, I have also requested Thailand, through the Foreign Minister, to assume the function of investigating any incidents that might occur during the cessation of military activities and report back to the parties. The technical details for this activity are in the process of being worked out and will be publicly announced later. My mission has now been completed.

The next stop was London to report the results of his talks and assuage hurt feelings in the British Foreign Office. Sukarno did not make Kennedy's job easy. Only hours after the Attorney General had left Djakarta, the Indonesian President publicly stated that the "confrontation to crush Malaysia" must continue, although "tactics may change." In the face of this, Kennedy still maintained in London that he thought President Sukarno was "genuinely willing" to try to resolve the dispute and added, "I never assumed, nor did I say, that President Sukarno had given up his opposition to Malaysia. But I hope that decision will be modified by conference and discussion. If Sukarno had given up his opposition, there would never have been the necessity for a conference. What he has given up is military confrontation and military activities against Malaysia while this conference goes on."

The British press was all but unanimous in their distaste for Kennedy's mediation. A notable exception was the London *Economist*, which praised his role and said he deserved congratulations and thanks for arranging a cease-fire.

The Attorney General's mission must be recorded as a success. He laid the groundwork for a summit meeting, although much water was to go over the dam before this could take place. The first step was a series of tripartite Foreign Ministers' meetings in Bangkok, mediated by the Thai government. These sessions failed to get anywhere.

The nut that could not be cracked was whether talks could continue while Indonesian irregulars remained on Malaysian soil. The Malaysian position was that they could not negotiate political concessions under the cover of a cease-fire unless the Indonesian military withdrew from Malaysian territory. But the Indonesians were unwilling to surrender the leverage that their military presence gave them, and insisted that actual withdrawal of Indonesian volunteers must accompany, not precede, any general political settlement. The agreed-upon cease-fire was therefore never fully implemented. Reports of new incursions into the territory began to come in.

A second Bangkok conference was convened on March 3 in an unsuccessful attempt to salvage the Kennedy program.

Meanwhile, Sukarno continued to exert pressure. On May 3 he issued an "action command" to "21,000,000 volunteers . . . to increase the revolution's vitality and help the peoples of Malaya, Singapore, Sarawak, Brunei, and Sabah dissolve Malaysia and attain national independence." As might be expected, this brought a sharp reaction from Washington. On May 5, William P. Bundy,[5] the new Assistant Secretary of State for Far Eastern Affairs, stated that if Indonesia continued or stepped up her campaign against Malaysia in Northern Borneo, it would be guilty of aggression. Under these circumstances, he warned, the United States might have to cut off all of its remaining aid programs.

Bundy's statement caused a stir in Indonesia. Meeting with Sukarno and Subandrio, I was told by the latter that relations between our two countries were approaching an all-time low. He said Indonesia would have to react strongly to Bundy's statement and suggested it might be in the interest of both parties for his government to announce that it would no longer accept any American assistance. I told the two Indonesian leaders that one day our aid program might have to cease, but now was not the time for either side to move in that direction. Despite the pressures of Congress and U.S. public opinion, the Administration had kept on course. As for Bundy's remarks, I pointed out that I had been telling them the same thing for months, which they admitted. What bothered them was not so much the substance of the remarks, but the fact that they had been made public.

"This is a very difficult period for us," Subandrio said. "If we want to keep United States–Indonesian relations on the present level of friendship, it will help very much if your people will not make public threats against us."

There were two sides to this, I retorted. It would be equally helpful if the Government of Indonesia put a brake on the anti-America campaign being conducted in Indonesia. And in any event, the best hope for improvement in relations lay in the peaceful settlement of the Malaysian dispute. So long as Indonesia appeared in the role of aggressor, things

---

5. I had known Bundy as a brilliant young lawyer with the prestigious Washington firm of Covington and Burling. He came to the State Department from Defense, where he had been Assistant Secretary for International Security Affairs, and consequently he knew his way around Washington. He was McGeorge's older brother, which gave him a direct pipeline to the White House. As the Vietnam crisis intensified, Bundy found it necessary to give the bulk of his time to Indochina, although he continued to have a hand in Indonesian policy. One of Bundy's deputies, Robert W. Barnett, gave considerable attention to Indonesia, especially in the economic realm.

would continue to be difficult, aid or no aid. Many people in America and elsewhere were convinced Sukarno was engaged in a drive for territorial expansion. I suggested that his actions had done little to dispel this suspicion. With a peaceful settlement of the dispute, not only would Sukarno's image improve, but he would be able to concentrate on his increasingly serious internal economic problem with the possibility of renewed friendly assistance from the outside world.

Subandrio used the latter comment as a springboard to charge that the principal reason for Indonesia's economic difficulties was the failure of the United States to fulfill its promises regarding balance-of-payments assistance. I took grim satisfaction in demolishing this accusation in Sukarno's presence, for I was dubious as to whether he had ever had an accurate picture of what happened. Subandrio beat a hasty retreat when I reminded him of how the Indonesian government had cut its own throat by establishing an economic blockade of Malaysia at a critical moment in the implementation of the stabilization plan. This was one of numerous instances in which I caught the devious Subandrio shading the truth to suit his own purposes in his reports to the President. It underlined how essential were my frequent talks with Sukarno in which I provided him with an accurate statement of U.S. policy, purpose, and manner of implementation. Subandrio had other fish to fry, and he was busy frying them.

The outcome of the conversation was an understanding that for the present, neither side would take action to cancel U.S. aid programs.

The Indonesian reaction to Bundy's comment confirmed what I had been telling Washington, that the Indonesians would never yield to threats; that an ultimatum was the quickest way to further disturb relations. At the same time, the character of Washington's response to Sukarno's May 3 announcement removed all doubt in Indonesian minds that the two nations were on a collision course. The unfortunate effect was to confirm the Indonesian suspicion that in spite of what we had been saying, the U.S. aid program did in fact have political strings attached.

Shortly thereafter, President Macapagal seized the initiative and appealed to both the Tunku and Sukarno to hold a second summit meeting in the spirit of the Manila accords and Maphilindo. The Tunku continued to insist that Sukarno must withdraw his guerrillas before he could talk; Sukarno maintained his position that talks must come first. Finally, however, the log jam was broken. Sukarno, after my repeated urgings, agreed to a token withdrawal of guerrillas to take place simultaneously with a resumption of negotiations. Complete withdrawal would follow, he said, "in accordance with the progress of the political talks." The Tunku, always ready to meet Sukarno halfway, agreed, provided that Sukarno recognize this as a "first" or "beginning" withdrawal, and not merely a "token."

Although this shift in the Indonesian position made possible a compromise, there were many details to be threshed out. Salvador P. Lopez, former Foreign Minister of the Philippines, was selected by President Macapagal to act as trouble shooter. Lopez shuttled back and forth between Manila, Bangkok, Kuala Lumpur, and Djakarta. This proved effective, for on May 23 the Tunku publicly agreed to a summit meeting. Sukarno kept his word. On June 18, simultaneous with the opening of the ministerial conference in Tokyo that was to precede the summit, some thirty-two Indonesian guerrillas walked out of the jungles at one of the agreed checkpoints.

Some time earlier, as the argument over the withdrawal of Indonesian guerrillas waxed hot, some wag in the American Embassy Djakarta had suggested that Indonesia had had so little success with its guerrilla activities that it would have to put guerrillas in if there were to be any to withdraw! Tending to confirm this speculation was the report that the thirty-two guerrillas appeared in fresh, well-starched uniforms, showing little evidence of jungle-survival wear and tear.

CHAPTER 6

Eyeball to Eyeball

At a Foreign Ministers' meeting, which preceded the June 1964 summit, Tun Razak put the issue bluntly, "So far as Malaysia is concerned, we have always wanted peace. To a small country like Malaysia, peace is dearest to our hearts and to live in peace with our neighbors is our most important objective. However, we cannot escape from the fact that there is a threat to peace in our region. And that this threat is not of our own doing. . . . I must say quite bluntly that this threat is solely due to confrontation. *There are troops in our country which have no right to be there.* So, if these troops are removed and withdrawal takes place, it will be very easy to solve our dispute and we can surely live in peace as neighbors." [1]

Subandrio's conciliatory opening statement urged the application of *"musjawarah,"* that is, discussion until a consensus is achieved, to reconcile the conflicting viewpoints. He did not address himself to the point raised by Tun Razak until after the recess, when he explained how Indonesia saw the question of guerrillas: "Tun Razak said that the only issue between Indonesia and Malaysia was the presence of guerrillas in Sarawak and Sabah. According to Malaysia, if the guerrillas are withdrawn there will be no trouble and our problem will be solved. But I hope Malaysia will try and understand why it is not so easy for us to say 'Withdraw' and to expect the guerrillas to obey our command. It is important that Malaysia should realize we cannot expect the guerrillas to obey our orders. . . . The guerrillas and volunteers have a deep political conscience. They are struggling for a political objective. They are fighting for the independence of those people there from colonialism and imperialism."

"But," Tun Razak complained, "we have agreed that there should be withdrawal before the summit. I cannot see how we can hold a summit if there is not going to be genuine withdrawal."

---

1. Quotations here and on subsequent pages are from the "Minutes of the Foreign Ministers Meeting."

Subandrio countered that this position made it very difficult. "Please try and understand that we are acting in good faith," he said. "Indonesia's standpoint is that withdrawal is not a physical matter but a political matter."

And so the argument ran throughout the meeting, with Subandrio laying the blame for all the difficulties at the door of the colonial powers, "It is the fault of the British, who interfered with procedures laid down in the Manila Agreement. . . . Therefore we have to return to the spirit of the Manila Agreement. This is our principle."

The summit meeting in Tokyo, which followed the Foreign Ministers' session, was short. It began and ended on June 20. Sukarno immediately picked up Subandrio's point and charged that Malaysia had not been established "in accordance with what we . . . agreed at the Manila meeting last year."

"Which part of the Manila Agreement do you think has not been implemented?" the Prime Minister of Malaysia asked. Sukarno cited the section on self-determination.

Throughout the meeting, the Indonesians kept referring to their feeling of having been humiliated. "You must understand," Subandrio said, "I am not blaming the Tunku. At the time of the investigations in Sabah and Sarawak, the British were threatening us and making all sorts of obstacles. They were doing their best to humiliate us. . . . For us Indonesians, it is not the result but the procedure of ascertainment which is important." Again he added, "We were humiliated and insulted."

Intervening in a discussion that seemed to be getting nowhere, President Macapagal proposed the establishment of an Asian-African commission to help resolve differences. Under the plan outlined by Macapagal, "each of us will select an Asian or African nation. Then these will unanimously elect one more. The four-man commission will be given a time limit. That is my humble way of perpetuating and expanding the Manila Agreement."

"We accept. There must be give-and-take," the Tunku responded.

"What is this give-and-take?" Sukarno asked.

Addressing the Chairman, the Tunku said, "As far as Malaysia is concerned, we have no quarrel. Why did they [the Indonesians] interfere in our affairs?"

Sukarno countered, "There is no interference. There is a *conflict* between the two countries."

"Do you consider that there is a dispute over the question of the formation of Malaysia?" the Tunku asked. "We cannot submit our internal affairs to a third party. How can we have peace and look into this question of Malaysia when all these acts of aggression are taking place?"

Macapagal noted that "before the commission reports, there must be favorable conditions." The Tunku, obviously taking "favorable conditions" to mean the withdrawal of guerrilla troops, said "that must be done before the formation of the commission."

Subandrio disagreed. "We must start from the existing conditions of the conflict," he said.

The argument continued, with the Tunku making clear that although the idea of the commission was a good one, he could not justify to his people acceptance of an agreement that would permit "foreign aggression" to continue indefinitely. "The question of withdrawal is a part of the condition of this meeting," he said to Sukarno, "and not to be treated as a concession in this dispute. . . ."

"Whatever condition or suggestion the commission makes, I shall accept," Sukarno said.

"There must be terms of reference and procedure, otherwise it will cause a lot more trouble than we have bargained for," the Tunku concluded. "Cease all acts of aggression, then I shall agree to the appointment of a commission."

At this point Sukarno, commenting that he understood the conflicting positions, and that no advantage would be gained by further discussion, announced that he had a television interview at 6:00 P.M. and withdrew from the room, returning later to sign the joint communiqué, which had the letter without the spirit of agreement. An Afro-Asian conciliation commission was to "be requested to study the existing problems between the three countries and to submit recommendations for their solution."

The plan unfortunately was never implemented. Although Sukarno on several subsequent occasions, public and private, repeated his pledge to accept whatever recommendations the commission came up with, as well as his willingness to attend another meeting "anywhere and any time," there was no response from Kuala Lumpur, which had laid down the condition of "cessation of hostilities."

Subandrio seized the tactical advantage he thought this gave him. "For us the result of the Tokyo meeting was satisfactory because from now on, we are no longer bound by the previous commitments we have given to Malaysia in order to facilitate the solution of this conflict. We now feel free to carry out this confrontation policy."

Seth S. King, reporting from Tokyo, wrote in the New York *Times* that the conference ended in failure.[2] But President Macapagal took the position that the summit meeting in Tokyo had not failed. On June 22, he wrote the Tunku from Manila urging the three Foreign Ministers to meet within two weeks to work out an acceptable formula for the formation of an Afro-Asian conciliation commission. The Tunku replied that his government shared the sentiment that the search for a peaceful solution should be urgently continued, "but we cannot be expected to succumb to any form of military pressure. As we found in Tokyo, Indonesia

---

2. June 20, 1964.

is not prepared to abandon the military pressure and its hard-line approach—a fact which resulted lately in the death of many of our military personnel and innocent citizens through military action. . . . The Indonesian Foreign Office is on record as having said June 23, reiterating Subandrio's statement of June 22, that the breakdown of the Tokyo talks freed the Indonesians from previous commitments on seeking a peaceful solution. This was followed by the statement of Army Colonel Sabirin Mochtar of the Combat Brigade that our 'volunteers now are free to enter Malaysian territory to support the military struggle of the people there'. . . . I am filled with foreboding for the future. It seems essential that some ground must first be prepared to provide for a reasonable chance of success and a time lapse of many months before any move is made to convene another meeting at the Foreign Minister level." [3]

I was now convinced that Sukarno was ready to call off confrontation if he could do so without being humiliated. And realizing that the British, now heavily involved militarily on the firing line in Borneo, would have a major hand in what formula might be arrived at, I therefore suggested in the fall of 1964 that we initiate exploratory talks with them. U.S. Ambassadors James D. Bell from Kuala Lumpur, William M. Blair, Jr., from Manila, and I arranged to meet secretly in Hong Kong to work out a plan.

We proposed jointly to the Department of State that Her Majesty's Government be encouraged to proceed with cautious talks with the Indonesians to explore the possibility of a settlement; that any U.S. initiative be deferred until the results of those talks were known; and that, in our view, a secret Tunku-Sukarno meeting, with or without a third party, offered the best bet after the talks had improved the atmosphere.

London's response was encouraging, and feelers were being put out when suddenly the Indonesians launched a new sea-borne landing on the mainland of Malaysia near the Malacca-Jahore border. Thirty-seven guerrillas participated, and in their repulsion, Australian troops were engaged for the first time. It killed any chance of a *démarche*.

At first professing ignorance of the attack, Sukarno later accused the British of attempting to encircle Indonesia, and said he would never withdraw "one single guerrilla." If the Tunku would agree to negotiate, however, the landings would cease, and he would try to calm his people down.

There was no give on either side, and no further meeting of Foreign Ministers to attempt to resolve the issues in the Malaysia dispute was ever held. Sukarno continued through 1965 his by now empty Crush Malaysia threats. But the palace-generated steam behind the movement

---

3. Interview, Howard P. Jones and Tunku Abdul Rahman, February 1969.

had long since been dissipated. The Malaysians and British were reasonably content to hold the line, confident that the passage of time would take care of the matter to the discomfiture of Sukarno. They were right.

Taken together, the Crush Malaysia campaign, the UN involvement, the Foreign Ministers' and summit meetings, the personalities of the leading role-players and their assessments of each other offer a rare insight into the problems that plague the peace-making process. Considering the atmosphere of the talks, the Tunku could hardly be blamed for not being responsive to the proposal for the establishment of a quadripartite commission to settle the dispute. Nevertheless, Sukarno's statement that he would accept any recommendation that the proposed commission came up with presented the Tunku with an unparalleled opportunity to settle the dispute or to show up Sukarno to the world as a man who did not keep his word. And he might have accepted the challenge without risk to his own position; indeed, with the cards stacked in his favor.

Why was Sukarno willing to take such a position? From Djakarta, the answer seemed self-evident. Wily politician that he was, he had gone so far with the anti-Malaysia campaign that he had to find some way to crawl back from the limb on which he was perched. Sukarno could have gone to his people and said, in his silver-tongued way, "Here is what our Afro-Asian brothers think we should do. I pledged my word that we would abide by what they thought was right. This, therefore, is the course we must follow." The fact that Sukarno did voluntarily pledge himself in advance to accept the commission's recommendations convinced me that he had reached the conclusion that it was time to liquidate the Crush Malaysia campaign, and that he had selected this method as the easiest way out.

Sukarno's unwillingness to withdraw his guerrillas from North Borneo was to have been expected. Otherwise, he would appear weak to his people and, more important, arouse vigorous protest from the very vocal far left, led by the PKI. He saw his guerrillas as the one card he had to play. It was his old tactic of ensuring action at the conference table by the threat or exertion of force.

The Tunku had nothing to lose at that stage. The mere existence of a quadripartite commission would have created a powerful moral suasion against Sukarno's further exploitation of guerrilla force. And finally, there was the very real possibility that by the time of the Tokyo talks, Sukarno no longer had any guerrillas to withdraw.

It must be remembered that Sukarno had built up the Crush Malaysia theme until it had achieved the status of a major nationalistic issue regarding which no patriotic Indonesian dared raise a question. Sukarno had nailed the flag of his own prestige to the mast of this issue. And the PKI, plastering Djakarta with anti-Malaysia, anti-Tunku, anti-American posters and billboards a block long, was not about to let him get off this particular hook. The army, "defending" Indonesia from the military threat of the "imperialist" forces marshaled on the nation's northern border, was stalemated. Without either challenging Sukarno directly on his pet issue or appearing unwilling to perform its function to preserve the nation's security, the army leadership could not protest the anti-Malaysia campaign. If it were to retain its influence in the country, the army had to remain in the van of this so-called struggle.

Sukarno's dilemma, in short, was how to extricate himself from the Malaysia issue without loss of prestige. The Tokyo conference showed him an exit through which he could walk with dignity. He apparently chose to use it. Tossing the issue to an Afro-Asian group to settle the dispute relieved Sukarno of the responsibility and gave him the perfect out.

Part of the trouble was that the British and Malaysians had no intention of supplying Sukarno with an easy solution. They felt they had this troublemaking Asian leader on the run. They also believed that an Afro-Asian commission could only come up with a compromise solution that would mean rewarding Sukarno for his aggression. They preferred to dig in and hold on. But, in taking no action on the commission proposal, the British and Malaysian leaders unwittingly strengthened Sukarno's position internally. He had assumed a position that was unassailable. To his people, the other side was being utterly unreasonable. They interpreted the lack of favorable response as a determination to humiliate Indonesia.

Long after, in February 1969, I talked with the Tunku in Kuala Lumpur. He told me he considered Sukarno's confrontation policy as that of a desperate man. He regarded Subandrio as the evil genius of confrontation. At the same time, he said, from the Malaysian standpoint, the break with Sukarno was "God sent." Confrontation united his own nation as nothing else could have. It eliminated what the Tunku termed "unreal loyalties." More than a quarter of the population of Malaya came from Indonesia, the Tunku pointed out, and still were bound by old loyalties. "A few years ago, traveling across the country, I would find pictures of Sukarno in schoolrooms and homes. Think of it! In my own country! I was quite jealous. I thought, Why should people be putting up portraits of a ruler of some other state? But all this disappeared with confrontation.

"Sukarno was acting more like Hitler than an Asian statesman," the Tunku observed. "At least Hitler built up Germany," he added tartly. He described Sukarno's dramatic entrance when he strutted into the Manila conference in a gleaming white uniform complete with gold epaulets and decorations. "The man's going mad!" the Tunku had exclaimed.

There were people in Washington and elsewhere who agreed with the Tunku and suggested that strong measures would bring Sukarno into line. But Sukarno had always been more susceptible to flattery and persuasion than to threats. My own closeness to the President and my seeming patience continued to be questioned. I was not advocating a policy of expediency or appeasing Sukarno at the expense of others, but simply recognizing Sukarno as a fact of life. Our influence over Sukarno was limited; yet we were one of the few nations in the free world that had any significant continuing dialogue with him. In my discussions with Sukarno, I aimed at achieving tangible results rather than simply registering indignation. We endeavored to exert pressure on Sukarno without driving him into a position he would regard as humiliating. Given a choice between humiliation and war, or humiliation and a break in relations, those who knew Sukarno had no doubt about what his decision would be.

Our contacts with the Indonesian Army were excellent in this period. On the Malaysian issue, it had no choice but to follow Sukarno's lead. Except for this, our points of view on the requirements for maintaining a free and independent Indonesia seemed to be identical. We thought we could count on the military leadership to restrain Sukarno from going to extremes, not because they were influenced by us, but because their assessment of the interests of the country and the direction it should take happened to coincide with ours.

In pursuing my course, I had the comforting knowledge of Averell Harriman's support. His roles from 1961 to 1969, first as Assistant Secretary and then as Under Secretary for Political Affairs, gave him a familiarity with the Indonesian scene that was exceptional. He had seen the West Irian issue through to its solution; he had witnessed the birth of the Malaysian dispute and been in on all our attempts to bring the contending parties together. Consequently, his voice was a strong one in Washington on the subject of Indonesia. Through the years, he and I had seen pretty much eye to eye on Indonesian problems. This was especially true of the Malaysia dispute. We both felt that military aid to Malaysia was unnecessary, since the British did not require this assistance, and that our granting it was almost certain to destroy what little influence we had left in Indonesia.

I did not question the fact that primary responsibility for instigating the dispute and elevating it to the dangerous level it finally reached lay with Indonesia. During this period, the United States government fully supported Malaysia's sovereignty, and was convinced that if there were to be a peaceful settlement of the dispute, it would have to be based essentially on some program of acceptance of Malaysia by Indonesia. At the same time, viewing the Indonesian-Malaysian dispute in the context of Southeast Asia and the Far East as a whole, two important elements deserved consideration. A free pro-Western Malaysia represented one of the important elements of the West's security arrangements in the region. The British bases must remain. Equally if not more essential to Western interests was that Indonesia not go Communist. Indonesia was destined to play a leading role in the affairs of the region and it was vital that that role not be played against the West. It seemed clear to me that there was every reason for our maintaining good relations with both of these countries. "Mad" or not, Sukarno occupied center stage. Access to him was important.

CHAPTER 7

Stabilization Scuttled

With Sukarno roaring "Crush Malaysia!" from Djakarta, with Britain rushing naval vessels, planes and troops to Borneo to defend the borders of the newly created state from an anticipated Indonesian attack, with the entire area upset with the threat of war, "we set about," as Roger Hilsman put it, "to pick up the pieces." [1]

One of the pieces that could not be picked up was the economic stabilization plan drawn up to deal with Indonesia's chronic economic ills. Ever since Sukarno and President Kennedy had met early in 1961, we in the American Embassy and the AID mission in Djakarta had been working closely with Prime Minister Djuanda in an effort to develop a practical program for the solution of Indonesia's economic difficulties.

There was no question in informed circles that the Indonesian economy was headed for real trouble. The country desperately needed foreign exchange for raw materials and spare parts. Indonesian factories were operating at about twenty per cent of capacity. Prices were rising intolerably.[2] In a land less endowed with fertile soil and benign climate, where few people were hungry no matter how hard the pinch, political uprisings must have been anticipated long since.

On President Kennedy's initiative, a team of economic experts led by Professor Don D. Humphrey of the Fletcher School of Law and Diplomacy at Tufts University, had been sent out in August 1961 with instructions to analyze Indonesia's new eight-year development plan, determine the areas of the Indonesian economy where U.S. aid should be concentrated, and recommend ways in which the U.S. could be of assistance to Indonesia, particularly in regard to the execution of the develop-

---

1. Roger Hilsman, *To Move a Nation* (Garden City, N.Y.: Doubleday & Company, Inc., 1967), p. 405.
2. The rupiah, Indonesia's currency, was ten to the dollar at the official rate in 1954. Inflation had brought it to approximately 400 to the dollar at this point. The price of rice had skyrocketed from 7.5 rupiahs a kilo in 1954 to 350 rupiahs a kilo ten years later.

ment plan. The team's report, submitted to the U.S. and Indonesian governments upon completion, noted that while Indonesia was still in a very early stage of economic development, there was a growing sense of commitment to policies that would promote it. This, combined with the native ability of Indonesians and the presence of rich natural resources, made the outlook for economic progress promising.

The team expressed its conviction that Indonesia had the necessary potential to strengthen its ability to maintain independence through foreign assistance, and that aid should be designed to give effective long-term support. To accomplish this, the report concluded:

> Our national interest calls for strengthening the economy of Indonesia. As the first means of doing so, the United States should commit itself to a sustained program of loans and grants, concentrated on training people and building institutions, on improving the nation's infrastructure, and on assisting the Indonesians to use their natural resources effectively. At the same time, we must be prepared to expand this initial commitment later into a larger loan program aimed at forwarding the economic progress of this vast country, while making it clear that such an expanded program cannot be carried out until Indonesia makes greater progress in putting its house in order.[3]

The Humphrey team recommended new aid programs in the amount of between $325 million and $390 million over a five-year period, with approximately one-third to be multinationally financed and the rest picked up by the U.S. By mid-1962, the American government had made clear its willingness to help if the Indonesians did their part, and Washington had received assurances of cooperation from Japan, England, Germany, Italy, and other Development Assistance Committee countries. A meeting of DAC to discuss final arrangements was called for the last week of October 1963, following approval by the International Monetary Fund (IMF) of Indonesia's plan for stabilization.

The key to success or failure of any development plan was President Sukarno. His silver tongue could make or mar any program. "The country will respond to your leadership in this field, as in all others," I said to Sukarno again and again in urging him to make economic development a first priority. But economics to Sukarno was "a dismal science." He frankly admitted that he knew nothing about it and his interest was not challenged. There was no excitement in an economic program; nor was there sufficient emotion to supply fuel for the fires he wanted to light for his people. "Give me men with flames in their eyes," he said to me once. Economists did not have flames in their eyes.

---

3. United States Economic Survey Team to Indonesia, "Indonesia, Perspective and Proposals for United States Economic Aid, A Report to the President of the United States" (New Haven, Yale University Southeast Asia Studies, 1963) p. 160; also known as the "Humphrey Report."

The eight-year development plan that Indonesia had adopted on March 28, 1961, was, for all practical purposes, to remain a plan. Aside from Sukarno's signature establishing it as Presidential Decree No. 107, there was no effective program for its implementation. It remained a pile of manuscript six feet high, too formidable for any one person to read— an ornament of state to be pointed to with pride, like the collection of paintings on the palace walls or the new fountain in the middle of the circle.

But Prime Minister Djuanda understood the problems, and in his plodding, determined way he gradually brought the President around to accept, albeit with a noticeable lack of enthusiasm, the new 1963 plans for economic stabilization and even make a few speeches on the subject. Djuanda knew that economic recovery required the making of hard decisions. Taxes can't be increased, expenditures reduced, credit curtailed, without a strong reaction from those adversely affected. It was the nineteenth-century British economist Walter Bagehot who likened the science of taxation to the art of plucking a goose—the object was to get the most feathers with the least squawk! But some squawk invariably accompanies the process.

Djuanda knew that the architect of any deflationary stabilization plan would be unpopular, at least during the early phases. It was a measure of his patriotism that he assured Sukarno of his willingness to assume full responsibility for the program. When the pressures became too great to bear without a government reaction, he would be willing to resign and take full blame for what happened. To Sukarno's credit, he refused the offer. Ironically, it was Sukarno's violent reaction to the formation of Malaysia that was to destroy the stabilization program, and Djuanda, destined to die of a heart attack later in the year, was a sacrifice on the same altar.

But in May 1963, Djuanda's stabilization plan was adopted, and many of us were encouraged to feel that at long last this potentially rich country had settled down in a serious effort to concentrate on its major problem. By midsummer the decisions taken by the government under the plan appeared to be succeeding beyond all expectations. Prices generally had declined, and all those who had worked on the plan were much encouraged that Indonesia was finally on the high road.

Internal politics, however, was playing behind the scenes. The Communist Party was doing its utmost to discredit the stabilization plan. It wanted no successes in the economic sphere except its own. And the party appeared to have an ally in Foreign Minister Subandrio, who was unsympathetic to this program, either because he had already begun to develop his ties with the PKI and consequently was playing their game, or he did not wish Djuanda to gain any credit. Subandrio in turn was supported by Governor of the Central Bank Sumarno, who was essentially opposed to large-scale foreign credits, or at least Western credits, and expressed a preference for "eating rocks if necessary." As the economic measures of May 1963 and the IMF standby arrangement of July 1963, which provided Indonesia with interim credits, moved forward, Sumarno agreed only to the exchange rates and credit ceilings that were established, but not to the overall concept of the stabilization program.

It had been decided that an IMF team would proceed to Djakarta by about the first of April for consultations and, with the Indonesians, work out the basis for a financial stabilization program. Then DAC members of the Indonesian Working Group—the Western donor-creditor countries and Japan—would meet in Paris to agree upon a program of grant aid, debt relief, and new credits to cover the Indonesian foreign exchange deficit for a year, and, with DAC assurance of a covered Indonesian foreign exchange deficit, the IMF would approve a standby arrangement with a loan to Indonesia.

The key to a timely conclusion of this sequence of events was the favorable report of the IMF team, but it could not go to Djakarta until invited. The invitation was delayed, and delayed again, with the result that the IMF team did not arrive in Djakarta until the middle of June and, even by compressing its work, was unable to make its report to IMF Washington before about July 10, 1963. Two and a half months were thus lost. The strategy of Subandrio and Sumarno appeared to be to generate a sufficient delay in the invitation to the IMF to defeat Djuanda's effort to obtain cover for the Indonesian foreign exchange deficit.[4]

Clues to the machinations involved accumulated gradually in the spring of 1963. In April, the Indonesian Ambassador in Washington thought that the IMF should not become involved until there was a "change in the Cabinet" in Djakarta, but apparently he had reported to his government that the IMF did not want to become involved until the Cabinet changed, a position the IMF would certainly not have taken since that institution scrupulously avoids involvement in domestic affairs. The Ambassador appeared to be lined up with Subandrio, as might have been expected.

In Djakarta we were bringing pressure on the government to get out the invitation. Finally, First Minister Djuanda told me the telegram had been sent, and I so cabled Washington. More than a week went by before it was delivered. Djuanda had signed the telegram inviting the team but sent it through Sumarno as the proper channel for messages to the IMF. Sumarno, playing ball with Subandrio, apparently held the message in Djakarta as long as he felt he could. As it was, because of the delay in delivery of the IMF report, the first meeting was not held until July 26. All plans for the second meeting were dropped when Indonesia launched its confrontation of Malaysia in September.

Indonesia's mounting of a trade blockade against Malaysia only weeks

---

4. Memorandum, Clifford C. Matlock to Howard P. Jones, March 15, 1969.

before the stabilization loan would have been granted was the final, fatal blow. The Indonesians were cutting their own economic throats by halting trade with Singapore, the entrepôt through which some twenty to thirty per cent of their trade flowed. In the early stages of the blockade, Indonesia had a serious problem as goods piled up in the ports of Sumatra with no ships to carry them. Indonesians consoled themselves by saying that the crisis they faced was a blessing in disguise because it forced them to make changes they should have made years ago. It was perhaps understandable that the Indonesians, peering across the Straits at prosperous Singapore and concluding that the port's prosperity was based on profits from Indonesian goods, wanted to keep those profits at home. Thus a decision to bypass Singapore could be defended as a rational economic policy. Nevertheless, this period of economic stress and strain was hardly the time to embark on such a program. To succeed, it would have required the establishment of facilities to enable Indonesia to service its export trade as efficiently as did Singapore. This would have taken years. Indonesia had products the world wanted; now it was cut off not only from the warehousing, handling and processing facilities for these products but, even more important, experience in marketing, financing and insurance.

Certainly, no stabilization program could have succeeded under these conditions; nor could any nation have been expected to put up money to support Indonesia, since any external assistance would have been regarded as supporting Indonesia's Crush Malaysia campaign. Plans that had envisaged some $400 million in financial assistance to Indonesia had to be scrapped. It would take years and a political cataclysm before another serious economic program would be mounted. Sukarno failed to crush Malaysia, but he succeeded in crushing the economy of his country, already laboring under a load too heavy to bear.

CHAPTER 8

"To Hell with Your Aid"

Nineteen sixty-three was generally a most unsatisfactory year for Indonesian-U.S. relations. By November, when I was called to Washington for consultations, the list of dissatisfactions had grown to the point where some in the Capitol believed that a major Sukarno objective was dominion in Southeast Asia by gaining control of all the adjoining Malay-populated areas. For evidence they pointed to Indonesia's drive to break up Malaysia, to convince the Philippines of the advantages of adopting a foreign policy in line with that of Indonesia, and the campaign to eliminate Western bases from the area. The termination of British military power in Surabaya and Malaya was viewed as a preliminary step toward forcing U.S. military power from the Philippines, after which Indonesia would presumably have little difficulty in annexing all the Malay states, including the Philippines. There was also impressive historical evidence to support this view: in 1945, part of the committee charged with drawing up Indonesia's Constitution favored the inclusion of the present Malaysian territories in Indonesia; in 1954, the Indonesian government was allegedly providing covert support to Pan-Malayan extremists in Malaya. Tan Malaka, founder of the Murba Party, was known to favor an Indonesia that would include the Malaysian territories and at least part of the Philippines.

But this hypothesis was too unrealistic when put in the context of today's world. Even had Sukarno's "grand design" envisaged such a program (and none could deny this as a possibility), the social and political environment no longer was such as to render possible an Indonesian expansionist program of this type. A voluntary federation like Maphilindo had much to offer all concerned; even so, it had proved to be too sophisticated a concept for the times.

There were other questions to be attacked: the U.S. had accomplished little with its policy of forebearance. Would not a tougher policy have produced more positive results? Should we not experiment along that line, at least to the extent of some measure of disengagement as a warning to the Indonesian government that there are limits to our patience?

To both of these my answer was no. I continued to emphasize, as in the past, that we were playing for the long haul in Indonesia, that we could afford to shrug off the "slings and arrows," that pique and petulance were no basis for the policy of a great nation. I was certain that getting tough would only result in resentment and withdrawal on the part of a proud people; the "lion killer," Sukarno, was quite capable of turning such a posture to his own advantage and discrediting the very democratic elements that we were concerned to strengthen. I could offer no guarantee; it was simply the only policy that had a chance. The test was not now; it would come in the post-Sukarno era.

Indonesia's flirtatious posturing with Communism was perhaps the toughest pill to swallow. Were we not, in effect, "shoring up" a government that made no secret of its interest in Communism, while it disregarded the welfare of its people and turned a deaf ear to American approaches and remonstrances?

Our assessment of the situation was that, although there was no immediate danger of a Communist takeover in Indonesia, the government's foreign and domestic policies were detrimental to our objectives in that they were obviously serving the long-range interests of the Communists. The economic stagnation, the increasing strength of the PKI,[1] the trend toward police-state methods, and the evolving anti-Western posture were all symptoms that gave us grave concern. At the same time, we would have to gain hope from what we knew as fact: anti-Western attitudes were not held generally by Indonesians, particularly not by the youth.

I returned to Djakarta saddened by the tragic death of President Kennedy, uncertain of the future. But I knew that I had the support of such key men in the Department of State and the White House as Roger Hilsman, Averell Harriman, and Mike Forrestal. Dean Rusk would accept their judgment and mine.

The war of words continued. In December, Sukarno demanded another survey of public opinion in the Borneo territories as the price for abiding by the UN verdict and agreeing to accept Malaysia. Subandrio told a mass rally in West Kalimantan, "One hundred million people and their armed forces are behind you," and introduced Azahari as the

---

1. By November 1963, the embassy was reporting that "the PKI is the largest and best-organized political party in Indonesia. . . . It also effectively controls, has heavily infiltrated, or otherwise exerts a dominant influence on other political parties. It has a young, vigorous, astute leadership. Above all, it has a reputation that is scarcely approached in other non-Communist countries." At the same time, we recognized that much of the membership "was undoubtedly not 'hard core' " and lacked a basic understanding of party principles.

"Prime Minister of the North Kalimantan Unitary Republic." With others making similar exaggerated statements, the overheated atmosphere in Djakarta boded ill for a peaceful settlement. A high point was touched on March 25, 1964.

On the occasion of a building dedication in Djakarta, President Sukarno began his speech by quoting from an editorial in one of the leading American weekly magazines that stated Indonesia was on the verge of economic collapse, and advised that Sukarno be notified that the U.S. would stop all aid to his country unless he pulled his guerrillas out of Malaysia and stopped his aggression.

Sukarno first ridiculed the idea that resource-rich Indonesia could collapse economically, and then stated, "We receive aid from many countries, and we are grateful for such aid. But we will never accept aid with political strings attached. When any nation offers us aid with political strings attached, then I will tell them," he paused a moment, then burst out in English, "Go to hell with your aid!" He had really done it this time.

Newspapers all over the United States, indeed, all over the world, headlined this story. More than one wondered why I had stayed there and taken the insult. And Senator Birch Bayh of Indiana, quoting newspaper reports, presented the United States Senate with a strong attack on President Sukarno:

> Despite his personal failing, despite his aggressive attitude toward his neighbors in Southeast Asia, we have continued aid.
> So at a public meeting in Djakarta on March 25, where more than 2,000 people had gathered, President Sukarno pointed at Ambassador Howard P. Jones and said:
> 'There is one country threatening to stop its foreign aid to Indonesia. That country thinks it can scare Indonesia. I say go to hell with your aid.'

He wound up with the following statement:

> But I do not believe in throwing good money after bad. I do not believe in continuing to ask the American people for their tax dollars to support a man who is arrogant, insulting, incompetent, and unstable—a man who, by his own foul admission, despises the very people whose energy and hard work make it possible for many of his people to eat and to ward off the ravages of malaria. It is absolutely imperative for the Senate to determine that when our foreign dollars are spent, they are spent for the cause of perpetuating freedom, and not spent as they have been spent in the past years in Indonesia.

I know Senator Bayh as a sincere and intelligent man. Had I been in his place, with the information in his possession, I undoubtedly would have felt precisely as he did. But the aid program in Indonesia had never been postulated on shoring up Sukarno. Quite the contrary. We were scrupulous in avoiding projects that would support the charismatic Indonesian leader—we were attempting, rather, to build a foundation for Indonesian economic stability and political independence. And Sukarno had not pointed his finger at the American Ambassador and said "to hell with your aid." With all his faults, Sukarno was not one deliberately to embarrass the representative of another nation.

Coming on the heels of Sukarno's statement, Secretary Rusk's testimony before Congress that no new aid would be forthcoming for Indonesia unless the Malaysia question were solved drew heated comment from all sections of the Indonesian press. Richard Nixon, traveling in Southeast Asia at the time, made clear that Americans were not divided on this issue. In his remarks indicating support for Malaysia, he of course also drew fire from the Indonesian press.

A diplomat struggling to counteract an unfavorable atmosphere in the country to which he is accredited frequently finds his efforts nullified by the press. Thus on March 30, the Philadelphia *Inquirer* published the following editorial under the heading "While Sukarno Dreams of Empire":

> Famine in Indonesia is a tragic irony.
>
> A hundred million people are confronted with a critical and worsening shortage of rice. Thousands of the hungry lie in the streets, some of them already dead or dying of starvation.
>
> President Sukarno, fat with power and bloated with a seemingly endless stream of hundreds of millions of American foreign aid dollars, continues to drain the wealth of his nation into military ventures that are designed to soothe his insatiable appetite for empire.
>
> Although adverse weather conditions have cut the rice harvests in Indonesia the plight of the country is man-made. Sukarno is the culprit. He has squandered treasure for armaments to wage war and threats of war against Dutch New Guinea, now fallen into Sukarno's hands, and against Malaysia. Rice and other foods could have been produced abroad to ease the suffering of the Indonesians but Sukarno has exhausted the patience of his creditors by his reckless spending for arms.
>
> He is akin to a drunkard who uses the grocery money to buy a bottle while the family at home waits in vain for something to eat.
>
> There is mounting danger that the Communists, already strong in Indonesia because of Sukarno's friendly encouragement, will utilize the food crisis as a springboard to a complete takeover of the reins of Government in Jakarta. It is a situation filled with peril, in an extremely sensitive area where the Red Chinese are trying, as in nearby South Vietnam, to extend their sphere of domination.
>
> The central figure in this Indonesian tragedy, which could explode into a world crisis, is a dictator who rose to power on the wings of American aid.

It may be a little late, but Washington should be reviewing its policy on Sukarno.

The very day this was published and relayed to Djakarta, I was asking Sukarno to express appreciation for our assistance through the years in an effort to calm the rising tempest in both Djakarta and Washington! My request was in a very real sense a test of Sukarno's intentions. He had let off steam five days before with his "Go to hell with your aid" blast; I was offering him a way of backing off. He could still insist he would accept no aid with political strings, but at the same time express his thanks for our aid through the years. Locally, I knew such a statement would be a signal to his people to continue cooperation with our AID Mission; otherwise the combination of PKI attacks and official disapproval would put serious psychological if not actual barriers in our way. Sukarno had agreed to do so. It might take him a few days, but he would find an occasion. Editorials such as the foregoing, however, changed his mind. Instead, he reiterated his challenge.

The situation reminded me of an experience told by a news correspondent. Enroute to Djakarta, he had run into a Dutch reporter who informed him that conditions were so serious in Indonesia that Sukarno had come out with a new slogan for his people: "Eat less rice, eat more mice." The American was impressed, and as he traveled around Java, he searched for evidence of starvation conditions but saw only a people on the whole happy and well fed. Once, during an evening meal of rice, corn, fish, bananas and other fruit, he inquired of his Indonesian host what had happened to Sukarno's slogan.

The host looked puzzled for a moment. Then he hooted. "Mice, mice. You mean *maize, maize* ["ai" pronounced as "i"]! That is what we call corn! That is what Sukarno said, 'Eat less rice, eat more maize.' And that's what we're doing. See?" He pointed to the corn on the table.

Indonesia's economic plight over the years was serious, and the editorial did have some basis in fact. Indonesia was in the difficult period between rice crops traditionally known as the time of "the small hunger." This year was worse than usual. An AID staff man sent to check out the situation reported evidence of slow starvation along the coastal plains of West Java and generally through Central and East Java, and Bali. An embassy doctor visiting Bali noted that in North Central Bali, 60,000 out of a population of 300,000 were severely undernourished, and there had been a number of deaths from starvation in Singaradja, Bali's principal port. The Indonesians were so sensitive on this subject, however, that Deputy Minister of Health Madame Subandrio (the Foreign Minister's wife) publicly rejected 600,000 pounds of skimmed-milk powder donated by UNICEF for distribution in connection with hunger-edema cases. Subsequently, Mrs. Subandrio privately accepted the milk but refused to allow UNICEF to assist in its distribution, a silly decision and one bound to affect the efficiency of the operation.

Intemperate, exaggerated press statements can seriously effect delicate international situations and are ever-recurring problems for diplomats. Yet, having served in countries where the press was controlled, I'll take a free press every time! The remedy is not governmental control; it is a broader understanding, and a greater sense of responsibility, on the part of journalists who are dealing with international topics.

The go-to-hell incident, combined with our disagreement with Indonesia's position in opposing the formation of Malaysia and our inability to move ahead with the balance-of-payments assistance, only served to heighten emotions on both sides. In the wake of the burning of the British Embassy on September 18, 1963, and the subsequent Indonesian embargo on all trade relations with the new state of Malaysia, American policy toward Indonesia had stiffened. Not only did the United States cancel plans to organize a free-world consortium to aid an IMF stabilization program in Indonesia, but we suspended our own bilateral aid program. In practice, this meant that the U.S. government undertook no new commitments of assistance, although it continued with ongoing programs. The Indonesians accused us of welching on our promises; denunciations of Sukarno reverberated within the halls of the United States Congress.

The force of these criticisms had been demonstrated on July 25, 1963, when the House Foreign Affairs Committee approved an amendment to the Foreign Aid Authorization bill offered by Representative Broomfield of Michigan. Among the most scathing attackers of Sukarno was Senator Wayne Morse of Oregon, who lashed out at the Administration's justification of its relatively mild response to what the New York *Times* liked to call "Sukarno's rampage." Totaling up United States aid to Indonesia over the previous fiscal year, Morse found $17.6 million in military aid and $123.3 million in economic aid for a grand total of $140.9 million. He said:

> This is what we sank into that rathole last year alone. There is plenty more scheduled to go into Indonesia in fiscal year 1964. . . . In my judgment, this is a country which ought to be dropped from the list completely. I say we should wipe it off the aid program. So long as the present regime is in power in Indonesia, we shall never be able to help the Indonesian people with American aid. We shall only be strengthening the tyrant who dominates them.

Men like Senator Morse, with the best of motives, overlooked entirely the lack of wisdom in abandoning such strongly anti-Communist elements as the Indonesian army and the police brigade. By maintaining our modest assistance to such groups, we fortified them for a virtually inevitable showdown with the burgeoning PKI. Despite the passage into law of the Broomfield Amendment, the Administration managed to continue selected military aid and technical training throughout 1964, albeit on a reduced level.

Sukarno continued to protest his treatment by the American press, particularly in reference to his personal life. "No one in a Communist state ever says anything like that about me," he would protest. And when I reminded him of American free speech and free press, he would invariably counter, "But has your government no *influence* with these people?" Once, he was prompted to give me an illustration of what he meant. "A German magazine was printing bad things about me," he said. "I went to Adenauer. 'Can't you do something about that, Mr. Chancellor?' I asked. Did he say, 'No, we've got freedom of speech here'? And they have, you know," Sukarno inserted parenthetically. "Certainly not! Adenauer said, 'Mr. President, you leave that to me.' He called the magazine editor in, and no more insults were published. I don't see why your government can't do the same."

The answer, he assumed, was because the Administration agreed with what was being said or did not consider him important enough to bother about. Either conclusion was enough to raise the hackles of this emotional man.

As congressional and press criticism continued, he came to believe that America's paternalistic attitude toward him bordered on the patronizing; the kind of attitude embodied in the phrase, "Papa knows best," or, "Mend your ways, my boy, and everything will be fine and dandy." He knew that in Washington he was regarded as a troublemaker. All right, he would make trouble. Or, more accurately, he would let others, *i.e.*, the PKI, make trouble on his behalf.

Our Consulate in Medan reported that a major demonstration was being planned by the PKI in North Sumatra and the presence of the Seventh Fleet, on a courtesy-call operation in the Indian Ocean, was to be exploited as a threat to Indonesia. Under cover of this trumped-up issue, the Communist labor unions—in the name of Indonesian nationalism—planned to take over the rubber estates in North Sumatra owned by Goodyear and United States Rubber. I informed Sukarno of the report, and requested him to take whatever steps were necessary to prevent this from happening. It was one of the many occasions on which Sukarno was instantly responsive. He ordered an aide to communicate an alert order to the Army Chief of Staff, General Yani.

Action and reaction between Djakarta and Washington continued throughout 1964. In May, the National Front established an "Action Command to Boycott American Movies." One theater owner reported that the Communists had told him, "If you show any American films, we won't raid your theater. We'll set fire to every automobile that is parked in your parking lot!" Protests to President Sukarno were of no avail, despite the fact that American movies were his favorites. Of course, he did not deprive himself. American films were shown at the Palace at least twice a week. He was noncommittal about taking action. "My people are angry at America," he told me. Read: Sukarno was angry.

The situation rapidly grew worse as those elements hostile to America took their cue from the passive attitude of the Indonesian government, which in most instances failed to express regrets for damages suffered by the United States government or its citizens. When USIS libraries in Djakarta and Surabaya were attacked, the government went so far as to virtually sanction violent action by publicly announcing that it could "understand the feeling of the youth" involved. In fact, since the National Front was an arm of the central government, and since permission from the police was required before demonstrations could be held, there was every reason to assume that the central government's blessing, including Sukarno's passive or active endorsement, had been given to such actions.

By mid 1964, however, there were growing signs of anti-Communist feeling in both the body politic and the press. Led by B. M. Diah's *Merdeka,* several non-Communist papers were demonstrating a vigorous spirit of attack. Seldom mentioning names and sometimes talking in riddles, they spoke out against PKI advances on the domestic front, the principal issues being Communist incitement of landless peasants against landlords, the PKI's efforts to inject its ideas and personnel into the education system, and the anti-Communist suggestion that Indonesia should have only one political party.

By June, *Merdeka's* dispute with the PKI newspaper, *Harian Rakjat,* over the one-party concept had gone far beyond the scope of the original question. *Merdeka* accused the Communists of distorting the ideas of President Sukarno and using Stalinist tactics by bitterly denouncing any opinion contrary to theirs. Editor Diah charged further that the Communists wished "to seize the leadership of the revolution by gaining the power of the masses," and that they did not truly accept the ideology of the state. As in the past, the one-party proposal, designed to submerge the PKI in a larger political grouping, floundered amid the dissension of the major non-Communist parties. As part of a government attempt to halt this display of disunity, the President disavowed the one-party suggestion and issued instructions ending the press polemic. Although some compromises were made, the net effect was to encourage the PKI to push harder towards its objectives.

Efforts by "moderates" and intellectuals to confront the PKI demonstrated that there was a substantial anti-Communist presence determined not to be downed. The first of these efforts, in August 1963, had centered around a document called the "Cultural Manifesto" (*"Manifesto Kebudajaan"*), which drew support and inspiration from Indonesia's leading intellectuals, including Soedjatmoko, who, throughout this

period, played a role of continuous encouragement of those forces opposed to captivity of individual freedom, the kind of role the Germans
describe as *intellektuelle Seelensorge* (intellectual care of the soul). The
Manifesto called for some degree of artistic freedom and objected to
creativity used solely in the service of the state. By early 1964, more than
500 individuals and representatives of about fifty organizations had
signed it.

The Communist Party was not slow to take up the challenge. The
PKI attacked the Manifesto and bestowed upon it the name *"Manikebu,"* an abbreviated form of *Manifesto Kebudajaan.* The Communists
succeeded in attaching an emotional stigma to *Manikebu*, similar to that
possessed by such words as *imperialism* and *colonialism*.

President Sukarno, too, was alert to the danger that the call for freedom posed to his regime. He seized an opportunity to show his feelings
by ignoring his scheduled speaking engagement at the Moderate Writers
Conference, organized by supporters of the "Cultural Manifesto" and
sponsored by Islamic and other moderate groups for the first seven days
of March 1964. It was almost openly supported by Minister of Defense
Nasution, who provided behind-the-scenes support from the army. The
government, following Sukarno's lead, cold-shouldered the conference.
Minister of Basic Education and Culture Prijono, also scheduled to
speak, instead sent a message in which he questioned the participants'
loyalty to the state. First Deputy Prime Minister Subandrio and Minister of Information Roeslan Abdulgani sent messages emphasizing the
need for writers to work with other groups to carry out revolutionary
goals. Only two Cabinet Ministers showed up—General Nasution and
Minister of Religion Zuhri. Nasution's speech was mild. Zuhri indirectly
attacked the Communists, pointing out that culture should be based on
religion. In May, Sukarno decreed the Manifesto illegal—an act that,
needless to say, the Communist press greeted joyfully—and the movement died.

Manikebu had hardly been buried when the seeds of a new movement
took root in a speech by Abdulgani on May 9, during which, in the
course of interpreting Sukarno's philosophy as expressed in *Manipol-
usdek*, he used the term "Sukarnoism." [2] Under that title, a series of
articles by PNI moderate Sajuti Melik appeared, beginning in early July,
in *Berita Indonesia*—the Murba Party organ—and was picked up by
dozens of newspapers throughout Indonesia, including *Merdeka* and
Warta Berita, an independent paper. The aim of the articles was not to
attack the PKI or refute Marxism; instead, they stressed the importance

---

2. Sukarnoism was described by one of its supporters as an essentially defensive measure designed to isolate President Sukarno from the Communists,
restore the balance of power between left and right, and rescue Indonesia
from the danger of being irrevocably committed to a pro-Communist
course.

of religion in the national philosophy and made the subtle point that since Indonesian socialism was now established under Sukarno, no necessity existed for a movement further left. It was a new approach that, without openly challenging the PKI, offered a rallying point for those opposed to its activities; it became a major issue in the press polemics, mentioned earlier, led by Diah's *Merdeka*.

There were a few other encouraging signs in the early spring of 1964, such as the closing down of the Communist-controlled Bank of China, in accordance with the government policy of eliminating all foreign-controlled banks. We welcomed this, particularly since the Bank was suspected of being one of the main channels through which financial support reached the PKI.

The internal atmosphere seemed to be somewhat improving, enough so that when, in June, I asked one of Indonesia's leading intellectuals what he thought of the increasing trend toward the left, he challenged the basic assumption. He said that he, and others like him, had the distinct impression that Sukarno felt the PKI was gaining too much power and that cutting it down to size was one of his principal motivations for finding a peaceful solution to the Malaysia dispute. My source also had concluded that further *rapprochement* with the Chinese Communists, as well as increased power for the PKI, would result only if Sukarno's hand was forced by events such as an escalation of the Malaysia military conflict or hostile actions taken by our government.

Anti-American actions, however, did continue. In June, the government banned the USIS magazine, *Aneka Amerika*, which had a nationwide circulation in Indonesia, and four U.S. magazines of general circulation.[3]

The Russians, with all their military and economic backing of Indonesia, were worried, too. The PKI had ungratefully moved toward the Chinese side of the Sino-Soviet dispute, and something had to be done about that. Soviet Deputy Premier Anastas Mikoyan arrived on June 22 with an impressive delegation. Their reception was decidedly cool, the PKI failing to turn out the usual noisy crowds. Mikoyan's long sessions with Aidit and other PKI leaders, designed to persuade them to return to the Soviet fold, were wholly unsuccessful. And the coolness persisted all during the visit. I was present at a major speech Mikoyan made; the only times he seemed to impress his audience were those when he played on nationalist themes like the Malaysia campaign. In supporting the Indonesian position, he reminded his audience of the Soviet military support and boasted of Soviet military superiority over the United States. But his mission was partly successful. Subandrio told me that the Indonesians would support the Soviet claim to be an Asian country for the purpose of

---

3. Despite the attacks on America, the embassy had been receiving up to 50,000 letters a month seeking information about the U.S.

the Afro-Asian Conference, although Soviet attendance probably could not be guaranteed.

Such was the life of an Ambassador in Djakarta at this time that the need for what I called "creative diplomacy," that is, assisting a new nation in the solution of its problems of poverty and economic development, was continually being obscured by the more short-term demand for diplomatic fire prevention. And as time went on, this became more and more difficult. Any one of these fires could, of course, cause a conflagration that would do serious harm to our relations with Indonesia. Indeed, so cocky did Aidit become that by late 1964, he was boasting of pressing matters to the point where the United States would be forced to break diplomatic relations with Indonesia within a year. To give the devil his due, he almost achieved his objective!

CHAPTER 9

The Diplomatic Community

An embassy operation today in most countries is a far cry from the teacup-balancing, cooky-pushing stereotype. Our day in Djakarta started at 7:00 in the morning, to match the hours of the Indonesian government. I held a daily 8:00 A.M. meeting for all top embassy staff and members of the "country team," the head of the economic aid program, the head of the military assistance group, the military attachés and representatives of the other government agencies. We discussed current developments and what American policy was applicable to them, and we handed out assignments as necessary.

Representing the American government in Indonesia was, of course, the primary assignment of the embassy, and this involved a continuing series of interviews and consultations with public officials at all levels. Keeping the United States government informed of political, social, economic and military developments in Indonesia was the second major task of the embassy. Few people realize that this reporting aspect of an embassy is almost as fast-moving an operation as a daily newspaper; an embassy has to analyze events in depth and feed Washington a constant stream of facts behind the news, evaluating their significance. Embassy political reporters thus have to be ahead of newsmen and correspondents in anticipating the flow of events and providing information on the basis of which policy may be formed. When an embassy does not see clearly and interpret accurately the trend of events, it has failed in its job.

The Indonesian government hours were from 7:00 in the morning until 2:00 in the afternoon, when officials and staff called it a day and went home to lunch and a siesta, utilizing the late afternoon for sports, relaxation or, in the case of higher officials, additional meetings and conferences. The American Embassy observed both Indonesian and American hours!

The diplomatic corps in any country is a world unto itself; a strange kind of dual world where an individual is less appraised and judged by his own qualities and capacities than he is by the posture and attributes

330

of the nation he represents. Often, of course, it works the other way, too: a nation may be judged by the inadequacies of a blundering representative or the adequacies of a competent one. The point is that a diplomat's significance is directly related to that of his government. What he says is taken not as a personal view but the expression of his government's attitude. He thus becomes more than a person, and yet to some extent is depersonalized by this very fact.

A diplomat is constantly being sought after for and seeking new information about developments on the international scene, the subtle changes in attitudes of nations, nuances of policy on the part of other nations toward the government of the country to which he is accredited, shifts in emphasis of that government's policy or its implementation.

It is an active, articulate, busybody world; each diplomat is probing the other, exploring, testing, analyzing, comparing information he has with that of others. It is a world of cocktail parties, receptions and dinners, of talk, talk, talk. Gossip reigns supreme, and it is the task of each diplomat to attempt to sift the wheat of truth from the chaff of rumors and misinformation.

The diplomatic community is thus a group of small State Departments or mini–Foreign Offices abroad. The relations, good or bad, between two nations are reflected in the actions of their ambassadors. Yet there exists a certain shared professionalism among diplomats, as there is among scientists, historians, musicians, artists, physicians, because each understands and makes allowances for the framework in which the other is operating.

According to former Under Secretary of State Herbert B. Prochnow, "A diplomat leads a terrible life. When he isn't straddling an issue, he's dodging one." There is a modicum of truth in this witticism, for if a diplomat knows his job, he is constantly on the alert to prevent conflict and confrontation, unless an issue is one of principle. But I would not wish to give the impression that sophisticated urbanity is the desirable quality for a diplomat. Much more important is sincerity and a genuine attempt to understand the point of view of the people among whom you are living. This means studying in depth their history, culture, language, mores, society and attitudes; the things of which they are proud, the things which make them ashamed, the things that, in the language of the modern generation, "turn them on."

Many people have asked me how I managed to retain the confidence and friendship of President Sukarno over such a long period, especially when the policies of our respective governments were sharply opposed and there were very few occasions when I was not either protesting specific actions or disagreeing with his policies. I can only assume there were two reasons. I always told him the truth, however unpleasant it might be. Also, he knew I loved his country and its people, and was genuinely interested in helping them attain their legitimate objectives. Although most of our frequent talks were carried on in a spirit of friendly give-and-take, occasionally we ended up shouting at each other. Fortunately, these encounters were "under four eyes" and caused neither of us embarrassment.

In Djakarta, as Dean of the Diplomatic Corps[1] the last three years I was there, I presided over a group of diplomats representing some sixty-one nations. The three largest missions in Djakarta were the American, Soviet, and Communist Chinese. Counting the Economic Aid Mission, the United States Information Service, the military and other attachés, and the U. S. Military Technical Assistance Group, the U. S. Embassy family was about 300 in number, excluding dependents. The Soviet Embassy was equal in size, and considerably larger when it was amplified by large numbers of technicians, military and economic. There was no way to ascertain the size of the Communist Chinese Embassy; its personnel and operations were enclosed within high walls and barbed wire.

All the Western European nations were represented except the Netherlands during the break in relations. My British, German, French, Swiss, Italian and other Western colleagues were consistently helpful in the various crises we faced—as were the ever-active Australians, just coming into full realization that they were part of Asia, and determined to maintain a solid friendship with their big Asian neighbor. Japan was rebuilding its damaged relations with Indonesia with tact and skill.

Aside from the leaders of the two world blocs, the Asian embassies were of keenest interest to Indonesia in view of Sukarno's ambitions to head the Afro-Asian bloc. All Asia was represented by active missions, as well as the Middle East. Sukarno, determined to put Indonesia on the map, pressed nations to establish diplomatic missions in Djakarta even when there was little mutual political interest and no commercial relations whatever. Thus Brazil and the Argentine were represented by Ambassadors who had little to do but collect *objets d'art*, a pastime I heartily envied them. The Panamanian Consul General, however, was a busy man, keeping track of the hundreds of vessels of Panamanian registry plying between Djakarta and other ports.

All of the Communist bloc countries except Albania were represented. Thus much could be learned about Communist attitudes and relations with other countries, often merely by observing their conduct at receptions. When the first signs of coolness developed between Russia and China, the entire pattern of social conduct altered. In "warmer" days, at

---

1. The status of Dean of the Corps, I should hastily add, is not an elected one; it is achieved by staying power alone. Protocol prescribes that diplomats in a country are ranked—and seated at a table—on the basis of seniority so earned. As Ambassador in Indonesia for seven and a half years, I automatically became Dean when I reached the top of the seniority ladder and, incidentally, acquired the record for the longest service at a single post by any American diplomat in the post–World War II period.

a reception or cocktail party, the Sino-Soviet bloc was conspicuous by the way in which all its members gathered into a huddle, forming a ring into which it was difficult to break. Then suddenly, there were two rings, one big and one small. The big ring was composed of the Soviet Ambassador and all his satellites. The Chinese Ambassador began to look rather lonely. He had few satellites—the Mongolian Ambassador (who was actually resident in New Delhi) and the North Korean and North Vietnamese Consuls General were about all. But Western diplomats whose governments recognized China, such as France, Great Britain and Canada, took advantage of the new situation to talk with him through an interpreter. And, varying with the state of relations, other Asian diplomats such as those from India, Pakistan, Burma and Cambodia would be seen courting the Chinese.

The three governments represented in Djakarta with which the United States had no relations—North Vietnam and North Korea had only consular representation—were China, Cuba, and the Republic of Outer Mongolia. The rather childish practice, universally indulged in, is for diplomatic representatives of such nations to totally ignore each other's presence. Many is the time I have sat next to the Chinese Ambassador at breakfast, lunch or dinner without so much as exchanging the courtesy of a "Good morning" or "Good evening." Once, at a Presidential Palace receiving line, I encountered the Chinese Ambassador. Automatically, I extended my hand. He ignored it and appeared absorbed in studying the ceiling until I had passed along. Another time, President Sukarno mischievously called me to him at a reception. Placing his right arm around the shoulders of the Cuban Chargé d'Affaires and his left around mine, he said, "Do you two know each other?" The poor Cuban turned pale and tightly clutched his hands behind him as I held out my hand. He apparently felt that shaking hands with the American Ambassador was equivalent to a ticket home. He need not have been so upset. I was Dean of the Corps and it was quite proper for him to acknowledge me in that capacity.

At one point, the Cuban Ambassador and his wife not only spoke briefly but made very clear their personal friendly feelings toward America. The Ambassador's wife was a beautiful brunette with flashing black eyes who had remained an ardent Roman Catholic. Whenever my wife and I met her at a reception, she would press our hands, give us a meaningful look, flash a brilliant smile, and then pass quickly along. Her manner as well as his seemed to convey a message. One day we heard that the couple had gone to Singapore and there were rumors they were not returning. Our relief was great when we had word that they had broken through the curtain and been given political asylum in Canada.

My long tenure in Indonesia overlapped the terms of three Soviet ambassadors. Cordiality characterized our relationships, in some cases to the point of personal friendship. The experience of one of them, Ambassador Wolkov, illustrated the ruthlessness of the Soviet system even as applied to its own public servants. The first night of Premier Khrushchev's 1960 Indonesian visit, Wolkov was giving a large reception in his honor. My wife and I were greeted not by the Soviet Ambassador but by his wife and the Counselor of Embassy. When we inquired about her husband, her eyes filled with tears. She told us he had gone back to Moscow that afternoon.

There were conflicting reports as to the reason. One rumor had it that when the Soviet leader's plane landed at Kemajoran Airport and the Soviet Ambassador reported to him certain changes in plan for the visit,[2] he flew into a rage, blamed Wolkov for deceiving him, and ordered his Ambassador to board the plane and fly back to Russia. Others said that the recall was demanded by General Nasution because of improper Wolkov pressure on Sukarno to reduce army influence in the government. Whatever the facts, we never saw Ambassador Wolkov again. His wife left Djakarta within a few days, and a few months later we heard he had died in a hospital.

Sukarno, a master at orchestrating the internal political chords and discords, was almost equally skillful in playing on the sensitivities and moods of the members of the diplomatic corps in ways that produced the kind of playback he desired. The Khrushchev visit was no exception. In a well-publicized statement to the *Pravda* correspondent, published January 19, Sukarno said that the Soviet leader was coming to Indonesia at a crucial moment in history. The visit, he maintained, had a significance "transcending" promotion of Indonesian-Soviet understanding.

Recalling Indonesian efforts to ease international tensions (a recollection greeted by jeers in some sections of the diplomatic community), abolish mass-destruction weapons, and promote the Bandung formula for settling world problems, Sukarno said Khrushchev's "position and strength" would make possible their realization. He expressed the hope that the visit would fortify Khrushchev in his search for univeral peace. "Should Eisenhower visit Indonesia, he would be given a similar message," the President concluded. The statement, portraying the Soviet leader in the role of peacemaker, pleased the Soviets. The reference to Eisenhower, apparently a friendly nod toward the West, was actually a pointed reminder of his disappointment at Eisenhower's failure to visit Indonesia on his Asian trip.

From Sukarno's point of view, Khrushchev's visit was a great occasion —the first time the head of state of one of the great world powers had visited the new nation. Sukarno was determined to do everything he could to return the lavish hospitality and courtesies extended to him during his visits to the Soviet Union, and to impress his vistor with the

---

2. *e.g.*, Khrushchev's failure to address the Youth Congress in Bandung or receive an honorary degree at Gadja Mahda University.

dynamic spirit and ancient culture of Indonesia. Among the invitations was one to address the Youth Congress in Bandung, and another to receive an honorary degree at Gadja Mahda University in Jogjakarta. Unfortunately for his plans, Sukarno had apparently assumed his wish was law, and had not consulted those concerned.

When the Youth Congress convened and the news spread that Khrushchev would appear before it during his visit, the leader of the Moslem youth rose to his feet and proposed a resolution to the effect that the Youth Congress refuse to invite Premier Khrushchev to address them. At this, pandemonium broke loose. Communist members of the Congress roared their protest, tried to attack the speaker physically, and created such a disturbance that the chairman was unable to put the motion. After five or ten minutes of this, the Moslem youth leader stood up and indicated he was prepared to withdraw his motion. The clamor momentarily subsided. "I withdraw my motion," the young man shouted, "but in so doing I have just one thing to say. When Mr. Khrushchev walks into this hall, every member of my organization will walk out!" As the young man controlled at least fifty per cent of those in attendance, Premier Khrushchev never appeared at the meeting.

At the University of Gadja Mahda the faculty met and discussed the President's proposal to confer an honorary degree on Premier Khrushchev. After some debate, they calmly decided there was no basis on which to confer the degree, and voted not to proffer it.

The build-up for Khrushchev's arrival was also somewhat smothered by the visit of the King and Queen of Thailand, continuing preoccupation with the Chinese dispute, and the deteriorating economic situation. The night before Khrushchev's arrival, some of the welcoming billboards for the Thai monarchy still had not been removed. The two major Moslem parties issued rather hostile welcoming statements, stressing Soviet atheism, fake peace movements, and the subservience of all Communists to Soviet Russia.

Khrushchev's visit was of critical interest to the United States for what it might mean to Indonesian-Soviet relations. In private comments to me, Foreign Minister Subandrio insisted that Indonesia's foreign-policy posture would not be altered, although further Soviet aid would be welcomed. The chief danger to our interest, we thought, lay in the possibility that Sukarno would commit Indonesia to more than the responsible members of his government anticipated in an effort to counter the growing army strength. A flood of reports had reached the embassy that Sukarno was planning to make major concessions to the Soviets in return for major political, economic, and military aid. The deal supposedly involved massive Soviet aid for the financing of the food and clothing program, the five-year plan, and the construction of a complete naval base at Ambon, in exchange for Sukarno's taking the PKI into the Cabinet and cutting back the power of the military. The contacts I made with Nasution and Subandrio about these reports made it seem clear that if Sukarno did have a private plan for a deal with Khrushchev, he faced stiff opposition from the army and Djuanda. The uproar had served to establish army-navy unity on the issue, as well as bring embassy relations with the army, navy, and other non-Communist elements closer together in a common cause.

At the end of the visit Khrushchev signed a joint statement with Sukarno (on March 1) announcing agreements giving the Indonesians $250 million over a seven-year period for projects including a steel mill, a chemical industry, atomic energy, textile plants, and aid to agriculture. Besides a cultural agreement, there was also the expected endorsement of efforts to extinguish "all manifestations" of colonialism, particularly in Africa; the nuclear test ban; the Soviet disarmament proposal; elimination of the cold war through a series of summit meetings; and, of course, the Indonesian claim to West Irian.

Notable was the lack of any reference to the Chinese Communists or their entry into the UN. I reported at the time that at receptions, Khrushchev was noticeably cool to the Chinese Communist Ambassador. Since the Indonesian position on Communist China's entry into the UN was well established, it could be inferred that it was the Russians who had decided to omit mention of the issue.

Aside from the favorable impact of the loan agreement, the propaganda effect of the visit was probably disappointing to the Soviets. The PKI was prevented from major exploitation of the visit by stern army measures, and the public reception of the Soviet leader was far from effusive. According to reports, there was little rapport between Sukarno and Khrushchev. The Indonesian President was apparently irritated by the bluntness of the latter's remarks.

Whatever the political consequences of Khrushchev's visit, socially it came close to being a disaster. The reaction of the gracious, courteous Indonesians to what they considered Khrushchev's crudeness and clumsiness can be appreciated with these two instances.

One evening, Sukarno's youngest daughter, then about nine or ten, was on the stage at the Presidential Palace dancing for the assembled guests, which included the visiting Soviet party. Khrushchev was sitting in the front row next to Sukarno; my wife and I a row or two behind.

Suddenly a tall blond aide to Khrushchev strode down the aisle bearing a large batch of copy. Bending down over the Soviet Premier, he proceeded to read key dispatches in a rumbling Russian that could be heard throughout the hall. Khrushchev, meanwhile, turned himself around in his seat so that he was no longer facing the stage or the little dancer. This went on for several minutes to the amazement and shock of not merely the Indonesians present.

When Khrushchev was in Jogjakarta, the center of Javanese art and culture, he was presented with a beautiful handmade batik cloth, representing perhaps six months' work. According to one of my Indonesian friends who was present, he said, "But why don't you make this stuff by machine?"

One final footnote illustrates the political and psychological differences between the two leaders. According to a high-ranking Indonesian official, the two men were discussing the economic-development program of the country, and Khrushchev asked Sukarno for budget and production figures—apparently stressing the necessity for cutting back on consumer expenditures. When Sukarno waved the question airily aside, Khrushchev, shocked by the President's lack of concern with such details, almost shouted at him, "You're no Socialist! Socialism is figures, figures, figures! You've got to know where you are every minute of the day or night."

Angered, Sukarno reportedly answered, "I'm no robot! I will never do anything that will bring tears to the eyes of the mothers of Indonesia."

The next Soviet Ambassador to appear on the scene, Mikailov, was an old-line Communist and a good friend of Khrushchev's. He had been a member of the Central Committee since 1935, one of the few members to have survived the purges of the Stalin era. He had also been Minister for Cultural Affairs, which gave him a somewhat special status and undoubtedly contributed to his self-confidence in dealing with me. With him I had a unique arrangement: once a month we would lunch together, alternating between my residence and his, and exchange views, question each other about our countries, and discuss foreign-policy trends. These were extraordinarily frank sessions, and while I am sure he never veered from the party line, his replies supplied insights into Soviet motivations and valuable keys for understanding what the Russians were up to.[3] On the widening gap between Russia and Communist China, Mikailov was invariably silent—as he was also about their competition for a sphere of influence in Indonesia, particularly *vis-à-vis* the Indonesian Communist Party.

As the Sino-Soviet rift widened, it became increasingly apparent that it was clearly not in the Soviet interest to see Indonesia wind up a Communist state dominated by Communist China—which, interestingly, made Soviet desires very much coincident with our own.[4] Soviet compe-

---

3. It was clear to me that some of our conversations were being recorded. I could guess when this was the case because of the more formal, flat, even provocative statements of Soviet policy that he would make, obviously, it seemed, designed for the record. Some of his questions would be so needling that I felt certain he had been instructed to get my answers. At other times, he would be much more relaxed.

4. In 1965, when U.S. relations with Indonesia had deteriorated to the point where the U.S. began to withdraw its aid programs, I could hardly believe my ears when the Soviet Ambassador strongly urged us to stick it out! He insisted that Indonesia needed all the help it could get from both our

tition with Communist China within Indonesia thus became even keener and of greater import than her competition with us, since it involved not only Russian national interests but its determination to dominate the Communist bloc—from within which the Kremlin could not tolerate an ideological challenge.

A somewhat parallel situation existed with regard to Southeast Asia generally. Although the Soviet Ambassador himself never discussed Vietnam in this context, I was repeatedly approached in 1964 and 1965 by Ambassadors from other bloc countries, who deplored the escalation of the war in Vietnam, urged us to get out, and stressed that we were playing into the hands of the Communist Chinese by forcing North Vietnam into their arms. The Soviet concern at the time seemed clearly to be directed toward keeping Southeast Asia quiet for the all-too-obvious reason that the Chinese had the more advantageous position for exploiting a chaotic situation there.

Not all was sweetness and light in our relations with the Soviet Embassy in Djakarta, however, as clearly indicated by the experience we had in connection with the visit of Admiral Frost in the spring of 1958. One morning, I was startled to see on the front page of the Communist newspaper *Bintang Timur*, a three-column replica of a letter allegedly written by Admiral Frost and referring to American-government assistance to the Sumatra rebels. It was not until years later revealed—in a book written by a former Soviet diplomat[5]—as a project designed and fabricated in the Soviet Embassy in Rangoon, Burma. This was a sharp reminder that the Soviets would stop at nothing to achieve their objectives.

The Djakarta diplomatic community's views of American policy ran the gamut from solid support to intensely hostile opposition. In the period when West Irian was a major issue, the diplomatic corps was sharply divided between the representatives of the colonial powers, who generally supported the Dutch, and those in the corps who tended to favor the Indonesian position. When the United States assumed a stronger military posture in Vietnam, the common talk among Djakarta diplomats was that the U.S. had made a deal with Britain—we would hold the fort in Vientam if she would save Malaysia. Among those who had no ties on either side of the disputes then raging, American policy was criticized, under both Republican and Democratic Administrations, for not taking stronger initiatives in Asia in the political and economic areas. Time after time during the long drawn out West Irian affair, diplomats would say to me, "Only America has the power to settle this

---

countries. Such a statement would have been inconceivable only a few years earlier; the Soviet Union would have been only too glad to have the economic-aid field to itself.

5. Aleksandr Kaznachev, *Inside a Soviet Embassy* (Philadelphia: J. B. Lippincott, 1962).

dispute. You are the acknowledged leader of the free world. Why don't you do something?" This came from both Asians and Europeans. To the standard reply, "We're neutral on this issue," the retort invariably was, "A leader can't afford to be neutral. If he has no position, he must at least take the initiative in providing machinery for settling a dispute that might lead to war."

Occasionally, the American Ambassador was criticized for being too patient, too forbearing. During the time of the greatest violence, our home was assailed by a mob. Hundreds of panes of glass in the French windows and doors on all sides of the house were broken, some of our furniture burned. Heaps of broken glass and stones were piled up in the rooms; the refrigerator, stove and freezer were overturned. Fortunately, the police arrived before more damage could be done. When I went to a nearby colleague's home, which had also been visited by the mob, I found the Ambassador standing in the midst of his shattered living room, looking up through the ceiling at the blue sky. The rioters had climbed onto the roof and tossed the tiles into the street. He was at once sad and seething. When I offered him the shelter of our home, he declined with thanks. Then he said, "You don't seem upset. How do you maintain your equanimity under these circumstances?"

Without thinking I replied, "It's tough. I guess you have to simply say, with Jesus, 'Father, forgive them; they know not what they do.' They are nice people who are being used. It's happened throughout history."

"I wish I could be so charitable," he replied tartly.

I relate this conversation not to picture myself as a meek and humble man, which I am not, but rather to illustrate the necessity for understanding in the most difficult of circumstances the inwardness of what is happening. I knew the Indonesian people as gentle and lovable. An Ambassador endeavoring to understand a situation in which such people are being exploited cannot afford to permit himself to be embittered or disheartened. Most members of the diplomatic corps understood this. Those who were not involved in the unpleasant conflicts arising from the new "diplomacy by window smashing," counted themselves fortunate.

Perhaps the strength to believe in the concept of man's releasing himself from the tyranny of violent means to achieve his goals lies in remembering the faith of those great leaders who have given their lives in pointing the way to nonviolence. The latest in a long line from Isaiah to Gandhi is Martin Luther King. He clung to and was strengthened by a larger vision: "We have of this world a neighborhood—now we must make it a brotherhood."

CHAPTER 10

The Watershed

International affairs are a complex of action and reaction between nations and between the elements of the societies within nations. And there is another complicating dimension in that the internal and external reactions to events inevitably work upon each other.

During the period from the beginning of 1963 to the end of August 1964, Indonesia was an interesting illustration of this. Sukarno's twin ambitions to undermine Malaysia and to attain leadership of the Afro-Asian world had driven him closer to Communist China and thereby alienated the West. Naturally, then, the Chinese interpretation of world events became more and more acceptable to Sukarno. And when the Communist Party of Indonesia took the Chinese side in the Sino-Soviet dispute, the power and influence of the PKI inevitably rose, just as that of the moderate forces diminished. The free rein given by Sukarno to the PKI emboldened the Communists to step up their harassment of American-government installations and of private enterprise. The fact that Indonesia was virtually at war, and that British troops were mobilized on the borders of Indonesian Borneo (even though their presence was obviously Indonesia's fault), lent credence to Sukarno's appeal for unity in the face of the enemy; anti-Communism was labeled unpatriotic because it led to disunity.

Yet what many observers of Indonesian collaboration with the Chinese failed to appreciate was that Sukarno was in no sense yielding his leadership to Mao, or Indonesian goals to Chinese ambitions. He had simply come to the conclusion that in the achievement of his long-cherished aims, the Chinese were temporarily the most logical partners. I do not share the conviction of many that Sukarno was always a Communist and forever plotting to make his nation so. He was one of the most pragmatic of men in the choice of ways and means; but he was also often a victim of his emotional biases. They became electric charges that derailed his judgment, as when he pulled out of the UN and when he confronted Malaysia.

Some time during the years of Guided Democracy, however, Sukarno had come to the cold conclusion that the PKI was the only political party with the necessary dynamism to support his ambitions and help in the ultimate unification of his people. He had long believed in a one-party system and had once hoped the Nationalist Party would emerge as the party of Indonesia. Time and time again, he railed at the lack of leadership and fire in the Nationalist Party. "Where are the young Sukarnos?" he demanded at one annual party conclave. Repeatedly, he complained to me of the placid posture of their leaders. "Why don't they get out in front?" he said to me once. "Why don't they give the PKI some competition?"

His decision to work with the PKI brought him into association first with Russia and then with China. Both were adept at pandering to Sukarno's vanity. More important, they told him that his objectives were theirs, giving not only lip service but material and political support to the goals closest to this heart. They encouraged him in his self-glorification as the leader of the Afro-Asian world. And all the while, Aidit and the Communist palace hangers-on, aided and abetted in the latter years by his trusted Foreign Minister, Subandrio, were filling his ear with inventive and ingenious suggestions that appealed to his craving for dramatic action and limelight and confirmed in him a growing conviction that the Communist leadership, at home and abroad, spoke his language and represented the new forces of the world with which he must work to accomplish his ends.

Also, Sukarno's Communist engagement period provided him with a counterweight to the power of an internal force he could not control. He regarded the army as a constant threat to his own authority, frustrating his efforts to achieve the socialist unity he sought. During my Indonesian years, the army was certainly loyal to the President. But it was engaged in a conscious effort to harness him, to direct his fantastic energy and leadership capacity into constructive channels. This meant army resistance to the continuing leftist course of the government. To Sukarno it represented resistance to his fundamental aim of national unity, one that he had preached long before independence but that latterly had manifested itself in his Nasakom concept. Perhaps because of his overweening confidence in his capacity to control people and events, Sukarno disregarded the lesson of history: there had never been a coalition with Communists that had not resulted in Communist domination. Sukarno was not less aware than we were that unless he managed to gain control of the army, its leadership would prevent a coalition. As a last resort, these men would move to take over the government. This was the brake on Sukarno. But as time passed, the brake linings wore thin.[1]

---

1. For a recent in-depth discussion of this whole subject and its relation to U.S. policy, see Frederick Philip Bunnell, "The Kennedy Initiatives in Indonesia, 1962–1963" (Thesis, Cornell University, September 1969).

America had always been difficult for the Indonesians to understand and classify in their world catalogue. There was an ambivalence in their attitude toward us. We did not quite fit into Sukarno's neat division of the world into "the new emerging forces and the old established forces." To the Indonesian Marxist—and Sukarno identified himself as such, while denying he was a Communist—we were a capitalistic country. Yet it was not too difficult to prove to an Indonesian that, in terms of the objectives of Indonesian socialism, the United States was more socialist than Indonesia. True, there was a serious imbalance in the black-white equation; but we did have social security, minimum-wage laws, unemployment insurance, government insurance for savings deposits, Medicare, and a host of other programs to which socialist countries aspired.

In the recent past, the Indonesians had wooed America, hoping against hope it would respond. Our relations had survived the strains of the 1958 rebellion, when Sukarno had told Louis Fischer, "I love America, but I'm a disappointed lover." In Kennedy, America had a young, progressive President. Indonesians, as well as the rest of the less-developed world, did not miss the significant note in his acceptance speech that "more energy is released by the awakening of new nations than by the fission of the atom itself."

But as of November 22, 1963, the young American President was tragically gone from the stage, and people of Asia were warily watching the words of the new Administration in Washington. The new President was a Democrat, to be sure, but he was known also to be a wealthy ranch owner as well as a consummate politician. The major question, then, was whether President Johnson would have the same sympathy for the new nations, whether he could be counted on to understand and support the rising expectations, or as Sukarno put it, "rising demands" of two-thirds of the human race. Specifically, Sukarno's question was, Will President Johnson remain neutral in the Indonesian-Malaysian dispute, or will he support Great Britain and Malaysia against Indonesia?

Sukarno's behavior had not been such as to have endeared him to the American people, or to induce an American President to go all out to reach an accommodation with him. Most people in Washington felt that it was up to Sukarno to make the first move—and preferably, that move would be to settle the Malaysia dispute peacefully.

In July 1964, just as the improving internal situation seemed to justify undramatic albeit hopeful expectations that U.S.-Indonesian tensions would be eased, the boom was lowered. On the twenty-third, President Johnson, in a joint communiqué with Malaysian Prime Minister Tunku Abdul Rahman, agreed to begin a program for training Malaysian military personnel in the United States and "to consider promptly and sympathetically" credit sales of military equipment to help Malaysia in its current defense efforts against Indonesia. The President also "reaffirmed the support of the United States for a free and independent Malaysia."

Later the same day, the Tunku told Washington *Post* reporter War-
ren Unna that from reading between the lines of the communiqué, he
thought the United States was more than sympathetic to Malaysia's
cause, although Malaysia couldn't count on America's coming completely to its side, since the Americans thought they could have a moderating influence on Sukarno. But he was satisfied. Then, at a National
Press Club luncheon, the Tunku compared Sukarno to Hitler, "He must
be stopped before he causes lasting harm to us and the rest of Southeast
Asia, just as Hitler did in Europe." He warned that Sukarno, in serving
the cause of Communism and its "expansionist ambitions," threatened
new imperialisms more fearsome than those suffered under colonialism.[2]

This did it, I knew. For the United States to proffer military assistance
to Malaysia at this critical juncture was waving a red flag in front of a
bull. Embassy Djakarta had not been consulted on these plans. In publicly moving us over to Malaysia's side, the communiqué would confirm
all of Sukarno's suspicions and prejudices.

Why were we in Djakarta not consulted on the Tunku's visit to
Washington, or at least on the substance of the communiqué, when any
gesture toward Malaysia was bound to affect relations with Indonesia? I
can only speculate on what happened. Visits of heads of state are ordinarily arranged more than a year in advance. It is quite possible that no
one in Washington had considered the unfavorable impact such a visit
might have on Indonesian-American relations at this particular moment
in history. Had someone thought of it, it is equally possible that the
insensitivity Washington had been displaying toward Indonesia might
have produced the reaction, "So what? It is time we stopped babying
Sukarno." Bypassing Embassy Djakarta might therefore have been deliberate in order to avoid the bothersome input from us that would be
certain to come. At this point, neither the White House nor the State
Department had much patience with Sukarno. Ours in Djakarta was also
running thin, but we saw no percentage in deliberate provocation.

We awaited the reaction we knew was bound to come—but none did.
Silence was even more ominous. Sukarno was holding his fire. For what?

On August 17, 1964, in the middle of a much-needed rest in Nan-
tucket, the summons came. I was to meet with Secretary Rusk immediately. In Washington, I discovered that a full-dress conference was about
to begin. Sukarno had found the dramatic moment for expressing his
reaction to the communiqué: the traditional Independence Day speech.
In *"Tavip,"* [3] as it later came to be popularly called in Indonesia, he
chose *"vivere pericoloso"* (Italian for "to live dangerously") as his

---

2. The Washington *Post*, July 24, 1964.
3. *"Tahun Vivera Pericoloso,"* "The Year of Living Dangerously." The Italian
   Ambassador observed drily that the meaning was clear even if the grammar
   was faulty.

theme, and launched an all-out attack on the U.S., praised our enemies, and topped it off with recognition of North Vietnam and North Korea as the legitimate governments of those countries. Unquestionably, the speech was the most alarming diatribe he had made in many years.

In the name of his believing himself to be "a friend of the nationalists, the revolutionary nationalists [and] of the Communists because the Communists are revolutionary people," he made a violent attack on pretenders to *Manipol*, "who think that the fate of Indonesia lies in their hands, people who think that Indonesia cannot exist without them." Although the objects of the attacks were not identified, it was obvious Sukarno was referring to persons in high places and undoubtedly PKI opponents. The assumption of most members of the diplomatic corps was that the Defense Minister, General Nasution, was the principal target. Speculation was widespread that this time Subandrio had succeeded in convincing Sukarno that Nasution was plotting the President's overthrow.

Sukarno showed himself to be in almost complete alignment with the PKI on the internal issues of land reform (he indicated that unilateral actions by peasants were justified in the event of delay), education (he supported leftist Education Minister Prijono against moderate critics), and the role of political parties, a major subject of debate in the Djakarta press in May and June.

His attack on the U.S. could not be faulted for indirectness:

> I have to address a few words also to the Government of the United States. This is more than I wish, and should there have been no Johnson-Tunku Communiqué then I would have never voiced these words. On the part of Indonesia, the desire to be friends with the United States is already very clear. Even after the attempt to land the Seventh Fleet at Pakanbaru, even after the bombing by Alan Pope, even after the insults by Avery Brundage, even after the incorrect behaviour of Michelmore, the Government of the Republic of Indonesia was still willing to forgive those events. But as was recently explained by Deputy Premier/Foreign Minister Subandrio—the question of R.I.-U.S.A. relations does not depend solely on the Republic of Indonesia, the question also depends, and mainly, on the Government of the United States of America. Has the U.S.A. Government thought twice before putting its signature to the Johnson-Tunku Joint Communiqué which is full of hostile words against the Republic of Indonesia? Have they thought of the consequences? Have they not remembered the ancient wisdom, that to hurt someone's feelings is easy, but to heal the hurt is difficult? With a heavy heart I have to state that the Johnson-Tunku Joint Statement is really *too much*. It really exceeds all bounds!

This time Sukarno was not indulging in mere rhetoric. Growing dissatisfaction with the political results of Borneo guerrilla activity led to more dramatic methods in the Crush Malaysia campaign. On August 17, the same day Sukarno spewed *"Tavip,"* some thirty to forty Indonesian guerrillas landed on the Malayan peninsula. The Indonesian press remained mute about these activities, although the foreign press and Kuala Lumpur were outraged. When questioned, Subandrio told foreign reporters he considered these landings "merely a fabrication of Kuala Lumpur." [4] But increased terrorism and infiltration activity continued.

Since the previous September, we had been continuing various AID and Civic Action programs, the training of Indonesian military officers, and a reduced flow of military materiel, with the overall objective of maintaining contact with the army and other constructive elements in Indonesian society that in the post-Sukarno period could be counted on to resist a Communist takeover. Now the question before the conference to which I had been summoned on August 17 was how to preserve these contacts—via continuation of the programs—in the face of a rapidly deteriorating political situation in which both Sukarno and Subandrio had already suggested termination of all U.S. assistance programs as a means of removing an irritant to our relations. It was a delicate matter. There was a face-saving necessity to react to the speech, but if we began a formal close-out of the military-assistance program, Sukarno in his present mood might well follow through on his suggestion to terminate all programs.

If we took no action toward reducing aid, some felt, it might seem to indicate to the Indonesian army a readiness to tolerate Indonesian actions and policies that in fact we opposed. But I did not take this too seriously. On the firing line in Djakarta, I had too often made our position clear to the military leadership.

What seemed obvious to me was that, while Sukarno's speech might well mark the watershed in our relations, he was merely reacting to the American posture, as he interpreted it. And this became the basis of my argument that we continue the current policy. Sukarno, I pointed out, had been waiting for many months for an indication of the attitude of the new Adminstration toward Indonesia. The invitation to the Tunku to visit the White House was a clear sign to the ever-suspicious leader that we were about to shift our policy and support his enemies. When, immediately following this visit, we announced a promise to sell military equipment in the amount of $5,000,000 to Malaysia, his interpretation was confirmed. However, Sukarno's reaction was not, in my opinion, irrevocable. Knowing Sukarno as well as I did, I was convinced that if we were willing to make a genuine gesture of friendship toward him, unconnected with the Malaysia dispute, we could perhaps soften his reaction. A visit by a high Administration official, a personal message from the President—something of this nature would help.

---

4. The Djakarta press first mentioned the news about the infiltration on August 20, on the inside pages featuring Subandrio's statement.

As for the recognition of North Vietnam and North Korea, was it a deliberate slap at the United States? Not necessarily. One interesting aspect of Indonesian policy toward Communist China was the gradual and systematic cultivation of the Chinese satellites. This might appear as a move away from us; but it might just as well prove to be the opposite. The North Vietnamese and North Koreans feared and probably hated the Chinese. And Indonesia was thinking ahead to the day when Djakarta might well be an opposite pole to Peking in its attraction for Asian countries not anxious to be swallowed up by China. When that day came, it would be important for Indonesia to be in or closely aligned with the free world.

Such a reading of the situation could only argue against reassessing our policy. Now was distinctly not the time to withdraw aid. I reminded the group that this assistance was a matter of placing our bets on the next generation, not on Sukarno. Up to now, this had been not only my own opinion but that of the Johnson Administration, and I saw no realistic alternative. Assistant Secretary Bundy had made this amply clear. When he testified before Congress a few months before,[5] he told the House Foreign Affairs Committee that our "assistance programs to Indonesia have never been intended to reinforce the prestige or the political position of President Sukarno personally. His eccentricities as a national leader, his vanity, his recklessness, his sudden changes of direction, have made it particularly difficult to maintain aid relations, which we consider important to preserve with the people of Indonesia and with key leadership groups, including especially the armed forces. . . . This program has been carefully weighed against Sukarno's confrontation policy with Malaysia. Obviously, Indonesia's present conduct in Borneo is unacceptable and we have made clear our strong opposition to it. We might, by now, have decided to terminate our assistance to Indonesia were it not that Indonesia, Malaysia, and the Philippines and Thailand, supported at every juncture by our diplomatic representatives in the field, are seriously engaged in negotiations to get Indonesian forces completely withdrawn and to settle the issue peacefully."

Bundy noted that our program had been cut back eighty per cent. "What remains is, even more clearly than before, an investment in people and institutions rather than in the purposes of the government itself . . . our aid is intended to support an effective American presence in Indonesia and to preserve, so far as possible, the influence of our own diplomatic establishment in Djakarta, whose moderating influence upon Sukarno's excesses has, we believe, been a crucial factor in forestalling, up to this moment, the outbreak of serious hostilities between Indonesia and Malaysia."

I felt that there was one more fundamental point that I must urge at

---

5. April 7, 1964.

the conference. If, because of Sukarno's intransigent attitude on Malaysia—an issue on which we professed to be relatively neutral—we were willing to sacrifice our very real stakes in Indonesia, we would be making a grave mistake. Our interest lay in assisting Indonesia in the maintenance of its non-committed posture, not in taking some action that would enhance its dependence upon the Communist bloc. Sukarno was only one man and a man who would not be on the stage forever. Could we, as a world leader, not afford to shrug off attacks that represented emotional reactions? Certainly Sukarno was moving the wrong way. But let us not take action that would accelerate his course. When all the arguments were in, there was one test question we might apply from now on, before finalizing any new policy or program—Will the Communists welcome it or will they oppose it?

It should be understood that no specific policy proposal was before this State Department conference; it had been convened to consider only whether we should have a major review of our policy toward Indonesia. In the general discussion following my remarks, there was some support for the position I had taken, although the majority present seemed to feel that taking cognizance of Sukarno's speech by some retaliatory action and a review of our policy was necessary.

We needn't have bothered. Sukarno did it for us.

On August 24, Sukarno announced that the Cabinet would be reshuffled in accordance with *"Tavip."* That moderates like General Nasution and Roeslan Abdulgani would be removed from the Cabinet seemed a foregone conclusion. Sukarno might even go so far as to establish what he had been aiming at for some time—a Nasakom Cabinet.

I did not share the general pessimism, convinced as I was that Nasution and Yani would not let Sukarno get away with a major reshuffle. Nevertheless, news of the actual changes, when it came on August 27, was bad enough. New Minister of Labor Sutomo was a crypto-Communist from the Partindo Party. And Politburo member Njoto was appointed, in a kind of liaison capacity, as Minister of State attached to the Presidium. Although this did not technically make him a member of the Cabinet, he would still be in a strategic position to influence policy and strengthen the party's ability to control Subandrio. I was right on one thing—the more extensive changes originally contemplated had to be abandoned because of army pressures to keep Nasution in the Cabinet. His powerful position as Minister of Defense made it difficult to alter substantially the *status quo.* That Sukarno had considered the time ripe for the appointment of so prestigious a Communist as Njoto to so important a position, however, boded ill for the future.

The day after my return to Djakarta, I called on President Sukarno. "Why did you do it?" I asked him. "Why did you make that speech?"

"I had no choice," he replied. His expression was grim. "When your government announced that it was going to give military aid to our enemy, Malaysia, this meant that you were joining Britain and Malaysia against us!"

"But Mr. President," I protested, "that announcement meant no such thing. My government stands ready to sell military equipment to any friendly nation for self-defense purposes. We sell this equipment for dollars and charge interest if the sale is financed by a loan. You have been the beneficiary of this policy yourself!" Sukarno remained unconvinced. He had made up his mind that the American offer to the Tunku constituted a deviation from our stated policy of relative neutrality in the Malaysian dispute. And, it must be conceded, the offer was indeed intended as a friendly gesture of support for Malaysia and a not-so-gentle admonition to Sukarno.[6]

In the wake of Sukarno's August 17 speech, mounting anti-Americanism was expressed in a series of hostile acts, including the landing of approximately forty more Indonesian paratroopers on the Malaysian mainland. In retaliation came instructions to prohibit Indonesians' going to the United States for education training. What also came was a strong message to me from Secretary Rusk, portions of which I quote:

> The escalation policy Sukarno is now following will have most serious consequences. To achieve an atmosphere in which problems can be worked out in the Maphilindo forum and the spirit of the Manila meetings, we believe there must be a "cooling-off" period. . . . In the event of U.N. consideration, we are firmly convinced Indonesia would receive support only from Communist countries and be completely isolated from a great majority of the newly developed nations. If Sukarno should put himself entirely at the mercy of Communist countries internationally and in the U.N., under these circumstances we feel the PKI influence would increase tremendously and that they might even try to make him a prisoner within Indonesia itself. . . .
>
> We have consistently tried to help Indonesia develop as a stability force in Asia and Sukarno's chance of becoming a historical world leader will be eliminated entirely if he follows a course leading to a humiliating defeat in and probably strong censure by the United Nations. . . . The principles of the U.S. would leave it no choice but to support Malaysia if a threat to peace in the area is brought to the U.N. because of Indonesia's policy towards Malaysia.
>
> Explain that these views are set forth in a spirit of friendship and cooperation and that we are anxious for Sukarno to be fully aware of the consequences of his current policy. We wish to achieve a real "cooling-off" period in which we are ready to discuss any ideas or suggestions with him which he may have on reestablishing communications with his neighbors. If you feel it advisable, tell him we would offer our help

---

6. Ironically, Malaysia later took umbrage at our charging five-per-cent interest on the loan when, in their view, they would be defending the free world with these weapons. Cries of "Shylock!" went up from Kuala Lumpur, and our friendly gesture turned sour.

in obtaining the cooperation of the Philippines and Malaysia to hold a Maphilindo meeting at the ministerial level if he will follow a policy creating an atmosphere conducive to the success of such a meeting.

Shortly after receiving this message, I passed on its contents to Sukarno. He obviously did not like it, but he agreed to a cooling-off period if the Tunku would.

Rusk's expectation was correct. Malaysia took the controversy to the United Nations on the basis that Indonesia's aggressive actions represented a threat to peace. As the UN debate proceeded, Indonesian military action slowed down; the Indonesians were beginning to realize that Rusk's assessment was correct—the world was not on their side. Both Sukarno and Subandrio separately assured me that Indonesia was not currently planning further military action, and Nasution publicly stated Indonesia was not escalating toward open warfare. Sukarno re-emphasized, in private discussions with me, that he stood ready to abide by the recommendation of an Afro-Asian conciliation commission and to meet with the Tunku again at a summit.

Things were fairly quiet until, toward the end of September, the Indonesian Parliament, spurred by the PKI, presented a package resolution that (1) strongly condemned the Tunku-Johnson communiqué; (2) criticized the "Malaysian attempt, backed by the United States and Britain, to distort facts in its complaint to the U.N."; (3) protested the "Anglo-American plan to establish radio relay stations in the Indonesian ocean"; (4) condemned "U.S. aggression" against North Vietnam as part of an "Anglo-American intrigue to besiege independent countries of Southeast Asia"; (5) demanded that the U.K. and the U.S. withdraw troops from Indochina and Southeast Asia; (6) urged Southeast Asian governments to liquidate foreign military bases on their territories, and (7) urged the nonaligned Cairo Conference to firmly oppose world-wide U.S./U.K. imperialism. It was the first official and unanimous condemnation of the United States by Parliament.[7] Slightly rippling the waters at this time, too, was the national congress of sobsi in Djakarta, which added to its normal anti-American barrage a demand for my expulsion from the country.

The conclusion of the Cairo Conference[8] on October 10 was hailed in Indonesia as a pronounced personal and ideological victory for Sukarno, for the militant tenets of the parliamentary resolution, and for the Indonesian international position that the struggle of the "new emerging forces" to overthrow the domination of the "old established forces" was

---

7. The Communists had unsuccessfully attempted to ram through similar resolutions in July. Indonesian sources attributed their success at this point to the altered political atmosphere induced by Sukarno's August 17 speech.
8. The second conference of nonaligned leaders. The first was held in Belgrade in 1961.

more important than peaceful coexistence. The contrary view was ascribed to India, Yugoslavia and the United Arab Republic. Widely publicized was Tito's announcement that he would soon meet with Sukarno to discuss the "question of peaceful coexistence, the true meaning of which is not clear to certain people." The PKI organ, *Harian Rakjat*, called India and Yugoslavia "U.S. lackeys with backward-looking views," out of step with the revolutionary spirit of the conference.

The truth was that the Cairo Conference was somewhat disappointing to the Indonesian leadership. Subandrio stated that it was more progressive than the 1961 Belgrade nonaligned conference, but was "still clearly under the domination of the great powers, to the point that their views sometimes were placed above those of the countries which participated."

In early November came the news of President Johnson's re-election. Sukarno sent him a friendly telegram of congratulations, but more indicative of the Indonesian reaction were Subandrio's comments to me. He emphasized the American failure to recognize the concept of the "new emerging forces" and added that "Indonesia . . . and the whole progressive world surely hope that U.S. policy under President Johnson will be adjusted to new developments." The comment illustrated the chasm that still existed between the Indonesian and American leadership.

The next major outbreak came in early December, following a statement by Subandrio on November 30, which condemned the U.S. for its part in rescuing hostages held in the Congo by rebel armed forces. The extent to which Indonesian suspicion of American motives carried over to events outside the immediate neighborhood was illustrated by the reaction to this combined American-Belgian operation to rescue the 2,300 captives. The press accused the United States of helping Tshombe oppress his own countrymen in return for a gain by the whites. It was ready grist for Sukarno's mill, and although I managed to persuade him to avoid the subject in an upcoming major address, it was not long before he broke loose and denounced what he termed "white intervention" in the Congo. And, like Mary and her little lamb, where Sukarno went, the left-wing and nationalist groups were sure to follow. Press attacks and demonstrations began again. After a meeting of the Youth Front on December 4, several thousand youths wrecked the USIS cultural center, desecrating the American flag and seal, and smashing a picture of the President of the United States. In answer to a formal protest, Sukarno expressed regret at the violence and told me he had ordered that full compensation be paid. However, no public mention of Sukarno's regrets was ever made by Indonesian sources. This meant to us that the trouble was not over.

The UN discussion of the Malaysia confrontation had a somewhat sobering effect upon the Indonesian leaders, although the Indonesian public never knew the full story. The Soviet veto of the mild Norwegian resolution was hailed in Djakarta as a failure on the part of Malaysia to brand Indonesia an aggressor. The veto, Subandrio commented, showed continued Soviet support for the Indonesian struggle against "colonialism, neo-colonialism, and imperialism." Nevertheless, the sympathy with which the Malaysian complaint was received gave Indonesia pause, and Sukarno's return to the idea of a possible Afro-Asian conciliation commission solution made it seem that he was ready to liquidate the Malaysian adventure and turn to something else.

In Embassy Djakarta, we marked 1964 as the watershed year in Indonesian-American relations. The Johnson-Tunku communiqué lighted fires of fury that we could not quench so long as Sukarno remained President.

Reflecting on this time of trouble, I was reminded of a parable once recounted by Sukarno:

> Once, one stone-cold night, I saw a flock of porcupines grow numb with cold in a zoo. Because of their being cold, they jostled each other in search of warmth. However, as they jostled too roughly, they pricked one another with their prickles; they felt pain and parted. Then, however, they grew cold again, and jostled again. Again they were pricked by one another's prickles, again they parted, again they grew cold, again they jostled—this process of going away and approaching one another continued on and on, until at last they found the most appropriate distance among them; everyone of them got the warmth needed without prickling one another.
>
> This is a simple story indeed, but the simile goes deep. Too close international relations, from which interference with the internal affairs of one of the other nations may ensue, may lead to colonial domination. . . .
>
> This, brothers, is the wise simile of the simple story about a flock of porcupines in a cold evening!

Sukarno violated his own admonition. He got too close to the Communist porcupine.

CHAPTER 11

The Moderates React

Indonesia's moderates had been alarmed but not disheartened by the trend of events since the 1964 Independence Day address. After a brief lull—and Sukarno's departure from the country—they surfaced again in September and organized the BPS (Badan Pendukung Sukarnoisme, "Body to Support Sukarnoism").[1] Comprised of newspaper editors and publishers, it had as its purpose the rescue of Sukarno's ideology from Communist distortion. The use of Sukarno's name lent a certain dignity and served to distinguish the body from any Marxist classification.

The term "Sukarnoism" was carefully chosen for a concept that was to be a unifying vehicle for non-Communists as well as to play up to Sukarno's ego and make it more difficult for the Communists to attack the movement. Functionally, the BPS became little more than a distributing agency for anti-Communist news copy. But symbolically it was the nerve center of the anti-Communist movement and stimulated the formation of "Sukarnoist" movements among youth and labor.

Sukarnoism also drew strong support from leaders of the Murba Party, several key Christian and Moslem leaders, functional groups allied with the army, many newspapers, and the moderate wing of the PNI. Of the major parties, only the PKI and the official wing of the PNI joined in opposition to Sukarnoism, the latter in part because they saw it as a rival to their own version of the President's philosophy, Marhaenism.

Minister of Defense Nasution proved himself a shrewd and prophetic observer of the Indonesian political scene with his comments about Sukarnoism. "Do not think this movement will become a power element in the Indonesian scene within the near future," he told me. "The thing important about this is that it is a real grass-roots movement. It did not come from the top—or from any of the power centers—but from the bottom. It will probably not succeed this time, but it represents a major

---

1. Although its formation was publicly announced November 9.

force in Indonesia, which will have its impact on events at some time in the future."

The great question about the movement in the early stages was whether it had Sukarno's blessing, and if not, would he give it at least tacit support. Most of its leaders with whom I talked, such men as Malik, then Minister of Trade, Abdulgani, Diah, Chairul Saleh, Third Deputy Prime Minister and head of all economic affairs, thought Sukarno would give the movement free play. According to their reasoning, with which I agreed, the Communist Party was becoming too powerful and had no effective political opposition. The army was anti-Communist but withholding itself from *overt* political activities in this period, and it was in Sukarno's interest to keep the army out of politics. Sukarno had on numerous occasions chided the non-Communist political leaders for their lack of vigor and revolutionary tactics. Now they were not merely vigorous but were adopting his own words as their political creed. Most observers who knew Sukarno well thought he would welcome a counter political force to the increasingly powerful Communist Party.

The Sukarnoism leadership had thought it unnecessary to check out the use of his name with the President. They believed he would be pleased to recognize a movement that might conceivably become the major anti-Communist political party of Indonesia. And of course if it failed, he could always disavow it. Meanwhile, he would keep his hands off. So ran the thinking of the movement's sponsors.

Malik, who had consistently opposed the PKI on the film boycott and other anti-American measures, lashed out against the Communists in a speech on October 12. He accused "obstinate groups" of endeavoring to lead the Government of Indonesia into abandoning its active independent foreign policy and aligning itself with "certain countries," meaning Communist China. He charged them also with attempting to enmesh the Indonesian government in the Sino-Soviet split, poisoning the people with lies, and endangering valuable support from the Soviet Union. It was the strongest anti-PKI statement by a public figure in many years. It demonstrated moral courage of a high order because, since Sukarno was cooperating more and more with the Communists, Malik's opposition to the PKI ultimately meant opposing Sukarno himself.

The PKI was outraged by the attacks of the Sukarnoists, clearly led now by two Cabinet ministers, Malik and Saleh, and protested to Subandrio who, in the absence of Sukarno, was Acting President. The wily Subandrio had no intention of getting into the middle of this controversy. However, as the debate waxed hotter, he felt compelled to call in Murba and NU leaders to stress to them the need for unity and cessation of the controversy. But the split in the country had reached such proportions that nothing Subandrio could do would stop it.

Sukarno was now in Paris resting; he would return about November 1. In January, he would go to Vienna for an operation to remove a large stone from his only functioning kidney. According to Subandrio, the President had reached the point where he realized he must slow down and, if he followed Subandrio's advice, play more of a father role. Whether the Foreign Minister went this far in counseling the President is doubtful, but his confiding this to me was clearly an opening gun to put me on notice that he intended gradually to assume as much of Sukarno's mantle of power as possible.

That Subandrio had the succession very much on his mind was further revealed by an extraordinary speech delivered on October 25, when he asked how the revolution would be continued if Sukarno were no longer able to lead. Subandrio said it must not be through a clash of forces or playing at *coups d'état,* but through making the entire public "progressive." The statement was made in the course of defining the Indonesian revolution as leftist and democratic and denouncing rightists as the principal enemies of the revolution. It was a clear play for PKI support as Sukarno, for health reasons, appeared to be walking off the stage. In another speech Subandrio went so far as to assert that the Indonesian revolution was entering its "second stage," a judgment that even the Communists had not yet made.[2] Naturally, these comments stirred considerable talk. The consensus was that he must be very sure of himself and his position, or at least of Sukarno's deteriorating physical condition, to go so far.

Sukarno was returning in early November. Could the moderate forces present him with a strong enough front so that he would be prompted to halt or slow down the Communist advance? There was some hope for this, particularly if the army were willing to take a strong position. General Nasution was trying behind the scenes to weld together an alliance of army elements with religious and other moderate groups. Army Chief of Staff, General Yani, was known to be sympathetic to the moderates.[3]

---

2. This was undoubtedly intended as a sop to the Communists. What Subandrio meant was that Indonesia was approaching socialism. The implication was that the government had nationalized enough sources of wealth and so developed the institutional apparatus that the situation was ripe for the Communists to take power. This was simply politically motivated jargon, for Subandrio was beginning to build his power base on Communist support. As Bertram D. Wolfe points out, nowhere in Marx's writings does he clearly spell out what he meant by socialism or, for that matter, capitalism or feudalism. See *Marxism: 100 Years in the Life of a Doctrine* (New York: Delta, Dell Publishing Company, Inc., 1965).

3. At a reception at the Presidential Palace in September, I started over to have a few words with the President, who was sitting in a corner talking with General Yani. As I neared them, I realized I would be interrupting a serious conversation and backed off. Yani was leaning over and talking heatedly, shaking his finger at the President; evidently, they were having an argument. A few days later, reports came in confirming this. Yani apparently had complained to Sukarno about not being consulted on the September 2 Indonesian landings on the coast of Malaya (which had so disturbed us).

General Yani told me the movement had the army's sympathy and support, although it would not join the front line. He was convinced that Sukarno was not opposed to the movement, and implied the President would welcome increased political opposition to the PKI. Yani, a Javanese, noted that an important aspect of the movement was the fact that much of the strong anti-Communist reaction was coming from Central Java, territory regarded as a PKI stronghold.

Malik, by this time the principal engineer and manager of the moderate coalition, told me on November 19 that President Sukarno now realized the breadth of the movement's support. He was beginning to tacitly encourage them—witness his approval of the Minister of Religion's undertaking a speaking tour through Java on the coalition's behalf. Malik considered Subandrio among the movement's most dangerous opponents. It was vital to act now, he said; in "another six months" it would be too late. In the Cabinet and out, there appeared to be wide agreement with Malik's assessment that the coalition was now too strong to be stopped by anything short of escalation of the Malaysia dispute.

By November, eight non-Communist labor federations had joined together to provide undercover support for the movement, and non-Communist student groups had formed an umbrella organization in a number of cities. Sukarnoism had become the most serious challenge to the PKI in many years. Now, the movement might stand or fall on an almost totally unrelated issue—the Malaysia dispute. Confrontation was the PKI's trump card in stirring up the nation against the external enemy and in attempting to suppress the coalition of moderate forces inside the country. A cry for unity in face of the enemy was one Sukarno could not resist. But there were no responses from the British or Kuala Lumpur to my recommendations that we pick up Sukarno's apparent willingness to talk seriously about reviving the idea of an Afro-Asian commission to settle the dispute.

The moderates' hopes soared when Sukarno returned and, despite appeals from the Communists, failed to take any action against the Sukarnoist movement. He also passed up several subsequent opportunities to take a public stand, for or against, and the moderates concluded that they had at least his tacit blessing to go ahead.

But Nasution's prediction proved correct. In December the ax fell. On the seventeenth, without warning, the President issued two decrees, and an "announcement," which dissolved the BPS, gave the governmental

---

He considered small-scale infiltration of that kind militarily unwise and likely to provoke British retaliation.

A day or two later, when I attempted to communicate with Yani, I was told by his office that he was "sick" and had gone to the mountains for a rest. Subsequently, the embassy heard from apparently reliable sources that Sukarno had censured Yani and ordered him to go away for a month's sick leave. Not ready to confront Sukarno publicly, Yani had bowed to his will.

purge organ KOTRAR responsibility for propagating the President's teachings, and prohibited further interpretations of the President's philosophy. It was a severe setback, catching the Sukarnoists totally off guard, but the BPS did not yield without a struggle. "One cannot clap with one hand," said Murba Party leader Sukarni, which Indonesians understood as meaning the government needed the support of all groups and was therefore wrong in banning the BPS. The anti-Communist elements began talking about regrouping. But another heavy blow fell, on January 6, 1965, when the Murba Party, political home of several prominent leaders of Sukarnoism, was banned. Sukarni was subsequently arrested.[4] Although this did not completely silence the moderates, it did throw them into confusion. Whose head would roll next?

The moderate press fell victim to Sukarno's ire. In response to a demand by the PWI—left-wing press group and virtual PKI instrument—that Minister of Information Achmadi stop the BPS press, the order was given by Sukarno "to ban whatever newspaper, whatever organization, whatever tool became a BPS puppet." During a revolution, he said, there cannot be press freedom.

The politicians began to run for cover. Chairul Saleh, swashbuckling leader of the '45 Generation and former guerrilla, suddenly changed his tune, denied that he was a Murba member or anti-PKI.[5] And even Roeslan Abdulgani, right-wing PNI leader, who in May of 1964 had given the name "Sukarnoism" to the movement, joined the rest of the PNI leadership in denouncing it.

But Adam Malik stuck to his guns. He was shortly thereafter removed as Minister of Trade, although he continued in the Cabinet as Minister without Portfolio. This meant he was actually out of a job, but Sukarno wanted to keep him in the official family, probably because he did not want to lose this able and articulate leader to the opposition.

Some observers felt that Sukarno took these actions in the course of following Mao's tactics: let "one hundred flowers bloom" but cut them

---

4. The Murba Party had influence disproportionate to its small size. Organized by Tan Malaka, it was regarded as a national Communist party opposed to the PKI and not responsive to either Moscow or Peking. Until banned, it was active, vocal, and well represented in the Cabinet. As contrasted with the PKI, which claimed a 1965 membership of 3,000,000, Murba reported about 200,000 in February 1961, when a declaration of membership had to be made to the government. Its size at the time of banning was estimated at less than 250,000. Approximately two-thirds of the membership was located in West Java.

5. I shall never forget having been summoned to his office following the publication of a New York *Times* story in which he had been so characterized. Saleh was quite upset and read me a lecture on how publication of this kind of identification in an American newspaper could hurt him. After I left, he told the Indonesian press he had formally protested to the American Ambassador and hotly denied the allegations.

down as soon as they can be clearly identified. But it was my feeling that Sukarno saw the moderates moving the country toward the center rather than toward the left, destroying the unity of the nation and attacking the most effective political force in the country, which by now Sukarno had come to regard as his own chosen instrument; and they were doing this in his name!

At the time, I thought that settlement of the Malaysia dispute—or at least the creation of an Afro-Asian commission for that purpose—might have saved the Sukarnoism movement. But with the benefit of hindsight, I have some reservations. It now seems to me that Sukarno had gone so far in committing himself to a pro-Communist position that he had come to look at the world through Aidit's eyes. The simplistic Marxian approach to the complex phenomena of a new nationalism appealed to him. It was ready made for the "government by slogans" of which Sukarno was a master. The principal and perhaps fatal weakness of the Sukarnoists was the fact that their major acknowledged aim—to suppress the PKI—in such a highly nationalistic atmosphere, branded them as traitors. Under Sukarno's Nasakom doctrine, anti-Communist actions were regarded as attacks on national revolutionary unity.

By the end of 1964, there were Communists in the Cabinet, and the most promising non-Communist movements since the Democratic League of 1960—the Cultural Manifesto and the Body to Support Sukarnoism—had collapsed. The most open expression to date of Sukarno's leftist political ideology had been delivered in the *Tavip* speech. The recognition of North Korea and North Vietnam brought with it a strengthening of relations between Djakarta and Peking. Perhaps most dramatic of all the year's events was the announcement on New Year's Eve of Sukarno's decision to cut Indonesia's ties with the UN, which proved to be a signal for acceleration of the leftist onslaught. By early 1965, the PKI and its allies were moving more openly and aggressively against the West, particularly America, and Indonesia's actions internally and abroad had isolated the nation from most responsible world powers. The sole encouraging sign was the fact that there still existed within Indonesia, despite years of harassment, significant leadership elements. Their well-nigh fatal weakness, however, was the fact that they were unwilling at this stage to directly oppose Sukarno.

American policy[6] had as its purpose the strengthening of the nations of Southeast Asia to enable them to stand on their own feet; it could only succeed if Indonesia remained free of the Communist bloc. To ensure that independence meant establishing an identity of interest with

---

6. What was often called a "soft" policy toward Indonesia was designed to retain the American presence there at a time when the Communists were doing their utmost to force us out of the country. Its implementation required patience, forbearance, and persistence.

that country, *i.e.*, working with Sukarno in the attainment of any of his goals that we considered consistent with our own. In this we were only partially successful: we were able to provide some Indonesians with enough exposure to a free society, through education and training in the United States, so that they came to know what they wanted and moved toward it when the chance arose.

I had been optimistic longer than most Americans that even with his offensive "noisy diplomacy," Sukarno would finally come around. By 1964, our expert Sovietologist, Robert J. Martens, had concluded that the pattern of Sukarno's actions demonstrated that he was consciously leading his country into Communism and must himself be regarded as a crypto-Communist. But I still could not see Sukarno, even spurred as he was not only by the PKI leadership but by the éminence grise of Indonesia, Subandrio, ever willingly subordinating himself and becoming a captive of the Communist Party.

By the end of that year, however, it was no longer necessary to make allowances for his intentions; Communism was the direction in which the Niagara of his policies was propelling him.

CHAPTER 12

Farewell

Sukarno's dramatic withdrawal from the United Nations in January 1965 caught most if not all of the Indonesian leadership by surprise.[1] Even the Indonesian Mission at the UN had not been aware of his plans. Taken by Sukarno in anger and pique at Malaysia's accession to the Security Council for a one-year term, the decision appalled members of the Indonesian Foreign Office, the diplomatic community, foreign governments, and influential segments of the Indonesian public.[2] Indonesia's artful Foreign Minister was equal to the occasion, characterizing the move as "carefully considered and designed to safeguard the revolution." The usual echoes from politicians and the tamed press followed. But the statements were hollow. People looked at each other questioningly, as if to say, "Has Sukarno gone mad?" None was ready to take up the challenge. But the seeds of doubt, long since sown, were beginning to sprout, and the conviction soon developed among the Indonesian elite—which I shared—that Sukarno had to go. Typical of the attitude of many former supporters of Sukarno was one Indonesian leader's comment to me, "I love that man, but the time has come when we have to choose between our country and Sukarno." Reaching that conclusion intellectually, however, was a long way from coming to the point of doing something about it. The Indonesians generally were in-

1. Ironically, at the moment of one of Sukarno's greatest mistakes—withdrawal from the United Nations—he almost simultaneously announced in his New Year's Eve proclamation what must go down in history as the greatest single accomplishment of Sukarno's period: his country's freedom from illiteracy. This represented one of the outstanding educational achievements of the century anywhere in the world. An estimated six per cent of Indonesians were literate when Indonesia became independent in 1945. Nineteen years later, there were schools in almost every village, and those in cities like Djakarta were operating on three shifts; virtually all Indonesians between the ages of thirteen and forty-five could read and write.
2. Deputy Foreign Minister Suwito could hardly believe it. He told me that the maximum action ever discussed was a temporary walkout.

359

clined to let Sukarno's periodic ill-health take care of the matter. "He will not be able to be active much longer," was the consensus.

Sukarno continued to plunge unhindered on his irrational course. In a major speech to the Consultative Congress on April 11, the President hit directly at Soviet Russia. Emphasizing the need for Indonesia to "stand on its own feet" economically, in view of the current transition from "national democracy" to a socialist state of revolution, he charged that the "concentrations of strategy in the international economic struggle in the form of common markets in Western Europe, Comecon in Socialist Europe, and the system of Commonwealth Imperial Preference, compel developing countries to unite their efforts and their economic forces internationally, in order to repel and resist the Nekolim gang." A week later, at the Bandung anniversary celebration, Sukarno lumped the Soviet-occupied Kurile Islands with Okinawa, Taipei, South Vietnam, South Korea and Malaysia in a category of "unfree" areas of Asia and alleged that an "accommodation" between the U.S. and the USSR had been reached, which supposedly outweighed the fact they led NATO and the Warsaw Pact respectively.

America, however, was his main target. In speech after speech he continued to attack the United States and to identify himself more and more with Communist ideology, in particular with the Chinese. Sukarno passed another milestone in his vilification of the U.S. in his twice-repeated charge that the CIA, in its efforts to oppose Communism, had backed the BPS, and was also behind two rebel movements and the banned Masjumi Party. He charged, in effect, that the CIA had instructed the BPS to kill him. Sukarno "explained" he had "secret, true information" that the CIA used BPS because it feared Communism. The U.S. role in Vietnam was likened to that of Hitler, who during the Spanish Civil War viewed the "field of struggle between fascism and progressive forces as an ideal opportunity to test and perfect weapons and tactics."

Pressures mounted against the American community. There were demonstrations in Djakarta; "takeover committees" made threatening gestures against American-owned rubber plantations in Sumatra; apparently on the initiative of the Communist-dominated unions, a mail boycott was instituted against our embassy, the AID mission, and our consulate at Surabaya; electricity and gas service to U.S. installations in Djakarta were suspended, and telecommunications personnel refused to handle copy for U.S. newsmen. Repeated protests to the Foreign Minister and the President were of no immediate avail.

Although the accelerated turn to the left in Indonesia in early 1965 was not going totally unchallenged by less radical elements—there was, for example, an increasing number of violent clashes between Moslem and Communist groups in East Java and parts of Sumatra—the opposition was ineffectual in slowing down the PKI.

In March, the annual meeting of United States Mission chiefs in the mountain resort of Baguio in the Philippines brought together such top policy men as W. Averell Harriman and William P. Bundy, and ambassadors and consuls general from the East Asian region to discuss American policy, programs, and problems in the area. It was a sad time for me. Decisions were reached to reduce the American presence in Indonesia, to close down USIS, to withdraw the Peace Corps, to liquidate AID except for the university contracts and Indonesians still studying in the United States under previous arrangements. Beyond consideration for the safety of American personnel and response to congressional pressures was fear of the potential damage to other U.S. programs throughout the world if we failed to take prompt action to demonstrate our displeasure at the Indonesian government's encouragement of anti-American actions. These were arguments with which I was thoroughly familiar and which I recognized I could no longer oppose. I knew that it was out of character for Indonesians to attack foreigners physically. Nevertheless, I did not discount the possibility that an emotionally aroused mob, driven to frenzy by screaming orators, might break over the line and injure some of our American personnel. Also, there was always the chance that, well disciplined as they were, some American career people might lose their heads and do or say something provocative, which would bring instant retaliation.

As for the judgment that failure to liquidate the AID programs to Indonesia would, in the present mood of Congress, have an adverse effect on other AID programs around the world, I had no reason to think otherwise; nor was I in any position to make a special plea for Indonesia as against all the other developing nations needing help. I did know that whenever I had an opportunity to explain to a Congressman that we were not propping up Sukarno, that we were betting on the new generation and investing in the future of a country that was bound to be an important factor in Asia, the comment was usually, "I see. I didn't understand that. That's different." Reluctantly, therefore, I went along with the reduction of American presence in Indonesia, maintaining to the last, however, that it was vital for us and for our friends there to maintain as much American presence as possible for as long as possible.

I was convinced that things were not as they seemed in Indonesia. Despite the noise made by the Communist youth, I knew from my own contact with other Indonesian youth that Sukarno had lost touch with the rising generation. The radical fringe was with him but not the bulk of sober-minded university students.

The bitter ideological conflict between Communism and anti-Communism was hot lava under the surface of Indonesian society. I was certain of its inevitable precipitation, probably when Sukarno was about to walk off the stage, maybe sooner.

...

I had been urging for some time that our government make some positive gesture to halt the deterioration in relations, for instance, a personal visit by someone who could speak directly for President Johnson.[3] In response to this, the White House sent Ambassador Ellsworth Bunker, who, as mediator in the West Irian dispute, was highly regarded by the Indonesians and an ideal choice.

By the time he arrived, in early April, virtually all U.S. economic assistance to Indonesia had been terminated, with the exception of four university technical-assistance contracts. The American Military Assistance Program (MAP) had practically ground to a halt. Begun on August 17, 1958, it had provided an annual sum of between $10,000,000 and $20,000,000, which was devoted to equipment for the army, navy and air force—though mostly for the army—the training of army officers in the U.S. service schools, and the assignment in Indonesia of a small MILTAG (Military Training Assistance Group).

During the course of his fifteen-day visit, Ambassador Bunker had four meetings with President Sukarno and two meetings with First Deputy Prime Minister and Foreign Minister Subandrio, in the course of which he redefined the U.S. position on several counts: that we had no territorial or other ambitions in the Far Eastern region; that Sukarno could rest assured that the United States government was not working against him personally and did not seek his removal from power; that although the two nations differed on a broad range of world issues, it was the wish of our government that these issues not control our relationship —however much it seemed to us that the Indonesian government had deliberately allowed this to happen. We did understand that the PKI desired to disrupt relations between the two countries, but we did not assume that this was true also of Sukarno and other Indonesian leaders.

In his reply, Sukarno dampened his assertion that he seconded our wish for a practical friendship by repeatedly bringing up third-country issues and giving every indication that Indonesia would continue to let our relationship be dominated by them. He and Subandrio constantly reiterated that what they termed American support of Malaysia could only constitute a serious obstacle to the improvement of relations between us. The President sought to obtain U.S. endorsement of his proposal that the Malaysian issue be settled along the lines of either the Manila Agreement or the Tokyo Declaration, and asserted that American support would permit his government to support, promote, and im-

3. Many times I have been asked why the American Ambassador, who was, after all, the official representative of the President of the United States, could not manage whatever messages were necessary or desirable. There are times when a special emissary, in touch with the President's current thinking, can be most helpful. This was especially true in this case, since it was known I would be departing shortly.

prove bilateral relations. Nor did he fail to bring in North Vietnam, North Korea, and the Congo as examples of differing approaches having an effect upon our bilateral relations. Sukarno saw Afro-Asia as an "integrated political whole," a concept on which he sought—but did not get —Ambassador Bunker's agreement.

Sukarno acquiesced to the removal of the Peace Corps from Indonesia but also, in the joint communiqué, publicly affirmed his desire that AID-financed university-contract teams be continued.

It was curious that Sukarno, with all his suspicion of the West, never felt threatened by programs that sent Indonesian students to America to be educated. I attributed this partly to his sense of urgency regarding the desperate need for educating Indonesians, and partly to his own appreciation of the dynamism of America, which he hoped would rub off on the Indonesians.

In his talks with Minister of Defense General Nasution, Bunker was strongly advised that American programs be removed for the time being. Since Indonesian officialdom had taken an anti-American line publicly, it was difficult if not impossible for the military and police to support or protect these programs adequately. Nasution predicted a one- or two-year period of tense relations.

Adam Malik, however, expressed a totally different point of view by urging that the United States avoid reducing its presence in Indonesia on the grounds that it would encourage the Indonesian Communists and make them appear much stonger than they actually were.

In his conclusions and recommendations to the U.S. government, Bunker strongly supported the positions I had been taking and advised that a major effort be directed toward influencing long-range developments in Indonesia. In dealing with the present regime, we should accept the fact that our present bilateral relations were unsatisfactory and, to the extent possible, continue to work with Sukarno and maintain the dialogue between him and Johnson. At the same time, we should endeavor to make and keep as much contact with as many other elements in Indonesia, of both current and potential importance, as circumstances permitted.

Bunker suggested some ground rules: avoid taking actions that appear to be punitive; quietly but effectively use wherever possible the agency of third countries in opposing Indonesia's efforts to turn the Afro-Asian and Latin American countries into an anti-American bloc; because the ideal of national unity is an overriding obsession with practically all Indonesians, avoid becoming involved in harebrained efforts to split off Sumatra or other areas from Indonesia, and avoid direct involvement in both the military and diplomatic aspects of the Malaysian problem.

As for specific programs, the recommendations were: that we not contemplate further deliveries under the Military Assistance Program except to complete the unfulfilled commitment to the Indonesian Army; finish the Fixed Communications System project, on which the Indonesian Army had already expended some $10,000,000, in order not to place General Yani, Army Chief of Staff, in a vulnerable position and affect his prestige (a point that I and the embassy had been stressing for some time, but without success); proceed with the harbor construction project, for to default on this would not only reflect unfavorably on the United States but put in jeopardy some $500,000 worth of equipment owned by an American company; that the embassy pursue and if possible expand an information program, with the objective of keeping a window open for U.S. influence with Indonesian leaders, particularly the young.

Ellsworth Bunker's departure from Djakarta was completely ignored by the Indonesian government. Destiny decreed that he go from the frying pan into the fire. To him fell the task of dealing with the Dominican crisis. The landing of American troops in the Caribbean republic in April 1965 sent tidal waves that rocked the Indonesian boat. Here again was the United States interfering, as the Indonesians saw it, in the internal affairs of another country.

Preparations for the Tenth Anniversary of the Afro-Asian Bandung conference occupied much of the Indonesian press during this period; the meeting itself convened the day following Bunker's departure. Despite the excellent administrative arrangements, welcoming arches, nighttime illuminations, and the general clean-up of Djakarta, blatant efforts made by the Indonesians to convert the ceremonial into a propaganda device serving Indonesian and Asian Communist aims brought expressions of disapproval from the Indians, Japanese, Thais, Turks, Filipinos, Tunisians, Ethiopians, and even Pakistanis. Of these, the most dramatic was the walkout of Thai Foreign Minister Thanat Khoman. He had been refused permission to answer an hour-long tirade of the North Vietnamese, who attempted, with Indonesian backing, to obtain a formal condemnation of U.S. actions in Vietnam. This was of a piece with Indonesia's blackout of other delegates' statements that did not support the Indonesians' pet themes and objectives.

Behind the scenes, the Indonesians were also waging a battle to prevent Malaysia from attending the Algiers Afro-Asian conference scheduled for June 29. The Indonesians, as so often was the case in this period, overplayed their hand, thereby diminishing enthusiasm for Sukarno's proposed "Conference of New Emerging Forces" and enhancing the prospects for Malaysia's admission to the Algiers meeting. Only the Communist and the Somali delegations expressed support for CONEFO, and there was some reason to believe that the latter was misquoted.

The Afro-Asian world was rapidly becoming polycentric and the appeal of meetings of what Sukarno used to think of as the Third Force in the world was fading. Bilateral, regional, and continental problems and

relationships were beginning to dominate the thinking and foreign policies of the Afro-Asian nations. Sukarno's insistence on always occupying
the center of the stage and his exploitation of Afro-Asian and nonaligned
meetings thwarted their real purposes and resulted in the increasing reluctance of other non-Communist leaders to cooperate with him.

It was an interesting fact, although I do not suggest a causal relationship, that as the American position in Indonesia deteriorated, so did the
prestige of Sukarno's government abroad, not only in the Western world
but in Asia and Africa as well.

Before leaving Djakarta, I made one more attempt to break through
the log jam holding up a settlement of the Malaysia dispute. Recognizing that at this point any formula would have to include something for
both Sukarno and the Tunku, I proposed to Washington the following
trade—the departure of British forces from Borneo in exchange for a
guaranty of the integrity of Malaysian territory. Within the framework
of the Maphilindo concept, it could perhaps establish a new relationship
between the parties concerned. Since in the prevailing state of emotionalism, it was too much to expect either the Indonesians or Malaysians to
indulge in much long-range thinking, perhaps we could do it for them
behind the scenes.

I recognized the potential objections to any suggestion that would include withdrawal of British troops from Sarawak and Sabah. For one
thing, Malaysia would find difficulty in being a party to any formal
agreement that would treat the East Malaysia States as separate from the
rest of Malaysia or appear to abridge Malaysia's sovereign right to invite
the assistance of a friendly power to repel aggression in any part of its
territory. For another, it might appear to give Sukarno a victory, since he
had been demanding their removal.

We all recognized, however, that the British military presence in Sarawak and Sabah was primarily in response to Indonesia's paramilitary
confrontation and that in the normal course of events it would be reduced or eliminated as tensions were removed. Therefore, it might be
possible to convince Malaysia that for the sake of a settlement, it would
be wise to privately express to Indonesia the point that British troops
would not be needed in East Malaysia if *konfrontasi* ended, and that the
Malaysian government would expect to thereafter maintain security in
the area; then the British forces would naturally be returned to their
normal bases on the Malaysian mainland. If assurances could be extended that this would take place relatively quickly following a settlement of the dispute, it would thus allow Sukarno to take public note
that Indonesian concerns were being met: the British forces were leaving
northern Borneo. However, the Indonesians would have to accept that
this could not be publicized as a "condition" of settlement, because the
Government of Malaysia could not publicly accept an allegation that not

only would be politically damaging but also appear to imply that Indonesia had the right to insist that Malaysia not reintroduce British forces into Borneo at some future time. But this suggestion fell on stony ground; I record it mainly to show the complex elements entering into any attempt to establish common ground between two antagonists when a substantial measure of "face" is involved on both sides.

The time had come for my wife and me to say farewell to Indonesia. I had accepted the chancellorship of the East-West Center[4] in Honolulu the previous October but the situation in Indonesia had been so touch and go that the Department of State did not wish to replace me. Now, my resignation finally accepted, I made arrangements to leave the country on May 24. President Sukarno, while making no secret of his displeasure at my departure, gave a dinner for us and the last two weeks of our stay were largely occupied with farewell dinners, luncheons, and receptions.

Aside from official farewell occasions such as the Foreign Minister's luncheon in our honor, it was politically dangerous for any top official to pay special attention to us. Yet both Adam Malik, now Minister without Portfolio and under heavy pressure, and Admiral Martadinata, head of the Indonesian Navy, insisted on doing so. I told Malik I would not go along with this, much as I appreciated his thought, because I knew such a gesture might hurt him. We were old friends, and this friendship did not require another proof. Malik looked at me and said, "You must let me do this. As a favor to me. I would not feel right in here," putting his hand over his heart, "if I let you leave without at least giving a luncheon for you." Such was the character of this man.

The press virtually ignored my departure. The brightest spot was an editorial in the Foreign Department–controlled *Herald*, which observed that while I was a political opponent, "we see in his departure the loss of a great and sincere personal friend." Perhaps the comment I appreciated most came from my stanch friend and beleaguered colleague, Sir Andrew Gilchrist. In a personally penned farewell note, he wrote:

> Dear Howard, I have only just heard of your very distinguished award[5]—hard-earned but very well merited during a spell of service

---

4. The East-West Center was established by Congress in 1960 as a national institution in cooperation with the University of Hawaii to foster better understanding among the people of the United States, Asia and the Pacific Islands area. Located on the University of Hawaii campus in Honolulu, the Center each year provides grants for up to 1,000 students, senior scholars and technical-training participants from more than thirty countries and territories. I considered the East-West Center to be the most vital experiment in international cultural communication through education going on anywhere in the world.

5. I had been given the Distinguished Service Award by the Department of State for my service in Indonesia.

more sophisticated in its approach and more successful in its results than either your friends or your enemies are apt to give you credit for!

My wife and I loved Indonesia and were sorry to leave. There was no bitterness in our departure, for we had shared the struggles of the Indonesian people over a period of eight and a half years. We understood them, and we also understood the conflicting forces in which they were engulfed. We had confidence that they would surmount their present difficulties, and hoped that our long presence there had contributed something to the ultimate solution of their problems.

PART IV

Back from the Brink

Democracies are most commonly corrupted by the insolence of demagogues.

—ARISTOTLE

There is no power in the world that can halt the masses when they have risen.

—D. N. AIDIT

Communism is not love. It is a hammer with which to strike our enemies.

—MAO TSE-TUNG

CHAPTER 1

Gestapu

Hawaii deserves its reputation as the crossroads of the Pacific. After 1966, Indonesians, whose access to America had been reduced to a trickle by Sukarno, came through Honolulu in ever-growing streams. Few neglected to visit me at the East-West center and share with me the story of their homeland's changing scene. Honolulu is also the site of CINCPAC, and I took full advantage of this to review the cable traffic dealing with Indonesian developments. The East-West Center itself again gathered increasing increments of Indonesian students, scholars and notables, including former Vice-President Hatta and Ambassador Palar, last representative to the United Nations in the Sukarno regime. Americans with long experience of Southeast Asia also found the Center a congenial place to sort out and set down their thoughts. Among these were Roger Hilsman, Arthur Goodfriend, John M. Allison, George Kanahele, Sam P. Gilstrap, and Samuel P. Hayes. Thus, in my new post as Chancellor of the East-West Center, and in frequent trips to Asia on Center business, I was able to keep close to Indonesia's heartbeat.

The account that follows, covering the period from 1965 to 1969, is drawn from data gathered through these diverse channels,[1] sifted by time, and capped by a sentimental journey to Djakarta in January 1969 to meet old friends, examine firsthand the post-Sukarno era, and contemplate the future of this fascinating land.

On an early morning in the fall of 1965, five months after our departure from Djakarta, an event occurred that dramatically altered the

---

1. In addition to Indonesian sources, I am indebted to the Department of State for providing access to its records for much of the information in this account of the events that followed my departure from Indonesia. See as well: John Hughes, *Indonesian Upheaval* (New York: David McKay Company, 1967); Robert Shaplen, *Time Out of Hand, Revolution and Reaction in Southeast Asia* (New York: Harper & Row, 1969); Arnold C. Brackman, *The Communist Collapse in Indonesia* (New York: Norton, 1969).

course of Indonesian history. Forces that had been churning beneath the surface of Indonesian politics long before independence were liberated. Through the interaction of these forces, a country that had well-nigh been written off by Westerners generally and the American government in particular as inevitably and inexorably marching toward Communism, suddenly reversed its course, slaughtered some 300,000 Communists (although estimates vary from around 150,000 to 500,000), including most of those constituting the basic cadres, banned the Communist Party, gently but firmly edged out of power its charismatic leader, rejoined the United Nations, and turned toward the West externally and more democratic freedoms internally.

The event was an abortive *coup d'état,* named by the conspirators the "30 September Movement," aimed at eliminating the top army leadership and, by changing the composition of the Cabinet, establishing a government more acceptable to the left-wingers and the pro-Communists within the armed forces. The attempt by Communists and disaffected army elements to take power failed and in its failure sparked a reaction that emasculated the world's largest Communist Party outside the bloc.

The full story of this so-called coup has yet to be told; indeed, it may never be. But the following facts have been established. I refer to it as a "so-called coup" because, contrary to popular assumption at the time, it does not appear to have been directed against Sukarno but rather at using him as an instrument of Communist and dissident will for the remainder of his political life. There is also considerable evidence to indicate that Sukarno had made himself party to the plot in order to rid himself of those army leaders who were opposed to his policies.

The plot was simple and diabolical. In essence, it was to remove from Djakarta, by one means or another, all the officers of the Indonesian Army who had command authority and might oppose the conspirators' aspirations for power. The resulting situation would make it necessary for President Sukarno, as Commander-in-Chief, to step in, reassure the country, and appoint a commander and government sympathetic to the objectives of the coup group. Removal of the commanders was to be accomplished by various means: assassination, exiting them from the country at the critical moment on various pretexts, and liquidation or transfer after the government was in new hands.

The leaders of this 30 September Movement, now generally referred to as "Gestapu," [2] mounted simultaneous raids on the homes of seven

---

2. Gestapu was not an adaptation of the German "*Gestapo,*" appropriate as that might have been. It was an acronym derived from *Gerakan September Tiga Puluh,* literally translated "Movement September 30." "Sjam," one of the chief planners of the coup group, gave the movement this name at their meeting of September 29.

generals at approximately 4:00 A.M. on October 1, 1965. With one exception, the generals were either killed on the spot or kidnaped and subsequently murdered. The military action was over in a matter of hours. It involved, besides the raids, the securing of a few vital objectives —the Presidential Palace in Djakarta, the Radio Indonesia station, the Central Telecommunications building, and an air base just outside Djakarta. The staging ground for the attack was an abandoned rubber plantation that was within the confines of Lubang Buaja, literally, "Crocodile Hole," a small hamlet on the edge of Halim Air Force Base approximately seven miles from the Presidential Palace in Djakarta. It was a remote area that could be easily sealed off.

What happened at the home of Army Chief of Staff Yani at that early morning hour was typical of the action. The rumble of military trucks echoed in the quiet streets. One swung into General Yani's driveway, and an officer, accompanied by two enlisted men, jumped out, told the guard he had an urgent message for the General from President Sukarno. The guard told him the General was asleep, but the officer entered the house, went upstairs, and pounded on the General's bedroom door. When Yani opened it, the officer said, "President Sukarno wants to see you!" He was armed, and his manner disrespectful.

"Put that gun away and salute when you address me," the General snapped. (One report said he slapped the man's face.)

The officer pulled the trigger of his automatic as Yani's small son came out into the hall to see what was going on. Madame Yani was not home that night. It was her birthday, and she was celebrating it Eastern fashion by staying up all night with some friends and relatives.

The soldiers then carted the bleeding body down the stairs and tossed it into the truck. Whether the General was dead or alive, no one knows.

In similar operations, five other generals were killed. Unfortunately for the conspirators' plans, they missed Nasution, the Minister of Defense, and for some reason did not include on the list Major General Suharto, chief of the Strategic Command (KOSTRAD), perhaps because he was a former commander of the Diponegoro Division, or perhaps, as Suharto himself said, "They didn't think my command that important."

The 100-man assassination squad assigned to General Naustion's home on tree-lined Tcuku Umar was the largest of all. The Nasutions, awakened by the commotion outside, concluded someone was trying to kidnap the General. While troops were struggling to get in the front door, Mrs. Nasution pushed her husband out a side door where a high masonry wall separated them from the Iraqi Ambassador's residence. As he left, Nasution heard a scream. Looking back, he saw his beloved five-year-old daughter Irma fall before a spray of bullets. His first impulse was to return and face the soldiers who shot her, but his wife implored him to jump and save himself. Nasution scrambled over the wall and dropped on the other side, breaking his ankle in the fall, and landing on brambles in his bare feet. He remained hiding in the bushes until he was rescued by General Umar Wirahadikusumah around 5:30 A.M.

Meanwhile, in the dark and confusion, the kidnapers met a man on the stairs they thought was General Nasution. But it was Nasution's aide, Lieutenant Tendean, who physically resembled his chief. And on that night, he had donned the General's jacket and cap. When asked if he was General Nasution, he replied, "Yes," and was seized and thrown into the truck. By that one mistake, the entire movement was irrecoverably jeopardized.

The six key generals assassinated that night were: Lieutenant General Achmad Yani; Major General Parman, chief of Army Intelligence; Major General M. T. Harjono, Third Deputy Army Chief of Staff; Major General Pandjaitan, fourth assistant to the Army Chief of Staff and in charge of logistics; Major General Suprapto, Second Deputy Army Chief of Staff; and Brigadier General Sutojo, inspector, military tribunals. It was a fantastic operation. Perhaps never before in history had the top command of an army been cut down in one night.

Grim irony entered into the assassination of General Parman. On September 14, he had presented a report on the security situation to General Yani in which a plot to assassinate the army's top leadership was mentioned. September 18 was the date specified. Yani is reported to have shown the report to Sukarno. It included Suharto, Mursjid and Sukendro among the generals to be assassinated. The army took special security precautions on the night of the eighteenth, placing tanks in front of the threatened generals' homes, but nothing happened.

Toward the end of September, the former military attaché in Peking, Brigadier General Sudono (in a good position to obtain interesting intelligence) is reported to have informed Major General Harjono that a number of generals would be abducted within a few days. Harjono, doubting the report, nevertheless called a staff meeting at army headquarters on September 30 to consider what Sudono had to say. He was only laughed at.

No one knew right away what had happened to the kidnaped generals. As reports began to pour in, it became clear that a major conspiracy was under way. But by whom and against whom was still a mystery. At 7:00 A.M. on October 1, coup forces took over Radio Indonesia and announced that a movement "directed against the generals who are members of the Council of Generals" had occurred that morning. The statement stressed that this action was purely an internal army affair. The generals were said to be under arrest. A relatively unknown officer of Sukarno's Palace Guard, Lieutenant Colonel Untung, announced that, as commander of the movement, he had assumed full responsibility for what he termed "preventive action against a plot by the Generals' Council, a CIA-sponsored subversive movement . . . which planned to stage a coup on 5 October." [3] Sukarno was announced to be safe and under the 30 September Movement's protection.[4]

At noon, Untung issued Decree No. 1, announcing the formation of a revolutionary council that would take charge of the government. Sukarno was not mentioned in the list of members. But Untung and his group had not reckoned on Suharto, Nasution, and other loyal military leaders. General Suharto saved the day. After a conference with General Nasution, who, as Minister of Defense and his superior, had instructed him to take command, Suharto went into action. Within hours he had gathered around him elements of his own division and loyal units of other commands and set out to neutralize the rebels, who had taken over the palace and radio stations. Determined to avoid bloodshed, Suharto's strategy was to talk the rebels into surrender, Indonesian-style—via bluff, threat, negotiation, and cajolement. Emissaries shuttled back and forth between Suharto and his aides at KOSTRAD headquarters and the acting commanders of two rebellious batallions. Major Sukirno of the 454th and Major Bambang Supeno of the 530th were inside the palace, where they had gone earlier that morning with General Supardjo to report to Sukarno. Learning he was not there, they decided to remain, believing that they were positioned to protect Sukarno from a coup by the Generals' Council. Suharto finally got into the palace, assured them there was no council, that they had been tricked and were actually protecting a coup movement. Suharto's strategy of talk was successful with the 530th battalion, but just as he had almost convinced the 454th's deputy commander to surrender, Major Supeno returned and ordered his men to stand firm and continue working in the service of the coup.

At 6:00 P.M. Suharto issued an ultimatum to the 454th battalion: either they evacuate their positions by 10:00 P.M. or he would blast them out. This was actually a bluff—Suharto's position was not so strong at that moment to ensure his success if there were to be a confrontation. But it worked. As they withdrew, a horde of armed Communist youths straggled into Djakarta from Lubang Buaja. It appeared as though the PKI and their front groups had resorted to arms and an attack was imminent. Suharto and his troops wasted no time; the youths were quickly arrested,[5] and by 8:00 P.M. Suharto was in full control of Djakarta.

During the afternoon, Suharto had received word via presidential couriers that Sukarno and the coup-group leaders were at Halim Air Base. Until then, Suharto had not known where the President was, and now his suspicions were aroused. Sukarno was obviously not a prisoner,

---

3. This was pure fabrication. The CIA was a convenient scapegoat.
4. Actually, Sukarno was not then with the coup forces.
5. Later evidence revealed that they had been kept at Lubang Buaja as a "reserve force." Apparently, they played no role in the coup until their march—except as witnesses at the murder scene, where they had spent the morning and most of the afternoon.

since he was able to send couriers to Djakarta. Suharto sent word to Sukarno via Leimena that he would soon have the base surrounded and was preparing to attack. He asked that Sukarno depart as he did not wish to endanger him.

Sukarno's whereabouts in the hours before, during and after the coup were not wholly clear. At first, after hearing the report of what had happened from Colonel Saelan, deputy commander of the presidential guard, he was persuaded to go to the home of Harjati, one of his wives, who lived in the center of the city. He is said to have stated that the whole thing came as an "absolute surprise." Later, Sukarno decided to go to Halim Air Force Base and arrived there around 9:30 A.M. From then until General Suharto's message came, Leimena told me, "Nobody knew what the situation was." It was then decided Bogor Palace would be the safest place for him, and, continued Leimena, "I took him by the hand and led him out to the car. He seemed bewildered and not to know what was happening. We drove to Bogor and spent the night in the Bogor Palace." [6]

Aidit and Air Marshal Dhani separately flew to Central Java early in the morning of October 2—Aidit to Jogjakarta, Dhani to Madiun. General Suharto closed in with his troops and seized the air base without a casualty. It was all over by 6:10 A.M., October 2. Suharto had suppressed the coup attempt.

The bodies of the assassinated generals were discovered the next day stuffed down a deep well at the edge of the military airport grimly named the Crocodile Hole. They appeared to have been badly mutilated. Indonesians have so much respect for the body after death that autopsies were illegal. Mutilation violated their deepest sensibilities: nothing the Communists could have done would have been so certain to arouse the resentment of the people.

Some observers found it difficult to believe the Communist Party was behind the coup. They had been doing so well under Sukarno; why should they want to unseat him? These analysts concluded that the entire conspiracy was an intra-army affair, as the PKI wanted everyone to believe. As time passed, however, the trials of the participants in the plot and the capture of key Communist leaders gradually etched a clearer outline of the objectives of the coup group and those directly involved.

The conspiracy consisted of the Communist leadership, dissident army officers, Marshal Dhani, and Communist youth groups trained and armed by the air force. It had Sukarno's blessing. The immediate objective, on which all—including Sukarno—were agreed, was to purge the army of its anti-Communist leaders.

Beyond this, however, objectives appear to have varied. The Commu-

6. Howard P. Jones interview with former Deputy Prime Minister Johannes Leimena, February 7, 1969.

nist Party was undoubtedly out to exploit Sukarno's popularity by leaving him titular President for the length of his usefulness, and to manage a gradual takeover of the government. Having known Sukarno as well as I did, I find it difficult to believe his objectives would have been the same. Rather, he would have been judging the situation in terms of the instruments of his own control over the country.

Between them, Subandrio and the PKI leadership seemed to have convinced the President that a so-called Generals' Council was plotting to get rid of him. Although no basis appears to have existed for this,[7] Sukarno, having survived seven assassination attempts, had become a highly suspicious person prone to believing anything, particularly about those who had been endeavoring to thwart his leftward thrust. Once Sukarno accepted the existence of an army plot to oust him, he would have had reason enough to go along with the plans of the coup group; indeed, reason enough to be the chief architect of the conspiracy.[8]

But why should the PKI, thriving under Sukarno's protection, have been interested in taking the extraordinary risks involved in such an operation when power via the democratic process seemed almost within its grasp? The basic assumption underlying the question provides the answer. The Communists had no choice but to attempt a coup at any time it appeared that the protective mantle was threatened. Thus it is possible that Aidit and the PKI leadership actually believed the story of the alleged plot and acted upon it.

The so-called Generals' Council was an informal group for discussions of political defense against what the army considered were a series of menacing moves by Sukarno. In April 1965, Sukarno called a special meeting of military commanders and ordered them to get in step with

---

7. In January 1965, General Yani and some of his closest colleagues began meeting in secret to discuss the deteriorating political situation. Yani referred to this group as his "brain trust"; Aidit termed it the "Generals' Council." There is no evidence that these secret meetings were for any purpose other than discussion. No indications of a coup plan have been discovered.

8. An instance of duplicity occurred in 1965, when Sir Andrew Gilchrist was alleged to have written a letter to the British Foreign Office reporting a conversation with me concerning U.S. and British plans for overthrowing the Indonesian government, in collusion with military leaders (Gilchrist's supposed reference was "our local army friends"). The letter was made public in Cairo by Subandrio in July 1965, on his way home from the abortive Afro-Asian conference. A covering note said the Gilchrist letter was found in Bill Palmer's house when it was raided by the PKI in early May. At his trial, Subandrio said he had been convinced of the letter's authenticity, and had given it to Sukarno on May 26, 1965. The President's reaction was one of genuine alarm. The letter proved to be a cleverly contrived forgery designed to arouse his suspicions of the U.S., the British, and the army leadership.

the revolution and "turn the wheel to the left." This meant revising the army's defense doctrine and aiming it at Nekolim, *i.e.*, the West, instead of Communist China. The army had reason to be alarmed. In a speech to the National Defense Institute in which he endorsed the idea of a "fifth force," that is, the arming of the peasants and workers, Sukarno ordered the institute placed under civilian control and the addition of pro-Communist courses to the curriculum. The idea of arming peasants and workers to fight against Nekolim had first been suggested by Aidit in January of 1965, but Sukarno had publicly rejected the proposal.

Deeply concerned, General Yani and a number of senior army generals quietly formed a group for the purpose of providing political guidance to the military and resisting the President's open effort to convert the military to his views, which now coincided with those of the PKI. In late May, Aidit requested Sjam, chief of the PKI's secret Special Bureau, to develop a plan of operations against the alleged council.

Sjam—whose real name was Kamarusman—was a member of the Central Committee, headed by Aidit, and apparently at this time a "deep-cover" agent for the PKI. In November 1964, he had been made head of a new covert organization, which was to carry out special duties, among them the infiltration of the armed services. The existence of this Special Bureau was a secret even within the PKI, and Sjam apparently worked directly under Aidit, whose colleagues on the Politburo were not taken into his confidence.

Aidit's next move was to propose that Nasakom councils be formed to advise all military commanders, from the top echelon on down to the military districts. It was a carbon copy of the political-commissar system in Communist China. The army possessed an extremely effective intelligence arm. Aidit must have known that the top rank of his organization was being penetrated, but not by whom.[9] He had to play almost a lone hand.

After the failure of the conspiracy, some American observers privately concluded that it could not have been a PKI operation because it would have been better organized. But this overlooked two important factors. First, knowledge of any plans had to be trusted to an inner circle. Any plot involving widespread action and many individuals could not have been kept secret. Second, the PKI wanted to keep its options open. Communist coups had failed three times before in Indonesia. This one must be so designed that failure could result in disclaimer. The PKI hand would not show in the coup glove until it was a pronounced success.

---

9. General Parman, head of Army Intelligence, used to boast quietly that he would know of any important PKI decision within four hours after it had been reached. He was one of those assassinated.

The Special Bureau (*Buro Chusus*) was an autonomous unit completely free of the control of the Central Committee or the Politburo. This was in accordance with standard Chinese Communist doctrine on the "Coordination of the Legal and Illegal Struggle": "The very existence of a secret or covert Communist organization must be unknown, its personnel must be unknown as Communists, its work carried on in complete anonymity. It is unknown not only to hostile security forces and the general public—it is unknown even to all except a few of the overt party. . . . Only the topmost leadership of the legal party knows of even the existence of the secret party. . . ."

Sjam, captured in 1967, admitted under interrogation that the Special Bureau "was the special apparatus of Comrade Chairman of the CC/PKI, Aidit." Its primary job was to prepare for armed struggle, which was not the policy of the PKI at the time. Each of its members worked with—the Communist word was "managed"—key officers in the armed forces.[10] Thus Sjam was in direct contact with General Supardjo and other army officers who became active in the coup group; "Pono," with officers of the First Infantry Brigade of KODAM V in Central Java; and "Walujo," directly with Marshal Dhani, the Palace Guard, and particularly Colonel Untung.

We in the embassy were aware that the PKI had plans for a coup and we assumed these plans would be implemented when, as, and if Sukarno was about to be gone from the political stage. For, given the existing army leadership, a crackdown on the PKI was certain when Sukarno was no longer around to protect the party. On August 3, 1965, Sukarno collapsed and later in the month had a setback. Aidit took the matter seriously enough to discuss it at a meeting of the Politburo on August 13. The Generals' Council's threat to the party was sufficiently great, it was decided, to warrant "preparations in anticipation of the possible death or incapacitation of Sukarno." On August 28, the Politburo met again and decided to launch a military movement against the council. Aidit entrusted its planning to the Special Bureau.

Meanwhile, Sukarno was preparing his Independence Day address. Probably viewing it as his last major policy speech to the Indonesian nation, Sukarno undoubtedly exerted every effort to chart his nation's future course. Convinced the army leaders were plotting against him, he selected the army as a special target. It turned out to be the most vehement attack on the anti-Communist position and the highest laudation of the Communists, in and out of the country, that Sukarno had ever

---

10. Central Bureau leadership included Sjam; his deputy, Marsudidjojo, always referred to as "Pono"; Subono, called "Walujo," whose job was finance. The Special Bureau had ten branches: Djakarta, West Java, Central Java, Bali, South Kalimantan (Borneo), North Sumatra, South Sumatra, West Sumatra, the Riau Archipelago, South Celebes.

made. "The revolutionary offensive" must be intensified in all fields in the near future, the President insisted, and especially in the army. "Even though you were generals from the PETA, who boast of your revolutionary services, if you now try to upset the Nasakom offensive, you are reactionary forces!" Sukarno shouted.

He expressed his annoyance at the army resistance to the "fifth force" concept, saying "Every time I suggest something, there is always a reaction. . . . In this case, they accuse me of copying others [the militia system of Communist China]. But our Constitution gives every citizen the right to defend the nation. After studying this matter further, I, the Supreme Commander, will make the decision." (Sukarno is on record as having stated that Chou En-lai originally suggested the "fifth force" system.)

In the field of international affairs, he warmly praised the countries of Eastern Europe for having established "People's Democracies" after World War II. He listed North Korea along with North Vietnam and Communist China, as the logical allies of Indonesia. He called for the creation of a Djakarta-Phnom Penh-Hanoi-Peking-Pyongyang axis as a fulfillment of the demands of history.

In the midst of these attacks, Sukarno singled out General Adjie and the Siliwangi Division of West Java for special praise. On August 28, Sukarno bestowed on the Siliwangi, the SAM KAYA LURHAA (equivalent to the U.S. Presidential Unit Citation) in an apparent attempt to secure the division's loyalty by honoring Adjie, its commander. Later, however, it was learned that on the twenty-fifth of August, Sjam of the PKI Central Committee held a meeting in Bandung attended by General Rukman, former Chief of Staff of the Siliwangi Division; General Supardjo, also former Siliwangi officer; and Colonel Sukardi, Mayor of Bandung. At the meeting, it was agreed that through the combined efforts of General Rukman and Colonel Sukardi, the Siliwangi would be immobilized. Sjam reported the meeting to Aidit on August 28, the day of the ceremony honoring the division. Convinced that the famous unit would be immobilized, Untung and the PKI thought they could hold Djakarta with only a few battalions. Apparently as part of the plan, a section of General Suharto's strategic reserve had been sent to Northern Sumatra and General Sarwo Edhy's paratroopers were presumed on their way to Kalimantan. As it happened, Adjie was on a hunting trip and not in Bandung on October 1. The Siliwangi did not play a significant role in the events of that day. During the following months, Adjie remained close to Sukarno, but it is assumed by current army leadership that Adjie's closeness was out of a personal loyalty to Sukarno and not in any way indicative of Adjie's support for the coup. In 1966 Adjie was sent to London to be the Ambassador.

In assessing Sukarno's role in the conspiracy and the extent of his cooperation with the coup group, his activities in late August, September, and during the sixteen hours of October 1 before the issue was resolved are of significance. For instance, to what "internal political developments" was he referring when he gave his reason for canceling an early September trip to Vienna for medical treatment? If there were a political crisis in Indonesia, it still lay under the surface. Did he mean the reports he had received of the plans of the Generals' Council? Or the plans he knew about to counter them?

And then there are the speeches. In one, Sukarno lashed out at the army as he had never done before, challenging Yani directly, telling him "the people will crush you" unless he became more revolutionary-minded. In another, he identified himself with the 1926 abortive PKI revolt against the Dutch. Sukarno had always been associated with the "third generation," which formed the nucleus of the PNI, the Nationalist Party that Sukarno founded. At no time had there ever been reference to his involvement with the Communists in the 1926 revolt. Yet he said, "I was always a member of the second generation. After the 1926 revolt, when the PKI leaders were in jail, they smuggled letters to me, urging me to carry on the struggle [against the Dutch]. . . . The third generation . . . I was never one of them. They were revisionists, collaborationists. . . . You can't do anything gradually. You have to seize power by force." Unless the historians are quite wrong, this was Sukarno rewriting history. There is no evidence that his commitment to the PKI had been so strong.

Taking courage and his line from his chief, on September 2, Foreign Minister Subandrio publicly attacked the army. Two days later, Colonels Untung and Latief were separately approached by their PKI contacts and told to attend a meeting on September 6. It was the first time the military officers who were to be involved in the coup got together with each other and their Communist associates. On September 19, Untung was told he had been selected as coup leader; at the same meeting, Sjam presented a list of the generals who were to be liquidated. Meanwhile, PKI organizations in Djakarta were instructed to provide volunteers for a crash military-training course at Lubang Buaja, to be given by the air force. Subandrio attacked the army in several more speeches, at one point charging that some former "heroes have turned into traitors." He also announced that an operation to eliminate "capitalist bureaucrats" was imminent. In a public address, Aidit mentioned a "child who will definitely be born," an apparent allusion to the birth of socialism in Indonesia. A few days later, clearly marking his common cause with the PKI, the President presented Aidit with the Order of Mahaputra Star.

It was a busy month. Marshal Dhani flew to Communist China on a secret mission for President Sukarno. Only Aidit and Subandrio apparently were informed of the trip, and although its purpose has not yet been pinned down, all evidence points to its having been undertaken to obtain weapons to arm peasants and workers. On September 20, Sukarno summoned Nasution and Yani to the palace and apparently told them he had reliable information that several generals were plotting against the government, but he would not divulge names. Nasution and Yani countered with the accusation that it was the PKI that appeared to be preparing for a coup.

On September 2, Aidit announced he was canceling his plans to attend the Chinese National Day celebrations in Peking on October 1. This was a curious decision, inexplicable except in light of what followed. Indonesian representation was scheduled to be the largest ever. The PKI delegation would still be a large one, but it would be distinguished by the lack of prominent personalities. Not only would Aidit be absent—no member of the Politburo would be there.

September 27 was important in other ways. PKI Politburo member Sudisman was approached by Brigadier General Sugandhi. The conversation, according to Sugandhi's testimony later, was as follows.

> Sugandhi: Man [abbreviation for Sudisman], what is going on with all these preparations and digging of wells in the villages?
> Sudisman: Why don't you just join us?
> Sugandhi: That is impossible, Man. I cannot possibly join the PKI, because I am a religious person.
> Sudisman: If you do not want to, it is because you have been listening too much to Nasution.
> Sugandhi: No, it is not a matter of listening too much to him, it is a matter of ideology. If you continue with your plan, you will be crushed and destroyed.
> Sudisman: No, that is impossible. We will have the initiative. Whoever begins and strikes the first blow will win. Have trust in us. We have made thorough calculations.

And later that day, Sugandhi had this conversation with Aidit:

> Aidit: Have you talked with Sudisman? We will start in a short time, in two or three days. Bung Karno [Sukarno] knows all this. It would be better for you if you join us.
> Sugandhi: Sudisman already talked to me, but I do not want to join the PKI. The PKI wants to stage a coup. I have my own doctrine, the Soldier's Oath.
> Aidit: Bung, do not say 'coup.' That is an evil word. The PKI is going to improve the revolution which is being subverted by the Council of Generals. We will start within two to three days. Will you join us or not? I have already informed Bung Karno about all this.

Three days later, Sugandhi talked with Sukarno:

> Sugandhi: The PKI is going to stage a coup. Do you know about this? I have been contacted by Sudisman and Aidit themselves.
> Sukarno: Don't be a communist-phobe. Don't you know about the

existence of the Council of Generals? Don't you know that these generals are hopeless? Be careful when you talk.

Sugandhi: If there are hopeless generals, why don't you just dismiss them? Isn't that your authority? There is no Council of Generals. There is a Rank and Post Review Council. It is an evaluation council to assist the army minister/commander to evaluate colonels who are to be promoted to generals, and not for any other purpose.

Sukarno: Don't you interfere. Shut up. You must have been listening too much to Nasution.

Sugandhi: It is true, Bapak. There is no Council of Generals. Pak Yani said so himself and declared to Bapak that there is no Council of Generals. Isn't Yani a man who is loyal to you, somebody who may be called your right hand?

Sukarno: Don't talk too much. Don't meddle. Don't you know that according to Thomas Tonly in a revolution a father can eat his own children? Don't you know?

Sugandhi: If that is the case, you must have joined the PKI.

Sukarno: Shut up, or I will slap you till you faint. Go home, and be careful.[11]

On the basis of these reported conversations, Nasution stated publicly on February 13, 1967 that "the President gave the coup his blessing and assistance." He cited a January 19, 1967 central-investigation team report stressing "the importance and the validity of the Sukarno-Sugandhi conversation of 30 September as proof of the President's advanced knowledge and involvement in the 30 September affair."

Thus a clear picture emerges in which the PKI leadership, the air force chief, certain pro-Communist elements in the army, officers in Sukarno's palace guard, and Sukarno himself were all involved in a conspiracy to liquidate the top military leadership of the country and move the nation farther left.

Sukarno's behavior following the failure of the coup is inexplicable unless viewed in the light of his participating in it. On October 1, before the body of General Yani had been found, and thus presumably before Sukarno could have known of the assassination unless he were in on the plot, he appointed General Pranoto Reksosamudera—cooperative with the PKI—as Acting Chief of Staff of the Army. Sukarno then summoned Omar Dhani from Central Java, where he had fled, and kept him at the Presidential Palace for his protection. He also reportedly harbored Lukman and Njoto, first and second deputy chairmen of the PKI respectively, in his Bogor Palace, as well as Subandrio when he was threatened. Flanked by Subandrio and Njoto, he faced the press and publicly defended the PKI.

At no point did Sukarno ever express public appreciation for what Suharto had done for the country, and only appointed him Army Chief

---

11. A. H. Nasution, *Menegakkan Keadilan dan Kebenaran* (Djakarta: Seruling Masa, 1967) vol. II, pp. 30–32.

of Staff after the army refused to accept anyone else. Never did he express any remorse over the assassinations of the generals, nor did he condemn the PKI or the Gestapu generally.

In three major speeches following the Gestapu affair, Sukarno kept insisting upon a return to Nasakom, but his golden voice was no longer heard.

CHAPTER 2

The Volcano Erupts

On a sunny day in February 1963, 800 Balinese men, women and children were praying in the great temple of Bekasih that their sacrifices —beautiful gold and silver towers bearing flowers, fruits, and vegetables —would be acceptable to the god of the Mount Agung ("King") volcano so that another hundred years of quietude would be ensured.

As they knelt, the god of the volcano found his voice. A rumbling sound came from deep within the great mountain cavity. The people on their knees prayed harder. Did this mean the god was angry? Or was he simply acknowledging their gifts? The rumbling became a fierce roar, and they knew the answer. And then came the explosion that rocked the earth beneath them as though the world were coming to an end. As they looked tongues of fiery red lava licked out of the huge mouth above them. The tongues grew longer and longer until they became great rivers of fire, pouring down the mountain toward them. The people had time to escape, but no one moved. The liquid fire was closer now, and its hissing drowned out every other sound. They continued to pray; the god could save them if he would.

The molten lava rushed over and through the temple, burying the people at prayer. They never stirred.

Three major eruptions of Mount Agung occurred during the months of February, March, and May 1963, claiming a total of more than 11,000 lives and a third of Bali's farm land. They left 85,000 people homeless and destroyed rice paddies that supported more than 200,000 people. The Balinese agreed the god was angry. Some said it was the people's way of life. They had grown too pleasure loving, like their President, and had put material things first. Others said no, it was the fault of the Communists who had invaded their paradise. These god-denying folk had come into power in Bali, and too many people had turned away from the gods. An incubus had fastened itself upon them. They must get rid of it. But how?

The volcanic explosions were prophetic of the societal eruptions, which came in December 1965, following the abortive coup. The blood-bath in Bali was the worst of all. Proportionately more people were killed there than anywhere else in Indonesia, not excepting the Communist-dominated areas of East and Central Java. Whole villages known to be in the Communist camp were wiped out. In typical Balinese fashion, these killings were carried out ceremoniously, with a certain dignity and grim implacability. An anti-Communist village would invite its antago-nists to a feast, each side knowing what was in store. After the feast, the invited guests would be slaughtered, either on the scene or on the way home. In most instances, as in the temple on Mount Agung, there was no resistance. This seems not to have been mere fatalism but rather a shared guilt complex. Those who had associated themselves with the Communist cause were convinced that they had done wrong and the gods they once denied were angry; their lives were given in expiation of their sins.

There were other explanations, less mystical, of the Balinese reaction. Sukarno was half Balinese, and he visited Bali frequently. The political parties which he favored—first the PNI, then the PKI—grew rapidly on the island in the sunshine of his smile. But the golden glitter of that smile's promise had tarnished in the economic and political realities of inflation and repression. The Balinese responded to the army's nod, kill-ing coldly, mercilessly cutting out what they considered a cancer in their body politic. In varying degrees of refinement and brutality, this cool, deliberate technique eliminated at least 300,000 Communists through-out Indonesia.

One of the most famous of the wajang plays makes clear how deeply rooted is the concept of the employment of violent means to counter evil forces and restore harmony and tranquility, which are ultimate values in the traditional Javanese world view.

Pre-eminent among the heroes of the wajang is Arjuna, brave, hand-some, clever, and lover of hundreds of beautiful women. Sukarno, in the eyes of the Indonesian masses, was Arjuna incarnate, which is why his peccadilloes, so disturbing to the West, had little significance for the majority of Indonesians. What they would resent in other men, they accepted in Sukarno. Another of the heroes is Kresno, wise adviser to the princes of the land. When Arjuna is driven from his kingdom by his half brothers, the evil Kurawas, he asks Kresno: "Is it good to win back a kingdom if, to do so, one must kill one's family? I would rather be a beggar than the murderer of my kin."

Kresno answers: "You are wrong, for in making such a choice, you exalt your own self, and place your personality above all else. The highest morality is to lose your personality, to submerge yourself, and to act without personal involvement or choice. You must kill your own family, but you must kill impersonally, without hatred, without passion, with complete detachment." Cold impersonal killing is sanctioned for a just cause.

This traditional Javanese cultural approach was but one of a blend of elements that, in varying proportions, were responsible for the violent eruption of social tensions at this time. Others included the religious pressures generated by Islamic groups for a "holy war" against the Communist infidel, economic dislocations such as the struggle for land in East Java, and political factors, which included the determination of the army to eradicate, once and for all, its major antagonist and competitor for power.

With varying motivations, the Indonesian people saw the purging of the Communists from their country as such a cause. They had been pushed around and intimidated much too long by the Communists. The killing of respected generals set off their long-smoldering fury. With the blessing, if not the nudging of the army, the people set out to even the score.

At long last, as sentient students of the Indonesian scene had so persistently predicted, the military overcame its unwillingness to take on Sukarno in a life-and-death struggle. The army reacted, and a new leader stepped on stage. General Suharto was no politician; nor, so far as anyone knew, had he ever had political ambitions. The story is told that once, during a tour of the military bases at the time of the West Irian campaign, Suharto stopped to rest with his staff in the jungle. Contemplating the fate of a soldier, Suharto asked, "Why should we men always make war, fight and roam the jungles?"

One of his subordinates commented, "General, who knows [but] that you may become President one day?"

Suharto replied emphatically, "That's impossible! What is my ability? Only to fight, to carry guns!"

The officer insisted, "God is always just." The General smiled but did not reply.[1]

In the diplomatic corps we put him down as an outstandingly able and strong commander, a modest and retiring man. He would not have been thought of as among the dozen men in the country who might succeed Sukarno. I doubt he had ever given it a thought himself. His patient persistence through the months that followed the fall of 1965 was the subject of much criticism by those who, while acknowledging he had saved the country on October 1, wanted events to move faster.

The slow process of cutting Sukarno down to size, however, was one of the most remarkable surgical operations in political history. The Russians could denigrate Stalin almost overnight, but not while he was alive.

---

1. *Indonesian Observer*, March 16, 1967.

The commander of military forces in Indonesia faced a much more difficult problem. He was legally under the direction of his President, a man
still presumably the idol of the masses. Suharto had to draw power unto
himself and exercise it with great skill and dexterity in order to avoid a
direct confrontation with Sukarno that would be unsuccessful. At the
same time, he had to gradually alter the image of the President and show
the people what he had become—an irresponsible mouther of meaningless slogans who had come close to turning his country over to the Communists.

For Suharto, this would have been impossible a short time before. He
was a loyal soldier. The thing that made the difference was the conviction on his part that Sukarno himself had played a leading role in the
Gestapu, in which six close friends and colleagues of Suharto's were
murdered. It was an unforgivable act of disloyalty.

The task Suharto had set for himself was not an easy one. Sukarno had
done his best to keep his options open. On October 2, before the generals' bodies had been discovered, he addressed the nation as if nothing
had been changed, and called "on all the Indonesian people to remain
calm. . . . The leadership of the Army is directly in my hands and I
have temporarily appointed Major General Pranoto Reksosamudra [a
leftist], assistant to the Minister/Commander of the Army, to carry out
the daily tasks of the Army. I have designated Major General Suharto,
Commander of the Strategic Command, to restore security and order.
. . . Brothers, let us firmly build a spirit of unity. Let our anti-Nekolim
spirit flourish. God is with us all."

The following day at midnight, the President delivered a second
speech over Radio Republic Indonesia in what listeners described as a
tone of anger.[2] He denied flatly that the air force was involved in the 30
September incident, and explained that "my trip to Halim Air Force
base early on October one was at my own volition because I thought that
the best place for me was near an airplane that could carry me at any
moment to another place if some undesirable thing should happen. We

2. These two speeches had been taped during the day but broadcast in the
small hours by Radio Republic Indonesia to the regional stations, typed by
them, and replayed the following day. Political Counselor Edward E. Masters
and his assistant, Robert G. Rich, Jr., were sleeping in the embassy at the
time because of the curfew effective immediately after the events of October
1. "I well remember hearing the first speech," Masters told me. "We had
left the radio on after the station had completed the day's transmission in
case there should be any late flashes. About 1:00 A.M., the announcer
started calling on the regional stations to stand by for an important announcement which they should transcribe. Soon came a voice, subdued and
even quavering a bit, which was unmistakably that of Sukarno. This was the
first clear evidence we had that he was alive and that it was not actually
his death or incapacitation which had triggered Gestapu."

must remain vigilant so that the Air Force and the Army are not pitted against each other to the profit of Nekolim and other groups. Therefore, I order that all members of the Armed Forces unite to safeguard the state and the Revolution."

Sounding like an apology for the September 30 Movement, the statement stirred considerable comment. His failure to mention either Nasution or Yani left the fate of these officers in doubt.

Immediately following Sukarno's talks, General Suharto directly challenged the President for the first time. In the face of Sukarno's announcement that General Pranoto would have charge of the army, Suharto stated that from now on the army would be led by the President and himself acting under Sukarno's authority. Suharto thanked the troops and the public for their cooperation and assistance, a gesture that was widely appreciated. Curiously, the radio immediately thereafter repeated the air force commander's October 1 announcement supporting the 30 September Movement, and followed this with a new announcement by Omar Dhani in which he denied the air force had participated in Untung's Revolutionary Council or had joined the 30 September Movement. This feeble attempt on the part of Dhani to regain respectability only served to anger the army leadership.

General Supardjo, known to have been deeply involved in the coup, was summarily dismissed from the army by General Suharto. Promptly making clear whose side he was on, Sukarno ordered Supardjo to take charge of the two rebel battalions still at Halim Air Base. Supardjo was no fool, though. Before the army could lay hands on him, he disappeared. When he was captured more than a year later, it was discovered he had been given a letter of protection by the President that had enabled him to evade detection and hide in home after home throughout Java.

At a Cabinet meeting at Bogor on October 6, Sukarno shocked the military as well as the country by calling the assassinations "just a very small ripple on the mighty ocean of our great revolution." He condemned the killing of the generals but did not blame the Communists or ban the party. He stated that he would not acknowledge the formation of the Revolutionary Council, and appealed to the members of his Cabinet to work together as if nothing had happened. Considering the political alignment of two of these men, Njoto and Lukman, his appeal was wholly unrealistic; Sukarno still had not learned it was impossible to mix oil and water.

Sukarno could undoubtedly have lived out his remaining years as titular President of Indonesia had he taken a different tack, condemned the coup group, and supported the New Order (*Ordre Baru*). But the posture he chose could only be interpreted as sympathetic to the coup group, and it represented the beginning of a struggle that Suharto had been anxious to avoid. The army's first clear-cut victory in that struggle was the announcement by Sukarno on October 14 that Suharto would replace Pranoto as Minister/Commander of the Indonesian Army.

The major event contributing to this victory was the discovery of the mutilated bodies in the Crocodile Hole on October 3 and their exhumation on October 4 in the presence of General Suharto and a large number of officials and members of the press. There were various versions of what happened. One was that those generals still alive had been tortured; that their eyes had been gouged out and their bodies otherwise mutilated, all in an effort to force them to sign a false confession that they were plotting a conspiracy against Sukarno. The horror aroused by the discovery was understandable. Grisly photographs of the corpses taken at the time of exhumation were widely distributed throughout Indonesia.

The murdered officers were given a state funeral on October 5, traditionally Armed Forces Day. Two extraordinary gaps in the attendance at the funeral were noted, and became the subject of general adverse comment. No representative of Communist China joined all the other members of the diplomatic corps. And President Sukarno, never known to miss a ceremonial occasion of national significance, failed to appear.

The people's shocked reaction to the discovery of the generals' bodies considerably changed Sukarno's tune. In a statement read to the general public by Subandrio after the October 6 Cabinet meeting, he condemned the murders, warned that action would be taken against those involved in the Gestapu, called for a halt in anti-Communist actions, assured the people he would seek a political settlement, asked the nation to remain calm, and appealed for national unity. But the change came too late. The lines were drawn: Suharto, the army, supported by the navy and the political moderates, on one side; Sukarno, Subandrio, and the PKI on the other side, supported for a time by the air-force leadership.

The dualism in government leadership continued for the next six months. The army acted; Sukarno ranted. Suharto did not confront Sukarno directly; his first job was to restore the security of the country.

At this time, a new force entered the lists. Perceiving the need for effectively coordinated action, and with army encouragement, the Indonesian youth organized themselves into two major groups. Kesatuan Aksi Mahasiswa Indonesia (the "University Students Action Command"), or KAMI, was a confederation of Indonesia's university-student groups. Its counterpart was Kesatuan Aksi Perhimpunam Perhimpunam Indonesia (the "Secondary School Students Action Command"), or KAPPI. The bulk of both memberships was made up of Moslem and Catholic elements, although the moderate wing of the Nationalist Party youth groups joined KAMI in the spring of 1966. The common denominators of the moderate youth groups were opposition to Communism and disillusionment with Sukarno. These organizations played a major role in the massive purge of the Communist Party and helped create the political climate that made possible the gradual curb of Sukarno's power.

The youth of Indonesia had been politically active since the early days of the nationalist movement. The revolutionary leadership had been made up largely of young men—Sukarno, Hatta, Sjahrir, Nasution, Adam Malik, Anak Agung, and many others—destined later to play a significant role in their nation's history and government. After independence, most of the groups were divided into three elements—those identified with the Moslem Party, the Nahdatul Ulama, or NU; the Indonesian Nationalist Party, and the Indonesian Communist Party. As President Sukarno moved the country further and further left, the PKI youth groups became more and more aggressive, and the moderate nationalist and religious groups found themselves increasingly on the defensive. This changed dramatically after the abortive coup, in which Communist youth groups were deeply involved.

The degree of unity within KAMI and KAPPI was remarkable, considering the diverse elements in their make-up—a baker's dozen of Moslem, Nationalist, Christian, and left-wing student and other youth groups, almost all of them divided on important political issues. But despite their differences, they managed to exert a major influence on events, supporting Suharto, at times pressuring him to ban the Communists, get rid of Subandrio and other left-wing Cabinet ministers, improve the economy, reorganize the government, and finally, oust Sukarno.

Their first move was to mount anti-Communist demonstrations in Djakarta and elsewhere. The Islamic Party (PSII) called upon Sukarno to disband the PKI and its affiliated organizations. There were mass arrests of Communists by the military in several areas, and Communist premises and property, including the Djakarta PKI headquarters, were sacked and burned by infuriated crowds. In October of 1965, virtual civil war existed for a time in East and Central Java, the stronghold of Communism. Communist forces mounted sporadic attacks on their opponents in the civilian population, mutilating and killing several hundred people, mostly anti-Communists, before General Sarwo Edhy and his paracommandos put an end to the carnage. Large-scale anti-Communist rioting continued in Djakarta between October 10 and 13, where predominately Moslem youths sacked and burned the homes of Aidit and other prominent Communist leaders.

The Indonesian Chinese, some pro-Communist, others not, were victims of the suspicion that Communist China had masterminded the coup. On October 15, a mob of Moslem youth burned the Chinese-owned Republika University charging it had been a "nest" for the coup movement. Some 250 people were injured in the two-hour riot, and a Chinese student was reported to have been beaten to death. In the face of a threatening protest by the People's Republic of China the disorder continued. On November 3, in the largest demonstration ever held in Medan, about 100,000 Moslem and other anti-Communists attacked the Chinese Consulate and tore down the Chinese flag. Periodic demonstrations were to continue into the spring of 1966. The Chinese Embassy in Djakarta was stormed and ransacked April 15, and some 2,000 Indonesian-born Chinese participated in an effort to demonstrate their loyalty to the government.

On October 18 (1965) the government announced a ban on the PKI in the Djakarta area; members were ordered to surrender at the nearest military post or police station. Most of the 1,334 people arrested the next day were believed to be Communists, and were charged with supporting the abortive coup "against President Sukarno," which was then the generally held assumption about the events of October 1.

On October 24, the same day SOBSI was banned, all Communist members of Parliament were "temporarily" suspended on instructions of the military authorities. From mid-October on, the army was, according to Djakarta broadcasts, reported to be heavily engaged against insurgent Communist forces, who were said to have spread their activities from Central and Eastern Java to include Celebes and Indonesian Borneo. On November 1, Sukarno placed Central Java under martial law because of the "grave danger" in that area.

On October 26, Sukarno's incredible October 6 address before the Cabinet and leading provincial officials was broadcast in its entirety. Referring to the importance of Nasakom, he called it "the first charm of the five charms of the Revolution, and I myself am the distillation of Nasakom. I never said that Kom had to be PKI and Aidit. . . . I said that Nasakom was a reality in our revolution . . . which existed in the hearts of the Indonesian people long before the PKI and Aidit.

"There are attempts to make us hate our Chinese friends. Never have I seen such a period when the struggle against Nekolim was so forgotten. Emotions are being aroused with lies that Djuanda died from drinking poisoned Chinese wine, that the Chinese Embassy refused to lower its flag and the like. Have we forgotten how much China helped us during the struggle to liberate West Irian and now during the struggle to Crush Malaysia?"

It was to be the prototype for his speeches throughout October and November in which he continued to uphold the Communists; attack Nekolim and the CIA ("They are extremely clever and can use us without our being aware of it. They have years of experience, as you will discover if you read the books, *The Invisible Government, The C.I.A. Story*, and Morris West's *The Ambassador*"); defend Subandrio, and scream irresponsible accusations against enemies of the revolution. Sukarno seemingly had no intention of making alterations in the state ideology and was determined to restore the Communists to respectability.

An army officer told me subsequently that the army leadership had pleaded with Sukarno at this time to stop insisting on Nasakom, because every time he urged it there was another wave of killings. As this officer explained, "People said to themselves, if we are going to return to Nasakom, we better get rid of so-and-so down the block"—"so-and-so" having been a part of the Communist apparatus intimidating the area.

The people and the youth were ahead of the army leadership, and by November were beginning to complain of delay in getting rid of Sukarno. They charged Sukarno's retention of Subandrio showed the President's disregard of public opinion. The Foreign Minister told Deputy Chief of the Embassy Frank Galbraith, who was making his farewell call on November 23, that the Indonesian Revolution would continue stronger than ever, and that above all, "it must not be permitted to go to the right." He noted also that the PKI had done a lot for the revolution, but he veered slightly with the wind by adding that he could not forgive the PKI its attempt to seize power and would never trust them again.

Sukarno, too, was veering with the wind. In December, he finally yielded to pressures from the army and youth groups and dismissed Subandrio as his deputy in KOTI and as head of the Central Intelligence Bureau, although retaining him as Foreign Minister and First Deputy Prime Minister. And also for the first time, undoubtedly taking his cue from Subandrio, Sukarno described the Communists as "rats that have eaten the big part of the cake and tried to eat the pillars of our house," in a speech to the People's Consultative Congress. "Now let's catch these rats," he said, "and I will punish them. But in catching the rats we should not burn the house."

"Let me handle things absolutely," he demanded, but "if you do not like me any more, tell me! I will quit! God knows I have done well enough for the nation! You may discharge me!"

This was only a flash in the pan, however. Soon he was heard saying that Communism will survive in Indonesia "because the teachings of Communism have been the result of an objective atmosphere, created within Indonesian society, just as in the case of nationalism and religion."

Yet whatever Communism's chance of survival in Indonesia, the career of Indonesia's Number One Communist had come to an end. On November 29, in reports somewhat contradictory and unclarified, the military authorities announced that Aidit was brought in for questioning and was killed "while trying to escape."

CHAPTER 3

The Showdown

Sukarno's counteroffensive to regain power continued into 1966. By February, he was speaking several times a day and seemingly regaining the initiative. He announced Indonesia's withdrawal from the International Labor Organization, violating Subandrio's earlier assurance that the break with the United Nations would not affect the ILO, and continued his attacks on America. During this time, demonstrations and other actions against the U.S. representation in Indonesia were stepped up. Beginning as protests against the bombing of North Vietnam, the main theme soon became the elimination of the U.S. presence from Indonesia.

The point of the spear, however, was aimed at Minister of Defense Nasution, upon whom the President blamed much of his trouble. On February 21, in a dramatic move, Sukarno announced that Nasution and Admiral Martadinata, head of the navy, were dismissed. It caused an international as well as local sensation. Few observers thought the President could get away with it. Insult was added to injury when, on behalf of Sukarno, Suharto announced on February 23 the reorganization of KOTI (which had served as an "inner Cabinet") into KOGAM, the Crush Malaysia Command formed by Sukarno to carry out military operations in Malaysia. The President made himself KOGAM's Supreme Commander, but no mention was made of Nasution, who had been Deputy Supreme Commander of KOTI.

Sukarno's dismissal of Nasution was the logical result of the longstanding conflict between the two men over Nasution's strong anti-Communist position. It had been brought to the point of ill-concealed hostility when Sukarno replaced Nasution with General Yani as Chief of Staff of the Army in 1962, elevating Nasution to the largely administrative position of Minister of Defense. To further ensure that Nasution was cut off from all direct authority over the military, he abolished the position of Chief of Staff of the Armed Forces, which Nasution also occupied, arranged for the army as well as the other military services to report directly to himself, and even moved Yani's offices to the palace area.

There were also petticoat politics involved in the hostile relations between Nasution and Sukarno. When I first arrived in Indonesia, Sukarno had just taken a second wife, Madame Hartini. This created a furor. His first wife, Fatmawati, was his wife of the revolution. Most of the leading women in Indonesia had fought side by side with her in the dark days of the Dutch capture of Jogjakarta. They were as loyal to her as they were to him, if not more so. But more was involved than personal loyalties. The Javanese women were strongly in favor of monogamy. Never mind the Koran's permission for a husband to take four wives if he could treat them equally. That was another era when other justifications reigned. The Indonesian women had fought in the jungles with their men. They were out in front. They were demanding equal status and, for the most part, getting it. When their President took a second wife, this was letting the women of Indonesia down. And the leading women of Djakarta, among them Madame Nasution, joined in refusing to acknowledge Sukarno's new wife or attend functions at which she was expected. They continued to treat Madame Fatmawati as the First Lady of the land.

Even Sukarno, the idol of the masses, knew enough not to take on the women of Indonesia. He never dared to introduce his second wife in Djakarta as his official hostess, even though he was separated from his first wife, and in the many years we were in Indonesia, Madame Hartini never appeared at the Presidential Palace in Djakarta. Neither did she live in the official Palace at Bogor, but the couple did entertain extensively there. Neither Madame Nasution nor her husband would accept invitations to these functions. The personal antagonism resulting from this can be well imagined. Madame Hartini was widely suspected of being a Communist plant in the palace. The local Communists as well as the Chinese and Russians made much over her at a time when nobody else was paying her much attention, and this may have affected her political sympathies. In any event, she had great influence with Sukarno. He loved her and was loyal to her in his own special way, which included resentment and retaliation against those of his associates who would not recognize her and treat her with the respect he felt due the wife of the President. Nasution not only boycotted the lady in Bogor himself but was in a position to influence the army officers and their wives to do likewise.

Sukarno, who had appointed Nasution as Chief of Staff of the Army in 1956, had come now full circle with Nasution's dismissal as Minister of Defense. The gauntlet had been thrown down. Would the army accept a decision, obviously unjust, that tossed aside the principal architect of army unity? Would Nasution bow to this action?

Sukarno had endeavored to save the Communist Party by taking the stand that there were two opposing actions connected with the October 1 affair: the Gestapu and the alleged conspiracy of the Council of Generals to overthrow Sukarno. He imputed equal guilt to both. His move against Nasution was made presumably on the basis that the Minister of Defense was the acting spirit behind the Council of Generals. It will never be known whether Sukarno really believed the army was plotting against him. My opinion is that he did, that the PKI over a long period had been successful in poisoning his mind.

And the obvious related question here is, was there in fact such a conspiracy? The army had become more and more disillusioned with Sukarno as he pressed his left-leaning policies and programs on Indonesia and gave the PKI an ever freer hand. But it was the PKI against which the army wanted to move, not Sukarno. I have seen no evidence whatever of an army conspiracy against Sukarno, but I am convinced that he believed there was one and blamed Nasution for it.

The internal pulling and hauling that went on reached the point of absurdity. Nasution and/or Suharto would issue orders; Sukarno would promptly countermand them. Here was not merely dualism but a government divided against itself. But the feeling of the people did not change. The youth organizations kept up pressure to outlaw the PKI, and KAMI sponsored public opposition to the President at a time when the military was still pledging loyalty to Sukarno. At one point he moved to form a military unit of his own—which might have resulted in civil war—the *"Barisan Sukarno."* But the territorial commanders moved in to prevent it.

Suharto protested vigorously the dismissal of Nasution, his old comrade-in-arms. But Sukarno stood firm. He said he could no longer cooperate with Nasution, and offered the position of Minister of Defense to Suharto, who refused it. Even by the nineteenth of February, when Suharto went to Nasution with the news he had done everything possible but Sukarno would not yield, the army leadership had not reached the point at which it was ready to challenge Sukarno directly.

The announcement on February 21 of an "Improved Dwikora Cabinet," in which Major General Hadji Sarbini was to take Nasution's place, sparked a major demonstration. On the morning when the Cabinet was to be installed, KAMI youths blocked all roads leading to the Palace. Some ministers walked. Some cycled. Others were brought by helicopter. The palace was surrounded, and the youths threatened to storm it. When the Tjakrabirawa, the Palace Guard, fired into the crowd, several demonstrators were wounded. One university student, Arief Rachman Hakim, was killed. He immediately became a martyr, and student attacks against Sukarno grew even sharper. The funeral demonstration was a deeply moving event. The killing of the student brought the youth and the people of Djakarta together for the first time. As the cortege made its way through the city, the people not only paid silent tribute but gave food and water to those marching in the procession. From this point on, the whole of Djakarta seemed to become emotionally involved in what the students were trying to achieve.

An enraged Sukarno strove to control the situation by ordering the KAMI outlawed and closing the University of Indonesia. Disregarding the ban, which the armed forces took no steps to implement, the youth moved to occupy key departments, among them the Foreign Office, prevented Subandrio and other pro-Communist ministers from entering, and demanded their dismissal. The mounting tension prompted Sukarno to try to mollify Nasution. Suharto came with the news that the President was still willing to appoint Nasution Vice Panglima Besar KOGAM (Deputy Commander in Chief of the Armed Forces). But Nasution would have none of it. Sukarno had gone too far this time.

During the Cabinet session on March 11, the President was handed a note apparently informing him that unidentified troops were moving on the palace. He signaled Subandrio and Chairul Saleh, and the trio left the session and flew to Bogor by helicopter. The showdown had come. Earlier that morning, General Suharto and General Andi Jusuf had agreed it was time to act. Suharto then sent General Jusuf, along with Generals Basuki Rachmat and Amir Machmud, to see Sukarno and tell him the only way to end this conflict was to turn over authority to Suharto.

General Jusuf, describing the interview to me later, said it was not an easy one. Sukarno stormed and threatened and accused. He pounded the table, shouted he was still President. But the generals insisted that there was no other way to avoid real trouble, the implication being that if Sukarno wanted to remain President, he had better listen.

They talked all day. They described the situation as it had developed, ultimately convincing him that he himself had been misled and misinformed, or else had not been following events closely enough to realize their inwardness. The generals were brutally frank about the President's peccadilloes, telling him bluntly that he had been spending too much time with women and had not bothered to keep himself up to date on the crisis confronting the country, which, they said, was on the verge of civil war. They also threatened to release testimony involving Sukarno in the planning of the coup.

Late in the afternoon, the President capitulated. Together they drafted the statement he finally signed transferring his powers to General Suharto. But Sukarno hesitated three times before signing. "Do you think that this is all right for me to sign?" he queried. "Read it over again, Bung Karno, and make up your own mind," General Jusuf answered. Sukarno finally signed, delegating power to Suharto to run the government. There was some question as to the extent of this delegation in the statement's emphasis on Suharto's taking "all necessary steps to guarantee security."

The next day the generals returned to Bogor to pick up the President and take him to the palace in Djakarta, where his powers would be transferred formally to General Suharto. Apparently Sukarno at first protested an action that for all practical purposes made Suharto Acting President, but the generals, perhaps with tongue in cheek, convinced him that he must participate in the ceremony in order to convince the people he was in fact still President.

General Nasution advised General Suharto to act immediately and form his own "emergency Cabinet." But one of the interesting things about this new leader of Indonesia was his preoccupation with the constitutional and legal basis for his actions. He wanted to preserve the democratic foundation of his government, and he was determined that the goals of the revolution would not be perverted by a military seizure of power. Even after the issuance of the executive decree of March 11, Suharto insisted that the MPRS, the Supreme People's Congress, reaffirm the decree by giving it their endorsement. This had another virtue—it made it much more difficult for Sukarno to change his mind! Thus Suharto, hewing to the legal line, insisted that the formation of the Cabinet was a presidential prerogative and he would recommend one to the President. His proposal of Nasution for Vice Prime Minister for Military Affairs of course enraged Sukarno and got nowhere. Finally, a Cabinet was established in which General Suharto, Adam Malik, and the Sultan of Jogjakarta became key ministers, with Leimena as Chairman of the Presidium and Roeslan Abdulgani and Idham Chalid also members. Subandrio, burned in effigy by the youth groups, was out. Nasution was later named to the position he had earlier refused, but for months he did not visit the palace.

Suharto maintained the momentum of his March 11 victory. At the time, some of his subordinates wanted to force Sukarno to leave the country. Suharto rejected this proposal, but he did make a number of dramatic moves that altered the power situation in his favor. He dissolved the Cabinet and arrested its eighteen crypto-Communists and corrupt pro-Sukarno ministers; banned the PKI as a political party; disbanded the Palace Guard Regiment, which had been Sukarno's personal elite guard; and restricted Sukarno's communications, actions and movements. In the same period, the pro-Sukarno Ali-Surachman wing of the Indonesian Nationalist Party was ousted, and increasing numbers of left-wingers were expelled from both the party and government positions. The pro-Sukarno Partindo headquarters in Djakarta and Surabaya were also taken over, and this Communist-oriented party was banned throughout Indonesia.

The MPRS met on June 20 and affirmed Sukarno's March 11 order to Suharto, specifying that the general would retain his broad powers until after the creation of a permanent MPRS by means of a general election. The decree clearly stated that Suharto derived his powers from the Congress, not from the President; it also removed the Sukarno-created ambiguity as to whether his jurisdiction was limited to maintaining internal security. The Congress also unanimously elected Nasution Chairman of the MPRS, thus making him in terms of protocol the Number Two man in the country, since the office of Vice-President still remained vacant.

An action of key significance was also taken by the MPRS in nullifying Sukarno's lifetime presidency, although he was confirmed in office until the Congress decided to take further action. The Congress also demanded that the President give an accounting for the causes of the 30th September Movement and the economic decline that preceded it, and placed Sukarno's teachings in abeyance until a special committee could study and screen them. The Congress ended as a victory for Suharto, with some typical Javanese face-saving for the President.

In his last Independence Day speech, delivered on August 17, 1966, Sukarno kept bleating that he was still Prime Minister and Supreme Commander of the Armed Forces as well as President, and denied what everyone knew to be the fact—that Suharto had been given real power by the action of the Congress. He refused to accept settlement of the Malaysia dispute as a *fait accompli*; demanded that re-entry to the UN be postponed until CONEFO (the Conference of New Emerging Forces) was held; condemned the "liberalism" of the 1950–1959 period and defended the innovations under Guided Democracy. He went so far as to implicitly defend the PKI, saying that it was necessary to retain "Nasakom, Nasasos, or Nasa—whatever other name for socialism." This declaration was jeered by some 2,000 students among the estimated half a million people, and the bulk of those present were silently hostile to much that Sukarno had to say. Senior officials present made no secret of their dissatisfaction with the speech, including General Suharto, who was described by one observer as being "obviously angry."

Suharto had ample reason. A day or two before, at the opening of the 1966–1967 Parliament, Suharto had outlined the "basic strategy" of the Cabinet as one involving a frontal assault on Indonesia's economic problems; he commented favorably on the end of confrontation with Malaysia, and called for increased cooperation among the nations of Southeast Asia. Sukarno's speech was a direct challenge to much of what Suharto had said. Sukarno also had addressed Parliament, delivering an arrogant, self-serving speech mainly devoted to empty reaffirmation of his own predominance in the governmental process; demands that CONEFO be held at all costs, and predictions that his own August 17 speech would be "a bombshell."

That speech came out of a dream world. It followed by a week Foreign Minister Adam Malik's flight to Kuala Lumpur with a fifty-member delegation to return Deputy Prime Minister Razak's visit to Djakarta the day before, when the two leaders had signed the peace agreement ending the three-year confrontation. The press was jubilant, and the atmosphere of the country was one of obvious relief. Sukarno attempted to save face by revealing the contents of a secret protocol that specified a reaffirmation of the desires of the people of Sabah and Sarawak before any formal exchange of diplomatic representatives. However, most Indonesians judged the legalistic distinction between *de facto* and *de jure* recognition, and the timing and steps in the process, as relatively unimportant. The stupid confrontation policy was over; this was what mattered. The period was added a few days later, on August 22, when KOGAM, the Crush Malaysia Command, was changed back to KOTI.

It was perhaps predictable, albeit tragic, that Sukarno would oppose such an abrupt and unrewarding ending to his long confrontation crusade against Malaysia. It seemed, indeed, that Sukarno was unable not only to accept his apparent loss of power; he could not even fully comprehend it. He had lost his balance, and with it the ability to distinguish between fantasy and reality. His will short-circuited at every turn by Indonesia's new masters, he continued to mouth the same sentiments and shout the same slogans.

The trials of the coup participants during 1966 contributed to the downgrading of the President in the public mind. The testimonies of ex-Foreign Minister Subandrio and former Air Force Marshal Omar Dhani were particularly revealing. Subandrio had ordered the burning of a secret letter to Sukarno from Aidit, but a copy of the letter was submitted as evidence. Writing from Central Java in October, Aidit had suggested several courses of action to Sukarno, some of which he had taken. Sukarno himself, although never summoned to testify in person, stated in writing that the violence of October 1 took him completely by surprise. It was also brought out that Sukarno had received the news of the coup's success and of the assassination of the generals casually, apparently without surprise. According to the official army report, he had patted General Supardjo, one of the coup leaders, on the shoulder and said, in Dutch, "Good job."

Other testimony had it that one of Sukarno's first questions on being apprised of the success of the coup was "What about Nasution?" He was assured that Nasution had been killed. When it came out later that this was untrue, Sukarno was reported somewhat agitated; it is thought by some that the fact Nasution was still alive contributed heavily to Sukarno's decision to choose the option of abandoning Aidit and the coup group and attempting to re-establish the pre-coup *status quo*.

The new leadership had done its best to preserve the tradition of Sukarno, "the Great Leader of the Revolution." There was not a man in the group who did not wish to see him walk off the stage with dignity. He had led them, after three and a half centuries of occupation, to freedom and independence. They were willing to argue, to temporize, to wait, to live with a situation in which the policies of their President were no longer the policies of the government; in which he who had so often represented himself as the voice of his people no longer spoke for them.

Years before, Sukarno had written: "And when I die, don't write on my tombstone, President Sukarno, doctor, engineer, leader of the Revolution . . . No! Just write on my tombstone, 'Here lies Sukarno, the voice of the people of Indonesia.' That's all." But Sukarno had effaced his own epitaph. A new order had replaced the old.

The old stag was not pushed out of the herd without a fight; but when the end came, it was to a figure bereft of dignity, tragi-comically beating his breast and still maintaining he was President as his world passed him by.

In March 1967, the dualism that had existed in the Indonesian government since October 1965 was over. The Provisional People's Consultative Congress removed Sukarno from presidential office and named General Suharto Acting President in his stead. Sukarno was not even permitted to attend the session. Until his death, he resided in a kind of luxurious house arrest in Dewi's villa on the outskirts of Djakarta. He was not permitted any outside visitors, only his family. An era had come to an end.

CHAPTER 4

The New Order

In January 1969, my wife and I returned to Indonesia on a "sentimental journey." We were welcomed with open arms. The press had a field day, good-naturedly lampooning my sentimental journey, obviously determined to make much more than that out of it. Jack W. Lydman, a close friend who was now Minister and Chargé d'Affaires, insisted that we stay with him and his wife for a few days, after which we moved into our old home for a few weeks, at the invitation of Ambassador Marshall Green, who was temporarily absent.

We had not been in Djakarta for more than three years. The physical alteration in the city was dramatic. The municipal busses had had their faces lifted. Shelters had been constructed for waiting passengers. One of the busiest four-lane boulevards in the city was the ribbon of road connecting Djakarta proper with its plush principal suburb, Kabajoran. It was as much as a man's life was worth to cross that street, with its traffic whizzing rapidly in two directions. Now, neat walkway bridges had been built so that pedestrians could get safely across.

Djakarta's rejuvenation program was the work of the city's energetic new mayor, Ali Sadikin, an old friend of mine. As soon as I could, I called on him.

"You've changed Djakarta," I said to him. "How did you do it?" In reply, he escorted me to a briefing room in the city hall, and we spent an hour together looking at charts, graphs, and slides showing the "before and after" picture in Djarkarta. The accomplishments were impressive. He had built more than 100 new schools, constructed new markets, and paved miles of roads.

The city had been in the red; he put it into the black. I had heard rumors of how this magic was accomplished, and I asked him about it. "We had to have revenue," he said, "and we couldn't get it from the national government. I looked around and decided to try legalized gambling." The city budget has been increased one-third by this and other ingenious money-producing schemes. Most of the gambling revenue has come from wealthy Chinese, who love playing for stakes. To ensure that Indonesians were not taught bad habits—gambling, like drinking, is contrary to the laws of Islam—the casinos were off limits to all but Chinese and foreigners.

Sadikin is popular in Djakarta. People say he has worked miracles. And he certainly has changed the face of the nation's capital. People are proud of their city today and speak proudly of their handsome mayor.

Djakarta's progress parallels what has happened to the nation. Under President Suharto's leadership,[1] Indonesia has chalked up an extraordinary record. It is difficult to exaggerate the international significance of this turnabout. For Americans, the impact goes far beyond the fact of a friendly government replacing a hostile one. It represents a major defeat for both Moscow and Peking; more serious for the latter since Chinese influence in Indonesia's Communist Party had superceded that of the Soviets. It is a blow, too, for the many in Asia who had casually accepted Communism as the wave of the future. Most important, it ensures that this important area of the world will not be caught in pincers between a Communist China on the north and a Communist Indonesia on the south—the two largest nations in East Asia.

In 1969, Indonesia was at long last on the way to realizing her potential. But how was this miracle accomplished? The credit goes to General Suharto and his team—Foreign Minister Adam Malik, Economic Minister Hamengku Buwono, Minister of Trade Sumitro; and a group of able economists, Widjojo, Sadli, Salim, and Finance Minister Ali Wardana, all with doctorates from American universities. Led by Suharto, whose only question was, "What is the best thing for the country?", these men made and stuck by all the hard initial decisions—and all the right ones— that were necessary to carry out a difficult rejuvenation program. And one of the happiest results of Indonesia's acting on its own is the *rapprochement* that now exists between that country and the United States.

At noon on August 11, 1966, almost three years of confrontation against Malaysia ended with the signing of the Bangkok Agreement at the Department of Foreign Affairs by Foreign Minister Malik and Deputy Prime Minister Tun Abdul Razak. It provided for the termination of hostile acts by both countries, immediate diplomatic recognition and exchange of representatives, and offered an opportunity to people in Malaysia "to reaffirm their previous decision about their status in Malaysia." On May 17, Malik had made clear the Government of Indonesia would not impose rigid preconditions for ending confrontation nor demand a Borneo referendum. Indonesia's only concern was that the will of the majority of people in Borneo be correctly interpreted.

---

1. In March 1966, Sukarno delegated his presidential powers to Suharto; in March 1967, Suharto was named Acting President, and in 1968, President.

In future, Malaysia and Indonesia would cooperate not only in economic and cultural affairs but also in military matters, including joint patrols in the Malacca Straits to stamp out piracy, and on the Malaysian-Indonesian border in Borneo against Communist guerrillas.

Within the country, settlement of the Malaysia dispute marked another major milestone in the process of downgrading Sukarno, and demonstrated that Suharto and his associates had the will and determination, as well as the power, to confront and defeat him on crucial national issues.

Suharto's next move was to rejoin the United Nations, correcting one of the most unpopular moves Sukarno ever made. Sukarno's Ambassador to the UN, Palar, exceeded his instructions—but correctly read the future—when faced with notifying the Secretary-General of his President's decision. He laid groundwork that would eliminate all red tape at the time when his nation would resume its place in the international body. Instead of having to proceed with all the formalities of application and formal readmission, a simple letter of notification was to do the trick. That letter was presented by Foreign Minister Malik to the Secretary-General on September 19, 1966, telling him of Indonesia's decision "to resume full cooperation with the United Nations and to resume participation in its activities." Sukarno opposed this to the last. Early in September, Malik told me, when he was in Belgrade enroute to the UN, Sukarno cabled him not to present the letter; Malik telegraphed back that the order had arrived too late. His action was a measure of the change in Sukarno's status. On September 28, the Indonesian Delegation resumed its seat in the UN General Assembly without any objections from other members.

The suspension of relations with Communist China came next.

Indonesia's relations with China may be divided into four periods: the courtship, the lovers' quarrel, the marriage, the separation. The courtship began with Bandung and continued until the Indonesian treatment of the Chinese minority aroused Peking's ire and led to a dispute over the status of the overseas Chinese. The lovers' quarrel reached its peak when Subandrio was snubbed and treated "as though Indonesia were already a satellite" on the occasion of his visit to the Chinese capital in October 1959. The marriage took place in the fall of 1964, when the Djakarta-Peking axis took on substance and form. The separation followed the Chinese support of Gestapu.

The Communist Party of Indonesia was never the pawn of either Moscow or Peking. Aidit maintained a cocky independence regarding the Sino-Soviet dispute, criticizing and praising each side in turn. Thus the PKI refused to follow the Soviets in condemning Albania at the CPSU

Twenty-second Congress in October 1961 [2] but lauded the "Program for the Development of Communism" put forth by the Russians, which the Chinese ridiculed. In December of 1961, at a time when the dispute with Peking over the status of Chinese in Indonesia was waxing hot, Aidit told the PKI Central Committee, "there is only one vanguard of the world communist movement . . . the cpsu." [3]

This apparently was the signal to Peking to alter its attitude and to start again to woo Indonesia. The Soviet retreat in Cuba and denouncement of China's border incursions against India had brought criticism from the PKI. And on February 10, 1963, Aidit's "Dare, Dare, and Dare Again" speech attacking revisionism was interpreted by both Peking and Moscow as placing him flatly on Peking's side in the Sino-Soviet dispute. The visit of Liu Shao-chi to Indonesia followed shortly, and by May of 1963 China was hailing the PKI for having adopted "the correct political line" in every respect.[4]

Rapprochement between Communist China and Indonesia, which had become a fact by the spring of 1965, thus did not develop overnight but, as Professor Mozingo points out, was "the culmination of a gradually evolving sense of the harmony between certain aims of Indonesian nationalism and Peking's drive to create a China-centered political order in the Far East that would exclude the presence of major Western powers, particularly the United States." [5]

The U.S. agreement to extend military assistance to Malaysia and the repudiation of Indonesia's views by the Cairo Conference in October 1964, tended to isolate Indonesia on the international scene and put Sukarno in a position where he badly needed support. He found it where he had known he would—in Peking. China's policies ever since the Bandung Conference of 1955 had tended more and more to coincide with Sukarno's strategy. The position of the PKI in the Sino-Soviet dispute, in which Aidit finally lined up on Peking's side, was an important element in Sukarno's shift toward China in the fall of 1964.

Marshal Chen Yi, China's Foreign Minister, suddenly arrived in Djakarta on November 27, 1964, shortly after Sukarno had been in Shanghai for a meeting with Chou En-lai. The Chen Yi-Sukarno talks appeared to have initiated a new stage in Sino-Indonesian relations. Their joint press release of December 3, 1964, revealed, as Professor Mozingo concluded,

2. See Donald Hindley, "The Indonesian Communists and the CPSU Twenty-second Congress," *Asian Survey* vol. II, no. 1 (March 1962), pp. 20–27.

3. D. N. Aidit, *Strengthen National Unity and Communist Unity* (Djakarta: Documents of the Third Plenum of the Central Committee of the Communist Party of Indonesia, 1962), p. 24.

4. D. P. Mozingo, *Sino-Indonesian Relations: An Overview, 1955–1965* (Santa Monica, Calif.: The RAND Corporation, 1965), p. 47.

5. *Ibid.*, p. v.

"the harmony of Sino-Indonesian political views with a candor that far exceeded anything found in previous diplomatic statements of either country." [6] The release stated that the two parties had reached "a common understanding and agreed that the struggles against imperialism, colonialism and neocolonialism [were] a single struggle [whose parts] cannot be separated from one another." Chen Yi reaffirmed the Chinese People's Republic's full support for Indonesia's struggle against Malaysia. He also offered Indonesia a credit of U.S. $50,000,000, of which $40,000,000 was for economic development and the rest for cash reserves.[7] This was the high-water mark.

There has been considerable speculation that Peking was behind Gestapu. It has apparently been documented that the Chinese shipped small arms into Indonesia inside packing crates of building materials to be used for Sukarno's CONEFO project.[8] These arms were presumably to supply the workers-and-peasants militia, but in fact were to arm PKI cadres secretly being trained at Lubang Buaja at Halim Air Base. In Peking on the morning of October 1, the Indonesian delegation was informed of the "attempted coup," and Chinese officials supplied a list of captured generals. Nasution's name was among them. Since Nasution had not been captured, the only logical conclusion was that the Chinese had had advance information of the plans. Thus, although the extent of Communist Chinese participation in the coup planning is not known, it is clear that close communication with those responsible for the events of October 1 had been maintained.

Relations between Indonesia and Communist China deteriorated throughout 1966 and 1967, owing primarily to the severity of restrictive measures placed upon the Chinese community in Indonesia since 1965. After the abortive coup, many Chinese lost their lives in the ensuing blood purge of Communists throughout Indonesia. Chinese government protests had no effect against hostile actions by Indonesian youth. Regional military commanders banned the Chinese from engaging in any kind of business and imposed a special tax on them. Further Indonesian outbursts continued, most of them turning into riots. It was reported on April 23, 1967, that 60,000 Chinese in Borneo were being evacuated to deportation camps in controlled areas.

After a number of Chinese nationals had been arrested in Djakarta for circulating pamphlets protesting the restrictive measures imposed upon the Chinese community, an elderly Chinese national died in prison. The Indonesian authorities attributed his death to suicide; the Chinese Communists charged he had been beaten and tortured. His funeral on

---

6. *Ibid.*, p. 70.
7. *Ibid.*
8. John O. Sutter, "Two Faces of KONFRONTASI: 'Crush Malaysia' and the GESTAPU," *Asian Survey*, vol. VI, no. 10 (October 1966), pp. 536–537.

April 20 became an occasion for a mass Chinese protest demonstration, which gave way to rioting. More riots followed on April 22 and 23.

Violent actions against the Chinese continued in Djakarta, and on October 1, the second anniversary of the abortive coup, about 1,000 Indonesian students stormed the Chinese Embassy before sunrise, ransacked the building, and stomped on portraits of Mao. Hand-to-hand fighting broke out, and several people were wounded. The climax came on October 9, when Indonesia formally suspended diplomatic relations with the People's Republic of China and ordered all Chinese representatives to leave the country. On the twenty-seventh, the Chinese finally announced that they were withdrawing their diplomats.

Unbalanced budgets had been the rule since 1951. In an ever-escalating pattern, expenditures were exceeding income three times over by 1966, and consumer prices had multiplied about 10,000 times.[9]

In September of that year, a stabilization and rehabilitation plan endorsed by the International Monetary Fund was put into effect. Suharto carried through a sophisticated program of budget balancing, increased taxes and revenues, credit restriction, and new exchange measures. Investors flooded into Indonesia, American, British, Japanese—and the Dutch. By January 1969, more than 320 applications for foreign investment had been received by the government. Many were from American corporations, most of whom have successfully negotiated agreements. A large number of oil companies are energetically exploring for petroleum under new arrangements; four oil strikes were reported in late 1968 and early 1969. Caltex is still the largest producer in Indonesia, with an estimated production of 700,000 barrels a day as of January 1970.

In 1969, a program to encourage exports was developed. The printing presses stopped turning out worthless money. Nationalized foreign properties were returned to their owners, and a law was passed that established a favorable climate for foreign investment. Though many of the deeply rooted ills surrounding the shortage of manpower in administration and in technical and skilled labor persisted, young men were once again obtaining engineering degrees on scholarship to American universities, or being included in extensive training programs to fit them for more demanding jobs. Some of these programs were sponsored by American industry.

America and the West, including Japan, took initiatives to help Indonesia get back on its financial feet. A roll-back of Indonesia's huge debt service was agreed to. A sticky point in relation to the latter was the question as to what the Soviets would do about the large credits they had

---

9. For a summary of the situation, see Roger A. Freeman, *Socialism and Private Enterprise in Equatorial Asia* (Stanford, Calif.: The Hoover Institution on War, Revolution and Peace, 1968).

extended to Indonesia. The U.S. and the West were not about to put in money which, directly or indirectly, would be used to pay Soviet debts. The Russians were invited to join the discussions but refused. The Indonesians, however, solved this difficulty by negotiating a roll-back of the debt owed to the Soviets. A consortium of Western nations plus Japan then extended credits of more than $200 million to help Indonesia with its balance of payments problems, enabling it to purchase required raw materials, spare parts, and finished goods. The United States put up a third of the total financial assistance, Japan a third, and the European nations plus Britain a third. This formula has been continued. Consortium conferences held annually from 1966 through 1970 reviewed the progress of the Indonesian economy and continued the financing of the rehabilitation program. Indonesia's record was so outstanding that the amount of assistance was increased to $325 million in 1968 and $500 million in 1969. The United States agreed to provide one-third of the non-food portion of the aid and a "fair share" of the food portion, provided the other donors made adequate levels of assistance available and that the IMF and World Bank continued to report satisfactory performance on Indonesia's part. At the meeting in Amsterdam in December 1969, the IGGI approved an Indonesian request for $600 million in economic assistance for a fifteen-month period beginning January 1, 1970. (The fifteen months was designed to bring the aid-pledging period into line with the new Indonesian fiscal year, which begins on April 1.) We reiterated our previous food and non-food pledge, subject to the same provisions.

What all this amounted to in terms of the American share was a total of $282.2 million put up by the United States in direct economic assistance to Indonesia between April 1966 and the end of September 1968, in addition to contributions made through such regional programs as the Asian Development Bank and the Southeast Asia Ministers of Education Council.

By the spring of 1969, the consortium, known officially as the Intergovernmental Group on Indonesia, could be satisfied with the result of their decisions. Instead of famine, there was now adequate availability of food from increased production and imports; effective fiscal and monetary policies, together with the inflow of foreign assistance, had brought about a substantial reduction of the rate of inflation. Indonesian debts from the Sukarno regime are still outstanding. The nation owed Soviet Russia and the Socialist-bloc countries $1.13 billion up to December 1968. The total debt to Western nations and Japan, including credits extended last year, amounted to about the same. Indonesia's total outstanding foreign obligations therefore had reached a minimum of $2.6 billion. It is a big load for a nation that still has to borrow to balance its international accounts. But hope is rising, both in Indonesia and abroad, that this resource-rich nation will make the grade.

Washington also quietly supplied Indonesia in 1967 with a substantial amount of surplus rice to meet the short fall and enable it to feed its people. To Washington's credit, as well as that of my successor and good friend, Ambassador Green,[10] the U. S. Government chose a course midway between holding back until Indonesia had fully proved itself both politically and economically (something it could not readily have done without help) and rushing in with massive bilateral assistance. The former would have been like standing on the shore when a drowning man called for help, and the latter would have led us to assume responsibilities rightfully Indonesian.

The attitude of the Nixon Administration was encouraging to Indonesians. The first American President to visit Indonesia, Nixon received a cordial welcome on July 28, 1969, and spoke glowingly of Indonesia's future. Even more meaningful to them was what he said to President Suharto during arrival ceremonies at Djakarta's Kemajoran Airport: "The people of the United States wish to share with you in this adventure in progress." It began to look as though President Nixon had made the decision to put his weight behind further economic assistance to Indonesia. If so, Indonesia could represent a test-case opportunity for America to prove it could help a nation economically, without sending in troops. If Indonesia could achieve political stability as the result of economic stability and stand on its own feet in the maintenance of its independence, this might serve as a pattern for a new approach to foreign aid (and one highly satisfactory from the standpoint of domestic politics). It would incidentially provide a well-deserved acknowledgment of an achievement without parallel in the postwar world.

In the political area, Indonesia's new leaders were moving more slowly, rightfully giving priority to the critical economic milieu where the Sukarno regime had badly bungled. Consequently, the general elections, which the Consultative Congress, the Republic's highest legislative body, had stipulated should be held by July 5, 1968, "at the latest," were postponed.

This was not wholly unexpected, or even undesirable. The struggle between Sukarno and the armed forces occupied the center of the stage during 1966 and the early part of 1967. After the new govenment took over in March of that year, the priorities were in the field of economic recovery, control of inflation, and plans for development. By July 1968, the new government would not yet have had a chance to prove itself, the issues facing the nation would not have been clarified. Precious time

---

10. Former Deputy Assistant Secretary of State for East Asian Affairs, Marshall Green had had extensive and rich experience in Asia. When he politely expressed some concern for "keeping up with the Joneses" in Djakarta, I told him he was like the man who slept on the floor. He couldn't fall out of bed!

would have had to be devoted by the new administration to the process of political organization and running for office. There was no question, however, that the Suharto government would have been returned to office with a mighty mandate.

There were other considerations that made the decision to postpone elections a wise one. The effective disenfranchisement of large sections of the population through the earlier banning of the Masjumi, Socialist and Murba parties meant that, until a new political channel had been created, or readjustment of older party organizations was accomplished, vital and progressive elements could not reach the people by way of the ballot box and consequently would go unrepresented.

In March of 1968, the Consultative Congress decided elections would be held by "July 5, 1971, at the latest" and President Suharto, discussing the matter with me in February of 1969, vigorously reaffirmed his intention to carry out this mandate. Despite this, I found a substantial segment in Djakarta political circles that took the position "let well enough alone" and argued that elections might better wait until the Economic Development Plan had had more time to make an impact on the nation. This point of view was not confined to military elements; it was also expressed by many civilians, particularly businessmen, who felt that the "patient" was recuperating rapidly but needed a period of convalescence before returning to the hurly-burly of an active political climate.[11]

The intellectuals did not agree, for the most part. They pointed out that the country had already wandered too long and too far from the path of democracy and the real goals of the revolution. Popular support should be demonstrated by the quantitative measurement of the ballot box, not based upon the trumped-up public expressions of the Sukarno era, the unchecked determinations of the military, or the actions of a rubber-stamp legislative body.

One of the questions in formulating the election procedures was the extent of participation of the armed forces. The army was more than a

---

11. However, on November 22, 1969, Parliament passed the long-delayed electoral law, and all indications are that elections will definitely be held during 1971. Also passed was a bill providing for the composition of the various parliamentary bodies. Parliament has 460 seats, and a super-parliament, the Constituent Assembly, twice that number; the latter is empowered to appoint the President and Vice-President, amend the Constitution, and overhaul the government structure. The government will appoint 100 of the parliamentary members and one-third of the Constituent Assembly, but must select them from the so-called functional groups, such as labor, women, and youth. The remaining seats in Parliament are to be elected according to a proportional-representation system within the provinces. A third bill in this series, regulating political parties, mass organizations, and functional groups, was scheduled to come before Parliament shortly.

security force; as the servant of the state, it had a vital role to play in safeguarding the goals of the revolution from extremes of right or left. It was therefore thought improper for the army to participate directly in elections, either by campaigning or voting. The Indonesians carried our Hatch Act—making it illegal for a civil servant to engage in political activities—a long step farther in the case of the military. U.S. officers and enlisted men can vote. But in Indonesia, the armed forces were denied this form of expression, and they insisted that their voices be heard in the legislative process. The solution finally reached was to give the military, including members in nonmilitary positions, 100 of the 460 seats in Parliament, or twenty-two per cent of the representation. Some observers think this goes too far toward ensuring military domination of any new government, regardless of its political complexion.

If elections were to be held on schedule, the government faced a problem of communication. Tired as the people were of Sukarno's golden voice endlessly repeating the banalities of the pseudo philosophy with which he had become entranced, they had felt in contact with the leadership during most of his regime. But there is no golden voice or silver tongue in the Suharto government. The President's sincerity and humble courage show through his rather uninspired speeches, and the people have confidence in him. But more is needed. In the marketplace, people are happier with the steadying or falling prices. But I heard no praise for the government in this regard. The people had not blamed Sukarno when the price of rice soared. The ups and downs of feast or famine, of plenty or shortage, had gone on through centuries. These were facts of life, acts of Allah, perhaps, but people saw no connection other than a moral one with the actions of a government. Thus if no blame had been put on Sukarno for the bad times, no credit would go to Suharto for the good—unless the relationship between decisions at the top and what happened in the marketplace were to be explained to the people. For this, Suharto needed a political instrument.

In discussing the problem of communication with many people in Indonesia, I thought it would be good for the nation if the elections could be focused on the genuine issues facing the country. Ideally, there should be a pro-government party, urging the virtues of the economic-development program, explaining why decisions had been taken and what the results were. Barring a degree of unanimity seldom achieved in human affairs, there should also be an antibody party; one either opposed to the government's program or critically focused on the failures and abuses. But in the spring of 1969, the political parties were mostly still absorbed in the ancient issues. None had a program to deal with today's difficulties. None had yet reached the point of adopting the Suharto program as its own. Young men of various political persuasions were keenly concerned with the success of the economic-development program, and were talking among themselves about the need for an

"Economic Development Group" that would bridge party lines and focus on the immediate concerns of both the government and people.

The Five-Year Economic Development Plan, presented by Suharto to Parliament in the spring of 1969, should have ample time to be tested by March 1973, the target date for the Consultative Congress to elect a President and Vice-President. Following the general elections in 1971, the Congress is to convene for this purpose, and also to determine the broad lines of state policy and approve a blueprint for a second five-year economic program.

Both politically and economically, Indonesia is on the way to solving its internal problems and safeguarding its newly acquired stability. The country no longer fits Herbert Luethy's harsh description of "a collective psychosis controlled by a charismatic leader." [12] It is working toward the application of rational solutions. As one General phrased it, "We've made some terrible mistakes. But we stopped the Communists ourselves. Now we are going to have to put the country back together again ourselves." [13]

There doesn't seem to be any foreseeable challenge to the Suharto government. One would guess, however, that the banned PKI is ever watchful for an opportunity to make a comeback; and should the Indonesian military leadership fall into the hands of ambitious men and a military junta ensue, the ingredients for such a comeback would be there. The sincere commitment of the present leadership to the democratic process makes me doubt this. Also, the Indonesian people are much too aware of what they want to accept for long a government based upon force and operating solely for the benefit of those in power. From left to right, I found in early 1969 no one who was not strongly in support of Suharto's objectives. Criticism of ways and means was refreshingly frank, but there was no question that the country was behind the hero who saved Indonesia from becoming a Communist state.

To say this, however, is not to ignore the very real problems confronting the army and the society of which the military has become an influential component. The determination of the army to preserve its influence in political and economic as well as security affairs must be recognized. It seems clear that the army intends to keep the balance of power in its own hands. While the nation's troubled history might well justify this position, the danger to what the Indonesian thinks of as the goals of his revolution—among them a just and prosperous society based upon a democratic, representative government—cannot be overlooked by military leaders responsible for nation building rather than merely selfish class or professional objectives. In this connection, these leaders

12. "Indonesia Confronted," *Encounter*, 25, no. 6 (December 1965), p. 80.
13. *Christian Science Monitor*, August 6, 1969.

must be alert to prevent a gulf from developing within the society between civilians and men in uniforms. This is not easy as power and
prestige accumulate in the hands of the latter. Even American promotion
of regional security arrangements among Asian nations under the Nixon
doctrine underlines the importance of the military and encourages its
neglect of internal political development. So long as the military is the
servant, not the master, of the state, its security role remains not only
an essential but positive one. But let the military leadership at any point
be tempted by the heady wine of power to exceed its basic function, and a nation that has shed so much blood on the altar of freedom could again be denied the rewards of its revolution with a consequent renewal of internal unrest and upheaval. A few voices are already
being raised in Indonesia deploring the dominance of the army.

"Today, nobody bothers to talk about a civil-military relationship.
One is resigned to the fact that the Army reigns supreme. . . . Nobody
believes any more in the possibility of the New Order," one reputable
Indonesian editor pessimistically commented.[14] This is perhaps too
sweeping a generalization, but it is a warning flag to be heeded by the
men who are shaping a nation.

To be sure, the army is not without its own endemic political problems. As disunity has plagued the nation, so, since the revolutionary
period, has the army been subject to divisive influences. "Indonesia's
chance to remain a nation depends upon the unity of the army," the
Sultan of Jogjakarta told me years ago. A major achievement of such
men as Nasution and Suharto has been in bringing ancient regional,
territorial and internal rivalries and tensions under control (such as the
long-standing rivalry between the Siliwangi and the Diponegoro divisions), and welding together a united army so vital to the security of
a rich, developing island nation.[15]

There are still many problems to be solved; the scars of the Sukarno
regime are still livid on the body politic. But I am convinced Indonesia
has the potential to become the Number One nation in Asia in economic development within the next thirty years, excepting only Japan
and perhaps that great question mark, China. The natural resources are
there. Equally if not more important, it has achieved freedom from the
mental limitations that continue to handicap other Asian nations as well
as some nations of the West.

In the field of religion, this is particularly evident. The country has
what Soedjatmoko, the Indonesian Ambassador to the United States,

---

14. Rosihan Anwar, "Dead End in Indonesian Politics," *The Pacific Community* vol. I, no. 3 (April 1970), 398.
15. I speak of the army, not to neglect the importance of the navy, air force,
marines, as well as the police, but in recognition of the fact that the size
of the army and its historical role make it the dominant force in the
maintenance of the security of Indonesia.

describes as "a layer cake with layer upon layer of cultural-religious sediments, some of them thick in some places while thin or entirely absent in others." [16] This syncretism of religious values makes for tolerance and open-mindedness toward others. Religious freedom, for which Sukarno fought, became one of the basic principles of the *Pantjasila*. This ecumenical quality was not at first observable after Indonesia became a nation because of fear and suspicion of Western motivation. Once Indonesia had begun to be successful in her search for her own identity, however, this relatively unwarped attitude of mind became apparent. It represents, I believe, one of Indonesia's greatest assets—one that was almost lost in the frenzy of the fifties and early sixties, when a new intolerance and a new bigotry were deliberately injected into the minds of the people. Sukarno and the PKI fanned the flames of nationalism and prejudice to the blazing point. The other parties parroted their slogans and pseudo philosophy. A secular creed is no less susceptible to the infection of dogmatism, hyperorthodoxy, and close-mindedness than is religion. The closed societies of the world—and the Indonesia of Guided Democracy—demonstrated this. But Indonesia, with the strength provided by its laminated layers of religion, never really embraced this secular substitute and, when the chance came, threw it off like an alien fever.

Unlike most Asian countries, Indonesia still has a frontier. Sumatra, which produces the greater part of the foreign exchange that keeps the country going, is still underpopulated. Four times the size of Java, its population is only 19,000,000, as compared with Java's 78,000,000. One can fly over Sumatra by the hour and see nothing but jungles and rivers, with an occasional lazy trail of smoke indicating human habitation of some kind. And Kalimantan (Borneo), the third-largest island in the world, has only about 4,000,000 people.

Sumatra is separated from Java by the narrow Sunda Strait, and one of the more obvious solutions to Java's population imbalance has been to move the people in large numbers to Sumatra. Unfortunately, there is not enough shipping available in the entire area to move the vast numbers necessary. Indonesia's population is increasing by 3,000,000 a year. Furthermore, even with the crowded conditions that obtain in Java, they hate to leave their villages. Indeed, the most successful mass-migration programs have involved the moving of whole villages. Traveling in South Sumatra, one can tell whether he is coming into one of these villages by the difference in dress and type of house. The maximum number of families the Indonesian government has been able to move in a single year is about 35,000, too few to make a dent in the problem.

I visited a number of these settlements in an effort to find out how successful they were and whether the transplanted Javanese were happy. Reactions varied, but it seemed clear that as a rule, when an entire vil-

---

16. Dillingham Lectures, East-West Center, Honolulu, Hawaii, 1969.

lage had moved, the experience was a successful one. I shall never forget visiting one of the young couples who had moved to the Sumatran jungles a few years earlier, lured by the promise of three acres of fertile land. They had cleared the jungle, built themselves a pleasant little split-bamboo house, and were quite content. They served us rice from their own rice paddies, papaya from their own papaya trees, coffee from their own coffee beans, coconuts from their own coconut trees, and bananas from their own banana trees. Smilingly, they pointed out the numerous varieties of tropical flowers in their garden.

I commented on how fresh and green everything looked. Not a leaf was marred by insect or pest. The young man looked pleased.

"Yes," he said, "you must remember that this was virgin jungle when we came here two years ago."

"You mean to tell me," I asked, "there are no pests of any kind here?"

"Not of the kind you are thinking of," he said. "Tigers and elephants bother us some."

This is the spirit of the new Indonesia. Tigers and elephants may be bothersome, but they are not permitted to interfere with the business at hand. Indonesia has turned the corner.

Indonesia's foreign policy ever since independence has been described as one of "active independence." Although it started out in the early fifties to be a good neighbor, it did not remain so. There was fear and suspicion of Sukarno and his motivations.

When ASA (Association of Southeast Asia) was organized on July 31, 1961, in Bangkok, Indonesia did not join Thailand, Malaya, and the Philippines. Responses from Burma and Cambodia were also negative.[17] Any regional economic organization that did not include the largest nation in the area, however, was bound to suffer limitations.

Indonesia, of course, did participate in ECAFE (Economic Commission for Asia and the Far East) and other regional groupings of United Nations agencies, but these were secondary-level operations in which Sukarno showed little interest.

Aside from the grandiose concepts of Bandung, CONEFO (Conférence of New Emerging Forces) and the like, which were to be regarded as "Third Force" movements rather than regional concepts, the only regional grouping in which Sukarno manifested any interest was Maphilindo, and this, most observers conclude, mainly for diversionary purposes in connection with attempts to settle the Malaysia dispute. But I am rather inclined to the view that Sukarno would have been pleased to mount Maphilindo and ride this horse to hegemony over the area. Be that as it may, Maphilindo is a thing of the past. Future regional group-

17. For an excellent review of the background of ASA, see chapter 6 in Bernard K. Gordon, *The Dimensions of Conflict in Southeast Asia* (Englewood Cliffs, New Jersey: Prentice-Hall, Inc., 1966).

ings will be on a broader base, not confirmed within a racial framework.

There is renewed hope in Southeast Asia today as a result of Indonesia's new posture. The foundation for genuine regional cooperation was established in what was an expanded version of ASA, the Association of Southeast Asian Nations. I found widespread evidence of a new attitude toward Indonesia during my 1968–1969 trip through Southeast Asia. Indonesia's neighbors were welcoming its new friendliness and expressing confidence in the new leadership.

Epilogue

Two decades are but a moment in time. Yet the last two decades have introduced change at a rate never before witnessed in human history. In this moment, new nations have been born or reborn. In this moment, one great people, the Indonesians, experienced the glory of standing tall in their own nationhood.

There were mistakes. They fought when there was no need to fight; they roared when quiet persuasion would have more readily gained them their ends. But they had suffered much. They have come through the tumult and the shouting and are on their way.

Mistakes were also made by those who became their enemies, and by those who wished to be their friends. There are lessons to be learned from this moment in time.

The West Irian issue and the belated mediation effort of the United States illustrate the importance of awareness and alertness in the identification of international problems and of prompt action in solving them. Had the nettle been grasped at an earlier stage, it seems quite possible that the one issue Sukarno could ride to power would have been neutralized. Even so masterful a political manipulator and creator and exploiter of issues as Sukarno would have been hard put to find a substitute with such an explosive emotional impact. For Sukarno used the West Irian issue to throw the Dutch out of Indonesia; to build a war machine and a war psychology; and to concentrate power in his own hands under the system of Guided Democracy.

The Kennedy initiatives to settle this matter came too late for the United States to gain even a little kudos; to the Indonesians, it appeared that their leader had, by the threat of war, forced America to diplomatically intervene. Coming more than a decade after the birth of the argument, the U.S. mediation effort has sometimes been termed a mistake, in that there were no tangible benefits for the U.S. Within a limited frame, this might perhaps be true. But I submit that had these initia-tives not been taken, the tempo of events in Indonesia would have been speeded up to the advantage of the forces that nearly took over the coun-try in 1965.

In the fifties and sixties, American efforts to exert a restraining in-fluence on Sukarno were often derided as exercises in futility. The unsuc-cessful attempts to dissuade him from courses of action he had already decided upon would seem to justify that description. But there is an-other aspect to consider. Sukarno had a wholesome respect for power. Specifically, he wanted and needed American support for his nation-building program. As long as Sukarno felt that there was a chance for this support—in education, economics, and international political goals —he moved with at least a degree of caution. Until convinced his suit had no chance of success, Sukarno was not ready to turn his back on America—the beautiful girl whom he alternately wooed and rejected. The United States, in turn, viewed Indonesia in a somewhat similar way. The net result was a sufficient passage of time to allow the con-structive forces within Indonesia to consolidate their position, even while—and to a considerable degree because—the Communist Party and its allies appeared to be steadily gaining. In terms of moral support alone, the American presence was vital to that process of consolidation.

The heritage of suspicion toward the West on the part of those who have lived under a colonial yoke is understandable. But wariness about American intentions is not confined to people of newly free nations. I recognize that a cynical view of U.S. operations abroad is popular in some circles on many American college campuses, *i.e.,* the United States has become an imperial power and intends to play a continuing role of this kind in the world. To these skeptics, our foreign-assistance programs are both an instrument of and a cover for this role. It is a simple step from this conclusion to a rejection of heretofore acceptable, legitimate aims of foreign policy. This leads inevitably to a new isolationism, one designed to protect not America but the alleged victims of American exploitation; or, to put it another way, to protect America from itself and preserve its purity by withdrawal from the temptations offered by participation in world affairs.

I cannot believe that this naïve, though sincerely held view will prevail, for it represents a distortion of history and, perhaps more important, is in opposition to major forces of our time that inevitably move us toward greater participation in world affairs and closer cooperation among peoples. The nation state is no longer a large enough entity to deal with the problems on its doorstep. Like the Hanseatic cities, it has become outmoded, and must make adjustments to the new world created by technology and instant communication.

■■■

In the field of foreign assistance, five principles emerged clearly from the Indonesian experience:

- The programs must be mutually planned—the goals, the design, and the implementation must come from shared concepts and be reflected in shared experience.
- In a world of mixed motives, the motivation must be pure. No political strings can be attached to an aid program, or, to say it another way, bribery has no place in the methodology of foreign policy.
- The motivation behind the expressed desire to help must be clear to the recipient nation. The host government knows, or thinks it knows, the help it needs. But in the *quid pro quo*, if there is apparently no *quo*, the government's leaders demand to know what is behind this sudden gust of neighborly good will. Centuries of colonialism have taught the lesson that this is too good to be true. The gift horse must be looked in the mouth.
- The personal relationships must be those that obtain between equals. This must be true at the top level; it must also be true at the day-to-day working level.
- With rare exceptions, aid should be on a loan, not a grant basis. Certainly this should be true of developmental assistance.

Another important lesson, perhaps most vital of all: economic development is not economics alone—it involves the total socio-political and religious attitudinal web and structure of society. The inclusion of religion may be a surprise. Actually, Hinduism is a key element in—often an obstacle to—the development process in India. The animist-Hindu-Buddhist-Islam layers in Indonesian culture are similarly a determinant of the directions of Indonesian society and the thrust (or lack of it) of development. The hinges on which motivations and conduct swing are likely to be more religious than secular in much of the East, certainly in Indonesia.

The relationship between an aid program in the field and Washington bothered me during the many years I was in Djakarta. The time lag between the identification of a "felt" need, the development of a program to fill it, the acceptance of the program at the Washington level, and the implementation in the country concerned has often been damaging to good relations, and occasionally fatal to the project. I have seen an AID technician identify a need and develop a program to meet it. So long was it held up in Washington that when approval finally came through a year or two later, neither the Cabinet Minister who had made the request nor the technician who worked out the program was still around.

I have been out of the government for some years now, and perhaps the situation has been improved. But I thought at the time—and said so—that this could be readily corrected by giving greater authority to the man in the field, who is familiar with local conditions. Money appropriated by Congress would be spent more effectively, and responsibility would rest where it should—on the shoulders of those best informed. The Ambassador, acting upon recommendations of the head of the AID mission, could make the necessary decisions and defend them before the Administration and Congress on the basis of the record. I recognize the reasons for the reluctance of any Administration to go along with such delegation of authority, but it would make all the difference in the effectiveness of our aid programs. A multilateral instead of a bilateral approach to foreign assistance, however, has become the logical answer. The problems of the world are requiring world solutions. Aid programs must be recognized as integral parts of the effort to build a world society in which a greater measure of economic as well as political justice obtains. Such an approach would have the advantage of insulating the United States from the criticism and suspicion so often directed at our aid programs, as well as relieving us of a responsibility that ought to be the concern of all developed nations.

The basic failure of American foreign policy in Asia in the period following World War II was in the coldness of our response to the new nationalism of Asia and Africa. This was not blindness; most Americans recognized that the day of colonialism was past. But we were too complacent, too preoccupied with our own affairs, too recently recovered from the shocks of World War II, and too involved in the complexities of the intimate relations with our Allies that had developed during that war to really hear the cry of peoples halfway around the world. They were men and women of different hue and strange religions, whose veiled origins in the Chinese-Mongolian mountains and plateaus had long since proclaimed them of a different race.

Our hearts and minds had been stretched in the process of helping to salvage Europe. But not enough. The country was "back to business as usual." We had not fallen into the trap of isolationism as we had following World War I—we had learned the vital lesson that events in far-off places can come suddenly to affect our daily lives. Yet we did not understand and made little attempt to comprehend the political, economic, and social revolution that was sweeping Asia and soon would engulf Africa as well. It took the fall of China to Communism four years after World War II had ended to jolt us into a realization that we had overlooked the forces that were stirring Asia. Then we moved defensively into the power vacuum we suddenly saw in Asia. We saw it, however, as just that. We saw the hammer and sickle marching in, and we prepared our response—which came to be known by George Kennan's term, "the containment policy." We were again involved in a world war, dubbed the "cold war" because it involved pressures, terror, and subversion rather than the use of military weapons. It was a world-wide chess game in the restrained application of power.

But we still were dealing with effects, not causes. We tended to see the spirit of the new nationalism in simplistic and hackneyed terms as the throwing off of the colonial yoke. Even when, in the case of Indonesia, we took active steps to assist the process, we did not fully comprehend what we were doing, although we came to.

This is not an "I told you so," for at the time few of us involved in policy making saw clearly the forces sweeping Asia. It is, rather, an attempt to take advantage of hindsight, to perhaps get at the blind spot in our policy, which was sincerely geared to the creation of an international environment in which all nations might pursue their purposes in an atmosphere of peaceful cooperation. We failed to realize that political independence was not enough for these people, that archaic societal systems, too, had to be overthrown if the aspirations of the common man were to be realized. The cold war is rapidly becoming outmoded, but if we look back at the situation then, it is quite clear that the Communists were riding the horse of nationalism the world over, bridling this powerful steed and turning him ever leftward. We remained afoot, to continue the metaphor, holding a bag of oats to tempt the horse in our direction.

It wasn't quite as bad as that, of course. And the successes of American policy in Asia have been overshadowed by the dramatic difficulties in Vietnam. The nations of Asia that were free in 1954 remain free, by and large. And we learned much as we went along. But the history of this part of the world, our relations with it, and our image would have been far different had we been aware of the aspirations of the Asian peoples and acted upon that awareness.

I realize that to make assisting the underdeveloped areas of the world part of our foreign policy is in some quarters regarded as highly idealistic and unrealistic. But as I see it, a narrow and restricted view of the national interest is distinctly not in the national interest. The basic concern of the United States from this point forward must be to create positive policies directed toward removing the causes of conflict. This is not an idealistic, impractical policy. It is, instead, the most practical of all policies; it is enlightened self-interest.

The Indonesians learned much from the United States and the West. We trained and educated many of their leaders and, perhaps more than any other nation, introduced them to the age of technology. The progress currently being made in Indonesia is due in considerable measure to the assistance programs of various kinds mounted by the United States government.

But we learned far deeper lessons from the Indonesians than they from us. For now we know that there are limits to power and intervention in the affairs of another country; that the myopia that has led us to look at the history of man through the restricted lens of Western history must be corrected; that greatness and glory have come to other peoples at other times, and unless we bring hearts and minds and understanding to these peoples, our time, too, "shall pass."

There is a new dimension in international affairs today that is vital to the solution of world problems. Regardless of how vigorous the effort, the abundance of resources, or the extent of outside assistance, progress can only be counted on if peace is preserved.

Twenty-two years ago, a great American President, Franklin D. Roosevelt, sat in his study one day writing a "fireside chat" for radio broadcast the next evening. He wrote in the knowledge that World War II was in its final phase. Millions lay dead; millions more wandered amid the rubble of their cities and farms, maimed in mind, body, and spirit. Worn thin by his burdens, aware of the power about to be unleashed by atomic fission, and agonized by the wastage of treasure that might, in peace, have banished poverty, illiteracy, disease and despair, the President searched for some compelling lesson he might pass on to his people.

"Today," he wrote, "we are faced with the pre-eminent fact that, if civilization is to survive, we must cultivate the science of human relationships—the ability of all peoples, of all lands, to live together and work together in the same world, at peace."

The date was April 11, 1945. President Roosevelt never delivered his message, for he died the next day. But I believe he was right.

Just as in Indonesia, where the nature of the people, their anxieties and aspirations, their habits of thought, their methods of self-expression, their history and psychology were all almost unknown or deemed to lie outside the realm of practical politics, so throughout Asia, Africa, Europe, North and South America, is the human aspect of political affairs largely overlooked. We cherish the physical sciences. We worship technology. We master the atom. We conquer space. But that which gives meaning to all else—the science of human relationships—continues to confound us.

Time and again, in Berlin, in China, in Indonesia, I have witnessed what occurs when reason is replaced by fear and suspicion, when decisions are based on prejudice, rumor, and propaganda, and when men react to each other without some shared experience, some common knowledge born of close association that assures each of the other's sincerity and induces trust and respect, if not always agreement. And I have come to conclude that, outlaw nations excepted, it is not a specific issue that brings nations to the point of war, but ignorance of each other's nature and the misunderstanding of each other's motivations.

If I seem to speak with some assurance on these matters, it is because, after years of living in foreign lands, I know that more valuable than any treaty or pact I have signed are the friendships I have formed with nationals of other countries. Emerson once said: "A friend is one with whom you can be sincere." In my heart I know that whatever differences may divide us and other countries, there is a core of human beings, of many races and sects, who have confidence in those virtues we discovered in each other, however alien our façades.

In the science of human relations lies the new dimension essential to the peaceful pursuit of international affairs. West must understand East, and vice versa. Each must appreciate not only the other's scientific and technical accomplishments, but its human aspects—modes of thought, culture, history, the things of which it is proud, its customs and mores. More important, both must recognize that they need each other, that alone neither is complete. The Constitution of UNESCO includes a most pertinent phrase: "Since war began in the minds of men, it is in the minds of men that the defenses of peace must be constructed."

In a dark day during World War II, President Roosevelt asked the American people to join him in this prayer of Stephen Vincent Benet's:

> God of the free, we pledge our hearts and lives today to the cause of all free mankind. Grant us a common faith that man shall know bread and peace, that he shall know justice and righteousness, freedom and security, an equal chance to do his best, not only in our own lands, but throughout the world. And in that faith, let us march toward the clean world our hands can make.

Biographies of Principal Characters

Dipa Nusantara Aidit

Aidit's shrewd policy was to ride Sukarno's coat tails to power. A cocky, strutting little man with bulging hypnotic eyes,[1] he was the designer and engineer of the remarkable Communist apparatus in Indonesia and its near-successful bid to take over the country. Born July 30, 1923, in Sumatra, Aidit spent seven years in elementary school, and then studied at a commerical high school in Djakarta. He began his political career at the age of sixteen as an active member of a youth organization, Persatuan Timur Muda (Eastern Youth Union). From 1940 until the Japanese occupation in 1942, he was one of the leaders of the youth corps of Gerindo, the major radical national-ist party of the time and a front for the Communist Party of Indonesia, which had gone underground. About the time of the Japanese occupation, Aidit began studying at the political training school of the Ang Katan Baru Indo-nesia (Indonesian New Generation) in Djakarta. There he first met M.H. Lukman, who was to become his chief deputy in promoting Communism in Indonesia. In the immediate postwar period, Aidit was active in various youth-farmers-workers organizations in Indonesia. In November 1945, when fight-ing broke out between the Indonesians and the British armed forces sent to Djakarta to secure the area, Aidit was captured by the British and handed over to Dutch military authorities, who imprisoned him for seven months.

Following the unsuccessful Madiun Rebellion, Aidit progressed rapidly in the party, being elected First Secretary early in 1951 and a Member of Par-liament at the age of twenty-eight. Sukarno appointed Aidit to numerous governmental bodies, including the Supreme Advisory Council in 1959 and the Central Board of the National front in 1960. From March 1962 until November 1963, Aidit served as Minister without Portfolio in Sukarno's Cab-inet.

Aidit always insisted he was not just a Communist but an "Indonesian Communist," and President Sukarno repeatedly emphasized in conversations with me that Aidit was an Indonesian first. Aidit was the principal theorist of

---

1. One of the tough members of my staff shudderingly described Aidit's eyes as "snakelike."

the PKI as well as its leader. His capabilities as an organizer and speaker served him well in directing the PKI's tactics of operating through a united-front coalition, an approach that fitted in with Sukarno's ideas.

For years Aidit worked closely with the Soviet Union representatives in Djakarta. With the advent of the Moscow-Peking rift, his initial reaction was to carry water on both shoulders, but he finally sided with Peking—while emphasizing that the PKI was still independent and would do what it thought best for Indonesia.

Aidit was listed as killed while trying to escape in October 1965, following the abortive Gestapu.

Anak Agung Gde Agung

Prince and former Foreign Minister, Anak Agung (literally, "son of the king") has had wide experience in government, serving in various ministerial positions and diplomatic assignments in Europe. He is presently Indonesian Ambassador to Austria. Intelligent, moderate, modern and Westernized in his outlook, he stated as Foreign Minister that while his government would continue its "active and independent" foreign policy, he hoped to develop close, friendly relations with the West, particularly the U.S. and the Netherlands. While in office, however, he failed to receive strong backing from the various parties in the government coalition, partly perhaps because of his former role as a leading proponent of federalism for Indonesia and his lack of rapport with Sukarno.

Born July 24, 1919, at Gianjar, Bali, the Anak Agung studied law at the University of Indonesia in Djakarta. As a young man, he participated in the negotiations that led to the founding of the Dutch-sponsored provisional State of East Indonesia, where he served both as Prime Minister and Minister of Interior (1947–1949). With the establishment of the unitary Republic of Indonesia in 1950, he was appointed Minister to Belgium, and in 1953, Ambassador to France, where he served until his recall in 1955. He was senior officer of the Ministry of Foreign Affairs from 1956 until 1962, when he was imprisoned without trial by Sukarno for political reasons. He was released in 1966 by the new Suharto government.

Hamengku Buwono IX, the Sultan of Jogjakarta

The Sultan is one of the most revered and influential leaders in Indonesia. He was active in the revolution; after independence was achieved, he presented his palace to establish the now well-known University of Gadja Mada. When he was appointed Fourth Vice Prime Minister for the Economic, Financial and Development Affairs Sector on March 27, 1966, he announced an impressive program that would include reorganizing the government's financial administration, increasing rice production, and creating incentives that would attract both private business and foreign investments. His appointment as First Minister for the Economic and Financial Sector on July 25, 1966, received wide popular acclaim.

Although a strong nationalist, the Sultan never joined a political party. His position as a religious leader in Central Java naturally brought him close to the Masjumi and other Moslem parties and groups.

Born in Jogjakarta in April 1912, he is descended in a thousand-year-old direct line from the ancient Javanese nobility. Both his secondary schooling and his university education were in Holland, where he studied law at the University of Leiden. He is the only Sultan in Indonesia to have supported the revolution, and a grateful nation permitted him to retain temporal as well as religious power. He succeeded his father in 1940 as Sultan and became Governor of an area of Jogjakarta having the status of a province and covering about 1,200 square miles with an approximate population of 2,000,000.

During World War II and the Japanese occupation, the Sultan remained in Jogjakarta, working with the resistance. After the war, he entered the Indonesian Army and became a lieutenant general, serving in various ministerial capacities during and after the revolutionary period. He served as Minister of State for Special Territories in the third Sjahrir Cabinet (1946–1947) and the first and second Sjafruddin Cabinets (1947–1948); Acting Prime Minister during The Hague Round Table Conference, when he accepted the transfer of sovereignty from the Dutch High Commissioner in Indonesia in December 1949; Minister of Defense in the second Hatta Cabinet (1949–1950); Deputy Prime Minister and Director of Internal Security in the Natsir Cabinet (1950–1951) and in the Wilopo Cabinet (1952–1953).

During the 1958 rebellion, the leaders of the PRRI demanded that Sukarno be replaced by former Vice-President Hatta and the Sultan. Buwono was in the United States at the time, and was not known to have encouraged the rebellion; but the rebels' demand reflected the great prestige he enjoyed throughout the country. In my talks with him in 1958 he expressed disapproval of the rebels' militant action. He considered unity to be vital to the new Republic, and was convinced that the issues between the central government and the regions were such that they could be settled by negotiations.

Sukarno undoubtedly regarded the Sultan as a potential rival and he maneuvered him into prestigious positions of little or no power. The President also moved to sever connections that might have led to the development of political power by the Sultan. One example of this was the abolition of the Boy Scout movement, of which Buwono was the national leader in Indonesia. In 1961, all Scout movements were merged into one organization, PRAMUKA (the Vanguards), with Sukarno as the supreme pioneer and the Sultan as his assistant.

Sumitro Djojohadikusmo

The able and articulate Dr. Sumitro, head of the Socialist Party, returned to Indonesia from exile to become Minister of Trade in the June 6, 1968, Development Cabinet. A brilliant economist and one of the most popular lecturers at the University, he trained a whole generation of young Indonesian economists, and is regarded as a high priest of the magic art of finance and economics.

Born May 29, 1918, at Kebumen, Java, Sumitro was educated in Indonesia and Europe, receiving his doctorate in economics in 1943 from the Rotterdam Commercial College in the Netherlands. During World War II, he was employed at the Netherlands Economic Institute and was a member of the anti-Nazi underground. In 1946 he returned to Indonesia, and was named adviser to the Republican Ministry of Finance. The following year he became director of the Banking Trading Company in Djakarta. Between 1948 and

1950 he was the Indonesian commerical representative in New York. He returned to Indonesia and in the next few years served variously as director general of the planning bureau in the Ministry of Welfare, Minister of Trade and Industry (1950–1951), government commissioner of the Java Central Bank (1951), and Minister of Finance (1952–1953 and 1955–1956). From 1951 to 1957 he was also dean of the Economic Faculty of the University of Indonesia.

In March 1957, the army began an anti-corruption drive, and Sumitro was summoned twice to explain his private financial affairs. When called for a third session in May, he decided not to go, convinced that this represented persecution rather than investigation. He fled to Sumatra, where he was shortly named by the dissident colonels as over-all economic and financial coordinator for the rebel government. After the PRRI was set up in February 1958, Sumitro was named Minister of Trade and Finance, and Acting Foreign Minister. In 1959, he was listed as Minister without Portfolio in the PRRI-proclaimed Federal Republic of Indonesia.

Sumitro appeared in Malaysia in 1963; in April 1964, he stated that he would not return to Indonesia while Sukarno was in power.

Mohammed Hatta

Indonesians have a gift for metaphor. Their revolution, they used to say, was born under the shade of two great trees. One of these was named Sukarno; the other, Hatta. In the early days of the struggle, each was the perfect complement to the other.

It would be difficult to find two men more different in character, philosophy, ethics, point of view, personality and method of operation. Hatta was the academician, Dutch-educated, intellectual, precise, rigid in his principles. He was articulate but unexciting, solid but unstirring. A professor of economics, he was sophisticated in an area that was a mystery to Sukarno. Hatta resigned as Vice-President in 1956 because he was no longer willing to be used as a façade for Sukarno's machinations.

Hatta was born on August 12, 1902, in Bukittinggi, Sumatra, whence came also Sjahrir and other revolutionary leaders. His family had high social standing. His father was an *ulama*, a Moslem scholar, who made certain his son had a thorough grounding in Islam religion and law before being sent off to school. An intellectually precocious child, he was one of the few Indonesians admitted to Dutch schools; he graduated with honors in 1921 from the top Dutch high school in Batavia (now Djakarta). From there he went to study in Holland and elsewhere in Europe, earning his doctorate in economics at the University of Leiden in 1932. Those ten years gave the young man a thorough background in Western culture.

Hatta was active in the Indonesian nationalist movement in his high-school days, joined the Perhimpunan Indonesia (Indonesia Association) in Holland and, upon his return to Djakarta, plunged into the work of organizing the Club Pendidikan Nasional Indonesia (Indonesian National Education Club). In no time, he, Sukarno and Sjahrir became marked men, iden tified by the Dutch as the three ringleaders of the Indonesian independence movement. Hatta was arrested by the Dutch in February 1934 and sent to the dreaded concentration camp of Tanah Merah in West New Guinea. In

1935, Hatta was transferred to exile on the Island of Bandanaira, where he remained until freed by the Japanese.

During the Japanese occupation, Hatta filled various advisory positions while working quietly on behalf of the Indonesian independence movement, his eye always on the day when the Japanese would no longer be present.

With Sukarno, Hatta signed the proclamation of Indonesian independence on August 17, 1945, and was chosen Vice-President by acclamation.

Popular confidence in Hatta was made clear when he was chosen Prime Minister in February 1948, in addition to his duties as Vice-President. In this capacity, he played a major role in suppressing the attempted Communist rebellion in the fall of that year. Hatta also led the Indonesian delegation at the United Nations–sponsored conference at The Hague, August 23 to November 2, 1949, which culminated in the relinquishing of Dutch sovereignty in Indonesia and the establishment of the Republic of the United States of Indonesia on December 27, 1949. During the first seven critical months of transition from a federal to a unitary state, Hatta again served as Prime Minister. He became one of Sukarno's severest critics during the period of Guided Democracy.

Djuanda Kartawidjaja

A dedicated public servant, former Prime Minister Djuanda, until his death November 7, 1963, had served in sixteen of twenty-one Cabinets since Indonesia's independence. I knew him as a man of unquestioned integrity and balanced judgment, and admired the effort and dogged persistence that went into his attempts to work out solutions to Indonesia's mammoth economic problems. During the years I worked with him, he always received me as a friend even though our respective governments might be disagreeing on policy.

Djuanda was born in 1911 at Tasikmalaja, West Java, and studied engineering at the Bandung Institute of Technology, graduating in 1933. He taught school for several years and was principal of the Mohammedijah school in Djakarta. In 1937, he was appointed to the Public Works Service of West Java.

During the revolution, he participated in many Indo-Dutch negotiations. After independence he was appointed head of the Indonesian Railway Service. Djuanda was appointed Prime Minister in 1957, and First Minister in 1959, after Sukarno became Chief Executive according to the readopted 1945 Constitution. He had served several times as Acting President in Sukarno's absence.

Although he had been a member of the Pasundan Party before the war, and in the 1955 election ran unsuccessfully as a nominee of Parki (a minor successor to the Pasundan Party, which won no seats), Djuanda considered himself a nonparty man.

Johannes Leimena

During the Japanese occupation, Dr. Leimena and a number of his friends were arrested and imprisoned. They were treated badly in an attempt to obtain information from them. After two weeks of severe torture, some went insane, but Dr. Leimena somehow managed to retain his sanity. Every day the guards told them they would be executed. They were forced to watch men being tortured, and they heard the screams of comrades who preceded them. Finally, the day came when they were told to stand up and depart. They all knew they were marching to their deaths. At that moment, a Japanese officer appeared and demanded whether there was a doctor in the group. Leimena said he was. At first the Japanese did not believe him, but finally he was led out to a senior Japanese officer who was seriously ill. After successfully treating the officer, he was given his own laboratory and office. His comrades were all executed within a few moments after he left the group.

Dr. Leimena, a devout Christian, was chairman of Parkindo (Indonesian Christian Party [Protestant]) and its perennial representative in various Indonesian Cabinets between 1946 and 1956, serving as Minister and/or Vice Minister of Health. He became Third Deputy Prime Minister in 1957, a post he held for more than two years before moving to First Deputy to the First Minister, and Minister of Distribution. In August and Ocober of 1961, he served as Acting President during Sukarno's absence.

Born March 6, 1905, in Ambon, eastern Indonesia, Leimena received his degree from the Medical College in Djakarta in 1939. Between 1930 and 1941, he was a government physician in hospitals at Djakarta and Bandung, and during the Japanese occupation (1942-1945) he served as director of the Christian Mission Hospital at Purwakarta, Java. It was because of his underground activities that the Japanese imprisoned him between August 1943 and April 1944. During the 1945–1949 revolutionary years, Dr. Leimena served with Indonesian delegations in all of the major Indo-Dutch negotiations, including The Hague Round Table Conference, which provided for the transfer of sovereignty to Indonesia in 1949. He was elected Third Deputy Chairman of the Constituent Assembly in November 1956. When not serving in a ministerial capacity, Dr. Leimena was an active member of Parliament. He was also vice chairman of the World Health Organization's Committee of Public Health Administration and of the Council of Churches in Indonesia. He became chairman of the Council of Curators of the College for Theological Sciences at Djakarta in 1955.

Dr. Leimena has published various medical treatises. He is married and has a large family. He speaks Dutch, English and French, in addition to Indonesian.

Adam Malik

Indonesia's able Minister of Foreign Affairs—and also at various times a journalist, revolutionary, politician, and statesman—was born July 22, 1917, at Pematangsiantar, North Sumatra. At twenty, he co-founded the ANTARA news agency in Djakarta, and later was its managing director. ANTARA became the organ of the nationalist movement (today it is Indonesia's national news agency), and the Dutch threw Malik into prison as a result.

Malik participated in various leftist political parties after 1932. He told me he had known Sukarno since 1932, and been associated with him in the old Partindo Party. In 1946, he was one of the founders of the Partai Rakjat, a small Marxist party that merged with two other groups in November 1948 to form the national (Communist) Murba Party, led by that colorful revolutionary, Tan Malaka, whom the Soviets labeled a "Trotskyite." Malik worked in Murba's political department until he was again arrested by the Dutch late in 1949. Afterward, he devoted his energy to managing ANTARA, doing Murba Party work, and traveling abroad.

During the Japanese occupation, Malik helped infiltrate the Japanese propaganda apparatus. After independence, he was party to a 1946 plot to change the new government by kidnapping Prime Minister Sjahrir and putting Tan Malaka at the top. Malik was imprisoned until late 1948.

From October 1959 until July 1963, Malik served as Ambassador to the Soviet Union and also to Poland (1959 to 1962). Upon his return, he told me, "If I had ever been inclined toward Communism, my service in the Soviet Union would have convinced me that this was not the path that Indonesia should follow."

In November 1963, Malik was appointed Minister of Trade. Though dropped from this post on March 31, 1965, he was retained in the Cabinet.

After 1963, Malik became increasingly disenchanted with Sukarno's policies and alarmed at the PKI's growing influence in the government's internal and foreign policies. He courageously initiated moves to blunt PKI boycotts and mass-action campaigns and to frustrate the Communist drive for power. He was also one of the architects of Sukarnoism, a movement designed to reinterpret Sukarno's views, which, its advocates claimed, had been distorted by the PKI.

By the time I left Indonesia in 1965, Malik was both anti-Communist and anti-Sukarno and consequently in a politically dangerous position. He had the backing of the army, however, and after the abortive coup, he became its principal civilian political adviser. Despite the fact that Malik was known at the time to be urging more drastic repressive measures against the PKI and Sukarno, he was appointed Coordinator-Minister to the President for Foreign and Economic Relations in February 1966. It was an empty position, however, since Subandrio continued to be the President's principal adviser in the field. But Sukarno was always ready to try to convert an opponent into an ally.

Following Suharto's elevation to Acting President in March 1966, Malik was named Interim Foreign Minister and Minister of Foreign-Economic Relations. In addition, on July 25, 1966, he was appointed Vice Minister for the Political Affairs Sector. Subsequently, President Suharto formed a triumvirate for a period, with himself, Malik, and the Sultan of Jogjakarta as the top governing body. In the Cabinet reorganization of October 11, 1967, Malik retained the portfolio of Minister of Foreign Affairs. He has been successful in bringing Indonesia back to the track of "autonomous and independent nonalignment" in her foreign policy.

Abdul Haris Nasution

One of the most powerful men in Indonesia during my stay there was General Nasution, who had a vision of the role a unified army must play in his country. A product of the revolution, he was a schoolteacher turned soldier. Born December 3, 1918, in Kotanopan, Tapanuli, North Sumatra, he was the son of an educated Mandailing Batak family. After attending a Dutch-operated teacher-training school near his home, he went to Central Java for further training and returned to Sumatra to teach in 1939. Presumably, his was to be a quiet academic career. But destiny has strange ways of selecting the instruments of its purposes.

The clouds of World War II were gathering and the Dutch saw the need for officers. The twenty-two-year-old teacher was chosen as a cadet to attend the Royal Netherlands Military Academy in Bandung. Two years later, he qualified for a commission as a subaltern in the Royal Netherlands Indies Army; schoolteaching was behind him forever. Now a member of a small but key group of Indonesians with prewar Dutch military training, he would be needed as the people of Indonesia moved toward independence.

During the rapid Japanese conquest of the Dutch East Indies in March and April 1942, Nasution was captured and imprisoned for several months. After his release, he worked in the civil branch of the Bandung Military Administration and also became the leader of the city's Japanese-sponsored paramilitary civil-defense corps, Barisan Pelopor. At the same time, he was associated with a small underground movement preparing for revolutionary action after the hoped-for defeat of Japan.

Following the outbreak of the Indonesian revolution in August 1945, Nasution emerged as the commander of the Indonesian Army's Third Division in Bandung. This division merged with several other military units, including irregular guerrilla bands, to form the Siliwangi Divison, which controlled the Priangan highlands of West Java and was to distinguish itself in later Indonesian history.

In September 1948, Nasution demonstrated his anti-Communist feelings, as well as his capacity as a military leader, when the Siliwangi Division played a crucial role in crushing the Madiun Rebellion, the first attempt of the Communist Party to take over the Indonesian government. The decisive defeat for the Communists represented not only a critical moment in the history of the young Republic but also the beginning of bitter antagonism between Nasution and the Communist Party.

In the curious "October 17th Affair" of 1952, Nasution reportedly turned his guns on the palace in an effort to force Sukarno to dismiss Parliament and return to the duumvirate of Sukarno and Hatta. Nasution, though only thirty-four years old at the time, had already reached the pinnacle of Army Chief of Staff (KSAD). When the attempt failed, he was forced to resign. Nasution remained in civilian life until 1955, when he was asked by the Cabinet to resume the position.

For a decade, Nasution led the army in its power struggle with Sukarno and the Communists. An able strategist and planner, Nasution has also written several books, one of which served as a basic guerrilla-warfare text for the U. S. Army.

Sjafruddin Prawiranegara

Sjafruddin's[1] remarkable career was characterized by his consistent and bitter opposition to Sukarno. As he told me in February 1969, "I knew Sukarno during the Japanese period and have hated him ever since. This was because of the way in which he sold the Indonesian people down the river.

---

1. Not to be confused with the pro-Communist Amir Sjarifuddin, who died during the Madiun revolt of 1948.

He was afraid that he would be treated as a war criminal when he had to face the Allied victors."

Sjafruddin's political and philosophical evolution differed widely from Sukarno's. His revolutionary career did not begin until the Japanese occupation. Prior to World War II, Sjafruddin was a content aristocrat who had a university degree, regarded himself as a political liberal, and held modernist Islamic ideas. His position in society was serene—"I had no reason to revolt against the Dutch." But when the Dutch abandoned Indonesia to the Japanese, he lost his complacence. "I had believed in them, and I was so disappointed. I decided that we must become independent." During the occupation, Sjafruddin worked with Natsir and other intellectuals in study clubs, whose above- and underground operations included spreading anti-Japanese, nationalist ideas and collecting information that was passed on to the larger nationalist organizations.

When the Dutch invaded Jogjakarta in December 1948 and Sukarno surrendered—a "double cross" to the Indonesian Republic in Sjafruddin's view—Sjafruddin proclaimed and headed the Emergency Provisional Government (under an earlier mandate granted him by Hatta in the event either Sukarno or Hatta should be captured). The Committee of Good Offices, however, chose to deal with Sukarno and Hatta rather than the Provisional Government when they began mediating between the Republic and the Netherlands. Sjafruddin believes that Sukarno misused his power to the detriment of the country. As he put it, "I fought against Dutch colonial rule and afterwards Sukarno colonial rule."

Sjafruddin found his political home in the Masjumi Party, and has served as Finance Minister in various Cabinets. I first met him in 1954, when he was head of the Central Bank of Indonesia and an advocate of sound policies for his country. Sjafruddin's position that the economy needed Dutch capital and know-how was anathema to the flamboyant President.

After the Dutch were thrown out of Indonesia in 1957, Sjafruddin, who had opposed the action, was more than ever convinced that Sukarno's economic policies would ruin the country. His vision of increasing difficulties resulting from the centralization of all power in Djakarta made him a thorn in the side of Sukarno and the PKI.

When I saw him in Djakarta before he fled to Sumatra, Sjafruddin was deeply concerned about the future of his country and worried about his personal safety and that of his family. Communist goon squads had been threatening their home at night, and repeated appeals to Sukarno for protection brought no results. In desperation he joined common cause with those who were convinced that a change in the central government had to be brought about.

On December 21, 1957, Sjafruddin went to Sumatra, originally, he said, for a rest. Lieutenant Colonel Barlian (commander of South Sumatra) had sent a plane for him because he wanted to talk. Sjafruddin stayed and within a few months was Prime Minister of the Revolutionary Government of the Republic of Indonesia (PRRI), proclaimed February 15, 1958.

After almost three years of jungle warfare, Sjafruddin surrendered. In 1961, he was granted amnesty but placed in "political quarantine" in different areas of the country, though reunited with his family. After one and a half years, at the time of the general arrests of political prisoners by order of Sukarno, he was thrown into a military prison in Djakarta. By the fall of 1965, he was completely free, after having first been under house arrest.

Today Sjafruddin claims to have left the political arena. When I last talked with him, he was organizing an association of Indonesian Moslem businessmen to promote the interests of the group.

Chairul Saleh

Aside from Sukarno, Saleh was the handsomest man in the government and easily the best-dressed man in Djakarta. A former guerrilla youth leader, he was tough-minded and self-confident, but he had a tendency to weaken in the clinches. I first met him when he was Minister of Veterans' Affairs, to which position he had been appointed by Sukarno in 1957 after his return from Europe. He made it clear in our first conversation that he did not intend to remain long in that office, but had higher ambitions.

Saleh was born on September 13, 1917, in Central Sumatra, and attended Sumatran secondary and law schools. During the Japanese occupation, he was a leading figure in a Japanese-sponsored youth organization, but was also involved in the underground anti-Japanese movement. Saleh was arrested because of his activities in postwar leftist youth movements and his association with a group attempting to overthrow the government and replace Sukarno. He was later released and, in 1952, banished from the country. It was a mild sort of banishment, however, since it consisted of studying politics in Switzerland on a government scholarship. He then went on to Leiden University in Holland, from which he was later expelled for political activity. He then proceeded to Germany, where he applied at the Indonesian Embassy for a new government scholarship. The late Mohammed Yamin, who was then Minister of Education and who had originally been responsible for springing Saleh from prison, arranged to have the scholarship approved. Saleh told his German professors he wanted to learn all that the Germans knew about the accomplishment of revolution by legal means.

While in Europe, Saleh met frequently with Indonesian students in the area; he told me he had headed a group that drafted an extensive memorandum to Sukarno recommending constitutional changes and government restructuring. According to Saleh, this formed the basis for Sukarno's thinking on the subject of Guided Democracy.

When Sukarno went to Western Europe in 1956, he met with Saleh and apparently liked the young man's ideas. Saleh shortly returned to Indonesia and was appointed Minister of Veterans' Affairs. After two years, he was reassigned as Minister of Construction and Development. In 1960 he was appointed Minister of Industries and Mining, an area on which he had long had his eye. By December 1961, he was a member of the National Defense Council.

Saleh had a hot temper that often got the best of him. On the golf course, I witnessed one of those occasions. During an altercation with a British businessman, Saleh struck him on the head with a seven iron.

Highly ambitious, Saleh regarded Subandrio as a rival for the president's favor. During the Malaysia confrontation, he advocated a tougher policy than did Subandrio, apparently in the hope of currying favor with Sukarno.

Saleh was chairman of an organization called the '45 Generation, whose members considered themselves the prime movers in independence. Saleh was a left-wing socialist and widely reported as a member of the Marxist-oriented Murba Party, which he publicly denied when it was under pressure in 1964.

Saleh was a tough negotiator and headed the successfully concluded talks with the American oil companies in 1963.

On November 13, 1963, Saleh became the Third Deputy Prime Minister and the Coordinator Minister for the Development Compartment. This involved the large responsibility of overseeing seven ministries and heading one of them, Basic Industries and Mining. At that time he also served as Chairman of the MPRS, the Constituent Assembly.

Saleh's luck ran out after the Gestapu. He was arrested in April 1966, charged with corruption and complicity in the abortive coup. He died in prison on February 8, 1967, of a heart attack, while awaiting trial.

Sutan Sjahrir

One of the original "big three" of the Indonesian revolution, Sjahrir was a small man of immense intellect. Sensitive, perceptive, articulate, he gave an impression of calm inner strength that inspired confidence. He is the author of *Our Struggle* and *Out of Exile,* two books that made a major impact on Indonesian thinking.

Despite the fact that Sjahrir had been forceably removed from the public eye in 1962, his funeral four years later was the occasion for an enormous turnout in honor of this Sumatran-born (1909) socialist intellectual. He was Indonesia's first Prime Minister (in three different cabinets), from 1945 to 1947. Western educated, Sjahrir became active in the independence struggle and, with Hatta, led the intellectual sectors of the movement. Both were imprisoned by the Dutch in February 1934 and released at the beginning of the Japanese occupation. Sjahrir went underground to help organize the independence movement, collaborating with Sukarno and Hatta, who remained visible.

After independence, he remained aloof from the new government until convinced of Sukarno's popular backing. Then he worked with the Indonesian President, but the differences in their principles and thinking set these two nationalists on a collision course.

Sjahrir formed the Partai Sosialis Indonesia (PSI), a moderate group that declined as a political force after the 1955 elections. He served as chairman until it was banned in August 1960. Sjahrir strongly believed in representative government, free political parties, and the positive elements of Western political and cultural values, seeing in them a means for melding his country into a democratic society. Sjahrir grew increasingly disillusioned with Sukarno's bend toward the left and his increasing authoritarianism. In 1962 Sukarno had him imprisoned. Because of ill health he was released in 1965 and taken to Switzerland, where he died in April 1966. His life style set an example for many Indonesians, and he is one of the Republic's most revered national figures.

Soedjatmoko

Indonesian Ambassador to the United States since May 7, 1968, Soedjatmoko, one of Indonesia's leading intellectuals, played a vital, behind-the-scenes role in moving his country in the direction it has now taken. Throughout the period I was in Indonesia, he was a leader of the moderate wing of the Indonesian Socialist Party (PSI), anti-Communist, liberal, pro-democratic, quietly opposing Sukarno's moves toward one-man rule and the appearance of unity that played into the hands of the PKI.

Believing firmly that social change can best be effected by giving political forces free play, Soedjatmoko consistently opposed Sukarno's efforts toward thought control and a closed society. He was a cofounder and member of the secretariat of the Democratic League, which in April 1960 made a valiant though unsuccessful effort to turn the rising tide of Communist influence and Sukarno domination. Soedjatmoko has been a key policy adviser in the Suharto government since its inception.

Born on January 10, 1922, in Sawahlunto, Java, Soedjatmoko attended the University of Batavia and the Medical School in Djakarta. When Indonesia proclaimed its independence in 1945, he joined the diplomatic service of the new nation at the age of twenty-three, and served in New York, London, Paris and Washington until July 1951, when he returned home. He then became editor of the socialist newspaper *Pedoman*, which the government closed in March 1958 because of editorials critical of government policy. In 1966, he was appointed deputy to the Indonesian Permanent Representative to the United Nations. Soedjatmoko is widely known in academic circles in America and abroad. He was a guest lecturer at Cornell University in 1961 and 1962, and has represented his country at many international conferences on economic and cultural topics.

Although his full name is Raden (Prince) Mangundiningrat Soedjatmoko, the Ambassador, like many Indonesians, prefers to use only his last name. Soedjatmoko's attractive wife, who formerly taught home economics, is a daughter of the royal family of Banjumas.

Subandrio

The "artful dodger" of Indonesian politics and diplomacy was Foreign Minister during the entire period of my ambassadorship. Clever, articulate, ambitious, capable of being "all things to all men," he was Sukarno's closest counselor in the latter years and one of the most politically agile men I have ever known. Convinced that he was the smartest man on the Indonesian scene, not excluding Sukarno, Subandrio's ambition knew no bounds. Like Aidit, but without Aidit's political power base, he was attempting to ride Sukarno's coat tails to the presidency.

Born September 15, 1914, in East Java, Subandrio became a prominent and reputedly skilled physician. As a medical student, he had participated in nationalist activities, and was later torn between a desire to practice medicine and enter politics. In 1945, he decided to join the Socialist Party, identifying himself with the organization's right wing under the leadership of Sjahrir. When the party split in 1948, Subandrio was stationed abroad and did not formally join the PSI subsequently organized by Sjahrir. He remained politically unaffiliated until 1958, when he reportedly joined the PNI, the party assumed to be most closely associated with President Sukarno.

In the meantime, Subandrio's views on international affairs had gradually altered. Until 1954, even if not naïvely enamored of the ussr, Subandrio appeared to be at least curious about the Communist system. He was one of the first leading advocates of diplomatic exchange between the Soviet Union and Indonesia. While stationed in London, he began studying Russian in anticipation of a possible assignment to Moscow. After receiving it in 1954 Subandrio attempted, with characteristic industry, to learn all he could of the ussr, but he was not overly enthusiastic about what he discovered. He told me he especially missed a free exchange of ideas in Moscow. He returned to Indonesia to serve first as Acting Secretary-General of the Ministry of Foreign Affairs (March–October 1956) and then as Secretary-General (1956–1957). On April 9, 1957, Subandrio was appointed Minister of Foreign Affairs in the Cabinet of Dr. Djuanda.

In November 1958, Subandrio attended a Colombo Plan Consultative Committee meeting in Seattle and met with Dulles and other U.S. leaders in Washington. He then visited London at the invitation of the British government, attended an Indonesian chiefs-of-mission conference in Vienna, and visited Prague and Moscow, meeting Prime Minister Nikita Khrushchev and Foreign Minister Andrei Gromyko in the Soviet capital. Upon his return to Djakarta, Subandrio created a small stir in diplomatic circles by announcing that "unanimity of views" had characterized his Washington talks, while his conversations in Moscow had been merely "useful."

By 1963, Subandrio was noticeably making an effort to ingratiate himself with the PKI, but this apparently had no ideological connotation. The Foreign Minister's relations with the army had been cool, and he presumably felt he had no choice but to make his peace with the only other significant political force in Indonesia. It seemed doubtful that he would have allowed himself to become a captive of the PKI, since in political agility, the highly intelligent Subandrio had few peers in Indonesia.

On numerous occasions, Subandrio emphasized to me that mainland China constituted the principal danger to Indonesia. He had received a graphic illustration of the harsh determination of the Chinese leadership when he visited Communist China in 1959 to discuss Indonesia's Chinese minority. He was coldly received and summoned at one o'clock in the morning to appear before the Chinese Foreign Minister. Subandrio told me that the Chinese had "acted as though Indonesia were already a satellite." It seemed extremely doubtful that Subandrio would wish to strengthen the PKI and thus enhance Communist China's fifth-column potential in Indonesia.

It was clear that Subandrio's ambitions extended beyond the First Ministry and that he planned to be Sukarno's successor. His chances were very slight; he had no popular backing, and without Sukarno's favor he would probably have fallen into political oblivion. The PKI alone might have found him useful, but if it had come into power, Aidit and no one else would have been President.

Under sentence of death, Subandrio has been confined to a military compound for the past few years.

Madame Subandrio

Subandrio's political career was ably abetted by his wife, Hurustiati, a brilliant, articulate, and politically active woman whose energy matched that of her husband. Born on July 19, 1917, at Lawang, East Java, Madame Subandrio received a Ph.D. in social anthropology from London University in 1952. She served as chief of the People's Health Education in the Ministry of Health, was active in Indonesian women's organizations, and later became Deputy Minister of Health. Madame Subandrio, who speaks English well, is the author of *Javanese Peasant Life*. (Her husband also published an English-language work, *The Last Chance*.) The couple had one son, Budoyo, born about 1942, who, interestingly enough in the light of subsequent developments, was sent by his parents to the University of North Carolina for a master's degree in economics and political science.

Suharto

The man whose prompt action frustrated the October 1 coup possesses a quiet dignity and strength. Indonesia's second President was born June 8, 1921, the son of a minor village official in Central Java. His parents were divorced when he was a child, and he went to live with an aunt in Solo, near Jogjakarta. His boyhood was spent in relative poverty, and his education ended in an intermediate school conducted by the Mohammedijah, a Moslem reformist social-welfare organization. He worked as a bank clerk for awhile, but did not find it to his liking.

In June 1940, Suharto began military training at the Royal Netherlands Indies Army military school, sponsored by the Dutch Colonial government, and discovered himself. He became a battalion commander in the Japanese-sponsored "Self-Defense Corps" during the war; in 1945 he entered the revolutionary Indonesian Army. He moved up quickly; as brigade commander, he took part in the attack to recover Jogjakarta from the Dutch in 1949. By 1956, he was chief of staff of the Diponegoro Division in Central Java, was appointed a full colonel on January 1, 1957 and became divisional commander a few months later. It was in this capacity that I first met him in 1958 in Semarang. He was transferred to the Staff and Command College in Bandung in 1959, apparently because he had desired to remove some pro-Communist officers from his command.

In 1962 he was promoted to major general and designated Deputy Chief of Staff of the Army for the East Indonesia Inter-Regional Command, and in this capacity served as "Mandala Commander for the Liberation of West Irian." When the Command was disbanded in May 1963, Suharto was appointed Commanding General of the Army's Strategic Command (KOSTRAD), the position he held at the time of Gestapu.

Appendix A

President Sukarno's Basic Ideological Formulations

Sukarno's Guided Democracy developed a terminology of its own that was in everyday use in Indonesia, but which was baffling to the outsider.

The Pantjasila

The basic official ideology of the Indonesian nation is the *Pantjasila* (Sanskrit for "Five Principles," *Pantja* meaning five and *sila* meaning principles). It was enunciated by Sukarno in a speech on June 1, 1945, two months before the declaration of Indonesian independence. According to the legend that has grown up around this formulation, the President "communed with God" under the stars for two nights before the speech. The principles were derived, according to Sukarno, via divine inspiration from the prophet Mohammed. They are: (1) belief in God; (2) internationalism; (3) nationalism; (4) sovereignty of the people, and (5) social justice. These principles received wide renown when they were endorsed at the first Bandung conference, in 1955, and publicized to some extent by Prime Minister Nehru of India. Sukarno, in a speech before the General Assembly in 1963, proposed that the UN also adopt them as a standard. Remarkably suited to the Indonesian environment, they represented a mix of democracy, Islam, mysticism, and nationalism. Although not stated in the form of principles as we would understand them, each of these had meaning for the revolutionary society for which they were designed. Something was there for everyone—everyone, that is, except the Communists. Because of the emphasis on belief in God, the *Pantjasila* was utilized by the religious and non-Communist elements in the Indonesia political scene in opposing the Communists, and also as an offset to the later formulations under Guided Democracy—*Manipol*-USDEK and Nasakom, which, stressed by Sukarno, were widely touted by the Communists.

"Sovereignty of the people" underwent considerable change in character over the years. In Sukarno's original speech in 1945, the emphasis was definitely on elections and representative bodies. As time went on, that connotation was obliterated and "people's sovereignty" became merely a dialectical abstraction theoretically embodied in the rubber-stamp consultative bodies that replaced the previously elective Parliament and Constituent Assembly.

439

*Manipol-*USDEK

In July 1959, Sukarno announced that the Indonesian nation had "gone astray," and that its Western-style political institutions were not adapted to the Indonesian environment. He dissolved the Parliament and Constituent Assembly, which had been drafting a new constitution, and declared that he was taking direct control of the government as his own Prime Minister and assuming the redirection of the course of the revolution.

Manipol is an abbreviated form of "Political Manifesto." It is the term used to describe Sukarno's speech of August 17, 1959, entitled "The Rediscovery of Our Revolution," officially designated by Sukarno as the "Political Manifesto of the Republic of Indonesia."

Five points were emphasized as the new course for the revolution to take. USDEK[1] is an acronym of the initial letters of the five concepts in the Indonesian language. The concepts:

1. Return to the 1945 Constitution. This was a rudimentary document used during the fight for independence; it gave the President supreme power in every field. Its adoption involved the abandonment of the parliamentary system of government and the substitution of a strong executive form, but without any system of checks and balances such as that included in the United States Constitution. The 1945 Constitution was originally intended as a transitional document until governmental institutions could be established; but widespread disaffection with the results of the parliamentary system and an almost mystical desire to return to the "pure" age of the revolution and the unity that obtained at that time gave Sukarno a ready-made opportunity to remove all restraints upon his own power.

2. Indonesian socialism. This represented a kind of visionary Marxism rooted in Indonesian customs but which presumably drew from the experience of all countries, West and East.

3. Guided Democracy. Sukarno-guided, this concept contrasted with liberal parliamentary democracy and, after July 1959, became an "anti-revolutionary" target of derision.

4. Guided Economy. A formulation of this concept was never set forth, but it involved the government's taking over all major enterprises.

5. Indonesian identity. This was a glorification of Indonesian culture and history, with emphasis on expunging alien, and particularly Western, cultural inroads into the society.

Although a nonrational, mystical pseudo philosophy, this combination of concepts served its designers well as the symbol of Indonesia's subsequent political development. Advocates of more moderate policies or of any check on government behavior were branded as "anti-Manipolist," a frequent charge used by the PKI against its enemies and equated with being unpatriotic.

Nasakom

Indonesian political unity must be a cooperative combination of all the major elements in the society, Sukarno declared. There were three: national-

---

1. The Indonesian words represented in USDEK are: *Undang 2 Dasar* 1945, *Sosialisme Indonesia, Demokrasi Terpimpin, Ekoni Terpimpin,* and *Keprioadian Indonesia.*

ist, religious, and Communist. Nasakom is an acronym of those three words. This was an asset to the Communists, which they fully exploited in demanding participation in bodies or activities from which they had previously been excluded. They branded any criticism of Communism as "anti-Nasakom" and therefore in opposition to President Sukarno and the state philosophy. The goal of the PKI for years was a Nasakom Cabinet, defined by PKI leaders as the sharing by the Communists in a ruling triumvirate, but it was never achieved.

Nekolim

This was an acronym standing for "neo-colonialists, colonialists, and imperialists," the combination viewed as the archenemy of the nation and opposed to the Indonesian revolution; during the Malaysian confrontation, all those who supported Malaysia were conveniently included in this grouping. "Nekolim" could be applied to any significant continuing relationship between a former colonial territory and a Western power that included major cultural interchange, foreign business investment, or military pacts. Thus Malaysia was described as a neo-colonialist arrangement because, although the British had given up political control of Malaysia, they were still economically dominant in the country and shared responsibility for the nation's self-defense.

"Tavip"

All of Sukarno's major speeches were given catchword titles. The 1964 state-of-the-nation address on Independence Day, August 17, was entitled *"Tahun Vivera Pericoloso"* ("Year of Living Dangerously"), nicknamed *"Tavip."* This speech represented a major new anti-Western shift in the Indonesian national policy and a much greater alignment with the Asian Communist regimes.

NEFO-OLDFO

These two acronyms—now disappearing from the Indonesian language —represented a crystallization of Sukarno's concept of the world. According to him, it was divided into two groups—the "old established forces" and "new emerging forces." Sukarno dismissed the East-West struggle, that is, Communist versus anti-Communist, as no longer significant for newer nations.

The incorporation of this idea into Indonesian political theory resulted in Sukarno's abandoning his earlier "independent and nonaligned" foreign policy as he concentrated his efforts on dominating the "new emerging forces." These forces were generally defined to include the less-developed nations of the world, and more specifically the nations of Africa, Asia, and Latin America, plus the Communist bloc. Sukarno had earlier concluded that peaceful co-existence was not possible between unequals and that confrontation and struggle were inevitable between the two groups until the "old established forces," *i.e.*, the exclusive source of imperialism and colonialism, were crushed. They were delineated in various speeches to include the United States and Western powers. A nation like Japan defied classification. Sukarno did concede, however, that there might be NEFO elements in the OLDFO nations (*e.g.*, Negroes in the United States, or Communists or left-wingers in some other country); hence his use of "forces" rather than "countries."

Sukarno maintained that since "neutrality is impossible," Indonesia had a sacred responsibility to struggle aggressively to achieve victory for the NEFO wherever they were threatened by Nekolim. The rejection of peaceful co-existence brought Indonesia into disagreement with other nonaligned countries, such as Egypt, India, and Yugoslavia, Indonesia's natural rivals for leadership of the Afro-Asian nations. Sukarno's reasoning fitted nicely, however, into Peking doctrine. In the latter years of Guided Democracy, until the unsuccessful coup on September 30, 1965, Chinese and Indonesian foreign policies exhibited a tendency to mesh closely.

(Note: CONEFO stands for "Conference of New Emerging Nations.")

Appendix B

Interview with President Suharto

On my most recent trip to Indonesia, I was privileged to be granted an interview with President Suharto, parts of which are presented here.

In January 1969, President Suharto received me cordially in Merdeka Palace, where I had so often seen President Sukarno. I ran the gauntlet of a battery of photographers, and flash bulbs popped as we shook hands. The large, impressive reception room was well furnished with overstuffed chairs and davenports in gold brocade. It was not the room where Sukarno had ordinarily received his visitors, and there were some paintings on the wall I had not seen before, although the Abdullah oils of the revolutionary struggle were still there.

Although the President obviously understood some English, he apparently did not feel completely at home in the language, as he spoke in Indonesian and used an interpreter. A handsome, stocky Javanese, he spoke rapidly, gesturing with his hands for emphasis. His lips closed in a determined line when he had made a point. His mouth showed a combination of strength and the sensitivity for which the Javanese are noted.

I observed that the political parties were weak, having been casualties of Guided Democracy, and wondered whether his government had plans to strengthen or reorganize them.

The President said that his government recognized the disorganized state of the political parties and was encouraging efforts to revive them and make them more effective. He was not interested in creating new parties; he seemed to think that prior to the time when elections would be held, the older parties could be revitalized.

I asked him what he envisaged as the political role of the military over a period of time.

In the security situation with which the country was faced following Gestapu and the establishment of the New Order, as he called it, military officers had been appointed to some twenty of the twenty-seven governorships of the provinces. He indicated that this was not a matter of the military taking power as such, but rather the assignment of men of known capabilities, who would know how to deal with a security threat. He did not mention the

443

increasing number of military men appointed to the executive positions in local government. The present security situation was satisfactory throughout the country, he said. Areas of heavy Communist penetration in Central Java and East Java were under control.

Why did he think former President Sukarno had continued to defend the PKI and insist on a continuance of Nasakom when it was clear that the PKI had been behind the coup and that its days were numbered?

His answer was pure Javanese. Sukarno had been favoring the PKI for a long time. When President Suharto was territorial commander in Central Java, the PKI was attempting to penetrate the Diponegoro Division. When he opposed this effort, he found himself shortly transferred to Bandung. In talking about the role of the military, the President continually used the word "pure," in the sense of returning to the pure motivation of the revolutionary period, and seemed to feel that the military had a special role in preserving and/or regaining the spirit of that time.

He expressed himself as highly satisfied with American-Indonesian relations.

On the subject of China, he felt that we could count on her continuing efforts to penetrate and subvert neighboring nations. China's neighbors had felt the pressure, sometimes in the form of direct military aggression, as in the case of India, more often in the form of subversion. He thought Asian nations must cooperate in resisting these efforts, which would intensify in the future. America's role should be to support the free nations of Asia in this defensive effort.

What about American bases, I asked, pointing out that I had heard a lot on this subject before I left Indonesia in 1965, when the Indonesian government had seemed determined to eliminate American bases from the Pacific.

United States bases must be held as long as they are needed, the President said, but should be removed when the situation permits. As for Vietnam, our bases there should be closed down when a settlement is reached, but not before. The President demonstrated the ambivalence that has always characterized Indonesian attitudes on our presence in Vietnam. He seemed to share the feeling of most Indonesians that Asia should be defended by Asians, and that our role should be a supporting one; but as a military man and anti-Communist, he recognized the practical necessity of the U.S. presence in Asia for the foreseeable future.

Index